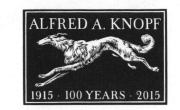

THE NEW TSAR

THE NEW TSAR

The Rise and Reign of Vladimir Putin

Steven Lee Myers

Alfred A. Knopf · New York · 2015

THIS IS A BORZOI BOOK
PUBLISHED BY ALFRED A. KNOPF

www.aaknopf.com

Knopf, Borzoi Books, and the colophon are registered trademarks of Penguin
Random House LLC.

Library of Congress Cataloging-in-Publication Data
Myers, Steven Lee.
The new tsar : the rise and reign of Vladimir Putin / Steven Lee Myers. —
First American edition.
pages   cm
"A Borzoi book"—Title page verso.
Includes bibliographical references.
ISBN 978-0-307-96161-7 (hardcover)   ISBN 978-0-307-96162-4 (eBook)
1. Putin, Vladimir Vladimirovich, 1952–   2. Putin, Vladimir Vladimirovich,
1952—Political and social views.   3. Presidents—Russia (Federation)—
Biography.   4. Soviet Union. Komitet gosudarstvennoi bezopasnosti—
Biography.   5. Political leadership—Russia (Federation)   6. Power (Social
sciences)—Russia (Federation)   7. Russia (Federation)—Politics and
government—1991–   I. Title.
DK510.766.P87M93   2015
947.086'2092—dc23
[B]   2015010720

Jacket photograph by Platon / Trunk Archive
Jacket design by Peter Mendelsund
Maps by Mapping Specialists, Ltd.

Manufactured in the United States of America
First Edition

For Margaret, Emma,
and Madeline

And in memory of my mother,
Nita Louise Myers

Oh, he understood very well that for the meek soul of a simple Russian, exhausted by grief and hardship and, above all, by constant injustice and sin, his own or the world's, there was no stronger need than to find a holy shrine or a saint to prostrate himself before and to worship.

—Fyodor Dostoevsky,
The Brothers Karamazov

Contents

PART FOUR

PART FIVE

PART ONE

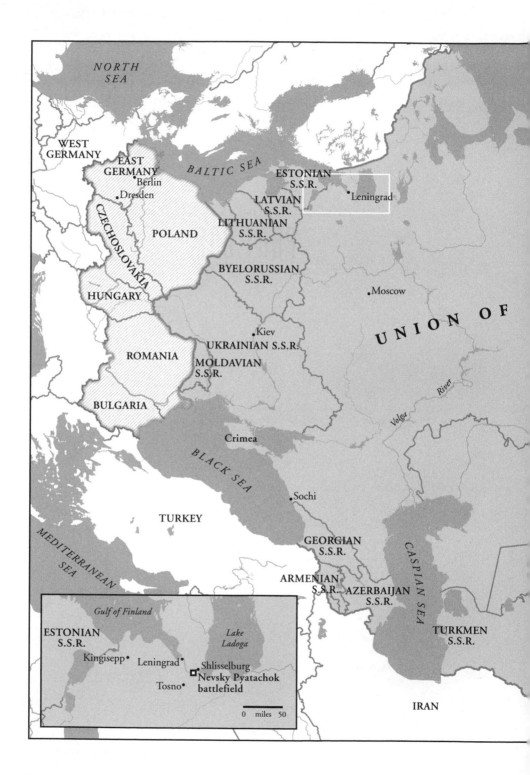

NORTH
SEA

WEST
GERMANY

EAST
GERMANY
•Berlin
•Dresden

CZECHOSLOVAKIA

POLAND

HUNGARY

ROMANIA

BULGARIA

BALTIC SEA

ESTONIAN
S.S.R.

LATVIAN
S.S.R.

LITHUANIAN
S.S.R.

BYELORUSSIAN
S.S.R.

UKRAINIAN S.S.R.

MOLDAVIAN
S.S.R.

•Leningrad

•Moscow

•Kiev

Crimea

BLACK SEA

*MEDITERRANEAN
SEA*

TURKEY

•Sochi

GEORGIAN
S.S.R.

ARMENIAN
S.S.R.

AZERBAIJAN
S.S.R.

UNION OF

Volga

River

CASPIAN SEA

TURKMEN
S.S.R.

IRAN

Gulf of Finland

ESTONIAN
S.S.R.

Kingisepp•

•Leningrad

*Lake
Ladoga*

Shlisselburg
Nevsky Pyatachok
battlefield

Tosno•

0   miles   50

KARA
SEA

THE SOVIET UNION

BEFORE 1991

Ob River

RUSSIAN S.F.S.R.

SOVIET SOCIALIST REPUBLICS

KAZAKH S.S.R.

UZBEK
S.S.R.

KIRGHIZ S.S.R.

TAJIK S.S.R.

AFGHANISTAN

Soviet Union
Warsaw Pact countries

0   miles   300

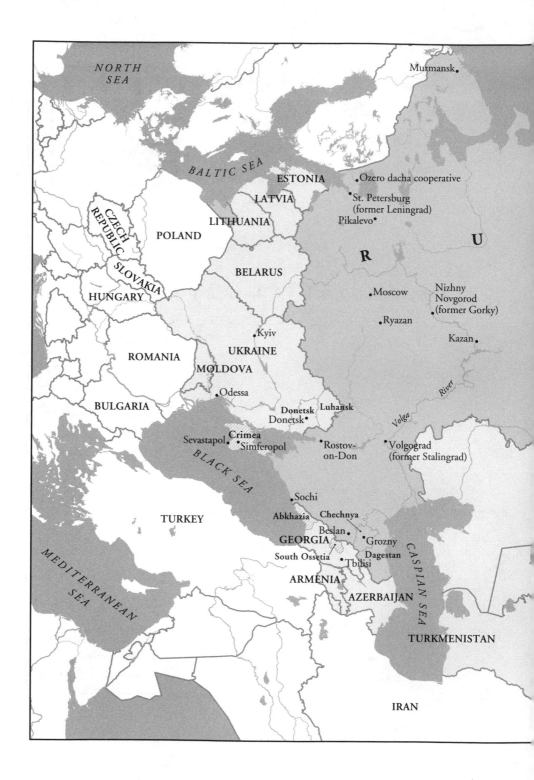

KARA
SEA

Norilsk•

RUSSIA

AFTER 1991

S   S   I   A

Ob River

•Nefteyugansk

•Yekaterinburg
(former Sverdlovsk)

KAZAKHSTAN

UZBEKISTAN

KYRGYZSTAN

TAJIKISTAN

AFGHANISTAN

Russia
Former Soviet republics
Disputed areas

0   miles   300

CHAPTER 1

Homo Sovieticus

Vladimir Spiridonovich Putin edged forward through the cratered battlefield beside the Neva River, roughly thirty miles from Leningrad. His orders seemed suicidal. He was to reconnoiter the German positions and, if possible, capture a "tongue," slang for a soldier to interrogate. It was November 17, 1941,[1] already bitterly cold, and the Soviet Union's humiliated army was now desperately fighting to avoid its complete destruction at the hands of Nazi Germany. The last tanks in reserve in the city had crossed the Neva a week before, and Putin's commanders now had orders to break through heavily reinforced positions defended by 54,000 German infantrymen.[2] There was no choice but to obey. He and another soldier approached a foxhole along a dug-in front, carved with trenches, pocked with shell craters, stained with blood. A German suddenly rose, surprising all three of them. For a frozen moment, nothing happened. The German reacted first, unpinned a grenade and tossed it. It landed near Putin, killing his comrade and riddling his own legs with shrapnel. The German soldier escaped, leaving Putin for dead. "Life is such a simple thing, really," a man who retold the story decades later would say, with a characteristic fatalism.[3]

Putin, then thirty years old, lay wounded on a bridgehead on the east bank of the Neva. The Red Army's commanders had poured troops across the river in hopes of breaking the encirclement of Leningrad that had begun two months earlier when the Germans captured Shlisselburg, an ancient fortress at the mouth of the Neva, but the effort failed. The Germans laid a siege that would last 872 days and kill a million civilians by bombardment, starvation, or disease. "The Führer has decided to wipe the city of Petersburg from the face of the earth," a secret German order declared on September 29. Surrender would not be accepted. Air and artillery bombardment would be the instrument of the city's destruction, and hunger would be its accomplice, since "feeding the population cannot and should not be solved by us."[4] Never before had a modern city endured a siege like it.

"Is this the end of your losses?" Joseph Stalin furiously cabled the city's defenders the day after the siege began. "Perhaps you have already decided to give up Leningrad?" The telegram was signed by the entire Soviet leadership, including Vyacheslav Molotov, who in 1939 had signed the notorious nonaggression pact with his Nazi counterpart, Joachim von Ribbentrop, which was now betrayed.[5] It was by no means the end of the losses. The fall of Shlisselburg coincided with ferocious air raids in Leningrad itself, including one that ignited the city's main food warehouse. The Soviet forces defending the city were in disarray, as they were everywhere in the Soviet Union. Operation Barbarossa, the Nazi invasion that began on June 22, 1941, had crushed Soviet defenses along a thousand-mile front, from the Baltic Sea to the Black Sea. Even Moscow seemed in danger of falling.

Stalin never considered surrendering Leningrad, and he dispatched the chief of the general staff, Georgy Zhukov, to shore up the city's defenses, which he did with great brutality. On the night of September 19, on Zhukov's orders, Soviet forces mounted the first assault 600 meters across the Neva to break the siege, but it was repulsed by overwhelming German firepower. In October, they tried again, hurling forth the 86th Division, which included Putin's unit, the 330th Rifle Regiment. The bridgehead those troops managed to create on the eastern bank of the Neva became known, because of its size, as the Nevsky Pyatachok, from the word for a five-kopek coin or a small patch. At its greatest expanse the battlefield was barely a mile wide, less than half a mile deep. For the soldiers fated to fight there, it was a brutal, senseless death trap.

Putin was an uneducated laborer, one of four sons of Spiridon Putin, a chef who once worked in the city's famed pre-revolutionary Astoria Hotel. Spiridon, though a supporter of the Bolsheviks, fled the imperial capital during the civil war and famine that followed the October Revolution in 1917. He settled in his ancestral village, Pominovo, in the rolling hills west of Moscow, and later moved to the city itself, where he cooked for Vladimir Lenin's widow, Nadezhda Krupskaya, at her official Soviet dacha in the Gorky district on the edge of Moscow.[6] After her death in 1939, he worked in the retreat of Moscow's Communist Party Committee. He was said to have cooked once for Grigory Rasputin at the Astoria and on occasion for Stalin when he visited Lenin's widow, beginning a family tradition of servitude to the political elite. Proximity to power did nothing to protect his sons from the Nazis; the entire nation was fighting for survival.

Vladimir Putin was already a veteran when the Nazis invaded the Soviet Union in June 1941. He had served as a submariner in the 1930s before settling down not far from Leningrad, in the village of Petrodvorets, where Peter the Great had built his palace on the Gulf of Finland. In the chaotic days that followed the invasion, he, like many citizens, had rushed to volunteer to defend the nation and was initially assigned to a special demolitions detachment of the People's Commissariat for Internal Affairs, or NKVD, the dreaded secret police agency that would later become the KGB. The NKVD created 2,222 of these detachments to harass the Nazis behind the front, which was then rapidly advancing.[7] One of Putin's first missions in the war was a disaster. He and twenty-seven other partisan fighters parachuted behind the Germans advancing on Leningrad, near the town of Kingisepp. It was close to the border with Estonia, which the Soviet Union had occupied the year before, along with Latvia and Lithuania, as part of the notorious prewar pact with Hitler. Putin's detachment managed to blow up one arms depot, as the story went, but quickly ran out of ammunition and rations. Local residents, Estonians, brought them food but also betrayed them to the Germans, whom many in the Baltic nations welcomed, at least at first, as liberators from Soviet occupation. German troops closed in on the unit, firing on them as they raced along a road back to the Soviet lines. Putin split off, chased by Germans with dogs, and hid in a marsh, submerging himself and breathing through a reed until the patrol moved on.[8] How exactly he made it back is lost to the fog of history, but only he and three others of the detachment survived the raid. The NKVD interrogated him after his escape, but he managed to avoid suspicion of desertion or cowardice and was soon sent back to the front.[9] It might have been courage alone that drove Putin, or it might have been fear. Stalin's Order No. 270, issued on August 16, had threatened soldiers who deserted with execution and their family members with arrest.

Inside Leningrad conditions deteriorated rapidly, despite efforts by the authorities to maintain a sense of normality. Schools opened, as always, on September 1, but three days later the first German shells landed inside the city.[10] With the blockade completed and the city now under regular assault from above, the authorities intensified the rationing of food.

Rations would gradually decline, leading to desperation, despair, and finally death. As Vladimir Putin fought outside the city, his wife, Maria, and their infant son were trapped inside. Vladimir and Maria, both born in 1911, were children of Russia's turbulent twentieth century, buffeted by World War I, the Bolshevik revolution, and the civil war that followed. They met in Pominovo, where his father had moved after the revolution, and married in 1928, when they were only seventeen. They moved back to Leningrad as newlyweds, settling back in Petrodvorets with her relatives in 1932. After Putin's conscription in the navy, they had a boy named Oleg, who died in infancy. A year before the war started, they had a second son, Viktor.

Maria and Viktor only narrowly avoided occupation in Nazi-held territories. She had refused at first to leave Petrodvorets, but as the Germans closed in, her brother, Ivan Shelomov, forced her to evacuate. He served as a first captain in the Baltic Fleet's headquarters and thus had military authority and what privileges still existed in a city under siege.[11] Captain Shelomov retrieved them "under gunfire and bombs" and settled them into a city whose fate was precarious.[12] Conditions became dire as the winter arrived, the cold that year even more bitter than usual. Maria and Viktor moved into one of dozens of shelters the authorities opened to house refugees pouring in from the occupied outskirts. Her brother helped her with his own rations, but her health faded nevertheless. One day—exactly when is unknown—she passed out and passersby laid her body out with the frozen corpses that had begun to pile up on the street for collection, left for dead, as her husband had been on the front. She was discovered, somehow, in this open-air morgue, her moans attracting attention.[13]

Vladimir's survival seemed no less improbable. He lay wounded beside the Neva for several hours before other Soviet troops found him and carried him back toward the regiment's redoubt on the bank. He might have died, one of more than 300,000 soldiers who lost their lives on the Pyatachok, except that an old neighbor found him on a litter at a primitive field hospital. He slung Putin over his shoulder and carried him across the frozen river to a hospital on the other side.

As it turned out, Putin's injury almost certainly saved his life. His unit, the 330th Rifle Regiment, fought on the bridgehead throughout the winter of 1941–1942. The battle, in scale and carnage, foreshadowed the terrible siege of Stalingrad the next year, a "monstrous meatgrinder," it was called.[14] The forces there endured relentless shelling by the Germans. The forested riverbank became a churned, lifeless landscape where nothing would grow for years. New recruits crossed the Neva to replace those killed or wounded at a staggering rate of hundreds a day until the spring of 1942, when the bridgehead collapsed and the Germans regained the ground on April 27. The 330th Rifle Regiment was entirely destroyed except for a major from its command staff, Aleksandr Sokolov, who managed to swim to safety, despite serious wounds.[15] It was one of the deadliest single battles of the entire war, and for the Soviet military command, a folly that squandered tens of thousands of soldiers and probably prolonged the siege instead of shortening it.[16]

Putin spent months in a military hospital, recovering in a city that was dying around him. By the time the last road out of the city was cut, three million civilians and soldiers remained besieged. Maria, who refused to be evacuated when it was still possible, ultimately found her husband in the hospital. Against the rules, he shared his own hospital rations with her, hiding food from the nurses until a doctor noticed and halted Maria's daily visits for a time.[17] The city's initial resilience succumbed to devastation, starvation, and worse. Essential services deteriorated along with the food supply. Corpses lay uncollected in mounds on the streets. In January and February 1942, more than 100,000 people died each month.[18] The only connection to unoccupied territory was the makeshift "Road of Life," a series of precarious routes over the frozen waters of Lake Ladoga. They provided minimal relief to the city, and the siege ground on until January 1943, when the Soviet army broke through the encirclement to the east. It took another year to fully free the city from the Nazi grip and begin the relentless, ruthless Soviet march to Berlin.

Vladimir and Maria somehow survived, though his injuries caused him to limp in pain for the rest of his life. In April 1942, he was released from the hospital and sent to work at a weapons factory that turned out artillery shells and antitank mines.[19] Their son, Viktor, did not survive. He died of diphtheria in June 1942 and was buried in a mass grave at Piskaryovskoye Cemetery along with 470,000 other civilians and soldiers. Neither Vladimir nor Maria knew where exactly and evidently made little effort to learn. Nor did they ever talk about it in detail later.[20] The war's toll was devastatingly personal. Maria's mother, Elizabeta Shelomova, died on the front lines west of Moscow in October 1941, though it was never clear whether it was a Soviet or a German shell that killed her; Maria's brother Ivan survived, but another brother, Pyotr, was condemned by a military tribunal at the front in the earliest days of the war, evidently for some dereliction of duty, and his ultimate fate was never known, and certainly not mentioned. Two of Vladimir's brothers also died during the war: Mikhail in July 1942, also in circumstances lost to history; and Aleksei on the Voronezh front in February 1943.[21]

These were the stories of the Great Patriotic War—tales of heroism and suffering—that Vladimir and Maria's third son would grow up hearing and that would leave an indelible impression on him throughout his life. From "some snatches, some fragments" of conversations overheard at the kitchen table in a crowded communal flat in a still-devastated Leningrad, he created his family narrative, one reshaped by time and memory, one that might have been apocryphal in places and was certainly far from complete. The Putins were simple people, unlikely to know much of the darker aspects of the war: Stalin's paranoid purges in the Great Terror that had decimated the army before the war; the connivance with Hitler's plans to conquer Europe; the partitioning of Poland in 1939; the forceful annexation of the Baltic nations; the chaotic defense once the Nazis invaded; the official malfeasance that contributed to the starvation in Leningrad; the vengeful atrocities committed by Soviet troops as they marched to Berlin. Even then, after Stalin's death in 1953, it remained dangerous to speak poorly of the state in anything above a whisper. The victory—and the Putins' small part in it—was an inexhaustible fountain of pride. What else could it be? One did not think of the mistakes that were made, the young boy would say later; one thought only of winning.

This third son, Vladimir Vladimirovich Putin,[22] was born on October 7, 1952, in a city still scarred by the siege, still suffering from deprivation, still consumed by fear. Stalin's megalomania, even in victory, had descended into paranoia and retribution. In the late 1940s, the city's wartime elite, both civilian and military, succumbed to a purge known as the Leningrad Affair. Dozens of party officials and their relatives were arrested, jailed, exiled, or shot.[23] Loyal citizens of the state refrained from speaking, out of either fear or complicity in the crimes that were committed, even descendants of a man trusted enough to cook on occasion for Stalin. Few people whose lives intersected with Stalin's, even briefly, "came through unscathed," Vladimir Vladimirovich Putin would later recall, "but my grandfather was one of them."[24] Not that he talked about it much. "My grandfather kept pretty quiet about his past life. My parents didn't talk much about the past, either. People generally didn't, back then." Vladimir's father was taciturn and severe, frightening even to people who knew him well.[25] The father's wartime experience—the limp he carried through his life, which always seemed worse when the weather turned cold—clearly made a great impression on his son. After the war, the elder Vladimir continued to work at the Yegorov Factory on Moskovsky Prospekt, which built the passenger carriages for the country's railways and subways. A member of the Communist Party, he became the factory's party representative, a blue-collar apparatchik ensuring rigor, loyalty, discipline, and, most of all, caution.

The job entitled him to a single room—180 square feet—in a decrepit communal apartment on the fifth floor of what had once been an elegant nineteenth-century apartment building at 12 Baskov Lane, not far from Leningrad's central avenue, Nevsky Prospekt, and the Griboyedov Canal. The Putins moved in in 1944 and after the war had to share the confined space with two other families. They would live there for more than two decades. The apartment had no hot water, no bathtub. A windowless hallway served as a communal kitchen, with a single gas burner opposite a sink. The toilet was in a closet jammed against a stairwell. The apartment was heated with a wood-burning stove.

Maria, like her husband, had limited education. She was ten days shy of forty-one when Vladimir was born. After so much suffering and loss, she treated her son like the miracle he seemed to be.[26] She toiled in various menial jobs, cleaning buildings, washing test tubes in a laboratory, and delivering bread, all jobs that left her more time to tend to him. An elderly couple shared one room in the apartment; an observant Jewish family, with an older daughter, Hava, shared the other. The younger Vladimir, the only child in the communal home, remembered the elderly couple fondly, and spent as much time with them as with his parents. They became surrogate grandparents, and he knew her as Baba Anya. She, like his mother, possessed deep religious faith. The Russian Orthodox Church, repressed by the Soviet regime, was allowed to function openly during the war to help rally the nation, though it would be severely repressed again when the guns fell silent. As Vladimir would later tell the story, on November 21, when he was seven weeks old, Baba Anya and Maria walked three blocks through the winter chill to the Transfiguration Cathedral, a yellow, eighteenth-century monument built in the neoclassical style of many of the city's churches, and there they secretly baptized the boy.[27]

Whether she kept the baptism secret out of fear of her stern husband or fear of official censure is not clear, though her son later suggested it might not have been as secret as she hoped. Little was ever secret in the Soviet Union. She took the boy with her to services occasionally but kept the apartment, with its lack of privacy, free of icons or other outward signs of practice.[28] Nor did she evidently discuss her beliefs with him then, certainly not in depth. It was only forty years later that Maria gave him his baptismal cross and asked him to bless it at the Church of the Holy Sepulcher in Jerusalem when he visited Israel for the first time. Faith nonetheless hovered in the background of the boy's life, along with his father's commitment to Communism's secular orthodoxy. He evinced little preference for either, though some who knew him would assert years later that his relationship with the Jewish neighbors instilled an unusual ecumenical tolerance and a disdain for the anti-Semitism that has long afflicted Russian culture.[29]

The building on Baskov Lane was Vladimir Putin's youthful universe. The gilded landmarks of tsarist Russia—the Hermitage, the Admiralty, the Peter and Paul Cathedral—were nearby but little more than distant monuments in the cityscape. He was a scion of the proletariat, not the Soviet intelligentsia or the political elite; only later, in hindsight, would he become conscious of the deprivation of his childhood. The stairs to the fifth floor were pocked with holes, fetid, and dimly lit; they smelled of sweat and boiling cabbage. The building was infested with rats, which he and his friends would chase with sticks. It was what passed for a game—until the time he cornered one at the end of a hallway. "Suddenly it lashed around and threw itself at me," he recalled. "I was surprised and frightened."[30]

He was always a slight boy. One of his earliest memories of venturing out of this cloistered childhood occurred on May Day in 1959, perhaps, or 1960. He found himself terrified of the bustle on "the big corner" at Mayakovskaya Street. A few years later, he and friends rode a commuter train to an unknown part of the city in search of adventure. It was cold and they had nothing to eat, and though they built a fire to warm themselves, they returned dejected, whereupon the elder Putin beat him with a belt as punishment.

The apartment building wrapped around an inner courtyard that linked with the neighboring building's courtyard to form an unkempt, treeless space, little better than the bottom of an airshaft. The courtyard attracted drunks and thugs, smoking, drinking, and otherwise whiling away their lives. By his own accounts and those of his friends, life in the courtyard and later in school made him rough, a brawler quick to defend against slights and threats, but it is more likely, given his size, that he was bullied. His parents doted on him, and when he was young, they refused to let him leave the courtyard without permission. He grew up in the overly protective, if not outwardly loving, embrace of parents who had miraculously survived and would do everything to ensure that their son did too. "There were no kisses," Vera Gurevich, a schoolteacher who became close to the family, remembered. "There was none of that love-dovey stuff in their house."[31]

On September 1, 1960, Vladimir began attending School No. 193, located a short walk away on the same street where he lived. He was nearly eight, Maria having kept him out of kindergarten, perhaps out of an overabundance of caution. He lacked the social adeptness he might have developed had he grown up around more children. He showed up on the first day carrying not flowers for his teacher, as tradition dictated, but a potted plant.[32] In school, he was an indifferent student, petulant and impulsive, probably a little bit spoiled. Vera Gurevich called him a whirligig because he would walk into class and spin in circles. He was highly disruptive in and out of class,[33] more inclined to hang out with boys she considered a bad influence, including two older brothers named Kovshov. He was caught in school carrying a knife, and was once rebuked for delinquency by a neighborhood party committee, which threatened to send him to an orphanage.[34] His behavior initially kept him out of the Pioneers, the Communist Party youth organization whose membership was a rite of passage; by the third grade, he was one of only a few among his forty-five classmates who had not joined. His father, as a party steward, could only have been dismayed at so conspicuous a failure, one that Vladimir later described as a rebellion against his father and the system around him. "I was a hooligan, not a Pioneer," he said.[35] Vera Gurevich, who met him in the fourth grade, eventually complained to his father that the boy was intelligent, but disorganized and uninterested.

"He's not working to his full potential," she told the senior Vladimir at the apartment on Baskov Lane, which she described as horrid, "so cold, just awful."

"Well, what can I do?" Vladimir Spiridonovich replied. "Kill him or what?"[36]

Vladimir and Maria nevertheless promised Gurevich that they would rein their son in. The father pressed him to take up boxing, though the slight boy quickly gave it up when, he said, a punch broke his nose. Instead, he turned to martial arts, apparently against the wishes of his parents, practing sambo, a Soviet style that mixed judo and wrestling and was more suited to his diminutive stature and "pugnacious nature."[37] One of his coaches became a decisive influence in his life. Anatoly Rakhlin worked at the Trud (or Labor) Club, not far from Baskov Lane, and in 1965 Putin, now in the fifth grade, joined it. Rakhlin had to reassure Vladimir's parents that "we do not teach anything bad to the kids."[38] The discipline and rigor of sambo, and later judo, intrigued the boy in a way nothing else had. The martial arts transformed his life, giving him the means of asserting himself against larger, tougher boys. "It was a tool to assert myself in the pack," he would say.[39] It also brought him a new circle of friends, especially two brothers, Arkady and Boris Rotenberg, who would stick by him throughout his life. The martial arts gave him an orthodoxy he found neither in religion nor in politics. It was more than mere sport, he believed; it was a philosophy. "It was sports that dragged me off the streets," he once recalled. "To be honest, the courtyard wasn't a very good environment for a kid."[40]

This made perhaps too much of his transformation. His claims to have lived the life of the jungle sounded more like bravado. The courtyard's squalor and abased occupants might have once intrigued him, but they also instilled a disdain for drinking and smoking, for sloth and disorder. Nevertheless, once he found his passion for the martial arts, he exhibited a steely determination to succeed. Since Trud required decent grades for membership, he made more effort in school, and by the sixth grade, his grades had improved. Vera Gurevich and his classmates resolved to get him into the Pioneers, belatedly appealing to the school's representative to make an exception for his previous lapses. His induction ceremony was held at Ulyanovka, a rustic village formerly known as Sablino, where Lenin's sister once lived.[41] Within weeks, he became the leader of his school's Pioneer branch, his first leadership position. By the eighth grade, he was among the first chosen to join the Komsomol, the Communist Party's youth organization. It was a necessary stepping stone to what he soon discovered was his life's calling.

In 1965, the twentieth anniversary of the victory over the Nazis arrived on a new wave of nostalgia and official celebration. One of the most popular novels of the decade was an espionage tale, *The Shield and the*

Sword. It first appeared as a serial in the literary magazine *Znamya,* or *Banner,* the organ of the Union of Writers. Its author, Vadim Kozhevnikov, served as a war correspondent for *Pravda,* and his experience gave the story a realistic skein, though it conformed dutifully to the narrative of Soviet propaganda. (Kozhevnikov, as head of the writers' union, was involved in the banning of a far more realistic account of the war, Vasily Grossman's *Life and Fate.*) The novel's hero, Major Aleksandr Belov, was a Soviet secret agent passing as a German in Nazi Germany just before the outbreak of the Great Patriotic War. Using the alias Johann Weiss, he rises through the ranks of the Abwehr, the Nazi military intelligence organization, and later the Schutzstaffel, or SS. Weiss is courageous in battle, stoic and unyielding, even when tortured. He is disgusted by the Nazis he has to outwardly serve, disgusted by the Nazi he has to appear to become, but obliged to endure the experience in order to sabotage the German war effort. "He had never supposed that the most difficult and torturing part of his chosen mission would be in this splitting of his own conscious self," Kozhevnikov wrote. "To begin with he had even been attracted by this game of putting on somebody else's skin and creating his thoughts and being glad when these coincided with what other people expected of this created personality."[42]

It was not Tolstoy, certainly. It was, to an impressionable teenage boy, much, much better. Three years after its publication, the book became a five-plus-hour film, with Kozhevnikov credited for the screenplay. It was the most popular movie in the Soviet Union in 1968, a black-and-white homage to the secret service—to what had by then become the KGB. Vladimir Putin, then almost sixteen, was enchanted. He and his friends watched the movie repeatedly. More than four decades later he could still remember the lyrics to the film's sentimental theme song, "Whence Does the Motherland Begin," redolent of birds and birches in the Russian heartland.[43] Vladimir promptly gave up his childhood dreams to become a sailor, as his father had, or maybe a pilot. He would become a spy, imagining himself as a future Major Belov cum Johann Weiss: handsome, fit, and empowered single-handedly to change history. "What amazed me most of all was how one man's efforts could achieve what whole armies could not," he recalled years later with the same romantic appreciation he had had in his youth. "One spy could decide the fate of thousands of people."[44]

He knew little about the KGB then or its inner workings. The father of one of his classmates had served in intelligence, but had already retired.

The film's release was part of the modernizing efforts of the KGB's new director, Yuri Andropov, who took over in 1967. Andropov intended to remake the agency's image, casting it not as a dreaded secret police force responsible for repression and terror, but rather as the defender of the great Soviet nation. In Vladimir's case at least, the propaganda accomplished its aims; sports may have dragged him off the streets, but the movie inspired his career. The day after he saw the first episode he told a classmate he would be a spy,[45] and soon after that, as he recounted the tale, he did an audacious and naïve thing. He walked unannounced into the office of the local KGB headquarters on Liteiny Prospekt, not far from his apartment, and volunteered his service.

The KGB's headquarters in Leningrad was known as the Big House, not merely because of its size. A sardonic joke circulated about its enormity, one told in variations in many Soviet cities: From St. Isaac's Cathedral, you can see all of Leningrad. From the Big House, you can see all the way to the Solovetsky Islands—the archipelago in the White Sea hundreds of miles to the north that included a notorious precursor of the Gulag's labor camps. Vladimir had to try three times before he found the right entrance at the Big House and an officer who would meet him. The officer indulged the boy, but told him flatly that the KGB did not accept volunteers. Instead, it sought out those considered worthy, those already in the army or at the university. Vladimir pressed. He wanted to know what course of study would best serve this new ambition of his. The officer, seemingly eager to get rid of him, suggested law school, and that decided the matter. He would go to university and study law, against the wishes of his parents, who thought his grades and temperament better suited him for a technical school, like the Academy of Civil Aviation, which he initially aspired to attend. Vladimir could be impulsive and unbending, though. His parents and his coaches were puzzled by his new purpose, as he had not told them of his journey to the Big House and thus the real motive for attending law school. One coach at Trud berated him when he learned his choice, presuming it would make him a prosecutor or police officer. A furious Vladimir exhorted, "I'm not going to be a cop!"[46]

His decision to join the KGB came amid the international tumult of 1968. Only days before he began secondary school in Leningrad, the Soviet Union invaded Czechoslovakia to crush the reforms of the Prague Spring. Vladimir seemed untroubled by the crackdown on dissent, either at home or abroad. Like many, he flirted with the forbidden culture of the West, listening to the Beatles on recordings passed between friends like contraband. "The music was like a breath of fresh air," he would say later, "like a window on the outside world."[47] Vladimir played the accordion for a while, and later, on a guitar his father gave him, he learned the folk songs of Vladimir Vysotsky and other bards of the era. Although the late 1960s in the Soviet Union were viewed as an era of repression and then stagnation, his teenage years were far more carefree than anything his parents' generation had experienced. The Putins were not part of the cosseted elite, but standards of living had risen after the war, and the family, too, became more comfortable. Vladimir and Maria even had a large black telephone at the apartment, which was still a rarity, and Vladimir and his friends would make calls from it.[48] By then, they were affluent enough to buy a three-room dacha in Tosno, a small village outside Leningrad, where he spent many of his teenage years with a core group of friends, outside the claustrophobic environment of the communal apartment. On the wall above a table in the dacha hung a printed portrait that one friend, Viktor Borisenko, did not recognize. When he asked about it, Vladimir explained that it was Jan Karlovich Berzin, a founder of the Bolsheviks' military intelligence branch. He was arrested in the Great Terror in 1937 and executed a year later, but he had been rehabilitated posthumously.[49]

Vladimir attended secondary school at School No. 281, a selective, specialized scientific academy intended to prepare students for university. He was not an overly popular student, but rather a brash one, obsessed with sports and almost militantly studious.[50] Although studying sciences might have guaranteed him a spot at a prestigious technical university, he pursued the humanities, literature, and history. He also continued lessons in German, which he began studying in the fourth grade with the encouragement of Vera Gurevich. This time his teacher was Mina Yuditskaya, who would describe him as a modest, though serious student. She would have a deep influence on him, and he would remember her decades later with a sentimental fondness.[51] School No. 281 tolerated, within limits, intellectual openness and debate. A popular teacher, Mikhail Demenkov, distributed samizdat, the banned literature circulated in carbon copies. A history teacher, Tamara Stelmakhova, held discussions on whether Nikita Khrushchev might ultimately have fulfilled his promise to build a truly communist state within twenty years.[52]

Although he joined the Komsomol in 1967, he rarely participated in its activities, devoting himself instead to sports and schoolwork to the exclusion of other teenage preoccupations. Vera Brileva, a girl two years younger, recalled him hunched over his desk, which stood in the communal living room next to a sofa and a buffet. She met him at the dacha in Tosno in 1969 and was smitten. She recalled a brief kiss during a game of "spin the bottle"—"I felt so hot all of a sudden"—but she soon found he had little time for girls, something even his teacher noticed.[53] Their youthful courtship ended one day when she interrupted his studies at the apartment by asking whether he remembered something or another. She had not finished the sentence when he cut her off. "I only remember things I need to remember," he snapped at her.[54] Interviewed many years later, she remembered his "small, strong hands" and sounded wistful about the rebuff.

Such assiduousness paid off. In his last two years of secondary school—Soviet education consisted of only ten years—he earned good, though not particularly impressive, grades. He did well in history and German, less so in math and science. In his last year, he devoted himself less to classwork than to cramming for the entrance exams that could earn him a coveted spot at Leningrad State University, one of the most prestigious in the Soviet Union. Vera Gurevich expressed doubts that he could get in and never knew the real reason he wanted to. "I'll solve that problem myself," he told her.[55] The chances of getting into Leningrad State were so low, with roughly one in forty applicants being accepted, that there has been speculation that he was accepted either because of his working-class roots or even, improbably, because of the silent hand of the KGB stealthily guiding his career without even his knowledge.[56] Nonetheless, he scored well enough on his exams and was accepted into the university's law department in the fall of 1970, just as the KGB officer had suggested two years before.

As a college student, he continued to study rigorously and devote much of his time to judo competitions, forswearing smoking and drinking in order to stay fit. He refused offers to join the Leningrad University judo team, remaining loyal to his coaches at Trud. He became a master in the sport in 1973 and competed in several city and regional championships. He still lived in the communal apartment, but he traveled more widely inside the Soviet Union. He attended judo competitions as far away as Moldova, cut timber one summer in Komi in the north, and spent two weeks in a student construction camp in Abkhazia, then a region of the Soviet republic of Georgia. He earned 800 rubles, or nearly

$600 at the time, buying a coat that he would wear for the next fifteen years and squandering the rest in Gagra, a resort on the lushly wooded coast of the Black Sea.[57] He and his friends managed to sneak onto a ferry headed to Odessa, with little money and only tinned meat to eat. For two nights he slept in a lifeboat, envying the passengers with cabins but also captivated by the night sky. "The stars seemed to just hang there," he recalled. "Sailors might be used to that, but for me it was a wondrous discovery."[58]

In 1972, his mother won a car after buying a thirty-kopek lottery ticket. She could have sold the car for 3,500 rubles, but indulgently gave it to her son. It only was a small, boxy Zaporozhets, but relatively few adults, let alone college students, had their own cars in the Soviet Union in the 1970s. For Vladimir, it was a status symbol, and a new diversion. He drove everywhere, going to his matches and giving friends lifts just for the sake of driving. He was also a wild and reckless driver. Once he hit a man who lurched into the road, though he claimed the man was trying to commit suicide. In some accounts, he chased the man as he stumbled away, but Vladimir denied it. "I'm not a beast," he insisted.[59]

He spent four years at the university before he was approached by a mysterious man, who, he later learned, served in the KGB division that oversaw universities. By then, he had all but given up on his teenage ambitions. He interned one summer with the criminal division of the local Transportation Ministry, taking part in the investigation of an airplane crash, and seemed destined to become an officer with the local prosecutor, as his coach had warned him would happen. The law appealed to Vladimir as martial arts did. It imposed rules and order, which he came to respect more than any ideology. He claimed he never worked for—or even heard from—the KGB as a student, though collaboration with the secret services was common among university students. Thus when the recruitment he had long coveted finally came in 1974, during his fourth year, it came, he would say, as a surprise. The man never really introduced himself. "I need to talk to you about your career assignment," he told Vladimir on the telephone, refusing to speak in detail. Vladimir sensed the significance of the encounter though and agreed to meet later in the university's faculty lounge. After arriving on time, he waited twenty minutes, angrily assuming he might be the victim of a prank. The man showed up and, breathlessly, apologized, something that impressed the young man deeply.[60]

Vladimir underwent a thorough background check. A last step involved an interview with his father, and in January 1975, a middle-aged officer named Dmitri Gantserov visited Vladimir Spiridonovich. The senior Putin was not very tall, Gantserov thought, a simple, honest, hardworking man who was proud that his son had gone to university and was now being considered for the security services. He understood the responsibility and difficulty of the tasks ahead of his son. He then spoke earnestly, almost pleadingly, to this stranger. "Volodya is everything for us," he told him, using the diminutive form of his son's name. "And all our hopes are tied only to him. After all, you know, two sons of ours died. After the war we decided to have a child. Now we live only Volodya's life. We already lived ours."[61]

Although his Volodya must have been aware of what the KGB did, the young man was untroubled by its history, by its role policing the enemies of the state, whether at home or abroad. On the contrary, he considered it the duty of a proper Soviet citizen to cooperate with the KGB—not for money, but for the security of the state. "The cooperation of normal citizens was an important tool for the state's viable activity," he said.[62] There might have been excesses, he understood, but the cult of personality around Stalin had been dismantled shortly after his birth, the victims of his terror gradually released from the Gulag. He did not give it much thought otherwise. As far as he was concerned, the crimes of the past that killed or ruined millions were old history, and he was not unusual in that. For many Russians, even those who suffered under his tyranny, Stalin remained the revered father of the nation who led the country to victory over the Nazis; the darker recesses of his rule were suppressed, either by fear, complicity, or guilt, leaving a conflicted legacy that would dominate Soviet society for decades. As he later recalled, he himself was "an utterly successful product of the patriotic education of a Soviet man."[63]

CHAPTER 2

A Warm Heart, a Cool Head, and Clean Hands

Vladimir Putin fulfilled his dream of joining the KGB in the summer of 1975, but he never became the secret agent of his childhood imagination. His induction was routine, aside from a comic miscommunication that occurred when he appeared that spring before the university employment commission that assigned graduates their careers in the Soviet system. An official from the university's law department announced that he would be joining the Leningrad bar after all. Only then did a KGB officer monitoring the assignments stir in the corner of the room. "Oh, no," the officer said. "That question has already been decided."[1] Vladimir did not even know his assignment, but he was delighted. "Let's go," he told his childhood friend, Viktor Borisenko, after picking him up in his car. It was clear to Borisenko that something important had happened, but Vladimir would not so much as hint at what it was. They went to a Georgian restaurant near the Kazan Cathedral, the colonnaded landmark on Nevsky Prospekt, eating chicken in walnut sauce and, to Borisenko's surprise, for his friend had never before allowed the indulgence, drinking shots of sweet liqueur.[2] Only much later did he learn that they had been celebrating his friend's acceptance into the KGB.

By the time Vladimir joined, the KGB had grown into a vast bureaucracy that oversaw not only domestic and foreign intelligence matters, but also counterintelligence at home and abroad, military counterintelligence, enforcement of the border and customs, and physical protection of the political leadership and government facilities like the country's nuclear sites. There were directorates that oversaw communications and cryptography, and that monitored telephone calls. The Sixth Directorate monitored "economic security" by policing speculation, currency exchanges, and other signs of deviant free-market activity. The

Fifth Chief Directorate, created in 1969 to "protect" the Constitution, enforced party loyalty and harassed dissidents in all walks of life. The KGB was more than just a security agency; it was a state within the state, ever in search of enemies within and without. It ostensibly served the interests of the Communist Party—and acted on its orders—but its vast powers also served as a check on the party's power.[3]

Vladimir went to work at the Secretariat of the Directorate, the personnel office of the KGB's Leningrad headquarters, housed in the same building on Liteiny Prospekt that he had visited as a teenager. Only now he was no Johann Weiss infiltrating the ranks of a foreign power. It was a time of relative peace, and the Soviet Union at the time was at war only with itself. He was a junior bureaucrat, twenty-three years old, pushing papers at work and still living at home with his parents without a room of his own. His was a drab office, populated by balding veterans of Stalin's times who were old enough to remember the Gulag, if not the Terror of 1937. The young agent claimed to question the old ways, but he never rebelled against the KGB, certainly not in a way that would undermine his budding career by, as the saying went, "sticking out his ears."[4]

After his initiation at a desk, he attended officer training at School No. 401 in Leningrad, one of the KGB's regional training academies. Located inside a heavily guarded, six-story building near where the Okhta River meets the Neva, the school was "a kind of submarine" where cadets immersed themselves in classroom studies and physical training, cut off from the rest of society.[5] For six months, he learned basic intelligence tactics, including interrogation techniques. The KGB's ranks had swollen under Yuri Andropov, who served as its chairman from 1967 until 1982, when he became the paramount leader of the Soviet Union. Andropov became one of Vladimir's heroes, a distant and yet revered leader. Andropov understood the limits of the Soviet system and sought to modernize it so it could catch up to the West, especially in economic affairs. The KGB sought out recruits who understood macroeconomics, trade, and international relations. Vladimir seems to have anticipated this with his studies at Leningrad State University, where he wrote a thesis on the principle of most-favored-nation status in international trade.[6] Andropov wanted to turn the KGB into an elite cadre, and Vladimir was a believer. He represented a new generation in the KGB, the post-Stalin generation of recruits who were thought to be less ideological, too young to remember the horrors of Stalin's regime.

Andropov was viewed, within the Soviet context, as a reformer, despite his involvement in repression at home and abroad. He had been the Soviet ambassador to Budapest during the Hungarian Uprising in 1956 and was haunted for the rest of his life by the swift violence that could erupt and threaten one-party rule. He "watched in horror from the windows of his embassy as officers of the hated Hungarian security service were strung up from lampposts."[7] This "Hungarian complex" shaped Andropov's belief that only force, wisely administered, could ensure the survival of the Soviet state and empire. Thus while Andropov might have wanted to modernize the Soviet system, he ruthlessly punished dissent against it. It was he who created the notorious Fifth Chief Directorate to combat ideological opposition, which led to the persecution of the physicist Andrei Sakharov and the author Aleksandr Solzhenitsyn. It was he who, in 1969, created a network of psychiatric hospitals to persecute dissidents by classifying opposition to the state as evidence of mental illness.

Vladimir, blinkered by official propaganda or by indifference, rationalized and romanticized the KGB's work. He believed the intelligence officer was the defender of law and order. In the summer of 1976, he emerged from the KGB's academy as a first lieutenant. He did not return to the personnel department, but rather to the counterintelligence department, the KGB's Second Chief Directorate. He took part in operations not against the enemy outside, but against the enemy within. He became an apparatchik who sought, above all, to maintain social order and political control, though very little was known about his activities at the time. His friends, and even his colleagues, could never be sure exactly what he did, and he went to great lengths for many years to keep the details of his work secret. An officer who worked with him later stated as a matter of fact that he worked for the Fifth Chief Directorate, but no one could be certain.[8] Although Vladimir would deny it, his colleague believed he was intimately familiar with the tactics the KGB employed against critics of Soviet power, including Solzhenitsyn and, later, Sakharov. Certainly, one of his closest friends in Leningrad, Viktor Cherkesov, became notorious for his work in the Fifth Chief Directorate against dissidents, including religious believers.[9] And he felt no remorse or reservation about the KGB's reliance on informants or collaborators. Although they sowed distrust throughout Soviet society, he believed that collusion with a feared police state not only was not wrong, but rather was essential to maintaining order. Ninety percent of the KGB's intelligence, he once claimed, derived from ordinary Soviet citizens willingly or otherwise informing on others, their coworkers, their friends, their relatives. "You cannot do anything without secret agents," he said.[10]

Vladimir, evidently, collected and controlled agents during his stint in counterintelligence in Leningrad, especially businessmen, journalists, and athletes who had traveled abroad or met with visiting foreigners. Though his activities remain shrouded in secrecy even now, he had become something closer to the "cop" his coach had warned he would become if he went to law school. He lived a double life, but a far less dramatic and dangerous one than that of *The Shield and the Sword.* It was among this cadre that he forged friendships with men who worked with him in the shadows and would do so for years to come: Viktor Cherkesov, Aleksandr Bortnikov, Viktor Ivanov, Sergei Ivanov, and Nikolai Patrushev. In this close, closed circle of friends—all men—he found camaraderie among like-minded officers who reinforced what would become a stark, black-and-white view of the world.

After six months in counterintelligence, Vladimir transferred to the KGB's First Chief Directorate, responsible for intelligence operations beyond the Soviet Union's borders. It was considered the KGB's elite branch. Of nearly three hundred thousand employees of the security apparatus, fewer than five thousand served in the department.[11] His study of German no doubt helped him land the post, and the KGB enabled him to continue to study two hours a day, three times a week.[12] Still, he did not become a spy, and he did not go abroad. He remained in the Big House on Liteiny Prospekt, responsible for shadowing foreign visitors and diplomats stationed in the city's consulates. Much of the work was analytical, and it was hardly demanding. As the Soviet Union's second city, Leningrad was not exactly a backwater posting, but it lacked the cloak-and-dagger intrigues that swirled around the capital, Moscow. The KGB itself had begun to succumb to bloat and sclerosis, its swelling ranks resulting in a reduction of efficiency. For many agents, the youthful enthusiasm for the world of espionage inevitably succumbed to tedium and bureaucratic inertia. "It's only in fiction that a lone man can take on the whole world," a contemporary, Yuri Shvets, wrote of the era.[13]

Vladimir seemed content to toil in the lower ranks. Though described by one of his superiors as meticulous in his work,[14] he displayed no driving ambition to climb through the organization. In 1977, his father retired from the train factory and, as a disabled war veteran, received a small two-bedroom apartment—not even three hundred square feet—on Stachek Prospekt in Avtovo, a newly reconstructed district south of Leningrad's historic district. The city's postwar housing crunch was such that many families still lived in communal housing—even officers of the KGB did not automatically qualify for an apartment—and yet now, at twenty-five, for the first time in his life, Vladimir had his own bedroom, his own "little corner," as Vera Gurevich called it.

With abundant free time, he careered around the city in the car his mother had given him and, according to his friends, continued to involve himself in street fights, despite the risk such indiscretions could cause his career. He was indifferent to risk and danger—he proudly recounted a poor performance evaluation that said as much—in part because his KGB service provided him some protection from the ordinary police. He bent the rules because he could. One Easter he took Sergei Roldugin, a classical musician who became a close friend, to a religious procession that he had been assigned to monitor, policing the faithful, people like his own mother. He impressed his friend by taking him to see the altar of the church, access to which was prohibited to laymen, suggesting that Putin had little reverence for the sanctity of the church. "Nobody can go there, but we can," he told his friend. He was reckless and temperamental. On the way home from their church tour, as Roldugin recalled, a cluster of drunken students at a bus stop accosted them for a cigarette. Vladimir, clearly an unintimidating presence, rebuffed them so rudely that one shoved him. Putin threw him over his shoulder as if it were a match in the judo club.[15]

He told his friends he was a police officer with the Interior Ministry, and many, it seems, believed it. Soon, though, it became harder to disguise his actual position. Roldugin, who met him in 1977, quickly discerned the truth. It made him wary. As a musician, he had traveled abroad on visits monitored by KGB operatives barely disguised as officials of the Ministry of Culture. Roldugin disliked these ideological minders and learned not to speak freely around them. And yet here he was, becoming friends with one of them. Vladimir disarmed him finally by admitting his true profession, though even then Roldugin found it impossible to draw him out further. "I play the cello," he once told his friend. "I could never be a surgeon—still, I'm a good cellist. But what is your profession? I know you're an intelligence officer. I don't know what

that means." Vladimir humored him, but only a little. "I'm a specialist
in human relations," he said cryptically, and then refused to talk about
it anymore.[16]

By 1979, Vladimir reached the rank of captain and was, at last, sent
to Moscow to attend the KGB's Higher School, which was named after
Felix Dzerzhinsky, the founder of the Soviet secret police. Dzerzhinsky remained a revered cult figure in the KGB, whose training manuals
quoted his description of the intelligence officer's essential characteristics: "a warm heart, a cool head, and clean hands."[17] At last, the First
Chief Directorate seemed to be grooming him for service abroad. And
yet, after a short course, he again returned to Leningrad and resumed the
task of monitoring foreigners—with uncertain success. One supervisor
described his work as "extremely productive," but the senior KGB official in Leningrad during his career, Oleg Kalugin, said that the agency
failed to uncover a single foreign spy on the loose in the city.[18]

His career seemed to stall just as the Soviet Union's relative period
of peace and détente began to face increasing turmoil at home and
beyond—in retrospect, the first signs of the decay and ultimate collapse of the Soviet Union. In December 1979, the Soviet Union invaded
Afghanistan after a bloody coup orchestrated by Andropov's KGB and
carried out by the military's elite commandos wearing Afghan uniforms.
The invasion began a futile operation to support the Communist government in Kabul that would cost the lives of thousands of soldiers,
whose bodies were brought home in zinc boxes known by the code name
CARGO 200 and kept shrouded in secrecy.

The election of Ronald Reagan as president of the United States
in November 1980 further inflamed Cold War tensions and pushed
the two superpowers ever closer to confrontation. The Kremlin and
the KGB soon became obsessed with what Soviet leaders believed to
be Reagan's plans to launch a preemptive nuclear strike against the
Soviet Union. At a conference in May 1981, an already ailing Leonid
Brezhnev denounced Reagan as a threat to world peace, while Andropov
announced that henceforth the ultimate priority of the security services
was to uncover evidence of Reagan's plan to destroy the country.[19] This
vast operation—code-named RYAN, after the Russian for "nuclear missile attack," *raketno-yadernoye napadenie*—became the principal intelligence effort of KGB bureaus around the world and remained a paranoid
obsession for the rest of the decade. Soon Vladimir Putin would play his
part in it.

In 1980, after he returned to Leningrad, Vladimir's personal life—and career—took an important turn. Unusually for Soviet society, he remained unmarried at twenty-eight. His bachelorhood was ill suited to the conservative KGB. The First Chief Directorate, in fact, refused to post single men abroad, fearing that sexual liaisons outside marriage could leave them vulnerable to exposure or blackmail.[20] Vladimir was not unattractive, with deep blue eyes. He was fit and quick-witted, if sardonically so. When it came to women, though, he seemed emotionally reticent, even stunted; he was far more at ease with the circle of male friends from his youth and the KGB. "I often used to tell him that he was terrible at making conversation," Roldugin said.[21]

Late in his university years, Vladimir had had his first serious relationship with a medical student. Her name was Lyudmila Khmarina, whose brother, Viktor Khmarin, was also a close friend. Roldugin described her as pretty and headstrong, inclined less to ask how Vladimir felt than to tell him when he was ill. They met at his family's dacha in Tosno and dated through graduation and the launch of his career. In 1979 they became engaged. They applied for a marriage license, and their parents bought rings, a suit, and a dress. And then suddenly he broke off the relationship. He decided "it was better to suffer then than to have both of us suffer later," but he never explained what happened, not even to Roldugin. He would only hint at "some intrigue," though it seemed not to have been especially bitter, since he would remain friends with her brother Viktor for years to come. Vladimir had grown used to the bachelor's life—perhaps preferred it, as a pampered son still living at home. He assumed he might never marry.[22]

In March 1980, however, he met another Lyudmila—Lyudmila Shkrebneva, a blue-eyed stewardess for Aeroflot who lived in Kaliningrad, the former Prussian province seized by the Soviet Union after the Nazi defeat. She was twenty-two and had blonde hair that flowed in waves to her shoulders. She and another stewardess, Galina, visited Leningrad for three days. On their first night in town, eager to take in as many of the city's sights as possible, they went with Galina's boyfriend, Andrei, to the Lensovet Theatre to see a performance by Arkady Raikin, an aging actor and satirist. Galina had invited Lyudmila, and so Andrei brought along his friend, Vladimir. Lyudmila was initially unimpressed, noting his shabby clothes and unprepossessing demeanor. Had she met him on the street, she recalled, she "would not have paid attention to him."[23] During the intermission, though, she grew bold and asked if he could help them acquire tickets to the musical performance the next night. He did, and by the end of the second night he gave her his telephone number. Andrei was shocked. "Are you crazy?" he asked his friend later. He had never before seen him give his number to someone he did not know well.[24] They met again the third night, and when she returned to Kaliningrad, she called the number.

When she flew again to Leningrad in July, they began a relationship. She joked that other girls took the bus or trolley to dates, while she flew to hers.[25] Soon she resolved to move to Leningrad. Vladimir urged her to return to college—she had dropped out of a technical college to become a stewardess—and she enrolled in the philology department at his alma mater, Leningrad State University. The stress of the move and the studies ruptured their relationship at first, and she broke it off until he flew to Kaliningrad and persuaded her to return. By October, she had settled in a communal apartment that she shared with a woman whose son had left to serve in the army.[26] Vladimir proved to be a demanding, jealous boyfriend; she felt he was always watching her, testing her, judging her. He would declare his intention—whether it was to go skiing, say, or for her to take a typing course—and leave her no room to argue. Unlike the first Lyudmila, she was more pliant. When Vladimir's mother met her, she was not impressed and, worse, told her so. Her son already had another Lyudmila, Maria huffed, a "good girl."

Lyudmila did not know he worked for the KGB. He had told her, too, that he worked for the criminal investigations branch of the Ministry of the Interior. It was a common cover for intelligence agents, and he had even been issued a false identification card.[27] Whenever she asked what he did during the day, he evaded her questions with quips. "Before lunch, we caught," he told her once, as if he and his colleagues had spent the day fishing. "After lunch we released."[28] It was not until 1981, after they had been dating for a year and a half, that she learned his true employment—and even then it was from the wife of a friend. She felt a tingle of excitement and pride. Unlike Roldugin, she had no reason to fear the KGB, or this young man. His taciturn manner now seemed understandable, explaining what had seemed elusive. When her friend told her, it was a revelation, but also an unsettling one. Being with him meant accepting that a part of him would always remain beyond her grasp.[29] It even occurred to her that the woman who had revealed his secret might well have been instructed to do so. She was never sure. Only then did she remember an odd encounter some months before.

She had agreed to phone Putin one evening at seven o'clock, as she often did. Because her communal apartment had no telephone, she went to a public telephone in a courtyard nearby. As it grew dark, she dialed his number, but he did not answer. She gave up, knowing his penchant for working late. As she was leaving, a young man approached her in the quiet, empty space. She turned to return to her apartment through the courtyard's arched entrance, and still he followed. He quickened his pace, and so did she.

"Young lady, please, I'm not doing anything bad. I only want to talk to you. Only two seconds." He seemed sincere, speaking from the heart. She stopped. "Young lady, it's fate. It's fate! How I wanted to meet you."

"What are you talking about?" she replied dismissively. "It's not fate."

"Well, please, I beg you. Give me your telephone number."

"I don't have a telephone."

"Then write down mine," he said. He was offering his number the way Putin had on their second date.

"I won't," she replied, before at last he let her go.[30]

The half-forgotten episode came back to her in a puzzling rush. Had the KGB—had Vladimir—tested her on the darkening street? If she were the type of woman who would strike up a relationship with any man on the street, that might provoke a husband's jealousy, exposing her or him to counterespionage or blackmail. Or maybe he was just a brash young man who hoped to get to know her. She was not unnerved exactly, but now she grasped what kind of life she would enter with this man. Some might be afraid of such a test, she assured herself, but it would be silly to let it upset her. She had nothing to hide, after all. She did not resent his work—"Work is work," she shrugged—but when she asked him about the encounter, more than once, he refused to answer, which did upset her. She knew he would never tell her anything about the other world he occupied, never put her mind at ease by explaining why he came home say at midnight instead of nine o'clock. She would worry, then grow angry, but always have to wait, alone and unknowing. His work at the KGB would leave its mark on her. She could never speak of his job or be open with people about her life or theirs together. Marrying Putin would be a "private ban" on her own life, she knew. She fell in love with the man, slowly, but it felt oppressive.[31]

Vladimir could be bold and impetuous, but in courtship, he dallied. He did use his position—and his salary—to travel with her. Twice they went to the Black Sea, which he had loved since his trip as a young student staring at the stars. They once drove with friends to Sochi, the resort town more than a thousand miles to the south. They stayed in a two-room apartment reserved for the guards of Bocharov Ruchei, the seaside mansion built on the orders of Nikita Khrushchev in the 1950s for the Soviet elite and that one day in the unforeseeable future would become the retreat of the presidents of a new Russia. Leonid Brezhnev convalesced there in the listless final years of his rule. From the balcony of their room, they could see the beach, but access to it was forbidden. In 1981 they returned to the Black Sea, this time staying two weeks in Sudak on the Crimea, their first trip alone.[32] It was hardly a whirlwind romance, though. When at last he asked her to marry him, it was April 1983, and she thought he was breaking off the relationship.

"In three and a half years, you have probably made up your mind," he told her at his apartment.

"Yes," she said, hesitantly, fearing the end. "I have made up my mind."

He seemed doubtful. "Yes?" he replied, and then added, "Well, then, if that's the way it is, I love you and propose that we get married."[33]

He had already settled on the date: July 28, then only three months away. They had a civil ceremony, not a religious one, which would have been forbidden for a KGB officer, and then two wedding celebrations. Twenty friends and relatives attended the first aboard a floating restaurant moored to the embankment beside Leningrad State University. A night later they held a different gathering in a more private space, a banquet hall in the Moscow Hotel. To Lyudmila, the first was warm and joyful; the second was more ceremonial, pleasant enough, but "a little bit different." In attendance were Vladimir's colleagues from the KGB who could not risk their confidentiality, even to the relatives and closest friends of one of their comrades.

They honeymooned in Ukraine, first driving to Kyiv, where they met friends who traveled with them, often sharing a room. They toured Moldova, then Lviv in western Ukraine, Nikolayev, and finally Crimea, staying in Yalta, all holiday landmarks of the vast Soviet empire. In Yalta, the newlyweds had a room of their own, and they stayed for twelve days, swimming and sunbathing on the rocky shore.[34] Crimea seemed a magical, sacred place to him. They returned, via Moscow so he could drop by the KGB headquarters—the Center, as it was known—and then they moved into his parents' two-bedroom apartment on Stachek Lane. He was thirty, she twenty-five, and together they settled into a happy, if constrained, marriage.

One colleague, Igor Antonov, believed Vladimir married to advance his career, knowing that bachelorhood would hold him back.[35] He certainly seemed to have thought it all out carefully, and his career break came a year later. The KGB promoted him to major after nine years of service and sent him to study in Moscow at the elite school of foreign intelligence, the Red Banner Institute. Founded in 1938, it was boot camp for the Soviet Union's foreign spies. The institute was not only ideologically exclusive, it also discriminated on racial and ethnic lines. Jews were banned, as were Crimean Tatars, Chechens, and Kalmyks. Religious practice of any sort was forbidden. His admission may well have resulted from the KGB's version of affirmative action. By the 1980s, the First Chief Directorate began to complain that too many of its cadets were "the spoiled children of privileged parents" who used their influence and connections in Moscow to gain entry. Instead, it wanted robust candidates with an aptitude for languages and absolute devotion to the Soviet cause. The directorate tried to expand its recruiting pool by increasing the proportion of cadets from the provinces, asking regional headquarters to nominate young officers.[36] Leningrad sent Vladimir Putin.

The institute was now named after Andropov. After his long reign at the helm of the KGB, he took over as the secretary general of the Communist Party after Brezhnev's death in 1982, raising the hopes of those who wanted to modernize the state under the firm hand of the security services. Instead, Andropov served only fifteen months before he died suddenly in February 1984, beginning a tumultuous turnover of geriatric Soviet leaders. Konstantin Chernenko replaced Andropov just months before Vladimir began attending the Red Banner Institute, and barely survived a year before dying in March 1985. The great Soviet nation suddenly seemed unable to generate new leaders, lumbering through a period of economic and political stagnation that left it falling ever further behind the West and the "main adversary," the United States. The Soviet war in Afghanistan had descended into a quagmire, and those in Vladimir's intelligence circles had the confidence to discuss truths about it that could never be uttered publicly. He was stunned by the revelations, having believed reflexively in the righteousness of the intervention.[37]

The institute was a secret facility located in a forest outside Mos-

cow, where it remains today under a new name, the Academy of Foreign
Intelligence. It offered courses that lasted one to three years, depending
on a cadet's education, experience, and expected assignment.[38] Lyudmila, now pregnant, remained in Leningrad, living with his parents. It
was here that Vladimir learned spy craft—how to recruit agents, to communicate in code, to conduct surveillance, to lose a tail, to make and
use dead-letter boxes. Above all, he was learning the art of deep cover.
Throughout the training, cadets adopted code names, derived from the
first letter of their names. Putin became Comrade Platov, protecting his
real identity even from other students. They wore civilian clothes, not
uniforms, preparing for their futures posing as journalists, diplomats,
or trade delegates in countries they would be expected to know intimately, before having visited them. Vladimir showed up in September
1984, wearing a new three-piece suit, eager to impress, even though it
was a warm fall day. "Look at Comrade Platov, now!" an instructor, Colonel Mikhail Frolov, told the other cadets, citing this slight young man
as a model.[39]

At last, after nearly a decade of tedium monitoring foreigners and
dissidents in Leningrad, he was learning the craft that he had imagined
as a youth. The institute's three main departments were headed at the
time by veterans of the KGB's "golden age" of espionage—the years
before, during, and after World War II: Yuri Modin in political intelligence, Ivan Shishkin in counterintelligence, and Vladimir Barkovsky
in scientific and technological intelligence. All made their reputations
as spies in London, and Modin was the last controller of the group that
became known as the Magnificent Five, the young Cambridge graduates,
including Kim Philby, who were recruited during the 1930s as agents of
the Soviet Union and ultimately penetrated the highest levels of British power. Although long since exposed and dismantled, the operation
remained "a model for young intelligence officers" at the institute.[40]
Comrade Platov was learning from the KGB's stars.

On April 28, 1985, while still completing her university degree,
Lyudmila gave birth to a daughter. She wanted to name her Natasha, but
Vladimir had already made up his mind. She would be named Maria,
or Masha, after his mother. He missed his daughter's birth, but after the
mother and child were released from the hospital, he received a pass to
visit and celebrated his new family with Sergei Roldugin, who became
Maria's godfather, at the dacha of Roldugin's father near Vyborg, by the
Finnish border. Though she did not know it, Lyudmila herself was un-

dergoing a thorough background check of her health and temperament; she learned of it only after she was summoned by the university administration office and told that she had been cleared of any suspicion.[41]

Vladimir was now an established family man at the most critical juncture in his life so far. His hopes for going abroad—for moving up to the elite work of foreign intelligence—depended on his success at the Red Banner Institute, and this was decidedly mixed. It was clear from his language immersion that he would serve in a German-speaking country. The only question was whether he would be assigned to the capitalist West—meaning West Germany, Austria, or Switzerland—or the Soviet satellite in the east, the German Democratic Republic. Serving undercover in the West would have required another year or two at the institute, with deeper and deeper training in local customs that often betrayed foreign origins—basic aspects of capitalist life, like mortgages, could stump and betray a Soviet operative.[42] Vladimir would later claim that he preferred to serve in East Germany, but the choice was not his to make.

The institute's graduation commission decided on assignments based on performance and personal comportment. And despite the stakes, his behavior put it all at risk. He was able to return to Leningrad for short breaks, and during one of them, he again got into a fight, during a confrontation on the metro with a group of hooligans, as he recounted to Sergei Roldugin. This time, he suffered as much as those he confronted, breaking his arm in the fight. He told Roldugin there would be consequences, and indeed he was reprimanded, though he never explained the punishment to his friend. "He has a fault which is objectively bad for the special services: he takes risks," Roldugin said. "One should be more cautious, and he is not."[43]

His evaluation at the end of his year in training was mediocre. He did not suffer from excessive ambition—the word "careerist" was practically a slur in the Soviet system—but Colonel Frolov noted several negative characteristics. He was "withdrawn and uncommunicative." While "sharp witted," he also possessed "a certain academic tendency," a polite way of describing his pedantic manner.[44] He did not have the family connections or background to grease the path to a prestigious posting. The fight on the metro in Leningrad almost certainly contributed to the abrupt end of his studies at the Red Banner Institute. Instead of continuing for another two years of grooming for the elite ranks of spy craft, he left at the end of the first. And when he received his assignment, it was not to West Germany, but to the East. It was not even to Berlin, a hub of Cold War espionage since the defeat of the Nazis, but rather to Dresden, the provincial capital of Saxony, near the border with Czechoslovakia. For the first time, he received a foreign passport. He was almost thirty-three and had never left the Soviet Union before.

CHAPTER 3

The Devoted Officer of a Dying Empire

O f all the socialist states established by the victorious Soviet Union
after the war, the German Democratic Republic seemed to have built
the workers' paradise Communism promised—only one managed by
oppression and terror as much as by ideology. The Ministry of State
Security—the Stasi—maintained a network of 91,000 employees, with
at least 173,000 informants, maybe more, in a nation of seventeen million people. "One can no more place a boundary around the Stasi,"
one historian wrote about the ministry's omnipresence, "than one can
encircle a scent in a room."[1] To Vladimir Putin, newly promoted to the
rank of major, it seemed he had moved backward in time. He considered
East Germany "a harshly totalitarian country,"[2] not so much a nation as
a pervasive security apparatus. He liked it very much.

The KGB maintained an enormous presence in East Germany. At
its base in Karlshorst in Berlin, where the Soviet army was also headquartered, it employed hundreds of workers throughout the Cold War.
The Stasi's officers—"dear friends," as their Soviet counterparts invariably called them—were both allies and rivals. The Stasi did much of
the KGB's political work, providing the majority of intelligence reports
cabled back to the Center in Moscow—not only from Germany but
from all of the Soviet bloc. The KGB also treated its "dear friends" with
patronizing wariness that the Germans resented. One of the KGB's biggest operations, begun in the 1970s in Brezhnev's time and code-named
LUCH, or "beam," furtively recruited German agents to monitor and
deliver reports on their own party leaders, government officials, and
ordinary people for disloyalty to the Soviet cause.[3]

The KGB residence in Berlin was the largest in the world. By contrast, the office in Dresden was a tiny outpost of the agency's worldwide
intrigue. The city, straddling the Elbe River, never had more than six

to eight KGB officers. Their office was located at No. 4 Angelikastrasse in a gray two-story mansion with a red-tiled roof in Neudstadt, across Dresden's famous bridges from the city's historic center. Here, in a corner office on the second floor, Major Putin would work for the next four and a half years.

Dresden, one of Europe's beautiful cities, was still disfigured by the shattered ruins of the Frauenkirche. The Baroque church remained unrepaired four decades after the firebombing of Dresden in February 1945 as a symbol of the horrors of war—and, for more contemporary propagandistic purposes, of Western barbarity. Angelikastrasse, across the river, was a short, pretty street, lined with trees and gardens that flowered each spring into a tapestry of colors, so unlike the crumbling monumental architecture of Leningrad. Across the intersection where it met the main road, Bautznerstrasse, there lurked a large compound that extended to a bluff overlooking the Elbe's wide, grassy estuary. After the war, the Soviet secret police, the NKVD, turned a small building there on the bluff into a military tribunal where they prosecuted not only the remnants of the Nazi regime but also opponents of the new Communist state.[4] The Stasi, after its creation, took over the compound and steadily expanded it. In 1953, it built a prison with forty-four cells, where over the years eventually more than twelve thousand prisoners would be held awaiting interrogation and imprisonment.

By the time Major Putin arrived, the Stasi headquarters had become a secret city-within-the-city. Inside were administrative offices, including a VIP guest house and enough apartment blocks to house three thousand people. There was also a building set apart from the rest, where officers pulled bulky headphones over their ears and listened to hours upon hours of conversations recorded by hidden listening devices across the city. The Stasi's chief in Dresden, Horst Böhm, had an office on the second floor of the main building, overlooking a paved courtyard where the Stasi officers played volleyball and soccer, sometimes with their KGB comrades from across the way.

So stagnant was life in the Soviet Union then that even a sclerotic socialist system like East Germany's seemed prosperous by comparison, dangerously full of temptations, especially for young officers of the KGB and the Red Army: women, money, and booze. All were dangerous paths to ideological degeneracy.[5] The Soviet officers and soldiers deployed to Germany scavenged whatever they could acquire—blue jeans, pornography, and even weapons—to sell or barter on the black market for vodka, then being restricted by the Red Army's commanders. Even among the KGB's elite cadre, officers and their spouses bought food, clothes, and electronics—luxuries in short supply back home—and shipped them home for others to peddle on a ravenous black market.

When he arrived in Dresden in August 1985, Vladimir had realized his childhood dream: he was a foreign intelligence officer sent abroad to battle the enemies of the state. And yet, his experience was far less cinematic than he had once imagined. He was not even undercover. He was a case officer, joining a dissipated, cynical staff in a provincial outpost of the KGB's empire. His colleagues promptly nicknamed him "Little Volodya," since there were already two other Vladimirs in the mansion on Angelikastrasse, "Big Volodya" and "Mustachioed Volodya."[6] Big Volodya was Vladimir Usoltsev, who had arrived two years before. He had trained and served in provincial offices of the KGB in Belarus and Krasnoyarsk and was by now deeply jaded.

When Konstantin Chernenko died earlier that year, before Little Volodya arrived, Usoltsev and his colleagues toasted to the illness that took him swiftly, rather than forcing the country to endure another prolonged period of uncertainty. Usoltsev mocked the bureaucracy, the insatiable demands from the Center, and its obsession, in his mind, with imaginary threats. He joked that "the most dangerous weapon" of the KGB spy in Dresden was the spike with which he punched holes in the reams of reports dutifully and uselessly sent to Moscow, many of them no more than a summary of political events reported in the local press.[7] "Volodya Putin came to the KGB for heroic romanticism," he wrote, "but in Dresden there could not by definition be any special romanticism, and by then he already understood that perfectly."[8]

Still Little Volodya fit right in. He almost immediately ingratiated himself with Dresden's station chief, Colonel Lazar Matveyev, who had served there since 1982. Matveyev was short, even shorter than Putin, softening around the middle and nearly bald except for two neatly trimmed fenders of white hair. Born in 1927, he was from the old school, a devoted Soviet intelligence officer whose father and mother had died in the Great Patriotic War. He took the young major under his wing, admiring his purposeful work ethic and his integrity. The year before Putin arrived in Dresden, the KGB began paying its officers there the equivalent of $100 in hard currency, a lavish sum distributed in dollars and marks. In Usoltsev's mind, a stint in East Germany was for most officers of the KGB "a unique chance to ensure their comfortable old age."[9] Not for Putin, though, nor for his wife. Matveyev adored Lyud-mila as a beautiful young mother who was not, like the others, "a mer-cantile woman." He made no secret among the rest of the KGB cadre on Angelikastrasse that Little Volodya was his favorite—above all because this young major showed no sign of being "a careerist" determined to outshine his superiors. He was a "crystal clear person" and a real "work-ing man," though not the sort of subordinate to overdo it by working day and night.[10]

At first, Lyudmila was still in Leningrad, finishing her degree. Little Volodya moved in briefly with a colleague on the top floor of a long, newly built apartment block at 101 Radebergerstrasse, a short five-minute walk from the KGB mansion. The building abutted a Soviet military barracks on one side and a forested park on the other, the northeastern edge of Dresden. Like most buildings in the neighbor-hood, it housed Stasi and Soviet officers and their families. It was a small, self-contained community of secret police and spies. The neighborhood included a military exchange, a store selling Russian products, schools for the children, a cinema showing Soviet films, and a *banya* (the Russian version of a sauna). Major Putin later moved into an apartment on the fourth floor above the first of twelve separate entrances to the building, each of which had its own stairwell, though there were no elevators. The apartment had only four rooms covering seven hundred square feet. It was not luxurious, but it was his first home of his own.

When Lyudmila arrived in the fall of 1985, cradling Masha, she found waiting on the kitchen table a basket of bananas, then a scar-city back home. At first, it felt to her that they had woken in a dream. The neighborhood was charming, the streets clean. The windows in the apartment were washed once a week. The German wives strung their laundry in rows on metal poles planted in the grassy garden outside, tidy and all very much alike.[11]

The Dresden outpost oversaw the KGB's work in four of East Ger-many's southern districts, Dresden, Leipzig, Gera, and Karl Marx Stadt. Major Putin and his colleagues involved themselves in intelligence oper-ations, counterintelligence, analysis, and another of the Center's growing obsessions, scientific and technical espionage—all focused principally on the enemy across the border, not far away. He shared a second-floor office with Usoltsev, who called the space their cell and Little Volodya his cellmate. The room had two desks, a safe for classified papers, and two telephones, though with only one line. Little Volodya initially feared answering the phone, embarrassed by his struggle with the German language, though he eventually improved to the point that he could adapt the Saxon dialect.[12] As a student, he had grown to love German culture, history, and literature, and now he immersed himself in it. "He sometimes knew more than I did," Horst Jehmlich, a senior aide to Böhm, Dresden's Stasi chief, recalled. The Russian often asked Jehmlich to explain idiomatic expressions in German, always hoping to improve his linguistic ability.[13]

Usoltsev was intrigued by his new colleague, his sense of humor and humble roots. His grandfather's brushes in the kitchen with the grandees of the October Revolution notwithstanding, Little Volodya had no "high" relatives who could have helped advance his career. He was the chief's pet and became the office's Communist Party representative, leading weekly discussions on political events, but he did so with what Usoltsev perceived to be feigned, even ironic piety. He enjoyed middlebrow variety shows on German television and yet also read the classics prodigiously, favoring Russian satirists, like Nikolai Gogol and Mikhail Saltykov-Shchedrin, who savaged the stifling and corrupt tsarist bureaucracy of the ninteenth century. *Dead Souls,* Gogol's masterwork skewering provincial venality and supplication, became a favorite novel. He joked irreverently about the loathsome traits of counterintelligence agents, which he had been, at least for a time. And he mocked Matveyev's anti-Semitism, which was pervasive in the KGB, though he never did so to the chief's face.

Little Volodya, Usoltsev thought, had a remarkable ability to adapt his personality to the situation and to his superiors, charming them and winning their confidence; it was a defining trait that others would notice. In their ample hours for discussion—often in the mansion's basement banya—Volodya would reveal glimpses of individuality and even perilous free thinking. On November 9, 1985, they watched the Soviet broadcast of the dramatic finale of the world chess championship between Anatoly Karpov and Garry Kasparov, which was seen as an ideological clash between the old and new guards. Almost all of the KGB cadre rooted for Karpov, the reigning champion and lauded hero of the Soviet Union. They thought that Kasparov, who was excoriated in the official press as the match unfolded, was an "extremely impudent upstart." Little Volodya, on the other hand, showed "dangerous sympathy" for Kasparov. He relished his ultimate victory and was not afraid to say so.

What intrigued Usoltsev most of all was his colleague's professed belief in God. In the KGB, it was "an inconceivable thing," and Usoltsev, truly a godless Communist, marveled at his willingness to acknowledge any faith whatsoever, though the young major was careful never to flaunt it. He was so discreet, in fact, that Usoltsev was never completely sure that he was not using God as just another intelligence tactic.[14]

Major Putin settled into life in Germany rather comfortably. For the first time in his adult life, he stopped practicing judo and gave up exercising regularly. Though never much of a drinker, he acquired a taste for beer, particularly Radeberger Pilsner, made in a small town near Dresden. He befriended a barkeep who would regularly fill his ration—a small keg—and he quickly added twenty-five pounds to his slight frame. Almost immediately after she arrived, Lyudmila became pregnant again, and their second daughter, Yekaterina, or Katya, was born on August 31, 1986. Usoltsev sensed that he was "slightly discouraged" that they did not have a son.

As a husband and father, he proved to be something of a chauvinist. He refused to help with shopping, cooking, or anything else to do with housekeeping, believing in a traditional division of marital roles. During a brief hospitalization when Lyudmila was pregnant in Dresden, he had been left alone for three days with Masha, and was nearly overwhelmed by the effort. He was "the provider and defender," as Lyudmila put it, and she had to handle the rest. He was such a picky eater, refusing to touch dishes he did not like, that she lost patience cooking for him. When she complained, he quoted a Russian aphorism: "Don't praise a woman, or else you'll spoil her." He never celebrated their wedding anniversaries.[15]

The demands on Major Putin at the office were not so onerous that they spoiled the couple's weekends. The Putins, with a Soviet-made Zhiguli at their disposal, spent many traveling with their Russian neighbors—all security agents and their spouses. He joined a fishing club and with Lyudmila visited the forests and parks of Saxony. At least twice they visited Czechoslovakia, another Soviet satellite, once with Colonel Matveyev and his wife, Yevgenia. The Putins bought a stereo from the West and later an early Atari video game. They never traveled to West Germany, though, and while they regularly hosted Russian and German friends in their apartment, their social life included only those within a narrow circle of German and Soviet intelligence agents. They became close to a couple, the Burkhards, who had a disabled child. When the couple later divorced, according to Horst Jehmlich, Major Putin helped the wife find work in Berlin. Compared to the people they knew back in the Soviet Union, the Putins lived a life of privilege and comfort, but one that was circumscribed. The wives were discouraged from making friends outside their immediate circle, which created an insular community that frayed nerves and fueled gossip and petty feuds. Their years in Dresden became "measured, settled, ordinary and monotonous."[16] Life became uneventful and, for Lyudmila, claustrophobic. Her husband never talked about his work at home, even though it loomed over everything. More than once he cautioned Lyudmila to avoid "undesirable" acquaintances she met. Even among the brotherly Germans, no one could really be trusted. Their real identities and intentions might not become evident for years, as the Putins would later find out when it was alleged that the West German foreign intelligence agency, the BND, had infiltrated the mansion on Angelikastrasse with a buxom agent who served as an interpreter. Her figure inspired her code name, BALCONY, and she was said to have befriended the Putins, and Lyudmila in particular. Lyudmila confided in her that theirs was a stormy marriage, that Vladimir was abusive and a serial womanizer.[17] Whether the interpreter was a spy was impossible to prove; it might have simply been part of the disinformation war between rival intelligence agencies. In the craft of espionage, truth was never really the point.

The KGB's objective in East Germany was to gather intelligence and recruit agents who had access to the West. Major Putin's part in this mission was routine, even tedious. The East Germans seconded two officers to the KGB's office, and together they scoured the applications of those hoping to travel to West Germany. The goal was to determine who among them had relatives near the American and NATO military bases in Bad Tölz, Wildflecken, and Celle and to see whether, in exchange for a visa, they would collaborate with the KGB by reporting back anything unusual they might see. In 1986, the KGB's leaders remained fixated on the risk posed by NATO, even as changes being introduced by a charismatic new Soviet leader, Mikhail Gorbachev, promised a de-escalation of Cold War tensions. Their orders in particular focused on an obsession with the location of the Green Berets in Germany, which Usoltsev thought ridiculous. The dull culling of lists for potential recruits was the Dresden office's "first task," he said, but eventually they abandoned it as a waste of time.[18]

Major Putin appeared in uniform on some days and in civilian clothes on others, depending on his tasks. He handled informants that he or others recruited in hopes of gathering information about economic, political, or military developments in the West and also within East Germany. The agents were the real spies, hiding their identities and activities and living in fear of betrayal; he was an administrator. He tracked businessmen or other foreigners passing through and paid particular attention to the city's only Russian Orthodox Church, Saint Simeon of the Wonderful Mountains, compiling a dossier on its cleric, Archpriest Grigory Davidov, and its small flock of believers.[19] Horst Jehmlich, the aide to Dresden's Stasi chief, Horst Böhm, recalled that Putin focused his recruiting efforts on students "who might become important in their home country one day," rising through the ranks of industry or government. That was how the KGB recruited Philby and the others at Cambridge to stunningly damaging effect, but Putin's success, as far as anyone ever knew, paled by comparison. People had once aided the Soviet Union out of ideological conviction, but now most betrayed their nations for money, as Aldrich Ames and Robert Hanssen were then doing in the United States. What else did the Soviet Union at that point have to offer?

For each potential recruit, Major Putin would prepare paperwork and submit it to Böhm's office for approval. "We had to guarantee that the people who were registered by our friends would not also be contacted by us," Jehmlich explained. Even then, he said, the Stasi did not know everything the KGB did. The Dresden outpost also analyzed political developments and party leaders in West Germany and East Germany, searching for signs of opposition to Soviet policies that under Gorbachev were experiencing profound change. Operation LUCH, the long-running KGB effort to monitor the East Germans, continued to feed the Center with reports on their "dear friends," even in the Stasi.

In 1987, Major Putin was promoted to lieutenant colonel and made one of Matveyev's assistants, then ultimately his senior assistant. He effectively became the deputy chief of the Dresden outpost. His administrative duties grew with his promotions, but they also took him further from the active work of the real agents and spies. He was, as in Leningrad, an enforcer, the equivalent of an internal affairs officer, ever vigilant for enemies inside as well as outside. A neighbor on Angelikastrasse, Siegfried Dannath, was once walking his dog when he stopped in front of the KGB office to engage in small talk with one of Putin's colleagues. When Dannath's wife photographed the men together with the mansion in the background, a Russian guard barked in alarm. He scolded the Russian and Germans alike, shouting that photography was strictly forbidden. Dannath quickly forgot about the encounter, but Lieutenant Colonel Putin sent a letter to the Stasi, requesting that the Dannaths be put under heightened surveillance as a precaution.[20]

In his official capacity, Putin had occasion to meet the East German leadership in Dresden, including Horst Böhm and Hans Modrow, the Communist Party secretary for the city, but his rank and position remained too low for familiarity. His duties included such mundane matters as seeing whether three visiting KGB officials could stay at a hotel at no cost (Moscow was evidently short on funds) or arranging free tickets for Soviet soldiers to watch a soccer match between Dresden's team and Spartak Moscow. His only known correspondence with Böhm was a letter requesting help restoring telephone service for an informant inside East Germany's wholesale trade enterprise. Putin seemed destined to remain an unprepossessing figure in the background.[21]

In 1987, the Stasi chief, Erich Mielke, signed a decree awarding Lieutenant Colonel Putin a gold medal on the occasion of the seventieth anniversary of the Russian Revolution. That night, November 7, he and twelve other KGB officers joined their Stasi colleagues in the ballroom at the headquarters on Bautznerstrasse—the same building housing the prison—to listen to a speech by Horst Böhm. Böhm was a notorious hardliner, and his tone was deliberate, somber, and terrifying in its ideological certainty. The Soviet leader might be seeking a less adversarial relationship with the West, but Böhm warned that night that the intelligence agencies of the enemies of socialism had not relented at all. "The imperialist secret services have stepped up their activities to obtain any information that is or might be significant for further action" against East Germany and the other socialist nations, he thundered. And yet a month later Gorbachev and Ronald Reagan signed the Intermediate-Range Nuclear Forces Treaty in Washington to eliminate some of the most dangerous weapons in Europe.

The Cold War was not over, but its thaw was foreseeable—just not to East Germany's leaders. They became ferocious critics of Gorbachev's perestroika and glasnost, their denunciations filling the KGB reports cabled back to the Center. The assuredness of its leaders' belief in East Germany's unshakable future never faltered until it was too late. Gorbachev understood that the Soviet Union was falling behind the West—economically, scientifically, and militarily—and falling apart. Gorbachev's first moves toward reforming the Soviet economic system, though endorsed by a newly "reformist" KGB leadership, began to expose dangerous fractures in the immovable state, and within the KGB itself. While his calls to modernize industrial and agricultural production had little immediate impact on the KGB's power or perquisites, his policy of perestroika, announced at the 27th Party Congress in 1986, promised initiative and creativity in government and tolerated criticism. It was the beginning of the end of the rigid orthodoxy of the Brezhnev years.

The cadre on Angelikastrasse watched these developments from a distance, and reacted cautiously. Colonel Matveyev did not like what he saw stirring in Moscow under Gorbachev, but the others, perhaps with the benefit of hindsight, would later say that they knew the Soviet system was cracking under the pressure released by perestroika and glasnost. "We were the young generation of the security service," Usoltsev recalled. "It was absolutely clear to us that Soviet power was marching inexorably into the abyss."[22] Lieutenant Colonel Putin, too, shared a grim view of the state of the Soviet Union. He thought the war in Afghanistan had become "senseless and in fact criminal."[23] He saw for himself the comparative wealth of the "decadent" West as he perused the catalogues of German department stores that were so coveted in the KGB office that they were bartered and sent back home to serve as fashion templates for seamstresses.[24] Scouring newspapers like *Der Spiegel* or magazines like *Stern* for tidbits to fill their intelligence reports to the Center, he and his colleagues could see for themselves the unvarnished reports of disasters, like the accident at the Chernobyl nuclear power plant in Ukraine in 1986, and know that the official version amounted to a lie. In a way, glasnost came to the security forces first, since they had access to what was forbidden then, but soon would spill into the public consciousness.

The little outpost in Dresden mirrored the divisions within the KGB as a whole over the tectonic changes under way at home, the divide between the hardliners and reformers, between the old guard and the new generation. At the end of 1986, the release of Andrei Sakharov from exile in Gorky prompted a tirade from Colonel Matveyev, but sympathy from his favorite underling. Lieutenant Colonel Putin would now and then express admiration for dissidents like Sakharov or Solzhenitsyn. The evening after Sakharov's release from exile, he surprised Usoltsev again. "Don't forget," he said, "only the obvious military superiority of the West can bring the unconstrained masters in the Kremlin to their senses."[25] In another instance, as early as 1987, he told a Red Army doctor who knew him in Dresden that he supported the idea of holding elections for the new president of the Soviet Union,[26] three years before it happened. His ambivalence was already evident. He sensed the need for political and economic change, but like Gorbachev and many other Russians, he favored evolutionary change, not radical reform. As many others, he never wanted the state to collapse.

The head of the First Chief Directorate in Moscow, Vladimir Kryuchkov, quickly adapted to Gorbachev's new thinking, at least on the surface. Kryuchkov was like Putin in many ways: a fitness fanatic, a workaholic, and a teetotaler who "caused dismay in the traditionally bibulous" ranks by banning drinking at farewell parties for officers about to go abroad.[27] He became one of Gorbachev's closest advisers, embracing a new openness in intelligence matters, and in 1988, he became the KGB's chairman; by then the KGB had already begun to sense that the bloc created in Eastern Europe was doomed.

From their Dresden outpost, Lieutenant Colonel Putin and his colleagues could also see that the government led by Erich Honecker, an obstinate old Marxist, was losing popular support. Honecker and his Stasi chief, Mielke, steadfastly refused to replicate Gorbachev's perestroika and glasnost, but ordinary East Germans sensed the change in the air; the latent desire for basic freedoms was awakening, as it was elsewhere in Eastern Europe. The country's "disappearance" was inevitable, Putin thought, but he had no idea it was imminent.[28]

In August 1989, Hungary opened its borders with Austria, allowing citizens to cross freely. East Germans, who could travel within the Soviet bloc, began heading there in hopes of emigrating onward. Protests appeared in cities across East Germany, energized by people demanding, at a minimum, what the Soviet leader was offering his own citizens: elections, freedom to criticize one-party rule, and market reforms that would offer greater material prosperity. The fear of the Stasi remained, but in that fervent year of revolution—from Lithuania to Tiananmen Square—it was no longer enough to keep people silent and fearful in their homes. In Leipzig on September 4, an opposition movement formed within the Church of Saint Nicholas and held a small protest after services that Monday night. The "Monday protests" grew with each passing week and spread to other cities, including Dresden. By October, tens of thousands had joined in the opposition movement, while thousands more had bolted for the West.

On October 2, Honecker issued orders to put down the protests by force, but a paratrooper unit dispatched to Leipzig never carried them out. The next day, Honecker's government tried to stem the flow of emigrants by banning travel to Czechoslovakia. When Gorbachev arrived in East Berlin on October 6, ostensibly to celebrate the fortieth anniversary of the founding of the German Democratic Republic, the end was already nigh. He pressed Honecker to address the protesters' demands, saying, "Life punishes those who delay," but the latter remained defiant. "We will solve our problems ourselves with socialist means," he declared in his speech with Gorbachev at his side. "Proposals intended to weaken socialism will not blossom here."[29]

Less than two weeks later, he was ousted, replaced by his deputy, Egon Krenz, in hopes of stanching the political upheaval. It was too late. The momentum of the protests became irreversible, and the increasingly erratic actions of the government hastened its own collapse. On November 9, a government spokesman announced that the Politburo had authorized East Germans to travel freely to the West and said, when asked, that as far as he knew the change took effect immediately. Tens of thousands of people promptly arrived at the Berlin Wall, overwhelming the border guards. With no clear instructions from the top, the guards let them through. They were greeted on the other side by euphoric West Germans. And together they began tearing down the most infamous symbol of the Cold War.

In Dresden, the tumult consumed the KGB office. Lieutenant Colonel Putin was deeply conflicted, or at least would later claim he was. He said he sympathized with the protesters' broad demands, but his heart was also with his Stasi friends. The Stasi, he thought, was "also part of society" and "infected with the same sickness," not an alien force that should be cast away with the decrepit political leadership. What he despised—what he feared—was the rule of the mob. And that is what he watched unfold around him. Worse, no one in Moscow seemed to care. He complained that the KGB, consumed with the internal struggles under way at home, ignored the warnings and recommendations that he and his colleagues were sending. Not only was the Soviet Union under duress, but now his own career appeared to have become an afterthought, a dead end. "The work we did was no longer necessary," he recalled later. "What was the point of writing, recruiting, and procuring information? Nobody at Moscow Center was reading our reports."[30]

The fall of the Berlin Wall in November did not end the protests. Nor did it immediately bring the government down. The Stasi's security network remained in place, though its authority began to erode. After the euphoria in Berlin, opposition groups formed and pressed their demands for free elections. The demands turned to the Stasi itself. In Dresden, an opposition group organized a protest outside the Stasi headquarters on December 5. A few hundred appeared at first, but soon they were joined by thousands. From a side balcony of the mansion on Angelikastrasse, the KGB's team could easily see the crowd swarming the Stasi compound. Lieutenant Colonel Putin ventured outside to its fringes to observe more closely. At five o'clock, overwhelmed by the size of the crowd and unable to calm the situation by fear alone, Böhm relented and ordered the gate opened. The protesters poured into the compound, milling through the buildings that until that evening had instilled only dread. Böhm, dazed and ashen, pleaded for calm as the crowd ransacked his headquarters. The takeover was largely peaceful, but in Putin's mind the crowd was deranged, consumed by madness. He remembered a woman shouting, "Look for the passageway under the Elbe! There are prisoners there being tortured in water up to their knees!" He knew it was nonsense—but only because he knew very well where the prison cells actually were.

It was dark by the time he retreated to the mansion. A new, more senior KGB officer, Major General Vladimir Shirokov, had replaced Matveyev earlier in the year. He had left the mansion that night at nine o'clock and was somewhere out in the city. As the crowds rummaged through the Stasi buildings, a small group broke away, turned up Angelikastrasse, and gathered outside the KGB outpost, its purpose and occupants no secret to those protesting. A security guard stationed in a small guard house scrambled inside to inform Lieutenant Colonel Putin, who was the senior officer on the scene, with only four others inside. He was angry and alarmed; responsibility for the KGB's property—its files, its secrets—was his now. He ordered the guards to prepare for an assault,[31] and then he telephoned the Soviet military command in Dresden, asking that reinforcements be sent to protect the building. An officer on duty told him he could do nothing because "there are no orders from

Moscow." He promised to inquire, though. When the officer did not call back, Putin called again.

"Well, so?" he pressed.

"I asked Moscow," the officer replied, "but Moscow is silent."

"And what will we do?" he asked.

"For now, there's nothing I can do to help."[32]

He was stunned. Whatever his doubts about the fate of the Communist system, he remained a dedicated officer of the state. Now the state was failing him at a moment of crisis. "I had the feeling then that the country was no more," he recalled, the bitterness still raw years later, "that it had disappeared. It became clear the [Soviet] Union was ailing. It was a deadly, incurable disease called paralysis—a paralysis of power."[33] He agonized over what to do. Even without an explicit declaration saying so, it was clear the Soviet leadership no longer intended to prop up East Germany's government, as it had in 1953, as it had by force in Hungary in 1956 and again in Czechoslovakia in 1968. Putin could not use force against the mob outside, and in fact he did not have the firepower to do much anyway. He thought of the files inside—the intelligence reports to the Center—and the almost unimaginable consequences if they fell into the hands of the rabble. The documents would not only betray the KGB's work but also affect the "the fates of concrete people," those who had collaborated with him and his colleagues over the years, people "who once trusted the security bodies" of the Soviet Union. He was sure he would face a military tribunal if the files were compromised, and yet he had no orders detailing what he could do to protect them. He thought of his career in the KGB and his family who relied on it. He sensed then that the Soviet Union would collapse and with it the only life he had known: his service as an intelligence officer.[34]

It was at this nadir, nearing midnight, that Lieutenant Colonel Putin committed the riskiest, most decisive known act of his KGB career. Dressed in his uniform, he went outside. Though he kept a KGB-issued pistol in the office safe, he did not retrieve it. He walked out alone to the mansion's gate, without his hat and without orders, and he bluffed.

The mood on Angelikastrasse was not aggressive so much as euphoric. A group of two dozen men gathered on the street outside the gate talking excitedly among themselves, amazed that the dreaded Stasi had crumbled without a fight. Siegfried Dannath, who had two years before had the encounter with his dog outside the KGB mansion, stood among them. Someone challenged the guard on duty to let them in, but he said nothing. After he disappeared into the house, they were not sure what exactly to do next. It was then that Dannath saw a short officer emerge from the front door, walk down the few steps, and approach. He said nothing at first and then spoke slowly and calmly.

"This house is strictly guarded," he said in German so fluent that Dannath was surprised. "My soldiers have weapons. And I gave them orders: if anyone enters the compound, they are to open fire."

He did not shout or menace. He simply spoke those few words, paused, and then turned and walked back into the house. The men on the street only murmured in response. Dannath felt the mood change. The protesters thought better of trying to storm the gates. No one wanted violence, and they had already toppled the Stasi. Taking on the KGB was another thing altogether. So they dispersed, drifting down Angelika-strasse to rejoin the throng milling about the Stasi compound.[35] A few hours later the Soviet base received some orders at last, and commanders sent two armored vehicles with soldiers who were no longer needed.

Legends grew out of this night, embellished according to author and agenda. In some versions, "hundreds" of protesters "stormed" the building. In others, guards positioned at the window pointed their AK-47s at the crowd, ready to shoot to kill. In one telling, the Russian officer brandished a pistol outside, or at the top of the stairs to the second floor, staring down a horde that pressed up toward him. Nothing so dramatic happened that night, and what did happen was overshadowed by the far more significant events unfolding in Berlin, including the resignation of the Communist Party's security committee and the detention of Erich Honecker. Egon Krenz resigned the next day, giving way to the first non-Communist leaders in East Germany's history.

Lieutenant Colonel Putin's role in the events surrounding the dissolution of East Germany was a small act in the face of uncertainty, if not danger. For a fleeting moment, he was indeed an intelligence officer standing alone in defense of his country, a single man able to affect the course of history—in Germany, no less—just as he had imagined as an impressionable young man two decades before. He acted with calm, stoic determination. He avoided a security breach and also bloodshed. And yet there would be no recognition of his actions that night, no commendation, no medal. *Moscow is silent.* The phrase haunted him for years afterward. He sensed that night that his career was coming to an end. So too was his country.

CHAPTER 4

Democracy Faces a Hungry Winter

It was bitter enough for Vladimir Putin to witness the collapse of the Soviet ideal in Europe, helpless to reverse the losses. He knew that a divided Germany could not endure, despite Erich Honecker's vow early in 1989 that the Berlin Wall would stand "in 50 and even in 100 years." For Putin, what mattered more was what he saw as an unconditional Soviet surrender, followed by a humiliating, chaotic, and catastrophic retreat. "That's what hurt," he said. "They just dropped everything and went away."[1]

The men and women he had worked with for nearly five years were cast aside, abandoned by their Soviet patrons, left to the mercy of West Germany and their own vengeful citizens. The Putins' neighbors and friends found themselves abruptly out of work, ostracized because of their employment in the Stasi. Katya's preschool teacher, an officer of the Stasi, was barred from working with children. One of Lyudmila's friends "cried for her lost ideals, for the collapse of everything that she had believed in her whole life," she recalled. "For them, it was the collapse of everything—their lives, their careers."[2]

The intelligence officers felt particularly betrayed. Markus Wolf, head of East Germany's foreign intelligence until 1986, resented Gorbachev's indifference after 1989, though he briefly received refuge in Russia. "There had been no great rush of comradely support from our Moscow friends during the past stressful months," he wrote. "Like us, they had been completely unprepared for what happened. The supposedly eternal brotherhood to which we had raised our glasses down the years was now a ragged band."[3] Horst Böhm, the Stasi chief in Dresden, committed suicide in his home on February 21, 1990, shortly before he was to testify before a commission on the future of the unraveling state, though rumors persisted that he was murdered to prevent him from appearing in a criminal trial of Dresden's despotic boss, Hans Modrow.[4] The East Germans soon learned the truth of the KGB's Operation LUCH, the decades-long effort to spy on them. Horst Jehmlich, Böhm's aide, felt betrayed by Putin personally. "They cheated and lied to us," he said.[5]

The KGB in East Germany was in disarray, scrambling to destroy or remove its intelligence files while severing or covering up its networks of agents and laying the foundations for new ones. The last chief in Dresden, General Shirokov, ordered the removal and destruction of twelve truckloads of documents from the headquarters of the Soviet armored division. They burned so many that the furnace designed for the task broke. A battalion commander then dug a pit on the grounds, dumped the papers, and ordered the pile doused with gasoline.[6] Lieutenant Colonel Putin, too, burned files—"all our communications, our lists of contacts and our agents' networks"—but he and his colleagues spirited the most important ones back to the KGB archives in Moscow. The real danger was the exposure of the KGB's secrets to the West and NATO, though there was little he or anyone else in the Dresden outpost could do to stop that now.

By the beginning of the new decade, Lieutenant Colonel Putin and his cadre had been recalled home, but he had one final mission as a Soviet intelligence operative. He continued to recruit informants, hoping to establish a new network of agents that would serve as a rear guard in the democratizing East Germany. He turned to his old friends and contacts, including an inspector in Dresden's police department and a Stasi officer named Klaus Zuchold, whom he had first met four years earlier. Zuchold had taken him on one of his first tours of Saxony—even before Lyudmila arrived—and visited him frequently. Zuchold apparently had never worked for the KGB until after the events of 1989. In January 1990, in one of his final acts, Lieutenant Colonel Putin formally recruited him, sending his Stasi file to the Center in Moscow for approval. He dictated Zuchold's letter of allegiance to the KGB, gave his daughter a book of Russian fairy tales, and toasted the occasion with Soviet brandy.[7] It proved to be a short-lived success: a year later, after the reunification of Germany in October 1990, Zuchold accepted an offer of amnesty and not only revealed his own recruitment but exposed fifteen other agents who had been in the KGB's Dresden network.[8]

The betrayal of agents—and the seizure of the Stasi's enormous collection of files by the West German BND and subsequently their public disclosure, which also exposed the extent of the KGB's activities—enraged

Lieutenant Colonel Putin. He later told his old friend Sergei Roldugin that the Stasi should never have turned over its archives, never have
betrayed those who had worked as informants. Roldugin rarely heard
him talk about his work and rarely saw him so emotional. "He said it was
equal to treason," Roldugin recalled. "He was very upset, extremely," but
also ashamed and remorseful. He had been powerless to help his German
comrades as their secret world imploded. "I felt it," he told Roldugin,
"like a fault of my own."[9]

In February 1990, packing boxes, each numbered and named, filled
the Putins' modest apartment. The apartment felt like a storage room.
The KGB's withdrawal, followed by that of the Soviet military, suddenly
freed up housing in Dresden. Jörg Hofmann, a young man whose wife
had connections in the city administration, managed to acquire the lease
to the apartment. He stopped by to see it while the Putins awaited the
movers. The walls were covered in tinfoil wallpaper, the windows decorated by cutouts of Russian nesting dolls, made by the girls. The Putins
were polite and friendly; the lieutenant colonel betrayed no outward bitterness or other emotion. He simply told Hofmann he was going home.[10]
On March 1, the Hofmanns moved in. In four and a half years, the
Putins had managed to save some of the hard currency he earned, and a
neighbor gave them a washing machine. It was twenty years old, but it
worked for another five years.[11] It was all they had to show for his career
as a foreign intelligence agent. Their belongings were packed in a ship-
ping container and sent to Moscow. The couple, with their two young
daughters, boarded a train, also to Moscow. On the journey back, a thief
made off with Lyudmila's coat and what rubles and marks she carried.[12]

The Putins had from afar followed the upheaval of Gorbachev's era—the
public excitement engendered by perestroika and glasnost—but whatever they expected, what they found when they returned disappointed
them. After the comparative comforts of East Germany, life at home
seemed a shock. "There were the same terrible lines, the ration cards,
the coupons, the empty shelves," Lyudmila recalled.[13] She feared going
to the store, unable to "sniff out the bargains and to stand in all the
lines. I would just dart into the nearest store, buy whatever was most
necessary, and go home. It was horrible." They had missed the liberating intellectual and political spirit of the era, the release of banned films
and previously censored novels like *The Master and Margarita*, Mikhail
Bulgakov's masterpiece imagining Satan's visit to Moscow, or Boris Pas-

ternak's *Doctor Zhivago*. The new freedom to read, to debate, to think openly, had been electrifying for so many, but they had returned to Russia at the moment when Gorbachev's liberalizing reforms were beginning to unravel.[14]

Lyudmila felt her husband "had lost touch with his life's real purpose."[15] His career as a KGB officer stood at a crossroads. He joined a mass repatriation of intelligence operatives from abroad, not only from Germany but from all of Eastern Europe and other far-flung battlegrounds of the Cold War, like Afghanistan, Angola, Mongolia, Vietnam, Nicaragua, and Yemen. They were defeated, dejected, and effectively out of work, displaced refugees of a crumbling empire. The Center in Moscow was the typical destination for officers returning from a posting abroad. Only nothing was typical anymore. For three months at the beginning of 1990, Putin was not even paid. The KGB initially offered him a position at the First Chief Directorate's headquarters in Yasenevo, the wooded, heavily guarded compound southwest of Moscow. His rank and appointment would normally have merited an apartment in Moscow, but none was available. With so many intelligence veterans in search of homes, he would have to wait, possibly for years. Lyudmila liked Moscow and wanted to move there, and he understood that whatever prospects he had for advancement existed in the capital, not in Leningrad, but his vague doubts about the Soviet Union's future had hardened. After fifteen years, his career was unspectacular, and no longer inspiring. In his last year in Dresden he sensed the disorganization of the organs of power, the breakdown of discipline, the theft and lawlessness within his own ranks.

He met his old station chief and mentor, Colonel Lazar Matveyev, who was then stationed at Yasenevo. "I don't know what to do," he told Matveyev in the graying colonel's apartment in Moscow. Matveyev, for all his affection for his former underling, did nothing to persuade him to stay in Moscow or even in the KGB. "Talk Lyuda out of it," he told him intimately, "and go to Leningrad."[16] There at least he had an apartment where they could live: his parents'. The elder Putins had moved into a larger place, this time on Sredneokhtinsky Prospekt, not far from the academy where Vladimir had first trained after joining the KGB. So he accepted a job as the assistant to the rector for international affairs at his old university, a KGB position intended to keep an eye on students and visitors. At last, he would be "undercover," though the true identity of officials in posts like that was, by intention, a poorly kept secret. It never hurt for people to know the KGB lurked everywhere. He now rejoined what Oleg Kalugin, the former deputy director of the KGB in Leningrad, described as "this absurd, stupendous ziggurat, this terrifyingly centralized machine, this religion that sought to control all aspects of life in our vast country."[17]

The university's rector, Stanislav Merkuriev, was a theoretical physicist appointed early in Gorbachev's tenure. He spoke English, German, and French and was determined to open the stifled system of higher education. By the time of his early death in 1993, he had earned plaudits for making the university one of the best in Europe.[18] He surrounded himself with like-minded professionals—and, as he surely would have known, one last minder from the KGB. For an aging KGB veteran, the university post might have been a sinecure, comfortable and undemanding, but for a lieutenant colonel, only thirty-seven and with years of service ahead of him, it seemed a dead end. He had little prospect now of securing another assignment abroad; the KGB was downsizing, and his achievements hardly merited a post. His career in foreign intelligence thus came crashing to an end. Not even Matveyev could reach down a hand to pull him up. He told Sergei Roldugin that he planned to leave the KGB altogether, though Roldugin had his doubts. "There is no such thing as a former intelligence agent," he said. He empathized with his friend's anger and confusion, but he also understood his mentality. "You can stop working at this organization, but its worldview and way of thinking remain stuck in your head."[19]

Leningrad had changed little outwardly, but perestroika breathed new life into the city's politics. In March 1989, while the Putins were still in Dresden, cities across the Soviet Union held the first competitive elections in the country's history to choose representatives to a new quasi-parliament, the Congress of People's Deputies. Instead of rubber-stamping Communist Party leaders, as Soviet elections invariably did, voters in Leningrad rebelled and rejected the top five candidates, including the city's party leader, Yuri Solovyev.[20] One of those elected instead was a tall, charismatic professor of law at Vladimir Putin's alma mater, Anatoly Sobchak. Born deep in Siberia and educated in Leningrad, Sobchak had already gained prominence as a critic of the Soviet system. He wrote widely, advocating market reforms and the rule of law; his doctoral dissertation had been rejected as politically incorrect. Sobchak's law school colleagues had unexpectedly nominated him to be one of four candidates from the university's district on Vasilievsky Island, which also included the sprawling Baltic shipyard and thousands of shipbuilders and stevedores. Despite the Communist Party's efforts to screen out opposition candidates, Sobchak managed to place second in a kind of political caucus held in the shipyard's Palace of Culture after delivering a late-night speech that, extemporaneously, evoked Martin Luther King Jr. "I dreamed of a time when our state would become law-governed—a state that didn't permit the granting of rights and privileges to some people at the expense of others," he wrote later.[21]

Though he had no electoral experience, Sobchak threw himself into politics. Like Gorbachev, he believed that the Soviet system could change with reforms, but he found himself and the country unprepared for the novelty of democracy after the decades of fear and suspicion that had fractured Soviet society. The peculiarities of the system—government-assigned employment, housing, and even vacations—meant that most people lived and worked within a narrow social circle and harbored a deep distrust of anyone outside it. "Never talk to strangers," the famous line from *The Master and Margarita*, was an article of faith in the Soviet Union. Sobchak lived what he admitted was the rarefied life of the intelligentsia, comfortable and "increasingly circumscribed," and when campaigning outside his milieu, he discovered how little he knew of how ordinary people lived.[22]

Once elected, Sobchak made an impression when the Congress of People's Deputies convened in the spring of 1989. He joined a bloc of reformist legislators that included Andrei Sakharov, the dissident physicist, and Boris Yeltsin, the bearish party official who had become the first secretary in Moscow, and he passionately and eloquently hectored the Soviet leadership, the military, and the KGB in public hearings that were transmitted across the vast country. Sobchak chaired an investigation into the killing of twenty people during an anti-Soviet demonstration on April 9 in Tbilisi, the capital of Georgia, exposing the mendacity of the official version of the military's crackdown there. The upheavals of 1989 had now spread to the Soviet Union itself—with unrest in Lithuania, Azerbaijan, and Armenia. Despite their last, violent efforts to contain the fervor, the Soviet authorities no longer wielded enough power to hold the system together.[23]

A month after the Putins returned, Leningrad elected a new city council. Enough reformers and independents won to break the Communist Party's monopoly on municipal power. The new legislators were earnest but also inexperienced, disorganized, and leaderless. A bloc of them appealed to Sobchak to run for one of twenty-five remaining vacant seats and then, assuming he won, to compete for the job of council chairman. Sobchak's prominence in the Congress of People's Deputies in Moscow raised hopes that he would be a unifying leader for the city. He won his election and in May became the council's chairman, effectively the city's top elected official. Sobchak "personified the transition to a new form of government," as one historian put it, where hope triumphed over reason.[24] He was a legal scholar, not an administrator, and whatever his charisma, he had no experience governing a city of five million people—let alone at a time of political upheaval, with a recalcitrant bureaucracy still controlled by the Communists. Sobchak needed allies and expertise, and he turned to the one institution where he thought he could find competent aides able to navigate what was becoming a treacherous political transition. He turned to the institution he had excoriated from the dais of the Congress of People's Deputies. He turned to the KGB.

Shortly after taking up his new position, Sobchak telephoned Oleg Kalugin, the former spymaster whose career fell afoul of KGB intrigue after his service in foreign intelligence, leaving him in "internal exile" in Leningrad. Kalugin had since joined the ranks of the democratic reformers and became one of the most prominent critics of his former agency. Now Sobchak had a favor to ask of him. Could he recommend someone inside the KGB whom he could trust as an adviser? He was suspicious of the bureaucracy. He needed a liaison to the security forces. Kalugin suggested a senior officer, a lieutenant general he trusted, but Sobchak dismissed the idea. Concerned that an outward alliance with the KGB might tarnish his democratic credentials, he wanted someone with a lower profile. A few days passed and Sobchak called again. He asked Kalugin if he had ever heard of a young officer named Vladimir Vladimirovich Putin.[25]

Some would assume the KGB had a hand in directing the young officer into Sobchak's office, but according to Kalugin, it was Sobchak who recruited him. Vladimir Putin remembered Sobchak from his lectures in law school but did not know him well. By his own account, a friend from law school had suggested he go see Sobchak, which he did with trepidation. He could hardly have agreed with some of Sobchak's most blistering criticisms of the KGB, and Sobchak's political future remained tenuous at best, like everything in the Soviet Union in 1990. Nevertheless, that May, he went to Sobchak's new office in the Mariinsky Palace, and Sobchak hired him on the spot. He said he would arrange his transfer with Merkuriev and told him to start the next Monday. First, though, Putin felt obliged to disclose his actual profession. "I must tell you that I am not just an assistant to the rector," he told Sobchak. "I am a regular officer of the KGB."

In Putin's recollection, Sobchak hesitated and then, to Putin's surprise, dismissed this issue. "Fuck it!" he replied.[26]

Putin insisted that he must inform his superiors and, if necessary, resign from the KGB. He agonized over the decision, his friends said. Although he had grown disillusioned, the KGB remained the institution he served loyally. In the event, whatever worries he had about the Center's reaction were misplaced. The KGB was happy to have its own agent working undercover in the office of Leningrad's rising political star. This new democratic experiment, after all, was a dangerous thing that required eternal vigilance. And so with the KGB's blessing, perhaps at its insistence, Lieutenant Colonel Putin remained in the service, continuing to earn his meager, if steady salary, which was more than he earned as Sobchak's adviser.

He was now living a double life, the life of the undercover agent at last—only inside his own country. He began to advise Sobchak even as he continued to work in a small office on the first floor of the university's red and white Twelve Collegia building. His task there was to monitor foreign students and visitors who were arriving in increasing numbers as glasnost eased travel restrictions. He no longer worked in the Big House on Liteiny Prospekt, but he still paid occasional visits, the purposes of which could only have been to keep his superiors informed of the changing politics of the day—at the university and in Sobchak's office. When a delegation from St. Petersburg Community College in Florida arrived in the fall of 1990 for an educational exchange, it was the lieutenant colonel who played host to the college's unsuspecting president, Carl M. Kuttler Jr.

Kuttler had met Putin's university adviser, Valery Musin, when he visited Florida and proposed establishing links between the two cities and the two universities. When Kuttler and his delegation arrived, Putin met them at the airport and spent the next ten days handling all the arrangements of their meetings, meals, and concerts at the symphony and ballet. He did so with a punctuality and efficiency that surprised Kuttler, given the deteriorating economic conditions in the city, including a critical shortage of gasoline that produced long, frustrating lines. When Kuttler went on an excursion out of the city, the government limousine was in danger of running out of fuel until Putin intervened and directed it to a city sanitation depot where it could find gas.

His dual careers increasingly began to intersect. He introduced Kuttler to Sobchak, and at a banquet on the last night Sobchak had a favor to ask of Kuttler. "Carl, would you do something for me?" he began. "We don't have much travel money." Sobchak had turned his sights to international travel and wanted to return again to the United States. "Would you pay for it?"[27]

Kuttler raised the money and Sobchak visited a month later. In Washington, he met President George H. W. Bush and senior congressional leaders. Procter & Gamble flew Sobchak's delegation to Cleveland for a day. And he stayed in Florida at Kuttler's house on the bay, where he marveled at the environmental restrictions that forbade him to fell a single tree without permission from the municipal authorities.[28] Putin credited the trip to America with Sobchak's decision to promote him to his permanent staff in 1991. He also remembered Kuttler's behavior at the banquet. When it came time to reciprocate a toast, Kuttler asked the surprised guests to hold hands, and he said a prayer. "You prayed for our university," Putin reminded him when they met again a decade later. "You prayed for our city. You prayed for our country. And you prayed for me." Kuttler suspected the young university assistant had never before heard a prayer on his behalf. He never imagined that his host was a KGB officer.[29]

Lieutenant Colonel Putin's future was now increasingly affixed to a man apt to quote classical poets and artfully articulate what were once heresies. "We are all infected to some degree by the system," Sobchak wrote only a year after his new adviser came to work for him, musing on Pushkin's "Bronze Horseman" and what he called the "system syndrome." "From birth we have been taught intolerance, suspicion and paranoid fear of spies." Sobchak envisioned a new Soviet Union that offered justice and hope, a democracy, a "normal, civilized state" in which "there is no need to slaughter half the population to make the other half happy."[30]

The two men made an odd couple. They differed in age, in temperament, and in philosophy. Sobchak was flamboyant, charismatic; Putin reserved, inherently suspicious, and secretive. He did not share Sobchak's hostility toward the Soviet Union, but he nonetheless served his new boss as loyally as he had his KGB commanders, and over time he began to absorb some of his superior's views. Even as other KGB officers resigned on principle or in pursuit of new ways of making money, Putin hedged his bets. He never broke with the agency the way Kalugin had; he did not regret his service and never would. One of his superiors in Leningrad who had also served in East Germany, Yuri Leshchev, said service in the KGB was to Putin "a sacred business."[31] And yet Sobchak drew him deeper and deeper into the new politics of the era. He worked for the old regime—and for those who would overthrow it.

Leningrad's city council, while democratic, proved inept. Its members quarreled endlessly among themselves and with Sobchak over the powers of the chairman, but did little to address the city's dire needs for housing, food, and transportation. By the summer of 1990, the Soviet economy was lurching on the brink of collapse, and Leningrad and other cities began to run out of basic foodstuffs; the shelves of its meager stores emptied first of tea and soap, then sugar, cigarettes, and even vodka. Shortly after returning from the United States—where he had visited a well-stocked Kmart in Alexandria, Virginia—Sobchak forced the council to introduce ration cards. It was hardly famine—not with a black market flourishing—but rationing brought back horrifying memories of the siege. "Democracy is facing a hungry winter," Sobchak said in defense of the plan. "It is crucial for democracy to survive this winter."[32]

By then the KGB and Soviet military leaders had already begun to make emergency plans for the imposition of martial law. In January 1991, Gorbachev ordered the military to restore Communist rule in Lithuania after days of protests, reversing the republic's declaration of independence the year before. The assault culminated with a tank attack on the television tower in the capital, Vilnius. Fourteen people died, but Lithuanian leaders continued to defy Moscow and pressed ahead with a referendum on independence in February, which Gorbachev declared illegal. In June Russia held its own presidential election, and Boris Yeltsin became a legitimately elected counterweight to Gorbachev's increasingly erratic and unpopular rule. The same month, Sobchak took advantage of the national election to win election to a newly created executive branch that would wield authority over the unwieldy city legislature. Only a month before, he had forced the council to create the position of mayor, which only he was in a position to win. The council's members were increasingly at odds with Sobchak's role as their chairman, and they hoped that by creating separate branches of government, they would be able to constrain his powers as the city's leader. Leningrad also held a nonbinding referendum to restore the city's prerevolutionary name, St. Petersburg. Sobchak had initially opposed the change, but he campaigned for the restoration of the city's name with savvy and tact. He described the change as the natural evolution of Peter the Great's vision of the city as a "window to Europe," and he offered to remove Lenin's waxy corpse from its Red Square mausoleum and bury him with his relatives in Leningrad, in keeping with the revolutionary's last will and testament. His offer respected those who still revered Lenin and appeased those who wanted to end the cult that still surrounded him.[33] When the election came, Sobchak won 66 percent of the vote, while a narrower majority—54 percent—voted to change the city's name.[34]

Vladimir Putin played no role in the politics of the collapse of the Soviet Union. He merited no appearance in the many contemporaneous memoirs and histories of the monumental events of 1991—not even Sobchak's, which he wrote in the year after Putin began working for him. He remained a young functionary, accustomed to working in the ranks and in the shadows. His loyalties and his fate, though, now rested with the city's undisputed political leader, a man often mentioned as a future president of all Russia.

After Sobchak's election, Putin ended his work at the university, and in June 1991 he joined the mayor's staff as the director of the city's new committee on foreign relations. He made himself indispensable: a quiet, level-headed, but stern presence, working in a sparsely furnished office. He worked so tirelessly and with such efficiency and "brute determination," as one colleague put it, that he earned the unflattering nickname "Stasi," only in part because of his tour of duty in East Germany.[35]

The KGB had not forgotten its officer in Sobchak's ranks. Coincidentally or not, Putin's colleagues showed up in his office one evening after Sobchak had rushed off on a trip and left his aide with three sheets of blank paper, each signed, to complete with assorted mayoral business. The officers who had come to him wanted one of them for some nefarious purpose he either did not know or never told. "Can't you see that this man trusts me?" Putin later claimed to have replied, showing them a folder with the papers in them.[36] Putin did not refuse outright, but they did not insist either. They simply apologized, and left.

On August 17, 1991, the Putins went on vacation, driving to Kaliningrad to stay in a resort on the Curonian Spit, a narrow crescent of beaches, dunes, and forests on the Baltic Sea.[37] Sobchak had spent that weekend in Lithuania to discuss his vision of a free trade agreement and then flown back to Moscow on the night of August 18 to take part two days later in the signing of a new Union Treaty that would effectively dissolve the central Soviet state. Mikhail Gorbachev, Boris Yeltsin, and the party leader in Kazakhstan, Nursultan Nazarbayev, had secretly negotiated the agreement to transfer functions of the central government to the individual Soviet republics, significantly weakening the central authority of the Kremlin.

The ceremony never took place. That night, inside the Kremlin, a group of hardliners had already set in motion a putsch, placing Gorbachev under house arrest at his vacation home in the Crimea and establishing the State Committee of the State of Emergency. The coup's leaders included Gorbachev's vice president, Gennady Yanayev; the prime minister; the ministers of defense and interior; and Vladimir Kryuchkov, the former chief of foreign intelligence and now the chairman of the KGB. Their formal orders to the military and the KGB to take control were issued at four o'clock the morning of August 19.

The Putins heard the news the way most of the country did, first through a series of radio announcements and then in special bulletins on state television that interrupted the broadcast of *Swan Lake*. Sobchak woke in his hotel room in Moscow when a friend telephoned from Kazakhstan to tell him the news. Tanks and paratroopers in armored vehicles had already poured into the streets of Moscow. Sobchak, with guards and a driver, went to Yeltsin's dacha, joining the leadership of the newly elected Russian parliament to organize the resistance. Sobchak's name, like Yeltsin's, was on the KGB's list of arrest warrants, but the arrests never began. Yeltsin urged Sobchak to return to Leningrad and lead the opposition to the putsch from there. Sobchak, along with a lone guard, made it to Sheremetyevo Airport and booked the next regularly scheduled flight to Leningrad. The putsch plotters, despite the declared state of emergency, allowed life to go on more or less normally, including routine air travel. The three KGB officers who met him in the airport lounge had orders to arrest him, but they simply disobeyed and waited with him until he boarded. "So now I had four guards, three with machine guns," Sobchak recalled.[38] The putsch that the reformers had long dreaded could happen was turning into a farce.

In Leningrad, the city's military commander, Colonel General Viktor Samsonov, had also received orders to deploy troops. He went on television at ten in the morning to announce the state of emergency, outlawing any demonstrations and public gatherings and dissolving all the political parties and social organizations that had sprouted like mushrooms in the previous two years. He also declared the formation of an emergency committee that would replace the city's newly elected government. The committee included local military and KGB leaders and the new Communist Party leader, Boris Gidaspov. Sobchak's name was conspicuously absent, but not that of the rear admiral Sobchak had selected as his deputy chairman and later vice mayor, Vyacheslav Shcherbakov. He too was at a seaside resort on the Black Sea, and after flying back to Leningrad, disavowed any involvement in the putsch. By the time Sobchak's flight from Moscow landed at two o'clock, however, no troops had entered the city. General Samsonov's order had not been carried out.

The city's police commander, Arkady Kramarev, sent a car that took Sobchak straight to the military headquarters on Palace Square, opposite the Hermitage, where the Leningrad emergency committee had convened. Kramarev was there already, openly resisting Samsonov's orders to clear the streets of the protesters who had begun to gather outside the city council's headquarters at the Mariinsky Palace.

Sobchak burst in and blusteringly accused them of an illegal conspiracy that would result in "a Nuremberg of their own." Sobchak ignored Gidaspov, the party boss who was to replace him as the city's leader, and focused his fury instead on General Samsonov. He cited specific instances of military commanders being used by corrupt or criminal party leaders, including the killings in Georgia he had investigated. Ever the lawyer, he challenged the legality of the general's orders on the technicality that they did not explicitly authorize a state of emergency in Leningrad. Kramarev later said that Sobchak berated the general in a tone he had almost certainly never heard in his years as an officer.[39] "If you take a fateful step now, everybody will remember you as a traitor, an executioner," Sobchak told him.[40] Whether because of Sobchak's anger or his logic, the general promised to reconsider the deployment of troops and dithered for crucial hours.

Sobchak then sped to the city's television station and spoke live on the air that evening, appearing with Shcherbakov and the provincial legislative leader, Yuri Yarov. Both of them had been announced as local leaders of the emergency committee, but now it became clear to the public that they had not supported the putsch. The national television channels in Moscow had been seized, but Leningrad's channels had not, and they still broadcast across much of the Soviet Union. The station manager let the broadcast proceed since Shcherbakov was there, assuming he was now in charge.[41] Millions heard Sobchak's remarks and could see that the putsch faced resistance. "Once again there is an attempt to block our people's path to freedom, democracy, and true independence," Sobchak began. He urged the population to gather the next morning in Palace Square. He referred to the putsch's leaders as "former" ministers and then simply as "citizens," as defendants in court were called.[42]

Throughout that first crucial day, Vladimir Putin remained at the beach resort more than five hundred miles away. He reached Sobchak by telephone the night of August 19 but did not return immediately, though he presumably could have. Instead he waited until the next day, when he caught a regularly scheduled flight from Kaliningrad.[43] He was, by all accounts, deeply ambivalent. A year and a half before, he returned from the crumbling Soviet empire in Eastern Europe dismayed by what he considered the abandonment of its comrade nations, the humiliating retreat of its troops and intelligence officers, and the triumph of NATO, the West, and capitalism. Now the Soviet Union itself was coming apart at the seams, its republics, including Russia, moving entropically toward independence. It meant the dismemberment of his country, and the putsch's leaders, he would later say, simply aimed to stop that. He considered theirs a noble purpose. The KGB chairman, Kryuchkov, widely considered a pompous, conniving bore, was in his mind "a very decent man."[44] Although Kryuchkov's intentions were clear, the KGB's loyalties were not. Many officers loyal to the new Russian government aided Boris Yeltsin and the putsch's opponents with intelligence and even a printing press. Some younger officers even drafted a statement denouncing the coup.[45] Lieutenant Colonel Putin, now working for one of the country's leading democrats, had to choose a side.

Shortly after dawn on August 20, Sobchak went to the sprawling Kirov factory, which produced tanks, tractors, and the turbines used in the Soviet Union's nuclear submarines and ice-breakers. The factory, the city's largest, was legendary in Soviet mythology because of its part in the Great Patriotic War, remaining open throughout the siege despite being only miles from the front. Sobchak wanted to arrive before the morning shift to rally the factory's thirty thousand workers. He spoke in front of a car with a loudspeaker, after which the factory's managers offered to allow workers to join the rally he had called for in Palace Square. The factory, the police, and most of the city's elected officials were now openly defying the putsch. Thousands of Kirov workers marched in columns up Stachek Prospekt to the center of the city. "They knew to what this might lead," a machinist among them said. "They felt that they were people, human beings. They had stopped being afraid."[46]

The crowd that gathered that day was the largest seen in Leningrad in decades. More than 130,000 people thronged Palace Square and adjoining streets for blocks around. Outside the Hermitage Museum a banner declared "No to the military putsch!" In contrast to the tense atmosphere in Moscow, where protesters braced for movements by the armored units in the city, the rally was orderly and hopeful, supervised by the police officers and KGB agents who were supposed to have prevented it from happening. According to one newspaper report, Sobchak had even discussed plans for the rally with the local KGB boss, Kurkov, agreeing that it would be conducted calmly.[47] Sobchak spoke briefly, followed by Dmitri Likhachev, a revered linguist, preservationist, and historian who had survived the Gulag and exile, who told the crowd that the people "can no longer be forced to their knees." That evening Sobchak appeared at a special session of the city council in the Mariinsky Palace. "The situation in Leningrad is fully under control of the bodies of lawful power," he declared. The putsch collapsed in Leningrad before it did anywhere else.

Putin arrived from Kaliningrad that afternoon but did not attend the rally in Palace Square. He joined Sobchak at the Mariinsky Palace and remained there. He had watched the new "acting president" of the Soviet Union, Gennady Yanayev, hold the news conference the night before—watched as Yanayev repeated the emergency committee's lies about Gorbachev's health and vowed to put an end to the "present Time of Troubles," alluding to the occupation, war, and famine that had followed the death of Boris Godunov at the turn of the seventeenth century. "Having embarked on the path of profound reforms and having gone a considerable way in this direction, the Soviet Union has now reached a point at which it finds itself faced with a deep crisis, the further development of which could both place in question the course of reforms itself as well as lead to serious cataclysms in international life," Yanayev said, but as he did his voice trembled and his hands shook. The journalists present began asking probing questions; they even laughed at his improbable answers.

Putin said he knew then that the putsch was doomed. No matter how deep his loyalty to the KGB, he would not follow the orders of this emergency committee, even if he supported their underlying intention of preserving the union. Their effort to reassert Soviet power meant the end of it. "Up until that time I didn't really understand the transformation that was going on in Russia," he recalled of his return from East Germany. "All the ideals, all the goals that I had had when I went to work for the KGB, collapsed." And yet siding with Sobchak would amount to a violation of his oath of office. And so, after sixteen years of service to the KGB, he wrote his resignation.

It was, he claimed, his second resignation. He said he had sent a similar letter a year before, though in far less dire circumstances. In the political turmoil surrounding the city council and later the mayor's office, Putin had confronted innuendo about his intelligence background; some people hoped for help from it, others threatened to expose it. Either way they wanted something from Putin, and he was "just sick and tired of that brazen blackmail."[48] He wanted to protect Sobchak and his reputation, as he had warned him when he first became his adviser. It was the hardest decision of his life, he said, but he drafted and sent his resignation. And then nothing happened. He never heard any more about his letter, which disappeared in the bureaucracy, if it ever reached it. Nor did he make any effort to follow up, a discrepancy he never would explain fully.

This time in the middle of the confused putsch, he told Sobchak of his decision to quit, making it clear to his boss and mentor that he had sided with him. Despite the huge public protest against the putsch, the situation in Leningrad remained unsettled. Yeltsin, acting as president of Russia, issued a decree naming Shcherbakov the military commander of the Leningrad district, effectively replacing General Samsonov, who was in fact quietly heeding Sobchak's warnings and staying on the sidelines. Putin organized the defenses at the Mariinsky, passing out pistols to Sobchak's advisers, though he later claimed he had left his KGB revolver in his safe, as he had in Dresden. A few thousand protesters remained in the square outside, keeping a nervous vigil behind makeshift barricades that would have served little purpose against a determined military assault. He once again found himself inside a building surrounded by a tense mob demanding freedom, only this time he was on their side of the barricade.

Rumors of imminent military action continued to swirl, including a report around three in the morning that elite special operation troops had been deployed from a secret location inside the city and would march on Sobchak's office. "They can polish us off in five minutes," Shcherbakov told Sobchak. For their safety, Sobchak and Putin fled and spent the night in the Kirov factory.

By dawn on August 21, though, the putsch had crumpled. Gorbachev had been freed from house arrest and was returning to Moscow. Boris Yeltsin, the public face of the resistance, would become the leader of the new Russian nation that emerged. Sobchak had led the resistance in Leningrad, and became one of that nation's most prominent new democrats. Not at all by his design, Vladimir Putin landed on the winning side of the collapse of the Soviet Union. And yet he did not share the euphoria that many Russians felt. On the contrary, the experience was for him a difficult one. Lyudmila and his friends described the period as the most trying of his life. "In fact," he said, "it tore my life apart."[49] Colonel Leshchev, who had been a superior in the Leningrad KGB headquarters, said Putin's resignation was more pragmatic than idealistic. "There were no prospects and in general it was not clear what would happen with the intelligence service."[50] It was a calculated risk. Had the putsch succeeded, he could have faced arrest. At a minimum, he would certainly have been unemployed after having resigned. As it was, he waited until the momentum had swung against the putsch. Leonid Polokhov, who studied law with him at Leningrad State University and later became a military prosecutor who exposed the terrible rituals of hazing in the Soviet military during the glasnost era, was simply stunned when he learned that his friend had left the service. "Volodya surprised me greatly two times: the first time, when he joined the KGB—and the second when he left it," he said.[51]

PART TWO

CHAPTER 5

The Spies Come In from the Cold

Igor Shadkhan spent four months in 1991 filming a documentary in Norilsk, the bleak, industrial city in the far north of Siberia. This place, above the Arctic Circle, was scarcely inhabitable, but underneath it lay some of the most valuable minerals on earth: nickel, copper, and other metals. Beginning in the 1930s, the Soviet Union built a prison camp and then a city to extract the wealth in the mines that extended for miles underground. Shadkhan was there to document a darker truth that would never have been revealed before glasnost: Norilsk was not a glorious Soviet conquest of nature; it was a desolate, frozen island of the Gulag Archipelago built on the bones of those who did not survive.

Shadkhan, fifty-one and all but bald, was a native of Leningrad. He achieved fame as the director of a television series, *Test for Adults,* that began in 1979 and was still on the air in 1991. In it, he filmed interviews with a group of ten children and their parents, charting the evolution of their lives over the years. Shadkhan's talent was his ability to converse; he elicited the hopes of his subjects in tender interviews that avoided topics which might have offended the censors during the Brezhnev years but seemed illuminating nonetheless. He planned to turn his interviews with the Gulag survivors in Norilsk into a new series, to be called *Snow: My Fate,* but the general director of his channel, Dmitri Rozhdestven-sky, had something else in mind for him first. He asked Shadkhan to profile the staff of Leningrad's mayor. Rozhdestvensky, who would go on to start a television production company called Russian Video, thought it would be good for business, since the mayor now effectively owned the station, and he suggested Shadkhan start with an aide who held an important position.

"Who is this Putin?" Shadkhan asked.[1]

When Shadkhan returned from Norilsk that fall, his hometown was suddenly a different city, under the control not of the Communist Party, but of the democrats. The collapse of the August putsch hastened the collapse of the Soviet Union, then in its final weeks of existence. The conspirators were arrested, including Vladimir Kryuchkov, the chairman of the KGB, which would itself subsequently be broken into disparate departments under the political control of Russia's new leaders. The Fifth Chief Directorate, which hunted dissidents, was abolished. Gorbachev returned to his post but as president of a country now devolving into fifteen separate states. The Russian parliament in Moscow—comprising the Congress of People's Deputies and a smaller Supreme Soviet with 252 members—was now the undisputed legislative power in the land. On September 6, it formally ratified the results of the referendum that Leningrad had held three months earlier. The city once again became St. Petersburg, as Peter the Great had christened it nearly three centuries before. Sobchak presided over a formal rechristening celebration on November 7, pointedly choosing the seventy-forth anniversary of the Russian Revolution as the date.

Boris Yeltsin, as president of the new Russia, had banned the Communist Party after the putsch, and Sobchak used every opportunity to bury the party in his city, too. He seized the party's power, assets, and infrastructure, including its headquarters in the Smolny Institute, the eighteenth-century convent and later girls' academy where Lenin had set up his Bolshevik government. The baroque landmark now became his office. The move symbolized "the victory of democratic forces" in a new Russia, but it also signaled "Sobchak's intention to grab real power for himself in the very beginning of the post-Communist era."[2]

Sobchak now appointed Putin to be the head of the city's new committee on foreign economic affairs, and Putin settled into a new office in Smolny. Following Sobchak's lead, he replaced the portrait of Lenin that decorated apparatchiks' offices with an engraving of Peter the Great. In his new capacity, Putin joined Sobchak in fighting the rearguard efforts of the Communist Party to throttle the city's new authorities, enforcing Sobchak's decrees that had usurped the party's perquisites. The House of Political Enlightenment, a modern marble-clad edifice across Dictatorship of the Proletariat Street from Smolny, had long been the Communist Party's property, but Sobchak decided to turn it into an international business center, which soon began to attract savvy Soviet entrepreneurs who had already seen the potential for trade and commerce in the new Russia. They included men like Dmitri Rozhdestvensky from the state television channel and Vladimir Yankunin, a former trade diplomat at the United Nations. Their liaison in the corridors of power would be the unprepossessing former KGB officer put in place by Sobchak.

The rump of the city's Communist Party continued to occupy a wing of the new business center, however, and its members defiantly raised the Soviet Union's red hammer and sickle from the roof. It was a symbolic act and nothing more, but Putin ordered the flag removed, only to have the Communists raise another the next day. Again Putin ordered it removed. Things went on in this way long enough that the Communists ran out of proper flags and began hanging handmade ones, one of the last more dark brown than red. Eventually, Putin had had enough. He ordered workers to cut down the entire flagpole.[3] Putin, echoing Sobchak, never had much patience for opposition.

The idea for a television documentary about the mayor's staff was Sobchak's. Understanding the role television played in his own rise to prominence in the Congress of People's Deputies, Sobchak believed that showing his managers at work would cement the idea that he, not the city council, was the central figure of authority in the new St. Petersburg. Shadkhan was not enthusiastic. He had just finished filming interviews with people who had spent years suffering in the Gulag because of an abuse of power. Now he was sent to the building that had until a few weeks before housed the Communist Party that had been responsible for their plight. He had been there only once before, he said, and found its corridors sterile and chilling. Now he found it bustling with clusters of people speaking not only Russian but also foreign languages—in the very seat of political power.

The man who greeted him in Putin's office on Smolny's first floor was Igor Sechin, whose lowly position and bearish demeanor belied his world travels and fluency in Portuguese.[4] A classmate of Putin's at university, he had worked in Mozambique and then Angola in the 1980s as a translator for Soviet military advisers, though many suspected he, too, worked for the KGB or for military intelligence. He became an inseparable aide to Putin, whose office—and soon Sobchak's—was full of men like Sechin, veterans of the Cold War, cast adrift when the Soviet empire caved in on itself. Putin explained Sobchak's idea for the documentary to Shadkhan and flattered him by praising his work on *Test for Adults,* but he also tried to set conditions, asking for the questions in advance. Shadkhan refused. "There is one rule: you should not know the questions—and I

the answers," he told him, and Putin relented.[5] The interviews continued over a number of days in November 1991. Putin looked younger
than the thirty-nine he was, his hair still blond, though thinning. He was
so short and lean, so diminutive, that he seemed out of proportion to the
grand committee rooms where Shadkhan filmed. In his office, though,
Shadkhan drew the camera claustrophobically close, focused on his deep
blue eyes and soft lips, his cheeks discolored by stubble. He began with
banal questions about his age, his family, his education, even his zodiac
sign. ("Libra, I think," Putin said, "but I'm not sure.") He asked about
his dog, his work, and the politics of a new Russia.

The obvious question, about his career before government, was soon
to come. Putin, years later, claimed he had arranged the interview himself to disclose his association with a loathed organization that was then
being dismantled. Sobchak's critics and others warned Putin that his
still-secret KGB background, once exposed, could be turned against him
or the mayor, and he believed that disclosing the fact on his own would
defuse the whole matter. Shadkhan obliged perhaps more than he had
expected. Being "a slave to metaphor," he filmed the young mayoral aide
driving his Volga and added to the scene a piano sonata from *Seventeen
Moments of Spring,* a beloved television miniseries from 1973 based on a
novel written, like *The Shield and the Sword,* with the cooperation of the
KGB.[6] Its hero was a double agent in Nazi Germany named Max Otto
von Stirlitz, and the series was another of the Soviet-era spy thrillers that
Putin adored.[7] When Shadkhan asked him about his vocation on camera, however, he sounded defensive and petulant.

"It seems that we cannot leave the subject," Putin said.

"You will agree, though, that one does not meet an intelligence officer
that often—well, at least one who admits being one," Shadkhan replied.

"You never know," Putin said cryptically. "You may be meeting them
quite often. He knows it, and you don't."[8]

His coming out continued with a lengthy interview published on
November 25 in the newspaper *Chas Pik,* or *Rush Hour.*[9] He did not
expunge his past, but he wanted to distinguish his career from the KGB's
crimes, from the ruthless crusades against dissidents to the abortive
putsch. He told the interviewer that the KGB had become "a monster"
that no longer carried out the "tasks for which it was created," that is,
the protection of the state from its external enemies. He insisted that
his work involved foreign intelligence and that he had no connection to
the KGB's internal repression. He also emphasized that no intelligence

agency in the world could work without secret agents. "So it was, so it is and so it will be." That past was behind him, he said, but he felt no remorse about the career he had chosen.

"You don't repent of your past?" the interviewer, Nataliya Nikiforova, asked.

"No, I don't repent," he replied. "I repent of crimes. I did not commit any crimes. And I don't justify, though to justify is easier than taking a decisive step." By "decisive step," he meant his resignation from the KGB, which he emphasized repeatedly.

Far from disqualifying him from public service, he said, his background, his experience, his fluency in German, and his familiarity with international economics would serve the city's needs and Russia's new democracy. When Nikiforova asked if the city's "international partners" would look askance at the presence of KGB spies on Sobchak's staff, he simply noted that the American president, George H. W. Bush, had previously served as director of the Central Intelligence Agency, and no one disqualified him from holding office.

Such were the heady days that followed the events of August. Everything was mixed up, and anything seemed possible, even to speak of secrets long hidden. Except for three deaths in Moscow, the people turned back the putsch, without violence, simply by refusing to accept the outcome of a power struggle in the high ranks of the Soviet hierarchy. This new Russia offered the exhilarating, disorienting opportunity to be free, to live without fear, to be honest and accountable, to remake oneself for the new era. Russia faced economic hardship, but the diminished heir of the Soviet Union could now establish a democratic government, end its Cold War isolation, and open itself to Europe and the rest of the world. In his first foray into the public spotlight, unthinkable only months before, Vladimir Putin portrayed himself as an avowed democrat. And yet even then, at the dawn of democracy in Russia, he warned that the imperative of the strong state—and the people's willingness to accept, even desire it—remained part of the collective Russian temperament. "No matter how sad, no matter how terrible it sounds, I believe that a turn towards totalitarianism for a period of time is possible in our country. The danger, though, should be seen not in the organs of law enforcement, the security services, the police, or even the army. The danger is in the mentality, the mentality of our people, in our very own mentality. It seems to all of us—and I will admit, to me sometimes as well—that by imposing strict order with an iron fist, we will all begin to live better, more comfortably, more securely. In actual fact that comfort would very quickly pass because that iron fist would very quickly begin to strangle us."[10]

Sobchak reached the zenith of his popularity and power after the putsch. He was Russia's second most prominent politician after Yeltsin.[11] His vision for his city was as grandiose as his personal ambition. He wanted to re-create the glory of the imperial capital, revitalizing the city's architectural masterpieces, its monuments, and its elegant canals. Having already proposed a free economic zone to attract foreign investment, he reimagined the old Leningrad as a glistening "new" European city, a financial and cultural capital that would rival Moscow for national and international preeminence. He met the U.S. secretary of state, James A. Baker III, who flew into the city on September 15, and five days later Sobchak flew to London, with Putin, to meet the British prime minister, John Major. It was Putin's first experience in the West: in October Sobchak traveled to West Germany for a meeting with Chancellor Helmut Kohl, with Putin serving deftly as his translator. Sobchak soon joined one of the eminent Cold Warriors, Henry Kissinger, as co-chairman of an international commission of experts and businessmen devoted to finding investors who would convert the city's moribund defense factories and other manufacturers into commercial enterprises. When Kissinger flew into Petersburg for a visit, it was Vladimir Putin who met him at the airport and took him to the mayor's residence, chatting about his KGB past. "All decent people got their start in intelligence," Kissinger told him, to his delight. "I did, too."[12]

Soon Sobchak was abroad as much as he was in Petersburg, an international celebrity, profiled by *Time* as one of the rising political stars who would turn Russia into a modern, thriving democracy and free market.[13] What happened instead disappointed and mystified those who invested so much hope in Russia's democratic future. Almost immediately, Sobchak squandered his enormous political capital with acts of arrogance and audacious folly. To the dismay of the city's liberals and intelligentsia, he filled his ranks with apparatchiks of the supposedly deposed Communist nomenklatura.[14] The now-discredited KGB, too, provided not only Putin but also a steady supply of veterans to fill the ranks of Sobchak's growing staff. For all his talk of democracy, Sobchak courted the security officials who remained in their positions. Viktor Cherkesov, a close friend and colleague of Putin's who was notorious for prosecuting dissidents for anti-Soviet crimes, took over the Petersburg branch of one of the security agencies that emerged from the broken-up KGB, the Ministry of Security.

Sobchak's motives for hiring the security veterans puzzled and alarmed the city's reformers, but he argued that the city needed experienced professionals to govern, even if it meant co-opting the political and security bureaucracy that he had once vowed to dismantle. To secure his power, he needed the apparatchiks, not the democrats. This would be a central dilemma in Russia for years to come. Young reformers like the economist Anatoly Chubais, who helped draft early proposals to establish Petersburg's free-enterprise zones, soon found themselves without positions or otherwise marginalized. Chubais left instead for Moscow in the fall and joined Yeltsin's privatization program, which eventually made him one of the most reviled figures of the new Russia.[15]

As he consolidated executive authority, Sobchak's relations with the city council soured even more than they had in the internal struggles before the Soviet Union's collapse. Many of its members, especially the most ardent democrats, were dismayed by his authoritarian tendencies. By early 1992, the council was already trying to impeach him, and the actions of his aide, Vladimir Putin, were among the reasons.

The city faced a multitude of challenges in the winter of 1991. Nothing worked, and the city was broke. The city's heavily militarized industries, already reeling, were atrophying with the collapse of weapons contracts. The dissolution of the Soviet Union severed economic links with neighboring and now independent republics that had once supplied Leningrad with food and gasoline. As winter arrived, the city had to tap a reserve of canned goods until four thousand tons of fresh meat arrived in January. Moscow, as the capital, had better supply chains and resources than Petersburg, and as a result the latter's shops would have only paltry stocks of food for years to come. Sobchak warned in November that the food shortages had become critical.[16]

And yet, inexplicably, one of his first decrees to revive the city's fortunes was to turn the city into a new Las Vegas, and he put Putin in charge. The result was a proliferation of casinos and gambling dens throughout a faded but beautiful city that had more pressing needs than slot machines. The Petersburg casino boom was not Sobchak's idea alone, but Russia's democratic transition soon had its enduring metaphor, the single most visible manifestation of the new capitalism Russians had been denied for decades. Sobchak's decree ostensibly sought to bring order to the newly emerging industry—with the "taxes to be used to finance top-priority social programs"[17]—but he also authorized the city to provide "the necessary facilities for housing casinos," an authority he used and abused in other industries as well. Sobchak distributed property rights like a tsar passing out land grants. For the next two decades Petersburg's cityscape, like Moscow's, would have a tawdry skein of neon lights and alluring billboards promising riches, and the authorities would fight an ongoing war with organized crime.

Putin did his homework; he studied the way the West regulated its gambling industry. Free now to travel beyond the borders of the Soviet bloc, he could experience life in places he knew only from intelligence reports. As part of his fact-finding that fall, he and Lyudmila flew to Hamburg, where with friends they visited the Reeperbahn, the city's famous red-light district and the location of one of its casinos. It was the friends, he insisted, who talked them into attending an erotic performance while there, and this introduction to the extremes of personal liberty—to indulge in vices without the moral stricture of state ideology and KGB scrutiny—left such a lasting impression that a decade later he described the performers in vivid detail, from their height to the color of their bare skin.[18]

His conclusion was that the profits of sin should belong to the state. Initially he favored creating a state monopoly to control the gambling industry, even though Russia's new anti-monopoly laws forbade it, hoping to break the state's grip on the economy. Putin's committee instead created a municipal enterprise that would buy 51 percent of shares in each of the new casinos the city licensed, and the dividends would fill the city's coffers. The city lacked the cash, and so acquired the shares in lieu of rent for the city-owned buildings that became the casinos. The lawyers advising Putin's committee were his university adviser, Valery Musin, and Dmitri Medvedev, a young lawyer who had campaigned for Sobchak when he ran for the Congress of People's Deputies. The enterprise proved to be a disaster, one giant racket that brought the city into alliance with shadowy figures said to include ex-KGB officers and mobsters.[19] The city's new company was called Neva Chance, and it founded two dozen casinos, most of which never received licenses from the new federal government being established in Moscow. And yet the profits the city hoped for never materialized. The managers simply laundered the proceeds of a cash business and reported losses to the authorities. The owners acquired property and made millions, and the city received almost nothing for it. "They were laughing at us," as Putin would put it later, defending his role.

The creation of a regulated market economy proved far more difficult than Putin, like many Russian officials, anticipated. The legal foundations for capitalism were not yet in place, and like most officials, he had no experience in managing economic affairs after decades of five-year plans and state control. "This was a typical mistake made by people who are encountering a market for the first time," he acknowledged. The people who suffered from the mistake were "pensioners, teachers and doctors,"[20] but he did nothing about the scandalous loss to the state's coffers then, or later. Others, meanwhile, quickly became rich, exploiting the immature legal and economic system with, some suspected, the complicity of officials like Putin.

The suspicions surrounding another of Putin's "mistakes" would have more lasting consequences, creating an aura of impunity in the city's governance and fueling his own distrust of public demands for accountability. On December 4, 1991, Putin wrote a letter to the federal Ministry of the Economy in Moscow requesting permission to barter abroad more than $120 million worth of products from what were still state companies—including 750,000 cubic meters of wood, 150,000 tons of oil, 30,000 tons of scrap metal, and smaller amounts of rare-earth metals, copper, aluminum, cement, and ammonium—for the equivalent in meat, butter, sugar, garlic, and fruit.[21]

For a second winter, the city faced severe shortages and imposed rationing again. The crisis worsened when the Russian government allowed prices to rise according to market forces at the beginning of 1992. Even where food was available, it was beyond the reach of poor Russians, which then included almost everyone except the most privileged. In the television documentary, Shadkhan showed Putin speaking on the telephone with Sobchak about preparations for a meeting with Yeltsin. When he hung up, eager to show the mayor's office was on top of the food crisis, he told Shadkhan that two and a half tons of sugar would soon be shipped from Ukraine. Already, though, he sounded jaded by the waste and corruption. "There is many a slip 'twixt the cup and the lip," he said.[22]

As the mayor's office negotiated the barter deals, Putin and a deputy, Aleksandr Anikin, signed dozens of contracts. Many went to companies whose owners, critics would later say, had links to the mayor's office and to Putin himself. The contracts were sloppily written, and the whole enterprise was legally dubious since some of the deals were negotiated before Putin had received permission to do so from the appropriate federal minister in Moscow. The contracts had unusually high commissions of 25 to 50 percent; these sizable profits ostensibly went to the city's coffers for what was supposed to be a crash project to stave off hunger, but most seemed to have mysteriously disappeared. Moreover, the contracts were priced at the official exchange rates, which undervalued the goods being exported. Worst of all, almost nothing was imported in return. The only contract reported to have been fulfilled delivered two tankers of cooking oil, which Putin duly reported to Moscow. The deal was a catastrophic failure at best. At worst, it was a scam.

The city council, perpetually at war with Sobchak, launched an investigation, led by Marina Salye, a gray-haired geologist and one of the council's most outspoken democrats. She and a colleague, Yuri Gladkov, focused on twelve contracts that they could establish with certainty had been signed by either Putin or Anikin, though they suspected there were still more hidden. There was no public bidding for these contracts, worth $92 million in all, though there were also no clear laws requiring public bids. From January until May, Salye and Gladkov gathered evidence, took depositions, and assembled a lengthy report that they submitted to the full council. Putin cooperated with the investigation but only grudgingly; he initially refused to provide some licenses and contracts, saying he had to protect commercial trade secrets. More likely, as Salye and Gladkov suspected, the documents would show who was already making money off the city's suffering.

Putin never explained how the contractors were selected, or who they were, but he defended himself aggressively, appearing before the council when summoned and holding press conferences to rebut the accusations.[23] He bristled at the very idea of legislative oversight, considering the inquiry nothing more than a politically motivated assault on the mayor's authority. On March 30, barely six months after the collapse of the August putsch, the council voted to oust Sobchak on the grounds that corruption riddled his government; evidence included the scandal over the food. The council had also compiled a list of one hundred properties Sobchak had already transferred to foreign and local businesses. Their effort failed because the council had no clear legal power to remove him, and Sobchak merely ignored the council's vote.[24]

Putin repeatedly came to his mentor's defense—and his own. He dismissed critics as "these innocent new people" and asserted that Sobchak's team consisted of the people "who knew what button to push to get things done."[25] Even so, he had to acknowledge that almost all of the contractors had failed to deliver the food. He lamented that they were shell companies and pyramid schemes beyond the reach of the courts, even though it had been his committee's responsibility to negotiate the contracts in the first place. Some of the companies had simply exported the materials and then folded as mysteriously as they had appeared, presumably stashing millions of dollars in banks abroad. And yet at least some of the businessmen who received contracts went on to become close associates of Putin's, including Yuri Kovalchuk and Vladimir Yakunin, who operated a new company that received a license to export aluminum and nonferrous metals.[26] Others went to a company called Nevsky Dom, controlled by Vladimir Smirnov, and to the export branch of a refinery with the unwieldy name Kirishinefteorgsintez, one of whose founding owners was Gennady Timchenko. None of these men ever faced any charges. Although they were little known at the time, they would grow close to the young official from the mayor's office and would ultimately, years later, become business titans in the new Russia. It was never proved that Putin himself profited from the deal, though some, like Marina Salye, said they suspected he did, but people around him clearly had, a pattern that would repeat itself in the years ahead. Putin's explanations seemed disingenuous. Instead of demanding an investigation, Putin for the most part deflected questions. He even suggested darkly that members of the council itself had wanted the contracts for themselves and did not want "a meddlesome KGB man" in the role of awarding them.[27]

The investigative committee's report stopped short of explicitly accusing Putin and Anikin of corruption, but it did charge them with "complete incompetence bordering on bad faith." The committee referred the entire affair to the prosecutor's office and called on the mayor to fire them both.[28] A team of investigators from the federal audit chamber traveled to Petersburg to investigate, but did not press charges.[29] The affair tainted Putin with scandal for the first time, but it would be largely forgotten for nearly a decade. Anikin did resign, and was replaced by Aleksei Miller, a young economist who would become one of Putin's closest aides. Sobchak did not punish Putin. Instead, he promoted him to deputy mayor and left him in charge of his greatest goal: attracting foreign investors to the city.

Putin had better success in that endeavor, in part because of his KGB career. His contacts and his fluency in German opened doors to investors from the newly reunified Germany. Even as the casinos and food contracts became mired in controversy, Putin traveled again to Germany—this time to Frankfurt—to announce an international banking conference in Petersburg. There he negotiated the opening of Russia's first foreign bank in the city, Dresdner Bank. The man sent to run it was Matthias Warnig, a former Stasi officer who had been assigned to work with the KGB in Dresden in October 1989, even as East Germany was unraveling amid the protests.[30] They both claimed they first met in Petersburg, though on at least one occasion, in January 1989, they appeared together in a photograph of Soviet and Stasi officers, along with another friend of Putin's involved in high-tech intelligence in Dresden, Sergei Chemezov.[31] Their three lives would soon be intertwined professionally and personally. They were like-minded intelligence veterans navigating the tumultuous transition to a new economic model, one they had operated against all their lives.

Dresdner's bank opened in January 1992, with the aim of creating the financial infrastructure necessary to integrate Russia's economy into the German market and to help privatize or restructure the vast Soviet state enterprises, vertical behemoths that were unlikely to adapt quickly to market forces. Its first project was to assist the Kirov factory, which was now in danger of going bankrupt, costing the jobs of thousands of workers who had supported Sobchak during the putsch in 1991. For Dresdner, it was a risky bet on the future of Russia. Not only were Petersburg's finances in disarray, so were its laws, regulations, and oversight. The entire economy, the entire country, was in chaos, and getting worse. "You really have to start with Adam and Eve," the bank's chief economist, Ernst-Moritz Lipp, said a few months later, explaining the dearth of expertise in banking and finance. "In St. Petersburg, maybe there are 10 people who can really have an effect."[32]

Putin made himself one of them, and Dresdner's early investment would reward the bank and Warnig spectacularly in the years ahead. Dresdner was followed by Deutsche Bank, Banque Nationale de Paris, and Crédit Lyonnaise. The Spanish candy maker Chupa Chups began making lollipops in Petersburg in 1991. Otis Elevator opened a branch, anticipating the renovation of the city's antiquated buildings. Procter & Gamble, which had invited Sobchak to its American headquarters the year before, opened an office in the city almost immediately after the putsch. Sobchak relished his role as city father, but Putin remained in the background, negotiating the deals with foreigners and seeing to the details. "Vladimir Putin was the person who was there to implement what Sobchak wanted," said Kaj Hober, a Swedish lawyer who dealt with him then. Hober spent weeks negotiating the sale of one of the city's landmarks, the Grand Hotel Europe—a sale forced by an onerous tax bill that many believe was meant to clear the way for another favored owner. Hober described him as a stubborn negotiator who would not "give up many millimeters" in their talks. "He certainly seemed at the particular time to be doing what he was supposed to do—that is, representing the interests of St. Petersburg."[33]

Macroeconomic policy—the debate over "shock therapy" to revive Russia's economy—was the province of Boris Yeltsin and his ministers in Moscow, but Sobchak wanted to make his city one of the friendliest to foreign investors in the entire country. Putin's committee oversaw the completion of a fiber-optic cable to Denmark, a project begun during Soviet times, giving the city its first modern international telephone connections. Later the committee would open industrial zones for foreign factories, including Heineken, Pepsi, Coca-Cola, Ford, and Wrigley. Sobchak had, with Putin's help, reopened the "window to the West" that Peter the Great had imagined his capital to be. The mayor traveled regularly abroad, often twice a month or more, tending to his international reputation as much as his job. He also continued to advise Yeltsin in Moscow, devoting hours of time and political capital to helping write Russia's new constitution, introduced in 1993.

Sobchak left the daily administration of the city to his deputies, including Putin, who after his brief star turn on television, tended to operate without public fanfare, or scrutiny. He avoided the cocktail circuit and diplomatic social life. Lyudmila complained that he worked long hours, returning home late at night, while she stayed at his parents' apartment with the children. He rarely had time for friends like Roldugin. Even when they did meet, Roldugin found him drained and preoccupied with the city's affairs.[34] Yet the new work—his "civilian life," as he described it—interested and challenged him. Before, as an intelligence officer, he had collected information to pass to superiors who made decisions on policy. Now he was the one making decisions.[35] Putin developed a reputation for competence, effectiveness, and absolute, ruthless loyalty to Sobchak. While others who worked for the mayor soon left, often acrimoniously, he remained steadfastly by Sobchak's side, his influence and authority growing, even as accusations of corruption swirled around the city's administration. At work, Putin appeared aloof, even imperious, rarely displaying emotion or sympathy—in contrast to the stormy political debates under way in the country. "He could be strict and demanding and yet never raised his voice," his secretary, Marina Yentaltseva, recalled. "If he gave an assignment, he didn't really care how it was done or who did it or what problems they had. It just had to get done, and that was that."[36] When Yentaltseva once broke the news to him that the family's new Caucasian sheep dog had been killed by a car, she was struck by the absence of any reaction at all.

He proved equally enigmatic in his interactions with the investors and politicians who swarmed Smolny, looking for deals and, as often, for help when deals turned sour in the lawless turmoil of Russia's transition to capitalism. Putin was the man to slice through the bureaucracy and opaque laws. "Although he was the principal official for dealing with the problems foreign investors encountered, the investors never felt that they knew him or had a sympathetic ear," wrote Arthur George, an American lawyer who worked closely with him then. "Putin picked his battles carefully and avoided controversy, never going out on a limb. It was difficult to decipher what he really thought."[37]

Putin became a wheeler and dealer, brokering investments and refereeing business disputes through personal connections, contacts, and threats. He continued to travel, with Sobchak or alone, to lure companies into the murky world of post-Communist capitalism. He became the "main enabler" for the city's economy, approving hundreds of licenses and ensuring the state shared in the wealth. He became the arbiter of business disputes in the city, working behind the scenes to settle conflicts that often turned violent. And yet despite Putin's efforts and Sobchak's dreams, Petersburg began to lag behind Moscow on most economic indicators, including production, foreign investment, and unemployment.[38] The city became notorious for its crime—for contract murders carried out by competing gangs and business interests, often with political motives, and for petty thefts from foreigners, which were so rampant that tourism dwindled after the initial influx inspired by the collapse of the Soviet Union.

The intersection of business and organized crime in Petersburg, as elsewhere in Russia, brought Putin into proximity with some of the city's most notorious gangsters. Golden Gates, a company he registered in 1992 for Gennady Timchenko to build an oil terminal, became entangled in a dangerous clash with a gang that escalated to the point that Putin sent his daughters, Masha and Katya, to Germany for safety until things blew over.[39] Putin's ties, through the foreign economic affairs committee and, some said, personally, also entangled him in accusations of criminality. A company he registered with Vladimir Smirnov in 1992, the St. Petersburg Real Estate Holding Company, would come under investigation for laundering money; one of its board members, Mikhail Manevich, would later be assassinated by a sniper in broad daylight on Nevsky Prospekt. The Company, known from its German abbreviation as SPAG, later drew the attention of investigators in Germany and Liechtenstein who suspected the company of laundering money, including proceeds linked to the Cali drug cartel in Colombia. Putin sat on the company's board for years.[40] Putin licensed another company, the Petersburg Fuel Company, which also involved Smirnov and the reputed head of the Tambov crime family, Vladimir Kumarin, whose activities were so notorious in the 1990s that he was dubbed the "night governor." It would receive the exclusive right to supply gasoline to the city.[41]

Despite his proximity to power and control over government transactions worth millions of dollars—unimaginable sums for a lowly former intelligence officer—Putin still lived modestly, at least not as ostentatiously as Sobchak and the generation of "new" Russian businessmen who were quickly amassing enormous fortunes and dressing the part. As a deputy mayor, he was assigned a state dacha in Zelenogorsk—it had previously belonged to the East German consulate, no less—and though it was more than thirty miles from the city's center, he moved his family there rather than continuing to live close to Smolny with his parents. Putin later acquired an apartment in the city on Vasilievsky Island—reportedly from Sobchak, who was accused of transferring hundreds of properties into private hands—and slowly set about renovating it. Lyudmila worked at the university, teaching German (though hers was far from perfect) and shuttling the girls to school, to the swimming pool, to the violin lessons they had taken up at Sergei Roldugin's insistance. It was a hectic life, but as secure as anyone's could be in Russia in the turbulent 1990s, when everything seemed to hang by a thread, even for the Putins.

The political euphoria that followed the collapse of the Soviet Union evaporated in barely a year. The "shock therapy" Boris Yeltsin's government imposed to introduce capitalism failed to stop the implosion of the economy; the gross domestic product fell by double digits in each of the first years of the new decade. Yeltsin sought to wrestle political control from the Congress of People's Deputies and the Supreme Soviet, then housed in the building on the embankment of the Moscow River known as the White House. In March 1993, Yeltsin imposed presidential rule and announced he would disband the congress until a constitutional referendum could be held in April and a new parliament elected. The deputies responded by voting for his impeachment. Yeltsin survived the vote, but was forced to back down. He narrowly won a national referendum on his leadership, but the vote did nothing to resolve the underlying political and legal struggles over power. By September, Yeltsin sacked his vice president, Aleksandr Rutskoy, whom he now saw as a rival, but the deputies refused to accept his decision. He then reappointed Yegor Gaidar, the reformist father of the economic policies that had infuriated and impoverished so many Russians, only for that appointment to be ignored, too. The untenable balance of power between the executive and legislative branches in the new Russia—between a presidential system and a parliamentary one—had reached a moment of crisis, and on September 21, Yeltsin acted at last, decisively, forcefully, and illegally.

He abolished the Supreme Soviet and the Congress of People's Deputies, where he had once served, and he scheduled a referendum on a new constitution that would create a new parliament with the State Duma, and a new upper house, the Federation Council, representing the eighty-nine provinces and republics that Russia had at the time. Elections would be held in December. Even Yeltsin regretted that his presidency—he was the first democratically chosen leader in Russia's history—had resorted to fiat.[42] A majority of the current deputies met in defiance of the decree, proclaimed Rutskoy president, and dismissed Yeltsin's ministers of defense, security, and interior. When they voted to hold simultaneous elections for president and parliament in March 1994, Yeltsin cut off electricity, phone service, and hot water at the White House, as public protests mounted and lawmakers prepared for a siege. Four days later he sealed off the building and ordered Interior Ministry troops to surround the building.

In Petersburg, Sobchak sided decisively with Yeltsin, going on air to appeal to the city's residents to refrain from demonstrations or strikes, but his vice mayor, Vyacheslav Shcherbakov, sided with the rebellious parliamentarians, appearing on television news to denounce Yeltsin's decrees as "anti-Russian and unconstitutional." Sobchak promptly fired him and locked his office in Smolny. A few protesters appeared outside the Mariinsky Palace, but not in the numbers and fury of the crowds that gathered around the White House in Moscow. The city council was in disarray. Its chairman, Aleksandr Belyayev, appeared with Sobchak in September to urge calm, but the council members passed sixteen resolutions or statements ineffectively criticizing Yeltsin's decrees. A journalist mocked the council for "impetuous brain-storming" at a time of grave political crisis.[43]

The protests in Moscow turned violent. On October 2, supporters of the parliament overwhelmed the police cordon around the White House, and this time they were armed. Rutskoy, from a balcony, called for an uprising. Yeltsin declared a state of emergency. The next night groups armed with rifles, grenades, and Molotov cocktails seized the mayor's office and stormed the Ostankino television tower, knocking state television off the air for several hours. There they were met by battalions of interior police officers, who fought them off, though at great cost of life. The violence there killed dozens, far more than the number that had died during the August 1991 putsch. Blood had not flowed in the streets of Moscow like that since the 1917 revolution. The Russian army equivocated—its commanders at one point complaining that their soldiers were too busy with the fall potato harvest to muster in force—but ultimately obeyed Yeltsin's orders after the minister of defense, Pavel Grachev, insisted that Yeltsin put them in writing.[44] By dawn Russian tanks had encircled the White House, crushing the makeshift barricades. At ten, in full view of television cameras, four tanks on the Novoarbatsky Bridge began firing shells into the upper floors of the building where Yeltsin had led the resistance to the putsch barely two years earlier. Soldiers occupied the building floor by floor, arresting Rutskoy and Ruslan Khasbulatov, the speaker of the Supreme Soviet, both former allies of Yeltsin, along with dozens of others. At least a hundred people died at the White House.

Putin's loyalties were never in doubt during the crisis: he followed Sobchak. On the night of October 3, he met the mayor at the airport with a detachment of guards that turned out to be unnecessary.[45] The next day, while the fighting raged in Moscow, a few hundred protesters reached Petersburg's television center, but did not confront the cordon of special police that surrounded the building. Seventy-two members of the city council adopted a statement condemning those who instigated the bloodshed in Moscow, without explicitly saying whom they blamed more for it. Sobchak managed to avoid violence in the city without military intervention, in part because the rebellion was limited to the capital, but also because his office took few chances with Yeltsin's opponents in Petersburg. The city's Ministry of Security—the descendant of the KGB that would ultimately become the Federal Security Service, or FSB—"introduced a number of measures advocating the arrests of extremists who were plotting provocations, planning to blow up things, or trying to destabilize the situation."

This was how Putin would later describe the events of October 1993. There may or may not have been provocateurs prepared to act in Petersburg. What mattered to Putin was that "there wasn't the same division between the law-enforcement agencies that there had been in 1991."[46] The security service's chief in St. Petersburg was Putin's old friend Viktor Cherkesov, who pledged his loyalty to Sobchak from the start of the crisis and ensured that at least in their city presidential authority would remain unimpeded. Sobchak later acknowledged that he had dispatched "a squad of special forces" to Moscow to help Yeltsin crush the rebellion when the loyalty of the army seemed uncertain.[47] The troops arrived at the end of September, and while they did not fight at the White House, they took part in clearing rebels from the Moscow mayor's office and the Hotel Mir.[48] The events affirmed Sobchak's early decisions to nurture ties with the security services; and they reinforced Putin's conviction that even in a democracy, law and order depended on the quiet, effective work of the secret services.

CHAPTER 6

Mismanaged Democracy

The turmoil of 1993 deepened Sobchak's dependence on Putin, and his trust in him. The newspaper *Kommersant* described Putin as "a man as close to Sobchak as Prince Menshikov was to Peter the Great," referring to the man who was the tsar's commander and confidant in the eighteenth century until he was exiled to Siberia after Peter's death.[1] Putin, Sobchak said, was a "courageous and decisive person,"[2] without designs on Sobchak's authority, or even on his position. As a result, he drew his deputy deeper into the city's management, not just in the field of foreign investment, but also into his fights against critics and prosecutors who began inquiries into Sobchak's financial affairs. In the fall of 1993, Sobchak asked Putin to manage the parliamentary campaign of Russia's Choice, a party created by Yeltsin's on-again-off-again prime minister, Yegor Gaidar. It was a puzzling order since Sobchak had created his own bloc, the Russian Movement for Democratic Reform—which failed spectacularly to win any seats when the vote was held in December—but Putin never questioned orders. He stood resolutely behind Sobchak, as loyal to his boss as he had been to his superiors in the KGB, even when it blinded him to their shortcomings. Putin worked tirelessly, with an obsession that seemed at times to inure him to hardship and tragedy, even those close to home.

On the morning of October 23, 2003, Putin drove his daughter Masha to school and then headed to the Astoria Hotel, where Sobchak had a special assignment for him. Lyudmila stayed at home with a feverish Katya, then seven. Katya pestered her mother to let her go to school anyway to rehearse her part in a play. She was going to be Cinderella, and though Lyudmila thought better of it, the girl insisted.[3] She drove a new Zhiguli, which, though modest, was the family's second car and a sign of rising prosperity. Just before noon, as Lyudmila neared a bridge that crosses the Neva, another car sped through a red light and smashed into the Zhiguli. The impact knocked Lyudmila unconscious; when she woke, she thought she could keep driving but found she could not. Katya, who had been asleep in the back, was bruised, though not badly hurt. Then for a long time, nothing happened.

The police arrived and bystanders gathered, but it took an ambulance forty-five minutes to arrive. Such was the decrepit state of basic services. A woman whose name and number Lyudmila later lost called the ambulance and a number that Lyudmila dictated to her. Putin's secretary, Marina Yentaltseva, answered but was unsure what to do. Putin's trusted aide, Igor Sechin, went to the crash site and brought Katya to the office at Smolny. Yentaltseva went to find Putin. The ambulance finally arrived and took Lyudmila to the October 25th Hospital, still named in honor of the first day (on the old calendar) of the Bolshevik revolution. "The hospital was horrible," she recalled later. "It was full of people who were dying. There were gurneys in the hallway with dead bodies on them." Worse, the doctors who treated her did not notice that she had broken three vertebrae in her spine and fractured the base of her skull. The surgeons sutured her torn ear and left her "naked on the table in freezing operating rooms in a terrible state of half consciousness."[4]

During all this, Putin was meeting at the Astoria with the American cable television executive Ted Turner and Jane Fonda, then his wife. They were in Petersburg to arrange the staging of the third Goodwill Games, the international sporting competition Turner dreamed up after the 1980 Olympics in Moscow were boycotted by the United States and other countries following the Soviet invasion of Afghanistan and the 1984 Olympics were boycotted in retaliation by the Soviet Union and most of its satellites. The first games had been held in Moscow in 1986, the second in Seattle in 1990. Turner wanted to return them to the new Russia in 1994, and Sobchak was eager to showcase the city, even if it could ill afford the necessary investments. Putin was shepherding the couple to a series of meetings when his secretary finally reached him at the hotel. He slipped out to go to the emergency room.

"Don't worry, she's not in any danger," the chief surgeon there told him. "We're just going to put a splint on, and everything will be fine."

"Are you sure?" he asked.

"Absolutely," the surgeon replied, and without seeing his wife, Putin returned to his meetings.

Meanwhile, Yentaltseva took Katya to a hospital and picked up Masha from school. Putin asked that Yentaltseva spend the night with them at the family's dacha. He also asked her to call Yuri Shevchenko, one of the city's most prominent physicians at the Military Medical Academy (who would later be a minister of health). It was evening before she finally reached Shevchenko, and he immediately sent a doctor from the academy's clinic. Lyudmila remembered waking in the operating room and feeling his warm hand holding hers. "It warmed me up and I knew that I had been saved." The doctor arranged her transfer to the military hospital, and an X-ray discovered spinal injuries that required emergency surgery. That night, between meetings, Putin visited her for the first time, meeting Yentaltseva and his children in the parking lot. He told her it was unlikely he would make it home because his discussions with Ted Turner were scheduled to continue into the night. She took the girls to the dacha and, unable to find the switch for the heat, huddled them in one bed with extra blankets. She was startled awake when Putin arrived home at three in the morning. By seven, he had already left again.[5]

Yentaltseva had grown close to the family, and she stayed with the girls until Lyudmila's mother arrived from Kaliningrad. She had become accustomed to Putin's stern, dispassionate demeanor, his reserved precision in dealing with the city's business, and his emotionless response when his dog was killed, but now he seemed rattled. "I can't say that he was thrown for a loop and totally at a loss and didn't know what to grab on to," she said. "That wasn't the case. I just sensed that he was trying to come up with a plan in his head." Lyudmila spent a month at the Military Medical Academy, where they later discovered the fracture at the base of her skull. After she was released, she had to wear a brace for months.

Putin's trust rested with those he knew best, many of them from the "power organs." These friends would become known as *siloviki*, from the word for "force," because of their backgrounds in the military or security services. In moments of crisis, these were the men who he knew would serve him selflessly. Putin distrusted almost everyone else. In the case of Lyudmila's injuries, Putin had relied on Igor Sechin, then Shevchenko, and then his new friend at Dresdner Bank, the former Stasi man, Matthias Warnig. It was Dresdner that arranged—and paid for—Lyudmila to receive at a clinic in Bad Homburg, Germany, the necessary medical treatment that Russia's deteriorating health-care system could not provide.[6] That Putin himself could not afford the cost of treatment abroad seemed to refute the claims of his critics that he, too, was personally enriching himself in Sobchak's administration. Still, he had a quintessentially Russian understanding that assistance, in crisis or not, came through connections, the exchange of favors. He always remembered acts of loyalty like Warnig's, just as he never forgave betrayals.

After Yeltsin's dissolution of the city council following the 1993 crisis, Sobchak's power in Petersburg seemed unassailable. A decree he authored—and Yeltsin signed—dramatically shifted authority from the council to the mayor's office as the city prepared to hold elections in March 1994. The decree created a new, smaller legislative body; instead of four hundred members, a new legislative assembly would have only fifty. In theory it was a democratic restructuring of the branches of power, but in reality Sobchak consolidated his control of almost all of the city's affairs. On March 16, four days before the elections, he restructured the city government, making himself the chairman of the government and eliminating committees that had once reported to the vice mayor, while consolidating others. The chairmen of the three most powerful committees—those overseeing finance, international relations, and operations—were promoted, and Vladimir Putin became one of three first deputies of Sobchak's new government, still in charge of foreign economic affairs.[7]

The legislative elections were a farce. Sobchak's office wrote the rules without any input or consent from the council members whose body was being restructured. When the polls opened on March 20, an overwhelming majority of people simply did not bother voting, risking the invalidation of the results since the law required a minimum turnout of 25 percent; in only half of the fifty districts did turnout meet the threshold. Twenty-five new deputies joined the assembly, but they lacked a quorum and could not function legally. As it was, Sobchak did not seem troubled by the turn of events. He did not schedule a new round of elections to fill the remaining seats until October; until then, he and his deputies would govern as they saw fit, without legislative oversight.

In the five years since the city council was first formed, the euphoric expression of popular will through the ballot box had devolved into disgust with the democratic process. Democracy in Russia had taken root in barren soil, and its growth was already stunted. Much of the blame lay with the catastrophic state of the new Russian economy, with the hardships of privatization, the corrupt amassing of wealth, and the surge in criminality that made Petersburg notorious as a swamp of violence and organized crime. The irony was that the man who had led the fight for democracy in Petersburg bore much of the blame. He had so assiduously belittled the council's work that voters no longer cared who served on it. A brilliant orator and terrible manager, Sobchak in his preoccupation with power and international prestige had ignored the workaday problems of his city. His instinct to strengthen democracy meant, in his mind, strengthening his own mercurial rule. Not long after the election, blaming the city's increasing crime, he forced the resignation of the city's police chief, Arkady Kramarev, who had defied the coup's leaders in 1991 and saved Sobchak from arrest. Having consolidated control of the city's television network, Sobchak made sure his coverage was adoring and that of his opponents nonexistent. After winning the right to host the Goodwill Games, he used a Soviet-era residency requirement, which the Constitutional Court had overturned, to drive unwanted migrant workers out of the city just before the games opened in July 1994.[8]

In that way, the Goodwill Games symbolized Sobchak's mayoralty: an improbable project to boost the city's prestige, undercut by the harsh realities of the country's halting transition. Having failed to turn Petersburg into a world banking capital or a thriving free-economic zone, Sobchak believed that playing host to an international sporting event would by itself attract investors who were increasingly shying away. The city, though, was ill prepared, short on cash, hotels, and sporting facilities. After draining money from the city's subway repair budget and pleading for more money from Moscow, Sobchak's office rushed to renovate the venues, pave roads, and polish up the facades of many of the city's palaces, churches, and monuments. By the time they began, the games were plagued by poor planning, logistical problems, and shoddy work. The indoor arena for ice skating—Turner's games mixed winter and summer sports—failed to ice over, and the swimming events had to be postponed for a day because the water in the pool turned brackish when a filter failed. Even then a greenish hue caused some swimmers to pull out.[9] Ticket prices were beyond the means of ordinary Russians, leaving many events sparsely attended, even when tickets were given away. The city and state invested $70 million in the games, and for most residents, the expense paid for little more than a Potemkin village, impressive to look at, perhaps, but really a facade concealing the city's woeful decay.

Sobchak's ambitions nevertheless emerged unchecked. He considered the games a rehearsal for the city's improbable bid to host the Summer Olympics of 2004. In the new Russia, as in the Soviet Union, the desire to hold the Olympics became an obsession directly proportional to the longing for international recognition, for legitimacy at home and abroad. The boycott of the Summer Games in 1980 had left an enduring bitterness that could only be forgotten when a great leader of the nation could once again bring the Olympics back. Sobchak would not be that leader. He was no longer even mayor when in 1997 the International Olympic Committee selected Athens as the 2004 host, having dropped St. Petersburg's bid, hastily prepared with Putin's help, before it reached the final round of consideration. Sobchak's hubris had blinded him to the most fundamental feature of the democracy he so eloquently promoted: the people have a vote. In 1996, Sobchak was up for reelection, and for Putin, the result represented a profound, personal betrayal.

Sobchak thought his reelection campaign would be simple: he would remind voters of his heroic leadership during the crises of 1991 and 1993, of the Goodwill Games and the bid for the Olympic Games for 2004, of the new businesses, the banks, the foreign investment, and his own meetings with foreign leaders, including, at the height of the campaign, President Bill Clinton. Sobchak proclaimed himself a democrat and statesman who stood in the way of the revanchists who would turn Petersburg back into Leningrad. In fact, the Communists were the least of his worries. His election was not a test of competing ideologies, but rather a referendum on his mayoralty, and he failed to see that the gravest threat came from within.

To coincide with the national presidential election, the city's Legislative Assembly set the date of the election for June 16, and changed the name of the position from mayor to governor, as it had been when the city's leader served at the pleasure of the tsars. Sobchak's campaign posters showed him sitting behind a desk, with the simple slogan "From Mayor to Governor," as if it were an inevitable transition. Even he thought the poster was insipid. "My campaign headquarters, unfortunately, was much less effective and efficient."[10] By now Sobchak had less faith in his deputy's political guile and left him to run the city's affairs, but even Putin sensed that Sobchak's political instincts and oratorical flair would no longer be enough to ensure victory. In the national parliamentary elections in December 1995, the party that Sobchak backed had fared poorly, even in Petersburg. Sobchak also underestimated his loss of support in Moscow, where his political ambitions were viewed as a threat among those conspiring to keep Boris Yeltsin in power as the presidential election of 1996 loomed. With the support of Yeltsin's influential chief of security, Russia's prosecutor general, Yuri Skuratov, had even launched an investigation into Sobchak's affairs at the end of 1995 that appeared intended to curb his political aspirations. It was a reversal of fortune as sudden and arbitrary as a Stalin purge, and it succeeded in sullying Sobchak's image. Skuratov formed an investigative committee that soon began to leak compromising details—known in Russian as *kompromat*—about the murky privatization of apartments by a company called Renaissance, including ones that went to Putin and other deputies. Putin saw the investigation as a raw use of prosecutorial power against the man he served, and the experience left him with a thirst for revenge.

"You know, you're on a completely different playing field," Putin recalled telling Sobchak. "You need specialists."[11] Sobchak agreed and turned to Aleksandr Yuriev, a political scientist at St. Petersburg State University, who warned him that his accomplishments, however great, no longer resonated with a weary electorate disillusioned with the crime and chaos that roiled the city.[12] In January, only a few days after agreeing to work for the campaign, Yuriev answered a knock at the door of his apartment. A pretty young woman stood there, and assuming she was a student delivering an assignment, he opened the door. Only then did he see a man in a mask, who hurled a vial of acid in his face. As Yuriev staggered back, the man fired a pistol, though he missed. When Sobchak visited him in the hospital, Yuriev's head was covered in white bandages. The police never found the attackers, or established a motive, but Sobchak had no doubt the attempt was part of a vast unfolding conspiracy to keep him from office.[13] The attack heightened tension so much that Putin began to carry an air pistol, which his old friend Sergei Roldugin noticed when he visited his dacha around the beginning of the campaign.

"Do you think an air gun is going to save you?" Roldugin asked him.

"It won't save me," he replied, "but it makes me feel calmer."[14]

Fourteen candidates ultimately qualified to challenge Sobchak, and they included some of his bitter personal enemies: the vice mayor, Vyacheslav Shcherbakov, whose dismissal after the 1993 events was still being contested in court; Yuri Shutov, a former aide turned unauthorized Sobchak biographer; and Aleksandr Belyayev, the former chairman of the city council Sobchak had disbanded. The man Sobchak worried about most, though, was Yuri Boldyrev, a prominent liberal who served as the head of the auditing authority in Moscow. It was Boldyrev who had investigated the first corruption accusations against Putin in 1992, and he had developed a reputation as a reasonably honest investigator at a time of staggering criminality.[15]

Sobchak was already under investigation, and Boldyrev's election would almost certainly compound Sobchak's legal troubles, and possibly Putin's as well. Sobchak tried to use lawyerly maneuvers to manipulate the race to his own advantage. In March, he amended the election law to include a residency requirement that would have excluded Boldyrev, a native of the city, on the grounds that he had been living and working in Moscow. It was a transparently desperate and undemocratic ploy, which Boldyrev successfully fought in court. Sobchak's next gambit proved to have more serious consequences. Although the date of the election was already set for June, Sobchak changed it. He claimed he did so at the insistence of Yeltsin, who had decreed that no other election except the mayor's race in Moscow should be held on the same day as the presidential election.[16] He initially suggested postponing the election until December, but his opponents fiercely denounced this as a naked attempt to extend his term. Instead he sent Putin to the Legislative Assembly in March to cajole the deputies. Promising jobs and threatening retaliation, Putin eventually pushed through legislation to hold the election on May 19, but only after mustering a highly suspect quorum.[17] Sobchak's challengers howled in protest. Not only was it a waste of city resources to hold separate elections, but the move cut short the time for them to make their cases with voters. The television networks controlled by Sobchak's office did not help either, lavishing attention on Sobchak while limiting his opponents each to a fifteen-minute program on air. The risk that Sobchak and Putin failed to consider was that holding the election before the presidential vote would almost certainly lower turnout and hurt his chances, as Yuriev had warned him.

Sobchak became uneasy. He suspected that his enemies in Moscow were conspiring against him. He even flew to Moscow in March to appeal to Yeltsin for support but instead found their friendship had dissipated. Yeltsin's own prospects for reelection that year were abysmal, and he and his aides feared challenges from all sides, real and imagined. It seems one of Yeltsin's deputy prime ministers, Oleg Soskovets, had told him that Sobchak, during a meeting with the German chancellor, Helmut Kohl, had expressed a preference for replacing Yeltsin with

Viktor Chernomyrdin.[18] Sobchak's paranoia was not misplaced. Within days of Sobchak's meeting in the Kremlin, the extent of the political intrigue against him became clear. Soskovets and Yeltsin's powerful chief of security, Lieutenant General Aleksandr Korzhakov, did have their own candidate in mind to challenge Sobchak in Petersburg. It was not one of the many already in the race, but Sobchak's own deputy, Vladimir Yakovlev. They had been secretly cultivating him for months, even as the prosecutors sharpened their investigations against Sobchak and his staff. On March 27, Yakovlev unexpectedly announced he was entering the campaign against his own boss.

Yakovlev, who at fifty-two was seven years younger than Sobchak, was a construction engineer, a former party apparatchik who had made the transition to the new democracy, like Vladimir Putin, under Sobchak's tutelage. He had remained a loyal Communist until the party was banned in 1991, even though in 1982 he had been fired from a regional executive committee for using his post to buy a car for his personal use.[19] He was working as chief engineer for a housing construction company when Sobchak hired him in October 1993. A year later he joined Putin and Aleksei Kudrin as first deputy mayors. Yakovlev had no more of a public profile than Putin, but he had more ambition and less loyalty, and he accepted the support Korzhakov and Soskovets promised to oust his own boss.

The announcement shocked Sobchak, who promptly fired Yakovlev. If Yakovlev had been man enough, he said, he would have resigned before announcing his challenge. Yakovlev's candidacy also infuriated Putin. He publicly called Yakovlev a Judas[20] and circulated a letter for all of Sobchak's employees to sign, declaring that they would resign in protest if Sobchak lost the election. With the bitterness of hindsight, Sobchak described Yakovlev's accomplishments as modest. He was not as intelligent as the "more educated, cultural and skilled people" on his team, like Putin. The staff disparaged him with the nickname "the plumber,"[21] a telling contrast to Putin's "Stasi."

Sobchak ignored Yakovlev along with the rest of his challengers and carried on with his official duties, as if that alone would prove his electoral worthiness. He campaigned more intently for Yeltsin before the presidential election, as well, hoping to prove his loyalty and restore the political alliance they had once had. On April 19, Bill Clinton arrived in Petersburg on his way to meetings in Moscow that the Americans, too, hoped would help Yeltsin beat back a challenge from the resurgent Communist Party. Sobchak met him at the airport and rode with him in the limousine to Tsarskoye Selo, the imperial estate south of the city. Perhaps mindful that his private conversations had a way of getting back to Yeltsin, Sobchak went out of his way to explain how Yeltsin would triumph over his main challenger, the Communist Gennady Zyuganov. Sobchak shadowed Clinton everywhere, relishing his appearance on television as a statesman in the company of a world leader. Clinton though complained that he had been "kept in a goddamn cocoon" during his trip. A meeting with students at the Hermitage had been canceled, his requests to stop the motorcade to shake hands in the street rebuffed. Clinton's aide, Strobe Talbott, blamed the overzealousness of the official who oversaw the details of the visit, Vladimir Putin, though he added that at the time the name "meant nothing to any of us."[22]

Yakovlev was not the natural politician Sobchak was, but he was charismatic in his own way and far more attuned to voters' desires. Tall and thin, he had a cherubic face with wide cheekbones prone to split into a goofy grin. He offered no real ideological alternative—he had no intention of reversing privatization of apartments or factories, for example—but promised that he would try to fix the city's myriad problems: undrinkable tap water, potholed streets, crumbling subways. He promised jobs, not the Olympics. Sobchak belittled his campaign promises as "bewitching fantasies for a gullible public," but he grossly underestimated his aide's appeal. In a city where people still lived in communal apartments, where basic services like ambulances were meager, the water was tainted with giardia, and sewage flowed untreated into the Baltic Sea, where for a month in September 1995 the city could not even heat its hospitals,[23] perhaps "a plumber" was just what voters wanted.

With an infusion of cash from his backers in Moscow, Yakovlev turned to professional campaign consultants, who helped him run a far more organized and effective campaign that filled mailboxes with leaflets, the airwaves with advertisements, all with the same simple message of restoring basic governance and services.[24] Yakovlev also had political support from a potent new ally, Yuri Luzhkov, the bald-headed, barrel-chested populist mayor of Moscow. Yakovlev fashioned himself as a Luzhkov for Petersburg, and Luzhkov publicly suggested new projects that would make both cities prosper. Sobchak's campaign, by contrast, ran out of money. Having played little role to this point, Putin now entered the fray, pleading for donations from the businessmen he had been working with for the past five years, something he viewed with undisguised disgust.[25] When he invited a group of them to a fundraiser, however, they refused to help—the very people who, in his view, had profited from the privatizations and investments that he and Sobchak had made possible. A local mobster had better luck, raising $2,000 each from small businessmen who thought better than to refuse a donation to the "Foundation for the Support of the Mayor."[26]

Sobchak's dominance of the city's politics since 1989, his charisma and prestige, no longer shielded him from withering personal attacks. Aleksandr Belyayev, the former council chairman, told a press conference that Sobchak—and Putin—owned property on the Atlantic coast of France. He said that Sobchak had been detained in 1993 at Heathrow Airport in London carrying a suitcase of $1 million in cash; he vowed that when he became governor, "Sobchak will be sitting in jail."[27] Putin responded to the accusations against him by filing a lawsuit accusing Belyayev of slander, but he filed it in the wrong jurisdiction and was mercilessly mocked in the press: "An Intelligence Agent Should Know Where His Defendant Lives," said one newspaper headline. Putin tried to defend himself, claiming he did not even know where the Atlantic coast of France was, which only intensified the public mockery.[28]

The campaign was wild, and it was dirty. It also was more or less free and fair. Elections in Russia could be riotous then, but they were democratic. When the ballots were counted on the night of May 19, Sobchak came out on top of the thirteen other candidates, but he received only 28 percent of the vote to Yakovlev's 21 percent. Since neither had accumulated 50 percen, a runoff was scheduled for June 2. Sobchak still hoped to prevail, but panic now gripped his campaign team and his staff. Putin "became noticeably more nervous," and threw himself even more directly into the campaign, "but by then it was hopeless."[29] Sobchak's vanquished opponents all endorsed Yakovlev. Worse, the investigation circling around Sobchak's finances and the apartments he distributed spilled into the public, confirmed by one of the local investigators, Leonid Proshkin. The news of the accusations was printed on flyers and distributed all over the city by Yakovlev's campaign—in one instance, they were dropped from a helicopter. Putin, indignant, wrote a letter to Yeltsin, Chernomyrdin, and the prosecutor general, Yuri Skuratov, whom he accused directly of engaging in a campaign of "persecution and slander." Proshkin, he fulminated, gave an interview "in violation of all procedural norms" to pro-Communist newspapers and thus spread "unsubstantiated material." Putin demanded "decisive action to end the use of the law-enforcement authorities for political purposes."[30]

The last two weeks of the election were fraught with tension, as both campaigns slung mud.[31] Yakovlev, worried about his own safety, rode around the city with two SUVs full of rifle-toting guards dressed in black. He confronted Putin with rumors that Sobchak had ordered his assassination. "What are you, crazy?" Putin replied. "You had better go look at yourself in the mirror."[32] Sobchak's last hope was a televised debate in the last week before the vote, but there his eloquence failed him. Yakovlev seemed at ease. He took off his jacket and spoke clearly and forcefully. Sobchak, sitting hunched in his suit, stammered and struggled for words. He had a fever before the debate, he later recounted, and felt his tongue thicken when it started. Spasms wrenched his throat. When asked about the suspicious provenance of a dacha, Sobchak could not answer. Only later, he said, did he learn the truth: Yakovlev's campaign team had brought a psychic into the audience! "I consulted experts, and they confirmed to me that a strong hypnotic effect often causes spasms in the throat, a heavy tongue, headache and a sharp rise in body temperature owing to the body's resistance to the influence of alien energy."[33] Sobchak was not just losing the election. He seemed to be losing his mind.

In the end, Yakovlev won with 47.5 percent of the vote; Sobchak received 45.8 percent. He was less than gracious in defeat. Never known for modesty, he compared his fate to Winston Churchill's, the "savior of the country, the symbol of victory," who was ousted at the ballot box in 1945.[34] He petulantly refused to attend Yakovlev's inauguration, held at Smolny ten days later, and yet Sobchak, for all his authoritarian tendencies, did what no other elected official of such prominence had done in Russia. He did not contest the results or otherwise try to block Yakovlev's victory; he accepted defeat and stepped down.

"I was not an addict to power, like Lenin or Yeltsin, and had I lost the election to a worthy opponent, the defeat would have been easier to accept," he wrote in a memoir he titled tellingly *A Dozen Knives in the Back*. "But in this case, it preoccupied me that I could lose to this obviously grey and primitive man, Yakovlev. I cursed myself that I failed to see it—the stealing from the government for private engineering offices—but what hurt the most was the apostasy or direct betrayal on the part of many of those who surrounded me."[35] He noted one exception: Vladimir Putin.

obchak's unexpected loss left Putin without a job, without a patron,
and without a purpose. It was like his return from East Germany all
over again. Despite the letter he and others had signed, he did not immediately resign, even though now he served at the pleasure of a new governor he had called a Judas. Yakovlev persuaded other Sobchak aides to
stay on, including Dmitri Kozak, a former prosecutor and friend, and
Mikhail Manevich, a young economist, who became a deputy governor.
Kozak would remain close to Putin for years, but Manevich was assassinated a year later by a sniper who fired eight bullets into his car as it
turned onto Nevsky Prospekt. Putin remained in his office at Smolny
through Yeltsin's unexpected reelection in the summer of 1996, but then
was asked "rather harshly" to clear out by the end of June.[36] The new
governor had not forgotten Putin's coldness and his comments during
the campaign. When an aide told him Putin was still waiting for word
on his fate, Yakovlev's face reddened. "I don't want to hear anything
more about that asshole," he said. [37]

Sobchak tried to help his loyal deputy land a new job, even appealing
to Yevgeny Primakov, an old spymaster who had headed the successor of
the KGB's foreign intelligence branch until he was appointed Yeltsin's
foreign minister in January 1996. "You'll be an ambassador," his former
boss told Putin. It was too ridiculous to contemplate, and Putin knew it,
though he could not bring himself to tell Sobchak. Others promised him
he would be needed somewhere, but nothing materialized immediately.
In July, he moved his family to a dacha he had built on the shore of Lake
Komsomolskoye, seventy miles north of the city on the Karelian Isthmus,
a part of Finland until the Soviet Union incorporated it after the Great
Patriotic War. A small village was nearby. There Putin joined a handful
of the businessmen he had befriended since 1991 in carving out what
would become a gated community on the lake's shore, incorporated later
that year under the name Ozero, or Lake. The shareholders included
Vladimir Yankunin, Yuri Kovalchuk, and the brothers Fursenko, Andrei
and Sergei. All had met through their work at the highly regarded Ioffe
Physical Technical Institute in Petersburg. They founded an enterprise
to turn their scientific work into commercially viable products, with
the help of Putin's committee for foreign economic affairs. Yakunin and
Kovalchuk became shareholders in a financial institution, Bank Rossiya,
which had been created in 1990 to handle the accounts of the Communist Party and, as was widely rumored, the KGB. The bank had become

a shell by the time Kovalchuk and his colleagues took it over, and it only survived because Putin steered the government's accounts to it. Another of Bank Rossiya's shareholders and executives, Viktor Myachin, also joined the dacha community, as did Nikolai Shamalov, who had been one of Putin's deputies on the committee for foreign economic affairs until he became the representative in northeastern Russia for the German manufacturer Siemens. Putin was the lone government official among these new businessmen, and it was never exactly clear how his meager salary covered the costs, though evidence would later surface that it came from Twentieth Trust, an organization Putin's committee had registered in 1992.[38] The company's activities, including numerous contracts from the city that bore Putin's signature, were among those that had drawn the attention of the investigators dispatched from Moscow to look into Sobchak's administration.

Putin's house on the property was made of red brick, paneled with wood inside. It had two stories, with an expansive view of the lake. Its size, only 1,600 square feet in all, was relatively modest, but it was on the lake's shore, isolated by the woods, a place where he could contemplate his suddenly uncertain future. Had Sobchak won the election, Putin certainly would have stayed at his side, but he had nurtured ties to no other politicians. He considered becoming a lawyer. He talked to an old judo partner, Vasily Shestakov, about working as a trainer at his club. Shestakov told him it was beneath him now, but if nothing else materialized, he could come.[39] It was a hard fall. He brooded, refusing to discuss his uncertain fate with Lyudmila. Whenever he sank into a funk, she knew it was best to leave him alone. Her husband was one of those "who does not love to lose," and the campaign gave him a bitter taste of the risk inherent in true democracy. "True, he never talked about it or even let on," Lyudmila said, "but I understood everything, felt it, saw it."[40]

August is a leisurely month in Russia, a season of late-summer languor, when most of the country retreats to their dachas. Having failed to find a new job immediately, Putin would have to wait until official business resumed in earnest at the end of August before he could seriously look again. On August 12, the Putins invited his former secretary, Marina Yentaltseva, her husband, and their daughter to visit the dacha. In the evening, the men retreated to the *banya* on the first floor, just inside the door. Putin called it "a wake for my former job."[41] He had just returned from a cooling plunge in the lake when he saw smoke. A heater inside the banya sparked a fire that soon spread through the house. Katya bolted out from the kitchen. Putin found his older daughter, Masha, and Marina on the second floor, and as flames climbed the stairs, he lowered them from a balcony using sheets as a rope. He suddenly remembered that he had a briefcase in his bedroom with his money—some $5,000. With the lights out and smoke choking the house, he felt around for the briefcase. Wrapped only in a thin sheet, he climbed from the balcony and, with his family and neighbors, watched the house burn like "a candle." Firefighters arrived, but they could do nothing because the truck had no water. "There's a whole lake right here!" Putin shouted. True, one told him, but they had no hose either.[42]

Vasily Shestakov marveled when he heard the news of the fire and the rescue of Putin's cash. Not only had Putin not built some opulent "stone mansion" but in five years as the "second man" in the city he had not amassed a fortune greater than $5,000. Such was the presumption of corruption among Russia's apparatchiks that Putin could have "stolen recklessly" without much fear of being singled out.[43]

The fire inspectors determined that the builders had improperly installed the banya's heater, and Putin forced them to rebuild it as it was—minus the banya. When workers cleared the debris, they found in the ashes the aluminum cross his mother had given him when he and Sobchak traveled to Jerusalem three years before. He had taken it off while they steamed in the banya and in the confusion of the fire forgotten about it. He considered it a revelation and later sometimes claimed that he never removed it.[44]

CHAPTER 7

An Unexpected Path to Power

Putin's salvation was not long in coming, and it came from an unlikely source: his boss's former ally turned foe, Boris Yeltsin. Yeltsin had fared better with the voters than Sobchak had; his winning the presidency a second time in the summer of 1996 seemed no less miraculous than the discovery of Putin's cross in the ashes of his dacha. Yeltsin's public approval rating at the end of 1995 had dropped to 3 percent. The war he launched to defeat the independence movement in Chechnya in 1994, which had promised to be short and glorious, had become a bloody, humiliating stalemate. The economy had continued its remorseless collapse, and so had Yeltsin's health. Late in 1995 he had the first of what would be a series of heart attacks, the severity of which was kept from the public. Yeltsin's closest aides—those who orchestrated Yakovlev's victory over Sobchak—conspired to either cancel the election in 1996 or back an alternative to Yeltsin: the deputy prime minister, Oleg Soskovets. Even Yeltsin's wife, Naina, urged him not to run. "Like wolves that gradually turn to a new leader of the pack, my closest friends had already found themselves a replacement," Yeltsin later reflected. "Even those upon whom I had always depended, who were my last resort, my resource, the spiritual leaders of the nation, even they had abandoned me."[1]

Not everyone had, though. Too many fortunes relied on Yeltsin. They included Russia's richest men, bankers and media moguls who the year before had acquired the state's controlling assets in major industries in exchange for loans to keep the country's budget afloat: Boris Berezovsky, Mikhail Fridman, Vladimir Gusinsky, Mikhail Khodorkovsky, and Vladimir Potanin. They were the pioneers of the post-Soviet gold rush, who through genius, guile, and grit cobbled together vast, diverse conglomerates that would almost certainly be at risk if Yeltsin did not remain in office. Although rivals in business, they found a common cause against Yeltsin's chief opponent, the Communist leader Gennady Zyuganov. Dull, heavy-browed, and shaped like a barrel, Zyuganov was by now a Communist largely in name only, but he and his party represented the enormous resentment that the collapse of the Soviet Union had wrought. With the party's strong showing in parliamentary elections in 1995—it won the most Duma seats by far—it was no longer inconceivable that Zyuganov could prevail, simply because of the unpopularity of the oligarchy that had come to define Yeltsin's chaotic presidency. Musing on the fate of himself and his wealthy supporters, Yelstin thought, "The Communists will hang us from the lampposts."[2]

When Zyuganov appeared at the World Economic Forum in Davos, Switzerland, in February 1996, he was greeted as a president in waiting. Something had to be done. Berezovsky, Gusinsky, and Khodorkovsky thus met over dinner with another banker, Vladimir Vinogradvov, and made the "Davos Pact" to ensure Yeltsin's reelection in June.[3] They offered Yeltsin's campaign millions in cash—and attached their strings to it. They insisted that Anatoly Chubais, Putin's former colleague in Sobchak's entourage and the author of the privatization programs that begot their billions, return to Yeltsin's team as his campaign manager. (Chubais had been fired as deputy prime minister that January, as Yeltsin lurched from scandal to scandal.) With Yeltsin's daughter, Tatyana Dyachenko, Chubais orchestrated an exquisitely Russian version of the modern political campaign, bankrolled by financial schemes so ingenious and convoluted that investigators never could track all the money spent, by some estimates as much as $2 billion.[4] Yeltsin's health and his erratic behavior were shielded from voters, his activities so carefully scripted as to almost appear normal. Berezovsky and Gusinsky controlled two of the country's most popular television networks, ORT and NTV, and they produced documentaries portraying Yeltsin as the genial, healthy leader he had once been.

When the election was held on June 16, Yeltsin narrowly won a plurality with 35 percent of the vote, two million votes ahead of Zyuganov, but not enough to avoid a runoff. Aleksandr Lebed, a decorated general who had resigned his commission the year before to enter politics and who opposed the war in Chechnya as a grossly mismanaged waste of lives, finished a surprising third, with 15 percent of the vote. Yeltsin's strategists had bolstered Lebed's campaign in the last weeks before the election with an infusion of cash and television attention in a successful effort to drain votes from Zyuganov, and now Yeltsin courted him and his voters. Yeltsin saw much to admire in Lebed. He was a "tough and unbeatable guy" who was "racing back and forth, searching for the certainty, precision, and clarity to which he'd been accustomed and couldn't find in our new life." Yeltsin had grown disillusioned with the country's post-Soviet generals, who were, he thought, missing "a certain nobility, sophistication, or some sort of inner resolve."[5] As early as 1993, he claimed, he fantasized about a new general who would appear on the political scene and guide the country with a steady, professional hand, not as a tyrant, but as a democratic leader. Lebed seemed at first to be that man, and Yeltsin considered him a potential successor as president. Two days after the first round of voting, he appointed Lebed the secretary of the Kremlin's security council, hoping to attract the votes he had received, but Lebed proved to be a disappointment from the onset. He was coarse and abrasive, impetuously clashing with other senior officials. Only days after his appointment, he berated a Cossack who asked him a question. "You say you are a Cossack," he interrupted the man. "Why do you speak like a Jew?"[6]

Still, Yeltsin clung to the notion of a military man as the political savior that he seemed to understand he himself would not be. "I was waiting for a new general to appear, unlike any other," Yeltsin mused. "Or rather, a general who was like the generals I read about in books when I was young." He would keep looking, and find his "general," though not in the Army, but in another security service.[7]

Yeltsin's actions before the presidential runoff exposed the rifts between his liberal advisers—his "sane forces"—and the conservative faction that included Soskovets and Yeltsin's "generals," Aleksandr Korzhakov and the chairman of the Federal Security Service. Yeltsin at last understood what Sobchak had tried to warn him about months earlier: the hawks in his camp "were spoiling for a fight in order to seize power in the campaign."[8] Korzhakov's presidential guards arrested two campaign aides, close associates of Chubais and Berezovsky, as they left the White House carrying a cardboard box filled with $100 bills—$500,000 in all. The arrests threatened to expose the campaign's secret financing. Yeltsin promptly fired his advisers, and a week later had another heart attack.

He spent the last week in a hospital bed installed in the living room of his dacha. His campaign canceled his scheduled events and pretended nothing had happened, his aides dissembling furiously when asked about the absence of the candidate. When the runoff was held on July 2, Yeltsin could barely cast his ballot, choosing a polling station near his dacha rather than the one in Moscow he would normally have used. He managed to speak to a small pool of journalists but only for a minute before guards hustled him back to bed.

And yet, in the end, Yeltsin beat Zyuganov convincingly, winning 54 percent of the vote, compared to 40 percent for the Communist. More than three million Russians, nearly 5 percent, voted "against all." Yeltsin had triumphed, but at an enormous cost to democratic values because of the dirty tricks, the lies, and the corrupting power of money. The outcome may have reflected the will of the electorate, but the campaign left ordinary Russians with a view of the country's democracy that was as jaded as the one they had of its capitalism. They might not favor a return to Soviet rule, but according to one exit poll, only 7 percent of voters approved of the democracy Russia had then.[9] Most Russians now associated their democracy with the dishonesty, criminality, and injustice they had long been conditioned by Soviet propaganda to fear. Russia had become, as one historian put it, a "nightmare vision of the West."[10]

Vladimir Putin, by all appearances, shared this view. He had helped run Yeltsin's reelection campaign in Petersburg, though he played too minor a role to attract much attention in Moscow. The furious power struggle after Yeltsin's victory, however, opened an unexpected path to the capital. Shortly after the second round ended in July, Yeltsin's hawkish chief of staff, Nikolai Yegorov, invited Putin to Moscow and offered him a position as a deputy. Two days later, though, Yeltsin fired Yegorov and replaced him with Chubais, a reshuffling that was seen to strengthen the influence of the Kremlin's economic reformers—and to repay the oligarchs for bankrolling his reelection. Chubais represented the Petersburg clan in Yeltsin's new administration, and he needed allies with experience dealing with officials and businessmen.[11] He turned to another man left adrift by Sobchak's defeat—not Putin, but rather the other deputy, Aleksei Kudrin.

Kudrin, who had overseen the city's finances and budget, was much closer to Chubais in temperament and experience than Putin, whom Chubais treated with a chilly distance. Chubais appointed Kudrin the chief of the Main Control Directorate, which served as the Kremlin's auditor, empowered to probe the finances of government agencies and the private enterprises with which they were increasingly entwined. As for Putin, Chubais eliminated the position in the administration that Putin had accepted from Yegorov only days before. The rebuff nurtured the animosity between the two men who had begun their public lives under Sobchak's tutelage. "He's so hard-nosed, like a Bolshevik," Putin would say later of Chubais.[12] Putin returned to his limbo in Petersburg that summer.

On August 18, three days after his dacha burned to the ground, Putin's fortune changed. Yeltsin's prime minister, Viktor Chernomyrdin, announced a new cabinet, appointing Aleksei Bolshakov, a former legislator from Petersburg who had been in charge of relations with the former Soviet republics, as the first deputy prime minister. Bolshakov once served on Petersburg's city council, but was forced to resign after the August 1991 putsch and "wound up almost on the street."[13] He was a twice-failed candidate for the congress of deputies and later the Duma, but then took over a shadowy company with plans to build a high-speed train to Moscow that never materialized, despite obtaining millions of dollars' worth of loans.[14] When he unexpectedly resurfaced in Yeltsin's administration, Putin treated him with obsequious formality during his working visits to Petersburg. "I never forced him to wait in the reception area," Putin said. "I would always stop what I was doing, kick everybody out, come into the reception area myself, and say, 'Aleksei Alekseyevich, right this way.' We were never close, but maybe he remembered me."[15]

In the palace intrigue triggered by Yeltsin's infirmity, everyone was competing to expand their influence by bringing in trusted appointees. It was Kudrin who persuaded Bolshakov to consider Putin for a job. At first Bolshakov agreed to appoint Putin to the Directorate of Public Liaison—making him effectively a spokesman. Though Putin did not relish the idea of working with the public, he accepted. He had traveled to Moscow at the end of August, and slept on Kudrin's sofa.[16] As the men drove back to the airport the next day, Kudrin called Bolshakov again, but now he had changed his mind. Bolshakov asked Putin to stay longer in Moscow, and the next day he arranged for him to meet a flamboyant bureaucrat named Pavel Borodin, who would be the man who introduced him to the inner workings of the Kremlin.[17]

Borodin was a jovial politician from Siberia who managed the Presidential Property Management Directorate. From that post, he looked after hundreds of buildings and plots of land, palaces, dachas, fleets of aircraft and yachts, hospitals, spas and hotels, art and antiques, and scores of state factories and enterprises that included everything from funeral homes to an Arctic diamond mine. By Borodin's estimate at the time—and it could only be a guess—the value of the Kremlin's assets exceeded $600 billion.[18] Borodin showed a flair for creative capitalism, diversifying the directorate's holdings in newly emerging sectors like banking and commercial real estate. He also used the position to replenish Yeltsin's patronage mill, dispensing gifts of apartments and dachas, travel and vacation vouchers. The press mockingly called his office the Ministry of Privileges.[19]

Borodin's pride—and folly—was an extensive renovation of the Kremlin itself, which Yeltsin began in 1994 when no one thought the country could afford the expense.[20] In August 1996, Borodin signed a contract with a Swiss company, Mercata, for the renovation of the Grand Kremlin Palace, the former home of the tsars that the Communist Party of the Soviet Union had refitted with all the charm of a factory auditorium. The project succeeded in re-creating tsarist splendor, but the contracts with Mercata and a sister company, Mabetex, would also entangled Yeltsin and his family in an international scandal involving accusations of bribes and offshore bank accounts.

Putin had met Borodin before when he once visited St. Petersburg in search of a northern dacha for Yeltsin. He also once helped when Borodin's daughter, a university student in Petersburg, fell ill.[21] The exchange of these kinds of favors—known as *blat*—had been a tradition of the tsarist and Soviet systems, where informal connections and networks cut through bureaucratic obstacles. Even in a free Russia, where money mattered more, *blat* remained a currency in Kremlin politics.[22] It also helped land Putin his first job in Moscow.

He was "somewhat surprised" that so elevated a bureaucrat, one with close ties to Yeltsin's family, would take an interest in him.[23] Borodin, in fact, was wary of having Putin installed in his office, as were others in the directorate "who suspected that Putin was loyal to other people and organizations."[24] Putin, for his part, was out of his element in the hothouse of conspiracy and infighting that consumed Moscow after Yeltsin's reelection and his (still secret) preparations to undergo heart surgery in the fall. Even his experience in Sobchak's government had not prepared him; he was an outsider in Moscow, and also something of a naïf. As he had when he entered public life in 1991, he arranged for a television interview showing him as he moved to Moscow. "Whose man are you?" was the interviewer's first jaded question to Putin as he waited to board a flight in a lounge at Pulkovo Airport. No one, after all, rose to positions of power in Russia without a patron, and the patrons in Yeltsin's "family," as in all unhappy families, were practically at war with one another. Putin, wearing an ill-fitting, luridly blue suit, demurred. He was his father and mother's son, he replied a little too earnestly, and no one's man. He insisted that he did not even belong to the "Petersburg clan" that was giving his political career a second act. "It's hard for me to imagine that some kind of group or faction even exists," he said. "I don't intend to concern myself with that. They brought me in to work."[25]

Lyudmila did not want to move. She finally felt they had a family life of their own in Petersburg, outside the cloying orbit of Putin's parents. She had no choice in the matter, though. "It always seemed to be the case that work came first for Vladimir Vladimirovich," she told a biographer with chilly formality, "and the family second."[26] Even Putin was reluctant to leave the familiarity of his hometown, but he felt that a job with Borodin "was the best way out of my situation."[27] Borodin's department, having the power to dispense favors, arranged for the Putins to move into a state dacha in Arkhangelskoye, a forested suburb west of Moscow. The house was old, but it had two stories with six rooms, more than enough rooms for both girls. Lyudmila soon fell in love with the capital and its bustle, the "feeling that life is in full swing."[28] By September 1996, Putin had moved into the vast presidential administration, settling into an office in a pre-revolutionary building on Staraya Ploshchad, or Old Square, near the Kremlin. With him came two of his closest aides from Petersburg: Sergei Chemezov, who had served with him in Dresden, and Igor Sechin, who had been with him on Sobchak's staff from the beginning.

Borodin put his new deputy in charge of the legal department and the Kremlin's vast holdings in seventy-eight countries: embassies, schools, and other properties that once belonged to the Communist Party of the Soviet Union. Putin's arrival coincided with a decree by Yeltsin that transferred control of the properties from the old ministries that had handled them in Soviet times, like the Ministry of Foreign Affairs and the Ministry of Foreign Economic Relations, to Borodin's directorate. Many of them were in former Soviet satellites or even former republics, like Ukraine, which claimed title to the Soviet properties in their newly independent territories. It fell to Putin to make sense of the legal morass, disposing of properties that were no longer worth having and reasserting Russia's sovereignty over those that were. Putin's inventory only underscored the disintegration of the Soviet Union and the scavenging of its carcass for profit. "Sometimes things came to light that made your hair stand on end," Putin's colleague, Sergei Chemezov, said.[29] Dozens of shadowy "corporations, proxy firms, and joint stock companies" that had been mysteriously created at this time began buying up many former Soviet properties abroad, according to a young debt collector, Filipe Turover,[30] who had uncovered some of them and, fatefully for Borodin, decided to share his evidence with prosecutors in Moscow and Switzerland.

Putin was a subaltern, as a Moscow newspaper wrote at the time in a profile of this new addition to the Kremlin apparatus. He was "absolutely a back stage person" whose greatest professional quality was his inconspicuousness.[31] This probably saved him when the power struggles surrounding Yeltsin exploded in public even as he began his new job. Aleksander Lebed, Yeltsin's national security adviser, negotiated an end to the war in Chechnya in August 1996 with a peace treaty that deferred but did not resolve the republic's drive for independence. Lebed then clashed publicly over the terms with Chernomyrdin and Chubais, who distanced themselves from an agreement that seemed to give away too much to the Chechens. The public squabbling became so intense by October that the interior minister, Anatoly Kulikov, accused Lebed of staging a "creeping coup" and put the national police on alert across the country. Chernomyrdin called Lebed "a little Napoleon." The next day Yeltsin fired Lebed, who then forged a political alliance with Yeltsin's ousted chief of security, Aleksandr Korzhakov, who in turn leaked a transcript of Chubais discussing efforts to squelch an investigation of the two campaign aides who had been caught with the box full of cash.

The clashes unfolded as Yeltsin underwent heart surgery in November, and Putin found himself pulled deeper into the Byzantine machinations. He had not even finished his inventory of the country's foreign properties, let alone dealt with them, when he was transferred to a new job in March 1997, after only seven months in Moscow. Aleksei Kudrin was promoted and became a deputy finance minister, and on his recommendation, Putin replaced him as the head of the Main Control Directorate. The assignment also made him a deputy chief of staff in the presidential administration, working out of a magnificent new office on Staraya Ploshshad.[32] A week after he assumed the job, a new presidential decree gave the directorate broader authority to investigate abuses in government spending throughout the country at a time when governors, state enterprises, and monopolies were taking advantage of the political and economic chaos to leech money out of the nation's coffers.

Putin's task was to restore order, to end the most rampant schemes that were dragging the government and the economy ever downward. The work exposed him to the corruption that gnawed at the country, but also to the political risks of exposing those in power. Putin learned quickly that service in the Kremlin required delicacy and discretion in interpreting how far to take his investigations. Within days of taking over the directorate, Putin publicly absolved Yeltsin and a former defense minister, General Pavel Grachev, of complicity in a scandal in which the military command in the Caucasus had from 1993 to 1996 transferred $1 billion worth of tanks and other weaponry to help Armenia in its war with Azerbaijan, despite a Russian law against arms sales to either side. To defuse the scandal, Putin granted interviews to the newspaper *Kommersant* and the radio station Ekho Moskvy. He confirmed that the transfers had taken place and said that investigators had found those responsible, though he coyly declined to name them.

"Did you find out who was connected with this supply personally?" the interviewer at *Kommersant* asked.

"Yes, we found their names," Putin replied.

"Can you name them?"

"I would prefer not to do this before the investigation by the Prosecutor General's Office and the Main Military Prosecutor's Office is complete."

"Are they officials of the Russian Ministry of Defense?" the reporter pressed.

"Yes."

"Is the name of the former minister of defense, Pavel Grachev, on this list?"

"No. In the course of the investigation that we carried out, we did not find any documents indicating that Grachev had given any direct instructions or directives on this score."[33]

Putin, as an intelligence veteran, understood how to calibrate his answers, speaking as if reluctantly while spooling out exactly the information he wanted to make public and no more. Grachev, whose corruption was so notorious that he was called "Pasha Mercedes" for acquiring luxury automobiles under unexplained circumstances, certainly knew too much for the Kremlin to alienate him entirely, despite dismissing him. An official from the military prosecutor's office, which had already questioned Grachev, complained anonymously that it was premature for Putin to exonerate anyone.[34]

Overseeing the directorate took Putin across the country and brought him into close contact with the general prosecutor's office and the security agencies, including the Federal Security Service, or FSB, which was the domestic successor of the KGB, responsible for internal security, counterespionage, and counterterrorism and still headquartered in the KGB's ominous building on Lubyanka Square. He discovered the extent to which Russia's government was failing on almost every level, its authority ignored, its resources wasted by governors and other officials who were conspiring with new entrepreneurs to pilfer as much as they could. Although he did not have prosecutorial power, he did have the authority of the Kremlin to scour budgets and contracts, to conduct investigations and compile thick dossiers of incriminating evidence for use when necessary. The information gave him power and influence. He became a modern-day *revizor,* the government inspector of Gogol's satirical play whose expected arrival in a village struck such fear in mendacious local officials that they heaped tribute on an unsuspecting fop in a case of mistaken identity. By the end of his first month on the job, Putin had declared a deputy transportation minister, Anatoly Nasonov, incompetent after "selective checks" in eighteen regions found that billions of dollars had been expropriated from the Federal Road Fund. By May 1997 he had expanded his inquiries to a third of the country's eighty-nine regions or republics, and charged 260 officials with malfeasance. By September he had announced disciplinary action against 450 officials and stressed the particularly "glaring evidence" of budgetary abuse in the Stavropol and Tver regions.[35] Putin impressed his superiors with his diligence in seeking to reassert Kremlin authority, albeit selectively, and with it replenish the government's coffers.[36] He also unnerved them at times. Boris Nemtsov, a young deputy prime minister whom Yeltsin appointed the same month that Putin took over the directorate, remembered Putin's delivering a report on theft and corruption his department had uncovered at a foundation created by Anatoly Chubais, who had passed him over for a job in 1996. The report ended with a salutation that Nemtsov, a reform-minded democrat, felt was the language of an intelligence operative: "Reporting at your discretion." Nemtsov called him for explanation, saying that if he believed that a crime had been committed, he should forward it to prosecutors instead of writing that. "What does it mean?" he asked his subordinate. Putin was not long in answering: "You are the boss, and you decide."[37]

Putin had been thinking about the country's economic problems for some time. In May 1996, while still in Petersburg, Putin had formally enrolled in a university to obtain the graduate degree he had first considered when he returned from Dresden. Advanced degrees always had a cachet in the Soviet Union and Russia, and Putin's decision to seek one reflected a desire to burnish his credentials, a need that became even more acute after Sobchak's defeat. As when he matriculated at Leningrad State with the goal of joining the KGB, Putin saw education as a means to an end, not an end in itself.[38] He did not return to the law department of his university for a higher degree, though. Instead, he chose the prestigious Mining Institute named after Georgi Plekhanov, a prerevolutionary theorist called the father of Russian Marxism. And he settled not on legal affairs but rather on a subject that he understood was vital to Russia's future: natural resources. He was not alone. Viktor Zubkov and Igor Sechin, both close associates in Sobchak's government, also enrolled at the institute, producing theses on the subject of Russia's natural resources; their interests stemmed from the city's many investments in fuel companies, pipelines, and ports.[39] As Sobchak's deputy, Putin had in 1995 drafted a report for the federal government on the need to improve the region's export of natural resources by restructuring Petersburg's ports, and that served as the basis for the thesis that Putin set out to complete.[40]

The product—218 pages long in the original Russian, with graphs and appendixes—was dry in tone and dense with facts and figures on the natural resources of the region surrounding Petersburg: not oil or gas, but bauxite, phosphates, clay, sand, gravel, cement, and peat. These resources remained underdeveloped after the Soviet collapse and needed strategic government investment in order to thrive. The thesis anticipated an economic policy focused on Russia's immense natural resources, grounded in the emerging free market. It argued for "appropriate regulatory and procedural recommendations," though not a reassertion of state control over economic development.[41]

Putin seemed to have neither attended courses at the university nor had the time to write a complicated thesis, given the demands of Sobchak's reelection campaign, his search for a new job, and the subsequent move to Moscow. He appears to have done what many Russians did at the time, especially busy public officials: he had someone else ghostwrite it for him. The estranged daughter of the institute's rector, Vladimir Litvenenko, would later claim that her father had written the thesis for Putin.[42] Litvenenko, who was an expert in mineralogy, went on to join the board of PhosAgro, one of the world's largest producers of fertilizers made from phosphates, which were found in abundance in the Petersburg region, as the thesis noted. He became a very rich man, though that would not become known for many years since the company's owners then remained secret.[43]

Whoever the author or authors, Putin's thesis lifted almost verbatim more than sixteen pages of text and six charts from an American textbook written by two professors at the University of Pittsburgh, which was translated into Russian in 1982—almost certainly at the behest of or with the approval of the KGB, which under Andropov was eager to find a way out of the Soviet Union's economic stagnation. The thesis's bibliography includes the textbook—*Strategic Planning and Policy*, by William R. King and David I. Cleland—as one of forty-seven sources, including papers and lectures by Putin at the institute, but in the text itself the work is neither credited explicitly nor are the lengthy passages lifted from its Russian translation acknowledged. Instead, the number 23, its place in the bibliography, is simply inserted between brackets in two places. The evident plagiarism would be grounds for failure at American or European universities, though it was an accepted practice in Soviet and Russian academia to cut and paste text with minimal citation. In any case, it was not detected for years.[44]

Putin seemed indifferent to the academic undertaking. He rarely mentioned it during the writing or afterward, though he did list it on his résumés, which had probably been the point in the first place. It is possible he was embarrassed by its academic unscrupulousness, or the improbable facility with advanced mathematics[45] that he had never displayed as a student. The thesis nevertheless showed an interest in the economics of natural resources that was a fixation for the circle of friends he had gathered in Petersburg (and later at the Ozero dacha cooperative founded in 1996). Putin defended the thesis at the Mining Institute in June 1997, and one of those critiquing his presentation described his defense as "brilliant."[46]

Now, in Moscow, he was in a position to influence the distribution of those resources on a national, not regional, level. An international commercial dispute over a gold deposit in Siberia, for example, prompted Putin to write a report in 1997 recommending the dismissal of the first deputy minister of natural resources, Boris Yatskevich. Yatskevich served in the ministry that granted mining permits, even as he served as chairman of the board of the company, Lenzoloto, which held the license to the deposit. Putin found the arrangement a flagrant violation of the law.[47] As was typical in Yeltsin's government, nothing happened; in fact, Yatskevich went on to become the minister of natural resources. Putin, though, began to formulate strong views about the necessity of reexerting state authority to put an end to the pilfering of the country's most precious assets. In an essay published in the Mining Institute's annual periodical two years later, he argued that natural resources would prop up Russia's economy for "at least" the first half of the twenty-first century, but they would require foreign investment and the strong guiding hand of the state in licensing and regulating the exploitation of the riches buried beneath the vast expanse of Eurasia.[48] Few academics ever have the chance to put their ideas so directly into practice, but Putin soon would. First, though, he had another piece of unfinished business in Petersburg.

Anatoly Sobchak's exile from power had not been tranquil. The investigation that had begun during his reelection campaign had not ended, not even after Yeltsin dismissed those who had plotted against Sobchak's reelection. They might have left office, Sobchak noted, but they had not left "the abyss in which they flew."[49] And they had allies in the parliament, which by April 1997 passed a resolution calling on the prosecutor general's office to finish the various investigations into "the heinous crimes" of Sobchak and several of his deputies.[50] Meanwhile, Sobchak's public commentary on political affairs won him no allies inside the Kremlin. In January 1997, he criticized Yeltsin's leadership, saying his illnesses had created "virtual anarchy" and the "criminalization of authority."[51] By July, one of his advisers, Larisa Kharchenko, was arrested and charged with negotiating bribes paid by the head of the construction company Renaissance, and Sobchak was summoned as a witness. The arrest of his chief of staff, Viktor Kruchinin, followed. All summer, leaks filled newspapers with details of the case and speculation that Sobchak himself was about to be arrested. He complained that his phone was tapped and that he was followed everywhere he went by agents of the

FSB, even as he ignored a dozen summonses to testify and denied he had done anything illegal in privatizing city property.[52]

He had reason to be paranoid: he was caught in Yeltsin's highly publicized, if not particularly serious, campaign against corruption, one in which Putin himself was playing a prominent role. On October 3, investigators and ten heavily armed special police arrived at Sobchak's office, now in the UNESCO headquarters, and arrested him as a material witness. While being questioned in the prosecutor's office, Sobchak complained of chest pains and was taken to the hospital. His wife said he suffered a heart attack, though no one believed it and the hospital's doctors did not confirm it. Either way, he was well enough the next day to fulminate to the news agency Itar-Tass that the investigators' work recalled the Great Terror of 1937. "Only in 1937 they would have killed me," he said.[53]

Sobchak spent a month in the hospital, his fate resting on the diagnoses of physicians. Even Yeltsin, whose antipathy for Sobchak had grown, felt the prosecution was going too far. He sent a message to the prosecutor general, Yuri Skuratov: "You can't harass a sick man."[54] But the prosecutors pressed on. They doubted Sobchak's claims about his health and arranged to have doctors from Moscow examine him. Before they could arrive, though, Putin intervened. Putin visited Sobchak in the hospital and arranged for his transfer to the Military Medical Academy under the care of Yuri Shevchenko, who had treated Lyudmila after her car accident and remained a close and trusted friend. Then he plotted Sobchak's escape.

On November 7, a holiday still although it no longer officially celebrated the Bolshevik revolution, Putin collected Sobchak's medical records and chartered an aircraft from Finland at a cost of $30,000—paid for, according to Sobchak's wife, by "friends," though some reports said the source was the cellist Mstislav Rostropovich.[55] Putin called on his old contacts in the local police and intelligence service to accompany an ambulance that quietly transferred Sobchak from the hospital ward to a waiting plane at Pulkovo Airport. Despite the warrants for Sobchak's arrests, the public furor over his case, and his own vows to remain in Russia to defend himself against the charges, he and his wife, Lyudmila Narusova, passed through customs on the tarmac, had their passports stamped, and flew to Paris.

Putin's involvement was certainly audacious and very likely illegal, even if the Sobchaks' documents were in order. As he had in 1991, he risked his own future out of loyalty to the charismatic, flawed leader who had been "a friend and a mentor."[56] Only in a country where the justice system had broken down could he have succeeded in spiriting Sobchak to safety abroad. Only in a dysfunctional political system could his brazen defiance of the law have earned him admiration—and not just among his close circle of friends.

Sobchak's flight created a furor, and Putin's role in the affair did not remain secret for long. "Putin understood the injustice of what was happening to his former boss and political mentor better than anyone," one admirer wrote later. Putin "sensed danger more quickly and acutely than others" and acted out of loyalty and nothing more. "When I learned that Putin had helped send Sobchak abroad, I had mixed feelings. Putin had taken a great risk. Yet I profoundly admired his actions." The admirer was Boris Yeltsin, and when he mulled the infighting and betrayals of his appointees, he felt awe at such a display of loyalty.[57]

CHAPTER 8

Swimming in the Same River Twice

After a year heading the Main Control Directorate, Putin grew tired of conducting investigations that yielded mixed results. He had uncovered corruption, only to have cases stall in a judicial system that he understood was easily manipulated. He had little power to challenge the vested interests of officials, and yet he also showed little zeal for crusading to change the system. "It was not very creative work," he recalled. He claimed later that he considered leaving Yeltsin's erratic government for the private sector in the winter of 1997–1998. He thought about creating a law practice, though he doubted he could make a living with it. What stopped him, indirectly, was the looming collapse of the new Russian economy, and very nearly the state with it.[1] By the beginning of 1998, Putin was swept up in what was described as the "revolution of unknown middle managers."[2] Yelstin turned to these faceless young apparatchiks in order to avert a national calamity and his own political demise.

The year after Yeltsin's reelection and convalescence following heart surgery, the country appeared to have stabilized after its lurch through its post-Soviet crises. Inflation eased, and the economy grew for the first time since 1989, although less than half a percent. No one was exactly optimistic, but the worst seemed to have passed. "Everyone was filled with hope, myself included," Yeltsin wrote in his memoirs. "I hoped that by the second half of 1997 and in early 1998 we would sense that something in the country was changing."[3] Something was, but not what he or anyone else imagined. The economic crisis that swept Asia in the fall of 1997 dragged down the world economy and, most critically for Russia, the price of oil. A barrel of oil at the end of 1997 sold for less than it cost Russia's oil companies to extract it; in the first three months of 1998, the industry that provided most of Russia's resources *lost* more than $1.5

billion.[4] Government revenues, already depressed by rampant tax evasion and capital flight into offshore accounts, plummeted, and Yeltsin's government soon drained its reserves trying to keep up.

On March 21, 1998, Yeltsin summoned his prime minister, Viktor Chernomyrdin, to his dacha, where he now spent more time than he did in the Kremlin. Chernomyrdin had served in the office for more than five years, proving to be a bulwark in the government through the worst years of political and economic turmoil. With Yeltsin increasingly weakened and a new election already on the horizon, some thought he could be the president's successor, an idea that tormented Yeltsin, who wanted someone "absolutely free of the influence of any political or financial groups."[5] So he fired Chernomyrdin and then offered vague and conflicting reasons for his action. He claimed the country needed a technocrat, but in truth he wanted a subordinate as prime minister, not a rival in waiting. Yeltsin's choice to replace him was Sergei Kiriyenko, a former banker from Nizhny Novgorod. He was thirty-five, nearly a quarter century younger than Chernomyrdin, and had arrived in Moscow only the year before to serve as energy minister. He only learned his fate the morning of the announcement and, according to Yeltsin, had "to collect himself and make sense of it all."[6]

The Duma twice rejected Kiriyenko's nomination, underscoring Yeltsin's waning influence and intensifying an atmosphere of political crisis. Chernomyrdin promptly announced he would seek the presidency in 2000, confirming Yeltsin's fear of his ambitions. Even some of the oligarchs who had backed Yeltsin two years before now threw their support behind Chernomyrdin, most importantly Boris Berezovsky. A short, balding former mathematician, Berezovsky had built a financial empire that included automakers, banks, oil, and a controlling interest in a state television network, ORT, which he wielded as an instrument of political power and vengeance. Yeltsin had appointed him to his Security Council after his reelection in 1996 and then promptly fired him. Berezovsky was mercurial and faithless; an ally was in his mind a "temporary phenomenon," a security official once said. "For Berezovsky, people are divided into two categories: a condom in its packaging and [a] condom that has been used."[7]

Berezovsky viewed Kiriyenko as a reformer in the mold of Anatoly

Chubais or Boris Nemtsov, the young liberals brought in to restructure Russia's economy. In other words, Kiriyenko stood in the way of his business interests.[8] He unleashed the full force of his television network against the nominee, allying himself with the Communists in the parliament who despised him as a rich tycoon. Yeltsin succeeded in pushing through Kiriyenko's appointment only by threatening to disband parliament, as allowed by the Constitution, if it failed to approve the nomination after three votes. Kiriyenko was narrowly confirmed on the third vote. Yeltsin's opponents in parliament consoled themselves by drawing up articles of impeachment.

The shakeup in Yeltsin's government created yet another opening for Putin. In May 1998, he took his third new job in the Kremlin in less than two years. He was never close to Yeltsin and was not then powerful enough to figure in his intrigues. And yet his competence and loyalty had enabled him to rise in the bureaucracy, often to the surprise of people like Chubais. This time Yeltsin appointed him the first deputy director of the presidential administration, putting him in charge of relations with the country's eighty-nine regions. The job was a natural extension of his work at the Main Control Directorate, where he had amassed files of corruption and malfeasance by regional officials. Russia is nominally a federation of its regions, and though the Constitution of 1993 gave the president broad, centralized authority, many operated as independent fiefs. By virtue of their local elections, the regional leaders also had independent political authority and thus posed potential threats to Yeltsin's preeminence. Yeltsin's distrust only intensified when Aleksandr Lebed, his challenger turned ally turned enemy, won election as governor in the Krasnoyarsk region of Siberia in May and made clear that his presidential ambitions had not diminished in the least.

Putin saw the fractured political system as a symptom of the country's ongoing dissolution. Chechnya's struggle for independence was only the most extreme example of Russia rotting from within. The *vertikal*, the chain of government authority, had been destroyed, he recalled, and "it had to be restored."[9] He told journalists that his main task now was to ensure that Yeltsin's decrees would be enacted at the regional level, but he emphasized that he did not intend "a tightening of the screws."[10] He never had time to do it. He would remain in that job for only sixty-one days—long enough to install a KGB colleague from Petersburg, Lieutenant General Nikolai Patrushev, in his old job at the Main Control Directorate, but not to accomplish much else.

Two days after Putin's latest appointment, Russia's stock market crashed. Shares had lost half their value from the beginning of the year, wiping out millions of dollars of wealth, though only among the elite who could afford to invest. The poor had nothing. Arrears in wages steadily mounted, and strikes soon spread. Foreign investors began to withdraw their capital, while wealthy Russians socked theirs offshore. The privatization of Rosneft, the last state-owned oil company, was canceled because no one would even bid for it. A $4 billion credit from the International Monetary Fund stabilized Russia's meltdown but only briefly. Yeltsin's government struggled to hold up the value of the ruble, but it was a losing battle. The government "resembled a major fire department that had to hastily deal with the outbreak of more and more new blazes."[11]

One of the blazes that preoccupied Yeltsin involved the loyalty of the FSB. Even as the country's economy imploded, Yeltsin fretted over the agency's power. Yeltsin, who had done more than anyone else to break the iron grip of the Soviet Communist Party, could never bring himself to purge the intelligence agencies with the zeal that the Germans had after 1989. He relied too heavily on the intelligence officers and their commanders, hoping to restrain their influence in politics and society by pitting them against each other.[12] For KGB veterans, the changes that occurred in the 1990s were disorienting and humiliating. Many left the ranks to serve as heads of security companies that were soon mired in violent battles for assets; others crossed into criminality, exploiting the government's weaknesses. Often it was difficult to tell which was which.

Shortly after his reelection in 1996, Yeltsin had appointed a KGB veteran, General Nikolai Kovalyov, as the director of the newly created FSB. He was the sixth head of the domestic security services since the collapse of the Soviet Union. Yeltsin considered him a competent administrator, but in office he developed "an enormous personal antipathy to business and all its representatives." "He simply despised people with large amounts of money," Yeltsin wrote.[13] He was not alone among the security officers who retained their paltry government salaries and, like many working Russians, watched as inconceivable fortunes landed in the hands of a privileged (and in their minds undeserving) few. Given the intelligence service's historic anti-Semitism, it is not surprising that much of their fury flowed toward the oligarchs who were Jewish. The

Jews "sold out Russia," they believed, manipulating the president and creating the economic crisis then unfolding.[14] What alarmed Yeltsin most was that under Kovalyov, the FSB began searching for these new "enemies of the people," collecting compromising material, *kompromat*, against the executives of banks and other companies, as its investigators had done against Sobchak. Now the FSB's zeal threatened people within Yeltsin's "family"—even Yeltsin himself. He decided he needed to rein in the agency. He needed his own man in the FSB.

Boris Berezovsky, whose control of Aeroflot had attracted the prosecutor general's menacing attention, lurched in and out of Yeltsin's circle. He nurtured his access to the president's advisers, though he met more and more rarely with the president himself. Valentin Yumashev, a close Yeltsin aide, told him that Yeltsin no longer trusted the FSB's generals and their "tightly knit clan." In early July, Yeltsin had announced plans to reorganize the FSB, including a sharp reduction in the number of officers at Lubyanka, but Kovalyov seemed less than eager to carry out the order. Yeltsin wanted to clean house, Yumashev explained, and asked if he had any thoughts about Vladimir Putin.

Berezovsky recalled a deal he had made in Petersburg years before. He wanted to open a car dealership and was surprised that Putin had refused even to consider a bribe, which presumably he was prepared to offer.[15] "He was the first bureaucrat who did not take bribes," Berezovsky said. "Seriously, it made a huge impression on me."[16] Whether or not Berezovsky's recollection was a factor, Putin had earned a reputation as competent and disciplined to the point of abstemiousness, though others noted his capacity for discretion. Yeltsin first noticed him when he served in the Main Control Directorate. His reports, he found, were "a model of clarity." In contrast to the endless chattering and scheming of his aides, Putin did not try to press any agenda on his boss—or even bother him with much small talk. In fact he tried to "remove any sort of personal contact" with Yeltsin. "And precisely because of that," Yeltsin said, "I wanted to talk to him more." He was wary of Putin's "coolness" at first but came to understand that it was "ingrained in his nature."[17]

After meeting at Yeltsin's presidential retreat in Karelia to make the final decision to fire Kovalyov, the youthful new prime minister, Sergei Kiriyenko, flew back to Moscow and summoned Putin to meet him at the airport when he landed. Neither he nor Yeltsin had consulted Putin about the job; he was then a mere pawn in the game of political chess that the president imagined as he lurched toward the end of his presidency. As he drove to the airport, Putin expected bad news and, in a way, for him it was.

"Hi, Volodya," Kiriyenko greeted him, familiarly. As young as Putin was, the prime minister was a decade his junior. "Congratulations!"

"What for?" he asked.

"The decree is signed," Kiriyenko said. "You have been appointed director of the FSB."[18]

Putin claimed he was surprised, though the possibility of his appointment had been rumored in the media nearly a year before.[19] He had even discussed the possibility with Lyudmila three months before during an evening walk at the dacha in Arkhangelskoye, one of the increasingly rare moments when he spared time for her. He told her he did not want to return to the "closed life" of the intelligence world, which he thought he had left behind in 1991. "I had no desire to step in the same river twice," he said.[20]

Lyudmila did not relish the prospect either. As the wife of a rising political appointee in Moscow, she lived a far more open and interesting life, traveling frequently to Germany and elsewhere, though often only with the girls, not together as a family. Basking in her new freedom, she remembered the oppressive strictures of the KGB spouse: "Don't go there, don't say that. Talk to that person, don't talk to this person."

Dutiful as ever, though, Putin did not refuse the appointment. He telephoned Lyudmila with the news while she was vacationing with their daughters on the Baltic coast.

"You be careful there," he told her, "because I've been returned to the place where I began."

Lyudmila was confused. She thought he had returned to Borodin's office—that he had been demoted somehow in the turmoil then roiling the country.

"I've returned to the place where I began," he repeated.

He had to say it a third time before she understood. She had to wait until she returned to Moscow to find out what exactly had happened to return him to the KGB's successor. "They appointed me, and that's it," he told her, and she asked no more questions.[21]

Kiriyenko introduced Putin to the FSB cadres at Lubyanka on the following Monday, July 27, 1998, and tried to placate Kovalyov, who

learned of his dismissal from the news reports on television. He had
served admirably, Kiriyenko said, but "conditions are changing, people
are changing."[22] At the announcement, Putin expressed his appreciation of the president's confidence and vowed not only to carry out the
restructuring Yeltsin had ordered, but also to focus on the government's
strategy for easing the economic crisis: prosecuting economic crimes and
tax evasion. He said he had "come home."

Kovalyov, although furious about his dismissal, handled the transition
professionally. He showed his replacement around and opened the safe
in his office. "Here's my secret notebook," he told him. "And here's my
ammunition."[23] Two days later Putin granted an interview to the newspaper *Kommersant,* in which he outlined his priorities and expanded the
agency's traditional domestic work to include the fight against political extremism and nationalism, against foreign spies, and against the
newly arrived and slowly expanding World Wide Web. "Of course, the
FSB is not going to take the Internet under its control," he said, already
expressing a wariness of the growing importance of the new medium,
"but it understands that modern tools of telecommunications can be
used to the detriment of the country's security."[24] Putin's appointment
caused grumbling among the FSB's veterans—also KGB veterans—who
viewed him as an upstart and an outsider. He was from Petersburg and
had served his entire intelligence career in provincial posts. He had never
risen above the rank of lieutenant colonel. It was an extraordinary, unan-
ticipated break for Putin—and an enormous advance in an unexpected
rise. He had leapfrogged over far more experienced and qualified generals, who considered him a parvenu sent to impose the Kremlin's control
over the agency—which is exactly what he set out to do.

On August 1, after returning abruptly from his vacation in Karelia to
deal with the looming economic crisis, Yeltsin summoned his new
FSB director to his dacha in Gorky, outside Moscow, to discuss the post.
Yeltsin wanted Putin to "make the service less politicized" and to restore
its prestige and authority, something that would send chills down the
spines of the dissidents for whom Lubyanka remained a source of fear.
Yeltsin proposed that Putin return to active intelligence service, with a
promotion to the rank of general. Putin refused, however, recalling his
resignation during the August 1991 coup. He also revealed to Yeltsin
that in the seven years since, he had remained in the reserves as the KGB

became the FSB. "I am a civilian," Putin told Yeltsin. "It's important that such a power ministry be headed by a civilian."[25] And so he became the first civilian to head the FSB—and the last.[26]

Putin moved into an ascetically decorated office on the third floor of Lubyanka. He did not move into the old executive office nearby that had been occupied by Soviet intelligence chiefs from Lavrenty Beria to Yuri Andropov. He turned that into a museum that some considered a shrine. On his desk he placed a bronze statue of "Iron Felix" Dzerzhinsky, who founded the Soviet secret police in 1917.[27]

As the loyal servant he had always been, Putin carried out Yeltsin's instructions to reorganize the agency and reduce the central staff—a task that became even more urgent as the country's economy and budget woes worsened. He ultimately reduced the number of officers at Lubyanka by a third, to four thousand from six thousand, at the cost of considerable discontent among those in the ranks who considered Putin's reductions a purge motivated by Yeltsin's politics. He also abolished departments he considered outdated and created new ones to address the most urgent security threats. They oversaw intelligence in the regions with a particular focus on seething Muslim areas, like Chechnya; computer security and telecommunications; and, ominously, the defense of the Constitution, a task that echoed that of the Fifth Chief Directorate, the KGB's agency that hunted dissidents in Soviet times. As he had since he arrived in Moscow two years before, Putin turned to lieutenants he could trust, the men he had known since his KGB days in Petersburg. Aleksandr Grigoryev, Viktor Cherkesov, and Sergei Ivanov, all generals on active duty, took up positions in the FSB's leadership. Yeltsin admired Putin's steely determination. "He did not allow himself to be manipulated in political games," he wrote. "In the insidious rumor mill of the government at that time, it was wise for even a seasoned person to avoid entanglements."[28]

Putin immersed himself once again in the life of the intelligence agent, where everything is secret and everyone is suspect. "If you were an intelligence officer, you were always the object of a potential vetting," he recalled. "They were always checking up on you. It might not happen very often, but it was not very pleasant." Even as director, he felt the "constant state of tension." He also shared the agency's paranoia. They "couldn't even go out to a restaurant!" he said of his cohorts. "They thought only prostitutes and black-marketeers went to restaurants. What would a decent officer of the security agencies be doing in such company?"[29]

The result was extraordinary discretion. When he once invited a pretty young reporter from the Kremlin press pool out for lunch at Izumi, one of the capital's new sushi restaurants, she arrived to find the new director of the FSB waiting for her alone, having cleared the place of other diners. The reporter, Yelena Tregubova, found him to be flirtatious, calling her Lenochka and encouraging her to join him in drinking sake. That she did not honor his discretion but rather included the scene in a book hardened his opinion of the media and reporters, who were in his view little more than vultures who sought to exploit or embarrass officials for personal gain.[30]

On the evening of August 20, less than a month after Putin's appointment to the FSB, a journalist in Petersburg, Anatoly Levin-Utkin, left the office of a recently created newspaper called *Legal Petersburg Today*. He carried a thousand rubles, then about $140, and a briefcase full of papers and photographs for articles in the next issue of the newspaper, which was only its third. Levin-Utkin was a deputy editor at the newspaper, which had already gained attention with articles delving into the city's banks and the competing spheres of influence. One of the investors noted was Boris Berezovsky, who had publicly clashed the year before with other oligarchs over the privatization of Svyazinvest, the country's largest telecommunications company. Another article concerned Anatoly Sobchak's escape from Russia and the activities of his deputy for foreign investments, now the director of the FSB. Its headline read "Vladimir Putin Became Head of the FSB Unlawfully." Levin-Utkin had written neither, but had contributed reporting for the articles. The newspaper's editor in chief, Aleksei Domnin, said that both articles had prompted vociferous complaints from their subjects. "Putin's people" met with him to complain, he said, though he did not say who. The meeting had "an obviously political nature" that he did not detail.[31] Complaints about press coverage were nothing unusual—and often warranted—and the furor over the articles would have quickly been forgotten, except for what happened next.

Levin-Utkin entered the foyer of his apartment building on Rednova Street and was checking his mailbox when two men approached from behind and beat him so badly they shattered his skull in several places.

The assailants took the briefcase and everything in his pockets, including his newspaper identity card. A neighbor found him unconscious in the foyer, and he was taken to the hospital. Surgeons operated twice, but he died on the morning of August 24, having never regained consciousness. Contract hits in Petersburg had become so common—happening at the rate of one a day for a while—that Levin-Utkin's murder would not have ranked highly if the journalists' organizations had not taken up his cause, appealing to the United Nations to press the Russian authorities for an investigation.[32] There was never any evidence linking either Putin or Berezovsky to the fatal beating; prosecutors doubted that the murder had a motive beyond simple robbery, though it was never clear that they seriously investigated the crime. It was the first time, though, that Putin's name, and Berezovsky's, surfaced in media reports in connection with the same death, and it would not be the last. The case, as it happened, was overshadowed by far more shattering events that August.

Three days before Levin-Utkin's murder, Russia defaulted on most of its debts and devalued the ruble, wiping out the savings of millions of investors and ordinary citizens. Russia was on the brink of total economic collapse. The crisis deepened the political turmoil surrounding Yeltsin, seemingly signaling the end of his political career. On August 21, the Duma called for his resignation. Two days later, he fired Kiriyenko instead. He had lasted a mere five months. Yeltsin then appointed as prime minister the man he had dismissed from the post five months earlier, Viktor Chernomyrdin. Yeltsin, the great democratic hope for Russia, had clearly lost his way. The "bold" moves he claimed to favor now seemed desperate. Four days later he appeared on television to declare that he would not seek reelection in 2000, and then all but disappeared for two weeks, making only six brief visits to the Kremlin at the height of the country's financial and political panic. The Duma, as it had with Kiriyenko's appointment, twice voted against Chernomyrdin's return, but this time Yeltsin no longer had the power to bluff since the parliament had prepared impeachment proceedings and under the Constitution the president could not dissolve parliament if an article of impeachment had been passed.[33]

A new confrontation loomed, as did rumors of a coup, fueled by reports that military units near Moscow had been ordered on high alert. The Communists in the Duma braced for a repetition of the siege of

1993; in fact, they seemed to dare Yeltsin to order it. Then, on September 1, Putin went on national television to deny that the Kremlin intended to use force to resolve a political conflict. He gravely declared in his televised remarks that the FSB would secure the interests of the people. "Those who violate the Constitution and try to undermine Russia's state system by unconstitutional methods and with the use of force will run up against appropriate resistance," he said. "This is something you can be sure of."[34]

Later, when a Communist member of parliament, Albert Makashov, denounced Jews as a scourge that should be removed from the country, Putin announced that an investigation had begun into his remarks, even as the prosecutor general's office and the Duma itself equivocated.[35] The controversy caused a furor in Moscow, with people taking to the streets during the Communist celebrations of the revolution to defend Makashov and his anti-Semitic rants. Putin made his announcement with Lubyanka in the background, sending a message not only to the protesters but also to the secret service, still infested with bigotry, that hateful expressions would not be tolerated. After just a few weeks on the job, he no longer seemed the inconspicuous aide he had always been, blending into the background. He exuded the full authority of the country's secret service and a fierce determination not to let political or popular unrest undermine the state's authority. As a grateful Yeltsin wrote, "I think his cold expression and the almost military precision of his formulations discouraged many people from causing trouble."[36]

Putin's public support did little to help Yeltsin, who had to abandon his nomination of Chernomyrdin. His aides, working with deputies in the Duma, settled on a candidate least objectionable to all: Yevgeny Primakov, who had been Yeltsin's foreign minister since 1996. Primakov was an old, genial Soviet academic, an Arabist by training, who had spent fourteen years as a journalist in the Middle East, working closely with the KGB. After the collapse of the Soviet Union, he took over the foreign intelligence service that had emerged from the ruins of the KGB, and where from 1992 to 1996 he all but disappeared from public view, trying to revive the agency in much the same way that Putin had its domestic counterpart.[37] Each was suspicious of the other. Primakov had far more experience in the world of intelligence, having been deployed undercover on missions not only to the Middle East, but also to the United States.[38] Eager to bring the FSB under his influence, he was among those who suspected Putin of packing the ranks with colleagues from Petersburg. Putin took "the whole FSB leadership" to meet with him to prove he had not conducted a purge.[39]

On September 11, the parliament voted overwhelmingly to install Primakov as prime minister, and the immediate political crisis eased. The desperate decisions of Yeltsin's government to default on bonds and devalue the ruble had sent shock waves through society but ultimately proved to be "a revitalizing tonic," allowing the economy to resume growing, aided by a recovery in domestic production and the beginnings of an oil boom.[40] Yeltsin's fortunes—and health—continued to decline, though. He was repeatedly hospitalized in the fall and winter, and the impeachment proceedings against him had not ended with Primakov's appointment. Meanwhile, a far more menacing threat to Yeltsin was emerging, and Putin's loyalty would prove decisive in defending against it.

Putin had not been long in Lubyanka when he found himself at the center of a public scandal greater than any he had faced before. On November 17, 1998, six men held a strange and sensational press conference in Moscow. Four wore masks and dark glasses. The other two, unmasked, were Aleksandr Litvinenko and Mikhail Trepashkin. All were veterans of the FSB, and before national and international journalists they sketched an alarming tale of corruption and conspiracy. The organized-crime unit they worked for, they said, had itself turned into a criminal enterprise, running rackets with Russian mobsters and Chechen independence fighters, extorting businesses they were supposed to protect and offering their services for hire, often with lethal effect. Their superiors, they said, planned to kidnap the brother of a prominent businessman, Umar Dzhebrailov. They had ordered the beating of Trepashkin after he was relieved of his duties for investigating wrongdoing. Most sensationally of all, they explained how they had been ordered by the officers at the agency now headed by Vladimir Putin to assassinate Boris Berezovsky.

Berezovsky, whose influence inside the Kremlin was never as great as he pretended it was, had privately told officials about the alleged plot against him. He even believed it to have been a factor in the dismissal of Kovalyov. Among Putin's first acts as FSB head had been to disband the organized-crime unit that these men were now accusing of having gone rogue. He had dismissed or transferred most of the unit's officers, but an internal investigation into the assassination order against Berezovsky failed to result in any criminal charges against the unit's commanders. (One prosecutor told Berezovsky that the order to kill him had been a joke.) The closing of the case prompted Berezovsky to go public. He appealed to Putin directly in an open letter published in *Kommersant* on November 13.

"Vladimir Vladimirovich," he wrote, "you have inherited a difficult legacy from your predecessors. Criminal elements and officials at various levels, whom they have corrupted, including officials in your agency, are striking out at people who are unwilling to go back to being cattle. Criminal terror is on the rise in Russia."[41] Berezovsky never explained the reason for his direct appeal; some officials and newspapers suspected he was now trying to discredit Putin or others in the Kremlin—or, contrarily, to regain some of the influence that he had once had inside it.

When the letter failed to accomplish much, the agents involved went public four days later. Aleksandr Litvinenko, the ringleader of the press conference, had worked for the KGB's military counterintelligence directorate in the late 1980s, and then for the FSB in the 1990s, focusing on terrorism and organized crime. He was never a spy or an undercover operative, but rather an investigator and enforcer. Like Putin, he was fit, patriotic, and loyal to the security services, rising to the rank of lieutenant colonel, but by then Litvinenko had grown disillusioned. He came to see the FSB as a rogue agency, especially the unit created in 1996 to fight organized crime, which was notorious for its ruthless brutality and corruption.[42] The line between service to the state, to the oligarchs, and to the mafia became less and less clear, and Litvinenko himself crossed it. In 1994, he had been assigned to investigate an assassination attempt against Berezovsky, who had just left his auto dealership in a chauffeured Mercedes when a remote-controlled bomb exploded, raking the car with shrapnel. The driver was decapitated but Berezovsky somehow survived. As Litvinenko collected evidence, he became enthralled with the ambitious tycoon and soon went on Berezovsky's payroll as his personal security guard and adviser, even as he continued to serve the FSB. Many officers, their meager wages often in arrears, moonlighted for the men with money; it was a symptom of the decay of the intelligence apparatus. When, according to his account, he received an order to kill Berezovsky in the winter of 1997, he refused and went to Berezovsky with details of the plot.

Litvinenko began the press conference by reading a statement, then emphasized that the corruption they were disclosing occurred before Putin's arrival at the FSB at the end of July, and he appealed to Putin to cleanse the agency. "We do not seek to compromise the Federal Security Service," Litvinenko said, "but to purify and strengthen it."[43] They had no proof other than their testimony, though they claimed otherwise. "I have made several attempts to get through to Vladimir Vladimirovich and present all these facts to him, but we did not have such an opportunity. We were simply denied access to him," he went on. And then he appealed directly to Putin. "I will take this opportunity. I think he will look at this taped press conference and I would tell him the following: I have proof that his deputies are deceiving him. I can provide documentary proof. If he calls me to his office, I will show him these materials."

The subsequent furor put Putin in an awkward position. He could not simply rebuff Berezovsky, who still claimed to have influence within the Kremlin; at the same time, the charges were scandalous, and they infuriated him. Putin responded to Berezovsky's letter with one of his own, sent to *Kommersant* the day of the press conference. "We are not afraid to wash our dirty linen in public," he went on, saying that internal investigations would be conducted into any accusations. Obliquely, though, he warned Berezovsky, "who is well known for his devotion to democratic values," that he was running a risk by interfering in FSB affairs. And he warned that if the allegations proved false, the FSB would have no recourse but to sue for slander—not only against Berezovsky, but also against the newspaper's editorial staff for printing his letter.[44] Putin proved to be exceedingly intolerant of criticism of his agency—and dissent within it.

At the end of the month, Putin quietly summoned Litvinenko to his office, just as Litvinenko had asked for him to do. Litvinenko arrived with an armful of documents, including a chart that in his mind linked all the names and crimes he and his colleagues had known of. Litvinenko, presumptuously, imagined Putin as another lieutenant colonel like him, "a mid-level *operativnik* suddenly put in charge of some hundred seasoned generals with all their vested interests, connections and secrets."[45] He was not sure how to address the man who now directed his agency—"Comrade Colonel"?—but Putin preempted him by rising from his desk to shake his hand. "He seemed even shorter than on TV," Litvinenko remembered thinking. The meeting was brief and, Litvinenko thought, chilly. Putin insisted on meeting him alone, without the two colleagues who had accompanied him. He politely declined to accept the dossier that Litvinenko had brought with him. Litvinenko described the meeting to his wife, Marina, as a disaster. "I could see it in his eyes that he hated me."[46]

Putin had compiled his own dossier against Litvinenko and the others. On the evening of November 19, he appeared on the state television network Rossiya and, though promising an investigation, insisted there was no evidence that any of the accusations against the FSB were true. He ridiculed the press conference as a specacle with "characters from a children's story," wearing masks even though they announced their names. The ex-wife of one of them—he did not say whom, but apparently he did not mean Litvinenko—had called him afterward, he said, improbably, to complain that he had fallen behind on alimony payments. "Perhaps this was the reason why he wore dark glasses." Then he turned the tables, and said that the agents themselves had conducted illegal operations.[47]

Yeltsin summoned Putin to his dacha again the next day and demanded that he resolve the embarrassing and escalating scandal. "Everyone knows what happens to people carpeted like this by a stern Yeltsin," one newspaper wrote about the meeting.[48] Putin did not relent, though; even if some of the agents' accusations were true, they were as complicit as their superiors. He considered that by holding a press conference the agents had betrayed their oath of office as intelligence officers. Instead of investigating their claims, he presented the president with the evidence he had compiled of their wrongdoing. And then he fired Litvinenko and his cohorts. "People like this cannot work in the FSB," he said.

Putin's handling of the affair did not earn him universal support in the Kremlin. Rumors floated that Yeltsin would sack him for incompetence—only four months into the job. The staff cuts at Lubyanka were not politically popular in the Duma, which continued to assault Yeltsin's presidency at every opportunity. Putin's position suddenly seemed precarious—all the more so after a prominent liberal deputy from Petersburg, Galina Starovoitova, was killed only three days after Litvinenko's press conference.

Starovoitova was an ethnographer who rose to prominence during perestroika as a champion of the rights of Russia's many ethnic groups. She and Putin were never close, but their paths crossed in Petersburg throughout the 1990s, and she knew Sobchak and his wife well. In September 1998 she appeared on a television program with an apt name for the era, *Scandals of the Week,* and suggested that the renewed leaks of criminal charges against Sobchak appeared to be an attempt to discredit the FSB's new director—that is, Putin. She noted that officially Sobchak remained only a witness in an investigation, not a suspect. Only a deeply cynical conspiracy could somehow scorch Putin himself she thought. "I don't rule it out, at least, although of course it is ridiculous."[49]

On the night of November 20, Starovoitova returned to her apartment on Griboyedov Canal with an aide, Ruslan Linkov. The assailants fired at least five bullets. Three struck Starovoitova in the head, killing her instantly. Two hit Linkov, who survived.[50] The gunmen dropped their pistols at the scene and drove off in a waiting car. The attack, with all the characteristics of yet another contract hit, provoked international condemnation. "To kill a woman—a woman in politics—that has not happened in Russia since Stalin's time," a supporter of hers, Sergei Kozyrev, said.[51] Yeltsin denounced the murder, calling it "a peremptory challenge" to "our entire society." He was so distraught by the news, an aide said, that he was hospitalized the next day.[52] He and Primakov ordered Putin; the interior minister, Sergei Stepashin; and the prosecutor general, Yuri Skuratov, to take "personal charge" of the investigation and demanded results. Starovoitova had recently declared her candidacy for governor of the Leningrad region (which, unlike the city, had not changed its Soviet name). She had denounced the nationalistic bile flowing in the parliamentary debates and amassed evidence of corruption in the Petersburg government. There was no shortage of potential motives and suspects—in fact the police arrested more than three hundred people in the weeks after her death[53]—and yet the motive for her murder would never be fully established.

Yeltsin, ill and frustrated, lashed out. He blamed the country's mounting problems that winter on "the outbreak of Communist hysteria," which included not only repeated denunciations of Jews, but also a call to return the statue of Felix Dzerzhinsky to its pedestal outside the old KGB headquarters where Putin now worked. Yeltsin was infuriated by the inaction of "our usually threatening Prosecutor General's Office" in the face of what he saw as criminal incitements to overthrow Russia's democracy.[54] Starovoitova's murder seemed like another crippling strike against the country, against him.

As the chief of the country's domestic intelligence agency, Putin shouldered at least some of the blame, in Yeltsin's mind. Putin's political fate now seemed tied to Yeltsin's unpredictable whim. Yeltsin summoned him again on December 15, this time to the Kremlin during one of his rare days at the presidential office. He wanted to discuss the Starovoitova case, the outbreak of racist statements in the parliament, the plot against Berezovsky, and Putin's progress in restructuring the FSB. Putin emerged from the meeting emphasizing that he had not lost the president's faith, while sounding like someone who worried he had. He accused those spreading the rumors, apparently from inside Yeltsin's warring camps, of wanting "to sow seeds of uncertainty among the administrative and executive staff of the service or weaken its control." At the base of the rumors "lies fear," he said, "fear of the security service." Putin seemed to be barely clinging to his position. He announced that when Yeltsin ended his term—then barely a year and a half away—he would resign to make way for a new intelligence chief under a new president. "It's clear that I'll have to go."[55]

CHAPTER 9

Kompromat

The next spring, late in the evening on March 17, 1999, the nightly news program on the state television broadcast a report preceded by a warning that it might not be suitable for anyone under the age of eighteen. Excerpts of a black-and-white videotape appeared. It was clearly taken by a surveillance camera, secreted in position above a double bed in what turned out to be a Moscow apartment owned by a banker of some renown. Two young women, described as prostitutes, move in and out of the frame in various stages of undress. Soon there appears a man who, as the announcer intoned, "very much resembles the Prosecutor General," Yuri Skuratov. The Kremlin's struggle with the prosecutor had intensified, and its counterattack had just taken a lurid turn.

All the major networks had received cassette copies of the video earlier in the week from an anonymous source. It lasted fifty minutes in all. Only the state television channel, RTR, chose to use it—at least at first.[1] The decision to do so was made, over the objection of some of the network's correspondents, by its general director, Mikhail Shvydkoy, who would later become Russia's minister of culture.[2] The source and authenticity of the videotape remained murky, and the quality was poor enough that no one could say absolutely that it was Skuratov cavorting with the two women, though when one of them asks his name, having refused to give her own, he replied "Yura," the diminutive of Yuri. The videotape had all the characteristics of the "honey traps" the KGB once used to embarrass or blackmail businessmen or politicians. A joke soon circulated that the source of the video was a man who "very much resembles the director of the FSB," Vladimir Putin.

According to Yeltsin, it was his chief of administration, Nikolai Bordyuzha, who first obtained the videotape. Shocked, Bordyuzha confronted Skuratov privately at the Kremlin on February 1, long before the scandal became public.[3] Skuratov promptly wrote a letter of resignation, citing the deteriorating state of his health, and checked into a hospital the next day. Yeltsin had just been released from his own hospitalization, undergoing treatment this time for a bleeding ulcer. Bordyuzha himself checked into a hospital a month later. It was as if a plague were sweeping the country's political elite. On February 2, Yeltsin returned to his Kremlin office for the first time since the end of 1998. He stayed only for an hour and a half, but it was long enough to dismiss four aides and to accept Skuratov's resignation. The reason cited in the announcement was Skuratov's health, which, since the sudden "illnesses" of Soviet leaders had long been a euphemism for deeper intrigues, no one believed.

Rumors of other dismissals, including Putin's, soon spread. No one knew what was unfolding behind the scenes. The upper house of parliament, the Federation Council, controlled by the country's governors, had the sole authority to confirm Skuratov's resignation; already eyeing the power vacuum that would follow the imminent end of Yeltsin's term, the council refused to consider Skuratov's fate as long as he was in the hospital and unable to explain himself.

Yeltsin claimed at the time that neither Bordyuzha nor his other aides had told him about the videotape before it became public. He was simply happy that Skuratov had resigned, and with ample reason. Skuratov had served as prosecutor general for more than three years, yet had distinguished himself only by a spectacular failure to solve the country's most notorious crimes, including the murder of Galina Starovoitova two months before. "The endless monotone of Skuratov's excuses was beginning to annoy me," Yeltsin wrote.[4] Skuratov, however, had not been completely idle. He showed more zeal investigating the president's affairs than the country's other notorious crimes, and in the months leading up to his dismissal, some of his investigations had suddenly gained new momentum. On the day in February that Bordyuzha confronted him with the videotape, Skuratov had delivered a report to the Duma accusing the Central Bank of Russia of secretly funneling $50 billion worth of foreign currency reserves through an obscure firm called Financial Management Co. Ltd. It was registered in 1990 in the Channel Islands, apparently by the KGB and the Communist Party, and used as an offshore account, though many of the details remained unclear, including who might have profited from what were clearly illegal transfers.[5] The next day, investigators from Skuratov's office, accompanied by masked special police officers, raided the Moscow headquarters of Sibneft, an oil company that was part of Boris Berezovsky's empire; a day after that they showed up at Berezovsky's security firm, Atoll, where the investigators found electronic eavesdropping equipment and tapes labeled the "Family," in reference to Yeltsin's inner circle of advisers, and "Tanya," Yeltsin's younger daughter and political adviser, Tatyana Dyachenko.

Despite his resignation, or possibly because of it, Skuratov's prosecutions suddenly shifted public attention—and outrage over corruption—to those at the heart of power in the Kremlin. After the wild abuses of privatization in the early 1990s, calls for justice grew louder, and sensing the political winds, the new prime minister, Yevgeny Primakov, announced at a cabinet meeting on January 28 that the government would amnesty ninety-four thousand nonviolent prisoners in order to free up space "for those who are about to be jailed—people who commit economic crimes."[6] It sounded very much like a warning that even the oligarchs around the Kremlin could no longer count on immunity in the wake of a Yeltsin presidency. Berezovsky, whose intense dislike of Primakov was reciprocated, responded by declaring that Primakov's threat sounded like a return to the Great Terror. The raids on his companies followed not long afterward.

Primakov's remarks had the rhetorical sweep of a politician ambitious to become Russia's next president. In his few months as prime minister, he had already built support in parliament and won over Moscow's powerful mayor, Yuri Luzhkov, who had once been a friend of Yeltsin's but now seemed to hover in wait for the president's demise. Yeltsin increasingly saw the political jockeying—and Skuratov's investigations—as an existential threat to his power and even his personal well being. He mused on the internal Communist Party conspiracy that had toppled Nikita Khrushchev in 1964, and now he was sure Primakov and Luzhkov were scheming with the prosecutor general to overthrow him. He had to do something to stop it.[7]

On the day the Federation Council finally took up the question of his resignation, March 17, Skuratov appeared to be in good health and now asked to keep his job—"if you extend your trust and support to me."[8] He explained to the lawmakers that he had resigned only under duress, and he blamed it on two former prime ministers and "well-known oligarchs." He did not mention Berezovsky, but he did discuss the raids investigators had launched against Berezovsky's companies. "These people were aware of my resignation no less than two weeks in advance," he said. He referred obliquely to people collecting information about his private life, but now seemed determined to hold on to his job.

It was then that the Kremlin sent the videotape of Skuratov and the women to members of the Federation Council who were preparing to vote on Skuratov's fate. The tactic backfired badly: the council's members were shocked and appalled, not by the videotape itself but by the use of such a crude trick to influence the outcome of its deliberations. They voted 142 to 6 to reject Skuratov's resignation and leave him in office. The videotape promptly aired a few hours after the council's vote. In the ensuing public uproar, it was impossible to say which was more morally compromising: the behavior on the bed or the decision to make it public.

The next morning Yeltsin summoned Skuratov to the hospital room where he was recovering, again, from a bleeding ulcer. By then, Yeltsin too had a copy, as well as still photographs. When Skuratov arrived, he found Primakov and Putin waiting in the room as well. He was not surprised by Putin's presence. Putin had visited him while he was hospitalized, told him that the "Family" had been satisfied with his quiet departure in February, and offered to make him the ambassador to Finland—an "honorable exile." Skuratov had refused.

"Then what would you like to be?" Putin asked.

Skuratov told him he wanted to continue "the very work I have performed."[9]

After Skuratov's release from the hospital in February, Putin tried new tactics to persuade him to resign. He called once and told the prosecutor he empathized with his quandary; he confided that "they say" there was a similar videotape of Putin himself! Perhaps it would be best to avoid scandal by stepping aside.[10] Putin visited Skuratov again at his government house in Arkhangelskoye—they were neighbors—and as they strolled in the wooded grounds, he worked him like a source or a recruit, alternately confiding and threatening. "Yuri Ilyich," he began, respectfully, "I am amazed that you managed to work three and a half years in this cesspool." He said he could not imagine surviving in his job until the end of Yeltsin's term. Then Putin's tone shifted abruptly. He pulled out a sheaf of papers and said there were irregularities in the renovation of Skuratov's apartment in Moscow. He insinuated that Skuratov was under fire now because of his investigation into Putin's former boss, Pavel Borodin.[11]

Through it all, Skuratov thought, Putin had been unfailingly polite, but the allusion to Borodin confirmed in his mind that his investigations had indeed struck close to Yeltsin and the "Family." Borodin's contracts with Mercata, the company that had renovated the Kremlin in 1994, and its sister company, Mabetex, had also come under the scrutiny of investigators abroad. There were suspicious transactions that suggested money laundering. In January, only weeks before the videotape appeared, investigators in Switzerland had raided Mabetex's offices in Lugano and confiscated records that appeared to show that the company had not only paid bribes to Russian officials to win construction projects but also paid off the balances of credit cards belonging to Yeltsin's daughters. Swizterland's chief prosecutor, Carla Del Ponte, had launched a prosecutorial campaign against the laundering of criminal profits in Switzerland, complaining the country was threatened "by dirty Russian money,"[12] and the evidence against Mabetex surfaced as a result. Even as the Skuratov scandal was unfolding in March, she traveled to Moscow to pursue her investigation, offering to share the Swiss evidence in exchange for Russian cooperation. In two days of private meetings, she and Skuratov discussed the investigations, including, he claimed, details of bank accounts belonging to several Kremlin officials. Now that the Kremlin was trying to force him to resign, Skuratov had the leverage to fight back, confident that the Federation Council would side with him in the power struggle of Yeltsin's political twilight.

When Yeltsin confronted Skuratov at the hospital the morning after the Federation Council's first vote—the morning after the videotape aired—he tapped his fingers on a copy of the videocassette. "You know, Yuri Ilyich," Yeltsin told him, leaning back in his chair and breathing deep. "I have never cheated on my wife . . ." Yeltsin then promised to stop showing it on television if Skuratov would write a second letter of resignation. This was "elementary blackmail," Skuratov thought, but he also knew that it was pointless to debate its authenticity now. Skuratov protested that he had launched an investigation into Mabetex, which Yeltsin interpreted as a form of blackmail in return.[13] "We're talking about something else now, Yuri Ilyich," Yeltsin told him. "After what's happened to you, I don't think you should remain in the post of prosecutor general. I won't fight with you. I won't try to persuade you. Just write your resignation letter. I will no longer work with you."

Yeltsin pushed a pen and paper toward him. Skuratov turned to Primakov, expecting support from the prime minister who had pledged to fight corruption among the country's oligarchs. He received none.[14]

Putin said nothing, though Skuratov sensed him observing him throughout. Skuratov signed the letter, resigning for the second time in less
than seven weeks, though Yeltsin agreed to his request that the letter be
postdated until April and the next scheduled meeting of the Federation
Council. As Skuratov left the hospital and returned to his office, he contemplated his next move. He envisioned his fight with the Kremlin as a
game of chess: his position was tenuous, but he had just avoided check-
mate.[15] Now he must counterattack. While driving, he called a television
reporter and made the Mabetex investigation public.[16]

Of all the political controversies surrounding Yeltsin's presidency, the
investigation that Skuratov and the Swiss had launched into Mercata
and Mabetex posed the direst threat yet to the president and his "Family." Yeltsin himself acknowledged that this was the one scandal that had
"legs" and could even bring his presidency to a premature end. The day after
his confrontation with Skuratov, Yeltsin checked out of the hospital and
returned briefly to the Kremlin. He fired his chief of staff, Nikolai Bordyuzha, with no public explanation, though many later assumed it was because
of his failure to remove Skuratov quietly. Bordyuzha, a former military
officer, received an "honorable exile" like the one Putin had offered to
Skuratov, becoming the ambassador to Denmark. Yeltsin replaced him
with Aleksandr Voloshin, a former business partner of Boris Berezovsky.
Ten days later he promoted Putin to secretary of the Security Council.

It was then that Putin intervened in a way that would deepen Yeltsin's
trust in him. Although Putin denied that his agency recorded Skuratov's tryst, he did make it clear that the FSB had intimate knowledge
of its provenance. On April 2, he announced that the videotape was in
fact genuine—first to the Federation Council "with eyes downcast," as
Skuratov described it, and then again in remarks to waiting reporters.
As embarrassing as that was, it was not enough by itself to force Skuratov, but Putin had found a legal technicality that trumped the council's
obstinacy. He went on to announce that there had been other "parties,"
like the one in the video, and that they had been paid for by criminals
trying to influence Skuratov's investigations. If shown true, this would
be a grave crime, and since any civil servant under criminal investigation had to step down pending the resolution of the charges, Putin's
announcement did what nothing else had so far. In the middle of the
night, the Kremlin called in a deputy prosecutor in Moscow, presented
him with the FSB's evidence, and ordered him to open an investigation.

Now Skuratov had no choice but to step aside until this new case against him was resolved.

Yeltsin then announced that he had suspended Skuratov. He removed his personal security detail, cut his office phone lines, and ordered his office sealed. "Russia without a prosecutor general was the lesser of two evils," Yeltsin would write.[17] Putin's maneuver was technically legal—assuming there was some basis to the accusations of influence buying—but it was also ruthless. A grateful Yeltsin once again took note. A week later, he announced that Putin would remain director of the FSB, even as he presided over the Security Council. He had demonstrated his loyalty to the president, impressing him with his quiet efficiency; others might promise, but Putin achieved results. After only two and a half years in Moscow, Putin now stood at the center of Yeltsin's administration, no longer a mere deputy, but one of the most powerful officials in the Kremlin.

Putin rose through the ranks as the Yeltsin era seemed to be in its death throes. The unfolding Skuratov scandal aided efforts by the Communists to impeach Yeltsin, a step that would have made Primakov acting president until new elections could be held. The president, ailing and fearful, no longer exerted much control over events, but instead reacted to them, often erratically.

On March 5, 1999, the Interior Ministry's special envoy to Chechnya, General Gennady Shpigun, was kidnapped as he boarded a plane in the region's capital, Grozny. Kidnappings had become the principal postwar industry in Chechnya, with hundreds of people held for ransom between 1996 and 1999, but the abduction of a senior envoy was too brazen for the Kremlin to ignore. The peace talks that ended the war in 1996 had given Chechnya a great deal of sovereignty, but nearly two years of fighting had devastated the region and left its economy in ruins. The war had killed as many as a hundred thousand Chechens, as well as nearly five thousand Russian soldiers, according to official records that some doubted were complete. Having survived the Russian counterassault, Chechnya after the war descended into chaos and criminality, undermining efforts by the region's elected president, Aslan Maskhadov, to restore order and win international recognition for its secession from Russia. Soon the lawlessness was spilling over Chechnya's borders. On March 19, the day after Skuratov's second resignation, an enormous bomb exploded in a market in the southern city of Vladikavkaz, the capital of North Ossetia, another of the republics along the Caucasus, not far from Grozny. The blast killed more than sixty people. Yeltsin ordered Putin and the interior minister, Sergei Stepashin, to Vladikavkaz to oversee the investigation.

Two days later, Maskhadov narrowly survived an assassination attempt. A former artillery officer from the Soviet era, Maskhadov was a committed nationalist and separatist, but he was one of the few Chechen leaders the Kremlin could negotiate with. For much of the year planning had been under way for Maskhadov to meet with Primakov or even Yeltsin himself to finalize Chechnya's transition to independence, as allowed in the peace accords of 1996. Now Maskhadov suggested that "certain forces" in Moscow had conspired to kill him as a pretext for declaring a state of emergency and avoiding a resolution of Chechnya's fate. Putin angrily denounced the accusation.[18] The peace accords that had suspended the first war had been a humiliation to Russia. They now no longer offered much hope for resolving the republic's ultimate drive for independence. The Kremlin's security men, including Putin, began drafting plans for a new war instead.

The renewed turmoil in Chechnya unfolded as Russia was facing a war waged by the Soviet Union's archenemy, NATO, against the country's Slavic brothers in Serbia. After the breakup of Yugoslavia in the 1990s, Serbia turned its nativist fury on the once-autonomous Muslim region within its own borders, Kosovo. At the end of 1998, Serbia's president, Slobodan Milošević, launched a campaign to crush separatist militias in the region; within months, the campaign looked more and more like the ethnic cleansing that had occurred in Bosnia only a few years before. Europe and the United States, shamed by their dithering over the earlier killing, responded aggressively.

The prospect of a NATO military intervention to protect Kosovo infuriated Russia in ways American and European leaders failed to appreciate. Serbia and Russia shared Slavic roots, religion, and culture, but Russia's concerns went deeper. The conflict in Serbia inflamed Russia's wounded pride over its deflated status since the collapse of the Soviet Union. The new Russia lacked the ability to shape world events, which made the American-led actions even harder to swallow. Yeltsin berated President Clinton, insisting that an intervention was forbidden by international law, only to be ignored. Russia resented the fact that the United States and its expanding NATO alliance were acting as if they could impose their will on the new world order without regard to Russia's interests. Even worse, the conflict in Kosovo had striking parallels to the one in Chechnya, and even Russians not prone to paranoia could imagine a NATO campaign on behalf of Chechnya's independence movement.[19]

NATO's air war, which began on March 24, 1999, lasted seventy-eight days, and each bomb or missile that fell on Serbia was perceived as an attack on Russia itself. Popular sentiment raged, with violent protests outside the American embassy and virulent denunciations in the Duma. The war stoked the nationalistic sentiment that Yeltsin had endlessly struggled to contain for his own political survival. He dispatched his former prime minister, Viktor Chernomyrdin, to act as a mediator with the United States and NATO. He did so at the suggestion of Putin, who considered it his "own small contribution" to resolving the war.[20] After weeks of relentless bombardment, Milošević had finally given in to NATO's demands and agreed to withdraw Serbia's forces from Kosovo to make way for an international peacekeeping force. Now Russia demanded to be part of the force but refused to be in any way under the command of NATO's generals. Putin, newly appointed as the head of the Security Council, took part in negotiations to resolve the impasse over the peacekeeping mission. "I was struck by his ability to convey self-control and confidence in a low-key, soft-spoken manner," Strobe Talbott, then the deputy secretary of state, wrote of his first meeting with Putin, on June 11, the day before NATO's peacekeepers were to move into Kosovo from Albania and Macedonia. "He was physically the smaller of the men at the top—short, lean and fit, while all the others were taller and most of them were hefty and overfed."[21] Putin had prepared for his meeting with the American, referencing details of the poets Talbott had studied as a student, Fyodor Tyutchev and Vladimir Mayakovsky. He had clearly read Talbott's intelligence profile.

During the meeting, the Americans received a note that Russia was threatening to send its peacekeepers into Kosovo without NATO coordination. Putin soothingly told Talbott that nothing had changed in the agreements they had reached and that "nothing improper" would happen. Something did anyway, and Talbott came to believe that Putin had known all along that it would.[22] That evening a Russian paratroop unit stationed in Bosnia—part of an earlier, now seemingly naïve sign of post-Soviet cooperation with NATO—loaded up and drove from its base to the airport in Kosovo's capital, Pristina. When British troops arrived at the airport on the morning of June 12 in a heavy downpour, roughly two hundred Russians were already there in armored vehicles. As General Michael Jackson, the newly appointed British commander of the peacekeeping effort, landed there and prepared to announce the successful launch of the mission, one of the Russian vehicles rumbled through his impromptu tarmac news conference. A Russian squad commander stood halfway out of the turret, with a discernible smirk on his face.[23] NATO's supreme commander, General Wesley Clark, implored Jackson to somehow block the Russian deployment, but Jackson refused. "Sir," Jackson told Clark, "I'm not starting World War III for you."[24]

In Russia, the reaction to the deployment was ebullient, but the improvised intervention at the airport nonetheless showed the disarray of the country's civilian and military commands. Putin, who a day before had said nothing would happen, acted as if nothing had when Talbott met him again the next day. He claimed total ignorance of the military's preemptive rush into Pristina, but explained "slowly, calmly, in a voice that was sometimes inaudible" that the country's "pre-election struggle" had pitted the hawks and doves against one another. Putin suggested it had been a mistake, but nonetheless the operation boosted the president at home. "No one in Russia," Putin told Talbott, "should be able to call President Yeltsin a puppet of NATO."[25]

Putin's remarks about the "pre-election struggle" underscored the extent to which the end of Yeltsin's presidency had become an overriding obsession of Russia's political elite. The country, after centuries of tsarist and then Communist rule, had never democratically transferred political power from one leader to another. The personification of power ran so deep in Russian culture that it seemed inconceivable. Even at this late stage, Yeltsin toyed with the idea of running for reelection. Though he had been elected twice already, the country's new Constitution, which limited a president to two consecutive terms, had taken effect only in 1993. He could argue that legally his reelection in 1996 began his first term, allowing him to run again in 2000, but all that was fantastical. He was already sixty-eight, frail, and politically crippled. He had not yet resigned himself to leaving the Kremlin, but he knew it was inevitable. He thought hard about how to ensure a transition that would both preserve the political transition from Soviet rule and protect himself from the vengeful purges that had followed the removal of every leader since the Romanovs. Retirement had never been kind to the country's leaders.

In the midst of the Kosovo conflict, Yeltsin had moved decisively to lay the groundwork for his life after the presidency. In May, he sacked his fourth prime minister. Primakov had proved a stabilizing force during his eight months in office, calming the panic of the August default in 1998 and navigating the parliamentary impeachment proceedings. He had been nothing but honest and decent and loyal, Yeltsin admitted. His greatest failure as prime minister had been to become more popular than Yeltsin. Now, a year before the 2000 presidential elections, Primakov and Moscow's mayor, Yuri Luzhkov, were the presumed front-runners to take over the country, and that was something Yeltsin could not accept. He was concerned by Primakov's remarks about freeing up prison space for "economic criminals" and by the fact that the Duma had completed five articles of impeachment and scheduled a debate for May. If any one article passed, Yeltsin would lose his authority to dissolve parliament for as long as the impeachment proceedings moved ahead; even if he could successfully delay or defeat impeachment, he would lose the leverage that had allowed him to push Kiriyenko through as prime minister the year before. Primakov could remain as prime minister and continue to amass political allies. Yeltsin, searching for an heir, thought Primakov did not have the temperament to be president. Russia needed "a person of a completely different mind-set, another generation, a new mentality." Primakov, he believed, "had too much red in his political palette."[26]

Without question the impeachment proceedings were politically motivated, pressed by the Communists and their allies in what was, arguably, the last great political battle over the collapse of the Soviet Union. Yeltsin's crimes, according to the articles, began with the agreement that dissolved the Soviet Union in 1991. They went on to include the violent confrontation with the parliament in 1993, the war in Chechnya, the erosion of the military, and the "genocide of the Russian people" caused by the economic crises of the 1990s. As matters of constitutional law, they were dubious, but they resonated deeply with a frustrated public, for whom the end of the Soviet Union had brought little but suffering and shame. Yeltsin's impeachment became a referendum on Russia's transition to democracy. And each article had the support of a majority of lawmakers.

On May 12, the day before the impeachment debate began, Yeltsin dismissed Primakov and nominated Sergei Stepashin, a loyal if colorless police commander who had served in various ministries under Yeltsin since 1990, most recently as interior minister. He had been appointed a deputy prime minister only two weeks before, the post being a prerequisite for anyone appointed acting prime minister, and during a government meeting Yeltsin made an embarrassing show of ordering Stepashin to move his chair closer to his own in order to, as he put it, "whip up the sense of expectation."[27] Yeltsin treated these shakeups as tactics in a game, and in truth they were all the power he had left to influence politics. "A sharp, unexpected, aggressive move always throws your opponent off balance and disarms him, especially if it is unpredictable and seems absolutely illogical," Yeltsin wrote.[28] He hoped that this latest reorganization could somehow derail the impeachment vote, but "absolutely illogical" is all it seemed to be.

The impeachment debate lasted two days, while Yeltsin's aides frantically tried to count—and buy—votes. When the votes were held, 94 of the 450 deputies failed to show up, making it more difficult to reach the 300 votes required to adopt each article of impeachment. Even so, 283 of those present voted to impeach Yeltsin for the war in Chechnya, which liberals had opposed with almost as much passion as Yeltsin's conservative opponents; 263 voted for the article pertaining to the events of October 1993. The other articles lagged, but all received an overwhelming majority of those present, and only narrowly failed to impeach him.

Yeltsin's gambit with Stepashin had not affected the outcome of the debate as much as he thought it might, but when the dust settled, on May 19 the Duma voted, surprisingly and overwhelmingly, to accept Stepashin's nomination as prime minister. The deputies calculated that he would be nothing more than a caretaker prime minister under a fatally wounded president until parliamentary elections were held in December. And if the prime minister's job was a springboard to the presidency in 2000, they had little to fear from this meek, apolitical administrator. Yeltsin's endorsement was a kiss of death anyway, and Yeltsin seemed to know that. He later claimed he had low expectations from Stepashin—and he had one last gambit to unveil. He wanted to wait until the time was right.

On the day of Stepashin's appointment, Putin met with Yeltsin in the Kremlin and presented a plan to increase the FSB's authority across the Northern Caucasus. The plan meant to improve "the coordination and means which are available to the federal organs of power"—in short, to prepare for war in a region that was careering out of control, not only in Chechnya, where Moscow effectively had no authority, but also in the neighboring republics like Karachayevo-Cherkessia, where local elections in May threatened to provoke a bloodbath between rival ethnic groups. Putin had had no experience dealing with the Caucasus before he moved to Moscow and dealt with the region's problems first as the inspector for the Main Control Directorate and then as the director of the FSB. Since Catherine the Great's conquests, the mostly Muslim lands stretching from the Black Sea to the Caspian had been restive subjects of the Russian and later the Soviet empires. Stalin expelled entire Caucasian populations to Siberia during the Great Patriotic War, fearing they would embrace the Nazi invaders. The collapse of the Soviet Union unleashed old grievances, which culminated in Chechnya's declaration of independence and the disastrous war from 1994 to 1996. In Putin's mind, this amounted to the dismemberment of Russia itself, aided and abetted by nefarious foreign influences. Apparently, he meant the victors of the Cold War, principally the United States.[29]

The debacle of Kosovo, and the near clash at the airport, prompted Yeltsin to order the Security Council to meet weekly to better coordinate national security strategy. The meetings further raised Putin's public profile. He began granting regular interviews to newspapers and television channels, answering the questions of the day—from a new nuclear doctrine to American complaints about Russian espionage, from a proposed reunification of Russia and Belarus to the coming political campaign. Yeltsin's continued infirmity fueled rumors of unrest and even of a coup by hardliners. In an interview with *Komsomolskaya Pravda*, Putin deflected a question about the possibility of a coup by the security services with a sardonic aside: "Why should we stage a coup if we are in power as it is?" he asked.[30] His comment sent chills through the country's liberals and Yeltsin's opponents, who did not take the threat so lightly.

By the end of July, Yeltsin cut short a vacation and returned to the Kremlin. He complained that a heat wave had made vacationing impossible, but he had a more pressing matter that for the time being only he knew. The precipitating cause was an election alliance revealed the day before between his banished prime minister, Yevgeny Primakov, and Mayor Luzhkov of Moscow. No longer close to Yeltsin, Luzhkov was now unleashing virulent attacks on the president's administration and his ties to the oligarchs. The media, including newspapers and a television station funded by Luzhkov's government, published report after report on Yeltsin's "Family" and the corruption around it. Yeltsin complained that the most slanderous stories had been bought by or leaked to the same newspapers the KGB had used in Soviet times (even though his man Putin was in charge of its successor). NTV, which had once supported Yeltsin against the Communist threat, turned against him with a vengeance after his chief of staff, Aleksandr Voloshin, tried to stop government loans to its owner Media-Most, the holding company of Vladimir Gusinsky, one of the oligarchs who had bankrolled Yeltsin's 1996 reelection effort.

Yeltsin convinced himself that the Primakov-Luzhkov juggernaut was a plot not simply to win the parliamentary elections, but to abolish the presidency itself. In several meetings over the summer, he pleaded with Stepashin to do something, *anything*, to stop governor after governor from pledging support to Luzhkov's party, called the Fatherland, which was now allied with Primakov's All Russia bloc. Yeltsin brooded, increasingly isolated from all but his inner circle, the "Family" that was now in as precarious a position as ever. "He was simply unable to understand what was going on in Russia," a Russian historian, Roy Medvedev, wrote, "and was thinking not so much about holding onto power but guaranteeing his own personal security."[31] Eight years after his heroic resistance to the putsch, Yeltsin had lost the admiration of a nation that was breaking free after decades of Soviet ideology. His memoirs did nothing to hide the self-pitying state he had reached. He felt abandoned, distrustful, and almost certainly afraid. "I tortured myself with worries. Who would support me? Who was really backing me?"[32]

Yeltsin claimed he had decided on his next course of action months before, though given his reactive and improvisational leadership, that seems doubtful. Even if he had thought of it earlier, no one else knew what he had decided to do, not even his closest advisers, until the announcement was imminent.[33] It certainly seemed impetuous, not planned. On August 5 he summoned Putin to his dacha outside Moscow for a secret meeting.

"I've made a decision, Vladimir Vladimirovich," Yeltsin told him, "and I would like to offer you the post of prime minister."

Putin said nothing at first; he simply stared attentively at Yeltsin, digesting the news. Yeltsin explained "the state of affairs," the brewing trouble in the Caucasus, the economy and inflation, and the thing that obsessed him most: the Kremlin's need to manufacture a parliamentary majority in elections that were now just four short months away.

Putin, he believed, would act where Stepashin had dithered on the most existential issue facing the Kremlin: Yeltsin's fate in the event Luzhkov or Primakov became the next president. Putin had already shown that he would act. As Luzhkov's political momentum built in the spring, Putin had launched an investigation into the company controlled by his wife, Yelena Baturina. Her company, Inteko, had managed to win contract after contract, making her the first woman billionaire in Russia, a rags-to-riches tale that helped leave the millions of Russians impoverished by the collapse of the Soviet Union deeply embittered about this new capitalism and democracy—and not a little bit envious. Luzhkov bellowed in protest when investigators began poring through Baturina's finances; he was no longer afraid to challenge Yeltsin and his senior security adviser. The FSB, Luzhkov protested, "unfortunately, works for the Kremlin today, not for the country."[34]

Yeltsin was now asking Putin to take on a far more important role. He was asking him to build and lead a political party that could defeat those who had almost completely abandoned the president. When he finally spoke, Putin asked the obvious question: How can you build a parliamentary majority with no supporters in parliament?

"I don't know," Yeltsin replied.[35]

Putin reflected for an unusually long time in silence. His quiet demeanor had attracted Yeltsin, but now it seemed like hesitation.

"I don't like election campaigns," he finally said. "I really don't. I don't know how to run them, and I don't like them."

Yeltsin assured him that he would not have to run the campaign himself. Campaign tactics were the least of his worries. Experts could master political technologies. He must simply project what now eluded Yeltsin: confidence, authority, the military bearing he believed the country craved. In his desperation, the latter was very much on Yeltsin's mind. Putin replied with "military terseness," he recalled.

"I will work where you assign me."

Yeltsin's next remark nonetheless surprised him. "And in the highest post?"

For the first time, Yeltsin said, Putin seemed to comprehend the full intent of his plan. He was not being offered a sacrificial position, like the previous three prime ministers, who lasted only months in the office. Yeltsin was suggesting him as his heir as president, an endorsement that had eluded so many of Yeltsin's senior aides.

A silence fell between the two men. Yeltsin felt the tick of the clock in his office. He found himself contemplating Putin's blue eyes. "They seem to speak more than his words," he thought.[36]

He asked him to think about it, and then summoned Stepashin, who took the news of his dismissal as prime minister badly, pleading with Yeltsin to reconsider. Yeltsin, who preferred the quick execution of his decisions, uncharacteristically sympathized with his prime minister, who had been loyal to him throughout his presidency. Yeltsin agreed to think about it, a forbearance he immediately regretted. Anatoly Chubais, who had first worked with Putin in 1991, tried to talk Yeltsin out of his decision to appoint Putin as prime minister, appealing to the chief of staff, Aleksandr Voloshin, and to Yeltsin's daughter. Chubais had always been cool to Putin, regarding him as a security man with little political savvy and, rightly, no political experience. Chubais had left Yeltsin's administration for a final time and by then headed the state electricity monopoly, but he had masterminded Yeltsin's comeback in 1996 and his political instincts were surer than Yeltsin's at this point. There was little obvious advantage to replacing Stepashin with Putin. Neither had ever been elected to anything. They were the same age. Both came from Petersburg, and neither had any independent political base that would shore up Yeltsin. Chubais warned him that another reshuffling of his government would be seen as yet another act of madness that would bolster the Communists and the emerging alliance between Luzhkov and Primakov.

Even as Chubais was pleading his case however, events in the Caucasus hardened Yeltsin's resolve. On August 7, a large force of Chechen fighters crossed the republic's border and encircled three towns in the neighboring republic of Dagestan. Russia's military and interior police had prepared for months for an incursion, but the Chechen forces again acted with impunity in the rugged borderland. They were commanded by two fighters: Shamil Basayev, a ferocious rebel commander, and a shadowy figure with the nom de guerre Khattab. Khattab, a Saudi, was a veteran of Islamic insurgencies dating back to the war against the Soviet Union in Afghanistan. He was a conduit for the foreign influence that Putin had warned about. Stepashin, whose handling of a similar intrusion in 1995 had led to his dismissal as the head of the FSB, flew to Dagestan the next day with the military's chief of staff, General Anatoly Kvashnin, to oversee what turned into a full battle between the Chechen fighters and Russian troops. Stepashin declared that there would be no repetition of the mistakes of the Chechen war, and Russian artillery and rockets began hammering the villages occupied by the Chechen forces. When Stepashin flew back to Moscow the next day, Yeltsin went ahead with his plans and fired him, nominating Putin as the next prime minister.

"I have now decided to name a person who in my opinion can bring society together," Yeltsin said in a television speech on August 9. "Relying on the broadest political powers, he will ensure the continuation of reforms in Russia." Yeltsin did not explicitly name Putin as his anointed heir, but he did mention the election scheduled for June 2000, expressing hope the voters would also find confidence in this diminutive, still relatively untested leader. "I think that he has enough time to show his worth."

"This is the kiss of death," a prominent Communist strategist, Leonid Dobrokhotov, declared at the time, referring to Yeltsin's endorsement. "Given the universal loathing of him in the country, any recommendation by him of any politician, even the best, points the way to the grave."[37] The Duma's speaker, Gennady Seleznyov, also declared that Yeltsin had ended Putin's political career, saying that deputies should "not waste weeks" debating the nomination since "he could be fired in the next three months." Even Putin himself doubted his future as a political leader, a future he had not considered for himself, as anyone who knew him well understood.

It had already been a difficult summer for Putin. His father's health had deteriorated badly, and despite his ever increasing responsibilities at the FSB and security council, Putin traveled to Petersburg at least once a week to see him. His mother, Maria, had died the year before. Both had lived long enough to see him rise through the ranks of the city and federal governments that emerged out of the ruins of the Soviet Union. Putin's relationship with his father had never been close, but the taciturn old veteran's pride was palpable. On his deathbed, he exclaimed, "My son is like a tsar."[38] He died on August 2, and Putin had just returned from the funeral in Petersburg when Yeltsin offered him the post of prime minister.

Putin knew, despite what Yeltsin would later claim, that the president might discard him as quickly as he had discarded Stepashin, Primakov, and Kiriyenko. He calculated he had two, three, maybe four months before he too would be dismissed. Now, at the age of forty-six, he felt he had been given his "historical mission," and only a short time to complete it. The violence on Chechnya's border with Dagestan seemed like a continuation of the dissolution that had begun in 1991 when the Soviet Union collapsed. The war in Chechnya had been a humiliation. Russia's leaders had reacted timidly to what was an existential threat to the nation. He felt the country was coming apart as Yugoslavia had and as East Germany had. "If we don't put an immediate end to this, Russia will cease to exist," he recalled thinking. The war in Chechnya had been profoundly unpopular, dragging down Yeltsin's reputation and prompting a vote on his impeachment. He knew a new conflict would be risky too. "I realized I could only do this at the cost of my political career," he said. "It was a minimal cost, and I was prepared to pay up." He recalled being a tiny kid in the courtyard who the bullies were sure "was going get his butt kicked." Not this time. In the Caucasus, he was going "to bang the hell out of those bandits."[39]

CHAPTER 10

In the Outhouse

Dagestan is the southernmost part of Russia, an ethnically diverse land that borders the Caspian Sea and rises into the mountain peaks of the Eastern Caucasus at its border with Chechnya. Like Chechnya, it is predominantly Muslim, but it is also one of the most heterogeneous places in the world, with dozens of ethnicities and languages. It first came under Russian rule at the beginning of the nineteenth century, and had joined the other republics of the Caucasus to form a briefly independent state after the Bolshevik revolution. With the collapse of the Soviet Union, however, it did not join Chechnya in declaring its independence from Russia. Secession had little public support there among the various peoples, though the idea of unifying with Chechnya was debated for much of the 1990s.

The commander who led the incursion from Chechnya on August 7, Shamil Basayev, declared his intention to create an Islamic state of Dagestan, hoping to expand his political and ideological campaign of violence and terror in order to bolster his own power in Chechnya. Along with the Saudi fighter Khattab, he led a force of two thousand fighters who seized the small villages along the mountainous border. The exact goal of the raid remained unclear, but thanks to the tensions that had been rising ever since General Shpigun's kidnapping (his body would later be found), the Russian military was better prepared. As interior minister and, after May, as prime minister, Sergei Stepashin had drafted plans for a police and military operation that would restore federal order in Chechnya; Putin, as FSB chief and head of Yeltsin's Security Council, was involved in shaping those plans. Stepashin would later claim that they had settled on the timing of the operation—August or September—long before Basayev's incursion.[1] Stepashin's plan had limited military objectives: to seize the plains in the northern third of Chechnya, the lowlands up to the Terek River, creating a cordon sanitaire that would contain the radicalism and criminality in the republic's mountains.

In the wake of Basayev's incursion into Dagestan, Putin now had something far more ambitious in mind. He asked Yeltsin for "absolute power" to coordinate all the security ministries and conduct military operations—authority that officially belonged to the president as commander in chief. Yeltsin agreed, the first time he had delegated so much of his presidential prerogative to a prime minister.[2] The day after his appointment in August, Putin declared that Russia's commanders would reestablish control in Dagestan, and he gave them a deadline of two weeks. His nomination had not even been confirmed yet. By August 13, Russian bombers and helicopter gunships bombarded the villages occupied by the Chechen fighters, and Putin threatened to carry the air war into Chechnya itself. The next day the Russians did exactly that, bombing villages that the incursion forces were using as bases.

On August 16, the Duma took up Putin's nomination and by only a narrow margin confirmed him after a debate that focused more on the election campaign than on his qualifications for the post or the violence unfolding in the south. He received 233 votes, only 7 more than the minimum needed, and far less than Stepashin, Primakov, or Kiriyenko had.[3] Putin seemed a transitional figure at best, soon to be swept aside. In his brief, clipped remarks before the parliament, Putin pledged to restore discipline in the government, and he reminded Russia's generals of the deadline for repulsing the invaders in Dagestan. "They have one week left."

And a week later Basayev's fighters withdrew, having miscalculated the ferocity of the Russian reprisals and the dearth of local support in Dagestan for an Islamic uprising. Although Dagestan had adherents to a radical strain of Islam, the republic's myriad ethnic groups remained far more loyal to the Russian state than the Chechens.[4] Local police and paramilitary forces had joined the federal troops in resisting the invaders, and by August 26 they had raised Russia's tricolor flag over the villages that had been occupied and then destroyed in two weeks of air strikes. The next day Putin flew to Dagestan, accompanied by newspaper and television journalists who were not told their destination until they landed at the regional capital, Makhachkala. With heavy security and complete secrecy, the entourage then boarded a helicopter and flew to Botlikh, a mountain village at the center of the invasion, only five miles from the Chechen border. Putin, dressed casually in slacks and a jacket, addressed a group of Russian and Dagestani fighters and passed out fifty medals. He announced that three Hero of Russia medals, the nation's highest military honor, would be awarded later in ceremonies at the Kremlin. A fourth would be granted posthumously. By the official count, nearly sixty Russian soldiers had died during the fighting—no one announced the rebel or civilian casualties—but Putin was there to proclaim their cause just, the losses worthy. He began to offer a toast to those who died but stopped in mid-sentence.

"Wait a second, please," he said. "I would like to drink to the health of those injured and to wish happiness to everyone present, but we have a lot of problems and big tasks ahead of us. You know it very well. You know the plans of the enemy. We know them, too. We know about the acts of provocation to be expected in the near future. We know in which areas we should expect them and so on. We have no right to allow ourselves even a second of weakness. Not a single second. For if we let our guard down, then those who died will seem to have died in vain. Therefore I suggest that today we put the glass back on the table. We will definitely drink to them, but later."[5]

Putin's flash visit was political theater from a political novice, but the contrast with Yeltsin was profound: youth and vigor versus age and infirmity. A dejected, divided nation could now relish a military victory, presided over by a prime minister most considered a little colorless, if they knew much about him at all. And yet Putin's remarks also contained the seeds of caution—and, some believed, forewarning—that the conflict had not ended with Basayev's retreat back into Chechnya.

Less than a week later, on the night of September 4, an enormous explosion leveled a five-story building in Buinaksk, about forty miles south of Dagestan's capital. The building housed Russian soldiers and their families, many of whom had settled in front of their televisions to watch a soccer match between Ukraine and France. The explosion, possibly a car bomb, killed sixty-four people. The next day Chechen militants again crossed into Dagestan, this time near Khasavyurt, the city where the peace accords ending the first war had been signed three years earlier. Yeltsin exploded in anger at a September 6 meeting of the Security Council. "How did we lose a whole district in Dagestan?" the president thundered. "This can only be explained by the carelessness of the military."[6] Yeltsin had extended sweeping authority to his new prime minister, and after an initial success, disaster struck anyway. The predictions of Putin's quick demise seemed prophetic.

Then, on September 9, the carnage of the Caucasus came to Moscow. Just after midnight, an explosion ripped through the center of a nine-story apartment complex at 19 Guryanova Street, not far from a wide bend in the Moscow River. The force of the blast, equivalent to hundreds of pounds of TNT, cleaved the wide rectangular building in two, as if it had been split by a giant ax. Those asleep inside were crushed in a burning pile of debris. At first investigators thought a gas leak might have been the cause, but by the next day officials began to suspect an act of terrorism, the worst ever in the Russian capital. An anonymous caller telephoned the Interfax news agency and said the explosions in Moscow and Buinaksk were deliberate acts of retaliation for the Russian strikes in Chechnya and Dagestan. The same or another caller, with "an accent of the Northern Caucasus," had warned Deutsche Welle's office in Moscow days *before* the explosion that there would be three bombings in the city to punish Russia. "If it is confirmed that this is a terrorist act, and everything is leading that way, we shall have to acknowledge that the echo of war in Dagestan is sounding in Moscow," Mayor Luzhkov declared, pledging to tighten security.[7] Ninety-four people died as a result of the bombing, and hundreds more were injured.

On September 11, even as emergency workers continued clearing the rubble from Guryanova Street, Putin flew to New Zealand to attend the annual Asia-Pacific Economic Cooperation forum in place of the ailing Yeltsin. The forum gathers the leaders of twenty-one nations, and Putin's attendance amounted to his debut on the international stage. The leaders were curious to meet Yeltsin's fifth prime minister in the last eighteen months, though few expected he would last any longer than the others. The violence around Chechnya that summer had already raised alarms in the West, and President Clinton used his meeting with Putin to gently raise concerns about the humanitarian tragedy in the region and to urge a political resolution that could include allowing international observers on Russian soil. Putin began politely, expressing confidence that the strains over Kosovo earlier in the year were behind them and hoping for a mutual understanding of the shared threat of international terrorism. When Clinton pressed on Chechnya, though, "Putin's mouth tightened, his posture stiffened and a hard-eyed look came over his face."[8] He drew a map on a napkin, explaining to Clinton the plans that had already been drawn up for the limited incursion, halting at the Terek River. He stressed that the fighting in Dagestan was not merely an isolated raid, but the beginning of an invasion of Russia, supported by international terrorists, including Osama bin Laden. He told Clinton that Bin Laden, whose Al-Qaeda network had orchestrated attacks on the American embassies in Kenya and Tanzania the year before, had financed Chechnya's Islamic fighters and even visited Chechnya (though the Americans were never able to confirm that).[9] Putin confided to the American president what he had not yet told his own countrymen: Russia's military was about to intervene again in Chechnya.

Putin was still in New Zealand on September 13 when an explosion destroyed another apartment building, this time on Kashirskoye Highway in southern Moscow, not far from Guryanova Street. The death toll reached 118, and the country's fear turned to hysteria. Reports of possible motives were confused and contradictory. Putin himself had hesitated after the first attack, stopping short of calling the bombing a terrorist attack. Now he reacted angrily, saying it was impossible to imagine that both bombings could be accidents. "Those who have done it cannot be called humans," he said. "They cannot even be called beasts."[10] He cut short his first international visit as prime minister and returned to Moscow. Who exactly the beasts were, however, was far from clear. Dagestani extremists had reportedly claimed responsibility for the bombing in Buinaksk, but Chechen leaders, including Shamil Basayev, whose fighters were still in Dagestan, denied involvement in the Moscow bombings, even as Basayev reiterated his vow to carve an Islamic state out of Russia's southern rump.[11] A hardline Communist leader, Viktor Ilyukin, told Itar-Tass that the first attack was linked not to the Caucasus but rather to the political feuds between supporters of Yeltsin and Mayor Luzhkov. The bombings, he said, were a pretense to cancel the parliamentary elections scheduled for December. "Political hysteria is being fanned artificially," he said.[12] Aleksandr Lebed, now governor in Krasnoyarsk, told the French newspaper *Le Figaro* that the Chechens had little to gain from such attacks, but that Yeltsin and his "Family" did. "A goal had to be set—to create mass terror, a destabilization which will permit them at the needed moment to say: you don't have to go to the election precincts, otherwise you will risk being blown up with the ballot boxes," Lebed said.[13]

The panic in Moscow led to police checkpoints and sweeps that arrested hundreds of people for little other reason than appearing to be from the Caucasus. Citizens mounted their own patrols. The police discovered seventy-six sacks of explosives in a shed at a building site in the Kapotnya district. The sacks, marked as sugar from a factory in Karachayevo-Cherkessia in the Caucasus, contained enough material to destroy several more apartment buildings.[14] The discovery ended the bombings in Moscow, but on September 16, the fourth bombing of an apartment building occurred, this time in the southern city of Volgodonsk, hundreds of miles from either Moscow or Chechnya. The attack differed from the others only in the details. The blast happened at dawn when most people were home asleep. The explosives were loaded in a truck parked outside the building, rather than hidden inside, which might have minimized the damage. The force sheared off the facade of the building, but did not collapse it. This time seventeen people died. The death toll from the wave of terror had now reached nearly three hundred.

Russia's limited air strikes inside Chechnya continued, but Putin now escalated the conflict. On September 23, Russian aircraft for the first time bombed deep inside the republic, striking Grozny's airport and an oil refinery, which burned out of control because the local authorities had little equipment left to fight fires. The strikes were more punitive than strategic. The attack on the airport destroyed one of Chechnya's two functional aircraft: an old biplane of no military significance. Putin, making an official visit to Kazakhstan, pledged that Russia would defend itself from "gangs of foreign mercenaries and terrorists," but he insisted he did not plan a new war in Chechnya. When he was questioned about the purpose of the air strikes, his temper flared. The laconic manner that Russians had seen in their dour, ascetic new prime minister vanished. He sounded like a street fighter. His answer was blunt, his language salted with the slang of the underworld. "I am tired of answering these questions," he responded testily. "Russian aircraft are only striking terrorist camps. We will go after them wherever they are. If, pardon me, we find them in the toilet, we will waste them in the outhouse."[15]

It was a bombing that did not happen that called everything about the events that summer into question. On the evening of September 22, the night before Putin's soon-to-be-famous remark about the outhouse, a bus driver who lived in Ryazan, southeast of Moscow, noticed a white Lada parked outside his apartment building. A young woman, clearly of Russian ethnicity, stood nervously at the entrance of the building, on Novosyelovaya Street. A man sat inside the car. Soon another man emerged from the building, and the three drove away together. On edge because of the previous bombings, the bus driver called the police. Initially the police seemed uninterested, but when officers finally arrived, panic erupted. In the basement, a police corporal, Andrei Chernyshev, found three sacks marked sugar, just like the cache found in Moscow, and a device that appeared to be a detonator. A timer had been set for 5:30 in the morning. The police frantically evacuated the twelve-story building, while a local explosives expert, Yuri Tkachenko, was summoned to defuse the timer. He tested the substance in the sacks with a gas analyzer. It was not sugar, but a military explosive, hexogen, like one known to have been used in at least one of the Moscow bombings.[16] By the next morning news reports announced that another catastrophic bombing had—miraculously—been averted.

The mood in Ryazan was not celebratory, but the residents and local police received praise. "I want to thank the population for their vigilance," Putin said in televised remarks. As the city's rattled residents contemplated what might have been, police investigators appeared to close in on the would-be bombers. They found the Lada abandoned in a parking lot and briefly stopped two men resembling those spotted outside the apartment building, but they showed FSB identification cards and were released. That evening a local telephone operator overheard a caller saying there was no way to get out of the city undetected. The voice on the other end of the line told them to split up and make their way out as best they could. The operator informed the police, and the police traced the call to Moscow. To their astonishment, the number belonged to the FSB.

By that evening, the FSB's spokesman began was casting doubt on everything that had apparently happened in Ryazan, claiming that a preliminary test showed no explosive traces among the materials, which the FSB had by now confiscated and brought to Moscow. There had also been no detonator, he said, just parts of one. The next day, the FSB director, Nikolai Patrushev, spoke to reporters after attending an emergency government meeting to discuss the bombings. Patrushev, Putin's KGB colleague from Petersburg, had followed his friend to Moscow and rose through the ranks with him. He took over as director of the FSB when Putin became prime minister in 1999 and remained one of his most trusted lieutenants. He declared that the entire episode in Ryazan had simply been a training exercise, meant to test preparations for a bombing exactly like those hitting Russian cities. He said the exercises had been conducted in several cities—where they obviously did not work since nothing like Ryazan happened elsewhere—and complimented the city's residents and police "for the vigilance they showed when they discovered these supposed explosives."

"And at the same time," he added, "I want to apologize to them."[17]

Patrushev's statement was reported straightforwardly by newspapers in Moscow and beyond, but it stunned and confused people in Ryazan. Perhaps the residents and the police would not be informed of a test of their vigilance, but even the local FSB department said it had no knowledge of any training; neither did the mayor or the governor or anyone else. The day-and-a-half delay in informing the city's terrified residents seemed inexplicable, especially since the Interior Ministry had mobilized 1,200 officers in a dragnet to catch the suspects and search for more bombs. And the officers involved in defusing the bomb knew what they had seen. The FSB's drill was either so convincing a test of preparedness in the face of terror or a hoax itself. That evening a caller telephoned Ekho Moskvy, then as now a radio station that encouraged reasonably open political discussion. Identifying himself as a security officer, though not giving his name, he expressed puzzlement over the FSB's explanation. It seemed so improbable, he said, that people might start to think the FSB was somehow involved in all of the bombings.[18]

On September 29, Putin expressed a willingness to negotiate with Aslan Maskhadov, Chechnya's president, but only on the condition that he condemn all terrorism, expel the armed militias in the republic, and arrest and extradite the most wanted criminals, with Basayev, Khattab, and other commanders presumably at the top of the list. It was an ultimatum, not an offer. Maskhadov had denounced the incursion into Dagestan and the bombings in Russia, but his authority as president was too weak to exert control over Basayev or Khattab, let alone arrest them and turn them over to the Russians. "I cannot simply have Basayev arrested," he told a journalist two days before Putin's ultimatum. "People here would not understand that. After all, we fought together for our country's independence."[19] On the day of Putin's offer, Maskhadov had planned to travel to Dagestan to meet with its president to explore the possibility of talks with Moscow, but he had to cancel, because protesters in Dagestan blocked the road.[20] It was too late anyway.

The next day the Russian army and Ministry of the Interior soldiers poured into Chechnya. Despite Putin's disavowals, a full invasion had begun. About 40,000 troops had taken part in the first war in Chechnya, many of them unseasoned conscripts, but now Putin ordered in more than 93,000, roughly the size of the Soviet force that invaded Afghanistan, a country nearly forty times as large.[21] On October 1, he declared that Russia would no longer recognize Maskhadov's government; instead he recognized a regional parliament that had been elected in 1996 during Russia's military occupation. Its members were now mostly in Moscow or elsewhere, having fled when the Russians withdrew after the first war. The declaration ended whatever slim chances existed for a negotiated settlement. Putin did not really want one anyway. Maskhadov joined Basayev and the other more radical commanders in a bloody defense of the Chechen homeland. By October 5, Russian troops occupied the northern third of Chechnya, up to the Terek River, as the secret planning that began in the spring had intended. A week later they crossed the river and moved toward Grozny.

Putin vowed not to repeat the mistakes of the first war, which many took to mean he would not launch an all-out ground offensive to seize control of the entire republic. But that is exactly what he aimed to do—only this time he deployed the full force of Russian air power to minimize the loss of life to the Russian troops, irrespective of the toll inside Chechnya. "The difference is that this time we will not thoughtlessly send our boys to absorb hostile fire," he told the newspaper *Vremya*. "We will act with the help of modern forces and means and destroy the terrorists from a distance. We will destroy the infrastructure. And special troops will be used only to clean up territories. There will be no frontal assaults any more. We will be protecting our men. Of course, this will require time and patience. Availing myself of this opportunity, I urge your readers and others to understand this and to realize that either, as in the past, we rush into the attack with screams of 'Communists, forward!' heedless of our losses, or we patiently and methodically destroy them from the air." And if the air strikes failed? "We will succeed," he told the interviewer. "There will be no 'if.' "[22]

On October 20, as the fighting raged, Putin traveled in secret from Moscow to Chechnya on a journey that included a short flight on a Sukhoi-25 jet. As he had in Dagestan, Putin again handed out medals to pilots at an airbase, and he met with village elders in Znamenskoye, a village just inside Chechnya's border, now liberated by the Russians. He lamented the Chechen government's failure to pay salaries and pensions and its failure to keep clinics and schools open, despite budget funds from Moscow that had never stopped flowing. Russia's goal was to restore order, he said, by ridding the territory "of those bandits who are not only up to their elbows but up to their shoulders in blood." "One of the aims of my visit here today is to show you that we and you are a single whole, so that anti-Chechen and anti-Caucasian feeling is not whipped up in Russia, so that the whole country knows and can see that there is nothing so bloodthirsty here."[23] The next day a Russian rocket landed in Grozny's central market, killing scores of people, mostly women and children shopping for dwindling supplies of food.

Despite the furor over the apartment bombings, and an eruption of anti-Chechen sentiment in Moscow and elsewhere in Russia, the war until then did not have universal political support, especially among the politicians jockeying for power in the coming post-Yeltsin era. The memory of the first war remained raw. By the middle of September more than two hundred Russian soldiers had died in the fighting along Chechnya's borders; the toll inside Chechnya was far higher, probably in the thousands. Yevgeny Primakov, who with Luzhkov was a front-runner to replace Yeltsin, expressed support for "pinpoint" strikes against terrorist camps, but not a new invasion. "I am strongly against large-scale operations that can develop into events we have seen in the past," he said. "We shouldn't be going back to that."[24] Luzhkov responded to the attacks with thinly veiled racism and the reinstitution of Soviet-era residency requirements. His proposal to resolve the conflict was to build a Berlin Wall along Chechnya's border, not to reconquer the territory. Several of Yeltsin's liberal supporters publicly raised doubts about the efficacy and morality of a military campaign that was killing civilians who were, for now at least, citizens of Russia. By the end of September more than a hundred thousand Chechens—mostly the elderly, women, and children—had fled for safety into neighboring Ingushetia, creating a refugee crisis that Russia was ill-prepared to handle.

The country was again awash in rumors that Yeltsin would resign, that he would dismiss Putin and his new cabinet, that the parliamentary elections scheduled for December would be canceled. Putin was forced to deny them all. Among Russia's political elite, Putin was widely assumed to be committing political suicide by lauching a new ground war in Chechnya. "Putin behaved like a political kamikaze, throwing his entire stock of political capital into the war, burning it to the ground," wrote Boris Yeltsin, the man who could never bring himself to throw the full might of the Russian military into the first war.[25] Putin acted as if he were indifferent to the politics of the war, perhaps because he had no experience with the first war in Chechnya, perhaps because he simply did not doubt his "historic mission." He was not responding to popular opinion or political expedience; as Yeltsin noted, he "didn't expect his career to last beyond the Chechen events." His actions seemed defiantly apolitical, even deeply personal, as if the incursion into Dagestan was an affront that he had to avenge.

Yet, to the surprise of Yeltsin and many others, Putin's conduct of the war proved to be immensely popular. The first war had been unpopular, but given the public's reaction to the second, that was because the prosecution of the first war had been halfhearted; because the Russian army, the remnant of the great Red Army, had been ill-prepared and ill-equipped; because the Russians had lost to a bunch of lawless Chechens from the mountains. This war, under this prime minister, seemed different. The political elite, looking ahead to the coming elections, feared the consequences of a war, but now it seemed that ordinary Russians wanted, as Putin, to "bang the hell out of the bandits."

Vladimir Putin had been largely unknown to Russians when Yeltsin appointed him prime minister. Now, even though he had not yet had time to articulate any policies or programs, his actions in Chechnya began unexpectedly to lift his approval ratings in the polls. In August, when he was appointed, a mere 2 percent of those polled favored him as a possible presidential candidate; by October, 27 percent did, only one point behind Primakov. Yeltsin kept his promise to Putin about the coming parliamentary elections: he did not have to concern himself with them. Yeltsin's political strategists created a new party, called Unity. Like Putin himself, the party had no discernable platform or ideology, but fashioned itself as a patriotic front, adopting the bear as its symbol, an idea that Boris Berezovsky claimed had come to him in a feverish dream while he was hospitalized with hepatitis.[26]

Unity seemed to have little chance to win. By the end of October it barely registered in the polls, far behind the liberals of Yabloko, the Communists, and the front-runners, the Fatherland–All Russia alliance between Luzhkov and Primakov. What Unity did have was the full resources of the Kremlin and the oligarchs who poured cash into the campaign. Even Berezovsky, who felt increasingly estranged from Yeltsin, used his television network to savage Luzhkov and Primakov whom he loathed, and to glorify Putin's role as de facto commander in chief. Berezovsky gave a prime-time television show to a flamboyant commentator, Sergei Dorenko, who week after week accused Luzhkov of corruption, hypocrisy, and even murder.[27] The accusations were extreme to the point of libel, but they were extraordinarily effective.

Given Yeltsin's paranoia about political challenges, Putin's rising popularity provoked a new wave of rumors about his imminent sacking. Those rumors gained momentum in November, when Putin affirmed his intention to run for president in 2000. People assumed that Yeltsin would fire him, as he had fired Primakov, not knowing that the aging president had invested his hopes for his legacy—and personal security— in this young prime minister. By the end of 1999, Yeltsin's physical and legal problems had left him weaker than ever. Yuri Skuratov, still fighting his suspension as prosecutor general in court, continued to dribble out accusations surrounding the investigations of Mabetex and its ties to Yeltsin's "Family." His efforts were aided by a decision in Switzerland to freeze fifty-nine bank accounts linked to Russian officials. In October the Federation Council refused for a third time to fire Skuratov, who was angling to retain his post as prosecutor general under a new parliament and the next president. "Of course the 'family' is afraid," he said in an interview at his dacha outside Moscow. "Now they control the situation, but it may get out of hand."[28]

Putin's rising popularity also began to attract the attention of Yeltsin's opponents. On November 20 Primakov and Luzhkov, Yeltsin's bitter rivals, met him privately in hopes of negotiating a political accomodation. Both began to suggest publicly that their alliance might support his nomination for president, effectively abandoning their own ambitions. Putin's rise was as astonishing as it was unexpected. He seemed to represent a new, independent political force. And it was not solely because of Chechnya. In the muck of Russia's politics, he alone seemed untainted by the intrigues of politicians and oligarchs that had consumed Russia for the previous eight years. Although he owed his career to Yeltsin and the "Family," the fact that he had mostly worked on the margins of public scrutiny since 1996 meant he was not associated with the Kremlin's multiple failings and scandals. His blunt public statements, even the coarse ones, seemed refreshing after the confusion and obfuscation of Yeltsin's administration. The newspaper *Nezivisamaya Gazeta* wrote in November that within a precious few weeks "a completely unknown,

fairly colorless functionary" had become a leader willing, "unlike his predecessors," to tell people what he intended to do. It went on to call this
"one of the rare cases in our political history."[29]

By then, Putin's approval rating exceeded 40 percent, and now he had
the political clout to influence the parliamentary election in December. He had not joined the Kremlin's new party, Unity, which despite
the government's resources, favorable coverage on state television, and
donations from the oligarchs ranked so low in the polls that it risked not
reaching the threshold to win any seats in the Duma at all.[30] On November 24, his one hundredth day as prime minister, Putin rescued Unity
from political oblivion with an endorsement—of a sort. "As the prime
minister, I would not want to discuss my political sympathies," he said,
"but as an ordinary voter, I will vote for Unity."[31] Most political analysts concluded that Putin was risking not only his own political future
but the party's as well by linking it too closely with the Kremlin. What
they misunderstood was the party's essential appeal as a new force that
eschewed the tired ideology of right or left and embraced the patriotism
of unity, not division, especially at a time of war.

Yeltsin, hospitalized twice in the fall, still agonized over his fate.
"Authority in Russia had always been transferred through natural death,
conspiracy or revolution," he wrote of his thoughts during the period.
"The tsar ceased to rule only after his death or after a coup. It was exactly
the same with the general secretary of the Communist Party. I suppose
the Communist regime inherited the inability to transfer power pain-
lessly." He reflected on Khrushchev's ouster in 1964 and lamented that
his death in September 1971 had been announced "in a tiny, obscure
notice in the newspaper."[32] On December 14, five days before the election, Yeltsin summoned Putin to his residence at Gorky-9 for a secret
meeting. They met alone.

"I want to step down this year, Vladimir Vladimirovich," Yeltsin said
he told him. "This year. That's very important. The new century must
begin with a new political era, the era of Putin. Do you understand?"

Putin did not understand. His reaction made Yeltsin's heart sink.
There had been rumors throughout the autumn that Yeltsin might step
down and, according to the Constitution, pass power to the sitting
prime minister. As recently as September, Putin had ruled out the idea
as preposterous. "If I am absolutely sure about anything, it is that the

president has no intention of going," he said. "No resignation what-soever."[33] And yet now Yeltsin explained to him that that was what he intended to do, playing the last "trick up his sleeve."[34]

The new, untested Constitution gave Yeltsin considerable control over the timing of his departure. Were the president to resign, the prime minister would become acting president until elections could be held ninety days later. Although that left little time for an election campaign, it would give the "incumbent" enormous advantage over his rivals.

The two men sat in silence as the realization dawned slowly on Yeltsin that Putin felt unprepared for the presidency. "I'm not ready for that decision, Boris Nikolayevich," Putin finally replied. "It's a rather difficult destiny."[35] Yeltsin, trying to persuade him, explained that he had arrived in Moscow to work when he was already over fifty—older than Putin—but "an energetic, healthy person" nonetheless. Now, he realized, his political life was exhausted. "At one time, I, too, wanted to live my life in a completely different way," he told Putin. "I didn't know it was going to turn out this way." Yeltsin claimed, improbably, that he would get back into construction or move back to Sverdlovsk, where he had begun his career. He looked out the window at the gray, snowy landscape, lost in thought. After an interlude, he returned to the matter at hand.

"You haven't answered me," he said to Putin, looking him in the eye.

Putin, at last, agreed. No one else knew of their conversation, according to Yeltsin, or the momentous decision they had made.

When the votes were counted on the night of December 19, after an election that was fiercely contested and considered more or less fair, Unity had achieved a stunning upset. The Communist Party had won a plurality of 24 percent, consolidating its base, but Unity came in second with 23 percent. The Luzhkov-Primakov alliance, which had seemed poised to coast to power only months before, lagged behind with only 13 percent of the vote, its leaders battered by negative television coverage—and badly beaten. Yabloko and a new liberal coalition that allied with Yeltsin, the Union of Right Forces, which Putin had also "endorsed" with a few polite words, together won nearly as much. Yeltsin drank champagne on election night in anticipation of a victory, but went to bed worrying as the unofficial results trickled in. When he woke, he felt his trust in Putin had been vindicated.[36] Yeltsin boasted that he had maneuvered Putin "from obscurity into the presidency over fierce resistance" from the political elite, inside and outside the Kremlin. "It really was very hard, getting Putin into the job—one of the hardest things we ever pulled off," Yeltsin's daughter Tatyana later said.[37]

For Yeltsin, this would be his parting legacy, one that would reshape the country he had nurtured out of the ruins of the Soviet Union. For the first time in his turbulent presidency, Yeltsin could rely on a pro-government majority in the new Duma, ending the paralyzing political clashes over Russia's transition. He could have cemented his policies and even introduced new ones in his remaining six months as president. Instead, he resigned.

On December 28, Yeltsin sat in front of a decorated tree in the Kremlin's reception hall and taped the president's traditional New Year's address. When he finished he complained that his voice was hoarse and he did not like the remarks. He asked the television crew to come back in three days and, despite their protests, record a new address. It was a ruse, though apparently only he knew it then. He returned to his residence and that evening summoned his current and former chiefs of staff, two of his closest advisers. What he said stunned them; he planned to resign on New Year's Eve. Yeltsin had one last grandiose, impetuous surprise to unleash on the country. He would end his presidency with the old millennium and let Vladimir Putin usher in the new one. The next morning he called Putin to the Kremlin and told him the timing of what they had discussed in the abstract fifteen days before. "I immediately had the impression that he was a different man," Yeltsin thought when the prime minister arrived.[38] The discussion that followed was practical, detailed, and unemotional. They discussed the decrees that Yeltsin and then Putin would issue, the rerecording of the New Year's address, the notification of the military and security agencies, the transfer of the "suitcase" carrying the codes to launch Russia's arsenal of nuclear weapons. When they finished, they emerged from Yeltsin's office, constrained by the public setting. They said nothing, though Yeltsin felt the urge to say more. Instead they shook hands, then Yeltsin wrapped Putin in a bear hug and said good-bye. Their next meeting was on New Year's Eve.[39]

On December 30, Putin filled in for Yeltsin at a reception in the Kremlin. The aging president's absence was noted but, given his frequent bouts of ill health, assigned little significance. Despite the festive occasion, Putin focused his remarks on the war in Chechnya, which was turning into a gruesome bloodbath as Russian forces surrounded Grozny. The city was reduced to ruins the likes of which had not been seen in Russia—or anywhere else—since the Great Patriotic War. Thousands of civilians remained trapped inside, cowering in basements with no electricity, heat, or running water. Chechnya's rebels continued to hold much of Grozny, killing hundreds of the Russian soldiers trying to seize it. Aslan Maskhadov reiterated his calls for a negotiated ceasefire, even as he vowed to keep fighting. "Even if the war lasts 10 years, Russia will not manage to subjugate Chechnya and its people," he declared.[40] As the fighting worsened, Russia faced mounting criticism from Europe and the United States about the unfolding humanitarian crisis, including evidence that Russian soldiers were conducting summary executions in "cleansing" operations in liberated areas. "Soldiers in Russian-controlled areas of Chechnya apparently have carte blanche to loot and pillage; many people have returned briefly to their homes to find them stripped bare of household goods and other valuables," Human Rights Watch wrote in a letter to the United Nations Security Council, calling for an international investigation into war crimes.[41] At the Kremlin, Putin brushed aside misgivings about the brutality of the war, saying it was the country's duty to crush the "brazen and impudent" rebels at all costs. "Unfortunately," he told the assembled guests before lifting a toast to the New Year, "not everyone in Western nations understood this, but we will not tolerate any humiliation to the national pride of Russians or any threat to the integrity of the country."[42]

Yeltsin woke early the next morning, and before he left for the Kremlin, he at last told his wife, Naina, of his decision to resign. "How wonderful!" she exclaimed. "Finally!" Still, only six people knew as he rode to the Kremlin for the last time as president, not even his presidential guard or his aides, who left his mail, his schedule, and his other documents on his desk. Voloshin, his chief of staff, arrived with the decree stating that the resignation would take effect at midnight. Yeltsin summoned Putin, who arrived on time at 9:30, and then read the decree aloud. He looked at Putin, who "gave a slightly embarrassed smile," and then shook Yeltsin's hand. Now Yeltsin taped a new address, and Yumashev accompanied the recording in an armored car to the Ostankino television tower with orders to broadcast it at noon. As the new millennium began in the Pacific and marched hour by hour across each time zone, Yeltsin addressed "my dear friends" one last time.

"I have heard people say more than once that Yeltsin would cling to power as long as possible, that he would never let go," he said. "That is a lie." He said that he wanted to create "a vital precedent of voluntary transfer of power to a newly elected president" but that he would not wait until the presidential election scheduled for June. "Russia should enter the new millennium with new politicians, new faces, new people who are intelligent, strong and energetic, while we, those who have been in power for many years, must leave."

Yeltsin rubbed a speck from his eye and finished with a strikingly personal appeal to the country he had led for eight years. "I want to ask your forgiveness—for the dreams that have not come true, and for the things that seemed easy [but] turned out to be so excruciatingly difficult. I am asking your forgiveness for failing to justify the hopes of those who believed me when I said that we would leap from the gray, stagnating totalitarian past into a bright, prosperous and civilized future. I believed in that dream. I believed that we would cover that distance in one leap. We didn't."[43]

Lyudmila had not watched Yeltsin's address, but five minutes after it ended, a friend telephoned. "Lyuda, I congratulate you," she said. "And I you," Lyudmila replied, thinking they were exchanging best wishes for the New Year.[44] Her friend had to explain that her husband had become the acting president of the country. Putin had not divulged Yeltsin's secret after their first meeting on December 14, or the timing after the second on December 29. She heard it along with the rest of Russia. Her husband's rise in Moscow had left her marveling at times that she was married to "a man who yesterday was really just an unknown deputy mayor of Petersburg."[45]

As she had feared when he returned to the FSB, her family's life became constrained. The girls, now fifteen and thirteen, had to stop going to the German school they had been attending since they arrived in Moscow; they were tutored at home. Security guards accompanied them on their rare excursions to the theater or cinema. When asked, Lyudmila said she had only three close friends. When Putin returned to the FSB, she had had to end a friendship she had developed with the wife of a German banker, Irene Pietsch, while they were in Petersburg. "She was not happy at all," said Pietsch, who went on to write *Delicate Friendships*, a titillating book about the Putins that described a stormy marriage.[46] In it Lyudmila complained that her husband would not let her use a credit card—no doubt worried about the scandal surrounding Yeltsin's daughters—and joked that his lifestyle was like a vampire's. "This isolation is dreadful," Lyudmilla told Pietsch when she ended the friendship.

"No more traveling wherever we want to go. No longer able to say what we want. I had only just begun to live." Her husband, too, could be cutting, and dismissive of her opinions. He once told Pietsch during a weeklong visit to their dacha in Arkhangelskoye that anyone who could spend three weeks with Lyudmila deserved a monument.[47] Now, Lyudmila was about to become first lady, a modern, Western role that Russians viewed ambivalently. She cried when she learned of her husband's new job, she said, because she "realized that our private life was over for at least three months, until the presidential elections, or perhaps for four years."[48]

Putin, after Yeltsin's announcement, presided over a meeting of the Security Council, which he had led until becoming prime minister only four months before. Its members included the leaders of the Duma and the Federation Council, as well as the ministers of defense and the interior and the intelligence chiefs. Those in the room had been in Moscow far longer than he had and had far more experience in government and politics. Now they listened as he outlined his priorities. He pledged no change in Russia's foreign policy but signaled a new era in military affairs: Russia had to improve its weaponry and address the social problems of its conscripted ranks, an "aspect that has been neglected recently." He noted the conspicuous absence of the prosecutor general, Yuri Skuratov, whose investigations had done as much as anything to propel him to his post, but then pointedly added that the acting prosecutor, Vladimir Ustinov, seemed "to be doing a good job." His remarks were brief, almost perfunctory given the occasion. He urged vigilance for the New Year given the fear of potential Y2K computer glitches that around the world had been the biggest news of the day—until Yeltsin's resignation.

Putin then recorded his own New Year's address, the one that Yeltsin would normally have delivered, to be broadcast at midnight in Moscow. He began with his own embellishment, saying that he and his family had planned to gather around the television that night and listen to Yeltsin's speech, "but things took a different turn." He assured listeners that there would be no power vacuum—"not for a minute"—and vowed to continue his efforts to restore law and order. "I promise you that any attempts to act contrary to the Russian law and Constitution will be cut short." He ended by offering his gratitude to the nation's first president. "We will be able to see the true importance of what Boris Yeltsin has done for Russia," he said, "only after some time has passed."

As Yeltsin prepared to leave the Kremlin, he paused in the hallway outside his office—now Putin's—and extracted from his pocket the pen he had used to sign his last decree. He gave it to Putin as they walked out to the door of the Kremlin, two men so different in temperament and physique. Their relationship, Putin said later, had not been "particularly close." It was never warm in the way that he remembered his feelings for Sobchak. "I can say that only when he began to discuss the question of his resignation with me did I sense a certain warmth in him," Putin recalled later.[49] Now Yeltsin wanted to say "something important" about the burden he would now face. "Take care," he told him, "take care of Russia." A soft, gentle snowfall surrounded the Kremlin's grounds as he twisted his large frail frame into the armored car that would take him home. Bill Clinton telephoned on the drive back to his dacha, but Yeltsin had an aide tell him to call back later. He went home and took a nap.[50]

That evening Putin signed his first decree. It was seven pages long, having been prepared by Yeltsin's aides in the previous two days, though Yeltsin would claim he was not aware of it until it was completed.[51] It granted Yeltsin an array of benefits and privileges as a former president, including a salary, a staff, and the use of the dacha where he had spent so much of his second term convalescing. It also made Yeltsin immune from prosecution, protecting his assets and papers from search or seizure. With a sweep of the pen Yeltsin passed to him, Putin ended the threat that Skuratov had exposed and that very nearly brought Yeltsin to ruin.

Putin then carried out his own New Year's surprise. He and his successor at the FSB, Nikolai Patrushev, along with their wives and a popular singer, secretly flew to Dagestan. The Putins told the girls that they would be gone that night but not where they were going. They had already given the girls their presents—their first computers—and left them in Moscow with Lyudmila's sister and one of Masha's friends. After arriving in Dagestan, Putin and the others boarded three military helicopters and flew toward Chechnya's second-largest city, Gudermes, recently liberated from the Chechen rebels. The weather was so foul, with visibility so limited, that the helicopters had to turn back. When the New Year and the new millennium arrived, they were still airborne, but they opened two bottles of champagne and passed them around, drinking from the bottles since they had no glasses. When they landed in Dagestan's capital, Makhachkala, they climbed into military vehicles under heavy escort and drove two and a half hours back into Chechnya. It was nearly dawn when Putin greeted the Russian troops there. "They looked tired and a little disoriented—as though they wanted to pinch themselves," Lyudmila recalled. "Were they dreaming?"[52] It had been a quiet night in Gudermes, but only twenty-three miles away, Grozny endured one of the heaviest nights of bombing to date. Putin, dressed in a turtleneck, again handed out medals and ceremonial knives. "I want you to know that Russia highly appreciates what you're doing," Putin told the soldiers mustered there. "This is not just about restoring Russia's honor and dignity. It's about putting an end to the breakup of the Russian Federation." The Yeltsin era was over. The Putin era had begun.

PART THREE

CHAPTER 11

Becoming Portugal

Vladimir Putin, who had never before been elected to political office, barely campaigned before the election, which because of Yeltsin's resignation was moved forward to March 26, 2000. As prime minister, he painted his vision for Russia only in the broadest strokes. His only real campaign platform or agenda appeared in a manifesto on the government's website on December 28, the eve of Yeltsin's surprise appointment. The document was prepared by the Center for Strategic Development, a think tank founded by German Gref, an economist who was another of Putin's colleagues in Anatoly Sobchak's administration.[1] In this five-thousand-word manifesto, called "Russia at the Turn of the Millennium," Putin frankly acknowledged the country's diminished social and economic status in the world. The country's gross national product had dropped by half in the 1990s, and was now a tenth that of the United States and a fifth that of China. It would take fifteen years of substantial economic growth just to reach the level of Portugal or Spain.

"Russia is in the midst of one of the most difficult periods in its history," the document said. "For the first time in the past 200 [to] 300 years, it is facing the real threat of slipping down to the second and, possibly even third, rank of world states. We are running out of time to avoid this."[2] The prescription was to restore national unity, patriotism, and a strong central government—not "the restoration of an official state ideology in Russia in any guise," but a voluntary social pact that placed the authority of the state over the messy, divisive aspirations of its subjects. Its tone seemed almost religious, as if Putin were sharing a "personal revelation" of the middle road Russia would take between its authoritarian history and its democratic future.[3] "Russia needs strong state power and must have it. I am not calling for totalitarianism. History proves all dictatorships, all authoritarian forms of government, are transient. Only democratic systems are lasting."

With the duties of the presidency already his, Putin eschewed overtly political events during the short campaign. He held no rallies, gave no speeches, and refused to participate in debates with his challengers. Reflecting his dour character and disdain for retail politics, he was redefining the modern campaign in Russia in his own image and in ways that would stifle the democratic future the fall of the Soviet Union had seemed to usher in. Within days of becoming acting president on New Year's Eve, Putin had co-opted his main potential rivals, tilting the playing field sharply in his favor. By the end of January 2000, the Unity bloc in the Duma had orchestrated an alliance not with the democrats or liberals, but rather with the Communists. Unity and the Communist Party divided up committee chairmanships among their members, while shutting out Yevgeny Primakov, as well as Sergei Kiriyenko, who had won a seat after his dismissal as prime minister, and Grigory Yavlinsky, the leading liberal in Russian politics. Their supporters promptly boycotted the Duma, and as a result a majority loyal to the Kremlin coalesced without regard to ideological differences. The country was learning that ideology mattered less to Putin than an orderly, pliant legislative majority.

A week later Luzhkov, who had been reelected as Moscow's mayor in December, announced he would not compete against Putin for the presidency. Primakov, who had announced his candidacy on the eve of parliamentary elections, also gave up, pulling out of the presidential race two weeks later with bitter resignation. "I sense how far our society is from being a civil society and from a true democracy," Primakov said.[4] By early February, Putin's most serious rivals—the ones who had terrified Yeltsin in the dying days of his presidency—had simply melted away before the official campaign began. One by one, regional governors then threw their support to Putin, even the man he had denounced as Judas four years before, Vladimir Yakovlev of Petersburg. The election, which had consumed Boris Yeltsin's final months in office, turned out to be not much of a drama at all. It was not a democratic competition among candidates so much as a referendum on the man already holding the post. Only one governor, Vasily Starodubtsev, the Communist from Tula, declared support for one of Putin's rivals, a fellow Communist, Gennady Zyuganov. "If there are no rivals, then there is no democracy, and if there is no democracy, then what was the point of demolishing the country?" he asked.[5]

Putin had told Yeltsin that he did not like election campaigns, and now he dismissed campaign promises as unachievable lies told by politicians and denigrated television advertisements as unseemly manipulation of gullible consumers. Visiting the textile city of Ivanovo, he announced that he would refuse the official television time allotted to all candidates to present their biographies and platforms. "These videos are advertising," he said, belying his appreciation of the importance of television in shaping his public image. "I will not be trying to find out in the course of my election which is more important, Tampax or Snickers." Behind the scenes, Putin's aides nonetheless recruited a campaign staff, led by the young aide he had brought with him from Petersburg, Dmitri Medvedev. They conducted a sophisticated operation to shape Putin's personal and political image, with all the tested techniques of modern politics but little passion for actual democracy. The result was an image not of a politician, but of a man above politics; Putin's strategists succeeded beyond expectations. State television conducted a long biographical interview with him—which in his mind might not have amounted to a commercial, though that is what it was—and his campaign released a series of interviews conducted over six days by three journalists.

In book form the interviews were called *Ot Pervovo Litsa*, literally "From the First Person," a phrase that also in Russian suggests "The First," that is, the leader or the boss. Boris Berezovsky, who still controlled the first state television channel, paid for the printing of the book, eager to ingratiate himself with Putin after his influence within the Kremlin had fallen dramatically. (He and Yeltsin had not met since 1998.) When the Election Commission banned the commercial sale of the book as a violation of campaign laws, Putin's headquarters simply purchased the first run in bulk and distributed the copies to voters at no cost.[6]

Putin, along with Lyudmila and others who had known him for years, recounted his biography in a folksy, occasionally frank manner that shaped his image as an ordinary guy, but also as the undisputed, virtually unchallenged ruler of a vast, once-great nation emerging from its latest "time of troubles." Putin managed at once to express pride in his Soviet upbringing and his KGB career while distancing himself from the failures of the Soviet Union. He offered everyone something to cling to, a cipher committed both to the past and to the new democracy, both a patriot and a religious believer. And no one knew for sure what he stood for, because he seemed to stand for everything. In his short months in prominence, the question "who is Putin?" became the refrain of journalists, academics, investors, foreign governments, and their intelligence agencies, including the Central Intelligence Agency, which set its analysts hurriedly to work to compose a profile, interviewing those who had had occasion to meet Putin during his years as an obscure underling.[7]

The strategy of Medvedev's campaign team was simply to let Putin carry on with his official duties as prime minister and acting president. It was no coincidence, of course, that those duties took him across the country for (televised) encounters that would appeal across the entire spectrum of Russian society. He visited Russia's space center outside Moscow one day, an oil rig in Surgut the next. He presided over meetings of his security advisers and an official visit from Britain's prime minister, Tony Blair. He pledged to pay all wage arrears by the end of spring. He raised pensions first by 12 percent, and then again by 20 percent, actions that contributed to his rising approval ratings at least as much as the war in Chechnya.[8] Putin would not deign to debate his challengers, but his remarks on the government's work received far more airtime than anything they ever said. He was not *promising* anything; he was delivering.

Once the month-long campaign officially opened, he published a letter to voters in three major newspapers that amounted to a public break with Yeltsin's Russia. "The state machine is coming apart," he wrote. "Its engine—the executive branch—sputters and hiccoughs as soon as you try to get it started."[9] He vowed to combat crime and declared that the war in Chechnya was a fight against "the criminal world," not against an independence movement with historical claims to self-determination. In a barely veiled reference to Primakov's threat to clear the jails to make way for those accused of "economic crimes," he made clear he did not intend to reverse the messy, inequitable privatizations of the previous decade, but rather to reinforce the state's control over the market in order to end "a vicious circle" of corrupt businessmen paying bribes to government workers and sapping resources from the budget that were needed to lift the poor out of poverty. "Millions of people in the country can barely make ends meet; they are skimping on everything, even on food," he wrote. "The elderly, who won the Great Patriotic War and made Russia a glorious world power, are eking out a meager existence or, worse, begging in the streets." Putin coined a slogan for his vision of a new, rule-abiding Russia that was secure and prosperous. It embodied the internal contradictions of his ideology, of his background as a lawyer and intelligence officer, and of his temperament. He felt it so deeply he used it twice in one letter. Russia, he declared, would be "a dictatorship of the law."

The biggest threat to Putin's popularity before the election, ironically, seemed to be the war that had propelled him to the Kremlin's highest post. The lightning push to the Terek River in the fall of 1999, cheered on by the public, now bogged down over the winter in gruesome street fighting for control of Chechnya's capital, block by ruined block. By the end of January 2000, when Russian troops pushed into Grozny, the military had acknowledged the deaths of 1,173 soldiers, though many accused the government of underreporting combat casualties by not including Russians from outside the military and Interior Ministry, including the FSB, or those who died of wounds later.[10] The Russian troops suffered shortages of equipment, uniforms, food, and ammunition—and could not trust that they would not be killed by their own bombs.[11] The heady burst of patriotic fervor that greeted the initial attack now faced the reality of a conflict that would be longer and bloodier than most Russians had expected.

Putin's response was not to shift tactics but to make sure that most Russians would not know the truth of what was happening. As the fighting ground on, the Kremlin strictly limited the access of journalists in the field, forcing Russian newspapers and television networks to cover the "counterterrorist operation" almost exclusively from the perspective of the Russian side. Romanticized coverage of the Chechen fighters in the first war had bolstered their cause and sapped morale in Russia, and Putin was not going to let that happen again.

News of the ferocious fighting, the indiscriminate slaughter of civilians, and the growing evidence of war crimes by Russian troops continued to trickle out, especially in opposition newspapers and foreign news reports, but the Kremlin's control of state television kept the most dismal news off the air. Reporters who dared to report the Chechen perspective on the conflict—or without official accreditation from the Russian military—faced arrest, or worse. When Andrei Babitsky, a reporter for the American-funded Radio Liberty, was captured by Russian forces in January, the military did not simply charge him with violating the rules on reporting from Chechnya and expel him from the area. It turned him over to masked Chechen rebels in exchange for five Russian prisoners of war, as if he were himself an enemy combatant. Babitsky's fate caused an outcry at home and abroad, prompting sharply critical stories about Putin and his KGB background.

Putin never sounded defensive; he sounded defiant, blindly so in some cases. He brushed aside any criticism of the war as an attack on Russia itself. "What Babitsky did is much more dangerous than firing a machine gun," he said when the reporters in *First Person* protested that journalists in a war zone were not combatants.[12] Pressed on the point, he simply replied, "We interpret freedom of expression in different ways."

The American secretary of state, Madeleine Albright, raised Babitsky's case when she visited Moscow and met Putin in February, but after a three-hour meeting, she nevertheless emerged sounding charmed by Russia's new leader. It was not the last time Putin's foreign counterparts would come away with a view they would later regret. "I found him a very well-informed person, a good interlocutor, obviously a Russian patriot who seeks a normal position with the West," Albright said.[13] Privately, she warned Putin that he was "riding a tiger" in Chechnya and again urged him to seek a negotiated settlement, something he never had any interest in pursuing. "I do not think we are any closer to a political solution in Chechnya," she declared. She was right then, but he would be proved right in the end.

By late January, Chechnya's rebel commanders, battered by the aerial assaults on their redoubts in Grozny, abandoned the city and began a treacherous withdrawal into a trap. A Russian counterintelligence officer who had previously arranged the exchange of prisoners accepted a $100,000 bribe to aid the escape of a large group of fighters through a settlement near Alkhan-Kala. On the night of February 1, the main force found the assigned route heavily mined. As they struggled through with devastating losses, Russian shells rained down on them. Hundreds of Chechens were killed. Among those badly injured was Shamil Basayev, who after the incursion into Dagestan was now Russia's most vilified foe. A mine shredded his right foot during the escape. The Chechens released a gruesome videotape of a surgeon amputating the foot, apparently to demonstrate to the rebels and others that, although injured, Basayev remained alive.[14]

On February 6, Russian forces captured Grozny—at least what was left of it. No building remained undamaged; most were destroyed and uninhabitable. Russian military commanders raised a Russian flag above the city's administrative office, but amid the devastation, they could not find a building sufficiently sound to serve as a military headquarters. The

Russian authorities airlifted food and medical supplies for residents who had spent the winter in their basements. "The people should understand that they are not a defeated people," Putin declared. "They are a liberated people."[15]

The war was not over by any means however. Thousands of Chechen fighters retreated into the mountains to join others, as many as seven thousand altogether. Maskhadov still remained at large, as did other commanders. Basayev vowed to continue to wage war "on the whole of Russian territory," and he would keep his promise.

On March 20, only six days before the presidential election, Putin visited Grozny for the first time. With Russian troops continuing to suffer losses in guerrilla attacks outside the capital, he braced the country's voters for a longer war than anyone in the Kremlin had dared to acknowledge. The war had stalled the stunning rise in his popularity over the winter, but with coverage stifled, it had largely disappeared as a campaign issue. While Russian forces had destroyed the "majority of large illegal armed groups," many threats remained, Putin said. "It is the reason why we should not pull out all troops from Chechnya but leave enough of our forces here to deal with current problems." Most Russians never learned the dark side of Putin's all-out war and did not seem to care if they did. Putin had arrived in Grozny aboard a two-seat attack fighter built in Soviet times. He emerged at the military airfield dressed like a character out of a war movie, swaggering in a pilot's flight suit. Stunts like this would soon become a staple of Putin's politics, the careful cultivation of the leader's televised image that one author would christen a "videocracy."[16] The television coverage of his visit to Grozny was so fawning that many actually believed that Putin had piloted the jet himself.

By election day, the outcome was a foregone conclusion. The only suspense was about the turnout, since anything less than 50 percent would render the results invalid. Putin faced ten other candidates, but most were little-known regional leaders or politicians like Yuri Skuratov, who was still fighting his dismissal as prosecutor general without ever revealing all the incriminating information he claimed to have against Yeltsin's inner circle. The most prominent challengers remained those who had opposed Yeltsin four years before: Gennady Zyuganov of the Communists and Grigory Yavlinsky of Yabloko. They were almost entirely ignored by the Kremlin and its state television networks until Yavlinsky faced a late barrage of campaign ads and news reports attacking him as a candidate supported by Jews, gays, and foreigners. The attack, appealing to the lowest common denominator of Russian popular sentiment, reflected a fear that Yavlinsky would draw enough of the country's liberals out of Putin's column to force him into a runoff. Either the fear was misplaced or the tactic worked. Putin won 53 percent of the vote in the first round, crushing Zyuganov, who received only 29 percent, and Yavlinsky, who finished with less than 6 percent. There was evidence that Putin's totals—and turnout—were aided by ballot stuffing,[17] but no one really cared. Putin was indisputably the people's choice in what would be the last election in Russia that could still arguably be called democratic.

Putin's ascension to the pinnacle of power was so rapid, so unexpected, so astounding, that a prominent Russian historian described it in otherworldly terms, as the act of a higher power bestowed on a battered, grateful nation. Yeltsin, the historian Roy Medvedev wrote, had released his grip on power "without revolution or bloodshed, without a palace coup or plot of any kind. Russia entered the new century with a new leader, Acting President Putin, and almost all the population perceived this, not as a cause for alarm, but as a providential New Year's gift."[18]

Only days before the election the lingering puzzle of the apartment bombings and the events in Ryazan—colored now by the brutality of the fighting in Chechnya—began to gnaw at Putin's opponents. They believed that there had to be a conspiracy at work, with this small, dull man merely a puppet of larger forces. The independent newspaper *Novaya Gazeta* published a series of articles that deepened the mystery about the "training exercise" in Ryazan. The articles quoted the police corporal who had first entered the apartment building and the officer who tested the sacks of "sugar" and defused the detonator. The newspaper also found a paratrooper from the 137th Regiment, which was stationed at a base near Ryazan, who had been ordered to guard a warehouse. Inside he and another soldier found dozens more sacks labeled sugar. "Tea made with this 'sugar' turned out to be foul, and not at all sweet," the newspaper wrote. The soldier informed his platoon commander, who had an expert he knew test the substance. It was an explosive, hexogen. The paratrooper was identified only as Aleksei P.,[19] and the evidence was purely circumstantial, but the newspaper suggested that the events in Ryazan and the bombings in Moscow and Volgadonsk might not have been acts of terrorists against the state but rather terrorist acts by the state.

"Why was hexogen kept at a special-service base, and why was it packed into sugar bags?" the newspaper asked. "According to sappers, explosives in such quantities are not transported or stored like this because it's too dangerous. Half a kilo is enough to blow up a small building."[20] Putin's rise, the newspaper insinuated, might not have been a providential gift after all, but rather the result of an unspeakable sin. On March 16 a cyberattack destroyed the next day's edition of the newspaper.

The same day the FSB, which had remained largely silent about the bombings since the fall, held a press conference to announce that its investigation had established the vast network of insurgents who had been involved in the attacks, which, a spokesman insisted, had been organized inside Chechnya.[21] The FSB also altered significant details in its new account, especially those involving the explosives. Instead of hexogen, which is produced and closely guarded by the military, the FSB said, the terrorists used a more common mixture of fertilizers that were widely available. The FSB's confusing and shifting accounts challenged even those inclined to believe that terrorists were responsible. Putin, in the campaign interviews collected in the book *First Person,* dismissed the suspicions as madness. "No one in the Russian special services would be capable of such a crime against his own people," he said. "The very supposition is amoral. It's nothing but part of the information war against Russia."[22] Who exactly was waging this war? Putin did not explain.

Zyuganov and Yavlinsky raised the lingering questions on the campaign trail. NTV, the independent part of the Media-Most conglomerate owned by the oligarch Vladimir Gusinsky, also echoed the accusations. NTV held a town hall debate in which residents of Ryazan questioned an FSB spokesman and mocked his unconvincing answers. At one point the spokesman held up a sealed box that, he insisted, contained all the evidence, though of course he could not open it. It was a preposterous performance. Despite the official denials, the media and some in the opposition began to piece together odd incidents and reports into the shape of a conspiracy to propel Putin to office. Local and foreign newspaper articles in the summer *before* the bombings—largely ignored at the time—seemed now to have eerily predicted them, though the presumed motive at that time was to declare a state of emergency and cancel the parliamentary elections, not to start a new war in Chechnya or propel

Yeltsin's security council director and FSB chief into the Kremlin. In July 1999, for example, a retired army colonel turned journalist, Aleksandr Zhilin, had published an article in *Moskovskaya Pravda* with the headline "Storm in Moscow," predicting "terrorist attacks" against government buildings, the goal of which was allegedly to discredit Mayor Luzhkov.[23]

Berezovsky's close contacts with Chechen and other rebels in the Caucasus—which he had cultivated during and after the first Chechen war—suggested to his many enemies that he might have been involved in the hopes of blocking the Luzhkov-Primakov alliance. Berezovsky, who ran for and won a parliamentary seat from the nearby Caucasian republic of Karachayevo-Cherkessia, acknowledged meeting Chechen fighters and making large payments to them, including Basayev, to free kidnapped hostages. A transcript purporting to be of Berezovsky's telephone conversations with a Chechen leader, Movladi Udugov, suggested they had haggled over the incursion into Dagestan, presumably as a provocation to justify the invasion. Berezovsky said the tapes had been edited but did not dispute that the conversations had taken place. Berezovsky's critics believed he had as much at stake in the post-Yeltsin transition as anyone else and would stop at nothing to retain his wealth and influence. "Berezovsky saw the world through the prism of his personal interests," the financier George Soros wrote. Soros had worked closely with Berezovsky until they fell out over a telecommunications auction, and he viewed the man as a con, as did many of Berezovsky's erstwhile business partners. "He has no difficulty in subordinating the fate of Russia to his own."[24]

There were counterarguments that supported the FSB's version of the bombings. It was not beyond the Chechen extremists—and their like-minded fighters in the other Muslim republics—to commit acts of terror, after all. The political logic of the conspiracy also ignored the fact that the political elite had deeply opposed a new war for the reasons that now seemed prophetic. Launching a war was in the summer of 1999 seen as a liability, not an asset. And now after the early military successes and all of Putin's tough talk, the war had become a drag on Putin's broader popularity, not the ballast it had been at the beginning. A survey of Russian voters found that the war in Chechnya was ranked as the worst decision of his first eight months in power. (Nearly as many ranked Putin's moves to increase pensions and wages as his best.)[25] Moreover, any conspiracy would have had to be set in motion before anyone, even Putin himself, knew he would become prime minister, let alone Yeltsin's anointed successor.

The evidence for either version was ultimately never decisive, in large part because the FSB under Putin reverted to Soviet-like secrecy and almost certainly covered up aspects of the bombings and the events in Ryazan. Only days before the election, the Communist and Yabloko blocs in the Duma drafted a resolution requesting an official investigation into what had happened in Ryazan, but only 197 deputies voted in favor, short of the 226 needed. All of Putin's supporters voted against. Strangling a parliamentary inquiry to untangle the conflicting theories only sowed deeper and darker doubts. At the inception of Putin's presidency lay an enduring mystery that would shadow Russia for years, one that did not stop claiming lives. Independent lawmakers and journalists who pursued the question died with such disturbing regularity that it was difficult to consider their deaths mere coincidence.

Even some close to Putin struggled to understand the facts of the horrendous bombings. "I don't know," Mikhail Kasyanov, a Finance Ministry official through the end of the Yeltsin years, said more than a decade later. On January 3, two days after becoming acting president, Putin had offered Kasyanov the job as prime minister, though it was not made official until after his election. Putin made the ground rules very clear: Kasyanov would tend to the government, the budget, and the economy, but the security services would remain in Putin's purview. The idea that bombings that killed some three hundred innocent civilians could have been the work of the government that he had joined under the new president, or even of rogue elements inside it, was simply an inconceivable evil to Kasyanov. "I don't know, and I don't want to believe that it could be true," he said.[26]

Putin built a political team out of a circle of people he could trust—that is, his friends, which he admitted were few. "I have friends, of course. Unfortunately, or perhaps fortunately, they are not so many," he told the journalist Mikhail Leontyev during an interview for the biographical documentary that state television ran before the election. "Because then, you value the friends you have more. These are the people with whom I have been friends for many years, with some of them from my schooldays, with some from university days. The character of our relations is not changing. I haven't been able to meet them often recently, but the meetings still take place regularly."

During the election campaign, he lost one of those few. Anatoly Sobchak had returned to Petersburg in the summer of 1999 after his exile in France; he was greeted like a prodigal son. Now that Putin had reached the heights of power, the criminal cases that had chased Sobchak abroad suddenly evaporated. Sobchak tried to regain the glory of 1991, running for a seat in the Duma in December, but his political star had faded and he lost. He nonetheless threw himself into Putin's presidential race, campaigning actively for his former aide. He was in Kaliningrad when he died suddenly in his hotel room on the night of February 18, apparently of a heart attack, though rumors darkly swirled of other causes, perhaps even poisoning.[27] Putin himself fueled the speculation with his rage and sorrow over Sobchak's death. "Anatoly Sobchak did not just die," Putin told Baltika radio in Petersburg. "He perished because he was hounded." Putin's severity in ensuring Yuri Skuratov's defenestration now seemed understandable, since it was Skuratov who had launched the first investigations into Sobchak's affairs. Putin's role in the prosecutor's fall might have had a political purpose, but it was also deeply personal. At Sobchak's funeral, Putin delivered the eulogy. He called him "our master" and "one of the last romantics." For the first time, Russia saw its new leader shed tears.

In May 2000 the Kremlin's protocol chiefs faced a logistical problem as they considered the inauguration of a new president of Russia. Since the 1960s, the Soviet Union's new general secretaries had taken the oath of office in the modern glass-and-concrete Palace of Congresses, an architectural anachronism that marred the historical integrity of the Kremlin. The tsars had been crowned in the fifteenth-century Cathedral of the Assumption. Boris Yeltsin, when he won reelection, considered abandoning both and erecting an outdoor stage, only to have to move it into the old Soviet palace because of his frail health. Yeltsin was so ill, walking stiffly and speaking shakily, that he did not deliver an inaugural address and read his oath from a teleprompter.[28] Putin decided to hold his inauguration in St. Andrew's Hall in the Grand Kremlin Palace, the former imperial residence built on the orders of Nicholas I. The Kremlin's planners knew precisely how many spectators could fill the Palace of Congresses but had no idea how many would fit into the Grand Palace. To find out, they bussed in soldiers to line up at attention and counted them.[29] They could not afford to overlook any detail.

On May 7, fifteen hundred people witnessed a new president swearing an oath amid the gilded, neo-imperial splendor that Putin's first boss in Moscow, Pavel Borodin, had renovated in the 1990s, bringing scandal onto Yeltsin and his entourage. Borodin could hardly have imagined that the suspicious, dour deputy sent to his office less than four years before would someday be the man with his hand on the new Constitution in that hall. At every turn, the contrast between Yeltsin and Putin was seared into the consciousness of the millions watching either in the hall or on state television. Putin remained a political novice; he seemed like an actor in his stage debut. He arrived at the side entrance to the Grand Palace in a midnight-blue Mercedes, emerged alone, saluted a ceremonial guard at the door, and then strode up the fifty-seven steps of the palace's monumental staircase. He moved deliberately, but not hurriedly, along a red carpet through the palace's grand hallways. The cameras tracked him in an elaborately crafted pageant that passed applauding guests crowded behind red ropes, as the soldiers had been. Putin seemed tiny in the enormous halls. He wore a dark suit and gray tie. His left arm swung confidently, but his right—possibly because of the fracture he had suffered during the fight in 1984 that clouded his KGB career—hung at his side. It gave his gait a distinctive swagger as he covered hundreds of yards, something that Yeltsin in his heartiest days would not have dared to attempt under the scrutiny of live television cameras.

The official guests included the members of parliament, governors, senior judges, and the clergy of Russia's four official religions—Orthodox Christianity, Islam, Buddhism, and Judaism. Mikhail Gorbachev, whom Yeltsin had conspicuously snubbed for his inauguration in 1996, attended like an apparition of another era. So did Vladimir Kryuchkov, the KGB chairman who had led the abortive coup to overthrow Gorbachev. The symbolism of their joint attendance signaled Putin's desire to project unity after the tumult of the previous decade. Yeltsin, looking pale and puffy, appeared with him on the dais to witness the oath, which was administered exactly at noon. During the elder man's short address, the lights of his teleprompter flickered, forcing him to pause long enough that the audience applauded, thinking he was done.[30] Putin, two decades younger, spoke crisply and sweepingly, focusing on the history of the moment, which he called the first peaceful, democratic transfer of ultimate authority in the country in its eleven hundred years (failing even to hint at the orchestration that Yeltsin had devised).

The ceremony blended the conflicted history of a country divided over the meaning of its past and thus its future. Putin, in his remarks, glossed over "both tragic chapters and great chapters," leaving it to the listeners to decide which was which. As the ceremony ended, cannons fired a salute from the bank of the Moscow River. Inside, a choir sang the finale from Mikhail Glinka's *A Life for the Tsar,* written in 1836 to celebrate a soldier's death in the war against Poland and rewritten in Soviet times as *Ivan Susanin* to remove the homage to the tsar. For Putin, the choir sang the Soviet verses.

After leaving the Grand Palace, Putin watched a military parade inside the Kremlin grounds. He met Aleksy II, Patriarch of Moscow and All Rus, the head of the Orthodox Church. He then laid a wreath at the Tomb of the Unknown Soldiers, located just outside the Kremlin walls. It felt like a coronation as much as a democratic transfer of power. Russia had a new leader, consecrated by the ballot, and yet little idea of where he intended to lead it.

Putin's rise to power constrained his family life. He allowed his daughters, Masha and Katya, then sixteen and fifteen, to grant interviews for the campaign biography, but afterward they disappeared from public life, their privacy fiercely guarded by the Kremlin. Photographs of them rarely appeared, not even with their parents; there was never an official portrait of Russia's new first family. The girls studied at home with tutors, learning not only German but also French and English. In the interviews, they came across as ordinary teenagers who enjoyed foreign movies like *The Matrix,* but only ventured out in the presence of bodyguards. Their parents bought them a white toy poodle, named Toska, the family's first dog since the car accident had killed their Caucasian sheep dog in Petersburg. Lyudmila said her husband spoiled the girls lovingly but acknowledged that "they see him more often on television than at home." They had servants and a cook, which saved Lyudmila the frustrations she had felt when she first cooked for him as a newlywed. Their life together, however, was no longer anything she could control. "I don't make plans anymore," she said. "I used to make them, and when they fell apart, I would get very upset and offended. But now I understand it's easier not to make plans for shared vacations or holidays or time off, so as not to be disappointed."[31]

Russia, like the Soviet Union, had little experience with the leader's wife assuming a public role as first lady. Gorbachev's stylish wife, Raisa, had accompanied him often on his travels and took up public causes, but this was still a novelty that was not universally welcomed. Yeltsin's wife disdained publicity and largely avoided it, and so did Lyudmila. In 1998 and 1999, she had briefly worked as Moscow representative for a communications company, Telekominvest, that had roots in Petersburg and links to a family friend, Leonid Reiman, who would serve as Putin's telecommunications minister. She earned the equivalent of $1,500 a month but gave up the job when her husband became prime minister, though some said she continued to be involved in business deals.[32] Now as first lady, she joined her husband at official events, especially with visiting dignitaries, like Tony Blair, the first Western leader who met with Putin after his unexpected ascent. The Putins took the Blairs to the Mariinsky Theatre in Petersburg to see a performance of Sergei Prokofiev's opera *War and Peace*. It seemed at first that she would play a more public role. After the inauguration, she embraced the issue of literacy, promoting reading and languages, and she founded the Center for the Development of the Russian Language, which organized projects with the aim of "enhancing the prestige" of Russian culture around the world.[33] Except for the humanizing interviews, however, Lyudmila had no role in her husband's campaign and none in his governing. Putin himself bristled at even the most benign questions about their life together. When Mikhail Leontyev asked gently if he had time to see his family, Putin replied curtly, "I see them," and the remark was followed by a noticeable cut in the interview. At the time, Leontyev was struck by the state of the Putins' home, which had been used by prime ministers for the previous decade. After six months in office, boxes remained unpacked, and he noted that it had the air of a temporary residence. "We have been living in temporary dwellings since 1985," Putin replied. "And so we constantly move from place to place and we think of our dwellings as if they were barracks—admittedly, very nice barracks. You can live quite comfortably here, but it is temporary. A temporary abode. We live as if we were sitting on our packed suitcases."

In his financial declaration, required by law, Putin reported that he owned three properties, including the dacha outside Petersburg that had been rebuilt after the fire and incorporated in the cooperative with the other businessmen from Petersburg, including the two who were involved in the early food scandal, Vladimir Yakunin and Yuri Kovalchuk. The cooperative faced a legal challenge from villagers in the area,[34] but the eight succeeded in securing title to the lakeside expanse and turned it into a gated community—reportedly with a shared bank account that any of the owners could use to deposit or withdraw cash.[35]

Putin declared a little more than $13,000 in various savings accounts, which by Russian standards made him a reasonably wealthy man, but hardly a high-flying tycoon. (Like the savings of most Russians, his had lost a lot of value when the ruble was devalued in 1998.) He may have omitted some assets in his disclosure, as many politicians habitually did since so much of Russia's wealth remained in the shadows of the unofficial economy, but before his presidency at least, the Putins had lived seemingly modest lives. Until then, they seemed to have no more guarantee of the future than most Russians, who feared that one day everything could simply become worthless again. Putin saw in his personal experience the fate of all Russia. "Over the past 10 years the whole country has been living like that," Putin said in the television interview with Leontyev. "And that brings us back to the problem we started with, the problem with stability."[36] It was stability he promised and had now found for himself. Indeed, the family's circumstances had now changed irreversibly. In May, the Putins moved to a new residence in a wooded compound abutting a winding river called Novo-Ogaryovo. The estate, built in the 1950s, had served as a government guesthouse until it became Putin's official residence. The area around it was called Rublyovka, and soon other mansions sprouted nearby. With buyers attracted by the proximity to power, it became one of the most expensive places in the world to live. The Putins remained there for years to come.

The men with whom Putin had worked in Petersburg under Sobchak now joined him in the upper echelons of the Kremlin. They included Dmitri Medvedev, who became deputy chief of staff, and Aleksei Kudrin, who had repeatedly helped him find his way in Moscow and who became minister of finance. His former KGB friends—Viktor Cherkesov, Viktor Ivanov, and Sergei Ivanov—all took up senior security positions. Putin installed so many friends from his hometown that his government became known as the Petersburg clan and was viewed suspiciously by the Moscow political elite, which was used to a monopoly on power and its perquisites. Many even speculated, with no basis in reality, that he would once again move Russia's capital to Petersburg, just as Peter the Great had. To protect himself from the Byzantine political intrigues of Moscow, Putin turned to those he could trust explicitly. It became a remarkable personalization of authority in the Kremlin, reflecting his deep distrust of the country's political elite. "I have a lot of friends, but only a few people are really close to me," he acknowledged. "They have never gone away. They have never betrayed me, and I haven't betrayed them either."[37]

He kept some prominent Yeltsin allies on his staff, including his chief of staff, Aleksandr Voloshin, and Anatoly Chubais, the reviled father of "shock therapy" who remained the chairman of the state electricity monopoly, but the character of the Kremlin hierarchy soon changed dramatically. On the day of his inauguration, he officially appointed as his prime minister Mikhail Kasyanov, who had risen through the ranks of the Soviet and post-Soviet economic and finance ministries and was known as a pragmatic negotiator respected by his counterparts in the West. The muckraking media nicknamed him Misha Two Percent because of rumors that he extracted a cut in the finance deals he negotiated with bankers—which he fervently denied—but his credentials as a market economist were unquestioned, and his appointment signaled Putin's careful but steady embrace of the privatization of the 1990s. More important after the political turmoil that had seen six prime ministers since 1998, Kasyanov's appointment did not provoke a new constitutional crisis with the parliament.

Putin's early policy choices reflected liberalizing reforms that were cheered on by big business at home and abroad. He imposed a flat income tax of 13 percent on individuals and cut the tax on corporate profits to 24 percent from 35, effective January 2002. He pledged that Russia would have lower taxes but also expect people—and businesses—to pay them, after a decade in which almost every Russian avoided them by any means available. Putin's new government adopted land codes that allowed private property to be bought and sold, and institutionalized labor rules governing private employment, removing some of the uncertainties that had paralyzed investment and invited corruption and lawlessness. Buoyed by rising oil prices and the slow recovery from the 1998 default, Russia for the first time balanced its budget. It began to pay off its debts to the IMF and others—ahead of schedule. Yeltsin's presidency had been erratic, but it had laid the foundation for an economic boom. The gross domestic product, which grew 5 percent in 1999, doubled that in Putin's first year in office and then averaged more than 6 percent for the next seven years.[38] The Wild West capitalism of the 1990s had created a decadent upper class and a host of shops, restaurants, and clubs that catered to ridiculously exclusive tastes, but now the fruits of a market economy began to trickle down to the middle ranks of society, especially in Moscow and other cities. Putin seemed to be the competent, efficient manager he had been as an underling in Petersburg and then Moscow.

He embodied the contradictions of Russia's progress, resting somewhere between a modern democracy and Soviet traditions it had not yet shaken. Putin's initial steps reflected both, and opinions on his leadership split according to which side of Putin one embraced. Putin himself seemed at times to struggle to decide which side he was on. Nevertheless, in a matter of a few short months, he offered Russians a break from the chronic chaos of the Yeltsin years. His goal was not to accelerate Russia's transition to capitalism and democracy but rather to move cautiously, to provide a modicum of what most people wanted, as he would say over and over: stability. And even as war raged in the distant Caucasus, he largely succeeded.

On May 11, four days after Putin's inauguration, dozens of FSB officers raided the downtown headquarters of Russia's largest private media company, Media-Most, which included the popular television channel NTV. They arrived in the morning, ordered the staff into the cafeteria, and for hours combed through the offices, seizing documents, computers, and, among other oddities, a decorative pistol belonging to the company's owner, Vladimir Gusinsky.[39] Gusinsky's early life had striking parallels to Putin's. He was born a day earlier, on October 6, 1952, and lived in a one-room apartment with his uneducated, loving parents; his father too was a veteran of the Great Patriotic War and a factory worker. Like Putin, he considered himself a "product of the street"; he learned to fight to defend himself against drunkards and thugs in the courtyards of a bleak Soviet apartment block.

The parallels ended there. Gusinsky's grandfather died in Stalin's purges, and though Gusinsky served in the army, he dabbled in black-market trades and eventually took up drama.[40] All of it—his education, his experiences as a Jew in the bigoted Soviet bureaucracy—made him a rebel against the system that Putin became so loyal to. He also became spectacularly wealthy, opening a consulting company at the end of the 1980s and befriending a city bureaucrat who oversaw the city's fruit and vegetable markets, Yuri Luzhkov. His business soon expanded into banking, housing reconstruction, and the media. His Media-Most, named after the automated banking network he had seen during a visit to the

United States, created a newspaper, *Sevodnya,* and later the network, NTV, which would ultimately provoke Putin's wrath.

NTV became Russia's first modern private television network, with a feisty news department that irritated Yeltsin's Kremlin with critical, often sensationalized reportage. Just as Berezovsky used the state channel, ORT, to attack Yeltsin's opponents before the election in 1999, Gusinsky wielded NTV as a cudgel against Yeltsin's "Family." The rivalry between the two television moguls was so personal and intense that Yeltsin's former chief of security, Aleksandr Korzhakov, claimed Berezovsky asked him to assassinate Gusinsky.[41] NTV kept up its critical coverage during Putin's campaign and aired a documentary about the apartment bombings that insinuated government involvement. Worse, from the Kremlin's perspective, its coverage of the war in Chechnya did not flinch from reporting the scale of brutality and suffering, as the state channels learned to do. NTV's owner and its journalists were slow to realize that the Kremlin's tolerance for criticism had diminished under its new leader. Putin had a particular dislike for the way he was portrayed on the channel's weekly satirical puppet program, *Kukly,* whose creator, Viktor Shenderovich, had been skewering the country's politicians since 1994. The caricature of Putin—jug-eared and bug-eyed, portrayed alternately as timid or malevolent—did not seem funny at all to the new president. In one episode after Putin's election in March, the puppet was portayed as a tsar, overwhelmed by a taller, plumper cooing bride representing all of Russia. "But she's so big," he whispered to his courtiers. "I don't have experience with anything of this scale." A puppet representing his chief of staff, Aleksandr Voloshin, replied, "Just do what we've all done to her."[42] Aides in the Kremlin promptly made it clear to the show's producers that the presidential puppet should no longer appear in its weekly satires.

The motives behind the police raid at Media-Most were not immediately clear, muddled as they were by contradictory statements from the tax police, the prosecutor, and other officials. Putin, however, strongly defended the action the following day, saying that no one would be above the law. It was clearly a signal, and it established a pattern that would become a familiar one. "There will be no such oligarchs as a class," Putin had declared on the eve of the election.[43] The raid did not immediately affect Gusinsky's media holdings, which covered the events with zealous outrage. Putin insisted there would be no limits on freedom of speech, but no one on Gusinsky's side believed him.

The prosecutorial assault on Media-Most coincided with the first
official visit by President Clinton to Moscow under Russia's new president. Putin had not made foreign policy the first priority of his presidency, though in April he succeeded in getting the Duma to ratify the
START II agreement negotiated by Yeltsin nearly a decade earlier to
reduce the nuclear arsenals of the United States and Russia. Clinton was
now eager to persuade the new Russian leader to accept American plans
to build a missile defense despite the limits imposed by the Anti-Ballistic
Missile Treaty, a crucial Cold War pact credited with preventing an
ever-esclating nuclear arms race. Clinton hoped to make missile defenses
one of his last achievements before stepping down, but ever since Ronald
Reagan first proposed his "Star Wars" vision of a missile shield, Soviet
and then Russian leaders had furiously opposed any proposals to allow
them. Putin would be no different, fearing that even the rudimentary
defensive system Clinton was considering could ultimately undermine
the last leverage Russia had as a superpower. Although Clinton wanted
to make a deal, Putin calculated that he would have better odds negotiating with the next American president. His wariness toward the Americans had been heightened by Clinton's admonishments over the war in
Chechnya. This time Clinton also raised objections to the assault on
Media-Most—with Putin and, pointedly, in an interview with a radio
station, Ekho Moskvy, that was owned by Gusinsky's company. Clinton
later paid a visit to Boris Yeltsin, whom after eight years in office he considered a friend. "Boris, you've got democracy in your heart," Clinton
told him. "You've got the trust of the people in your bones. You've got
the fire in your belly of a real democrat and a real reformer. I'm not sure
Putin has that."[44]

Clinton's visit ended inconclusively. He did not win Putin's support
for changes that would allow missile defenses. Nor did Putin heed his
encouragement to respect a free media. Nine days after he left, the new
prosecutor general, Vladimir Ustinov, summoned Gusinsky, ostensibly
to question him about the bullets for the decorative pistol found in his
headquarters. Gusinsky arrived late and was immediately arrested.

On August 12, during the lazy month of summer holidays, Putin finished a last round of meetings with his national security advisers at
the Kremlin and then departed with his family for Sochi, the Black Sea
resort beloved by Soviet leaders for decades. They stayed at the presidential dacha that he and Lyudmila had admired from a distance during

Brezhnev's rule. He would barely have time to rest. The next morning he received a telephone call from the minister of defense, Marshal Igor Sergeyev. The early hour could only mean bad news, and it proved to be the gravest test yet of his young presidency.

Russia's newest nuclear submarine, the *Kursk,* had lost contact with the Northern Fleet during a training exercise in the Barents Sea. Construction of the *Kursk* had begun in Soviet times and was completed in 1994, when the country's once mighty military reached the nadir of its post-Soviet decay. It was the pride of Russia's navy, a giant warship designed to battle American aircraft carriers. Now it had gone missing in territorial waters off Murmansk and no one knew why. Sergeyev, it seems, misled Putin about the severity of the crisis, perhaps because he had been misled himself by the navy. The commander of the Northern Fleet, Admiral Vyacheslav Popov, released a statement declaring the exercise a resounding success but made no mention of the disaster that was clear not only to Russian commanders, but also to American and other foreign militaries who had been monitoring this exercise closely.

Just before Putin left Moscow, an explosion had ripped through the *Kursk's* bow, triggered by a misfiring torpedo. The blast ignited a blaze in the fore compartments, which was followed two minutes and fifteen seconds later by a much larger explosion, which was detected by two nearby American submarines and seismic sensors as far away as Alaska.[45] The explosions sent the *Kursk* to the bottom of the sea, 354 feet below the stormy surface. The submarine had a crew of 113 officers and sailors, accompanied by five more senior fleet officers who were monitoring the exercise, the largest in the Barents since the Soviet Union collapsed. Most died instantly, but a group of twenty-three sailors managed to seal themselves inside a rear compartment, where they waited in the dark and cold for a rescue that was not forthcoming. A young officer, Captain-Lieutenant Dmitri Kolesnikov, gathered the survivors, took roll, and wrote notes to his commanders and to his wife. The last, scribbled on lined ledger paper, was dated August 12 at 3:15 in the afternoon, nearly eight hours after the first explosion. He folded it in plastic and put it inside his uniform.

> *It's too dark to write here, but I'll try blind.*
> *It looks like there is no chance, % 10–20.*
> *We will hope,*
> *That someone finds this*

Here is a list—of those in the compartments who are here on
the 9th and will try to get out
Hello to everyone, do not despair.[46]

The wrecked submarine was already at the bottom of the sea when Putin was told only that it was missing. He carried on with his seaside vacation, jet-skiing on Sunday afternoon in the calm, warm water of the Black Sea. No one outside of the military chain of command knew anything was amiss since the navy did not publicly acknowledge the *Kursk*'s fate until Monday, after which officials obfuscated and then lied day after day.

After finally acknowledging that an explosion had crippled the *Kursk,* officials falsely insisted that the cause had been a collision with a foreign submarine—almost certainly from the United States or NATO. Russia's military leaders reverted to a Soviet instinct for secrecy, and so did the Kremlin. The press office curtly noted on August 14 that the navy commander had briefed Putin on the rescue operation, but Putin himself said nothing until August 16 when he left Sochi—not to return to Moscow, but to attend a meeting of former Soviet states in Crimea.

On the sixth day of the crisis *Komsomolskaya Pravda* published a list of the 118 sailors and officers aboard, having paid a bribe worth $600 to obtain it. For relatives, the newspaper's report was the first confirmation that their sons and husbands were aboard—and by now almost certainly dead. Another headline in the newspaper directly challenged Putin: "The sailors on the *Kursk* fell silent yesterday. Why has the president been silent?" Putin found himself excoriated in the media. Another newspaper published a sequence of photographs showing a tanned Putin, along with Marshall Sergeyev playing billiards and the navy commander, Vladimir Korayedov. The caption read, "They don't sink." [47]

Putin's decisiveness in Chechnya, his bold promises to restore stability to the nation—these failed him in this new crisis. He seemed unable to control the military or an increasingly anguished and angry population, incited by television and newspaper coverage that displayed the sympathy and heartbreak that neither Putin nor his military commanders could seem to muster. Boris Berezovsky, who still harbored illusions of influence despite public disputes with Putin over his initial actions as president, telephoned Putin in Sochi on August 16 from his villa in Cap d'Antibes.

"Volodya, why are you in Sochi?" he said. "You should interrupt your holiday and go to that submarine base, or at least to Moscow." He warned him that he was doing damage to his presidency.

"And why are you in France?" Putin asked sarcastically.

Berezovsky pointed out that he was not the nation's leader. "No one gives a shit where I am," he said.[48]

Russia initially refused offers of international assistance from Norway, Sweden, Britain, and the United States. Putin only agreed after President Clinton called him in Sochi and pressed the offer. By agreeing to assistance, Putin had to overrule Sergeyev and the admirals whose highest concern was not the crew but the possibility that Russia's enemies would learn the secrets of its nuclear submarine fleet. When British and Norwegian divers—but not American—finally arrived with a rescue vehicle on August 21, they succeeded in opening the *Kursk*'s outer escape hatch in six hours, something the Russians had not managed in nine days. By then all aboard were dead. The waiting families, still clinging to hope, erupted in outrage that filled the newscasts not only of Gusinsky's NTV, but also of the channel Berezovsky controlled.

Putin had returned to Moscow quietly on the morning of August 19, but continued to say little about the crisis, leaving the media to declare the country leaderless in its time of tragedy. That morning Berezovsky discovered the consequences of critical coverage. Putin's chief of staff, Aleksandr Voloshin, told him flatly that the channel was "working against the president." Voloshin, who had once been a business partner of Berezovsky's, now told him he should give up control of the network or go the way of Gusinsky. Berezovsky insisted on a meeting with Putin in person, and when they met in the Kremlin on August 20, along with Voloshin, Putin's fury erupted. He claimed he had a report asserting that Berezovsky's reporters had hired prostitutes to appear in news reports claiming to be the wives or sisters of the sailors. "They are not whores, they are real wives and sisters," Berezovsky insisted. "Your KGB idiots are feeding you baloney."[49]

With that, Berezovsky's fate was sealed. Putin had come prepared. He opened a file and began reading about the mismanagement of finances at the state television channel.[50] Berezovsky sputtered in protest, but could do nothing. Putin was cutting him off from whatever influence he hoped to have in the Kremlin. It would be the last meeting between the two, one who portrayed himself as a modern Rasputin, and the other happy to be rid of an odious oligarch wielding the power of television.

On August 22, ten days after the *Kursk* exploded, Putin flew to Vidyayevo, a closed military city above the Arctic Circle; the *Kursk's* home port was in this dilapidated garrison town, weathered by the unforgiving climate. There the fathers, mothers, wives, and children of the submarine's crew had come from all over the country to wait as the tragedy unfolded, veering between hope and anguish, grief and fury. One of Putin's deputy prime ministers, Ilya Klebanov, had tried to placate the families four days earlier, only to encounter uninhibited wrath inside the city's officers' club. Klebanov, who oversaw the country's faltering military industries, looked shaken when one mother, Nadezhda Tylik, leapt from her seat, shouting, "Swines!" A nurse approached her from behind and plunged a needle through her coat sleeve to sedate her.[51]

Now, the relatives gathered once again at the club at five o'clock, this time to see the president himself. And they waited four hours until Putin arrived at last. Dressed in a black suit over a black shirt with no tie, Putin now faced the reality of suffering—not the "prostitutes" hired by unscrupulous journalists, as he had been told, but people genuinely bereaved. What he found was an angry mob. He had not finished his first sentence when he was interrupted by shouts. When he offered his condolences for the "appalling tragedy," a woman loudly shouted that he should cancel the day of mourning that he had announced the day before. Putin seemed unsure of himself. He acknowledged the sorry state of Russia's military, but sounded defensive. "There have always been tragedies," he said. "You surely know that our country is in a difficult position and that our armed forces are as well, but I too never imagined that they were in such bad shape."[52] When a man demanded to know why the Northern Fleet did not have a rescue submersible, Putin blurted out, "There's not a damned thing left in this country!"

The crowd angrily corrected him when he stated the salaries of sailors and officers, shouting over his answers and forcing him to plead with the audience to let him finish. He misstated the timing of the explosion and repeated the navy's obfuscation of the cause. "It could have been a collision, or a mine, or possibly an explosion on board, though specialists think this very unlikely." The meeting lasted nearly two hours and forty minutes, and it was never intended to become public. A television camera from one of the state channels—not Berezovsky's—filmed from a balcony, but the Kremlin released only the video without the sound so viewers never heard his misstatements or the crowd's angry protests. One journalist, however, managed to record the event unnoticed. He was Andrei Kolesnikov, one of the three journalists who had interviewed the acting president for *First Person*. In his telling, Putin ultimately tamed the fury, especially with his promises of compensation for the relatives—ten years' salary and apartments in Moscow and Petersburg— the details of which had occupied nearly an hour of the meeting. "Putin left it," he wrote of the meeting, "as the president of people who had been ready to tear him to pieces a short time earlier."[53]

It was a searing experience. Some in the crowd shouted that they did not want his money, they wanted their loved ones. Putin's political honeymoon had ended. The aura of invincibility—the charmed rise of the political neophyte who would restore Russia's greatness—was gone. Putin believed he knew why; it was not the neglected state of the military, or the Soviet-like obstinacy of the navy's commanders, who continued to blame the Americans. He refused to accept Marshal Sergeyev's offer to resign or to punish any of the commanders who had so clearly lied about the tragedy.[54] No, the cause of Putin's political misfortune was the media. "Television?" he erupted in the officers' club when asked why they had initially refused foreign assistance in the rescue, as widely reported. "They're lying! Lying! Lying! There are people in television who bawl more than anyone today and who, over the past ten years, have destroyed that same army and navy where people are dying today."

In case anyone had any doubt whom he blamed, he appeared on state television in Moscow the next day to address the nation for the first time. After expressing "a total sense of responsibility and sense of guilt for this tragedy," he angrily denounced those who would "take advantage of this calamity in an unscrupulous way." Without using their names, he referred to Berezovsky's pledge to raise $1 million for the relatives of the crew and mentioned the villas he and Gusinsky owned abroad. No one missed the allusions. "Let me put it more bluntly: attempts are being made to inflate the situation politically in order to make some kind of political capital or pursue certain interests of particular groups. And they are right who say that in the front ranks of the defenders of the sailors are people who for a long time were contributing to the collapse of the army, navy, and state. Some of them have even put together a million. A single thread from everyone, and there's a shirt for a naked man. It would be better for them to sell their villas on the Mediterranean coast of France or Spain. Only then they would have to explain why all this property is registered in dummy names and in the name of juridical companies. We would then ask them where the money came from."

Of course, Putin already knew. He had files already compiled. In the shady world of Russian business, few oligarchs could withstand scrutiny over their dealings, their murky acquisition, their tax dodges, their secret accounts offshore. As head of the FSB, he had established a monopoly on financial information,[55] and as prime minister and now president he knew where the skeletons could be found. This was, not incidentally, the method of the KGB once upon a time. The suspended investigation into Berezovsky's holdings in Aeroflot suddenly resumed the next month. When he was called to testify in November, Berezovsky ignored the summons and fled the country. In February he sold his shares in the television channel to his former partner, Roman Abramovich, who turned them over to the state. Gusinsky, who had been released on bail following his arrest in June, fled to his villa in Spain. In April 2001, Gazprom, the energy behemoth, seized control of NTV in a boardroom coup after calling in a $281 million loan it had given Gusinsky to weather the 1998 financial crisis. The channel's journalists occupied the studio in protest but gave up after eleven days, and new management took over. Many at home and abroad registered protest, to no avail. Putin from the start understood the importance of television to the Kremlin's authority—of its ability to shape not only his image, but the reality of Russia itself. Sergei Pugachev, a banker and friend who worked closely with him in the Kremlin at the time, marveled at how Putin would obsessively follow television news reports, even calling the channels' directors in the middle of a broadcast to challenge aspects of the reports. He considered the state networks a "natural resource" as precious as oil or gas. "He understands that the basis of power in Russia is not the army, not the police, it's the television," Pugachev said. "This is his deepest conviction."[56] Now, barely a year into his presidency, the three main television networks in Russia were firmly under the control of the Kremlin.

CHAPTER 12

Putin's Soul

On the afternoon of September 11, 2001, Putin assembled forty-eight journalists in the Kremlin to bestow upon them the honors of the state, a tradition from Soviet times. In his brief remarks before the television cameras, he singled out the war correspondents who reported from Chechnya and who thus confronted the "well-organized and generously paid propaganda warfare" of the rebels. "The peace process is gaining momentum there largely through your achievements," he told them. The man who had neutered the only private television network and the only state network that displayed independence then declared the media an important pillar of the new Russia. "Huge political and economic changes would be impossible in Russia without its free mass media," he said. The ceremony had just ended when his security aides summoned him to a conference room where they watched television reports of the commercial airliners that crashed into the World Trade Center and the Pentagon, an attack carried out by Al-Qaeda, the organization that the Russians had long argued provided assistance to Chechnya's rebels. Putin turned to Sergei Ivanov, his old KGB colleague and friend. "What can we do to help them?" he asked.[1]

Many later viewed Putin's response as cynical, but in the hours after the attacks he acted with alacrity and purpose to help a country he viewed with lingering suspicion. He tried to telephone President George W. Bush but could not reach him as Air Force One hopscotched the United States. When Bush's national security adviser, Condoleezza Rice, tried to call Ivanov, Putin immediately took the receiver. He assured her he would not increase Russia's military alert in response to the American move to a war footing; in fact, he lowered the alert and canceled a military exercise in the Pacific Ocean that had begun the previous day—simulating a nuclear conflict with the United States. "Is there anything else we can do?" he asked Rice. A thought flashed through her mind: *The Cold War really is over.*[2]

Putin was the first world leader to call the White House, even before the extent of the attack was clear. He later telephoned Prime Minister Tony Blair in Britain and Chancellor Gerhard Schröder in Germany, repeating that the world must unite against the scourge of terrorism. In contrast to his cautious silence after the *Kursk* disaster and other major events, Putin went on television and expressed his condolences to the victims of what he called "an unprecedented act of aggression." "The event that occurred in the United States today goes beyond national borders. It is a brazen challenge to the whole of humanity, at least to civilized humanity," he said. He made it clear that the tragedy was an opportunity to refashion international relations to fight "the plague of the 21st Century." "Russia knows firsthand what terrorism is," he said. "So we understand as well as anyone the feelings of the American people. Addressing the people of the United States on behalf of Russia, I would like to say that we are with you, we entirely and fully share and experience your pain."[3]

By the time Bush called back on September 12, Putin had decreed a moment of silence in solidarity, setting a tone from the top that for a time at least tempered the virulent anti-American sentiment that infused Russian politics. Only two years after the anti-American protests against the NATO war in Serbia, many Russians—though certainly not all—followed Putin's lead. They piled flowers outside the American embassy, and the tone of state television, where the Kremlin's mood increasingly manifested itself, shifted markedly. "Good will triumph over evil," Putin told Bush. "I want you to know that in this struggle, we will stand together."[4]

Putin's response seemed to validate Bush's initial impression of him, which no one had anticipated when the new administration began. During his campaign against Al Gore in 2000, Bush had denounced the war in Chechnya with as much vehemence as Clinton ever had, seeing it as a way of portraying the Democrats as having been soft on Russia. From Bush's very first days in office, relations with Putin's Russia appeared fraught. In January 2001, American border agents acting on an international warrant had arrested Pavel Borodin when he landed in New York. After taking office, Putin had quietly transferred Borodin out of his post overseeing Kremlin property and given him a largely ceremonial assignment as an envoy to the Union State of Russia and Belarus, an entity formed in 1996 but never realized. Russia's new prosecutor, Vladimir Ustinov, quietly closed the investigation of Borodin's activities, but the Swiss had not closed its case. Carla Del Ponte had circulated the warrant that snared Borodin, accusing him of accepting kickbacks of approximately $30 million from the contracts he had issued to renovate the Grand Palace at the Kremlin and the Accounting Chamber. The scandal that had tarnished the Yeltsin presidency now cast such a shadow over relations with the new American president that it was the subject of Putin's first phone call with Bush on January 31, 2001.

Within weeks relations seemed doomed to worsen. In February, the FBI finally uncovered a long-suspected mole within its ranks: Robert Hanssen, a senior counterintelligence supervisor, had spied for the Soviet Union and then Russia until the evening of his arrest. His exposure led to the expulsion of fifty Russian diplomats from the United States, followed by the tit-for-tat expulsion of fifty Americans from Moscow.

For a time the Cold War seemed to take on a new life, but when Bush and Putin met for the first time in June 2001 at Brdo Castle, a sixteenth-century villa outside Slovenia's capital, Ljubljana, both men seemed eager to defuse the mounting tensions. And both turned to their intelligence briefings in hopes of breaking the ice. Putin greeted Bush by mentioning rugby, which Bush had played for a year in college. "I did play rugby," Bush told him, knowingly. "*Very* good briefing."[5] Then as Putin got down to business, reading through his agenda from a stack of note cards, Bush interrupted and asked about the cross Putin's mother had given him to bless in Jerusalem. Bush saw the surprise in Putin's face, though it quickly passed. Bush explained that he had read about the story, without mentioning that it was contained in his own briefing book, prepared by the CIA. Putin recounted the story of the fire at his dacha, re-creating for him the moment when a worker found the cross in the ashes and presented it to him "as if it was meant to be." Bush, a believer, told him, "Vladimir, that is the story of the Cross."[6]

When the two emerged to meet the press after two hours of meetings, they had resolved few of their differences, especially over Russia's opposition to missile defenses, which Bush pursued far more aggressively than his Democratic predecessor, but they exuded a personal warmth that was striking given recent events. Bush called him "a remarkable leader," and, in contrast to what the Russians viewed as Clinton's carping, he made only passing mention of Chechnya or freedom of speech in Russia. When asked if Americans could trust Putin, given their differences over a plethora of issues, Bush said he would not have invited him to his ranch in Texas the following November if he did not think so. "I looked the man in the eye," Bush said. "I found him to be very straightforward and trustworthy. We had a very good dialogue. I was able to get a sense of his soul: a man deeply committed to his country and the best interests of his country."[7]

Neither Bush nor Putin mentioned the story of the cross or the fact that Putin was not wearing it that day, as he had told his biographers he did every day. (He did bring it with him when he and Bush met again at the Group of Eight summit in Genoa the next month.) Not everyone was convinced by this fledging partnership. "I can understand the strategy on rapport, but it went too far," Michael McFaul, an American academic who first met Putin in Petersburg before the collapse of the Soviet Union, told a newspaper. "I think there is plenty of good reason not to trust President Putin. This is a man who was trained to lie."[8]

Putin traveled to eighteen countries in his first year in office, often with Lyudmila. He projected the image of a new Russia eager to engage the world and erase some of the vestiges of the Cold War. After his initial focus on policies at home, he overhauled Russia's foreign policy in ways that Yeltsin never could, weakened as he had been by the Communists and nationalists still nostalgic for the lost superpower that was the Soviet Union. What Putin sought was nothing less than a rapprochement with the West—especially with Europe, but even with the "main adversary" he had been trained to fight as an intelligence officer. In 2001 he closed Soviet-era military outposts overseas, including a massive eavesdropping post in Lourdes, Cuba, and a naval and intelligence base in Vietnam, vowing that the new Russia should focus its resources instead on building up its military to counter the more pressing threat of Islamic extremism in the Northern Caucasus. After the attacks of September 11, Putin softened his public opposition to the enlargement of NATO, the next round of which would extend membership to Lithuania, Latvia, and Estonia, the three Baltic republics that had been annexed by the Soviet Union and still included sizable Russian populations. (As a candidate in March 2000, Putin had even suggested that Russia might one day join NATO.)[9] As the United States went to war against the Taliban and Al-Qaeda in Afghanistan in October, Putin provided not only Russian intelligence but also money and weapons to the Northern Alliance, the

Afghans who had continued to resist the Taliban after it seized power in 1996 and before that had fought against the Soviet invasion. Putin also acquiesced in the establishment of American military bases in Uzbekistan and Kyrgyzstan, the first deployment of American soldiers to any part of the former Soviet Union since the Great Patriotic War.

Putin's moves faced resistance from Russia's military, a hidebound bureaucracy that more than most parts of society had not shed its Soviet heritage. It was now a decrepit force—vastly reduced from the 2.8 million personnel at the end of the Soviet era to barely 1 million—and, after the 1990s, a deeply corrupted one. The majority of soldiers were conscripts subject to a brutal form of hazing by older soldiers known as *dedovshchina,* from the word for "grandfather." Conditions in the military were so bad that most Russian families did whatever they could, from bribes to faked illnesses to emigration, to keep their sons out of the draft. Crime and corruption infected the ranks from top to bottom, with commanders renting out conscripts as serfs and selling off their units' fuel, spare parts, and even vehicles.[10] Although he favored warships and fighter jets as backdrops for his popular image, Putin was not a military man. In Soviet times, the soldiers and officers of the Red Army had disdained the elite agents of the KGB, and the feeling was often mutual. The military, though, lay at the heart of Putin's mission to restore the nation, and he understood the sorry state it was in. Though eager to introduce a new military doctrine and turn the military into a leaner, more modern, and more disciplined professional force, Putin moved cautiously to impose his vision on the one institution that still had a measure of independence, despite its diminished standing.

Putin barely mentioned military policy in his first months in office, beyond the strategy for winning the war in Chechnya. Some military analysts in Russia pronounced Putin weak or aloof; others saw a Machiavellian strategy to allow rival commanders to batter themselves into such a weakened state that they would have to submit to Putin. "Putin prefers to deal with people who have been politically hamstrung, feel constrained and thus have to stay loyal to the president," a prominent military analyst wrote.[11] After the *Kursk* disaster, Putin resisted the expedient political move of dismissing the commanders whose incompetence and lies had dented his popularity. He proved far more calculating, building popular support and boosting morale by raising the salaries of soldiers and pledging more money for the military, even as he ordered a restructuring of the armed forces that would further reduce the number of troops. Putin restored the Red Banner as the army's standard, now with the tsarist double eagle, and the music of the Soviet national anthem, though with new words. (The anthem adopted after the collapse of the Soviet Union contained no lyrics, and athletes at the Summer Olympics in Sydney in 2000 had complained to Putin they could not sing along when they stood on the podium to receive their medals.)

Such moves proved deft. They appealed to the nostalgic patriotism of the military and large swaths of society, without restoring the Soviet ideology that many Russians were happy to put behind them. Putin might have been a political novice, but he found a balance between the conflicted past and the uncertain future—one that came naturally because it very much reflected his own views. He did not rail against the Soviet system the way Yeltsin had but instead co-opted the parts of its history that served his idea of the new Russia. During a call-in with voters in February 2000, he used an aphorism that has been widely attributed to him, but was not in fact his own. "Anyone who does not regret the collapse of the Soviet Union has no heart," he said. "And anyone who wants to see it re-created in its former shape has no brain."[12] Putin himself seemed suspended between his impulses. He kept Felix Dzerzhinsky's statue on his desk at the FSB but opposed public appeals to restore the man's bronze monument to the traffic circle where it stood in front of Lubyanka. He glorified the Soviet victory in the Great Patriotic War, but when asked to do so, he refused to restore the wartime name of Volgograd, the site of the terrible siege, far better known as Stalingrad.[13]

Despite Putin's criticism of the failures of the Soviet past, his embrace of some of its symbols raised alarms among intellectuals and liberals. A group of prominent artists and writers published an open letter to him, warning of the dangers of restoring the Soviet anthem. "The head of state must be clearly aware that millions of fellow citizens (including those who voted for him) will never come to respect an anthem that flouts their convictions and insults the memory of the victims of Soviet political repressions," they wrote.[14] Boris Yeltsin, criticizing his successor for the first time since he left office, said the music was associated in his mind with Soviet bureaucrats attending Communist Party congresses. "The president of a country should not blindly follow the mood of the people," Yeltsin told *Komsomolskaya Pravda*.[15] "On the contrary it is up to him to actively influence it." Putin did influence the mood, sampling the past as if from a buffet, picking and choosing a history that he presented to a society deeply divided over what it represented.

Putin had been in office a year before he moved, abruptly and surgically, to bring the recalcitrant military command under his control. The minister of defense, Marshal Igor Sergeyev, had already passed retirement age, but he extended his term annually by appealing first to Yeltsin and then to Putin in 2000. Sergeyev, then sixty-three, assumed that his reappointment in early 2001 would again be a mere formality.[16] Like Yeltsin before him, Putin favored secrecy and surprise in the timing of his announcements. Only his trusted advisers knew of his plan, and Sergeyev was not among them, otherwise he would not have miscalculated the level of support he actually had in the Kremlin. On March 28, Putin assembled his national security team at the Kremlin and announced that Sergei Ivanov would take over as minister of defense. Ivanov was so close to Putin that he was sometimes described as an alter ego. Thin and pale, his hair parted sharply on the left, his face perpetually pinched, he had joined the KGB after studying English and Swedish at Leningrad State University. He and Putin met in 1977 at the Big House, where they worked together for two years before Ivanov's career took off.[17] He attended the Red Banner Institute outside Moscow and by 1981 had emerged as a foreign intelligence operative who served under diplomatic cover in Soviet embassies in Finland, Sweden, and Kenya, and maybe Britain. That his résumé remained so opaque underscored the sort of spy he was—and Putin was not. Unlike Putin he never resigned, rising through the ranks of the post-Soviet foreign intelligence service to become the youngest general in the new Russia. When Putin became director of the FSB, he appointed Ivanov as a deputy; Ivanov later followed him into the Kremlin, where he joined Putin's inner circle of aides, attending the national security meetings held on Mondays, but also the less formal Saturday meetings and the purely social gatherings that occurred at Putin's presidential residence whenever the mood struck, often late into the night.[18] Ivanov was often portrayed as a hardliner, a *silovik,* who reflected Putin's own experience and conservative views. He certainly shared Putin's goal of remaking a bloated, inefficient military. Having retired from his military rank in the FSB, Ivanov became the first civilian to head the ministry in Soviet or Russian history. "As you can see, civilians are coming to take up key positions in military agencies," Putin said when he announced the appointment. "This is also a deliberate step. It is a step towards the demilitarization of Russia's social life."[19]

Putin's appointments signaled a break with Yeltsin, albeit a modest one. He appointed the first woman to a senior position in the Ministry of Defense, Lyubov Kudelina, putting her in charge of overseeing the military budget. He replaced the interior minister with another Petersburger, Boris Gryzlov, who headed the pro-Putin bloc in the Duma, but he did not demote anyone except the minister for nuclear affairs, Yevgeny Adamov, who was later charged in an American court for embezzling $9 million in funds earmarked to bolster security at nuclear sites.[20] The newspaper *Izvestia* declared that Putin's "team now really has been brought together like a 'fist.' "[21]

As defense minister, Ivanov watched the prospect of an American intervention on Russia's periphery with alarm. Three days after the September 11 attacks, Ivanov ruled out "even the hypothetical possibility of NATO military operations on the territory of Central Asian nations."[22] Putin, though, felt that the United States now understood the threat of Islamic terrorism and was gratified. He traveled to Germany two weeks later and addressed the Bundestag, beginning his remarks in Russian and then shifting to "the language of Goethe, of Schiller and of Kant." "Today we must state firmly and finally," he said, "the Cold War is over!" The German chancellor, Gerhard Schröder, reciprocated by declaring that the world should moderate its criticism of Russia's military operations in Chechnya (even as he pressed Putin privately to intervene in the most prominent military trial involving war crimes by Russian soldiers).[23] When Putin returned to Moscow on September 24, he went to the Ministry of Defense, a hulking white building on the Bulvar Ring in the city's center, and ordered the commanders to work with the Americans. He overruled Ivanov, who quietly dropped his public opposition to the American operations in Central Asia.

Putin expected something for his acquiescence to a post–Cold War order. He invested heavily in developing a personal relationship with Bush. Already the first Russian or Soviet leader since Lenin to speak a foreign language, he took lessons in English for an hour a day, learning the language of American diplomacy and commerce, and he used his rudimentary skill to speak privately with Bush and to break the ice. In Slovenia, walking in the garden, he remarked on the commonalities between them. "I see you named your daughters after your mother and your mother-in-law." When Bush replied, "Aren't I a good diplomat?" Putin laughed and said, "I did the same thing!"[24] In private, he felt he could be candid with Bush about their differences, trying to make him understand the difficulties that Russia—that he—faced in the transition from the Soviet ruins. He sought some kind of accommodation with the United States, even with NATO.

When he met Bush again on the sidelines of the Asia-Pacific Economic Cooperation summit in Shanghai in October, Putin proposed changes in the Anti-Ballistic Missile Treaty that would allow some tests of the American missile defense system that Bush coveted but leave the treaty's main provisions in place for another year or two. He considered the treaty critical to Russia's strategic defense, and a delay would give its scientists time to develop new weapons that would counter the American system. He also pressed Bush to agree to lower the number of nuclear weapons each country had, an essential step for Putin in reducing the costs of sustaining Russia's military. He considered his proposal a sensible compromise, and Bush promised to consider it, but his administration was feeling heady following the invasion of Afghanistan. The Pentagon dug in its heels, balking at Putin's proposal that Russia be notified in advance of each and every test and be allowed to monitor the progress of a defense system that, ultimately, could negate Russia's standing as a nuclear superpower. When Putin arrived in Washington in November for his first visit to the United States as president, he still imagined a grand bargain was possible, but any hope of one evaporated when he met Bush in the White House.

"My God," Putin blurted out when he entered the Oval Office on the morning of November 13, the light streaming through the south windows. "This is beautiful." Bush, like his aides, never stopped being confounded by the seeming contradictions contained by "a former KGB agent from the atheist Soviet Union"[25] and never seemed to imagine that perhaps an agent might use them to his advantage. Bush felt certain that they would overcome the differences of the past. The common cause they had forged over the attacks of September 11 bore fruit, in his mind, even as they met: the night before, the Taliban abandoned Afghanistan's capital, Kabul, and retreated in disarray. "This thing just might unravel like a cheap suit," Bush told him. Condoleezza Rice, who speaks Russian, could not be sure of of the exact translation but said Putin roared in approval.[26]

The next day the Putins flew to Bush's ranch in Crawford, Texas. The Bushes greeted them in a pouring rain, with Lyudmila handing Laura Bush a single yellow rose, a symbol of Texas lore. They stayed in the ranch's guesthouse next door to the Bushes, and arrived at dinner an hour early, forgetting the time change from Washington. When dinner finally began, they ate barbecue and listened to the pianist Van Cliburn and a country swing band playing songs like "Cotton-Eyed Joe." Lyudmila wore a dress with red, white, and blue sequins, and when Putin offered a toast, he sounded personally moved. "I've never been to the home of another world leader," he said, adding that the United States was "fortunate at such a critical time in its history to have a man of such character at its helm."[27] The down-home camaraderie continued when they met students at Crawford High School the next day, after which Putin flew to New York and visited the ruins of the World Trade Center, still smoldering two months after the attack.

Then, three weeks later, Bush telephoned Putin in Moscow and informed him he was withdrawing from the ABM treaty despite Putin's objections. The only concession that Putin wrested from him after six months of talks—and four meetings between the two leaders—was the courtesy of a week's advance notice before Bush announced the move publicly in the middle of December.

Throughout the debate over Afghanistan and missile defense, Putin managed to prevent any eruption of nationalist fervor over his quiet accommodation with Bush's actions and policies. Yeltsin had railed against the United States and the West in part to protect his political flanks. Putin instead co-opted those in Russia most critical of America, cementing his dominance of the parliament in the same slow, stealthy, and methodical way that he had done with the military. One of Putin's first legislative initiatives in 2000 had been a restructuring of the Federation Council, then comprising the governors of the country's eighty-nine regions and their representatives who, as they showed in the Skuratov affair, operated independently of the Kremlin. The move, along with the creation of seven regional envoys, faced opposition at first but ultimately succeeded in reining regional leaders under Putin's control. Over time, the upper house that had tormented Yeltsin became a rubber stamp filled with Putin loyalists. In Putin's first years in office, the Kremlin also controlled an unwieldy majority in the Duma; some of his early reforms—especially an effort to allow the privatization of agricultural land—still faced opposition. Putin disdained party politics and legislative jockeying, as he had as Anatoly Sobchak's deputy facing Petersburg's

Putin with his mother, Maria, in July 1958, when he was five.

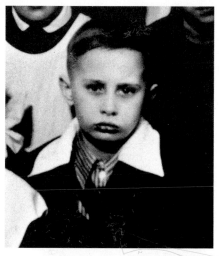

In September 1960, Putin began attending School No. 193 in Leningrad, located a short walk away on the same street where he grew up, Baskov Lane. He was nearly eight, having been held back by his mother.

In elementary school in Leningrad, Putin was an indifferent student—petulant, impulsive, and disruptive in class. One teacher, Vera Gurevich, called him a whirligig because he would walk into class and spin in circles. His studies improved when he took up the martial arts. Putin is in the back row, second from the left.

Putin joined the KGB in 1975 and was assigned to work in Leningrad, first serving in counterintelligence and later joining the First Chief Directorate, which oversaw foreign intelligence.

Putin spent a decade working for the KGB in Leningrad, rising rather slowly through the ranks. In 1985, the KGB sent him to East Germany, where he served in an outpost in Dresden. He appears here in 1980 with his superior in Leningrad, Yuri Leshchev, who was also sent to East Germany, but to the far more important KGB headquarters in East Berlin.

The KGB worked closely with East Germany's notorious secret police, the Stasi. In this photo taken in January 1989, Putin, then a lieutenant colonel, appeared with his colleagues from the Stasi, as well as the Soviet and German militaries at a reception in the 1st Guards Tank Army Museum in Dresden. Putin is second from the left in the first row, standing. In the back row, third from the left, is a Stasi officer who would become a close personal and business friend, Matthias Warnig. Another KGB colleague who would rise with Putin in government and business, Sergei Chemezov, is also in the back row, seventh from the left.

On July 28, 1983, after a prolonged courtship, Putin married Lyudmila Shkrebneva, a stewardess who worked for Aeroflot and lived in Kaliningrad.

Putin's first daughter, Maria, was born in Moscow in 1985. He and Lyudmila are shown here with their friends Sergei and Irina Roldugin.

The Putins' second daughter, Yekaterina, on the left, was born in Dresden in 1986.

After the fall of the Berlin Wall, Putin returned to Leningrad in 1990 and, while still in the KGB, went to work as an adviser to Anatoly Sobchak, one of the leaders of the nascent democratic movement in the Soviet Union. When the Soviet Union collapsed after the abortive putsch in 1991, Sobchak became mayor of the newly renamed St. Petersburg, and Putin became his deputy, overseeing foreign economic affairs.

Aleksandr Litvinenko, a former lieutenant colonel in the KGB and later the FSB, became a whistleblower while Putin was the FSB's director. Litvinenko appeared at a press conference in 1998, along with other agents, some of them disguising themselves with masks and sunglasses, and accused the agency of running rackets and ordering assassinations. Litvinenko ultimately fled to London, where he became a vocal and opportunistic critic of the Kremlin. In November 2006, he was poisoned by a dose of radioactive polonium-210 that investigators would trace back to Russia.

On August 27, 1999, only weeks after Boris Yeltsin appointed him prime minister, Putin flew to the southern republic of Dagestan to award medals to local and national police and military fighters who repulsed an incursion into the republic by Chechnya's separatist rebels. The fighting presaged Russia's second war in Chechnya following the collapse of the Soviet Union.

On December 31, 1999, Boris Yeltsin resigned as president, making his prime minister the acting president until elections were held three months later. Between the two men is Aleksandr Voloshin, Yeltsin's chief of staff, who remained in the post under Putin until a falling-out with the Kremlin in 2003. Moments after this photograph was taken, Yeltsin turned to Putin and said, "Take care of Russia."

Putin and his beloved black Labrador, Koni, during an interview with *The New York Times* in October 2003. Koni often appeared with him even during official meetings at his residence, serving as a humanizing prop or an intimidating one, as Chancellor Angela Merkel of Germany, who is afraid of dogs, learned when Koni circled her during her first meeting with Putin.

In 2003, the Kremlin launched a prosecutorial assault against Yukos Oil Company and its chairman, Mikhail Khodorkovsky, one of the oligarchs who had amassed fortunes in the 1990s. Khodorkovsky was charged with tax evasion, fraud, and embezzlement and convicted in 2005 after a trial that was widely denounced as politically motivated. He was tried and convicted in a second trial in 2010 but then amnestied by Putin at the end of 2013, before the Winter Olympics in Sochi.

Putin focused relentlessly on Russia's natural resources as the means of restoring the country's prosperity and prestige. He installed his close allies, most of them from his years in Petersburg, as chiefs of the most important assets. He shakes hands here with Aleksei Miller, an aide from Sobchak's administration, who became chairman of the state natural gas giant Gazprom. Between them is Igor Sechin, one of Putin's closest aides, who became chairman of the state oil company, Rosneft. Sechin was widely seen as a driving force behind the assault on Yukos.

Putin often disavowed manifestations of a cult of personality, but the Kremlin carefully crafted his image as a Russian Everyman, engaged in various sports or other activities, often outdoors. This photograph was taken by the Kremlin's official photographer during Putin's vacation in Siberia in the summer of 2007. In 2013, Putin's longtime spokesman, Dmitri Peskov, insisted Putin never intentionally posed shirtless.

After months of uncertainty and political paralysis before the end of Putin's second presidential term, Putin anointed his aide, Dmitri Medvedev, as the next president in December 2007. Medvedev, who, like Putin, had never run for office before, in turn appointed Putin as his prime minister. From that post Putin remained the country's paramount leader from 2008 to 2012. In this photograph, Medvedev addressed the nominating convention of the United Russia party at the end of 2007 as Putin listened from the dais.

During Putin's rule, some of his closest friends from Petersburg emerged from the margins of regional business to become the most powerful—and richest—men in Russia. They included Yuri Kovalchuk, Gennady Timchenko, and an old judo sparring partner, Arkady Rotenberg, shown here with Putin at the funeral of their coach from the 1960s, Anatoly Rakhlin.

Aleksei Navalny, a lawyer turned blogger, became famous for his online campaigns against corruption and cronyism in Putin's Russia. In 2011 and 2012, he emerged as a leader of large protests against the parliamentary and presidential elections—and promptly faced criminal prosecution on a variety of charges that were seen as attemtps to silence him. The sticker on his computer with Putin's face says "Thief."

In 2013, Putin and his wife emerged from a ballet at the Kremlin and announced that they would divorce after nearly thirty years of marriage. By Putin's second term as president, Lyudmila had largely retreated from public view.

Rumors swirled around Putin's relationship with Alina Kabayeva, an Olympic rhythmic gymnast who became a member of the State Duma. She is shown here in 2005 receiving a state medal. Although the depth of their relationship remained unclear for years, she was close to Putin's inner circle of friends, ultimately working for the media conglomerate controlled by Yuri Kovalchuk.

After the annexation of Crimea from Ukraine in 2014, Putin's popularity soared to new heights at home, even as he was isolated abroad for having upset the prevailing order that had largely kept peace in Europe after the Cold War. Flags with his image dominated a rally in March 2014 in Red Square, the theme of which was "We are together!"

city council. To him, the political blocs of the legislative branch should be instruments of the Kremlin's executive. He said he had no desire to re-create a single ruling party that would govern Russia as the Communist Party of the Soviet Union had; he intended to create several parties, all effectively reliant on the Kremlin. In July 2001, Putin signed a new election law to reduce the number of parties by requiring memberships of more than fifty thousand, dispersed through at least half of the country. Ostensibly the idea was to create a two-party or three-party system like those in Europe, the only difference being that all the parties would be loyal or at least pliant. Although he professed his commitment to democracy, he had little patience for debates with uncertain outcomes. Unity already shared control of the parliament's committees with the Communists, but to consolidate its power, Putin's aides orchestrated a merger with the party of Primakov and Luzhkov, unveiling it in a new congress on December 1, 2001. The new party was to be called United Russia, an organization filled with the officials and bureaucrats of Putin's "party of power."

The mastermind of the Kremlin's political strategy was Vladislav Surkov, a Chechen-born advertising genius with a background in military intelligence who in the 1990s had worked for the banks of three of Russia's oligarchs, including Mikhail Khodorkovsky. He joined Aleksandr Voloshin's staff while Yeltsin was still president, and more than anyone else he helped craft Putin's public image and engineered his political strategies. He was youthful and deeply cynical, a fan of American rap music—he kept a picture of Tupac Shakur next to one of Putin—and Shakespeare, whose work he considered a font of political inspiration. As a Russian novelist and activist, Eduard Limonov, once said, Surkov had "turned Russia into a wonderful postmodernist theater, where he experiments with old and new political models."[28]

In April 2002, Surkov overturned the Duma's leadership in what became known as the "portfolio putsch." The Kremlin's allies ousted the Communists from the committee posts that Putin had offered them shortly after the elections in 1999, while the Communist speaker, Gennady Seleznyov, threw his support to the Kremlin and abandoned his party colleagues. Putin, as aloof as a tsar from the petty squabbles of the dukes and boyars, had effectively decapitated the Communist leadership. Gennady Zyuganov, the party's chief, who had once seemed a serious threat to Yeltsin's Kremlin, could only sputter in protest. "Even when tipsy, Yeltsin had the courage to gather leaders of different factions in critical moments and look for a solution together, rather than starting a new war," he said bitterly.[29]

The motive for Putin's reshuffling of the legislative leadership became clear two weeks later when he delivered his annual address to the Federal Assembly, which comprised the upper and lower houses of parliament. In the Marble Hall of the Kremlin Presidium, Putin touted his accomplishments—a drop in unemployment, rising incomes, a balanced budget, Russia's return to its position as the world's second-largest oil producer—but he lamented the "large and clumsy" bureaucracy of the government, the unreformed ministries that still acted as "branches of a centralized economy." He needed a parliamentary majority not to debate the issues but to pass the legislation the Kremlin needed to impose solutions. And for an hour, he listed a host of liberal reforms intended to transform the judiciary, to create a mortgage system to expand the housing market, to end the draft and introduce a professional volunteer military, and to write regulations that would hasten Russia's membership in the World Trade Organization. It was an ambitious agenda, and he now had few obstacles to imposing it.

In his speech, Putin devoted barely a minute to the war that he had ridden to power, in part because it was no longer the triumph he had promised. In 2001, Putin announced that the withdrawal of the Russian military from Chechnya would soon begin, but the war was far from over. Federal forces controlled the republic's borders and most of its cities and villages, but only during the day. Attacks from the rebels continued to kill Russian troops, who retaliated with sweeps of villages that resulted in arrests, torture, and death.[30] Although the Kremlin had installed a former rebel commander and imam, Akhmad Kadyrov, as the republic's loyalist leader, the military and the FSB could not crush the insurgency. Its leaders remained at large, hiding in the mountains along the border or in villages that remained committed to Chechen independence.

The initial popularity of the war had faded; polls showed that most Russians no longer believed it was winnable. Chechnya threatened to become a quagmire that most felt should be resolved through peace talks. The mounting casualties threatened not only Putin's strategy but his presidency. The war remained a personal crusade for Putin, and the official propaganda was so successful that he "began to believe the sterilized versions of events, falling victim to his own spin."[31] It was only when disaster struck on an enormous scale that the Kremlin's propaganda could not conceal the devastation and Putin glimpsed the shortcomings of the strategy he had launched and the security bureaucracies he had enlisted to carry them out.

On August 19, an Mi-26 helicopter approached the main Russian military base in Chechnya, the sprawling airfield at Khankala, just outside Grozny. The helicopter, the world's largest, was designed to carry tons of equipment and as many as eighty passengers and crew, but by 1997, the Ministry of Defense had banned its use to ferry passengers, restricting it to cargo. On this day, there were 147 people onboard, soldiers and civilians, including the wives of several officers and at least one young boy, the son of an army nurse, who had hitched a ride. As the helicopter descended, a missile struck its starboard engine. The helicopter landed a thousand feet short of its landing pad—right in the middle of a minefield intended to protect the base's perimeter. Loaded with fuel for its return trip, it burst into flames. Most of the passengers who survived the crash landing were trapped inside the burning cabin; those who made it out tripped mines as they fled. The military, reflexively, lied about the cause and the casualties, which ultimately reached 127, including the boy and his mother. It was the worst helicopter disaster in history, and the single biggest loss of life in the war, a military catastrophe more deadly than the *Kursk*.

Putin, having learned the hard political lesson of the *Kursk,* immediately acknowledged the crash and promised an investigation with Sergei Ivanov in charge of it. Ivanov flew the next day to Khankala and relieved the commander of the army's aviation wing, Colonel General Vitaly Pavlov, who protested that he was being scapegoated. Pavlov complained about the maintenance of the helicopter fleet and said the order banning passenger transit applied to peace time, while the country remained at war. "If there is no fighting, why are our troops dying at the hands of militants?"[32]

Putin's frustration with his commanders flared. Two days after the crash, he met in front of television cameras with Sergei Ivanov in the VIP hall of an airport outside Moscow. Aside from his major addresses and press conferences, the televised tête-à-tête became Putin's signature means of communicating, a scripted setting in which he was the unquestioned leader praising, encouraging, or hectoring his subordinates, even a friend as close as Ivanov. "How could it happen that despite a defense minister's order banning the use of helicopters of this type from carrying people, people were still being carried?"[33] Putin demanded to know.

"There is no justification, Vladimir Vladimirovich," Ivanov replied, playing his part in the public censure. Two weeks later, he forced General Pavlov to submit his resignation and reprimanded nineteen other commanders, including twelve generals. The one thing Putin never considered in the wake of the disaster was any change in the war's strategy.

Although intermediaries had floated proposals for peace talks earlier in the year, Putin continued to rule them out. The only thing Putin would accept from Chechnya's rebels was unconditional surrender. The rebels' response came shortly thereafter in a videotape that showed a shoulder-fired missile downing the helicopter. Despite rumors of his death, the narrator was Aslan Maskhadov, surrounded by bearded men he referred to as "our mujahedin." He sat in front of Chechnya's green flag, which no longer bore a wolf, the symbol of the independence struggle for more than a decade. It had been replaced by a sword and a Koranic verse.[34]

We came to the capital of Russia to stop the war," a young man said, speaking thickly and slowly into a camera as he sat cross-legged in front of an open laptop, "or to die here for Allah."[35] The man speaking was Movsar Barayev, a rebel fighter and nephew of one of Chechnya's most ferocious commanders, Arbi Barayev. Russia's military command in the Northern Caucasus had triumphantly announced two weeks earlier that Movsar Barayev had been killed on October 10, 2002, ignoring the fact that his death had already been announced a year before that.[36] Now Barayev was in Moscow, barely three and a half miles from the Kremlin, where Putin, as was his custom, was working late in his office. Putin would not leave for the next three days.[37]

Barayev, three days shy of his twenty-third birthday, was the public face of a "special detachment" of fighters, twenty-two men and nineteen women, who had arrived in Moscow a month earlier, traveling individually or in pairs on trains and buses from Dagestan to avoid the scrutiny of police wary of travelers from the Caucasus. They came on the orders, he said, of Chechnya's "supreme military emir," Shamil Basayev, though they professed grudging loyalty to its putative president, Aslan Maskhadov. They spent weeks in Moscow preparing for an assault that would bring the bloody, brutal war to the capital. They wanted a public place that would ensure a mass hostage taking of ordinary Russians. They considered the parliament, but settled on a theater.

The one they chose was on Dubrovka Street in southwest Moscow, a hall still known by its Soviet name, the Palace of Culture for the State Ball-Bearing Factory No. 1. A part of the building housed a gay club— "frequented by members of parliament, prominent businessmen, and politicians," it was said—that was undergoing renovation. The fighters of Barayev's group disguised themselves as construction workers and made plans to storm the theater.[38] The theater was showing Russia's first Broadway-style musical: *Nord Ost,* based on a popular Soviet novel, *The Two Captains,* by Veniamin Kaverin. The story was a romantic melo-drama, spanning the first half of the twentieth century, the exploration of the Arctic, and the siege of Leningrad in the Great Patriotic War. The musical's creator, Georgy Vasiliyev, spent $4 million to produce it and promote it on billboards ubiquitously plastered across the city. He calcu-lated that Russia's new middle class—the beneficiaries of the economic boom that Putin was riding to popularity—had grown prosperous enough to afford the $15 ticket price. On the night of its 323rd perfor-mance, October 23, 2002, the Chechens moved in just as the second act began. The actors, dressed as pilots in vintage uniforms of the Red Army air force, were tap-dancing across the stage when a masked man in camouflage entered from stage left. The closest actor jolted in shock, but most of the audience thought it was a part of the performance—until the gunman fired his AK-47 into the roof and more camouflaged men joined him on the stage.[39] Barayev's fighters sealed off the main hall and wired explosives to columns supporting the theater's balcony. The women, dressed in black hijabs with Arabic inscriptions, took up posi-tions among the audience. They carried pistols and wore belts of what appeared to be explosives, which they threatened to detonate if anyone resisted or the authorities dared to storm the building. The women, as young as nineteen, became known as "black widows," the wives, daugh-ters, and sisters of Chechen fighters who had died in the war. In all the years of fighting in Chechnya, suicide bombings had been rare, and the women proved to be a terrifying portent of the turn the war in Chech-nya was taking. "We are on Allah's path," one of them declared. "If we die here, that won't be the end of it. There are many of us, and it will go on."[40] There were 912 people inside, including the cast and crew and foreigners from Europe and the United States. The siege unfolded over the next two days in a surreal, televised spectacle. Barayev told the cap-tives they could use their phones to call their loved ones and tell them that they would die if the authorities did not end the war in Chechnya.

Now Putin was besieged, too. He had vowed to wipe out Chechnya's bandits, but the war had ground on for three years, devouring Russian soldiers and thousands of Chechens. He had lost the popular support for the war he cultivated at the outset. The military had failed to subdue the insurgency. And now the FSB had failed spectacularly to stop a terrorist raid in the heart of Moscow. Putin canceled plans to travel to Germany, Portugal, and then to Mexico, where he was to meet George Bush again. Meeting the director of the FSB, Nikolai Patrushev, he ordered preparations for an assault on the theater, authorizing negotiations only if it would buy time. The FSB dispatched three teams of commandos to the scene. Only his prime minister, Mikhail Kasyanov, protested that a rescue could result in hundreds of deaths. Putin sent him in his place to the international gathering in Mexico, apparently to get him out of the way.[41]

Several prominent politicians, journalists, and officials, including the Chechen representative in the Duma, Aslambek Aslakhanov, telephoned the captors inside and eventually were allowed in to negotiate with them. Thirty-nine of the hostages were soon released, most of them young children. Grigory Yavlinsky, whose party, Yabloko, was sharply critical of the war, entered the theater that night after seeking approval from the Kremlin, which seemed unable to control the intermediaries going in and out, or the phone calls and later the video of the terrorists' demands. He was struck by how "very, very young" the fighters were; they would have been merely children when the Soviet Union collapsed and Chechnya declared independence in 1991.[42] He doubted they had ever gone to school. All they knew they had learned on the battlefields of the Caucasus. They could barely articulate their demands, let alone negotiate. When they demanded an end to the war, Yavlinsky asked, "What does this mean?" He left frustrated, but hopeful that incremental steps, including the release of more hostages, could at least minimize the casualties. Yavlinsky returned to Putin's office in the Kremlin and took part in a series of meetings with him on the progress of the negotiations. And yet it became clear to him that Putin also presided over a separate set of meetings, with Patrushev and other security officials, and people like him were not invited to attend.

On the second day of the siege, conditions in the hall became dire with the hostages succumbing to hunger, dehydration, exhaustion, and fear. The terrorists shot several people, including a woman who inexplicably ran into the building and an FSB commando who had approached from a patio outside. Even so, intermediaries continued to enter the theater, including Anna Politkovskaya, a journalist whose scathing reports from Chechnya had defied and infuriated the military and the Kremlin. She and a prominent physician, Leonid Roshal, managed to persuade a fighter who called himself Abu Bakar to allow her to return with boxes of juice for the hostages. Politkovskaya, born in New York to Soviet diplomats posted at the United Nations, was one of the most courageous Russian journalists who covered the war, and by then she had become an eloquent, impassioned critic of it. Her reports sympathized with all who suffered—Russia's conscripts, the rebels, and the civilians caught in between—but she loathed the military's inept and inhumane commanders and most of all the commander in chief who in her mind had orchestrated the entire catastrophe in the Caucasus. Her encounter with Abu Bakar made her legs "turn to jelly," but she persuaded him to let her meet two of the hostages. One, a journalist named Anna Adrianova, spoke of despair. "We are a second *Kursk*," she said.[43]

More releases seemed imminent. An American hostage, Sandy Booker, was allowed to telephone the American embassy. He told a diplomat there that Barayev had agreed to release the foreigners the next morning.[44] The Kremlin announced that it had summoned Putin's special envoy in the southern region, Viktor Kazantsev. The rebels believed that he would arrive at ten the next day, but he never boarded a plane to Moscow.

The storming of the theater began, on Putin's orders, shortly after five o'clock in the morning. The terrorists appeared to have relaxed, anticipating more negotiations the next day. Russian commandos had already infiltrated the building through the gay club, and inserted listening devices to learn the position of the terrorists. Fearing explosions that could destroy the building, they were to kill the terrorists, not capture them.[45] An odorless gas began to seep into the main hall, released through the building's ventilation system. It was an aerosolized derivative of a powerful anesthetic, fentanyl, developed by an FSB laboratory. The release of the gas caused confusion among the captors and hostages. Anna Adrianova, the hostage Politkovskaya had met, telephoned the radio station Ekho Moskvy and said that the terrorists seemed uncertain but not ready to execute them. "Can you hear us?" she said after shots rang out. "We're all going to be blown to hell."[46] Mysteriously, they were not. The gas put most of the hostages to sleep, while the commandos fought gun battles with terrorists who were not in the main hall or were otherwise unaffected by the gas. The fighting lasted more than an hour before Barayev was cornered on a second-floor landing behind the balcony. All forty-one captors died, most from bullets to the head.

The rescue seemed to be an unmitigated victory—except that the men who planned and carried out the raid had not given thought to the effect the gas would have on the weakened hostages. The succcessful raid turned into disaster. The first unconscious victims were brought out at seven o'clock and laid in rows on the theater's front steps, followed by more and still more. Some had already died, but many more were merely unconscious, left amid the growing piles of corpses. Rescue teams were overwhelmed. They were prepared to treat wounds from bullets or bomb fragments, not people choking on swollen tongues. The authorities had prescribed an antidote to counteract the effects of the gas, but there were not enough doses available. And neither the paramedics on the scene nor the doctors in the hospitals knew how much to administer. In the end 130 hostages died during the siege, only five of them from gunshot wounds. Of the latter, only two were hostages inside the theater. The other three were the woman who had burst into the theater the first day and two other men who were shot as they approached or entered the building during the siege.[47] A doctor who participated in the rescue described the confusion and chaos. "It wasn't an evil plot," he said. "It was just a Soviet mess."

Putin delivered a televised statement that night. He had appeared sparingly during the siege, shown only in brief clips of his meeting with his security advisers, members of parliament, and Muslim leaders. He was grave, steely-eyed, and seething with coarse fury, referring to the terrorists as "armed scum." He said he had hoped for the release of the hostages but had prepared for the worst. "An almost impossible thing was accomplished," he went on. "The lives of hundreds upon hundreds of people were saved. We proved that Russia cannot be brought to its knees." In Putin's mind, the rescue had been a victory, though he acknowledged it was a painful one.

"We were unable to save everyone," he said, before the authorities had disclosed the horrible toll. "Please forgive us."

The horrific siege hardened Putin's views that Russia faced an existential threat. The rebels fighting on the country's flank would, with international support, tear the country apart, and the only answer was to destroy them. Aslan Maskhadov, through a representative at a gathering of Chechens in Copenhagen, denounced the attack and offered to enter peace talks without any conditions, but the Kremlin refused. Instead Russia's prosecutors issued an international arrest warrant for Maskhadov's representative, an actor turned activist, Ahkmed Zakayev, who had been at the conference. Denmark arrested him, but refused to extradite him a month later, saying the Russians had fabricated the evidence implicating him in the siege. In Putin's mind the West was now harboring the avowed enemies of Russia.

A week after it ended, Shamil Basayev claimed responsibility for the siege, saying he wanted to give Russians "a firsthand insight into all the charms of the war unleashed" by the Kremlin. Instead of seeking to exploit the apparent rift between Basayev and Maskhadov, Putin refused even to consider the possibility of peace talks now. Some believed that might have been the point of the siege all along. A new round of conspiracy theories arose that Putin's cadre had either orchestrated or done nothing to prevent the siege, exploiting it as they had the apartment bombings three years earlier in order to undercut those calling for a negotiated truce. The FSB's opacity deepened the suspicion. Officials refused to discuss how forty-one fighters with arms and explosives managed to slip into the capital undetected. They refused to divulge the formula for the gas used to anesthetize those inside the theater. The Duma, under pressure from Putin, refused to authorize an investigation, leaving many of the mysteries forever unsolved. When survivors of the siege sought compensation through the courts, they faced harassment from the authorities and defeat after defeat until they won a measure of justice more than nine years later.[48]

The doubts—even the questions—infuriated Putin. The next month, after a meeting in Brussels with the European Union, a reporter for *Le Monde* asked him whether the use of land mines in Chechnya killed innocent civilians in addition to the terrorists they were intended to kill. Putin bristled visibly, arguing that Islamic radicals wanted to win Chechnya as part of a worldwide jihad targeting Russia, the United States, and its allies. "If you are a Christian, you are in danger," he replied, his indignation rising uncontrollably. "If you decide to become a Muslim, this won't save you either, because they think that traditional Islam is also

hostile to their goals." He went on, his language so crude that the inter-
preters did not bother to translate. "If you are determined to become a
complete Islamic radical and are ready to undergo circumcision, then
I invite you to Moscow. We are a multiconfessional nation. We have
experts in this sphere as well. I will recommend the operation be conducted so that nothing on you will grow again."[49]

CHAPTER 13

The Gods Slept on Their Heads

On February 19, 2003, Putin held another of his periodic meetings in the Kremlin with Russia's bankers, industrialists, and oil men: the oligarchs who so dominated the post-Soviet era. In their first meeting in 2000, Putin had come to terms with most of them—Gusinsky and Berezovsky notwithstanding—in an informal pact: they could keep their wealth as long as they stayed out of the affairs of the state. He would not reverse the controversial privatizations of the 1990s, leaving the oligarchs their prizes, as long as they ended their reckless, often bloody battles for still greater riches in deference to the Kremlin. "What then should be the relationship with the so-called oligarchs? The same as with anyone else. The same as with an owner of a small bakery or a shoe-repair shop," he wrote in his open letter to voters in *Izvestia* during his campaign.[1] When Putin came to power, journalists and political observers accustomed to the Kremlinology of the 1990s had looked for evidence of the influence of the oligarchs, misunderstanding that they would no longer be pulling the strings. Vladimir Gusinsky had fled the country. So had Boris Berezovsky, who presumptuously declared himself the leader of the opposition in exile. The rest adapted to the Putin era.

The agreement in 2000 was a negotiated truce; by and large both sides abided by its terms. Contrary to the popular perception, Putin did not insist that the oligarchs stay out of politics altogether—some, like Roman Abramovich, held elected office—but rather that they do nothing to oppose the Kremlin. The tycoons, in turn, agreed to pay taxes and avoid public disputes with Putin over policies that might affect their fortunes. They also dutifully joined the Russian Union of Industrialists and Entrepreneurs, which became the institutionalized forum for discussing issues facing Russia's economy. Their subsequent meetings with Putin had been low-key, devoted to taxes and legal reforms, the prospects for joining the World Trade Organization, and the fate of the struggling automotive industry.

Now, in 2003, two dozen of the country's richest men—their collective worth greater than many countries' entire economies—gathered again to discuss something far more sensitive, the intersection of business and government, that shadowy nexus where corruption flourished. In the Kremlin's Catherine Hall, an oval chamber of pale blue and gold decorated with allegorical sculptures called "Russia" and "Justice," Putin opened the meeting with an outline of his proposals for administrative reforms, which he had promised when they met the year before. "We spoke about random interpretation of law by some agencies, the arbitrary actions of bureaucrats and so on," Putin told them in the clipped managerial tone he used for his televised appearances. "In this connection the question of corruption and its tenacity in the country was repeatedly raised," he said, sounding like the reformer he had promised to be when he took office. "It is obvious that corruption cannot be eradicated only by punitive measures. Far more can be achieved by creating conditions in the market in which it would be easier to obey the rules than to break them."

The tycoons had agreed in advance on an agenda to present to Putin, and they expected it to be a fraught encounter. Aleksei Mordashov of Severstal, a steel and mining company, spoke first, reporting on the administrative obstacles to the development of small and medium-sized business. The second speaker was Mikhail Khodorkovsky. Only thirty-nine, he headed a banking and oil empire that included Yukos Oil, which he had acquired through a privatization deal as murky as most in the 1990s. He had been a member of Komsomol as a student in Soviet times, but he was too young to have experienced working in the Soviet system and "had never learned to fear it."[2] Khodorkovsky was an intense man with cropped, already graying hair. He was less flamboyant than other oligarchs of the 1990s who flouted the rules and flaunted their influence, though no less powerful. Having abandoned the shaggy style and mustache he preferred as a young man, he fashioned himself as a corporate ascetic, a Russian Bill Gates. He wore rimless glasses and preferred turtleneck sweaters over suits. He turned to foreigners, especially Americans, to provide expertise in oil extraction and to make Yukos a model of a modern, transparent international corporation. As a businessman he was ambitious—many thought ruthlessly so—but by the time of Putin's ascent his ambitions had moved beyond the mere accumulation of wealth. Like the robber barons of America in the Gilded Age, he turned to philanthropy to burnish his image, donating money for scholarships and assistance for disaster victims. In 2001 he created an organization called Open Russia, modeled on George Soros's Open Society Institute, to support community development, health and social welfare, and small business. Although many viewed him cynically, he imagined that he could create the kind of society that Komsomol never did in Soviet times: open, educated, freely swimming in the free market, and increasingly connected to the entire world.

Khodorkovsky did not know Putin well—they met only after the latter had become prime minister—and he had some doubts about him as Yeltsin's replacement. Still, he wanted to help Putin strengthen the legal foundations for modern capitalism. He believed in Putin's democratic instincts, though his first impression of Putin was of "an ordinary, normal person" whose upbringing in the courtyard in Leningrad and in the KGB left an indelible impression on him: he believed no one except "his own," meaning his people.[3] By the time of the meeting in 2003, Khodorkovsky had become Russia's richest man, and Putin had become its most powerful. A clash was probably inevitable, but on that winter day, no one saw it coming.

Beneath the dome of Catherine Hall, infused with the wan light of winter, Khodorkovsky delivered a speech on behalf of the industrialists' union, which another tycoon, Mikhail Fridman, was supposed to give, but refused. He read from a PowerPoint presentation with a searing title, "Corruption in Russia: A Brake on Economic Growth." Khodorkovsky did not appear overly confident. He looked "extremely nervous, pale," and his voice broke at times, as if the import of the words seized his throat.[4] He cited opinion polls and government statistics showing that corruption permeated the country, accounting for as much as $30 billion a year, roughly a quarter of the state's budget. Russians feared going to court because of the bribes required, he said, while young students rushed to the institutes that trained tax inspectors and civil servants—and paid bribes to get in—because a career in government was the surest way to enrich themselves in the same way. Putin interjected that his damnation of civil servants was too sweeping, but Khodorkovsky carried on, this time turning to the state's struggling oil company, Rosneft, whose president and chairman of the board were also in the room. He questioned its purchase of Northern Oil, a small producer on the edge of the Arctic, for a staggering sum of $600 million, far more than analysts and other companies, including his own, had estimated it was worth. He suggested that the overpayment amounted to little more than a kickback to Rosneft's executives—that is, to officials of Putin's government.

Khodorkovsky had gone too far. Putin's temper flashed. "Putin was not ready for this remark and simply blew up," his prime minister, Mikhail Kasyanov, recalled later. "And everything he said—it was not a prepared answer, but a pure emotional reaction."[5] In a cutting tone, Putin replied that Rosneft needed new reserves like any other company. Anyway, Yukos had "excessive reserves."

"How did it obtain them?" he pointedly asked. He also noted that Yukos had had tax problems in its checkered past and had worked with the government to resolve them, "but how did they arise in the first place?

"Maybe that's why there are five applications for every vacancy at the Tax Academy," he said. A smirk appeared on Putin's face, a reflection of satisfaction and confidence that he had shamed Khodorkovsky back into his place.

"I'm returning the hockey puck to you."

Those in attendance were surprised by the visceral, personal emotion that erupted over a relatively small sale that was of no real consequence for a company as large as Yukos or for the government itself. Another of Putin's economic advisers at the meeting, Andrei Illarionov, had never seen Putin so angry before. Illarionov himself was surprised by Khodorkovsky's accusation. He had assumed the inflated price of Northern Oil was a mistake or a bad investment. Maybe it even involved bribes and kickbacks, but what major contract in Russia did not?[6]

Putin's fierce defense of Rosneft made clear what some in the room had not yet discerned. Rosneft had more than Putin's blessing. It had a personal connection to him. Khodorkovsky did what no one had dared to do before, certainly not in remarks during a televised meeting in the Kremlin. "He didn't know," Illarionov said of Khodorkovsky. "That is the only reason why he started talking about that. He didn't think that Putin was involved. Otherwise he would never have said anything."[7] Khodorkovsky failed to appreciate the risk he took in criticizing the obscure purchase, but the consequences soon became evident to all. "It was clear to me that we had signed our own death warrants," Aleksei Kondaurov, one of Yukos Oil's executives, said afterward.[8] Khodorkovsky himself was advised to leave the country, as Gusinsky and Berezovsky had, but

he refused, believing that his power, his finances, his influence, and ultimately the truth would protect him.

"What did I say that was wrong?" he asked.[9]

What he had done was expose a strategy of Putin's whose roots reached
back to Petersburg more than a decade before, when Putin forged
his bonds with the cadre of aides and businessmen concentrated around
the Mining Institute where he had defended his thesis. By the middle
of the 1990s, Putin was meeting regularly for informal discussions on
the country's natural resources under the aegis of the institute's director, Vladimir Litvinenko, who had presided over Putin's dissertation.[10]
The ideas that Putin and his friends, Igor Sechin and Viktor Zubkov,
formulated in their discussions and academic work became the basis for
a strategy of restoring the state's command over Russia's vast oil and
gas resources. Litvinenko, a respected geologist, advocated greater state
control as a means not to revive its beleaguered economy but to restore
Russia's status as a superpower. "They're the main instrument in our
hands—particularly Putin's—and our strongest argument in geopolitics," he declared.[11]

Putin's strategy for extending the state's control over natural resources
had been judicious and incremental, carefully maintaining a balance
between the liberals and the hardliners in his own inner circle. In 2001, he
appointed another Petersburg aide, Aleksei Miller, as the chief executive
of Gazprom, the state enterprise that had never been officially privatized
though its shares had increasingly been acquired by its senior executives, leaving the state with only 38 percent ownership. He gave Miller,
only thirty-nine, "an absolute mandate for change," which over the next
two years meant bringing the vast company—and its shares—back into
the hands of the Kremlin.[12] He also reasserted the state's control over
Rosneft, the company Khodorkovsky was now accusing of corruption.
Created as a state company in 1992, Rosneft barely survived the 1990s,
when its best assets were raided by rivals, speculators, and gangsters.[13] It
had failed to sell at auction in 1998, when Yeltsin's Russia was desperate for cash, because it had already been thoroughly plundered. When
Putin arrived in the Kremlin, he threw his support behind the company
and set out to rebuild it. A driving force behind the effort—then not yet
public—was Igor Sechin, the man who used to carry Putin's bags and
greet his visitors at the mayor's office in Petersburg.

From the start, Putin toggled between liberalism and statism, between the reformers on one hand and the hardliners on the other. The team he trusted—almost all of whom were from Petersburg—contained both. They included economists and academics who pushed to open its markets and the *siloviki* who, like Sechin, came from the security services or judiciary and who favored strengthening the state's grip on society, business, and politics. Throughout his presidency, journalists and analysts parsed Putin's decisions to gauge the waxing or waning influence of either faction. In practice, the boundaries were never so rigid,[14] and while rivalries surfaced at times in public disagreements, these were rare. Three years into his presidency, Putin's inner circle remained remarkably united behind him and behind a unifying goal of resuscitating a greater degree of political control over the economy. Behind the scenes, though, the advisers had begun to struggle for power, and profits, requiring Putin's constant intervention and mediation.

The men whom Putin brought with him to the heights of power had been on the periphery of the profit-making of Yeltsin's era. Some had done well enough, but none had become billionaires, few even millionaires. They resented those who had not only amassed fortunes but also dictated policy. Yeltsin had tolerated—even encouraged and exploited—the headlong rush to capitalism as a necessary medicine to rid the body of the illness of Communism. Putin's aides more or less agreed on their boss's strategy to bring order to the market, even to increase state control over strategic natural resources like oil and gas. The confrontation with Khodorkovsky, though, revealed another motive that drove them. Sechin and others within Putin's circle "had missed out on the first post-Soviet division of assets in the 1990s and were determined not to miss a second one."[15]

The meeting in Catherine Hall was overshadowed by events in the world, especially the looming invasion of Iraq. Putin opposed the American-led war, despite President Bush's strenuous efforts to persuade his new friend to support the overthrow of the dictator Saddam Hussein (which, not incidentally, Khodorkovsky supported). Russia's deep ties in Iraq dated to the Soviet Union's cultivation of the Arab world and survived the Soviet collapse and the first Gulf War of 1991. Russia continued to purchase much of Iraq's oil exports as allowed under the United Nations "oil for food" program developed in the 1990s to ease the suffering of ordinary Iraqis—with profits and kickbacks amounting to millions going to Russian businessmen and politicians, including Vladimir Zhirinovsky; Putin's chief of staff, Aleksandr Voloshin; and a little-known oil trading company, Gunvor, whose owner Putin knew from the earliest contracts he had authorized in the winter of 1991.[16] Charles Duelfer, one of the United Nations inspectors, was convinced the deals implicated the highest levels of Putin's government, though the Americans decided against accusing Putin directly for diplomatic reasons.[17] Russia's oil companies, both private and state-owned, also had stakes in Iraq's undeveloped oil fields, including a deal worth $20 billion for a vast field in the southern desert. The deals remained frozen as long as the sanctions remained in place, but the overthrow of Saddam Hussein's government threatened to make them all worthless. "Vladimir Putin didn't consider Saddam a threat," Bush later wrote. "It seemed to me that part of the reason was Putin didn't want to jeopardize Russia's lucrative oil contracts."[18]

Putin tried to mediate, dispatching Yevgeny Primakov on a secret mission to persuade Saddam Hussein to resign. Primakov, the veteran diplomat and spy who had been Gorbachev's envoy to Iraq during the 1991 war, delivered Putin's personal appeal during a late-night meeting in one of the dictator's palaces in Baghdad. Hussein listened calmly at first, but then summoned his senior aides and in front of them denounced Putin's accommodation with Bush. "Russia has turned into a shadow of the United States," he told Primakov.[19]

With American troops already massing in Kuwait, Putin figured that he could do nothing more to stop the war, but despite Bush's endeavors to persuade him otherwise, he would do nothing to support it either. Only days before his meeting with the tycoons, he flew to Paris and joined President Jacques Chirac and later Chancellor Gerhard Schröder in publicly calling for the United Nations to intervene and stop the U.S. invasion. "There is an alternative to war," their joint declaration said. "The use of force can only be considered as a last resort."

For two years Putin had sought a new relationship with the United States through his friendship with Bush, but Russia had received little return on the investment. Chirac, who had personally greeted him at the airport in Paris, had as much to offer Russia and tended not to muddy cordial relations with criticism of rights abuses in Chechnya or elsewhere. Putin did not break with Bush outright, but Iraq was a turning point. To him, the war revealed the true ambitions of the United States. In his view, it wanted to dictate its terms to the rest of the world,

to champion "freedom" and use unilateral means to impose it, to interfere in the internal affairs of other nations. When Russia wanted to
build civilian nuclear reactors in Iran—a deal worth billions for Russia's
nuclear industry—the United States furiously fought to block it. Bush
pledged friendship and cooperation, but Putin also heard the voices of
others in Washington, liberals and conservatives, who criticized Russia
and seemed intent on keeping it in its weakened post-Soviet state. On
the fourth day of the war, the two men spoke. Putin made a point of
reaching out on a personal level. He did not reiterate his opposition or
even mention it. Putin, Bush thought, was simply worried about the toll
ordering a war would take.

"This is going to be awfully difficult for you," Putin told Bush. "I feel
bad for you. I feel bad."

"Why?" Bush replied.

"Because there's going to be enormous human suffering," he
told him.[20]

Bush appreciated Putin's remarks, all the more so because it was the
only conversation like it that he had with any world leader. He then took
the opportunity to berate Putin, warning him that Russian companies
continued to provide weaponry to Saddam Hussein's forces, including
night vision goggles, anti-tank missiles, and devices to scramble the navi-
gation systems of the American missiles and bombs then raining down
on Iraq.[21]

After the fall of Saddam Hussein, Putin made an effort to move past
his differences with the United States over Iraq, but he also began to
look increasingly askance at what he considered American hegemony. If
American military might was not explicitly directed at Russia's interests,
its "soft power" was—the money and influence that the United States
spent on assistance inside Russia, millions of dollars that had flowed after
the collapse of the Soviet Union to support civic organizations involved
in everything from health care to the environment. As the buildup to the
war intensified, Russia ended the work of the Peace Corps in the country and stripped the license of Radio Free Europe, calling both relics of
the Cold War. It expelled an AFL-CIO union organizer and ended the
mandate of the Organization for Security and Co-operation in Europe's
mission to observe the fighting in Chechnya.[22] Each step happened in
isolation, with lengthy, legalistic explanations, but a strategy emerged
out of the pattern. Putin began to see American conspiracies to isolate or

to weaken Russia, aided by a fifth column within that was increasingly in his mind the greatest threat to the state he was creating.

When Khodorkovsky began negotiations with two American oil giants, Chevron and Exxon, to sell a stake in Yukos or even arrange a merger with them, Putin at first welcomed the talks as international validation of Russia's growing investment potential, but when Khodorkovsky traveled to the United States and made pronouncements on Russia's foreign and economic policy, Putin began to fear that the Americans were seeking to dominate the country's national treasure as well. And, he thought, Khodorkovsky seemed a willing party to the takeover.

The confrontation in the Kremlin in February had not tempered Khodorkovsky's economic and political ambitions. In April, Yukos negotiated a merger with Russia's fifth largest oil producer, Sibneft, creating one of the largest oil companies in the world, with an output greater than Kuwait's. Sibneft's chairman was the youthful governor of the remote Arctic region of Chukotka, Roman Abramovich, the erstwhile partner of an embittered Boris Berezovsky, who the same year had used much of his fortune to purchase the Chelsea football club in England, spearheading the influx of Russia's new riches into the capitals of the West. The merger made Khodorkovsky an international celebrity; it was described as "a coming of age for Russian capitalism."[23] A week later Khodorkovsky and other executives met with Putin at his residence at Novo-Ogaryovo, even as he pursued negotiations with the American companies about expanding even more. Putin blessed the merger and told him to report back to him as the details took shape over the coming months. Putin did have other issues he wanted to raise with Khodorkovsky, but he asked to do so privately, after the public meeting had ended.

Putin's reelection was a year away, and while his own reelection seemed beyond doubt, he worried about the parliamentary elections that would take place in December 2003. Khodorkovsky, like many tycoons, had been pouring money into the parties in the Duma without regard to political ideology and with the Kremlin's approval; he financed the liberals, Yabloko and the Union of Right Forces, but also Putin's party, United Russia, and the Communists. The intimacy between business and politics was such that Khodorkovsky's own managers and executives served in the Duma, notably Vladimir Dubov, who was simultaneously an executive of Menatep, the bank that had made Khodorkovsky rich, and chairman of the Duma's tax subcommittee. Khodorkovsky used his influence to lobby against legislation that would hurt Yukos, at times brazenly. Now Putin wanted to rein in Khodorkovsky.

"Stop financing the Communists," he told him when they met privately. Khodorkovsky was taken aback; only months before, Putin's political mastermind, Vladislav Surkov, had given his blessing to the money Yukos was contributing to them. He did not argue, though. He did what Putin asked, but some of the candidates Yukos was bankrolling were also its own executives. The chairman of the company's Moscow subsidiary, Aleksei Kondaurov, even ran as a Communist. ("Today's Communist Party does not reject private property," he once said.) Khodorkovsky tried to explain to Putin that he could not stop other executives from running or supporting political parties, but Putin did not see the distinction.

Putin's concerns about the Communists betrayed a worry inside the Kremlin. Despite his popularity, his political program had lost momentum as the parliamentary elections of 2003 approached. The war in Chechnya, now nearly four years old, had become a quagmire, despite a referendum and an election that installed a loyal official, Akhmad Kadyrov, as the president of what was once again a constituent part of the Russian Federation. The harsh crackdown that followed the *Nord-Ost* siege did not end the terrorist attacks but intensified radicalization of the Chechen independence movement. Suicide bombings, almost unheard of in the first decade of fighting in Chechnya, became horrifyingly commonplace. On May 12, 2003, a truck loaded with explosives was driven into the security gate of a government compound in the town of Znamenskoye in Chechnya, killing four dozen people, many of them civilians in nearby houses crushed by the force of the blast. Two days later, two women approached Kadyrov himself during a religious festival commemorating the prophet Mohammed in a village east of Grozny and detonated explosive belts. Kadyrov escaped injury, but four of his bodyguards were among the fifteen killed. Another "black widow," as these female bombers became known, blew up her explosives as she boarded a bus in Mozdok in June, killing eighteen. In July two women did the same at an annual rock festival in Moscow attended by thirty thousand people.

Until Iraq descended into sectarian war in 2006, no other country in the world, not even Israel, had faced a terror campaign of such scale. Putin could do little more than reiterate his vow to destroy the bandits he had promised to "waste in the outhouse" back in 1999. Putin's decisive-

ness in ending the theater siege had, despite the avoidable deaths of so
many hostages, earned him support, but increasingly he seemed adrift.
The biggest successes of his presidency had come in his first two years,
but now he seemed to have lost energy. Russia's economy continued to
improve, expanding the opportunities of millions, but many workers
remained mired in Soviet-era industries—mines, factories, farms—that
resisted modernization. Russia had not yet become Portugal. The military reform he promised inched forward against institutional inertia.
The health care system functioned on bribes, while the life expectancy
of men continued to decline, as did the entire population, which shrunk
by nearly a million people a year. The Putin prosperity was benefiting
many, but mostly those already at the top, or clustered in the main cities.
Mikhail Kasyanov, his prime minister, dutifully carried out the domestic
and economic duties he had promised Putin but felt that the Kremlin
had no new initiatives to offer, and was backtracking on some that had
been launched.[24]

Even the head of Putin's party, Boris Gryzlov, who served as interior
minister, said the government he was part of had "largely lost the ability
to energetically and surely solve the most burning and painful problems
the country is facing."[25] Bereft of new ideas, Putin's team fixated on the
political risk posed by the parliamentary elections in December 2003, as
surely as Yeltsin had in the waning years of his presidency. United Russia's plurality in the Duma was no longer certain, and the Kremlin had
to make sure a new one would not challenge Putin's primacy. Above all,
the Kremlin could not let a new figure emerge, a new political force or
leader prepared to offer the country an alternative.

In late May 2003, a treatise circulating in Moscow created a public uproar. It was written by a group founded the year before, the Council
for National Strategy. The council included twenty-three experts from
across the political spectrum who seemed to disagree about everything,
including the treatise. Its ideological progenitors were Iosif Diskin, who
was close to the Kremlin, and Stanislav Belkovsky, a political strategist
once enmeshed in Boris Berezovsky's web. The work of a think tank
might have languished in obscurity, except that this one was brought to
Putin by two of his hardline deputies, Sechin and Viktor Ivanov, as evidence of the threat facing the Kremlin.[26] The treatise, titled "The State
and the Oligarchs," argued that some of the country's corporate titans
were conspiring to usurp Russia's government as they sought interna-

tional legitimacy for their riches. Their path to power lay not in directly challenging Putin, but in empowering the parliament and establishing a new form of government, a parliamentary system that would be led by the prime minister, not the powerful president ensconced in the Kremlin. "The front-runner of such a government, formed under a new constitution, is considered to be Mikhail Khodorkovsky," it warned.[27] The report ignored Russia's political realities, which made the very idea that a parliamentary majority could seize power from Putin implausible. Whether the plan was true, even in part, was beside the point. What mattered was that Putin believed it.

In June, he held his annual press conference in the Kremlin with local and foreign reporters, and the scripted event began with a question about the report and its warning of the ripening of "a certain oligarchic revolution." Putin answered in detail and at length, as if prepared. He said he did not believe a parliamentary system could govern a country as large and ethnically diverse as Russia. "Any state system other than a presidential republic," he said, "would be unacceptable and even dangerous." As for big business, he explained patiently, it had a natural influence on the country's life, as was to be expected with a growing market economy. Russia's new tycoons created jobs and revenue, developed new technologies, and provided examples of modern, effective management. "This does not mean, of course, that we should let certain representatives of business influence the country's political life with the aim of pursuing their own group interests." He ended by alluding to a line from Pushkin's *Eugene Onegin* about the Decembrists who revolted against Nicholas I in 1825 and ended up on the gallows or in Siberian exile. "As for those who disagree with this principle, it's like they used to say, 'Some are gone forever, and others are far away.' "[28] It sounded very much like a warning.

The legal assault on Yukos began unexpectedly—neither against Khodorkovsky nor against the company directly. In June 2003, the authorities arrested the company's head of security, Aleksei Pichugin, on murder charges, alleging that he had organized assassinations of company rivals. On July 2, less than two weeks after Putin's public remarks on the "oligarchic coup," a special police unit arrived at a hospital in Moscow where Khodorkovsky's business partner, Platon Lebedev, was convalescing after treatment for heart trouble. Although the law prohibited arrests of hospitalized patients, the police led him away in handcuffs. Lebedev was the chairman of Menatep, the bank that controlled 61 percent of Yukos's shares, but the prosecutors charged him with fraud involving an obscure 1994 deal to buy a fertilizer company called Apatit. Khodorkovsky was summoned two days later as a witness, and a week after that, the police raided one of Yukos's offices. The prosecutor general, Vladimir Ustinov, made no move against Khodorkovsky himself, but the pressure increased. Ustinov, formerly a middling prosecutor from Sochi, was not part of Putin's Petersburg circle, but he had proved his mettle by organizing the legal assaults that drove Gusinsky and Berezovsky into exile. And he grew closer and closer to Putin's court inside the Kremlin, especially to Igor Sechin, whose daughter married his son that year.

Khodorkovsky and his partners believed that Putin and Sechin had ordered the investigations into Yukos's affairs,[29] but they did not expect anything more than legal harassment that they would be able to fight off. Khodorkovsky believed that the importance of Yukos to the economy would protect him and the company. At a meeting of Yukos department heads, he warned that the company faced a prosecutorial assault and said that those who felt unprepared should leave, but he vowed to stay and fight.[30]

The "Yukos affair," as it quickly became known, created confusion and alarm. Putin obfuscated in such a way that no one knew if the investigation signaled the first salvo of the renationalization of the industries auctioned off in the 1990s, or something else. Officials and businessmen expected the worst. Russia's volatile stock market—a lucrative but never stable investment—plunged 15 percent in the first two weeks after Lebedev's arrest, wiping away $7 billion of Yukos's value, or nearly a fifth of it. On the day of the searches at Yukos, Putin met in the Kremlin with the parliamentary leadership and the heads of the councils of trade unions and the tycoons, represented by Arkady Volsky, who warned that the spiraling investigation would harm the economy. Putin did not address Yukos directly but warned that the Kremlin would not tolerate public organizations that did not put the public good "above their group, corporate, or personal interests." In televised remarks, he spoke cryptically: "I am, of course, opposed to arm-twisting and believe this is no way to resolve the issue of economic crimes. We cannot base our actions on wild applause at someone being put away in a cell." Within weeks, an orphanage sponsored by Khodorkovsky's Open Russia was raided.

Putin's chief of staff, Aleksandr Voloshin, did not even know Lebedev's name at the time of his arrest and believed that Putin did not either.[31] The president kept his fingerprints off the investigation, insisting that he did not involve himself in authorizing arrests or searches—only to contradict himself later when he acknowledged in an interview with American journalists that he had discussed Lebedev's arrest with the prosecutor general.[32] Putin's involvement grew as the affair unfolded haphazardly over a summer rife with speculation that recalled the Kremlinology of Soviet times. "The Yukos affair was not a Stalinist-type operation planned in advance and implemented methodically," as one historian wrote.[33] Instead Putin reacted as developments progressed and said virtually nothing in public, which only deepened the sense of intrigue. As late as September, he insisted that the investigation was an isolated criminal matter.

Khodorkovsky continued to clash with the Kremlin, not only over tax legislation but also over plans to build a pipeline to China, a decision that Putin believed should be a prerogative of the state, not a private company. Even as the investigation widened, Khodorkovsky pressed ahead with the merger with Sibneft and continued to court the American oil giants in the talks Putin had blessed. If Lebedev's arrest was a warning, Khodorkovsky paid no heed. He continued to travel, to conduct business, and to rail defiantly against the prosecutor's office.[34] He believed that the company's legal troubles were part of a struggle inside Putin's administration but bet that public pressure would bring the crusade to an end. "The probability of my arrest now is 90 percent," he told his lawyer, "but it's not 100 percent. To be 100 percent, it has to be sanctioned."[35] Putin certainly gave him hints. After Lebedev's arrest, Khodorkovsky tried to arrange a meeting with him through the director of the FSB, Nikolai Patrushev. Patrushev invited him to meet with Ustinov instead, but Khodorkovsky thought better of it.

By August 2003, Yukos had recovered some of its losses in the stock market, and Russia's antimonopoly agency approved the merger with Sibneft, quieting speculation among investors and analysts that the investigation would scuttle the creation of the new oil giant. The same month, the Kremlin approved a partnership between BP and TNK, a smaller Russian company, seemingly signaling its openness to foreign investment. In September Khodorkovsky attended an energy summit with oilmen from American and Russian companies in Petersburg and tried to close a deal to merge Yukos-Sibneft with Chevron. When that fell apart, he revived negotiations with ExxonMobil, whose chairman notified Mikhail Kasyanov of the talks.[36] The speculation about a deal drove the stock market to new highs.

The Yukos-Sibneft merger, valued at $45 billion once completed, became official on October 2. Khodorkovsky continued to travel and deliver lectures to students, journalists, and activists about his vision for a modern transformation of business and society that would free up the country's human potential by breaking the last chains of the Soviet mentality. In an interview in the company's gleaming headquarters in Moscow, he explained that Russia stood at a crossroads, its fate a choice not between capitalism and Communism, but rather between a democratic society and an authoritarian one. "It is not a matter of choice between the South Korean model and the North Korean model," he said, dismissing the old ideological divisions. "It is more like the choice between Canada and Guatemala," a modern, transparent, and accountable government versus a banana republic.[37] Such public musings infuriated Putin. He complained to John Browne, the chairman of BP, when they met in Moscow to finalize that company's investment in Russia. "I have eaten more dirt than I need to from that man," he said.[38]

Putin's anger at Khodorkovsky conflated his fears about the coming parliamentary election, scheduled for December 2003, and the disgust he and his closest aides from Petersburg felt toward this political upstart, this man who exploited the chaos of the 1990s to enrich himself and now felt he could use that wealth to dictate Russia's course. "We have a category of people who have become billionaires, as we say, overnight," Putin said in an interview with *The New York Times* as the investigations climaxed in October. It seemed a discordant answer; the question had been about criticism in the West of Russia's hesitant embrace of democracy, not about Yukos or Khodorkovsky. "The state appointed them as billionaires," he said. "It simply gave out a huge amount of property, practically for free. They said it themselves: 'I was appointed a billionaire.' Then as the play developed, they got the impression that the gods themselves slept on their heads—that everything is permitted to them."[39] A senior Kremlin official said that Putin saw it as his "historical mission" to thwart Khodorkovsky's ambitions not just to buy or influence politics, but to seize the country itself. Putin would use whatever means he had at his disposal to stop Khodorkovsky, the official said. "Unfortunately, that can't be done in a way that looks pretty."[40]

On October 23, a fax arrived at the Yukos headquarters in Moscow, signed by Vladimir Ustinov, summoning Khodorkovsky to answer questions about the company's payment of taxes involving the Apatit fertilizer company. Khodorkovsky had not seen the summons, his lawyer claimed,[41] and he flew to Siberia to continue his political barnstorming before the coming elections. When his private jet landed to refuel in Novosibirsk shortly before dawn on October 25, elite FSB commandos appeared, surrounded the plane, and then stormed aboard. Russia's richest man was forced to the cabin floor, handcuffed, hooded, and taken on a military aircraft back to Moscow.

Khodorkovsky's arrest rocked Russia's stock markets, sending shares lurching up and down all week as investors, and other political leaders, tried to make sense of what was happening. In nearly three years in office, Putin had presented himself as a reformer, a free-market champion who was bringing prosperity to the country. Now he seemed to have come down decisively on the side of the hardliners in his government, the *siloviki.* "Capitalism with Stalin's face," a headline in *Nezavisimaya Gazeta* screamed on the Monday after Khodorkovsky's arrest. Another newspaper, *Novaya Gazeta,* declared that the law-enforcement agencies had seized power, and "the president had done nothing to stop that coup."[42] The union of businessmen, which until that weekend had included Khodorkovsky, issued a statement condemning the arrest, saying it had "thrown the country backwards."

Putin met his cabinet two days after Khodorkovsky's arrest. As the country's stocks, currency, and bonds plummeted, he called for an end to the "hysteria and speculation." He rebuffed a plea from the business union to discuss the case, icily declaring that there would be "no bargaining on matters related to the activities of the law enforcement bodies" and warning the government ministers around the table that they should not involve themselves in the matter. He went on to say that he assumed "the court had good reasons to take this decision," though the final approval for Khodorkovsky's arrest had come from Putin himself.[43]

The "liberals" in Putin's camp, including Mikhail Kasyanov and his old Petersburg colleagues, German Gref and Aleksei Kudrin, were dismayed by the investigation, seeing it as a sign of the end of their reforming mission.[44] Kasyanov had adhered to his agreement with Putin from 2000: he oversaw the government's economic policies and left the security matters to Putin. Now Putin was very much involved in economic affairs, despite Kasyanov's protests. Five days after the arrest, the prosecutor general froze Khodorkovsky's and his partner's shares in Yukos. This represented nearly half the company, with a worth of $14 billion before their value collapsed with the rest of the market. A spokeswoman for the prosecutor general insisted the freezing was not a "confiscation or nationalization," but it would turn out to be exactly that. Kasyanov spoke out the next day, saying the seizing of assets was a "new phenomenon" whose consequences could not be predicted.[45] He was "deeply concerned," but he no longer had any influence over the events.

Only one among Putin's circle of advisers registered any real protest. Aleksandr Voloshin, the chief of staff who had stayed on from Yeltsin's administration and maintained close ties to the country's business elite, resigned on the day of Khodorkovsky's arrest. Putin tried to talk him out of it during a series of meetings in the Kremlin the following week, but Voloshin felt that the administration that had begun with such promise had exhausted itself and was now flailing about in search of enemies. When his resignation was announced, the Kremlin said nothing about the reasons behind it. Putin simply replaced him with Dmitri Medvedev, his young protégé, and elevated another ally from Petersburg, Dmitri Kozak, as Medvedev's deputy. Voloshin's departure thus only solidified Putin's team. When Voloshin and his colleagues gathered for a farewell drink at the Kremlin, Putin arrived late. He sat in the last empty seat at a long table and offered a toast, saying he thought it was a mistake for Voloshin to leave. Putin's presence caused long, awkward silences until he excused himself, saying he felt like he had interrupted.[46]

Kasyanov asked three times why Khodorkovsky had been arrested before Putin told him that the tycoon had crossed the line by funding his political opponents. Putin was not, as some feared, renationalizing the country's industry or even taking on the oligarchs so much as taking down a man he viewed as a political threat to the power he was accreting. Several days after Khodorkovsky's arrest, Putin told his economic adviser, Andrei Illarionov, that he had been protecting the tycoon for some time from those in his circle who wanted to punish him. Instead, Khodorkovsky had ignored repeated warnings and had "chosen to fight" the Kremlin. Putin told Illarionov that he decided then to step aside and let Khodorkovsky "solve his problems with the boys by himself."[47] It was an attack less violent than the ice pick that had killed Trotsky in Mexico City on Stalin's orders, but it was just as crude and just as effective.

Khodorkovsky was arrested only six weeks before the parliamentary elections in December, and for all the national and international condemnation, the blow to investor confidence and the losses on the markets, the
assault on one of Russia's oligarchs proved immensely popular among
Russians, the vast majority of whom had little or nothing invested in
stocks in the first place.

When the elections took place, Putin's bloc in the Duma, now
rebranded as United Russia, cruised to an overwhelming victory. It did
so despite having only the vaguest platform beyond supporting Putin.
Vladislav Surkov, the Kremlin's strategist, had begun his career working
with Khodorkovsky, but now he exploited populist sentiment against
the oligarchs by cynically associating them with the Communist Party.
He also orchestrated the creation of a new party, Rodina, or Motherland,
four months before the vote with the sole purpose of siphoning votes
from the Communists by appealing to nationalist and socialist themes,
as did Vladimir Zhirinovsky, the leader of the uproariously misnamed
Liberal Democratic Party of Russia, who was known for clownish antics
and xenophobic harangues.

It was a listless campaign, marked by growing apathy. What debate
there was rehashed Russia's economic collapse in the 1990s as if the electorate still wanted to exact its revenge on the corruption and chaos that
democracy brought. The whole of the Yeltsin era, the economic hardships and the oligarchs, including Khodorkovsky, came under blistering
assault on state television, the message driven home over and over: Putin
had ended the collapse. "If by democracy, one means the dissolution
of the state, then we do not need such democracy," he told a group of
foreign journalists before the election when asked about accusations that
democratic freedoms were being eroded. "Why is democracy needed?
To make people's lives better, to make them free. I don't think there are
people in the world who want democracy that could lead to chaos." The
chaos that continued to afflict Russia—including a suicide bombing on
a passenger train not far from Chechnya that killed forty-two people two
days before the election—was simply airbrushed away. The Organization of Security and Co-operation in Europe criticized the Russian state
media for exhibiting a clear bias in election coverage and cited evidence
of administrative abuses in the campaign that favored United Russia or
punished the others. The Communist leader, still the aging Gennady
Zyuganov, filed a formal complaint when 800,000 ballots showed up in
the republic of Bashkortostan already checked off for United Russia.[48]

Putin had a sleepless night before the election. Lyudmila explained why when they showed up early to vote at their polling station.[49] His beloved black Labrador, Koni, had given birth to eight puppies. Putin had received the dog as a gift in December 2000 after he visited a kennel where she had been trained for search and rescue. She was said to be descended from a Labrador once owned by Leonid Brezhnev. Koni joined the poodle Putin had given his daughters, Toska,[50] and quickly became his favorite, accompanying him even to official meetings at his residence, serving as a humanizing prop or an intimidating one.[51] When Bush visited Novo-Ogaryovo, Putin compared Koni to Bush's Scottish terrier, Barney. "Bigger, faster, stronger," he said.[52]

The news of the puppies received far more coverage than the opposition parties, who by the end of the day had been routed. United Russia, despite having no independent political identity, won handily with 36 percent of the vote, enough under the system for distributing seats to win an outright majority of seats in the Duma. The Communist Party won less than 13 percent of the vote, half their showing of four years before, when Putin's political career had only just begun. Yeltsin had narrowly beaten back a Communist resurrection in 1996, only five years after the collapse of the Soviet Union; Putin had effectively buried the threat for good.

The Liberal Democrats and the newly hatched Rodina won nearly as many votes, leaving Gennady Zyuganov seething. "This shameful farce which is currently being shown to us has nothing to do with democracy," he said.[53] Yabloko, the stalwart of liberal politics since the days of perestroika, and the Union of Right Forces, dominated by the liberal economic reformers who had protested Khodorkovsky's arrest the loudest, failed even to reach the 5 percent threshold required to win a bloc of seats. They had withered under the Kremlin's pressure and succumbed to infighting among themselves. Except for a handful of deputies who won individual mandates, the Duma would not have a bloc of liberals for the first time since the Soviet collapse. By the time the final ballots were counted and the seats apportioned, Putin could count on a parliamentary majority of more than 300 of the 450 seats—in other words, enough to adopt any legislation the Kremlin saw fit and even to change the Constitution, which people had already begun to note limited a sitting president to two terms in office. "We now have, again, a one-party parliament," Yabloko's leader, Grigory Yavlinsky, said glumly the morning after the vote, sitting in an elegantly rebuilt Kempinski

Hotel with a view of Red Square, a symbol itself of the prosperity that had begun to emerge in Putin's era. Even at the end of the Soviet era there had been a sort of legislative debate. "Russia has had no such parliament since Brezhnev."

Putin's Kremlin reveled in the electoral triumph. Vladislav Surkov gloated that the liberal parties that failed to win seats should "realize that their historical mission has been completed." Putin represented the end of the "old political system," he said. "A new political era is coming."[54]

CHAPTER 14

Annus Horribilis

On September 1, 2004, Putin was in Sochi on the Black Sea, trying not very successfully to spend the waning days of the country's traditional August holidays in the subtropical climate. By now he spent more time in the presidential compound there than in any of the Kremlin's other official residences outside Moscow. It was here that he frequently held meetings with foreign leaders, including one the day before with Jacques Chirac of France and Gerhard Schröder of Germany, the "troika" who had publicly opposed the American war in Iraq. Without exactly gloating, they felt their forewarnings of disaster had been affirmed as the swift American toppling of Saddam Hussein's government turned into a deadly insurgency. Putin had grown so close to Schröder that he expedited the adoption of a Russian orphan for him and his wife. Each leader, finding common cause with Putin against the swaggering policy of George Bush, muted his country's criticism of Russia, including the war in Chechnya.

Putin's August vacation had already been disrupted by an ominous string of tragedies. On August 21, a bold raid by insurgents in Chechnya killed at least fifty people. It followed a similar raid in neighboring Ingushetia in June that had killed nearly a hundred and came only days before Chechnya held a new election, which Chirac and Schröder would praise as evidence that Putin sought a political solution to the conflict, now in its fifth year. Then, on the night of August 24, two passenger airliners took off from Domodedovo Airport in Moscow, roughly an hour apart. Almost simultaneously, around eleven o'clock, they both exploded in midair, destroyed by suicide bombers, both women. One had paid a bribe of a thousand rubles to get on one of the planes after boarding had already closed. One plane was headed to Volgograd, the second to Sochi. Eighty-nine people died.

Sensing the gravity of the attacks, Putin returned to Moscow and ordered the creation of a task force to investigate, but by the weekend he had returned to Sochi and said nothing more until he appeared with Chirac and Schröder. He blamed the bombings—the worst terrorist act in the skies over Russia—on Al-Qaeda, which grossly misstated the facts. Only a few hours after he spoke, a woman blew herself up at the entrance to the Rizhskaya metro station in Moscow, only three miles north of the Kremlin. That attack killed the bomber and nine others, and injured more than fifty. The officials who rushed to the scene included Moscow's mayor, Yuri Luzhkov, underscoring the panic that was unfolding, not unlike that which had followed the apartment bombings in 1999. The police in Moscow announced that the bomber was Rosa Nagayeva, though that later proved false.[1] Her sister, Amanat, was suspected of destroying one of the two airliners; their roommate, Satsita Dzhbirkhanova, destroyed the other. The three shared a grim apartment in Grozny's shattered ruins with another woman, Maryam Taburova. They lived steps away from the city's muddied, fetid central market, where they sold clothing they shuttled in from Azerbaijan.[2] On August 22, two days before the attack on the airliners, the four had all left Grozny and taken a bus to Azerbaijan's capital, Baku. They were now involved in a new wave of terror. The authorities quickly pieced together their trail, but they did not know where Taburova—and, as it turned out, Rosa Nagayeva—had gone.[3]

Putin had begun 2004 seemingly at the peak of political power. The parliamentary elections had cemented his control of the legislature, and while the arrest of Khodorkovsky had rattled the stock market, it had not dented his popularity ratings, which hovered above 70 percent. Even wary investors seemed relieved that the attack on Yukos seemed to be a personal and political fight, not the result of a drive to renationalize industry. "People will forget in six months that Khodorkovsky is still sitting in jail," declared William Browder, the director of Hermitage Capital, one of the funds that rode the Putin boom.[4] The effects of an improving economy seemed to proliferate day by day in new stores and restaurants and apartment buildings, especially in Moscow and other cities. Oil prices had more than tripled since the fiscal crisis of 1998, and a new tax regime Putin imposed on the oil companies—based, ironically, on proposals drafted by Yukos—poured money into the state's coffers. The share of oil profits the government received had nearly doubled, and revenues had surged from less than $6 billion when Putin became prime minister to more than $80 billion.[5] The Russians now talked about becoming the world's largest oil producer, surpassing Saudi Arabia. The boom was not Putin's success alone, and his critics derided him as lucky, but as the undisputed leader of the country, he reaped the political benefits.

In early January the Kremlin pressed its case against Yukos, announcing that the company owed $3.4 billion in back taxes for the year 2000 alone. Prime Minister Mikhail Kasyanov voiced the lone public protest. In an interview he gave to the newspaper *Vedomosti,* he argued that Khodorkovsky and his partners had not cheated on taxes, but simply used loopholes that were then available to everyone but were now retroactively being declared illegal.[6] Putin took note of his prime minister's defiance, however mild it seemed. Kasyanov was careful never to speak directly against his boss, but the following Saturday, at a regular meeting of his Security Council, Putin asked the members to stay on after the regular agenda had been completed. The council included the country's most important officials, including the ministers of defense and foreign affairs and, of course, Kasyanov as the prime minister. Putin instructed the prosecutor general, Vladimir Ustinov, to read aloud the charges against Khodorkovsky, all of them, in the belief that the enunciation of Khodorkovsky's "crimes" would dispel any doubts and refute Kasyanov's dangerous line of questioning before anyone else took it up. Ustinov read the indictments monotonously, page after page, for more than an hour. "The Security Council members, not really understanding why this was being done, sat there with stone faces, not moving," Kasyanov recalled. He could not help but smile at "all of the absurdities and obvious inventions." Putin, at the head of the long oval table, scanned the faces of his aides, making note of the reactions: the blank, unaffected stares of most and Kasyanov's grin. When Ustinov finished, no one asked a question or said a word in response, "and everyone walked out silently."[7]

Putin's political dominance was such that there seemed to be little point in challenging him. Not even in the presidential election, held that March, did he face meaningful opposition. The political titans of the Yeltsin era—Gennady Zyuganov and Vladimir Zhirinovsky, men who had once seemed within reach of ruling all of Russia—pulled out before the official campaign even started. Instead, they assigned party apparatchiks to run token campaigns; in Zhirinovsky's case, his bodyguard, a former boxer named Oleg Malyshkin, carried the party's banner. Grigory Yavlinsky, so embittered by Yabloko's defeat in December, refused entreaties from the Kremlin itself to mount a third campaign for the presidency, to create the semblance of a democratic choice. When they vacationed together that winter, Boris Nemtsov, another reformer who had served under Yeltsin, tried to persuade Kasyanov to run as the candidate representing the country's economic liberals, but Kasyanov dared not seriously consider challenging his boss. In the weeks before the campaign, a poll found that 55 percent of respondents thought it would be better to cancel the election and save the money it would cost to hold it.[8]

Putin's reelection, the affirmation of the course he had chosen for Russia, seemed on the verge of collapsing, but in a way he and his aides had not expected. The "managed democracy" that Surkov had orchestrated had succeeded so well that it threatened to undermine Putin's own image as the democrat who had turned Russia around with the assent of the people. One of the first pieces of legislation in the new Duma called for amending the Constitution to extend the presidential term to seven years, allowing Putin to run for two new terms. It would have kept him in office until 2018, but he demurred, insisting that there should be no constitutional changes. He still sought a democratic imprimatur, though in a race in which he faced, by the Kremlin's own design, no genuine competition. The Kremlin was left having to recruit its own candidates to oppose him, including Yavlinsky and a former legislator from Petersburg, Sergei Mironov, who accepted the nomination of a small party with an impassioned plea to vote for the incumbent. "When a leader who is trusted goes into battle," he said of Putin, "he must not be left alone."[9] The liberals could not agree on a single candidate now any more than they had been able to unite as a bloc before the parliamentary elections. Irina Khakamada, a Russian of Japanese descent and one of the most prominent women in politics, ended up running a lonely challenge. Her own party, the Union of Right Forces, refused to endorse her.

From exile in London, Boris Berezovsky bankrolled another candidate, Ivan Rybkin, a former Duma speaker and Yeltsin ally. He ultimately dropped out, but not before injecting the most drama into the campaign by disappearing for four days in February, during which the authorities announced an investigation into his possible murder. When he resurfaced, he vowed to continue his campaign. He then promptly fled to London, where he met Berezovsky's aides, including Aleksandr Litvinenko, the former FSB officer who had gone public with his accusations against the agency. Litvinenko had fled Russia in October 2000 and settled in London with Berezovsky's financial patronage. Rybkin now claimed that he had been kidnapped and drugged in Kyiv, where he had gone on an invitation to meet the head of Chechnya's separatists, Aslan Maskhadov, the former president and now one of Russia's most wanted criminals. The implausibility of Maskhadov risking travel to Ukraine, where Russia's security services were deeply embedded, seemed not to have occurred to Rybkin.

Rybkin said he had fallen unconscious for four days after having sandwiches and tea in a Kyiv apartment. When he came to, two armed Russian men showed him a videotape that he declined to describe in detail except that it was made by "perverts" and was meant to humiliate him into silence.[10] Litvinenko claimed the drug Rybkin had ingested was SP-117, a truth serum used by Russia's foreign intelligence services. "Once you get SP-117, they can do whatever they want with you, drive you around, put you in bed with girls or boys, tape you, and so on," he said. "Then you get one pill of antidote and you are normal again and don't remember what happened."[11] No one took Rybkin's accusations seriously, not even his wife, who said she felt "sorry for Russia if people like this want to govern it."[12] His political career never recovered. Berezovsky, though, never tired in his campaign to discredit Putin, denouncing him regularly with increasing vehemence and a diminishing regard for the truth. It would not be the last time he and Litvinenko became entangled in a sensational drama involving spies and poison.

Putin ignored not only his challengers; he ostensibly ignored his own campaign, as he had four years before. He did not have to campaign overtly because the Kremlin's control of television meant his duties as president were dutifully and uncritically covered even more prominently on the evening news. Putin's challengers, if they were mentioned at all, were infantilized or denounced. When the first debate among the presidential candidates was held on February 12—at eight in the morning, the early hour ensuring the fewest possible viewers—Putin refused to attend. His twenty-nine-minute speech that day officially opening his campaign, however, aired repeatedly through the afternoon and evening. He ran no campaign ads, held no rallies, and offered no clear proposals for a second term except to continue to be the living embodiment of Russia's stability.

The paradox was that, four years into Putin's presidency, Russia's stability still seemed precarious, a disaster away from the turmoil of the 1990s that Putin often invoked. On the eve of the race, a bomb exploded at the door of Yelena Tregubova, the journalist Putin had treated to sushi while he was director of the FSB. In 2003, she had published a book on her experiences in the Kremlin's increasingly circumscribed press pool, *Tales of a Kremlin Digger*. It had been a best seller, describing in gossipy detail the Kremlin's efforts to manage the pool's reporting, including an incident where Putin scolded a boy who had been hit by a car. "From now on," he told the boy, "you won't be violating traffic regulations anymore." Tregubova assumed the bombing was somehow linked to the coming election. She was not injured, but she was rattled enough that she fled Russia. "It is becoming uncomfortable to live in this city," she said.[13] Four days later, a suicide bomber blew himself up on a metro train in the center of Moscow, killing forty-one and wounding more than two hundred. One of those accused of organizing it was later involved in the attack at the Rizhskaya metro bombing six months later.[14] On February 14, two days after the official start of campaigning, the roof of a popular new indoor water park in southern Moscow collapsed. Transvaal Park symbolized the amenities that Putin's economic boom was bringing to the country's emerging consumer class: an indoor tropical paradise in the frigid north. Twenty-eight people died in the disaster, which the building's designers blamed on a terrorist attack but that was in fact caused by a construction flaw. It was impossible to blame Putin directly for any one of the events, but they were collectively as sure a measure of his rule as the economic successes he happily took credit for. Ivan Rybkin produced a lacerating American-style attack ad that showed the subway and water park disasters, along with the sorry state of education and health care, but the state's television networks simply refused to broadcast it.[15]

Still, Surkov's political team left nothing to chance. The Kremlin issued orders to outlying regions specifying Putin's vote totals and voter turnout. The authorities in Khabarovsk in the Far East threatened to discharge hospital patients if they could not prove they had received absentee ballots to cast their votes. A housing official in St. Petersburg sent a letter to building superintendents ordering them to ensure 70 percent turnout.[16] Anticipating the Kremlin's wishes, local bureaucrats threw up obstacles to keep Putin's rivals from mounting campaigns at all. The police interrupted one rally in Yekaterinburg on the premise there was a bomb threat; the electricity was cut off at another in Nizhny Novgorod two days later. The campaign was so stripped of any electoral interest that the Kremlin's biggest worry now was that voter turnout would fall below the 50 percent threshold required to make the election legal. Anything below that would force a new election. That would be embarrassment enough, but Putin's closest advisers also began to see the seeds of a conspiracy to deprive him of power. By law, if a new election were required, the prime minister would step in to serve as acting president in the interim. That is, Mikhail Kasyanov. He had criticized the prosecution of Khodorkovsky, who, Putin was convinced, was trying to buy control of the state. He had vacationed with Boris Nemtsov, who had raised the possibility of his running for president, as Putin must surely have found out. The chances of Kasyanov maneuvering into power were infinitesimally remote, but Putin and his aides believed it, and they would not tolerate any risk.[17]

At a concert at the Kremlin on February 23, Kasyanov himself sensed Putin's coolness. He noticed him during an intermission, whispering in a corner with FSB head Nikolai Patrushev and otherwise avoiding him.[18] The next day, Putin summoned Kasyanov to his Kremlin office alone and fired him. Not only did he not explain why to the public; he refused to tell Kasyanov, who was so stunned by the news that he did not initially understand that Putin meant immediately, not after his reelection in March, when a new prime minister might have been expected.[19] It was Putin's most significant shakeup of his government, whose continuity had been held up as a measure of political stability, and like Yeltsin before him, he used surprise to maximize the impact and keep the media's attention on him. Not even other senior officials knew the move was coming. Putin said only that the voters deserved to know the composition of the new government before the election, which only underscored how predictable he knew the result would be. Putin did not immediately announce Kasyanov's replacement, though, and the delay touched off rampant speculation—not about the election in three weeks, but about the one in 2008 that would elect Putin's successor after he completed his second presidential term. Most politicians and analysts assumed Kasyanov's replacement would be Putin's choice as political heir, as Putin had ultimately become Yeltsin's, but they misunderstood Putin's intentions: he did not want to name an heir apparent who might emerge as a political figure in his own right. Doing so would create the idea of a Russia without Putin, and it was far too early to contemplate that.

Putin waited a week to let the mystery and suspense deepen. Speculation focused on the camps in Putin's Kremlin: the liberals and the *siloviki,*

led respectively by Aleksei Kudrin and Sergei Ivanov, who had their own
aspirations to ride Putin's coattails to power. Instead he announced a
nominee that no one predicted, not even those within the rival factions.
"The political elite were stirred," the journalist Anna Politkovskaya
wrote. "The guessing game about whom Putin would appoint took over
the television channels. The political pundits were given something to
discuss, and the press finally got something it could write about the election campaign."[20]

Less than two weeks before election day, meeting with parliamentary
leaders to create the appearance of consultation, as nominally required
by the Constitution, Putin proclaimed that the new prime minister
would be Mikhail Fradkov. "There was a silence," one of the meeting
participants told the newspaper *Vedomosti*, "because some of us could
not remember who Fradkov was."[21] Fradkov, a balding, jowly bureaucrat, had a long, obscure career that began in the Soviet Ministry of Foreign Economic Affairs; he had no patron, no political constituency, no
policy proposals that anyone could discern. He seemed as bland a choice
for prime minister as Putin had been in 1999. Even Fradkov seemed
stunned. Putin had first called him over the weekend, and he was still in
Brussels, where he served as Russia's envoy to the European Union, when
Putin made the announcement. When he arrived back in Moscow the
next day, he admitted he had little qualification or vision for the post.
He did not have to.

If Putin really meant the appointment to clarify the next government's course, it signaled nothing except that a cabinet of ministers
under Fradkov's command would be as pliant as the Duma and the Federation Council had become. Fradkov had no personal ambition, but
rather belonged to the cadre of former intelligence officers Putin assembled in Moscow during his presidency. Fradkov's scientific education at
the Moscow Machine and Tool Design Institute, a mysterious gap in his
résumé, his fluency in English and Spanish, and an assignment in the
1970s as an economic adviser in the Soviet Union's embassy in India
strongly suggested ties to the KGB. The fact that he never acknowledged or denied it suggested only that he operated undercover, as many
Soviet trade officials did.[22] In his announcement, Putin merely said that
Fradkov was a good administrator who had experience in the security
services. Throughout his first term Putin had favored the security men
in his appointments, by some estimates filling as many as 70 percent of
senior government positions with former military, police, or intelligence

officers, many of whom had the same background in the KGB. Fradkov fit the pattern. What few realized was that Putin had known Fradkov, this bland unprepossessing apparatchik, for years. He had served as
the Petersburg representative of the Foreign Trade Ministry in the early
1990s and with his boss, Pyotr Avon, now one of Russia's richest bankers, had approved the barter contracts Putin had signed in the scandalous scheme to provide the city with food in the first winter of the new
Russia.[23]

Kasyanov and, before him, Voloshin had represented a legacy of the
Yeltsin years. Officials with their own ambitions, interests, and constituencies, they were now gone. There were still rivalries and divisions inside
the Kremlin, but with Fradkov's appointment, Putin consolidated his
political supremacy by elevating a complete network of underlings that
would above all remain loyal to him. A mere five days after the appointment, the Duma confirmed Fradkov's nomination after a perfunctory
debate that included only nine questions. Fradkov offered only the vaguest platitudes about his policies. He was there to do Putin's bidding, and
everyone understood it. The vote was 352 to 58, with 24 abstentions.

Putin's reelection followed the script that Surkov's political team had
written for it. He won more than 71 percent of the vote. The little-
known Communist candidate, Nikolai Kharitonov, came in a distant
second with 13 percent. There was ample evidence of ballot stuffing and
suspicious tallying, but the Kremlin blocked investigation of the accusations. In several regions the turnout and Putin's total were incredible. In war-ravaged Chechnya, 92 percent voted for Putin. "I guess
only Maskhadov and Basayev did not go to the polls," Kharitonov
quipped, complaining bitterly about electoral irregularities, including
instances of votes cast for him being counted for Putin.[24] All across the
Northern Caucasus, the regions conquered by imperial Russia in the
eighteenth and nineteenth centuries, similar results were delivered to
Moscow like tributes to a tsar. In Dagestan, 94 percent voted for Putin;
in Kabardino-Balkaria, 96; in Ingushetia, 98. In some districts across the
country, the turnout and the votes for Putin exceeded 99.9 percent, and
yet no one in the Kremlin—or beyond—seemed particularly embarrassed about it.

The only drama of the night had nothing to do with the election.
Only minutes after the polls closed in Moscow, a fire started in the
Manezh, a neoclassical landmark across the Aleksandr Gardens from the

Kremlin. The fire spread quickly through the wooden rafters of the roof and soon consumed the entire building. The first images broadcast on television made it appear that the Kremlin itself was on fire, "not something the authorities would like Russians to see on the day of Vladimir Putin's triumph," as one newspaper wrote.[25] Putin watched from the roof of the Senate, the presidential office building inside the Kremlin. He had to postpone his victory speech, and even so the state channels could not avoid showing the fire in the background during their live reports from the city's center. When the building's roof collapsed in an exploding heap, sending embers into the sky like an unwanted fireworks display, the crowd on the street inexplicably burst into cheers. Two firefighters died when the burning rafters fell in on them. Officials blamed faulty wiring or perhaps a welder's spark, but since no one had been working there on a Sunday night, the suspicion of arson lingered and was never fully dispelled. In a deeply superstitious culture, the fire seemed a dark omen.

"I promise that the democratic accomplishments of our people will be unconditionally defended and guaranteed," Putin said when he finally made a brief appearance at his campaign headquarters on election night, dressed in a black turtleneck sweater. There was no victory party or celebration. No one seemed particularly excited. On the morning after his reelection, Putin received congratulatory telephone calls from George Bush, Tony Blair, Jacques Chirac, Gerhard Schröder, and Junichiro Koizumi, even as the international observers from the Organization for Security Co-operation in Europe gathered for the now-ritual postelection news conference and declared that the election "reflected the lack of a democratic culture, accountability, and responsibility."

Putin's reelection demoralized the country's democrats. The collapse of the liberal parties that had begun with the parliamentary elections prompted soul-searching over what went wrong. One of the few independent liberals elected to the Duma in 2003, Vladimir Ryzhkov, who represented Barnaul in Siberia, called it "the liberal debacle." The country's democrats, he argued, had been tarnished by the negative consequences of the Soviet collapse, the chaotic and criminal transition to pseudo-capitalism that left millions impoverished and pining for the stability of the Soviet state, if not its stifling ideological and economic stagnation. And Putin, who had worked for one of the country's first democrats and was the heir to the man who led Russia in the

1990s, somehow received all the credit for the economic recovery and the personal freedoms that still remained. Ryzhkov went on to lament that most of the democratic supporters of the liberal parties, Yabloko and the Union of Right Forces, had voted not for their party leaders, but rather for Putin, whom the party leaders blamed for stripping the election—and the system itself—of any real democratic character. "In the eyes of the majority of Russians, the country's number one democrat is none other than President Vladimir Putin himself."[26]

The most striking remonstrance, however, came from an unexpected quarter: the cramped prison cell of Mikhail Khodorkovsky. He had been incarcerated for five months already, meeting with his lawyers and poring through the hundreds of pages of documents the prosecutors had assembled for his coming trial. He had made only brief remarks at his intermittent court hearings, but he spent the hours in his cell contemplating the evolution of politics and business in Russia. He had invested his personal fortune bankrolling politicians who had now been routed in parliamentary and presidential elections by the man he had tried—audaciously, he now understood—to challenge. From notes cobbled together with his lawyers, he published a lengthy treatise in the newspaper *Vedomosti* after Putin's reelection. It was part prescription and part confession, a biting analysis of the sins of Russia's liberals, himself included.[27] Big business had pursued profit above the social good; it had perverted politics by sidling up to political power and lying about it to the people; the liberal champions of democracy had paid attention to 10 percent of the population and neglected those who suffered. "Today we are witnessing the virtual capitulation of the liberals. And that capitulation, indeed, is not only the liberals' fault, but also their problem. It is their fear in the face of a thousand-year history, mixed with the strong liking for household comforts they developed in the 1990s. It is their servility ingrained on the genetic level, their readiness to ignore the Constitution for the sake of another helping of sturgeon." He atoned for his own role as a financial sponsor of Yeltsin's reelection in 1996 and the "monstrous effect it took to make the Russian people 'choose with their hearts.' "

Khodorkovsky's letter sounded like a jailhouse act of contrition, a plea for leniency or clemency. It was also an acute analysis of Russia's politics and society. Putin, he wrote, "is probably neither a liberal nor a democrat, but he is still more liberal and democratic than 70 percent of our country's population." The man who jailed him was the man who would preserve the country until society developed a greater sense of

unity, communality, and equality. Khodorkovsky singled out one opposition candidate, Irina Khakamada, for suggesting in a full-page newspaper advertisement that Putin had been responsible for the *Nord-Ost*
siege. "We must give up the useless attempts to call the president's legitimacy into question. Regardless of whether we like Vladimir Putin or
not, it's time to realize that the head of state is not just a private person. The president is an institution guaranteeing a nation's stability and
integrity. And God forbid that we live to see a day when this institution
collapses—Russia will not survive another February 1917. The nation's
history tells us that a bad government is better than no government
at all."

September 1 is, by tradition, the first day of school across Russia, a ceremonial occasion called the Day of Knowledge. Parents and grandparents join their children as they assemble at their schools, everyone
wearing their best clothes and carrying flowers or other presents to their
new teachers. In the waning days of the summer of 2004, the celebrations once again took place across the country, including at School No.
1 in Beslan, a small city in North Ossetia, a predominantly Orthodox
region in the center of the Caucasus. More than twelve hundred people
had gathered in the school's courtyard at nine o'clock in the morning
when a military truck appeared and uniformed men leapt from beneath
a tarp that covered the cargo bed. They fired rifles in the air and shouted
"Allahu Akbar." The gunmen herded everyone first into a courtyard and
then into the school's gymnasium, which they wired with bombs they
hung above their hostages.[28] Among the camouflaged men were two
women, the roommates from Grozny who had been linked to the earlier
attacks on the airplanes and the metro in Moscow: Maryam Taburova
and Rosa Nagayeva. They were now part of a terrorist attack as barba-
rous as the *Nord-Ost* siege nearly two years before.

The Kremlin's strategy in Chechnya had suffered one setback after
another. On May 9, 2004, two days after Putin's subdued second inauguration, a bomb secretly cemented into a pillar at Grozny's newly rebuilt soccer stadium exploded as the republic's political elite assembled
for a Victory Day parade, commemorating the fifty-ninth anniversary
of the Nazi defeat. The blast killed thirteen people, including the newly
installed president, Akhmad Kadyrov.[29] Kadyrov, fifty-two, had fought
against the Russians in the first war in Chechnya, but he broke with
the republic's president, Aslan Maskhadov, during its brief period of

quasi-independence, opposed to the radicalized form of Islam that was taking root. As a mufti himself and a respected commander, Kadyrov had commanded enough respect to carry out Putin's plan to reunite Chechnya with the motherland. Now he was dead. In Chechnya's clannish society, the only obvious successor was his son, Ramzan, a thuggish fighter who had once served as his father's driver and then security chief, in charge of a group of fighters who became notorious for their brutal tactics against suspected militants. When Putin summoned Ramzan to the Kremlin on the day of his father's assassination, he arrived looking disheveled and wearing sweatpants. He was only twenty-seven, too young according to Chechnya's new constitution to become president, but Putin elevated him to the post of deputy prime minister and laid the foundation for him to succeed his father when he turned thirty. The rebels vowed to kill him too. "You don't have to be Nostradamus to guess the fate of Ramzan Kadyrov," they vowed on their website. Two days after the attack in May, Putin secretly flew to Chechnya to attend Kadyrov's funeral, and his own delusion about the progress that had been made became clear. He flew by helicopter over the ruins of Grozny, seeing with his own eyes the physical evidence of devastation that had been airbrushed out of official accounts of the war. When he returned to Moscow, he appeared before his ministers and declared that not enough was being done to rebuild the shattered republic. He stated what had been obvious to anyone who had to live in Grozny. "Despite all that is being done there," he said, "it looks horrible from a helicopter."[30] He sounded surprised.

In Beslan, the local authorities were overwhelmed. Police commanders initially reported having trouble reaching the terrorists inside the school, even though one of them answered the school's telephone and told Nikolay Khalip of *The New York Times* that the fighters were a unit under the command of Shamil Basayev, Russia's most wanted terrorist. "Wipe your sniffles," he told Khalip.[31] After a while a terrified woman emerged from the school with a note demanding negotiations with the leaders of North Ossetia and neighboring Ingushetia and the doctor who had mediated during the *Nord-Ost* siege, Leonid Roshal. The note also warned that the captors would shoot fifty hostages if any of their fighters were killed. By evening they escorted the men to a classroom on the second floor and began to execute them one by one anyway, heaving their bodies out the window.

On the morning the siege began, Putin woke and managed an early swim in the sea, but the unfolding crisis made staying in Sochi impossible. He flew back to Moscow, where a senior aide who met him described him as "terribly upset," complaining about the utter breakdown in security that could allow a group of heavily armed fighters to seize an entire school.[32]

Putin remained in the Kremlin during the following days, retreating periodically to the office's chapel to pray, it was made known, but also complaining that he did not have time for his daily exercise routine.[33] He appeared in public only briefly, on September 2, during an appearance with King Abdullah of Jordan, in which he vowed to protect the lives of the hostages above all. He spoke even as he ordered the FSB to dispatch ten "special purpose" groups to Beslan, each comprising elite officers trained for extraordinary crises.[34] Putin sought to convey a sense of calm authority, but the reflex of Russian officials to lie in the face of tragedy compounded the sense of panic and choas. The authorities in Beslan and in Moscow reported that there were only 354 hostages, even though everyone in the town knew there were more. Some of those outside the school angrily resorted to holding up signs in view of television cameras saying there were as many as 800 hostages and imploring Putin to intervene peacefully, knowing that would not be his reflexive instinct.[35] The terrorists inside were furious when they watched state television parroting the lie about the number of hostages; they threatened to shoot hostages until only 354 were left. Even some officials agonized over the lies they had to repeat.[36]

The authorities—the police, the Interior Ministry, and the FSB, all bolstered by Putin during his first term—seemed paralyzed. They worried as much about protecting the regime that Putin had created as about protecting the children and parents besieged inside the school. Anna Politkovskaya, who had negotiated with the terrorists at *Nord-Ost*, reached out to Chechnya's opposition leaders in exile to mediate again, but when she flew to an airport near enough to drive to Beslan, she fell ill during the flight; she was convinced that the tea she had been given was poisoned. Andrei Babitsky, the reporter whose capture during the early years of the war had led to a scandal, was detained at a Moscow airport, as well.[37] The authorities who had failed spectacularly to protect Beslan's school were determined to protect the city from unwanted reporters.

The officials in Beslan appeared uncertain and hesitant as the siege entered a second day. The tension was heightened by intermittent explosions and gunfire, the cause of which remained unclear to those outside. Putin had made himself the ultimate authority in Russia, but his "vertical of power" created paralysis in times of crisis: No one would risk taking an initiative that might provoke disapproval.[38] Putin had vowed never to negotiate with terrorists, but for the first time he allowed his aides to explore the possibility of a negotiated end to the siege, even as the Kremlin distanced him from the effort.[39] He instructed the region's governor, Aleksandr Dzasokhov, to make contact with Alsan Maskhadov's chief representative in exile, Akhmed Zakayev. He did so through Ruslan Aushev, the former president of neighboring Ingushetia. Aushev, a hero of the Soviet war in Afghanistan, had been sympathetic to Chechnya's struggle for independence, but he also made sure to keep his region out of the fighting. Aushev arrived in Beslan on the second day of the siege and took over contact with the terrorists. Within fifteen minutes, he was told he could enter the school, the first official allowed in.

What he saw inside was desperate. The terrorists had given the hostages no food or water. The commander of the group, who called himself Colonel, gave Aushev a handwritten list of demands: Russian troops should withdraw from Chechnya and grant it independence. The new Chechnya would join Russia in the Commonwealth of Independent States, keep the ruble as its currency, and work with Russian forces to restore order in the region. The note, scrawled on notebook paper, was addressed to "His Excellency, President of the Russian Federation" and written in the name of "the servant of Allah, Shamil Basayev." None of the demands would be acceptable to Putin, but Aushev promised to convey them if the terrorists would release the women with nursing babies. One of the terrorists told him there were 1,020 hostages inside the sweltering school. Aushev managed to persuade them to allow twenty-six hostages to leave with him—eleven women and fifteen babies.

When Aushev returned to the command center, he called Zakayev, then in London. Zakayev told him that he and Maskhadov were prepared to assist, but that if Maskhadov were to travel to Beslan to speak to the terrorists, Russia would have to guarantee safe passage.[40] Aushev knew that a plan had been drawn up to raid the school; in fact, two of the special units that Putin had ordered to Beslan were already training for an assault at a similar schoolhouse not far away.[41] He hoped he could win the release of more hostages in the meantime, however. On the morning of the third day, September 3, he reached an agreement

with the terrorists to remove the bodies of the men who had been executed and tossed from the classroom window; by then, their corpses had
begun decomposing. A four-man crew from the Ministry of Emergency
Situations pulled up in an ambulance at one o'clock and had just begun
picking up the bodies when a thunderous explosion rocked the school's
gymnasium. Twenty-two seconds later a second explosion erupted. The
blasts lifted the roof and rafters off the school, blew out the windows,
and ripped a hole in the gymnasium's wall.

Scores were killed immediately, but dazed survivors began to escape,
tumbling out of the shattered school. The soldiers outside and the terrorists inside—both unsure of what had happened—began a ferocious
firefight that lasted for ten hours. The roof caught fire and the burning
rafters collapsed on those still inside. A conspiracy theory later emerged
that the Russians had started the battle by firing into the school, but
none of those outside had appeared prepared to launch an assault on
the building when the assault began. Many did not have bullet-proof
vests. Nor had they established a security perimeter around the building. There were no ambulances or fire trucks on hand. Local men with
hunting rifles joined the fight, firing haphazardly and running into the
crossfire to carry children to safety.[42]

The horrific pandemonium unfolded live on international
television—though not on the Russian networks, which interrupted
their regular programming only for brief updates that continued to play
down the carnage as it worsened. Neither Putin nor any other senior
officials emerged to address the crisis. Prime Minister Fradkov carried
on with a government meeting convened to discuss the nation's privatization plans, even as the bursts of gunfire and explosions shredded the
school. The climax of the battle came that night at 11:15, when a Russian tank fired a shell into the school, killing three insurgents holding
out in the basement. Russia's state television networks had declared the
situation under control hours before.

When it was over, 334 hostages had died, 186 of them children. Ten
Russian commandos were killed trying to free those inside. Thirty terrorists died, including the two women, Maryam Taburova and Rosa
Nagayeva, whose roommates had launched the wave of terror by destroying the two airliners. One terrorist was captured and later tried in court,
but others were believed to have escaped in the chaos. Since the death
toll nearly equaled the number of hostages that had been repeated for
more than two days on state television, the lie could no longer be hidden.

The public distrust of official statements was such that many believed the government continued to lie about the number of dead, the fate of the terrorists, and the cause of the two explosions that had brought the siege to its horrible end.

Putin left the Kremlin early on the morning of September 4 and flew to Beslan. He arrived before dawn and visited the wounded in a hospital before making a brief statement with the region's president, Aleksandr Dzasokhov. "Today all of Russia suffers for you," he told him.[43] He offered no other words of comfort beyond his vow to hunt down those responsible for the siege. He was not there to comfort, but to create the image of having comforted. He did not hold a meeting—even one scripted for the cameras—with the people of Beslan. The anguished, frenzied, and traumatized crowds that had kept vigil outside the school demanded afterward that the government act, that the government stop lying. Instead Putin returned to Moscow and delivered a televised address to the nation.

When Putin appeared in the nation's living rooms that night, he looked uncharacteristically shaken. He stood alone in front of a wood-paneled wall and a Russian flag. "It is a difficult and bitter task for me to speak," he began. "A horrible tragedy happened in our land."[44] He asked all of Russia to remember those "who lost the dearest in their life," bowing his head slightly, but he offered no apology and accepted no responsibility. He did not use the occasion to defend, justify, or explain his policies in Chechnya. Nor did he offer any new approach. He did not even mention Chechnya by name. Putin instead offered a soliloquy on the country's history, one with a deep nostalgia for the unifying purpose and security of the Soviet Union, then already thirteen years gone. He had only suggested as much before, careful to honor the history of the Soviet past without embracing its failures and crimes, but now he seemed to blame the siege in Beslan on Russia's inability to preserve the strength that made the Soviet Union he remembered as a boy so strong and respected. "There have been many tragic pages and difficult trials in the history of Russia," he went on, lecturing patiently as a professor might. "Today we are living in conditions formed after the disintegration of a huge, great country, the country which unfortunately turned out to be nonviable in the conditions of a rapidly changing world. Today, however, despite all difficulties, we managed to preserve the nucleus of that giant, the Soviet Union. We called the new country the Russian Federation. We all expected changes, changes for the better, but found ourselves absolutely unprepared for much that changed in our lives. The question is why. We live in conditions of a transitional economy and a political system that do not correspond to the development of society. We live in conditions of aggravated internal conflicts and ethnic conflicts that before were harshly suppressed by the governing ideology. We stopped paying due attention to issues of defense and security. We allowed corruption to affect the judiciary and law enforcement systems. In addition to that, our country, which once had one of the mightiest systems of protecting its borders, suddenly found itself unprotected either from West or East."

Putin's remarks sounded almost like an indictment of his first years in office, a recognition that *he* had failed to deliver on the promises he had made over and over. The reference to Russia's "unprotected" borders revealed a blinkered understanding of the threat still emanating from Chechnya. He had long sought to link the war to the rise of Al-Qaeda globally, but despite a shared ideology of extremist Islam, the terrorism Russia faced was largely grown at home. Its roots reached back to the tsarist conquest of the Caucasus in the nineteenth century. Yet he believed that those who attacked the school had help from nations determined to punish Russia, to keep it weak and pliant. His tone was apocalyptic and defiant; he said the country had to unite to preserve its very existence. "Some want to tear off of us a juicy piece of pie," he said. "Others help them to do it. They help because they think that Russia, as one of the greatest nuclear powers of the world, is still a threat, and this threat has to be eliminated. And terrorism is only an instrument to achieve these goals."

Putin spoke as if he had experienced a great revelation, yet the war on terrorism was the one place where he had found common ground with world leaders. Despite occasional rebukes for the brutality of Russian tactics in Chechnya, no leader ever expressed sympathy for the terrorist tactics of Basayev and his followers. The only government that ever recognized Chechnya's declaration of independence after the first war was the Taliban in Afghanistan, who the United States, with Russia's blessing and assistance, had helped overthrow after the attacks of September 11, 2001. But now Putin blamed unseen enemies for abetting one of the most heinous terrorist acts in history. The country had grown lax and lazy in the face of this external threat, he said, and he vowed to take every possible measure to strengthen the state.

"We demonstrated weakness," he said, "and the weak are beaten."

The reforms that Putin promised in his national address after the Beslan tragedy were not long in coming. He did not shake up the intelligence services that had failed to anticipate the attack on a school. He did not fire the military or police commanders who had botched the attempted negotiations and the ultimate rescue. Instead, Putin announced that he would tighten the Kremlin's political control by further dismantling the vestiges of democratic government.

On September 13, ten days after the horrifying end of the siege, Putin abolished the elections of governors, mayors, and presidents of Russia's many regions and republics, who since the collapse of the Soviet Union had maintained their own constituencies and power bases outside of Moscow's direct control. He would now appoint them and submit his candidates to the regional parliaments for ratification. If they rejected his candidates, he could then disband them. He also abolished the representative district elections for the parliament, which accounted for half of the Duma's 450 seats. With opposition parties increasingly circumscribed, these elections provided the only independent and liberal members left in power after the 2003 elections.

The proposals shocked those who felt that for all of Putin's authoritarian instincts, the country was nonetheless making steady, if halting, progress toward democracy. *Izvestiya* called it the "September Revolution," while Putin's critics denounced the moves as unconstitutional, even though they were resigned to the futility of any legal challenge. The most prominent criticism came from Boris Yeltsin. In an interview with *Moskovskiye Novosti,* he recalled his promise to remain out of the nation's political debates in retirement, but said Beslan had been a watershed that had made Russia a "different country." "We will not permit ourselves to renounce the letter and, most importantly, the spirit of the Constitution that the country adopted at a nationwide referendum in 1993—if only because strangling freedoms and curtailing democratic rights marks, among other things, the victory of terrorists."[45] Privately, Yeltsin despaired over the leader he had elevated to power, seeing Putin's moves against the media, against opposition parties, and now against the governors as an erosion of his own legacy,[46] but the interview was the only time Yeltsin had voiced his concerns so sharply in public. By now, though, Yeltsin's moral and political authority had little force in Putin's Russia. His time had passed, and his heir was taking the country on a new path. Indeed, the Yeltsin era—the erratic lurch through the chaos of the 1990s—had become Putin's recurring justification for his decisions. Step by step, Putin erased the legacy of his predecessor, as surely as Stalin had Lenin's, as Khrushchev had Stalin's, as Brezhnev had Khrushschev's, as Yeltsin had Gorbachev's.

Even those most affected by Putin's new decree—the governors and mayors who owed their electoral legitimacy and authority to the ballot box, however compromised—stepped forward one by one to praise Putin's proposal. The proposals had been debated before in his administration, but he used the Beslan tragedy as the pretext to implement them. Popular will, in Putin's view, was the road to chaos. The people could not be entrusted with the power to choose their own leaders except in the most carefully controlled process. "The Russian people are backward," he would later tell a group of foreign journalists and academics invited to a retreat that would become an annual affair known as the Valdai Club, after the resort where it was first held. "They cannot adapt to democracy as they have done in your countries. They need time."[47] His remarks reflected condescension that bordered on disdain, but few in Russia spoke up to challenge the authority he now took upon himself. Within weeks, the Duma and the Federation Council enacted all of his proposals, willingly handing more and more powers to the Kremlin. "The only thing left is absolute prostration," Leonid Dobrokhotov, an adviser to the Communists, said in response.[48] And most of Russia's elite, either from loyalty or from fear, were happy to oblige.

CHAPTER 15

The Orange Contagion

On September 5, 2004, the night after Putin's Beslan speech, Viktor Yushchenko drove surreptitiously to an exclusive, gated dacha outside Kyiv. He was running for president of Ukraine, and he was certain someone was trying to kill him. Accompanied by his campaign manager but not his bodyguards, he met General Ihor Smeshko, the head of the Security Service of Ukraine, or the SBU, the country's own successor to the KGB. Smeshko had not wanted anyone else around. The host was Smeshko's deputy, Volodymyr Satsyuk, whose cook prepared a midnight meal of boiled crawfish and salad, washed down with beer, followed later by a dessert of fruit with glasses of vodka and cognac.[1] Nothing seemed amiss. Yushchenko posed for a photograph with the two security officials, and left at two o'clock in the morning. Later that day, he began to feel ill. His head hurt, and then so did his spine. His symptoms worsened in the days ahead and his handsome face was soon discolored and disfigured by an eruption of cysts. In pain, he traveled to Austria on September 10 for treatment, fearful of Ukrainian hospitals. After puzzling over his symptoms for weeks, the doctors there ultimately concluded that he had ingested, presumably at the late-night dinner, one of the highest doses ever recorded in a human of a highly toxic compound, known as 2,3,7, 8-Tetrachlorodibenzo-p-dioxin, or TCDD.

Ukraine's presidential election was scheduled for October 31, 2004. The winner would replace the president of the previous decade, Leonid Kuchma, an apparatchik who had been elected as a reformer in 1994, only to turn increasingly authoritarian and corrupt as Ukraine stumbled through its transition to democracy and capitalism. The country experienced the same chaos and corruption, poverty and criminality that Russia had, but there was a crucial difference. For many Ukrainians, the demise of the Soviet Union was not a catastrophe but a liberation—the rebirth of independence from Moscow that it had experienced only very briefly, in the chaotic years that followed the Bolshevik revolution in 1917.

With nearly forty-eight million people in 2004, Ukraine was the second largest and most important of the former Soviet republics, an agricultural and industrial heartland that had been devastated by the civil war; by the collectivization policies of Joseph Stalin, which produced a famine; and then by the Great Patriotic War, when it was occupied and ravaged by the Nazis and then retaken again by the liberating Soviet armies. Ukraine lost more than three million people during the war, more than a sixth of its population at the time, and the scars were deep. Ukraine's nationhood—its national identity—remained tenuous. It was deeply divided geographically and ethnically between Ukrainians and Russians, among others; between those who embraced the liberation that came with the collapse of the Soviet Union and those who lamented its demise. Ukrainians were close to Russia, historically and culturally, but the nationalistic spirit that emerged in the country's first years of independence resembled that of the former republics like Lithuania, Latvia, and Estonia, which had endured five decades of Soviet occupation and now were part of NATO and the European Union. They adopted Ukrinian symbols and Ukrainian names for cities, including the capital, which had been rendered in Russian as Kiev for centuries, but reverted in independence to the Ukrainian style, Kyiv.

Throughout his presidency, Kuchma balanced Russia on one side and the European Union, and even NATO, on the other. His government retained close economic and diplomatic ties with Russia, but also dispatched Ukrainian troops to Iraq as part of the American-led coalition that was then struggling to reestablish order after the overthrow of Saddam Hussein. Like the country itself, he seemed conflicted. To his many critics, he simply lacked conviction; he was a kleptocrat motivated by greed and power, beholden to the country's oligarchs. Yet he never had the will or the power to stifle politics the way Putin had, because the country's divisions ensured competing power centers. The country's oligarchs themselves had divided loyalties and ambitions and thus were never entirely subservient. Putin had tamed Russia's oligarchs, while in Ukraine they still threw their support—and cash—behind different political factions, depending on their financial interests.

Democracy in Ukraine was immature, unruly, and, at times, vicious, but no one man dominated the country's politics. Kuchma's opponents enjoyed the support of a television network, Channel 5, which had remained free of state control, permitting a diversity of news and opinion that in turn fostered political debate. When Kuchma was implicated in the murder of a prominent journalist, Georgy Gongadze, he could not easily suppress the anti-government protests that erupted, nor could he prevent opposition members of parliament from demanding an investigation. In 2000, Gongadze's headless body was discovered in a forest outside of Kyiv only months after he founded an online investigative newspaper that infuriated Kuchma's inner circle with its rollicking reports on corruption. Conversations secretly recorded in Kuchma's office caught him railing against Gongadze's reporting and urging aides to deal with him.[2] Kuchma denied ordering the murder, but his political career was in ruins. Many had feared that as his second term came to an end in 2004, he would try to revise the Constitution to extend his rule, but in the end Kuchma had no choice but to step aside. Unlike Russia's listless parliamentary and presidential elections in 2003 and 2004, Ukraine's remained passionately, fiercely contested, the outcomes uncertain.

Putin followed Ukraine's politics closely and found them worrisome. Kuchma's dwindling credibility raised the very real possibility that the opposition could win. Putin had already watched another former Soviet republic, Georgia, succumb to a popular, democratic uprising after a disputed election in 2003. It was a tiny country of five million people on Russia's new southern frontier, the spine of the Caucasus. The country's president, Eduard Shevardnadze, had been the former foreign minister of the Soviet Union, a close adviser of Mikhail Gorbachev, and a man many in Russia blamed for the collapse that followed perestroika. Shevardnadze returned to his native republic and stumbled into power following Georgia's violent birth as an independent state, fractured by wars, abetted by Russian fighters, which established the breakaway regions of Abkhazia and South Ossetia inside the country's internationally recognized borders.

After Georgia's parliamentary election in November 2003 was rigged, thousands of people poured into the streets to protest. They had the training and financing of international organizations funded by George Soros and the United States Congress, among others. When Shevardnadze tried to install the new parliament on November 22, the protesters stormed the building, led by the opposition leader, Mikheil Saakashvili. Shevardnadze had to appeal to the Kremlin for help. He telephoned Putin that night as the latter dined with his senior advisers in one of Moscow's most famous Georgian restaurants.[3] Putin ordered his foreign minister, Igor Ivanov, to fly to Tbilisi, the Georgian capital, to mediate, though with clear instructions not to let a mob overthrow an elected head of state. In the end, Ivanov failed, and Shevardnadze, misunderstanding the level of support he had from Moscow, resigned. The "Rose Revolution," as it came to be known, thrust Saakashvili into power. The parliamentary election was followed by his election as president in January 2004. Saakashvili considered himself Georgia's Putin, a strong leader determined to restore stability to the country. In one of his first acts in office, he flew to Moscow to meet Putin, fawning over him as a political inspiration. Putin, however, was alarmed by Shevardnadze's ouster and Saakashvili's westernizing instincts. Putin responded to the fawning with a tirade about the former countries of the Warsaw Pact becoming "slaves to America."[4] Georgia's relations with Russia went downhill from there.

For Putin, the stakes in Ukraine were much higher. Georgia was a rump state that posed no major threat to Moscow's influence. Ukraine, in contrast, had deep ethnic, cultural, and economic ties to Russia—and to Putin. It was the historical root of Russia itself: Kievan Rus, the medieval fief whose leader, Vladimir the Great, adopted Christianity in 988, and the frontier of the tsarist empires that followed—its name translated literally as the Ukraine, or "the border." Its borders had shifted over time: Parts of its western territory had belonged to Poland or the Austro-Hungarian Empire; Stalin seized some of it with his secret pact with Hitler in 1939 and the rest after the end of the Great Patriotic War. Ukraine's modern shape took form, but it seemed ephemeral, subject to the larger forces of geopolitics, as most borderlands have been throughout history. In 1954, Nikita Khrushchev decreed that Crimea, conquered by Catherine the Great in the eighteenth century and heroically defended against the Nazis, would be governed by the Ukrainian Soviet Socialist Republic from Kiev, not from Moscow. No one then—and certainly not Putin when he honeymooned there nearly two decades later—ever envisioned that Ukraine and with it Crimea would one day be part of another, independent nation. Even now, in 2004, it seemed a historical accident that Putin, like most Russians, would tolerate only as long as the new Ukraine remained firmly nestled in Russia's geopolitical embrace.

In July 2004, three months before Ukraine's presidential election, Putin flew to Crimea to meet with Kuchma and Viktor Yanukovych, who had been Kuchma's prime minister since 2002, when he replaced the man now running as the main opposition candidate, Viktor Yush-chenko. Despite reservations from Putin, who did not consider him the best candidate,[5] Kuchma had tapped Yanukovych as his political heir. Their meeting with Putin that July took place in Yalta—in the same building, the Livadia Palace, where the victors of the Great Patriotic War had divided the spoils of a soon-to-be liberated Europe. Putin, too, had "spheres of influence" in mind that summer, and as far as he was concerned, Ukraine remained within Russia's.

Putin pressed Kuchma to end his government's flirtation with the European Union and NATO. The latter was now particularly reviled in Russia as it crept further and further eastward. Only months before, in March, NATO had expanded its member nations from nineteen to twenty-six, admitting not only Bulgaria, Slovakia, Slovenia, and Roma-nia in eastern Europe but the three former Soviet republics of Lithuania, Latvia, and Estonia, each of which was home to a sizable population of Russians. Most American and European officials accepted as an arti-cle of faith that NATO's expansion would strengthen the security of the continent by forging a defensive collective of democracies, just as the European Union had buried many of the nationalistic urges that had caused so much conflict in previous centuries. Putin had grudg-ingly accepted NATO's plans to expand, but now NATO seemed to loom over Ukraine. Like many in Russia's security establishment, he had been trained to subvert and, if necessary, fight NATO, and a sense of enmity lingered. Officials often cited reassurances that Mikhail Gor-bachev believed he had been given during the reunification of Germany after 1989 that NATO would not expand to the east (though leaders of the United States and Europe insisted that no such reassurance had ever been made). It was humiliating enough that the Baltic nations had joined NATO, but influential American and European officials were now openly advocating the inclusion of still more former Soviet repub-lics, including Georgia and Ukraine. "The presence of American soldiers on our border has created a kind of paranoia in Russia," Putin's new for-eign minister, Sergei Lavrov, acknowledged in April 2004 when the cer-emonial raising of the flags of the new member states took place outside the alliance's headquarters in Brussels. There were in fact no Americans deployed to the Baltic states, merely a rotating squadron of European fighter jets to patrol the skies over the new territories, but it seemed to Putin as if the enemy had reached the gates. They had to be stopped, and Putin drew the line at Ukraine.

In Yalta, he and Kuchma discussed the integration of a proposed Common Economic Space, a loose economic alliance between Russia and Ukraine, along with Belarus and Kazakhstan, that over the years would take shape as a more formal customs union and finally an economic and political bloc intended to rival the European Union. Putin had floated the idea the year before, but now he wanted Kuchma's explicit public support for it. This meant reversing a formal strategy that Kuchma's government had published a month before calling for Ukraine to pursue membership in the European Union and NATO. Needing Russia's support in what was shaping up as a close election for his successors, one that could provide a tainted president with security after he left office, Kuchma succumbed to Putin's pressure. After their meeting, he announced that he had abandoned the strategy he had just announced and would only seek cordial relations with the alliances that dominated Europe—an abrupt reversal that stunned Ukraine's opposition.

Behind closed doors, Putin and Kuchma also struck a side deal: they created a new energy trading company.[6] It went by the unwieldy acronym RosUkrEnergo, and its ownership remained deliberately vague. Half was owned by a branch of Gazprom, the gas monopoly in Russia that had increasingly become part of Putin's vision of a greater Russia, controlled by the Kremlin and led by his closest allies from Petersburg. The other half was owned by a shadowy company whose partners remained secret, their share managed by an Austrian bank, Raiffeisen International. The new company was registered neither in Russia nor in Ukraine, but rather in Switzerland.[7] This murky deal underscored how Putin's concern about Ukraine's looming election extended far beyond politics alone, and how much financial concerns figured in most of his calculations.

Natural gas, even more than oil, had become Russia's most powerful tool in foreign policy. Oil trades freely, sloshing through the world's economy; gas requires fixed pipelines, linking the nations of Europe to Russia. The network of pipelines, dating to the Soviet era, gave Russia clout and, with rising energy prices, the prospect of the wealth that Putin nearly a decade before had argued in his dissertation was the core of the state's power. Ukraine, through which most of Russia's gas passed, represented a potential chokehold on Putin's ambitions. Putin was certain that he now faced a concerted effort to thwart his plans. When he appeared at Livadia Palace following his private talks with Kuchma and Yanukovych, Putin even used a KGB term for networks of agents and informants betraying the state on behalf of the countries trying to destroy it: *agentura.* "The *agentura,* both inside our countries and outside, are trying everything possible to compromise the integration between Russia and Ukraine," he said.[8]

L ook at my face," Viktor Yushchenko declared when he returned to Kyiv on September 21 from treatment in the Austrian hospital. The source of his poisoning, even the fact of it, was not yet clear, but he went directly to the Ukrainian parliament, the Supreme Rada, to accuse unnamed enemies of trying to stop his candidacy. His appearance was sensational. Yushchenko, a central banker who helped create the country's new currency, the hyrvna, had served as Kuchma's prime minister for two years before he was ousted by those opposed to his westernizing vision for Ukraine's future. He strongly supported the European Union and NATO. The fact that his wife was a Ukrainian-American from the diaspora in Chicago only confirmed the worst to his critics, including Kuchma, who was heard in the secret recordings coarsely ranting that she was an operative of the CIA.[9] (He also had them both followed.) Now Yushchenko stood at the Rada's dais and accused Kuchma's allies of conspiring to murder him. "What happened to me was not caused by food or my diet, but by the political regime in this country. Friends, we are not talking today about food literally, we are talking about the Ukrainian political kitchen where murders are on the menu."[10] Hidden under his suit, he had a catheter in his spine, pulsing sedatives to ease the pain he was experiencing. Four days later he flew back to Vienna for further treatment.

Yushchenko was not a charismatic politician, but his campaign was well funded and astute. It had chosen a simple message—*Tak,* or Yes— and adopted the color orange, plastering the city with flags, banners, and ads. He also forged an alliance with Yulia Tymoshenko, a formidable nationalist and energy tycoon who had manipulated the collapsing Soviet system to enrich herself as Mikhail Khodorkovsky had in Russia. Her ambition was astounding and, as a woman in a political milieu dominated by men, she unabashedly used her attractiveness as a political prop, braiding her hair in a trademark peasant's rope. With Yushchenko sidelined for treatment, she carried the campaign for him, delivering

blistering denunciations of Kuchma's rule and the prospect that Yanukovych would simply steer the country ever closer to Russia.

As the election neared, Yushchenko's campaign gained momentum. The intelligence reports that reached Putin each morning must
have confirmed his worst fears of Western nefariousness, detailing an
elaborate plan to encircle Russia. What was happening in Ukraine must
be a prelude to a final push into Russia itself. This plot owed much to
the febrile imagination of Russia's intelligence services, but the United
States, Germany, and other European nations fed the fever by supply-
ing money to organizations in Ukraine that promoted democracy, civil
society, legal reform, and environmentalism. Since the collapse of the
Soviet Union, these nongovernmental organizations (NGOs) had operated throughout Eastern Europe, even in Russia, with the aim of assist-
ing newly independent nations to make the transition from one-party
systems to open, multiparty democracies. In Serbia in 2000, then in
Georgia in 2003, they had provided support to peaceful political protests
that ultimately overthrew sclerotic governments. Though their funding
was modest, rarely more than a few million dollars or euros each, they
represented the *agentura* that Putin feared.

Russian businesses, under pressure from the Kremlin, countered with
pledges of cash for Yanukovych at the same meeting in Yalta. Roughly
half of the $600 million that Yanukovych's team was believed to have
spent—the equivalent of 1 percent of the country's GDP—came from
Russia.[11] Signaling the depth of his personal involvement, Putin put his
own chief of staff, Dmitri Medvedev, in charge of the Kremlin's political
operation in Ukraine. Medvedev, who had run Sobchak's and Putin's
campaigns in the past, dispatched trusted advisers, including Gleb Pavlovsky and Sergei Markov, to Ukraine. In August, the Kremlin's political operatives opened a space called "Russia House" in a central hotel
in Kyiv, ostensibly to promote good will between Russia and Ukraine,
but in reality to run the Kremlin's campaign on Yanukovych's behalf.
They orchestrated the same sort of operation that characterized Russia's
elections: uncritical coverage on state television of set-piece rallies for
Yanukovych and vicious attacks on Yushchenko as an agent of the West.
A cache of posters produced by Yanukovych's advisers showed Yushchenko's orange slogan under a picture of President Bush riding Ukraine like
a cowboy. Yanukovych's wife, Lyudmila, ranted at a rally in Donetsk that
the Americans provided Yushchenko's supporters with felt boots and

oranges laced with narcotics—remarks that were promptly remixed into a pop song that provided a sound track for the upheaval to come.

Putin, for his part, injected himself directly into the campaign, meeting with Kuchma and Yanukovych repeatedly. On the eve of the first round of voting on October 31, he traveled to Kyiv for a state visit that ostensibly celebrated the sixtieth anniversary of the Soviet Union's liberation of Ukraine from the Nazis in 1944. The night before the parade he even appeared during prime time on three state television channels for a call-in interview, in which he affected magnanimity and concern for the issues facing Ukrainians. He nodded to Ukraine's independence and sovereignty, but also made it clear that a historical mistake had separated the two brotherly nations from their natural alliance.[12]

Several of the questions, which were sent in by email or fax or called in live, lamented the demise of the Soviet Union. One questioner asked Putin to run for president of Ukraine. Putin demurred. It was impossible to rebuild the Soviet Union, he said, but Ukraine's future lay in tightening its economic ties to Russia. He never mentioned Yushchenko, but five times he praised Yanukovych's stewardship as prime minister. Putin, by now used to these formats at home, exuded charm and humility. The announcer exclaimed that there were six hundred calls a minute coming in on the phone lines. Putin recited—in Ukrainian—a fragment of a poem by Taras Shevchenko, Ukraine's national poet, although he had to admit that while he understood some Ukrainian, he did not speak it. A schoolboy named Andrei wanted to know if he could be photographed with him—"Vladimir Vladimirovich, do you believe in dreams?" he began—and the next day, Putin obliged, appearing with little Andrei in Kuchma's office and presenting him a laptop as a gift. During the military parade Putin stood beside Kuchma and Yanukovych on the viewing stand as thousands of soldiers goose-stepped past wearing vintage uniforms and standards of the Red Army. (At one point, Yanukovych tried to hand Putin a stick of chewing gum, prompting a look of astonished disgust at his coarse manners.)[13]

However transparently staged, Putin's appearances resonated with some Ukrainians, those who envied Russia's rising standard of living or harbored the same nostalgia that many Russians did for the Soviet era. Ukraine, however, was more pluralistic than Russia, and its democracy less "managed." State television served the power and assailed Yushchenko on a daily basis, insinuating that his illness was caused by sushi or syphilis, but Kuchma's control of the media was not absolute. Channel 5, owned by a chocolate tycoon, Petro Poroshenko, threw itself unabashedly behind Yushchenko. It became the voice of the opposition's campaign, prompting the government to try unsuccessfully to suspend its broadcasting license. Putin's unprecedented intervention in another country's election also played into the opposition's main argument: that a vote for Yanukovych would simply return the country to the empire from which it had gained independence. That anyone would ask Putin in earnest to become the leader of Ukraine was too much. The Kremlin's political apparatchiks never appreciated that, because Putin did not. Putin's strategists also miscalculated the degree to which the crude anti-Americanism that worked in Russia's politics would resonate in Ukraine.

When the first round of the election was held on October 31, Yushchenko collected 39.87 percent of the votes, edging out Yanukovych's 39.32 percent, with twenty minor candidates dividing the rest. Exit polls paid for by the Western *agentura* had Yushchenko ahead by an even larger margin, and with widespread reports of ballot stuffing and other irregularities, some in the opposition, including Yulia Tymoshenko, wanted to protest in the streets, as they had been preparing to do all summer. Yushchenko, though, was content to celebrate his unexpectedly strong showing and vowed that he would prevail in the runoff scheduled for three weeks later, on November 21.

After Yanukovych's lackluster showing, Putin redoubled his efforts. With both candidates courting the also-rans from the first round, Putin pressed Russia's Communist leader, Gennady Zyuganov, to use his influence with Petro Symonenko, the Ukrainian Communist candidate who had received 5 percent of the vote. Zyuganov agreed, but he had a price: the Kremlin had to provide financing to the Communist Party of Russia and end the relentlessly negative coverage of it on state television. The Kremlin did, for a while, but the tactic failed since Symonenko too was furious over the voting, believing that more than fifty thousand Communist votes had been stripped from him in the first round. Instead, he called on his party members to vote against both candidates in the runoff.[14]

Putin then traveled to Ukraine for yet another working visit, meeting Kuchma and Yanukovych in Crimea once again to inaugurate regular ferry service between the peninsula and the Russian mainland, and together they traveled down the Crimean coast to the Artek International Children's Center, a famous Soviet-era resort that was then hosting hundreds of schoolchildren who had survived the terror attack in Beslan. The Kremlin's political operatives, including Medvedev, remained confident of Yanukovych's victory, in part because Kuchma and Yankuvoych were. Still, Putin pressed Yanukovych to do more with the government resources at hand to boost turnout, a practice that had worked well in Russia.[15]

To prepare for the runoff, election officials padded voter lists with "dead souls," suspiciously inflating the turnout in the eastern areas that supported Yanukovych. In Donetsk, the turnout for the second round jumped nearly 20 percent to an incredible 96.7 percent. On the day of the runoff, voters were bused to Kyiv to vote after voting in their home districts; hundreds of them were caught in the act.[16] Yushchenko's campaign had anticipated fraud, but the flagrancy of it provoked outrage. By the time polls closed that night, his supporters, wearing orange and waving orange flags, poured into the streets around Kyiv's central public space, Maidan Nezalezhnosti, or Independence Square. The crowds had grown to tens of thousands by the next morning, when the election commission announced preliminary results that showed Yanukovych winning with 49 percent to Yushchenko's 46 percent, even though the exit polls paid for by NGOs from the United States and Europe showed the latter winning by 11 points. International election observers immediately raised questions about the conduct of the vote and the tally, but Putin, who had spent the previous three days in Latin America for a summit of the Asia-Pacific Economic Cooperation nations, promptly telephoned from Brazil to congratulate Yanukovych.

Yushchenko's supporters erected a tent city in the Maidan, vowing to remain until the election result was overturned. For all the outrage over the fraud, the mood of the crowd was festive. Pop musicians performed between the speeches of Yushchenko and his supporters. Kuchma's advisers were in disarray, divided over what to do. Journalists began revolting at the state television networks, including an interpreter for the deaf, who disregarded the official script of the anchor on the main state channel and began signing the truth. "The results announced by the Central Electoral Commission are rigged," she signed. "Do not believe them." When Kuchma's government made no immediate move to remove the protesters, more people poured into the square—not just political activists, but ordinary people, even parents who took their children to witness what they felt was a historic moment in Ukraine's young history. It was suddenly more than an outpouring of support for Yushchenko. For all the country's problems, its crippling Soviet legacies, Ukrainians, unlike Russians, were willing to take to the streets to demand fairness and accountability from their leaders. On November 23, Yushchenko took a symbolic oath of office, proclaiming himself the winner in a quorum-less session of parliament, only to have the election commission declare Yanukovych the official winner after the final tally the next day. Putin extended congratulations again, this time in a letter to Yanukovych, say-ing the Ukrainians had made "a choice for stability," but the crowds grew even larger, laying siege to the parliament and presidential building in a sea of orange. It was Putin's worst nightmare.

Putin flew from South America to Brussels for a meeting with the lead-ers of the European Union, most of whom had refused to recognize the election results in Ukraine and instead called for a investigation into the fraud. The chummy partnership that Putin hoped to develop with the Europeans—promising to expand cooperation on energy, secu-rity, trade, and travel—had grown increasingly strained, and Ukraine all but broke it. "I am convinced that we have no more right to incite mass disturbances in a major European state," Putin said after a tense private meeting with the leaders. He was accusing them of encouraging the peo-ple massed in the streets of Kyiv. "We must not make it an international practice to resolve disputes of this kind through street riots."

Putin's insistence that the outcome was "absolutely clear" left Russia with no alternative strategy, and the Kremlin struggled to keep up with the pace of events. Ukraine's parliament, sensing the political tide turning toward Yushchenko, voted to declare the election results invalid. Mem-bers of Ukraine's security forces, including the secretive successor to the KGB, began to break ranks and side with the protesters. Ihor Smeshko, the general who had attended the late-night dinner before Yushchenko's disfiguring illness two months before, now also swung against the Yanu-kovych camp, warning that the country's interior troops would resist any order to crack down. Putin had pressed Kuchma to resist the momentum toward a compromise, hinting strongly that he should deal firmly with the mass protest. "Putin is a hard man," Kuchma said later. "It wasn't like he was saying directly 'Put tanks on the streets.' He was tactful in his comments, but there were some hints made."[17]

Yanukovych retreated to Donetsk, his hometown, to attend a congress of political leaders from the eastern regions that remained deeply loyal to him and to Russia: Donetsk, Luhansk, and Kharkiv. Meeting in a skating rink in Severodonetsk, the congress voted unanimously to declare their regions autonomous if the chaos in Kyiv persisted. The regional assembly then moved up a vote on autonomy to the following week. Yuri Luzhkov, the mayor of Moscow, attended and seemed to lend the Kremlin's endorsement to the calls for separatism. He denounced the opposition leaders as a "sabbath of witches" pretending to "represent the whole of the nation." The Donbas, as Ukraine's industrial heartland was known, would split before agreeing to any compromise that would install Yushchenko.

On the night of December 2, Putin summoned Kuchma to Moscow; they met in the VIP lounge of Vnukovo Airport as Putin prepared to depart on a state visit to India. In Ukraine, the parliament continued to debate the mechanics of holding new elections, while the country's highest court heard Yushchenko's arguments for nullifying the results of the last one. Putin now embraced Kuchma's call for an entirely new vote as the best chance to head off Yushchenko's victory. "A rerun of the second round may also produce nothing," Putin declared. "What happens then? Will there have to be a third, a fourth, a twenty-fifth round until one of the sides obtains the necessary result?"[18]

The next day, after a week of hearings that were broadcast around the country, Ukraine's highest court intervened to order a new runoff, saying the second round had been so "marred by systematic and massive violations" that it was impossible to determine who had genuinely won. It was an unmitigated victory for Yushchenko, and the center of Kyiv erupted in celebration. For Putin, it was an unmitigated defeat.

Three weeks later a repeat of the runoff election was held. Between the court's ruling and the voting, Yushchenko's doctors in Austria had finally determined that he had been poisoned by dioxin. The accusations that Yushchenko's illness had been a stunt, exploiting some other illness to win voters' sympathy, now seemed a cynical cover-up of some dark conspiracy by a deeply corrupt system willing to stoop to poisoning to derail a candidate. When the second runoff was held, under even greater international scrutiny, Yushchenko won with almost 52 percent of the vote; Yanukovych trailed with 44 percent. Despite an investigation, the question of who poisoned him was never answered. Yushchenko himself showed an odd lack of zeal for the investigation despite the horrible disfigurement it caused.[19] He would later say that he suspected his host,

Volodymyr Satsyuk. Once Yushchenko was in office, Satsyuk was questioned by investigators and his dacha tested for traces of dioxin, but he
was never declared a suspect.[20] In June 2005, Satsyuk left Ukraine for
Russia, where he received citizenship. Yushchenko came to believe that
Putin was harboring his would-be killer.

The Orange Revolution, as it became known, was treated in Russia as a
humiliating defeat and in the Kremlin as an ominous warning. Putin
the tactician had been outmaneuvered in a geopolitical struggle, and he
nursed the experience like a grudge. The Kremlin responded by intensifying pressure on Russia's NGOs, by redoubling its hunt for foreign
spies, and by creating its own youth movement to contain any manifestation of youthful dissent. It was called Nashi, and its ideology and practices bore more than a passing resemblance to those of the Soviet Union's
Komsomol, or even, to critics, the Hitler Youth. Putin acted increasingly
defensive and increasingly suspicious of international rebukes about
Russia's record on basic democratic rights. He found them hypocritical,
especially coming from the United States, which under President Bush
was pursuing a hyperaggressive foreign policy that had overthrown governments in Afghanistan, Iraq, and now, he believed, Ukraine. His initially warm relations with Bush had cooled, and were about to get colder.

Shortly after Bush's inauguration for a second term in January 2005,
the two met in Bratislava, the capital of Slovakia. Bush had delivered
a speech that morning in the city's Hviezdoslav Square, only hours
before Putin flew into the city. He had made the advancement of
democracy—the "freedom agenda," he called it—a central theme of his
second term, and now he cheered the popular uprisings in Georgia and
Ukraine. The recent elections in Iraq, he said, were part of the inevitable
march of democracy that had begun with the Velvet Revolution in the
then-unified Czechoslovakia in 1989. He did not mention Russia, but
he declared that "eventually, the call of liberty comes to every mind and
every soul. And one day, freedom's promise will reach every people and
every nation."

In Slovakia the two presidents were accompanied by their wives, who
appeared with them for an official photograph in falling snow at the
entrance to Bratislava Castle. After tea, Lyudmila, whose public activities had perceptibly diminished after Putin's reelection the year before,
joined Laura Bush on a tour of the tapestries at the Primacial Palace in
the heart of the city's old center; together they listened to a boys' choir

sing in Russian and English.[21] When the two men met inside the castle, however, Putin dropped any pretense of good-natured friendship. When Bush raised his concerns about the arrest of Mikhail Khodorkovsky, the strangulation of the media, the "lack of progress" on democracy, Putin counterattacked. He compared his decision to end the elections of regional governors, announced after Beslan, to the use of the Electoral College in American presidential elections. The prosecution of Khodorkovsky was no different than the prosecution of Enron the Texas-based energy company that went bankrupt in 2001. It went on for nearly two hours. Putin's tone was mocking and sarcastic, irritating Bush to the point that he imagined reaching over to "slap the hell" out of the interpreter.[22] "Don't lecture me about the free press," Putin sneered at Bush at one point, "not after you fired that reporter." Bush was momentarily puzzled. Then he realized that Putin meant a scandal that had erupted over reporting by Dan Rather for CBS on Bush's service in the Air National Guard, which was based on documents that could not be authenticated. Rather had had to apologize and was forced to retire, and now Putin was citing it to accuse Bush of suppressing freedom of the press. "I strongly suggest you not say that in public," Bush told him. "The American people will think you don't understand our system."[23] Later, their joint press conference revealed how their differences could no longer be papered over for the sake of diplomacy. Putin repeated his assertion that the Electoral College was a fundamentally undemocratic practice. A Russian journalist chosen by the Kremlin then raised the issue that Putin had just discussed with Bush privately, asking Putin why he had not raised publicly the violation of rights in the United States. ("What a coincidence," Bush said he thought.) The partnership Bush had imagined when he looked into Putin's eyes four years before never really recovered. "Perhaps we should have seen it coming," Condoleezza Rice, now Bush's secretary of state, later wrote, "but this Putin was different than the man who we had first met in Slovenia."[24]

Ukraine's election, coming in the wake of Beslan, proved to be a turning point for Putin and for Russia. His initial instinct to bring Russia into closer cooperation with the West, if not an actual alliance, had faded as steadily as his political and economic power had grown. When he delivered his annual address to the Duma and Federation Council in April, he appealed for a new national unity against those who would challenge the state, inside or outside Russia. He began with a preamble that the country needed to consider "the deeper meaning of such values as freedom and democracy, justice and legality," and went on to utter a sentence that to many confirmed the worst about Putin's instincts: a lingering nostalgia for the glory of the Soviet Union.

"First of all," he said, "it should be recognized that the collapse of the Soviet Union was the greatest geopolitical catastrophe of the century. For the Russian people, it became a real drama. Tens of millions of our fellow citizens and compatriots found themselves outside Russian territory. The epidemic of disintegration also spread to Russia itself." Putin did not wish to restore the Soviet or Communist system—anyone who wants to, he had said, has no brain—but for the first time he began casting his leadership in a broader historical context. He meant to restore something much older, much richer and deeper: the idea of the Russian nation, the imperium of the "third Rome," charting its own course, indifferent to the imposition of foreign values. It was an old Russian idea, and he found the model for it in the history books he was said to favor.

Far less noted at the time than Putin's lament for the "catastrophe" of the Soviet collapse was his reference to Ivan Ilyin, a religious and political philosopher arrested repeatedly by the Bolsheviks and finally expelled in 1922. Ilyin's ideas provided an intellectual foundation for Putin's evolving understanding of Russia's revival and would become more prominent in subsequent political debates. As a White Russian in exile, Ilyin embraced a vision of an Orthodox Russian identity that the secular Communist system was bent on destroying. In his writings Putin found much to sustain the state he wanted to create, even the notion of "sovereign democracy." Putin was not lamenting the demise of the Soviet system, but the demise of the historical Russian idea. It was the first time Putin had quoted Ilyin, whose writings only began circulating openly in Russia after perestroika: "Let us not forget this," Putin said. "Russia is a country that has chosen democracy through the will of its own people. It chose this road of its own accord and it will decide itself how best to ensure that the principles of freedom and democracy are realized here, taking into account our historic, geopolitical, and other particularities and respecting all fundamental democratic norms. As a sovereign nation, Russia can and will decide for itself the timeframe and conditions for its progress along this road."

Putin's reference to a philosopher little known outside or even inside Russia coincided with the repatriation of his remains, along with those of General Anton Denikin, a tsarist commander on the losing side of the civil war. Ilyin had been buried in Switzerland; Denikin in the United States, but Putin supported the campaign to re-inter them in their homeland at the Donskoi Monastery in Moscow.[25] He was said to have personally paid for Ilyin's new headstone. All this led to a revival of interest in the man's works. The Central Intelligence Agency scrambled to prepare an analysis examining their role in Putin's thinking and what it might portend for the future. Ilyin advanced Orthodoxy, patriotism, the law, and private property as the foundations of a state. Writing from exile through Stalin's reign and the Great Patriotic War, he eulogized the heroes of the civil war with a reverence and romanticism whose echoes reverberated in the new Russia. Putin could find much to like in Ilyin's words. "The hero takes up the burden of his nation, the burden of its misfortunes, of its struggle, of its quest, and having taken up that burden, he wins—wins already by this alone, indicating to all the way to salvation. And his victory becomes a prototype and a beacon, an achievement and the call, the source of victory and the beginning of victory for everyone connected with him into one whole by patriotic love. That's why he remains for his people a living source of cheer and joy, and his very name sounds like victory."[26]

On May 9, 2005, the Kremlin celebrated the sixtieth anniversary of the victory in the Great Patriotic War with a ceremony more extravagant than ever. The grandiose plans included dozens of ceremonies and concerts and a military parade through Red Square, a tradition that Putin resumed after the years when Yeltsin played down Soviet holidays and traditions. The parade was attended by fifty-seven dignitaries, including the leaders of victorious and vanquished nations of the war—from George Bush to Gerhard Schröder, Silvio Berlusconi, and Junichiro Koizumi. For Putin, the war became the keynote of his new nationalism, one very much shaped by the memories he had of listening to his father's stories. The anniversary's approach had revived the debates over the Soviet subjugation of Eastern and Central Europe after the war, but Putin rebuffed calls for Russia to account for the darker aspects of the Soviet past, most notoriously the Molotov-Ribbentrop pact with Nazi Germany in 1939, which led to the Soviet occupation of part of Poland that year and the Baltic states a year later. The presidents of Lithuania and Estonia refused to attend as a result. The attendance of Latvia's president, Vaira Vike-Freiberga, prompted raucous protests by Nashi activists outside the country's embassy in Moscow. For his role in brokering talks during the election in Ukraine, Aleksander Kwasniewski of Poland was conspicuously snubbed, relegated to the back row of the viewing stand that discreetly covered Lenin's Tomb.[27]

Putin would no more concede Stalin's failures during the war—including the prewar complicity with Hitler, the useless slaughter of ordinary soldiers, the maurading countermarch to Berlin—than Soviet propagandists had. The war of Putin's new ideology was the war of his youth: honorable, righteous, unblemished, and unrepentant. "The battles of Moscow and Stalingrad, the courage of besieged Leningrad and the successes at Kursk and on the Dnieper decided the outcome of the Great Patriotic War," he said. "Through the liberation of Europe and the battle for Berlin, the Red Army brought the war to its victorious conclusion. Dear friends! We never divided victory into ours and theirs." He noted that the "common sacrifice" united the fifteen republics of the Soviet Union, now independent nations pursuing their own paths in the case of the Baltic countries, Georgia, and, much to Putin's frustration, Ukraine. The reconciliation of Germany and Russia, he said, should be a model of international relations for the twenty-first century. Not far from the Kremlin, though, the Pushkin Museum commemorated the sixtieth anniversary with a display of 552 ancient works of art, including Greek bronzes, Etruscan figures, and fragments of Roman wall paintings that the Soviet Union had seized from a bunker in Berlin and that Russia still refused to return.[28]

CHAPTER 16

Kremlin, Inc.

A week before the second runoff of Ukraine's presidential election in December 2004, Russia dismantled Yukos Oil. In his public remarks ever since the affair began, Putin had insisted that the Kremlin had no intention of doing so, and many people—the other tycoons, foreign investors, ordinary Russians—had believed him. They assumed that even if the entire prosecution stemmed from some animosity toward Khodorkovsky, Putin would not destroy the country's richest company. As the prosecutorial assault continued on Khodorkovsky and Yukos itself, however, it became harder for Putin to protest his innocence or to deny what was becoming obvious. He may not have initiated the criminal and tax charges against Yukos, according to one Kremlin official, but "at some point he moved from observer to participant, and then the leader" of the final demolition of the company and the redistribution of its richest asset, the crown jewel of its oil empire.[1]

Yuganskneftegaz was Yukos's main production unit. It was located on a tributary of the Ob River in western Siberia. The first wells were tapped during the Soviet oil boom of the 1960s, but production had steadily declined over time, grossly mismanaged in the years before and after the Soviet collapse. Khodorkovsky's bank acquired the project as part of the notorious "shares for loans" deal that protected Yeltsin's presidency. The bank's investors paid a mere $150 million for Yuganskneftegaz, and after a turbulent few years they brought in foreign expertise and technology to turn it around.[2] By the time of Khodorkovsky's arrest, it was producing 60 percent of the company's oil.

The Ministry of Justice announced that it would seize and auction off Yuganskneftegaz only five days after the trial of Mikhail Khodorkovsky and his partner, Platon Lebedev, opened in July 2004 inside a tiny, heavily guarded courtroom in northern Moscow. The prosecutors had not yet finished their opening arguments on the eleven criminal charges Khodorkovsky faced, let alone convicted him of any wrongdoing, but the expropriation of the company's most valuable asset would not wait. Khodorkovsky's supporters gathered outside to protest on the day his trial began and would reappear periodically for the next ten months, even though the proceedings already seemed a foregone conclusion. The trial was so riddled with procedural violations, including harassment of the defendants and witnesses, as well as their lawyers, that it was reminiscent of a Soviet show trial. And like those earlier trials, the prosecutorial spectacle sent an intended chill through the political and economic elite, silencing even the few voices willing to speak out after Khodorkovsky's arrest. Other major oil companies moved quickly to forswear the sort of tricks Yukos used to lower its taxes and instead took to boasting about how much in taxes they were willing to pay. Except for Khodorkovsky's supporters, his spokespeople, his investors, his lawyers, his friends and family, fewer and fewer dared to openly confront Putin's Kremlin on any issue. "I'm very scared to name names now," Arkady Volsky, the head of the industrialists' union, told a television network, saying he knew who was behind the Yukos affair. "I'm simply scared. I have six grandchildren, after all, and I want them to be alive."[3] For such candor, he was promptly replaced as the head of the union.

Publicly Putin maintained his distance from the proceedings, as if he did not approve them. The decision to seize and auction Yukos's subsidiary, however, made it clear that removing Khodorkovsky from public life was no longer the sole objective: the breakup of Yukos itself now seemed inevitable, and a decision of that magnitude could only be made at the top. The subsidiary's value far exceeded the $3.4 billion that the company allegedly owed the state for having underpaid its taxes. Yukos had already begun paying that debt in hopes of saving itself, but the tax authorities announced new audits and new fines for underpaying taxes in subsequent years and rebuffed efforts by Yukos's managers to negotiate any payment plan. The debt soon ballooned to $24 billion, more than the company's remaining worth. Putin had no interest in winning back taxes for the country's flush coffers;[4] he wanted the asset itself. On November 18, Russia's property fund announced the opening price for bids on Yuganskneftegaz at $8.65 billion, considerably less than the valuation of $18 billion to $21 billion made by a German firm, Dresdner Bank, at the government's request. And it set the auction for the earliest date possible under the law, December 19, and went ahead even though the date fell on a Sunday. The only question was who the buyer would be.

As the auction approached, Putin found himself mediating an avaricious struggle among the circle of loyalists whom he had lifted up to be the high officers of the state and industry. He no longer faced significant political challenges outside the Kremlin, but inside the factions closest to him maneuvered like the boyars had under the tsars. As with any court, the courtiers often were at odds, but in this case the conflict was not over ideology or vision between the "liberals" and the *siloviki*. This was about money and power. The courtiers circled the wounded Yukos like wolves, anticipating the profits that would come with the company's largest asset. They included some of his most trusted aides, Dmitri Medvedev, and a "politburo" of hardliners—Igor Sechin, Viktor Ivanov, and Nikolai Patrushev—who advocated for the strengthening of state control over natural resources.[5]

Medvedev had served as chairman of Gazprom since 2000, working to exert greater government control over a company that was technically private, though the state owned 38 percent of its shares. Putin wanted full control of this energy giant, which possessed nearly a fifth of the world's natural gas reserves and thousands of miles of pipelines that kept much of Europe warm, and his initial plan to accomplish that was to have Gazprom absorb Rosneft, the ailing state company that he had steadily favored with political support and licenses, especially in Chechnya, where no other company dared work after the second war began.[6] Since Rosneft was wholly owned by the state, the merger would give the Kremlin a controlling stake in an energy juggernaut as rich as Exxon and as pliant as Saudi Arabia's Aramco. The roots of the idea reached back to Putin's days in Petersburg, when he and his friends oversaw provincial business deals and oil trades and wrote academic theses about the necessity of the steady hand of the state. Now, only a few years later, they were on the verge of realizing their vision on a national scale.

Putin approved the deal to merge Gazprom and Rosneft in September 2004, the day after he announced the sweeping political changes in the wake of Beslan. It fit a pattern of centralizing control, a steady gathering of more and more power into Putin's hands. The merger proposal, though, delighted investors and analysts, especially foreigners, the same ones who had been so shaken by the tumult in the market as the Yukos case unfolded. The reason was not complicated: there was money to be made. As part of the merger, Putin promised that once the state controlled a majority share of Gazprom, he would lift the restrictions on foreign investors buying minority shares. Although Gazprom was seen as an unwieldy, inefficient behemoth, its monopoly power to sell natural gas and the Kremlin's doting patronage created the prospect of returns enormous enough to tempt even the most jaded investor. Few seemed troubled by Yukos's fate anymore. By some estimates, foreign investment would double Gazprom's market capitalization, with the rising value benefiting thousands of shareholders. A month after the merger was announced, John Browne of BP heaped praise on the direction in which Putin had taken Russia, brushing aside the trepidations many inside and outside the country had about the Kremlin's tactics. "Since Gorbachev a lot has happened in Russia," he said. "No country has come so far in such a short space of time." As for Yukos, he dismissed the prosecutorial assault on Khodorkovsky and his partners as an isolated matter "related to a person, place and a time," not to the country's economic future.[7]

Putin announced that the merger would be completed by the end of the year, and it became clear that he wanted the new company to bid for Yuganskneftegaz. When the auction and opening price were announced at the end of 2004, he turned to Germany's chancellor, Gerhard Schröder, to help arrange the as much as $10 billion in financing that would be required for the purchase.[8] The bank that led the consortium was Dresdner, whose managing director in Russia was Matthias Warnig, the former Stasi agent who had befriended Putin in the early 1990s and remained a liaison in the many deals being hashed out between German and Russian companies.

Gazprom, with another Putin aide, Aleksei Miller, serving as chief executive, did not seem as enthusiastic. The company remained skeptical about absorbing Yuganskneftegaz on top of merging with Rosneft; it was already struggling with debt and the looming expenses needed to modernize.[9] Igor Sechin, on the other side, had his own ideas about creating the energy giant that Putin favored. That July Putin had appointed him the chairman of Rosneft, then the country's fifth largest oil company, and now Sechin had grand visions to make it, not Gazprom, the country's leading energy company. That meant keeping it from being swallowed by Gazprom and acquiring Yukos's besieged assets for Rosneft alone. As soon as the merger was announced in September, Sechin and Rosneft's chief executive, Sergei Bogdanchikov, worked behind the scenes to scuttle it, and that is exactly what they managed to do, though not in the way anyone expected.[10]

Meanwhile, Yukos's shareholders and managers, many of whom were now safely abroad, had not yet given up their fight to block the auction and somehow preserve the company. Knowing they had little hope in the Russian courts, their lawyers filed for bankruptcy in faraway Texas six days before the auction of Yuganskneftegaz. It was an act of desperation, with only shaky legal grounds for a Russian company with little connection to Texas, but the next day a judge issued a temporary restraining order intended to block the auction until she considered the merits of the filing. The order could not stop the Russian government from proceeding, but it did affect the foreign banks lining up the loans for the auction. Like the ruling by Ukraine's Supreme Court barely two weeks before, the restraining order upset Putin's carefully calculated plans, and he reacted angrily, mocking the judge ("I am not sure this court even knows where Russia is," he said) and fuming at the audacity of an American court interfering in what he considered to be the internal business of the Russian state. To make his point, he cited, in Latin, the core principle of state sovereignty from ancient Roman law: *par in parem non habet imperium,* an equal has no authority over an equal. Putin's outburst betrayed a sense of grievance and anger that he had mostly kept in check on issues outside of Chechnya; now he was lashing out.

The judge in Texas ultimately dimissed the filing on jurisdictional grounds, but by then her order had had its intended effect. Fearing legal liability in the United States, the international bankers withdrew the financing they had lined up for Gazprom to buy Yukos's assets through a new company created in anticipation of the merger, called Gazprom Neft, which was then still just an empty structure. To protect itself, Gazprom officially divested itself from the new firm, but this shell company pressed ahead anyway when the auction took place that Sunday, even though it no longer had any cash to use for the purchase. At the auction, two officials from Gazprom Neft sat at one table, while at another table sat a man and a woman few people knew. They did not identify themselves, but they represented a company called Baikal Finance Group. The woman turned out to be Valentina Davletgaryeva, who had registered the company thirteen days before in Tver, a city southeast of Moscow. She listed its address as an old hotel that now housed a mobile phone shop and declared its capital at the equivalent of $359. (Three days before the auction, the company submitted a deposit of $1.7 billion.)

The auction itself was theatrical. The auctioneer wore a tuxedo with tails and a bow tie; wielding a gavel, he invited the first bid. Davlet- garyeva's companion, Igor Minibayev, raised his hand and offered $9.37 billion. Gazprom Neft's representative asked for a recess and promptly left the room to take a phone call. When he returned, he said nothing, and the auctioneer brought the hammer down. The whole thing lasted ten minutes.[11]

No one outside Putin's Kremlin knew who now owned Yukos's crown jewel, not even the head of the property fund who had just sold it. The auction recalled the murky privatizations of the 1990s; for all Putin's promises to the contrary, the state was resorting to the same tactics to divvy up property on the cheap, this time having seized it back from private hands. One of the sharpest critiques of the auction came from Stanislav Belkovsky, who only a year before had been one of the politi- cal strategists warning the Kremlin of an "oligarchic coup." Now he said the auction of Yuganskneftegaz was "just a deal for the redistribution of property by a criminal group with a mission to get control over the basic financial flows of the country, just as in the 1990s." He called Putin "the chief of this criminal group."[12]

Even more surprising was a rebuke from within Putin's administra- tion. Andrei Illarionov, the Kremlin's economic adviser, described the sale as a disturbing turning point for Russia, though he was careful to avoid criticizing the president personally. "For the past thirteen years Russia was seeking to return to the first world, to which it belonged until the Bolshevik Revolution. Now we see it has preferred the third world," he said at a press conference. "We have passed the crossroads—we are in a different country."[13] He was promptly demoted from his job preparing for the G8 meeting to be held in Scotland the following June.

For a couple of days afterward the fate of Yuganskneftegaz became a parlor game in Moscow. Many analysts assumed, wrongly, that Baikal Finance was a front to protect the ultimate buyer, Gazprom. Putin, in Germany for a state visit with Gerhard Schröder, spoke coyly two days after the auction, giving away nothing, though he acknowledged that he knew the company had been hastily created to help deflect the potential liability from the lawsuits swirling around Yukos.[14] "As is well known, the shareholders of this company are all private individuals, but they are individuals who have been involved in business in the energy sphere for many years," he said when asked about the mysterious buyers. "They intend, as far as I am informed, to establish relations with other energy companies in Russia which have an interest in their company." He was dissembling. The day before, Rosneft had sought and, with Putin's blessing, received authorization from Russia's anti-monopoly committee to purchase Baikal Finance Group. Rosneft, which only weeks before had seemed destined for absorption into Gazprom, now owned a vastly undervalued subsidiary able to pump a million barrels of oil a day.

On December 23, four days after the auction, Rosneft announced its purchase. It would take another year to untangle the complicated financing involved. The mysterious and short-lived Baikal Finance had received the advance for the auction from another oil company with close relations to Putin and the Kremlin, Surgutneftegaz; it was repaid once Rosneft acquired the auctioned asset, which even at its discounted price was worth more than Rosneft itself. Rosneft, in turn, struck a deal with China's state oil company, CNPC, to put up the cash as prepayment for the oil that Rosneft stood to derive from Yukos's seized assets.[15] The irony was that Mikhail Khodorkovsky had long advocated developing a strategic partnership with China, even building a pipeline to the country, only to be blocked by the Kremlin, which remained wary of the rising economic power of Beijing. Now Rosneft, with Igor Sechin on its board, had effectively acquired Yukos's confiscated asset for nothing except the promise to pay that asset's future profits to China. It was, as Andrei Illarionov called it, "the swindle of the year."

Facing a new storm of international criticism, Putin defended the auction with a swaggering confidence, calculating that the initial furor over Yukos would dissipate and that no one could do anything about it anyway. At his annual press conference that December, he smugly brushed aside questions with coy elisions and evasions. "Now regarding the acquisition by Rosneft of the well-known asset of the company— I do not remember its exact name—is it Baikal Investment Company? Essentially, Rosneft, a 100 percent state-owned company, has bought the well-known asset Yuganskneftegaz. That is the story. In my view, everything was done according to the best market rules. As I have said, I think it was at a press conference in Germany, a state-owned company or, rather companies, with 100 percent state capital, just as any other market players, have the right to do so and, as it emerged, exercised it." He lamented again the 1990s, when oligarchs "using all sorts of stratagems" managed to amass state assets "worth many billions." It was different now, he went on. "Today, the state, resorting to absolutely legal market mechanisms, is looking after its own interests." The last statement was widely quoted in the media, but the ultimate significance of it was little noticed at the time. Eventually, it would come to haunt Putin and cost Russia billions.[16]

Mikhail Khodorkovsky's trial dragged on for another five months, as prosecutors read through copious financial records and questioned witnesses. The evidence was scant and contradictory, and in some cases clearly fabricated. It did not matter; the outcome by now was preordained. The court repeatedly rejected the defense's motions, refused to allow subpoenas, and restricted its questioning. On April 11, Khodorkovsky stood before the court and made a final statement.[17] He declared his innocence and for thirty-nine minutes spoke passionately, defiantly, righteously. He called himself a patriot of Russia who was prosecuted not for any real criminal offenses but for being the "wrong kind of oligarch." Unlike the "modest businessmen" and government officials behind the Yukos affair, bureaucrats with lifestyles incommensurate with their official salaries, he said, "I have no yachts, no palaces, race cars, or football clubs." The destruction of Yukos "was contrived by certain influential people with the aim of taking for themselves the most prosperous oil company of Russia, or more precisely, the revenues from its financial flows." He suggested that Putin had been deceived into believing Khodorkovsky posed a political threat whose removal was necessary to protect the state's interests. "Those people who are busily plundering Yukos's assets today do not actually have anything to do with the Russian state and its interests. They are simply dirty, self-serving bureaucrats and nothing else. The entire country knows why I was locked up in jail: so that I wouldn't interfere with the plunder of the company." The "court of history" would vindicate him, he said. He finished by thanking those who had supported him, especially his wife, who stood by him courageously, "like a real Decembrist's wife."

Once the final verdict was read in full over two weeks in May, the historical allusion seemed apt. With his partner, Platon Lebedev, he was convicted and sentenced to nine years in prison, and like the military officers who rose up against Tsar Nicholas I in 1825, he was banished to Siberia, to a penal colony in Chita, a region bordering China and Mongolia, even though the law required prisoners to be incarcerated in the region where they committed their crimes. A few days after he arrived, his business partners paid for a full-page advertisement in *The Financial Times* with a defiant letter from Khodorkovsky. "They hope Khodorkovsky will be soon forgotten," it declared. "They are trying to convince you, my friends, that the fight is over, that we must resign ourselves to the supremacy of self-serving bureaucrats. That's not true—the fight is just beginning."[18]

The final acquisition of Yuganskneftegaz by Rosneft upended Putin's plan to create a single energy giant. Gazprom had lost the financing to allow it to take over the asset and worried about the legal risks of doing so. Rosneft, though, had no exposed assets outside of Russia that could be at risk if it violated the Texas court's ruling. Rosneft, now an oil giant on its own, worked assiduously to stay independent—that is, to avoid the merger with Gazprom. Putin ended up in the middle of an internal struggle over the state's most important assets, pitting Medvedev and Miller at Gazprom on one side versus Igor Sechin and Rosneft on the other. The unseemly conflict spilled into public view in a way few others inside the Kremlin had, and it ended only in the spring of 2005, when Putin decided on a compromise that allowed each faction to keep control of its respective company.

The dismantling of Yukos may not have gone exactly according to plan, perhaps, but it had proved remarkably successful. Putin weathered the warnings from outside economists, and even insiders like Illarionov, that the Kremlin's centralization of business would damage Russia's standing as a reliable place for business and foreign investment. He simply repeated that the country welcomed and encouraged investment even as the organs of the state expanded even deeper into the economy. The Yukos affair did taint Russia's reputation, sowing distrust and fear of the risks of investing in the country, but in the three years after the assault began, Russia's stock market had more than tripled in value anyway; the economy continued its robust growth, its gross domestic product surging 6 or 7 percent a year on average. Over time, the consternation over Khodorkovsky's fate—and that of Yukos—grew fainter and fainter. The potential riches Russia had to offer proved too irresistible to the world's energy and financial giants—and so to Putin's counterparts in foreign capitals. Despite their public remonstrations over the state of democracy or the rule of law, they could not afford to ignore Russia. Why should Putin worry if some questioned the state's methods?

"Russia is a dynamically growing market with large capacity," he told a group of American and other foreign executives inside a marbled conference room at the resplendent Konstantin Palace in Petersburg in June 2005, less than a month after Khodorkovsky's sentencing. "I am sure that we can provide investors, including yourselves, with good working conditions and impressive profits." Putin sounded like Russia's pitchman. Sanford Weill, the chairman of Citigroup, had conceived this meeting after a previous one with Putin in February. Among those attending were eleven of the most important chief executives in the United States, including Craig Barrett of Intel, Alain Belda of Alcoa, Samuel Palmisano of IBM, James Mulva of ConocoPhilips, and Rupert Murdoch of News Corporation. All had major investments in Russia and wanted more. Weill wanted Putin to clarify the "rules of the road" for investors,[19] but instead Putin chided the men for various restrictions that the United States imposed on trade with Russia, including export controls on space, computer, and military technology and an amendment passed by Congress in 1974 in retaliation for the Soviet Union's restriction of emigration by Jews to Israel. Russia had long since dismantled the barriers to emigration, but the United States in the 1990s never got around to taking off the books the trade sanctions it had opposed three decades before, even as president after president waived their use. "It would be funny, if it were not so sad," Putin told them. He encouraged an expansion of trade but placed on these men the task of straightening out the rules back home first.

When the meeting concluded, the executives gathered around to greet Putin and to pose for photographs, all smiling. Weill at one point turned to Robert Kraft, the head of the Kraft Group and owner of the New England Patriots, which had won football's Super Bowl in February. "Why don't you show the president your ring?" he urged him. Kraft did not often wear his but carried it with him in his suit pocket. The ring was a gaudy bauble, studded with 124 diamonds and engraved with Kraft's name. He handed it to Putin, who then slipped it on a finger. "I could kill somebody with this," Putin said, admiringly. As the photo session ended, Kraft held out his hand for the ring, but Putin slipped it instead into his pocket, turned with his aides, and left. Putin apparently assumed the ring was intended as a gift, and Kraft was flustered by the misunderstanding. He appealed to Weill and later the White House for help retrieving the ring, but by then articles and photographs had appeared in the media, and an aide at the White House, fearful of the growing strains with the Kremlin, explained that it would be best for relations if Kraft would say he had intended it as a gift. "I really didn't," Kraft explained. "I had an emotional tie to the ring. It has my name on it. I don't want to see it on eBay." The aide was silent for a moment and repeated, "It would *really* be in the best interest if you meant to give the ring as a present."[20] Kraft obliged with a statement four days after the meeting, saying the ring was a "symbol of the respect and admiration that I have for the Russian people and the leadership of President Putin." It was a cost of doing business in Russia, but the misunderstanding gnawed at Kraft for years afterward. ("Of course, his forebears were probably raped and pillaged by these people," his wife later said, referring to Kraft's Jewish ancestry, "but Robert had to make it sound good.")[21] Kraft had another ring made, and the original went into the Kremlin library, where gifts to the head of state are collected.

The Yukos affair did not, as some feared, augur the renationalization of all of Russia's newly privatized industries, especially those tapping Russia's natural resources, but it was a turning point—and a model for the steady encroachment of the state into the country's important industries. Putin identified scores of enterprises that, by law, could not be held in private hands and then began overseeing the creation of giant state corporations that would consolidate entire sectors and thus command the nation's economy. He put in charge of them the men he had brought with him from Petersburg, many of whom continued to serve as ministers in his government while carrying out their corporate responsibilities. Their corporate positions provided access to cash flows and the opportunity for patronage. In addition to Igor Sechin at Rosneft, suddenly Russia's second largest oil producer and within a year the largest, Sergei Ivanov, then the defense minister, took over as chairman of United Aircraft Corporation, created to consolidate civilian and military aircraft manufacturers. Vladimir Yakunin became the head of Russian Railways, sometimes called the country's third natural monopoly, after oil and gas. Sergei Chemezov, who had known Putin since they worked together in Dresden, took over the consolidated arms manufacturer Rosoboronexport. According to one estimate, by 2006 the revenues of the state companies accounted for a fifth of the country's GDP and a third of the value of its stock markets—and Putin's friends and allies controlled them.[22]

The most powerful of all remained Gazprom. Neither Dmitri Medvedev, its chairman, nor Aleksei Miller, its chief executive, was installed for his particular experience or expertise in natural gas management; both were chosen for their loyalty. Through them, Putin pulled the reins at Gazprom, involving himself in the minutiae of the company's budgets, pricing, pipeline routes, and even personnel, which he approved "down to the deputy level," sometimes without telling Miller about important appointments.[23] It became such an obsession of Putin's that many wondered whether he was preparing to take over the company when his presidential term ended. "Thank you for the job offer," he replied in January 2006 when a journalist asked him the question directly. "However, I am not likely to head a business. I am not a businessman, either by character or by previous life experience."

Gazprom may have lost the internal jockeying to seize Yukos's main asset but it continued its quest to expand, and did so with tactics more stealthy and subtle than the expropriation of Yukos. Roman Abramovich, having abandoned Sibneft's merger with Yukos in 2003 after meeting with Putin (while keeping the $3 billion Khodorkovsky paid him), also found his company facing new tax claims. Facing a $1 billion bill, he quietly negotiated a settlement in 2005 for $300 million[24] and promptly sought to sell his controlling stake of the company. He considered offers from Chevron-Texaco, Shell, and Total, but he was savvier than Khodorkovsky, or at least less confrontational, and he could read the writing on the wall.[25] In July 2005, Sibneft paid an enormous dividend of $2.29 billion to its shareholders—more than its entire profit two years before—in what was clearly a sign that Abramovich was cashing out and preparing the company for sale. Two days later, at the meeting of G8 leaders in Scotland, Putin confirmed the speculation and acknowledged that Gazprom was the suitor. He insisted that it was a private matter between businesses but also divulged that he had personally been involved in discussions with Abramovich. Gazprom did not have the cash to acquire Sibneft, but Putin announced that the government would buy enough of Gazprom's shares to give the state majority control, using funds from the state's coffers. Gazprom then used the infusion of cash to purchase Sibneft for $13 billion, a price so inflated that speculation swirled about the kickbacks that must have been involved.[26] The American ambassador at the time, William J. Burns, cabled the State Department that "only a quarter" was said to have gone to Abramovich himself.[27] Many others, it seemed, took a share, too.

———

By Putin's second term Gazprom, once a sclerotic behemoth, had emerged as the energy giant he dreamed of. It became one of the largest corporations in the world by market capitalization, bypassing stalwarts like Toyota, Walmart, and Sanford Weill's Citigroup. It had not become any more efficient or well managed, but Putin made it the country's most powerful business—and a powerful arm of the country's foreign policy from Asia to Europe. With Chancellor Gerhard Schröder, a leader and friend who had once called him a "flawless democrat," Putin orchestrated a deal to construct the longest underwater natural gas pipeline in the world, connecting terminals in Russia to those in Germany. The project, eventually known as Nord Stream, would bypass the old Soviet pipeline network through Ukraine, Belarus, and Poland, giving the Kremlin leverage in negotiations over transit fees in those countries and increasing Europe's dependence on Russia. It was deeply controversial. Poland's defense minister called it the energy version of the Molotov-Ribbentrop Pact,[28] while environmentalists along the Baltic Sea warned of the potential damage of running pipelines along a sea floor littered with munitions from both world wars.

When Schröder was ousted from office in elections that year, Putin appointed him chairman of the shareholders committee of the new subsidiary that would build Nord Stream, only days after the German had blessed the project with a secret loan guarantee worth 1 billion euros. Gazprom owned a controlling stake, along with Germany's two major energy companies, BASF and E.On, and Putin was in the position to dispense the perquisites. The managing director of the pipeline project, appointed with his blessing, was his old Stasi friend, Matthias Warnig. A week after hiring Schröder, Putin summoned Donald Evans, an oil man and confidant of President Bush who had served as secretary of commerce during Bush's first term, to an unexpected meeting at the Kremlin and offered him a similar position at Rosneft, hoping to give an international legitimacy to the company that now existed on the pilfered remains of Yukos.[29] Evans passed, but Putin had come to believe it was ultimately money that drove men and politics. In Europe especially many proved him right.

Despite disavowing any business acumen, Putin reveled in the details of the country's biggest deals, negotiating himself and mediating disputes. In July 2005, Royal Dutch Shell acknowledged a staggering cost

overrun in the oil and gas project on Sakhalin Island in the Far East—the
product of the country's first production-sharing agreement, signed in
the 1990s—only a week after signing a memorandum of understanding
with Gazprom to include the giant in the project. During a state visit
to the Netherlands in November, Putin publicly berated the company's
chief executive, Jeroen van der Veer, at a meeting with businessmen in
the home of Amsterdam's mayor.[30] Van der Veer had to plead for time
at the reception to meet with Putin privately, and the two spent twenty
minutes arguing in German about why a $10 billion project had bal-
looned to $20 billion, delaying significantly any profits the Russian
government would receive. Van der Veer tried to explain that the massive project, which included offshore platforms and hundreds of miles
of pipeline, required expertise and technologies for producing liquefied
natural gas that neither Gazprom nor other Russian companies had.
The project would still be profitable, despite the rising cost, but Putin
demanded that the agreement with Gazprom be renegotiated anyway.
When those talks dragged on for months, the Kremlin unleashed the
Ministry of Natural Resources's environmental watchdog, Oleg Mitvol,
who carried out a highly publicized assault on the project for its damage to the environment. That there was an environmental impact on
Sakhalin—to salmon estuaries and the breeding grounds of gray whales
in the Sea of Okhotsk—was certainly true, but preservation of wildlife
had never been such a priority before. Mitvol now threatened to open a
criminal case for every tree that had been cut down, making an outland-
ish estimate that Shell could face $50 billion in fines and fees.[31]

Shell, which owned the project with Mitsu & Company and Mitsubishi Corporation in Japan, took the hint. It not only acquiesed to
a new agreement, but sold a controlling share of the entire project to
Gazprom for $7.45 billion, considerably below market price. At Putin's
insistence,[32] Van der Veer then had to return to the Kremlin with the
executives of Mitsu and Mitsubishi to validate the agreement before the
cameras, a ceremony intended to show that Putin's mastery extended
beyond Russian officials and businessmen. "All of the world's largest
companies are benefiting from their work in Russia," Putin told those
gathered around a table in a conference room near his office. As for the
massive environmental damage, Putin said the issue would "be regarded
as almost settled in principle."[33] The foreign executives had lost control
of the project, but they kept the oil and gas reserves on their books and
millions in profits for their companies. And so, one by one, they wel-

comed Gazprom as the project's new owner and thanked Putin for his efforts to support international partnership, just as Kraft had.

Each new acquisition emboldened Putin. At the end of 2005, Gazprom hiked the price of natural gas it delivered to Ukraine from a heavily discounted $50 per 1,000 cubic meters to $230, in line with prices charged in the rest of Europe. The increase was transparent retribution for Yushchenko's flirtation with the West after taking power. Putin had negotiated the lower price ahead of the election, hoping to boost Yanukovych's prospects, but now with the contract up for renewal and Yushchenko orienting the country toward Europe, Putin would make Ukraine pay more. It was not politics, Putin insisted, just business, but he sounded spiteful. "Why should we pay for that?" he said of Ukraine's embrace of the West.

On New Year's Eve, Putin offered a three-month reprieve and a loan to help Ukraine cope, but when the country continued to balk, Gazprom shut off the gas on New Year's Day, with Putin's blessing. As a hardball tactic, it backfired. Since most of Russia's natural gas to Europe flowed through pipelines traversing Ukraine, the decision rippled across the continent at the height of winter. Instead of letting the rest of Russia's gas continue to flow to Europe, Ukraine siphoned off what it needed, causing disruptions in pressure in Austria, France, Italy, Moldova, Poland, Romania, Slovakia, and Hungary. Russia had principle on its side, but Putin's tactics rattled even those who had argued that Russia deserved respect. He also undermined his own strategy of showing Europe that Russia would be a dependable and indispensable energy source.

Putin had to retreat. He offered a compromise that would raise gas prices overall, but install as a middleman RosUkrEnergo, the shadowy trading company he had created with Leonid Kuchma in the months before the Orange Revolution. Gazprom owned half of it; the other owners, who remained secret then, included Dmitri Firtash, a Ukrainian businessman who acknowledged ties to one of the world's most notorious mob bosses, Semion Mogilevich.[34] Mogilevich, who was on the FBI's Ten Most Wanted list because of a fraud case, had deep contacts with Ukraine's government, including Yushchenko, and was said to have known Putin in the 1990s. According to one of the taped recordings of Kuchma, he lived in Moscow under a false identity with Putin's protection in exchange for having worked as an intelligence agent for the Russians.[35] The agreement gave Gazprom even greater control over

Ukraine's gas supply, which might have been the point of the dispute in the first place, securing Russia's control inside a country bent on turning away from it.

The terms of the deal and the murky ties between the middleman company and Yushchenko and his allies provoked a political furor in Ukraine that Putin easily exploited. When asked, he suggested that it was the Ukrainian leader who was behind the shadowy owners of RosUkrEnergo. "Ask Viktor Yushchenko," he said. "I don't know any more than you do, and Gazprom does not know either, believe me." Putin was having his cake and eating it too. Gazprom got half the profits of selling its own natural gas to Ukraine, while Yushchenko was tarred with the implication of corrupt ties to a deal that was so controversial at home that it split the coalition that had led the Orange Revolution. By the time Ukraine held parliamentary elections in March 2006, Yulia Tymoshenko, the "gas princess" who had her own experience with the energy trade in Ukraine, railed against the agreement and the president she had helped win office. As a result, Yushchenko's party fared dismally, forcing him to seek a new coalition with the man he had beaten, Viktor Yanukovych, who now began his political comeback.[36]

It was becoming unclear where the affairs of state and business diverged; people in Russia started to call the government Kremlin, Inc., with Putin as the CEO. He presided over not just Gazprom, but all the "national champions" at home, granting prerogatives that included protection from tax inspectors who were often unleashed against other businesses, small and large. And he lobbied for their interests abroad with a zeal that would have been unimaginable coming from Yeltsin in the 1990s.[37] By 2005, the extent of his control over the state's monopolies became evident, and it coincided with the elimination of the last political checks against his power in the parliament or the judiciary. Putin, who had vowed to eliminate the brash oligarchs as a "class," had become the patron of a growing part of Russia's economy. He did not dictate every business deal across Russia, but all the major ones required at least tacit approval from the Kremlin. The oligarchs from the 1990s who survived the transition to the Putin era showed their obsequiousness with acts of fealty and charity—as when Viktor Vekselberg bought and repatriated nine of the famous Fabergé eggs or the bells of the Danilov Monastery that rang for nearly a century at Harvard University's Lowell House.

There were certainly other acts few knew about, quiet exchanges of favors and gifts done to preserve their fortunes. One that had been meant to be secret would eventually leak out, providing a rare glimpse of how fortunes were made behind the scenes. In 2000, Nikolai Shamalov, one of Putin's colleagues in the Ozero dacha cooperative at Lake Komsomolskoye, struck a deal with the owners of a small medical supply company that Putin's committee in Petersburg had helped create in 1992. It was called Petromed, and though the city of Petersburg eventually sold its majority shares, the company had flourished. Shamalov arranged with its owners to accept donations from oligarchs who were "coming forward" to offer help to the new president. Roman Abramovich pledged $203 million, for example, while Aleksei Mordashov, the owner of the metal and mining conglomerate Severstal, offered $15 million. The donations would be used to purchase medical equipment, but part of the receipts would be funneled into offshore bank accounts that were then used to acquire other assets in Russia, including, allegedly, shares in Bank Rossiya. The arrangement started out relatively small and entirely secret, but by 2005, Shamalov told the owners of Petromed that the proceeds from the donations—estimated by then to amount to nearly half a billion dollars—would now be funneled from the offshore accounts into a new investment company in Russia, called Rosinvest. And its principal investment became the construction of a luxury home on the Black Sea coast near Sochi, where Soviet rulers had vacationed in luxury and Putin already had the run of the presidential retreat. The home would be a palace "fit for a tsar," with an estimated cost of $1 billion.[38] None of this became public at the time. It was known only to a few businessmen and government officials who were discreet enough or corrupt enough not to divulge what was going on. It was here in the murky nexus where the state met business that a new class of oligarch would emerge from the shadow periphery of the economy—and from Putin's past.

Yuri Kovalchuk, the physicist Putin had worked with in some of Petersburg's early experiments in capitalism, had continued to operate Bank Rossiya, an institution founded in the Soviet era. In the early part of the decade, it remained little more than a small provincial institution handling the assets of its shareholders with no discernible part in the economic boom that followed Putin's rise to power. The bank, however, united the circle of men Putin had befriended in the 1990s and with whom he remained close even after his political fortunes catapulted him far higher than anyone expected, including his partners in the dacha cooperative. Like their fortunes, the cooperative had grown with Putin's rise, expanding at the expense of neighbors, allegedly in order to install the necessary security measures. The owners faced legal challenges from neighbors who complained that their access to the lake had been expropriated. One complained that the cooperative's head, Vladimir Smirnov, whom Putin had appointed to head the nuclear export agency, had throttled her when she tried to exercise her right of way to the shore by crossing through a fence.[39] By the end of his first term, though, Putin was said to have sold his share, having far more ambitious plans for his own personal space.

Some of the dacha owners, like Smirnov, had followed Putin to Moscow to take on public roles in the government. Andrei Fursenko became a deputy minister, then minister of industry, science, and technology, and finally, in 2004, minister of education and science. Vladimir Yakunin took over Russian Railways in 2005. Others, including Kovalchuk and Nikolai Shamalov, who had worked as the director in Russia for the German manufacturer Siemens, kept a much lower profile. Their bank had lost its privileged access to the government coffers after Sobchak's defeat as governor nearly a decade before, but with Putin's accession things looked much brighter.

In Putin's first term as president, men like Kovalchuk and Shamalov, along with Gennady Timchenko, all remained largely unknown. Putin's first prime minister, Mikhail Kasyanov, could not recall ever having heard the name of either the bank or its owners in the many government deals he oversaw.[40] Kovalchuk's name surfaced in connection with Putin's only in 2004, coincidentally the month Kasyanov was fired, when the doomed presidential challenger Ivan Rybkin published an ad in *Kommersant* accusing Putin of being in business with him, along with Timchenko and Roman Abramovich. Rybkin's odd disappearance days later overshadowed his claims, and nobody paid much attention to these men, because on the scale of big business in Russia, they were inconsequential outsiders, minor players from the provinces. The bank reported scant profits the year Putin came to power, but like so much else in Putin's Russia, that would soon change.

Kovalchuk took over as chairman of Bank Rossiya in 2004 after one of the country's biggest oligarchs, Aleksei Mordashov of Severstal, deposited $19 million in the bank and then took an 8.8 percent share in exchange. It was then the equivalent of the bank's entire capital.[41] Many assumed Mordashov was trying to buy favor with Putin in the midst of

a struggle with a business rival, as he had happily donated funds to Petromed to buy hospital equipment. With its resources swelling, the bank
then quietly bought nearly half of Gazprom's insurance arm, Sogaz, on
the stock market in July 2004. The total sale was $58 million, which was
later argued to be significantly less than its value. It was the first sale by
Gazprom of one of its non-core assets. Officials and analysts had long
argued that the company should sell them, but this sale seemed puzzling,
especially since the bidding was closed and the buyers remained behind
the scenes. Putin intervened directly in the deal, ordering that the shares
go to Bank Rossiya. "Putin said, 'Bank Rossiya,' that's it," a former deputy minister during Putin's first term, Vladimir Milov, recalled later. The
liberals in his cabinet seemed shocked or confused,[42] as Bank Rossiya's
role in the purchase did not become public until January 2005. It now
controlled Sogaz through a series of shell companies, including one created in Petersburg in 2002 called Aksept, which was owned by Mikhail
Shelomov, the grandson of Putin's uncle, Ivan Shelomov, who had helped
evacuate Putin's mother during the Nazi invasion. To those in the know,
the bank clearly had a privileged status, with ties to the very top.

Now business simply flowed toward the bank. Sogaz soon became
the insurer of choice for major state companies like Russian Railways,
headed by Yakunin, and Rosneft, now controlled by Igor Sechin. That in
turn fueled a phenomenal expansion, as Bank Rossiya quietly acquired
more and more of Gazprom's assets, including its banking subsidiary
and ultimately its media holdings. The bank's expansion began as a
stealth operation, executed patiently and secretly, its ownership structure
obscured in layers of offshore companies stacked like matryoshka nesting dolls, hiding, some would suspect, Putin's personal stakes in them.

In his first term Putin had moved slowly to set the economy on its feet,
benefiting enormously from the unexpected surge in the price of oil
(which in turn affected the price of natural gas), but his second term
represented a significant shift, one that coincided with the departure
of some of his liberal advisers and the consolidation of the Kremlin's
control over the branches of government, as well as over the media and
business. Now, with the country increasingly solvent, he began to redis-
tribute the proceeds to a new generation of tycoons in waiting, those
who had not had the privileged, insider track to amass fortunes in the
1990s. None of them were billionaires then, flashing their wealth ostentatiously. They were a new generation of oligarchs, made in the Putin

model: dour, colorless, secretive, and intensely loyal to the man who brought them out of relative obscurity. Those who had not joined Putin in the ranks of government soon followed in business.

After Rosneft acquired the lion's share of Yukos, the contracts to trade much of its oil shifted to Gennady Timchenko, the trader who first made deals with Putin in the 1990s. When Arkady Rotenberg, who along with his brother Boris had learned judo at Putin's side when they were teenagers in the 1960s, formed a judo club in Petersburg in 1998 called Yawara-Neva; Timchenko provided sponsorship, and Putin became the club's honorary president. The club created a "judocracy" that would shape Putin's political leadership as much as the KGB did.[43] Vasily Shestakov, another judoka and founder of the club who had promised to hire Putin as a coach in 1996, entered politics and published books and videos on the sport, including one ostensibly co-authored by Putin.

When, on the eve of his inauguration in 2000, Putin established a state company to consolidate dozens of vodka distilleries in which the government still had a controlling interest, he turned to the judocracy to control it. He put Arkady Rotenberg in charge of what was called Rosspiritprom. In a country with a taste for the hard stuff, the enterprise would grow into a multimillion-dollar business, controlling nearly half the country's alcohol market, benefiting from new government regulations and raids on private rivals.[44] Rotenberg and his brother Boris parlayed the profits of Russia's national drink into their own bank, SMP Bank, which then began investing in pipeline construction of exactly the sort Putin was negotiating with the likes of Gerhard Schröder.

Unlike the get-rich-quick schemes of the 1990s privatizations, the accumulation of assets by Putin's friends was so slow and incremental that its significance only became clear much later. Putin had enabled his circle of friends to rise to the heights of the country's economy, enriching them while ensuring they would control the sectors of the economy—from natural resources to the media—that he considered vital to the nation's security. "He doesn't take the St. Petersburg boys to work with him because of their pretty eyes, but because he trusts people who are tried and true," Putin's first judo trainer, Anatoly Rakhlin, told *Izvestiya* in 2007.

On December 26, 2005, Putin gathered his advisers for a special meeting inside the Kremlin to discuss, among other issues, how to divide up the proceeds of Rosneft's extraordinary growth. Around the long oval table were the men who had been with him since Petersburg: Aleksandr Medvedev, Aleksei Kudrin, German Gref, Igor Sechin. It was an unusual meeting, smaller than a cabinet meeting but larger than the regular meetings devoted to economic matters. Andrei Illarionov, already demoted once, was also there, but by then he felt increasingly uncomfortable with the direction of the Kremlin's economic policy. Illarionov, trained as an economist, had been a pugnacious, strong-tempered adviser to Russian governments since the collapse of the Soviet Union. A libertarian and a free-marketer, he had never shied away from stating his mind. The first time he met with Putin, in February 2000, while the latter was still acting president, an aide passed a note informing Putin that Russian forces in Chechnya had captured the town of Shatoi, the last stronghold then still occupied by the rebels. He was ebullient, and when Illarionov responded by telling him the war was illegal and destructive for Russia, they argued for an hour before Putin icily cut him off. From that point on, he declared, they would never again discuss Chechnya—only economic matters.[45] For the first term of Putin's presidency, Illarionov felt vindicated by the economic course the country was taking. He endorsed the decisions Putin took to embrace the flat tax of 13 percent, pay off the country's debt, and create a stability fund of reserves, which had grown unexpectedly flush. The Yukos affair signaled something different, and he said as much. He now found that Putin no longer heeded his advice, first demoting him then steadily shrinking his staff in the Kremlin. In an interview with the Russian opposition newspaper *The New Times,* Illarionov said that Putin had divided those around him into distinct groups. One he called the "economics group," which involved his advisers on all matters involving the economy. The other group involved "business people," from which official advisers were generally excluded. It was with those people, he said, that Putin "would establish control over property and financial flows."[46] Just as Putin declared they would no longer discuss Chechnya, he no longer seemed interested in discussing the plans for Rosneft with Illarianov.

The meeting to discuss the company's initial public offering—on the London Stock Exchange and Russia's two exchanges—was the first Illarionov had been invited to on the matter, but it soon became clear to him that the plans were already well advanced. At this meeting Igor Sechin presented the proposal to raise $12 billion in capital by selling 13 percent of the company's shares and then using the proceeds to pay off debt and invest in new projects. One by one Putin's aides then endorsed the idea. "It's fine," Gref said. Medvedev said he had verified the legality of the deal. When it came time for Illarionov to speak, though, he objected. If the state were going to sell a share of its largest oil company, he argued, should not the proceeds return to the state's budget? Putin pushed back his chair, his face reddening. Illarionov knew that he had made him uncomfortable by pointing out the political risk involved. It was one thing to prosecute Khodorkovsky and seize Yukos's assets—Russians had cheered for that—but another altogether to not share the profits with the ultimate shareholders, the Russian people. Illarionov now understood that the matter had already been decided by everyone in the room. Nobody joined his argument. They stared silently at the table. Even worse, he told them, not all the proceeds were intended to shore up or expand Rosneft: under the proposal being ratified that day, $1.5 billion of the sale was earmarked for unspecified bonuses for Rosneft's management, presumably the company's executive and its board members, including Igor Sechin. This seemed to surprise Putin. He went pale and pulled his chair back to the table.

"Igor Ivanovich," Putin said, turning to Sechin, "what is this?"

Sechin bolted upright, standing like a conscript soldier in front of an angry officer, stammering Putin's name, according to Illarionov. He did not or could not explain the bonuses, and Putin simply thanked Illarionov for his contribution to the discussion. Illarionov, who believed that Putin had not known of the bonuses, resigned the next day, publicly criticizing the direction in which Putin was taking the country. "The state has become, essentially, a corporate enterprise that the nominal owners, Russian citizens, no longer control," he wrote in a blistering editorial in *Kommersant*.[47] Illarionov's opposition served to delay the IPO, as Sechin and Putin debated the terms and the timing, but not for long.

When the proposal was announced in early 2006, Rosneft said it hoped to raise $20 billion, though it later reduced its target to $10 billion. The government announced with fanfare that it would put individual shares up for retail sale through the state bank, Sberbank, and others, trying to portray this privatization as a benefit for ordinary Russians, who would also have the chance to share in the country's energy boom. The main focus, though, was on enlisting international energy companies, including BP, Petronas, and China's giant CNPC, who were enticed by the prospect of a new foothold in Russia's energy market, if only as minority shareholders. When the results of the offering seemed low, other Russian oligarchs, including Roman Abramovich, stepped in with large purchases, presumably at the prompting of the Kremlin, so that Rosneft would hit its target.[48]

The offering was as controversial as the Yukos affair—and a risk for Putin personally since it amounted to a test of the brand of capitalism he was managing. To float shares in London required a full disclosure of the risks to investors. Rosneft's disclosure in fact acknowledged the crime and corruption in Russia and the likelihood that Yukos-related lawsuits would hound the company into the distant future. It also made it clear that Kremlin, Inc. remained the ultimate arbiter of the company's fate. "The Russian government, whose interests may not coincide with those of other shareholders, controls Rosneft and may cause Rosneft to engage in business practices that do not maximize shareholder value," the prospectus acknowledged.[49]

Whether the bonuses Illarionov criticized were paid was never made public, and the interest of institutional investors remained lukewarm, but the offering was the fifth largest in history. It raised $10.7 billion, and at the selling price of the shares, Rosneft was valued at nearly $80 billion. The offering took place, not by coincidence, on the eve of the G8 summit, which was being held for the first time in Petersburg with Putin as the host. The Kremlin prepared an ambitious agenda that included Russia's place as the guarantor of energy security, despite the conflict with Ukraine and, later, Georgia and Belarus over natural gas. Rosneft's rise proved that Russia had righted itself again, and in the run-up to the summit, Putin exuded a confidence, even a swagger, that had appeared for a time to have been tempered by the horrors of Beslan, the contagion of popular uprisings, and the rising criticism of Russia's course.

"The market," Sechin declared in the company's next annual report, "has spoken."[50]

CHAPTER 17

Poison

Aleksandr Litvinenko was already dead when he publicly accused Vladimir Putin of having killed him. A radioactive isotope had slowly but inexorably destroyed his body over three weeks. It was as if "a little, tiny nuclear bomb" had gone off inside him.[1] His doctors, who initially suspected that he had eaten tainted sushi, would not pinpoint the cause of his mysterious illness until it was too late: a dose of the element polonium-210. He had ingested it, it seemed, in the wood-paneled bar of the Mayfair Millennium Hotel in London on November 1, 2006, after briefly meeting a cadre of visiting Russians he hoped to entice into his new business enterprise: trading information on Russian power and business, which had taken on new significance now that Putin commanded the center of it. When he got home that evening, he began to feel ill. Three days later he was in the hospital, where he agonizingly withered away. He died the night of November 23, only forty-three years old. The next morning, a friend and colleague, Alex Goldfarb, emerged before a circle of journalists and television cameras and read a statement Litvinenko had dictated in his dying days.

"I can distinctly hear the beatings of the wings of the angel of death," it went, in improbably elegant English, which Litvinenko had barely learned to speak during his years in exile. "I may be able to give him the slip, but I have to say my legs do not run as fast as I would like. I think, therefore, that this may be the time to say one or two things to the person responsible for my illness. You may succeed in silencing men, but that silence comes at a price. You have shown yourself to be as barbaric and ruthless as your most hostile critics have claimed. You have shown you have no respect for life, liberty or any civilized value. You have shown yourself to be unworthy of your office, to be unworthy of the trust of civilized men and women. You may succeed in silencing one man, but a howl of protest from around the world will reverberate, Mr. Putin, in your ears for the rest of your life."[2]

Litvinenko had not settled into a quiet exile after making a furtive escape from Russia in 2000, hounded by the agency he betrayed when he went public with his accusations at the surreal press conference in 1998, before the dawn of the Putin era. He had never fully integrated into English life, remaining within the insular world of "Londongrad," populated with exiles, émigrés, and itinerant tycoons. He did not mingle socially with the rich Russians then flooding London with their wealth—his means were far too modest—but rather with the shadowy, conspiratorial circles of Putin's fiercest critics. Chief among them was Boris Berezovsky, who continued to contrive plots to discredit the man he blamed for his fall from political favor and wealth. With Berezovsky's financing and inspiration, Litvinenko wrote a book with Yuri Felshtinsky, an émigré historian based in the United States, which made the case that Putin's FSB had been behind the bombings in 1999 that propelled Putin to power. They called it *The FSB Blows Up Russia,* and it was tendentious from its opening lines: "No one but a total madman could have wished to drag Russia into any kind of war, let alone a war in the North Caucasus. As if Afghanistan had never happened."[3] A film version followed, shown discreetly in Moscow and extensively abroad, a campaign Berezovsky financed as part of his vengeful mission to bring Putin down. Litvinenko followed up with a second book, *Lubyanka Criminal Group,* portraying the KGB's successor as little more than a mafia or terrorist organization, engaged in corruption and crime. Litvinenko was burning the bridges to his past, to his own career in the security services, with a recklessness that at times verged on madness. He became consumed with Putin and his rule, trading information with other KGB veterans and with intelligence agents in Britain and Spain, and possibly elsewhere. He was eager to pursue any morsel of information that he heard and willing to believe in vast conspiracies, which he knitted out of facts, rumors, and a furious imagination.

At the end of his short life, his interest was piqued by rumors that Putin might be gay or bisexual, based in part on a brief, unsubstantiated anecdote in the memoirs of Yuri Skuratov, the former prosecutor, recalling Putin telling him that he believed a videotape existed showing him in a sexual tryst. The videotape has become a legend among Putin's critics, including former officers purged when Putin took over the FSB in 1998, who claim that various copies have been secreted abroad for safekeeping. No one seems to have actually seen it, and the accounts vary between an encounter with a young man in 1984, when he trained as a KGB foreign operative, to a tryst later in the same apartment where Skuratov was taped.[4] In Litvinenko's mind, though, a mere probability could easily become an indisputable truth. On July 5, less than four months before his poisoning, Litvinenko published his insinuation about Putin's sexuality after Putin awkwardly lifted the shirt of a young boy visiting Red Square and kissed him on the stomach. His article appeared on the website of Chechnya's rebel movement, a cause Litvinenko increasingly embraced after befriending another exile in London, the actor turned rebel spokesman Akhmed Zakayev, who had moved into a row house on the same street as Litvinenko in North London. Oleg Kalugin, the spy in exile, warned him when they met only months before his death that peddling unsubstantiated innuendo was dangerous. "Sasha, it's too much," he told him.[5] Litvinenko, already a traitor in the eyes of the FSB, had lost any sense of caution in what he presumed was the safety of exile. Even his daughter thought he was "a little crazy." "Any conversation would end up with him going on about Putin's regime," she said. "He would wind himself up to such an extent he couldn't stop, as if he was out of his mind."[6]

Litvinenko continued to work for Berezovsky, but their relationship waned and by 2006 Berezovsky had reduced the stipend he had been giving him to support his family. In search of steady income, Litvinenko then offered his services as a private investigator and researcher for firms that advised businesses on managing risk in Russia. His knowledge of the inner workings of the FSB, his obsessive collation of material, and his willingness to share led him into a labyrinth of investigations in the heart of Putin's Russia. In April 2006, he traveled to Israel to meet with one of Khodorkovsky's former Yukos partners, Leonid Nevzlin, who later said that Litvinenko had passed on information that "shed light on the most significant aspects of the Yukos affair,"[7] though what precisely this consisted of was never made clear. A month later he was in Spain, where he met security officers and a crusading prosecutor, José Grinda Gonzalez, with whom he discussed the activities, and locations, of several figures in the Russian mafia. He presented a thesis, which Grinda later endorsed, that the Russian government, through the FSB and the foreign and military intelligence branches, controlled organized crime gangs and used them to smuggle arms, launder money, carry out assassinations, and otherwise do whatever the government "cannot acceptably do as a government." Grinda was on the trail of Russian criminals in Spain, including a reputed mafia boss named Gennady Petrov, who was in business during Putin's time in Petersburg and for a time had been a shareholder in the institution that united Putin's inner circle of friends, Bank Rossiya.[8] Litvinenko kept these visits secret, traveling on the British passport he had received when granted asylum, but then he consciously thrust himself into the public spotlight after what was, until his own death, one of the most shocking murders of a Putin critic.

On the night of October 7, 2006, Putin's fifty-fourth birthday, an assassin followed Anna Politkovskaya into the hallway of her apartment building and shot her four times as she stood in the elevator. The assassin dropped the pistol beside her, the signature of a contract hit. Her murder was intended to shock, and it did. Politkovskaya had never relented in covering the war in Chechnya, even as most Russians turned away from what had become a grinding counterinsurgency operation, now largely carried out by forces loyal to Ramzan Kadyrov, the son of Putin's anointed leader, Akhmad Kadyrov, who had been assassinated in Grozny in 2004. Two days before Politkovskaya's murder, the younger Kadyrov had turned thirty, making him legally old enough to take over as the republic's president. Putin had already made him the republic's prime minister, a post that was a mere formality, since Kadyrov and his fighters held absolute control in Chechnya.

At the time of her murder, Politkovskaya was preparing an article about the torture of a Chechen migrant from Ukraine, who was beaten and electric-shocked until he confessed to committing murders—another horrifying, though not exceptional, example of the brutality of Russia's war. (Her newspaper, *Novaya Gazeta*, published the article six days after her death.) Even she wondered whether these accounts of the war's atrocities had any impact on a population that tacitly supported the government's harsh tactics simply by not paying attention. Another article found in her computer was titled "So What Am I Guilty Of?" It amounted to a lament for what journalism in Russia had become. "I have never sought my present pariah status and it makes me feel like a beached dolphin," she wrote.

In the same article she pointedly criticized Putin's unblinking support for the younger Kadyrov. Putin, she wrote, appointed him as Chechnya's prime minister "with blithe disregard for the fact that the man is a complete idiot, bereft of education, brains, or a discernible talent for anything other than mayhem and violent robbery."[9]

And yet, Putin's strategy in Chechnya ultimately proved ruthlessly effective. Aslan Maskhadov, the elected president of the republic during the brief period of independence between 1996 and 1999, had been cornered and killed in March 2005 in a basement only twelve miles from Grozny. His replacement as the political leader of the rebellion, Abdul Khalim Saidullayev, was killed a year later—betrayed by an informer, Kadyrov taunted, for the price of a dose of heroin. Months later, in July 2006, an explosion in Chechnya's neighboring republic, Ingushetia, killed Shamil Basayev, the notorious military commander and self-professed terrorist who had organized the sieges of *Nord-Ost* and Beslan, among dozens of other attacks. The FSB claimed it was a special operation, while the insurgents claimed it was an accident, but the impact was indisputable. The string of killings decapitated the leadership of the rebellion that Putin had fought from the moment he rose to power, driving its adherents even deeper underground. The cost in blood and treasure was extraordinary, with thousands of Russian soldiers killed and thousands more Chechens displaced or "disappeared." The brutality, the violence, the impunity—the repressive political and security tactics that characterized all of Russia, but were amplified in the mountains on the southern border—would create disenfranchisement and grievance that would fester into an Islamic-tinged insurgency that the authorities could never snuff out. And yet, Putin's tactics—and his support of the younger Kadyrov—had succeeded in crushing Chechnya's independence movement. Three months after Politkovskaya's death, using the authority he imposed after Beslan, Putin appointed Kadyrov Chechnya's new president. He was little more than a satrap, but Putin repaid his loyalty to the Kremlin by giving him absolute sovereignty to run Chechnya as his fief, which he did with ruthless cruelty against enemies and critics, people like Politkovskaya. She was one of the last casualties of Putin's victorious war. In 2008, too late for her to wield her acerbic wit against it, Kadyrov renamed a portion of the main street in the battered capital Grozny, which was at last being rebuilt with a massive infusion of cash from the federal budget. In the center of a city that had been flattened on Putin's command, Victory Avenue became Putin Avenue.

Given Politkovskaya's prominence, her murder drew immense international attention—and conspicuous silence from the Kremlin. Since she had an American passport, having been born in New York to Soviet diplomats at the United Nations in 1958, the American ambassador, William Burns, delivered an official démarche expressing concern and demanding a thorough investigation of the death of an American citizen. The deputy foreign minister he met, Andrei Denisov, seemed shocked by the murder and insisted that "no one in a position of authority had anything to do with the crime," adding that "many individuals could have benefited from Politkovskaya's death."[10] Yet neither the Ministry of Foreign Affairs nor the Kremlin said anything at all. Few had any authority to speak out, especially on so sensitive a case, until the president himself signaled what the official line would be. And Putin said nothing until three days later, the day Politkovskaya was buried in a heavy rain with thousands of mourners lining up to pass her coffin.

Putin had arrived that day in Dresden, his old KGB posting, for an official visit with Angela Merkel, the new chancellor who had replaced Schröder, as well as with business executives, promoting Russia's ever-expanding energy prospects. When they appeared together, Merkel joined in the international condemnation of Politkovskaya's assassination, but Putin said nothing in his comments. He addressed it only when a German reporter followed up with a question. Putin called it "a horribly cruel crime," but he then belittled the journalist's work and suggested the true motive for her killing was to besmirch Russia's reputation. "This journalist was indeed a fierce critic of the current authorities in Russia, but as the experts know and as journalists should realize, I think, her impact on Russian political life was only very slight." Her murder, he said, dealt a greater blow to the authorities than anything she had written. He expounded on the theme later that night, when he told Russian and German officials meeting in the semiannual forum known as the Petersburg Dialogue that Politkovskaya's assassination had been orchestrated by enemies of Russia. This would become a recurring theme: the enemies of Russia, of Putin, were conspiring to discredit him. "We have reliable, consistent information that many people who are hiding from Russian justice have been harboring the idea that they will use somebody as a victim to create a wave of anti-Russian sentiment in the world," he told them.

This was exactly what Litvinenko sought to do. He considered Politkovskaya a friend—whenever she visited London, the two traded information about Chechnya and the security services working there[11]—and her death enraged him. On October 19, less than two weeks before he fell ill, he attended a panel discussion in London on Politkovskaya's murder and declared that Putin himself was culpable. He rose from the crowd to address the panel, beginning in halting English and then continuing in Russian as a woman sitting beside Akhmed Zakayev translated. After emphasizing that he had nothing to hide and repeating several times that the journalists there should feel free to quote his remarks, he said that Politkovskaya herself had received a warning that Putin had put her on a hit list. "I know very well that only one person in Russia could kill a journalist with the standing of Anna Politkovskaya—and that is Putin, no one else."

Thirteen days later, he collected the "evidence" he was sure would help him prove the case. An Italian security analyst, Mario Scaramella, who traded in the same secrets he did, shared emails that had been sent by another Russian in exile purporting to be the hit list of an association of KGB veterans called Dignity and Honor. Politkovskaya's name was on the list. So were Litvinenko's and Berezovsky's. And yet Litvinenko seemed to let his guard down when he left his lunch meeting with the Italian to meet the two Russians who would become the chief suspects in his murder: Andrei Lugovoi and Dmitri Kovtun.

Lugovoi, also a veteran of the KGB department that provided protection for government officials, had once run security for the television station controlled by Berezovsky. He now owned a security company called the Ninth Wave and remained in contact with Berezovsky. Kovtun was a childhood friend of Lugovoi's who served as a captain in the Soviet Red Army's military intelligence branch in East Germany and owned a business consulting company. Litvinenko knew Lugovoi through his connection with Berezovsky and was eager to bring him into his orbit of contacts, which included Erinys, a security company where Litvinenko sometimes worked as a consultant. Lugovoi introduced Kovtun during that visit in October, meeting at Erinys and afterward at a Chinese restaurant. The authorities in Britain later disclosed that the first attempt to kill Litvinenko had happened at the security company, using the same radioactive poison.[12] He felt sick afterward, vomiting that night, but he recovered.

The three met again on the November day he fell gravely ill. It was Litvinenko who urgently insisted on seeing them this time, before a meeting already planned for the following morning. He was eager to share what he had learned from the emails that Mario Scaramella had shared over lunch. Their meeting at the Mayfair Millennium's Pine Bar was short since Lugovoi, who was traveling with his family, had tickets to a soccer match between Arsenal and CSKA Moscow that night at Emirates Stadium. When his son arrived at the bar, he introduced him to Litvinenko, and then he left to change his clothes for the match. Kovtun thought Litvinenko looked strange, agitated, and, perhaps, unwell. "He didn't close his mouth," he said.[13] As Kovtun waited for Lugovoi in the lobby, Litvinenko clung uncomfortably close to his side. "I was standing too close to him," Kovtun said. "He kept talking and talking."

After the British authorities determined what poison had killed Litvinenko, polonium-210, they ultimately found residual traces of it everywhere the three men had been—not just on November 1, but during their previous meetings on October 16 and 17. It contaminated their hotel rooms, the conference room where they met at Erinys, the seat at Emirates Stadium where Lugovoi sat, the seat cushions at the Hey Jo strip club and a hookah at the Dar Marrakesh restaurant, which Lugovoi and Kovtun had visited. It irradiated two British Airways jets that flew between Moscow and London and even the couch in the house of Kovtun's ex-wife in Hamburg, Germany, which Kovtun had visited only days before he flew again to London to meet Litvinenko the second time, and where, according to testimony made public years later, he asked a friend if he could recommend a chef who might be able to deliver a dose of poison.

Polonium-210 occurs naturally in minute quantities in the earth's crust, in the air, and in tobacco smoke, but when manufactured it appears as a silvery soft metal. It was once used in the triggers of nuclear weapons and is produced in small amounts to eliminate static electricity in industrial machinery and to remove dust from film and camera lenses. It decays by emitting alpha particles that travel only a few inches and are easily stopped by a sheet of paper or a person's skin. The only health risk comes when it is ingested. Easily and safely handled and lethally toxic—it is an ingenious weapon. Ninety-seven percent of the world's industrial supply comes from Avangard, a Russian nuclear facility in the heavily guarded city of Sarov, where the Soviet Union built its first atom bomb.

As happened with Politkovskaya's murder, Putin was traveling when Litvinenko's death exploded into a global media frenzy. This time he was in Helsinki for a summit with the European Union that had already gone poorly, and as he prepared for the ritual press conference that culminated such meetings, Putin's spokesman, Dmitri Peskov, delivered the news about Litvinenko's deathbed accusation, knowing he would surely be asked to respond. Putin was livid, incredulous that he had been accused of being personally involved in Litvinenko's death.[14] The timing, he and his aides believed, could not be a coincidence; it could only be a provocation.

When he appeared with the prime ministers of Finland, Iceland, and Norway, along with the European Union's two senior officials, Putin's discomfort was palpable. He grimaced, shifted, and stared at the ceiling. His aides on the sidelines suggested to reporters that he had a cold,[15] but he seemed to be suppressing the fury that Peskov said he felt. None of the leaders who spoke from the dais pretended that the meetings had been a success, though they diplomatically expressed hope that the efforts to forge closer economic and social ties would continue. After they finished speaking, the first question was about Litvinenko: Would Putin respond to the accusation that he was responsible?

Putin, normally cocksure in these press appearances, answered awkwardly. "A person's death is always a tragedy," he began, and then offered his condolences to Litvinenko's family. As he had with Politkovskaya's murder, he tried to play down the victim and obfuscate the circumstances. The British doctors, he said, had not indicated that this was "a violent death." He suggested that the British authorities bore responsibility for protecting the country's citizens. He offered Russia's assistance *if* an investigation was warranted and urged the British not to "support any tendency to inflate any political scandals which are groundless." As for the note, he questioned why it had not been made public while Litvinenko was alive: if it was written after his death, Putin said, there was no need to comment. "The people who have done this are not God and Mr. Litvinenko is, unfortunately, not Lazarus," he said. "And it is very much a pity that even such tragic events like a person's death can be used for political provocations." As he had in Politkovskaya's case, Putin sought to deflect blame elsewhere, to his enemies. And yet nowhere in his short, awkward remarks did he come out and explicitly deny that the Russians had done it.

No direct evidence has yet emerged that Putin had any involvement in Litvinenko's death, or Politkovskaya's, or any of the other mysterious and unsolved crimes that bore the hallmarks of political assassination during his rule. By now, however, his standing in the West had sunk so low that few doubted that, at the very least, he had created a climate that made political murder grimly ordinary. In the wake of Litvinenko's poisoning, older cases suddenly took on new significance. Yuri Shchekochikhin, a member of parliament and a journalist who also worked for Politkovskaya's newspaper, died in 2003 after a sudden illness that suggested a poisoning; he had just written an article about a stalled investigation that now, three years later, was about to surface amid renewed intrigue. Another case involved the strange death of a man supposedly acting as a mediator in the Yukos affair in 2004; the victim, Roman Tsepov, an acquaintance of Putin's in the 1990s, died in a manner that eerily foreshadowed Litvinenko's case: he succumbed to radiation sickness only days after supposedly having been invited for a cup of tea at the FSB's headquarters in Petersburg.[16]

Litvinenko's poisoning had all the intricacy and intrigue of a John Le Carré novel, minus only a coherent motive and a climactic resolution. Back in Moscow, Lugovoi and Kovtun did not act like suspects. Lugovoi had called Litvinenko twice after learning he was ill, but before anyone knew of the cause. This did not seem to be the action of a murderer. When his name surfaced as one of those who had met Litvinenko on November 1, he presented himself at the British embassy, agreeing to meet the diplomats to clarify the situation and to be interviewed by British investigators. The chair he sat on was so irradiated with polonium-210 that the embassy sealed the room.[17] On the day after Litvinenko's death, he and Kovtun granted an interview to the radio station Ekho Moskvy, expressing bewilderment over the whole affair, and they continued to speak out for months afterward, denying any complicity. Later they insisted they were the intended victims—either with, by, or instead of Litvinenko. "To kill him, and more so in such an extravagant way, was absolutely beyond understanding," Kovtun said. If he and Lugovoi were hired assassins dispatched to London, Kovtun insisted, they would have been sent after the most-wanted men on Russia's list of enemies, not an insignificant one like Litvinenko. In fact, Lugovoi had met Berezovsky the day before Litvinenko's poisoning. "Lugovoi always had the chance to meet with Berezovsky, Zakayev, with all of them together. Since he had the chance to meet any of them, it would be easy to kill the more important target."[18] In the shadowy world they inhabited, the argument made a certain amount of sense.

Putin did his best to ignore the drama, but Russian officials vigorously tried to undercut the narrative taking shape around the world. They did so with more zeal than they showed in investigating the murder itself. When traces of polonium-210 were found in Kovtun's system, the prosecutor general's office announced an investigation into *his* attempted murder. A month later, it announced, without evidence or even explanation, that Litvinenko's death was linked, somehow, to ongoing prosecutions against Yukos. When Putin appeared at a press conference in February 2007, he dismissed Litvinenko as an inconsequential guard in the border troops who had abused his oath of office and then fled the country. "There was no need to run anywhere. He did not have any secrets. Everything negative that he could say with respect to his service and his previous employment, he already said a long time ago, so there could be nothing new in what he did later." Instead, he claimed, the enemies who sought to harm Russia were the "runaway oligarchs hiding in Western Europe or in the Middle East." He clearly meant Nevzlin and Berezovsky, suggesting, with as little evidence as those who accused him, that they somehow had a hand in Litvinenko's death. "But I do not really believe in conspiracy theories."

Russia, though, had become fertile ground for conspiracies, real and imagined, and the deaths of Litvinenko, Politkovskaya, and the others challenged the carefully cultivated impression that Putin presided over an era of progress, stability, and renewed national pride that left behind the violent chaos of the 1990s. Many theories centered on the end of Putin's second term as president, which was, by law, already on the horizon. Some saw the murders as a provocation to ignite a popular uprising before the election in 2008, the way Georgy Gongadze's murder in Ukraine hastened the end of Leonid Kuchma's rule. Others saw the dark hand of those inside Russia who wanted Putin to remain in power. By this logic, the opprobrium that would fall on Putin for orchestrating the murder of a critic in London would force him to remain in office to assure his immunity from criminal prosecution.

Putin had been asked about his intention to revise the Constitution and seek a third term as president even before he had romped to reelection for a second term.[19] Over and over he insisted that he had no intention to change the Constitution to erase the term limits on the powerful presidency, and over and over appeals were drafted to do exactly that. Regional parliaments proposed holding referendums on the issue from Primoriye in the Far East to Chechnya. The speaker of Chechnya's parliament, Dukavakha Abdurakhmanov, echoed Ramzan Kadyrov in his fealty by declaring that Putin should have three or four more terms as president—that he should rule for life, if possible. "The number of terms should not decide the end of his presidency but rather his age and health," he said.[20] With a simple signal from the Kremlin, any of the initiatives to extend Putin's rule would have passed easily, but Putin demurred, rebuffing the appeals, though he did not actively discourage them either. For the first time ever, the country had a legal, democratic mechanism for the peaceful transfer of power, but by Putin's own design, it had become impossible to imagine anyone else in charge.

Putin once said he had been thinking about his potential replacement from the moment he took office, but by his second term, the question of succession had begun to concern Putin and his court the way it had the ailing Yelstin—or the discredited Kuchma in Ukraine. He disclosed as much in December 2004 when he was asked at a press conference about his plans after leaving office and whether he would consider returning to politics in the following election, in 2012? He joked, "Why not in 2016?" His coy deflections never put the question fully to rest, but he acknowledged that, like Yeltsin before him, he had begun to think about the coming "milestone" of the 2008 election, which he cryptically called "a critical line" for the country.

The search for Putin's heir—"Operation Successor," it was called—began in earnest in November 2005 when the Kremlin announced that Putin had promoted two of his closest aides: Dmitri Medvedev, then his chief of staff, and Sergei Ivanov, the minister of defense. Putin elevated Medvedev to the newly created position of first deputy prime minister while Ivanov became a deputy prime minister in addition to minister of defense. Like Putin before his appointment by Yeltsin, neither man had run for elected office, but of the two Ivanov seemed the more likely heir. He was thirteen years older than Medvedev and had risen to the rank of general in the KGB. Medvedev, by contrast, was a boyish, bookish lawyer who had co-authored a legal textbook and lectured at St. Petersburg State University's law school before following Putin to Moscow as his trusted protégé. Putin told neither man whom he would choose, and in the following months, it seemed that both were being groomed for the role, slipped into the public spotlight to burnish their images, though they were "campaigning" for the only vote that mattered: Putin's. They both now took prominent roles in policy initiatives. Medvedev oversaw

$5 billion in spending on "national projects" in agriculture, housing, education, and health care; Ivanov, the restructuring of the military and by 2006 a new commission to oversee military procurement. Both began appearing more often in nightly news reports, certainly more than their nominal boss, the colorless prime minister who ran the government, Mikhail Fradkov, who in his first year in office had become notable for his lack of political significance. As the speculation mounted, both Medvedev and Ivanov faced repeated questions about their political aspirations, and they became artful in deflecting the issue. In Putin's court, no one dared to campaign openly, even if they harbored political ambitions of their own. They conspired instead.

The seeming solidity of Putin's political control belied a subterranean struggle to influence his ultimate choice. It was an extension of the struggle for control over the redistribution of assets that the Kremlin had orchestrated in earnest throughout Putin's second term.[21] As in any court, rivalries emerged. Igor Sechin, whose power had increased with the acquisition of Rosneft, disliked the prospect of either of Putin's aides becoming president. He favored the prosecutor general, Vladimir Ustinov, who had played an important role in the Yukos affairs and whose son had married Sechin's daughter. Unfortunately for both men, a transcript of one of their conversations was said to have landed on Putin's desk in the spring of 2006.[22] It had been taped surreptitiously by a deputy in Russia's drug enforcement agency, which was then headed by Viktor Cherkesov, Putin's KGB colleague from Petersburg. In the wiretapped conversation, Sechin was said to have suggested, improbably, that Putin was weak and Ustinov would make a suitable replacement. Whether it was true was not the point: Ustinov was nakedly ambitious, chairing meetings of prosecutors with "a presidential air," which was a dangerous presumption.[23] Emboldened by the takedown of Khodorkovsky and with Sechin's blessing, he vowed publicly in May 2006 to prosecute "high-profile criminal cases" involving government officials, including, some argued, against Dmitri Medvedev.

Putin dismissed Ustinov on June 2. The decision surprised the Federation Council, which still had the final authority to install or remove a prosecutor general, though no longer the independence it had under Yeltsin to debate doing so. In an indication of how much the balance of power had shifted in the seven years since the scandal over Yeltin's removal of Yuri Skuratov, the council voted the same day to affirm Putin's decision. There was no debate, and the vote was virtually unanimous, with only two abstentions. Sergei Ivanov hinted that there were "good reasons" for Ustinov's departure, but Putin offered no public explanation. No one understood then that the dismissal was the first ripple from the political turmoil beneath the surface. The murders of Politkovskaya and Litvinenko soon followed. The hidden battle over Putin's heir would not explode into public, however, until the following year over an investigation into the furniture store Tri Kita, or Three Whales. It was the case Yuri Shchekochikhin had been circling around in his reporting when he died mysteriously.

At the height of the furor over the Litvinenko investigation, Putin dispatched Medvedev to the annual meeting of the world's business and political elite at Davos, Switzerland, in January 2007. A little awkward, with a thick mat of brown hair and a musical taste for early American and British heavy metal, Medvedev projected a gentler image of a Russian politician than Putin had of late. Then only forty-one, he was a child of the intelligentsia with no known background in the security services. He came of age as perestroika took root, representing a new generation less hardened by Communism and the Cold War. He even spoke a smattering of English, picked up from his abiding passion for the music of Deep Purple. In his keynote speech, he reassured the audience that Gazprom was no bully—only weeks after it had suspended supplies to Belarus. He claimed that Russia had every intention of being a reliable partner in trade and investment—despite the Kremlin's role in squeezing investors like Royal Dutch Shell. He even took issue with the slogan Putin's political strategist Vladislav Surkov had popularized: "sovereign democracy." Democracy, Medvedev said, needed no adjectives, and he was confident that Russia's version was genuine enough. "We are not trying to push anyone to love Russia, but we won't allow anyone to hurt Russia," he said. "We will strive to win respect both for the citizens of Russia and for the country as a whole. Moreover, this shall be achieved not by using force but rather by our behavior and by our achievements." Medvedev's prominence at an international forum—Davos being a rite of passage for aspiring political leaders everywhere—was by and large well received, and it seemed to confirm his emergence as Putin's heir apparent.

Medvedev's defense of Russia did not diverge substantively from Putin's, but the tone lulled the Davos attendees into believing him to be a different kind of leader. Less than two weeks later, however, Putin made it clear at another international forum that he was taking a much harder line against his detractors in the West, and above all in the United States. The furor over the Politkovskaya and Litvinenko murders stoked Putin's anger, but the precipitating impulse for the speech he was about to deliver was President Bush's decision to negotiate the establishment of bases for the American missile defense system in Poland and the Czech Republic. In his mind, they were all of a piece. Putin had fiercely opposed Bush's decision to abandon the Cold War treaty prohibiting the deployment of national missile defenses, but he had acquiesced somewhat, reassured by the pledges to forge a new, more constructive friendship between the two countries. Instead they had drifted further apart. Now the United States wanted to put radar stations and interceptor missiles on Russia's flank. In the view of Putin and his military commanders, the deployment challenged the core of the country's nuclear deterrent, the one thing that had survived the collapse of the Soviet Union and preserved Russia's great power status. "I've had enough," he snapped at his aides.[24]

To express his vexation, Putin chose a forum often called the Davos of the national security world: the annual Munich Security Conference. At the February 2007 gathering, following an opening address by German chancellor Angela Merkel, Putin strode to the podium and began with a warning of what was to come. "This conference's structure allows me to avoid excessive politeness and the need to speak in roundabout, pleasant, but empty diplomatic terms. This conference's format will allow me to say what I really think about international security problems. And if my comments seem unduly polemical, pointed, or inexact to our colleagues, then I would ask you not to get angry with me. After all, this is only a conference."[25] He jokingly hoped the conference's moderator would not turn on the red light warning him his time was up. A smattering of uncomfortable laughs followed. Merkel, sitting in the front row, forced a smile.

The end of the Cold War, Putin went on, left the world "with live ammunition, figuratively speaking." He meant "ideological stereotypes, double standards, and other typical aspects of Cold War bloc thinking." The collapse of the Soviet Union ended the geopolitical division of the world, but the resulting "unipolar" power was creating new divisions, new threats, and sowing chaos around the world. "It is a world in which there is one master, one sovereign," he went on. Instead of easing the world's tensions, "unilateral and frequently illegitimate actions" have resulted in more war and more deaths than in the divided world. "Significantly more," he repeated. "Significantly more."

"Today we are witnessing an almost uncontained hyper use of force—military force—in international relations, force that is plunging the world into an abyss of permanent conflicts. As a result we do not have sufficient strength to find a comprehensive solution to any one of these conflicts. Finding a political settlement also becomes impossible. We are seeing a greater and greater disdain for the basic principles of international law. And independent legal norms are, as a matter of fact, coming increasingly close to one state's legal system." If anyone missed the point, he then singled out the United States, which had "overstepped its national borders in every way. This is visible in the economic, political, cultural, and educational policies it imposes on other nations. Well, who likes this?"

Merkel watched with a stony face, as did the American delegation sitting in the front to her left, including President Bush's new secretary of defense, Robert Gates, and two senators who were regular fixtures at the gathering, John McCain and Joe Lieberman.[26] Viktor Yushchenko of Ukraine, whose election he so vigorously fought, was to Merkel's right. Putin's speech went on for thirty-two minutes, a public dressing-down of the West over a catalogue of grievances from arms control treaties to the expansion of NATO, the development of missile defenses to that of weapons in space—all, in his mind, caused by the unchecked hubris of a superpower bent on dominating the world on its own terms. Other international organizations had to bend to its demands. Negotiations to admit Russia to the World Trade Organization became entangled with unrelated demands for greater freedom of speech. The Organization for Security and Co-operation in Europe, which had criticized elections under Putin, had become "a vulgar instrument" to interfere in the internal affairs of others. The reaction in the hotel ranged from stunned to furious. The American response came the next day. Gates defended American actions and, as a former intelligence officer himself and director of the CIA who said he had evolved in the decades since 1989, offered a gentle rebuke to the man who seemingly had not. "One Cold War was enough," he said.

Putin's speech became a landmark in Russia's relations with the West, interpreted by many as a defining moment as significant as Winston Churchill's speech in 1946 that gave the world the phrase the "Iron Curtain." Putin, as he had certainly intended to do, tapped into the global anger and anxiety about the United States under George Bush: the prison on Guantánamo, the rendition of prisoners in secret detention centers, the torture of terrorist suspects, the war in Iraq. Putin might be criticized for his tightening grip at home, for Russia's own atrocities in Chechnya and elsewhere, and even for the poisoning of Litvinenko, but many around the world—including some even in Europe and the United States—agreed with his assessment and openly cheered a country and a leader willing and able to provide a counter to unbridled American power. Russia was no Venezuela or Iran or some other enemy whose anti-Americanism could be easily brushed aside as the ravings of the weak and irrelevant. The German newspaper *Süddeutsche Zeitung* wrote after the speech that Putin's was a warning worth minding: "The mother of all failures has been the paternalistic way in which the winner of the Cold War has treated the loser."[27]

Putin had not closed the door on working with the Americans entirely—he would make one last bold gambit to co-opt Bush's missile defenses—but in the seventh and last year of his presidency, Russia had regained its international swagger, emboldened by surging revenues from oil and gas. Medvedev had said as much in Davos, but in a soothing reassurance that now, only two weeks later, seemed weak. Putin was charting a new foreign policy that would be far more defiant, even hostile, toward the United States in particular but also, in the wake of the Litvinenko murder, to Britain too. He went from Munich to Saudi Arabia, once a vehement enemy of the Soviet Union, and then to Qatar, seeking to expand Russia's energy power with an OPEC for natural gas. Joining him on the trip was Sergei Ivanov, whose hawkish views hewed far more closely to Putin's rhetoric than Medvedev's. Medvedev's debut in Davos had been warmly received by the same international elite Putin had just dressed down. He had been seen as the front-runner in the unofficial primary race for the coming presidential election, but when Putin returned to Moscow a week later, it was Ivanov whom he promoted. There were now two first deputy prime ministers, and Ivanov was the one who seemed much more in tune with Putin's mood.

Putin's jeremiad in Munich also reverberated through the Russian military and security establishment, leading to an upsurge of threats and hostile acts not only against the United States but also against the Europeans. The commander of Russia's strategic missile forces warned that he would retarget the country's nuclear weapons at Poland and the Czech Republic if they went ahead with the deployment of American military hardware. In April, Putin announced that Russia would suspend compliance with the treaty on conventional armed forces in Europe, a pact negotiated at the end of the Cold War to limit the number of armored vehicles, artillery batteries, and attack aircraft deployed across the continent. Putin's deliberate turn in Munich was like a whistle to a nation that shared his feelings of betrayal and besiegement; it unleashed a suppressed fury toward foreigners, even diplomats. When Estonia relocated a Soviet war memorial from a park in its capital, Tallinn, in April 2007, the country's computer network faced a crippling wave of cyberattacks that Estonian officials traced to computers in Russia, including one with an Internet Protocol address inside Putin's presidential administration.[28] It was described as a cyberwar, launched furtively by an increasingly bellicose Russia that no longer respected the sovereignty of its neighbors—exactly what Putin accused the United States of doing.

In Russia, Nashi, the militant youth group created and nurtured by the Kremlin, laid siege to Estonia's embassy. Bodyguards for Estonia's ambassador, Marina Kalijurand, had to use pepper spray to escape Nashists who rushed her as she departed a press conference trying to calm tensions over the monument. Her car was attacked as it left, as was the Swedish ambassador's when he tried to visit the Estonian embassy. These breaches of diplomatic protocol were tolerated by the usually zealous Russian police. Nor did Putin let up on his public criticism of the American hegemon; at the annual Victory Day commemoration in Red Square on May 9, he compared the United States to the Third Reich with its "same contempt for human life" and its same desire to rule the world by diktat. The stability of international relations and the security architecture constructed after the Cold War—an era that augured a new peace for the continent—was unraveling in a convulsion of mutual reproach.

It was at this point that Britain's Crown Prosecution Service brought to a head its investigation of the poisoning of Aleksandr Litvinenko. In May 2007, it announced that there were sufficient grounds to accuse Andrei Lugovoi of the murder. The prosecutors did not make their evidence public then, but the British had concluded that only the Kremlin could have authorized such a brazen and risky operation. Russia defiantly refused to consider Britain's appeal for Lugovoi's extradition. Russia cited its own constitutional prohibition on extraditing its citizens—and the hypocrisy of Britain's repeated rebuffs of its own numerous appeals to bring Boris Berezovsky to justice in Russia. In April, Berezovsky had told *The Guardian* that he was actively financing an effort to foment a new revolution in Russia among the political and business elite, who he believed were the only hope of change, not the coming election for Putin's successor. "It isn't possible to change this regime through democratic means," he told the newspaper. "There can be no change without force, pressure."[29] The Kremlin declared Berezovsky's threat a violation of the new law on extremism and renewed its demand for his extradition. Lugovoi held his own carnivalesque appearance before the press, mocking the indictment and accusing instead MI6 (the British foreign intelligence service, which had tried to recruit him), the Spanish branch of the Russian mafia (presumably in retaliation for Litvinenko's meeting with the authorities there), and Berezovsky himself of the murder of the man he had once supported financially. He had himself been tainted with polonium-210, he said, "for the future use in a political scandal."[30]

The spectacle heightened suspicion in Russia that Litvinenko's murder, like Politkovskaya's and the others, was part of an elaborate conspiracy to dictate the outcome of Russia's political transition. The only questions that remained were whether the conspirators were inside Russia or outside, and whether they were conspiring to keep Putin in power or to force him from it. In June, two days after Britain expelled four Russian diplomats in retaliation for Russia's refusal to extradite Lugovoi, the British police detained a mysterious Russian who had arrived in London on false papers. Suspecting him of intending to kill Berezovsky, they expelled him from the country.[31] In July, the Royal Air Force fighter jets had to scramble to intercept Russian TU-95 strategic bombers, testing British air defenses as the Soviet Union had done in the Cold War. It was as if the bear that was the Soviet Union had woken from two decades of hibernation.

CHAPTER 18

The 2008 Problem

In July 2007, Putin flew to tiny Guatemala on a personal mission that would assuage an international slight that dated to 1980, when the Soviet Union hosted the Summer Olympics in Moscow and much of the West boycotted to protest the invasion of Afghanistan. Bringing the games back to Russia became an obsessive quest that Putin had pursued from the time Sobchak made an improbable bid for Petersburg in the 1990s. As an avid sportsman and fitness obsessive, a judoka, a skier, and a swimmer, Putin loved the Olympics; as a leader, he saw hosting them as the means to affirm Russia's return to its rightful place on the world stage. In 2001, not long after he assumed the presidency, he went on a skiing trip to St. Anton am Arlberg in Austria, accompanied by an oligarch of the Yeltsin era, Vladimir Potanin, and Boris Nemtsov, the liberal who had initially thrown his support behind Putin. Seeing the resorts nestled in the Alpine scenery, Putin lamented that the new Russia had none. "I want to get one European-style winter resort," he told his companions.[1]

The oligarchs beholden to Putin, old and new, obliged. In January 2006, Yuri Kovalchuk's Bank Rossiya opened a ski resort called Igora fifty-two miles north of Petersburg on the highway to the Ozero dacha Kovalchuk shared with Putin, with seven trails, though a vertical drop of less than four hundred feet. Potanin, whose holding company Interros controlled the metal giant Norilsk Nickel and kept him at the top of the list of Russian billionaires, drafted blueprints for a far more ambitious project on a ridge called Rosa Khutor in the mountains above the Black Sea resort of Sochi. Putin, who regularly vacationed at Sochi's presidential retreat, visited the remote site above the forlorn mountain village of Krasnaya Polyana, and thus a legend was born. "He came to see this road," Anatoly Pakhomov, who would later become Sochi's mayor, said, referring to the precarious, potholed route that wended beside the Mzymta River. And Putin said, "This beauty, these riches in Krasnaya Polyana, should belong to all the people."[2]

For Putin, the projects were not investments in the purest business sense. In fact, they were economically dubious. Rather, they were patriotic endeavors carried out for the greater public good, which he believed he best understood and which he alone decided. Soon Gazprom, firmly under Putin's control, began a similar resort in an adjacent valley near Rosa Khutor. The two projects were the foundation for the new bid Putin was flying to Guatemala to present to the delegates of the International Olympic Committee.

Sochi's bid was submitted by Russia's Olympic Committee in 2005, but despite Pakhomov's hagiographic recollection, the idea of staging the games there did not originate with Putin. He was carrying on an ambition that the country's leaders had harbored for decades. In the wake of the Moscow Olympics, the geriatric Politburo in the Kremlin secretly debated a bid for the Winter Olympics, reviewing four possible locations across the Soviet Union. The dream had to be abandoned, as the leadership was overtaken by the rapid succession of general secretaries in the 1980s and finally by the promise and upheaval of perestroika.[3] Three of the cities they had reviewed—Almaty in Kazakhstan, Bakuriani in Georgia, and Tsaghkadzor in Armenia—were no longer part of Russia at all. Only Sochi still was. While it had been a favored seaside resort since Stalin's days, it lacked any of the modern facilities required for the Olympics, beginning with a lack of functioning ski slopes. In 1995, during Yeltsin's erratic presidency, the Russians had submitted a bid for Sochi for the 2002 Winter Olympics, but it failed even to make the short list. Putin tried again in 2005, bidding for the Summer Olympics. Moscow went up against New York, Madrid, Paris, and London for the 2012 Summer Games and finished last in the final balloting. The International Olympic Committee's evaluations pointedly questioned whether Russia had the capacity to organize the games in its own capital. How could Russia two years later possibly make the case that Sochi, a decaying resort without a single Olympic-standard facility, would be ready for the Winter Olympics of 2014?

Sochi was competing against Salzburg in Austria, and Pyeongchang, South Korea, the favorite going in to the final vote, having narrowly lost the previous bid. Few gave Sochi much chance.

The 119th session of the International Olympic Committee took place in the Westin Camino Real in the heart of Guatemala City. Putin had prepared intensely, rehearsing his speech in stilted, heavily accented, but nearly perfect English. Among the officials presenting the final bids, he spoke first in the morning. "The Olympic cluster in Sochi will be the first world-class mountain sports center in the new Russia," he began, making it clear he had absorbed the Politburo's review from the 1980s and the consequences of the Soviet dissolution. "Let me point out that after the breakup of the Soviet Union, Russia has lost all of its sports venues in the mountains. Would you believe it?" He sounded incredulous, even offended by the cruel historical turn. He highlighted the novelty of Sochi's location on the Black Sea, abutting the peaks of the Caucasus. "On the seashore you can enjoy a fine spring day, but up in the mountains, it's winter." He pledged to spend $12 billion to erect the venues—a staggering sum that exceeded what Vancouver planned to spend in 2010. He promised "a safe, enjoyable, and memorable experience" and even joked that he would ease the city's chronic traffic jams. He finished with a flourish of stilted French, thanking the committee for its consideration.

And then he left the hotel. He had staked so much of his prestige—and Russia's—on the vote, but he refused to stay for it, as if he anticipated an unhappy outcome and feared the embarrassment of having to witness the delegations of Salzburg or Pyeongchang celebrating. Instead, he boarded his presidential jet and began the long flight back to Moscow.

By now, Putin was vilified in much of the West, and yet his remonstrations to the bullying Americans—and the fact that he was not wrong about the bloodshed in Iraq—won him grudging admiration in some quarters, and there were those who thought that played a role in the voting, which began while Putin was over the Atlantic.[4] Sochi came in second in the first round of votes, receiving thirty-four votes, compared to thirty-six for Pyeongchang; Salzburg won only twenty-five and was eliminated. When the second round finished, though, Sochi drew more of Salzburg's votes, edging Pyeongchang by four votes. Russia had won; Putin had won. "He was nice," Jean-Claude Killy, the French ski champion and a member of the International Olympic Committee, explained after the vote. "He spoke French—he never speaks French. He spoke English—he never speaks English. The Putin charisma can explain four votes."[5]

The deputy prime minister who remained in Guatemala, Aleksandr Zhukov, telephoned Putin on the presidential plane to inform him of the committee's choice. Putin in turn called the chairman of the International Olympic Committee, Jacques Rogge, and thanked him for what he called an "impartial decision." At home, Putin's popularity soared even higher. When he returned triumphantly to Moscow, he stepped out of his jet and met assembled reporters at the VIP hall of Vnukovo Airport. "It is, beyond any doubt, a judgment of our country," he declared. Only in a country desperate for affirmation could the choice of an Olympics have loomed so disproportionately large. "Russia has risen from its knees!" German Gref declared in Guatemala City.

And yet through the summer and fall, those inside the Kremlin's walls were consumed by a fear that without Putin Russia might fall back down. Uncertainty gripped the political and business elite because, at the height of his political powers, the end of his presidency suddenly loomed. Putin's repeated assertions that he would not amend the Constitution so he could serve a third term had finally sunk in. The elite had come to the unhappy realization that these were not simply coy deflections. Putin had created his own problem: he wanted to adhere to the strict letter of the law and assure a smooth transition to a new president, but he was determined that it be one that he alone controlled. His strategy was unquestionably authoritarian, but he sought the patina of legitimacy, fearing that a reprise of a color revolution—fomented by his enemies abroad—would destroy the system he had spent nearly eight years building.

Sergei Ivanov still seemed the presumptive front-runner in the undeclared campaign to replace Putin, trailed closely by Dmitri Medvedev, though periodically Putin would drop teasing hints that others might be considered: perhaps his old friend Vladimir Yakunin of the Russian Railways, or even, for diversity's sake, the governor of Petersburg, Valentina Matviyenko. None dared declare an ambition for the post, which would usurp Putin's prerogative. Ivanov had quietly assembled an advisory council to prepare policy positions,[6] though, while Medvedev's work on the "national projects" assured him a conspicuous public role. Both gathered informal supporters, and opponents, in the deliberations that swirled through the government, but by the end of summer, Putin had not yet signaled a choice. He was in no hurry; a designated heir might steal attention from him, rendering him a lame duck, which seemed not only inconceivable, but also unacceptable. As a result of his irresolution, the ranks of the bureaucracy became paralyzed, unwilling to make decisions that would last beyond the end of Putin's presidency or affect their place in whatever administration was to come.[7] His irresolution also created dangerous tensions that spilled indecorously into the public.

Putin stoked the speculation further when on September 12 he revealed the latest act in the theater of managed democracy. Mikhail Fradkov, the loyal, functional prime minister since 2004, walked into Putin's office in the Kremlin and, cameras rolling, unexpectedly resigned. "I understand the political processes taking place at the moment and I would like to see you have as free a hand as possible in making decisions," Fradkov said. He did not sound like a man stepping down on selfless principle as much as an actor who had not rehearsed his lines enough. He looked forlorn and troubled. Putin at least made the effort to seem thoughtful and considerate. "Perhaps you are right," he replied, thanking him for his service, though he went on to point out that some mistakes had been made. He said it was important to reflect on how the new nominee would affect the political situation before the parliamentary elections in December and the presidential election in March. A few hours later he announced an even more unexpected choice to replace Fradkov: Viktor Zubkov.

No one outside the Kremlin and few inside it understood Putin's decision. Even Sergei Ivanov did not know it was coming.[8] If Putin was following Yeltsin's model of designating his successor, tapping a new prime minister on the eve of the presidential campaign, he had opted for a man who by design had kept a low profile. Zubkov, born in the early months of the Great Patriotic War, was part of the cadre of men whose bonds with Putin had been forged in Petersburg in the 1990s. After the early barter-for-food deals created a scandal in the winter of 1991, Zubkov, a former collective-farm boss, had assisted Putin by using his influence among regional farmers to resume supplies of produce to the hungry city.[9] He became one of Putin's most trusted associates, taking over the city's taxation enforcement and later joining him and Igor Sechin in producing dissertations at the Mining Institute in the 1990s. He followed Putin to Moscow, where for seven years he had quietly headed the new Russian Financial Monitoring Agency, a department that gave him—and Putin—exclusive knowledge about the flow of money in and out of the country's businesses, information that was invaluable in enforcing loyalty and thus maintaining some sort of equilibrium among the rival financial empires being established, many of which had connections to the state itself. "Not once, I would like to emphasize, did Viktor Zubkov abuse this trust," Putin later explained.[10] After his announcement, Putin then flew off to the regions of Chuvashia and Belgorod to see how Medvedev's "national projects" were reviving the nation's agriculture, leaving the political elite to ponder the meaning of his unforeseen gambit. Had Putin decided against Medvedev or Ivanov after all? He certainly wanted to signal that the decision was still an open one. On September 14, he said there were at least five serious candidates for the presidency, but he would not reveal them.[11]

Zubkov's nomination, swiftly rubber-stamped by the Duma two days later, did little to calm the behind-the-scenes power struggle that had been unfolding all through Putin's year of uncertainty. This struggle, which had become known as the "war of the clans," erupted unexpectedly on October 2 when a special detachment of the FSB ostentatiously arrested a senior official of the country's anti-narcotics agency, Lieutenant General Aleksandr Bulbov, as he arrived at Domodedevo Airport. Because Bulbov traveled with his own security detail, the arrest very nearly erupted into a shootout in the terminal. Bulbov, a decorated veteran of the Soviet war in Afghanistan, was a senior deputy to Viktor Cherkesov, one of the KGB men Putin had known since the 1970s. On Putin's orders, Bulbov had been assigned to the long-stalled investigation of smuggling at the furniture store Tri Kita, as well as at a second one called Grand. The case had begun in 2000 when customs officials confiscated a shipment of furniture from China and discovered that the owners of Tri Kita had evaded duties and taxes with the complicity of senior officials in the FSB. Vladimir Ustinov, as prosecutor general, had suspended the investigation, but the controversy lingered, seemingly leaving a trail of victims, including Yuri Shchekochikhin, the parliamentary deputy who had written about the case for *Novaya Gazeta*. After dismissing Ustinov, Putin had ordered a more vigorous prosecution, but now the man heading it was under arrest by the FSB, accused of authorizing a series of wiretaps of businessmen, journalists, and, it seemed, Cherkesov's rivals inside Putin's court: the *siloviki* allied with Igor Sechin.

From the beginning, Putin's courtiers had pursued shifting alliances and ambitions, but Putin had enforced at least the public appearance of unity. Now with the end of the presidential term in sight, the tensions threatened to become open conflict. The foundation of Putin's power, the men he had installed throughout the ranks of government, no longer seemed as solid as it had. The arrest of a deputy and four other officers from his agency compelled Cherkesov to speak out, perhaps because he could no longer reach the president, access to whom was controlled by a rival allied with Sechin. A devoted, even romantic operative who was unapologetic about his KGB past, Cherkesov wrote an extraordinary open letter that appeared on the front page of *Kommersant,* detailing what had until then been the subject of only speculation and rumor about the inner workings of Putin's Kremlin. He wrote that a war had broken out in the ranks of the special services that had been the salvation of the nation but that now cynically pursued commerce and profit. He all but accused the FSB of arresting his deputy to cover up its complicity in the Tri Kita schemes. "Do not try to be a merchant and a warrior at the same time," he wrote, seeming to address all the former and current intelligence officers in Putin's court. "It cannot happen. It's either-or."[12] The struggle within Putin's ranks could not be won, he went on; it was a war that would end in the complete dissolution of what Putin had built. Curiously, though, he did not call it the state. He called it the corporation.

The internecine fighting continued through the fall, and neither Putin nor Zubkov seemed able to control it. In November, the long-forgotten—or possibly suppressed—report on Putin's malfeasance in the export scandal in Petersburg sixteen years before resurfaced. The "clan war" now seemed aimed at discrediting Putin, who soon faced the first public accusations that he had amassed a fortune himself by using as fronts his closest friends from Petersburg, Yuri Kovalchuk and Gennady Timchenko. Rumors of a coup d'état rumbled through Moscow, just as they had in the last summer of Yeltsin's presidency, though in this case it was never clear whether the intent was to overthrow Putin or overthrow the Constitution and keep him in office. An appeal for calm appeared in the nationalist newspaper *Zavtra* in the form of a letter by five former directors or regional directors of the Soviet KGB, including Vladimir Kryuchov, the man who had led the abortive putsch in 1991. "Trust our experience," they wrote. "A great disaster could happen."[13]

Putin said little about the struggle, seeking to maintain an equilibrium between the competing factions, though some suspected him of orchestrating it to preserve his ultimate authority as arbiter.[14] He chastised Cherkesov for airing "these kinds of problems" but went on to expand the authority of the drug-enforcement agency Cherkesov oversaw.[15] He also kept his ultimate plans for the succession to himself, waiting for the outcome of the parliamentary elections in early December.

Russia's elections by now had become desultory affairs so thoroughly controlled by the central authorities that they lacked genuine competition and therefore suspense. The party of power, United Russia, had all the advantages of the Kremlin's resources, leaving the tolerated opposition—the Communists, the nationalist Liberal Democrats, and a new party headed by one of Putin's political allies from Petersburg, Just Russia—little oxygen to breathe. Putin's liberal and democratic critics, led now by Putin's former prime minister, Mikhail Kasyanov, and the former world chess champion, Garry Kasparov, mounted determined but quixotic protests, but they and other potential candidates were simply disqualified from the ballot on bureaucratic pretexts. One who did not face administration hurdles was Andrei Lugovoi, who, basking in the limelight of his notoriety as a murder suspect, joined the candidate slate of the Liberal Democrats, assuring himself a seat in the Duma and thus immunity from prosecution (which hardly seemed necessary given Russia's refusal to extradite him).

To Putin, the unruly leaders of the opposition represented a conspiracy against Russia itself. Kasparov, who had retired from chess in 2005 to devote himself to loosening Putin's grip on power, proved to be a perfect foil. He was arrested for organizing protest rallies in Moscow, Petersburg, and other cities the weekend before the parliamentary vote, and sentenced to five days in detention. When Kasparov, a polyglot, shouted something in English as he was manhandled into a police bus, Putin, who had once admired the young champion's brash victory in 1985, responded dismissively. "Why did Mr. Kasparov, when arrested, speak out in English rather than Russian?" he asked *Time* magazine, which despite his vilification in and of the West had just named him Person of the Year. "Just think about it. The whole thrust of this thing was directed toward other countries rather than the Russian people, and when a politician works the crowd of other nations rather than the Russian nation, it tells you something. If you aspire to be a leader of your own country, you must speak your own language, for God's sake."[16]

Putin still had not joined the party of power, United Russia, but heading into the parliamentary election, he sat at the top of its candidates list, clearing the way for him to remain the party's leader, should he choose to be. Some believed he would step down from the presidency but use the party leadership to remain the ultimate political authority.

He campaigned for the party no more than he had in his own elections, but merely presided over the state, portrayed on the nightly news as Russia's savior. On the eve of the election, he delivered a nationally televised speech that sounded very much like a valedictory address. "We have done a lot of work together," he said in his firm, clipped style. "The economy is growing steadily. Poverty is in retreat, albeit slowly. We are going to step up the fight against crime and corruption." He made the rare acknowledgment that not everything had gone well, but moved on to the rationale of his presidency. "Let's remember what we started with eight years ago, the kind of pit we had to drag the country out of." Russia had a long way to go, yes, but it could not succumb to "those who have already tried unsuccessfully to govern the country."

The phrasing was discordant. Whom did he mean? Yeltsin who had lifted him to the Kremlin? The Communists of the Soviet era? The Communists' platform called for greater social justice for pensioners but not, significantly, a radical break from the economic boom over which Putin had presided. Putin's enemy was the mysterious "other," the frenzied barbarians at the gates about to storm the walls with the sole intent of destroying Russia. "Today such people would like to rehash the plans for Russia's development, to change the course that the Russian people support and return to times of humiliation, dependence, and dissolution."

When the votes were cast on December 2, United Russia officially won 64 percent of the vote, though few believed the validity of the tally or, as before, the suspiciously high turnout in some regions. And yet no one poured into the streets as they had in Ukraine to demand a recount or a revote. By now, as Kasparov had warned in his campaign, it was impossible to challenge the legal mechanisms that ensured a preordained victory. The other parties, led by the Communists, trailed badly, though the Liberal Democrats did well enough that Andrei Lugovoi won a seat. The day after the vote, Putin declared that the outcome signified the maturity of the country's democracy.

With the presidential election now only months away, Putin's future remained unclear, even to those closest to him. He faced the defining choice of his political career. His greatest legacy—after the conquest of Chechnya, the economic boom, the winning of the bid for an Olympic Games—would be a transition of power. In Russia's long history, only an enfeebled Boris Yeltsin had stepped down voluntarily, and now Putin stood at the same crossroads. With an obsequious constitutional majority, he could easily, even at that late hour, ram through a revision of the Constitution and remain in office. There would have been few protests in Russia, where his popularity remained astonishingly high, and the rebuke that would surely come from the international community would only affirm his case that the country's enemies refused to accept its destiny as a restored power. Or he could hand power to a new leader and retire, the unexpected mission he had been given by Yeltsin eight years before—"Take care of Russia"—having arguably been accomplished far beyond anyone's expectation at the time.

It was eight days after the parliamentary vote, and barely three months before the presidential election, when Putin at last made his choice clear with one final bit of political theater before the prolonged winter holidays. On December 10, the leader of United Russia, Boris Gryzlov, joined the leaders of three other parties in Putin's Kremlin office. *They* had deliberated over the possible candidates for the nation's highest office, Gryzlov told Putin, and wanted to discuss with him in detail their recommendation. The meeting played as if it were a consultation, not a decision of Putin's that had already been made. It was politics as performance art, with not very good actors. Gryzlov explained to Putin that he and the other party leaders were unanimous in their choice: not Ivanov or Zubkov or any of the other unnamed candidates who had been touted by Putin himself, but rather the one whose star had seemed to wane over the last year: Dmitri Medvedev, the diminutive protégé who had worked loyally at Putin's side now for seventeen years.[17] Medvedev just happened to be in attendance as the television cameras suddenly panned back to reveal Putin, turned to him in feigned ignorance.

"Dmitri Anatolyevich, have you been consulted on this?"

"Yes," he replied, playing his role as dutifully as the others. "There were preliminary consultations and they were positive. We will continue these discussions today and tomorrow."

Putin then complained that there were "a lot of political events crammed into a rather short period of time" before the New Year, "but life has to continue and the law requires that we begin the presidential campaign." He sounded put out, as if the election were a chore that had to be tended to. Instead of explicitly announcing his heir as Yeltsin had, Putin wanted to create the impression that his own choice had been made for him, with the consent of a "broad spectrum of Russian society" represented by the party leaders in the room. Putin, with the reins of power in his hands, wanted to preserve the pretense of a pluralistic choice, a "managed" democracy, not an authoritarian writ. For all his bluster and dark ridicule of the West, he still sought its validation, something a constitutional grab for power would have precluded. Putin, legalistically minded, sought a way to ensure his succession within the strict letter of the law, if not the spirit.

Among the Kremlin's clans, Medvedev seemed the least divisive choice, acceptable to the various factions arrayed beneath Putin, with the exception perhaps of Sergei Ivanov and Igor Sechin.[18] He was not viewed as a serious threat to any of them, least of all to Putin himself. Medvedev had his allies in government—the other "liberals" and reformers—but he had no power base of his own. Putin at the end of his presidency had orchestrated a barely plausible transfer of power in a resurgent super-power, but even then did not unveil his own fate. The final act in his political theater came a day later. Medvedev, addressing the nation as the presumptive president in waiting, declared that for the sake of stability, he would, *if elected,* nominate as his prime minister . . . Vladimir Putin. The arrangement would come to be known as the "tandem," and it reassured those who had been most worried about Putin's departure from the Kremlin. After eight years at the helm of state, Putin would not really be leaving after all.

On April 11, 2008, a few weeks before Dmitri Medvedev's inauguration as president, a relatively new tabloid newspaper, *Moskovsky Korrespondent,* printed a short article that dared to test the limits of the political era that many hoped the new president would usher in. The article, by a veteran reporter named Sergei Topol, was only 641 words long, and its tone was neither particularly salacious nor slanderous. Rather, it was sympathetic when it came to the delicate matter of Putin's private life. It was not entirely true, but it lifted the veil of secrecy that had enveloped Putin's family for eight years. "The Sarkozy Syndrome," the headline declared, referring to the French president's recent divorce and his marriage to his third wife, the model and pop singer Carla Bruni. Putin's personal life, Topol wrote, was the inverse. He had remained married through his first two terms as president, but now that he was stepping down from the highest post, "there is little that binds the first couple." The "demobilization," as Topol put it, freed him now to "find time to resolve his personal matters."

And then, four paragraphs into the article, came the supposed bomb-shell: The Putins had secretly divorced in February, and according to "our informer" he planned in June to remarry. The bride would be Alina Kabayeva, a world champion rhythmic gymnast, winner of the bronze medal in the Sydney Olympics in 2000 and a gold medal in Athens four years later. Kabayeva, then not quite twenty-five, was one of the most glamorous celebrities in Russia. By 2001, with her sporting career taking off, she had become the public face of the political party that would become United Russia; in the elections in December 2007, she even stood as a candidate on the party's slate, recruited as part of an effort to make the party more attractive and duly assigned a seat in the Duma when it swept the vote.

Despite having lived in the public eye for eight years, Putin had shielded details of his private life from virtually any scrutiny or public discussion. His daughters, especially, disappeared into a sheltered world of pervasive security, shaped by their father's fears and paranoia. "I have taken my wife and children away and hid them," he once told his old friend, Sergei Roldugin, Masha's godfather.[19] In the beginning, at a time when the war in Chechnya struck the very heart of Moscow, Putin feared for their security, and few questioned his motives. Unlike the children of other Russians, politicians and businessmen, Putin's daughters did not use the advantages of birth to propel their careers or celebrity. They simply vanished, accepting the lives of comfortable, if constrained, anonymity. Except for the early interviews they gave— intended to hone his image as a doting, if stern, father—he never again used them in the way politicians elsewhere use their children as props. They finished school in the isolation of tutors behind maximum security. They both learned to play piano and violin, encouraged by Roldugin and Putin's own interest in music. Roldugin believed they could have become professional musicians "if they had a different fate." They attended their father's alma mater but under assumed names; even their acquaintances were unaware of their relation to the nation's leader. Over time, Putin's relationship with them became more distant, consumed as he was by the duties of power. Together, they once recorded a CD for their father of their music that included Bach's Concerto in B Minor. After they moved on to university, Putin would listen at night, silencing anyone who tried to interrupt when he listened. By the time they reached adulthood, no one outside their family circle even knew what they looked like.

Lyudmila had never settled comfortably into the public life of a politician's wife. Early in her husband's presidency, she had granted occasional interviews and accompanied him on his state visits, appearing beside the first ladies of the United States and Britain, among others, but only as protocol dictated, but later on less and less. She curated an organization called the Center for the Development of the Russian Language, devoting herself to the promotion of reading and education and the unifying bonds of the language in the *Russki mir,* or "Russian world," including those who, as Putin would often point out, found themselves abandoned beyond Russia's borders when the Soviet Union collapsed.[20] Putin adopted the theme more explicitly after the humiliation of the Orange Revolution in Ukraine and created a government organization, the Russian World Foundation, to champion the rights of the diaspora and keep them, at least culturally, in the motherland's embrace. Lyudmila's influence on her husband's policies, though, was inconsequential, even in private. "She never meddled in Putin's politics," Roldugin said, and Putin never asked her to. They were rarely seen being affectionate, or even cordial, in public. Their appearances together bordered on the uncomfortable and had become less and less frequent by Putin's second term. Privately, they lived together, dined together with their daughters when they were still at home, and rarely quarreled openly, according to Roldugin, but they ceased to be intimate.

The Kremlin's grip on the media, of course, ensured that even the most benign scrutiny of his private life was taboo. He was no different in that than most previous Russian and Soviet leaders, who were traditionally portrayed as preeminent and thus remote figures. He was the father of the nation as much as father of his own family, an image the Kremlin relentlessly crafted. A film that appeared in February was seen as a new effort to portray Putin as a dedicated husband at a time when the rumors to the contrary were becoming more persistent. Its title, *A Kiss Off the Record,* came from a scene in which an influential politician very much resembling Putin kisses a woman very much resembling Lyudmila before a phalanx of photographers and playfully admonishes the journalists not to publicize the encounter. The producer-director, Olga Zhulina, insisted the film was fictional, but the details came straight from Putin's life: his KGB service in Dresden, Lyudmila's car accident, his unexpected rise to power. The film's hero even went by Platov, Putin's code name from his days in the KGB academy, a knowing allusion to the ultimate inspiration for the project. It departed from Putin's life only in depicting Lyudmila's role: in the dramatic climax, she fills in for Platov when he is late to an important press conference abroad, showing such poise and intelligence that she earns a standing ovation from the press. One interpretation of the film—that it was intended to "feed the fantasies of Putin's female admirers"—suggested that its underlying message was that the political fate of the country rested on the stability of the Platovs' marriage.[21]

The real reporters in the Kremlin pool knew not to ask, let alone write, about Putin's family. By the end of his presidency, though, it was impossible not to notice what Topol called the widely discussed rumors that "all was not well with the second half" of the first couple. "The fact that Vladimir Putin, as well as any healthy man, is not indifferent to beautiful sporty women is well known in his inner circle," Topol wrote, and then went on to mention the "gossip" that linked him with other women, including a well-known anchor of the state television news on Channel One, Yekaterina Andreyeva, a former basketball star. He even alluded to the journalist Yelena Tregubova and her story of Putin's taking her to an emptied restaurant for sushi. The article referred to the personal relationships and "scandals" of other world leaders—from Sarkozy to Bill Clinton to Václav Klaus of the Czech Republic—and suggested that perhaps the Russian public, too, was prepared to accept a leader's divorce as the normal state of affairs, rather than the mythology that the Kremlin had created of the contented domicile.

As speciously sourced as the article was—Kabayeva's spokeswoman denied it, and the marriage in June did not, in fact, take place—the article created a sensation, titillating the foreign press and terrifying the Russian journalists who knew it had gone further than any had dared before. The article spread on the Internet, which was then still outside the control of the Kremlin's minders, testing the once-ironclad shield erected around Putin's personal life. Dmitri Medvedev's presidential election campaign had promised a more open Russia, a freer place, and perhaps now it was possible to speak of issues that had long been forbidden.

After a week of churning rumors, it became impossible for Putin to avoid the matter any longer. He had to address the matter during a press conference in Italy, with Silvio Berlusconi, whose own personal proclivities provided endless material for the freewheeling Italian press. Berlusconi, who had just won the latest round of elections, had a deep admiration for Putin and his political style, and the feeling was mutual. Putin took to wearing suits made by Berlusconi's tailor, and they became close in business and in private, negotiating deals and exchanging visits and lavish gifts, including a four-poster bed with curtains that would become fodder in Berlusconi's much-publicized tryst with an aggrieved prostitute, Patrizia D'Addario. The Italian leader called it "Putin's bed."[22]

The question came from a Russian reporter, Nataliya Melikova of *Nezavisimaya Gazeta*. She was careful to note that the rumors had reached the Italian press, but she appeared trepidatious anyway. She began with a question about the purpose of the visit, but tacked on one about the rumored divorce and whether the Putins' eldest, Masha, had in fact moved to Germany and married. After a short aside, Putin emphasized that he did not intend to duck the more incendiary question. "The first thing I want to say is this: there is not a word of truth in what you said," he replied. It was clear he was familiar with the article because he went on to mention Andreyeva, too, and rumors of other relationships, even though the reporter had not. He then tried to make light of it. "I think that nobody will be surprised if I say that I like them all, just as I like all Russian women. I think that no one will be offended if I say that I personally believe that our Russian women are the most talented and the most beautiful. The only women who can compare with them in this regard are Italian women." After the translation, the Italians chuckled in approval, as Berlusconi beamed and nodded. Then Putin turned icy. "I am, of course, aware of the cliché that politicians live in glass houses, and people, of course, have a right to know how those who are involved in public activities actually live, but even in this case there have to be some limits."

He went on: "There is such a thing as one's private life with which nobody should be allowed to interfere. I have always reacted negatively to those who, with their snotty noses and erotic fantasies, meddle in other people's lives." Then he changed the subject, citing the growth of the economy under his presidency. Russia had reduced the number of those who lived in poverty twofold; real incomes were growing; and at least "no one is asking about Chechnya anymore." The answer proved revealing: his public accomplishments were what mattered, not his personal life. Berlusconi shook his head as Putin spoke: he, above all, could empathize. As his friend finished, he put his two hands together to mime the firing of a machine gun, pointing directly at the young journalist who had asked the question.

On the same day, back in Moscow, the owner of the newspaper announced that he was closing it. He cited its low circulation, but no one believed that.

The depth of Putin's relationship with Kabayeva, or any other women, would remain unknown to any but his closest friends. And yet there was more than a passing political acquaintance between the two. She had clearly moved into the circle of friends from Petersburg who had emerged during Putin's second term. Only a month before her name surfaced in connection with Putin's, she had joined the advisory council of the newly formed National Media Group, a holding company controlled by Yuri Kovalchuk, whose banking empire had expanded to include some of the country's most prominent television stations and newspapers. Sergei Fursenko, the brother of Putin's minister of education, Andrei, and like him a founding member of the Ozero dacha cooperative, took over as the director of the company, which would continue to expand its media holdings, forming an ever more potent instrument of the propaganda that girded Putin's power. Kabayeva's inclusion signaled an intimacy with the clique—if not with Putin personally—that had quietly enriched itself during his presidency. Only at the end of his presidency, as he grappled with the 2008 problem, did the veil of secrecy lift a bit. The rumors of their relationship, some thought, might have been a symptom of the struggle under way.

In February 2008, on the eve of Medvedev's election, two of Putin's most prominent critics, Boris Nemtsov and Vladimir Milov, had published a seventy-six-page pamphlet that for the first time detailed the business connections that united Putin's circle, including the stunning rise of Yuri Kovalchuk's fortunes.[23] The acquisitions that made up National Media Group, they wrote, included the media assets of Gazprom, purchased in 2005 for $166 million, which Medvedev himself valued two years later at $7.5 billion. As former ministers Nemtsov and Milov did not come from the radical fringe of Russia's opposition, but they struggled to have an impact. They hoped the pamphlet would at least encourage a political debate before Medvedev's election; perhaps Medvedev would even listen to the litany of problems they intended to highlight. Nemtsov, with a doctorate in mathematics, had served as a governor in Nizhny Novgorod and a deputy prime minister under Yeltsin. He had been an early supporter of Putin's, even skiing with him in the Austrian Alps when the Sochi Olympic dream took root. Milov had been a deputy energy minister under Putin. Both had grown disillusioned, however, with the authoritarian trends that followed Putin's early reforms. The pamphlet,

Putin: The Results, challenged the very foundation of Putin's valedictory speeches, in which he claimed to have resurrected the country from the ashes of the 1990s, working, as he himself would put it, like a "galley slave." The authors acknowledged the stunning rise in GDP and average incomes, the drops in unemployment and poverty, but they argued that Putin's economic miracle was a Potemkin mirage, erected with the profits from rising oil prices and papering over structural problems and a numbing growth in corruption. When Putin took office Russia ranked 82nd in Transparency International's annual list of the least corrupted countries; by their writing, it had since plummeted to 143rd, putting it in the company of countries like Angola, Guinea-Bissau, and Togo. The disclosure of $90,000 in book advances during Yeltsin's presidency had created a political scandal that led to the dismissal of Anatoly Chubais and other presidential aides, but "today's practitioners of corruption laugh at this pathetic sum," they wrote. "Today theft by civil servants is measured in billions and is hidden from the eyes of the people: large share-owners cover for dozens of secret beneficiaries, 'friends of president Putin,' hiding behind their backs. Information on who the real owners are is carefully protected by the secret services, and the subject of corruption in the higher echelons of power is taboo for the Kremlin-controlled media."

The pamphlet, like the *Moskovsky Korrespondent* article, sought to break the *omertà* that permeated the Kremlin in Putin's time, especially when it involved the most secret parts of the president's biography. The authors not only detailed Kovalchuk's rise, but questioned the offloading of Gazprom assets, the profits of Roman Abramovich, the murky business of the gas middleman in Ukraine, RosUkrEnergo, and the furtive consolidation of lucrative exports by Gennady Timchenko, founder of Gunvor, the trading company based in Switzerland. With the exception of Abramovich, these new tycoons had remained relatively unknown throughout Putin's eight years as president. They were barely mentioned in the media, and when they were it was usually with abundant caveats about the sources of the information. Timchenko's companies now handled the contracts for nearly a third of Russia's oil exports, including most of those of Rosneft since its takeover of Yukos's assets. Timchenko, lean and silver-haired, shared Putin's love of energy markets and politics, as well as judo, but he remained so secretive that suspicion lingered that he had a KGB past, which he would later deny. He carried a Finnish passport as well as a Russian one, and lived in Cologny, Switzerland, in a villa overlooking Lake Geneva. Few photographs even existed of him then, and he granted even fewer interviews. (When he finally gave one to *The Wall Street Journal* four months after the pamphlet appeared, he did so on the condition that he would not be photographed and the location of his company headquarters would not be disclosed.[24]) Timchenko denied having more than a passing acquaintance with Putin, insisting, falsely, that they were not friends, and even sued *The Economist* for suggesting otherwise in an article titled "Grease My Palm."[25] Yet as their fortunes grew, it became harder for the Putin oligarchy to remain secret. Kovalchuk and Timchenko both debuted on the *Forbes* list of billionaires the month after the pamphlet appeared. The Rotenberg brothers followed not long after that.

Stanislav Belkovsky, the impish, bushy-bearded, bespectacled political strategist who had authored "The State and the Oligarchs" report on the eve of the assault on Yukos, went even further than Nemtsov and Milov. He claimed that Timchenko acted as a proxy and a partner for Putin, who owned at least part of Gunvor, as well as shares in Gazprom and Surgutneftegaz. He estimated—speculated, really—that Putin's net worth amounted to $40 billion, a figure that was close to a secret estimate by the Central Intelligence Agency a year before, perhaps because its analysts were assessing the same sources as Belkovsky's, or Belkovsky's own claims.[26] Belkovsky insisted his sources were Kremlin insiders—and his previous associations with Igor Sechin and others made this seem plausible—but he also acknowledged he had no documentary evidence. That his critiques of Putin over the years had not endangered him lent some credibility to the claims.

Putin responded with humor and then with seething contempt when asked about the allegations at his last press conference as president, held the month before Medvedev's election that March. Was it true that Putin was the richest man in Europe? "This is true," he replied. "I am the richest person not only in Europe but in the world: I collect emotions. I am rich in that the people of Russia twice entrusted me with leadership of such a great country as Russia. I believe that this is my greatest wealth." He then dismissed Belkovsky's allegations, which he acknowledged having read, as "rubbish." "They dug it all out of their nose and smeared it on their papers."

If the paper trail of Putin's personal wealth was impossible to trace, it was becoming harder for the Kremlin to dismiss the evidence of the interlocking connections among his circle of friends, including Kabayeva.

Only weeks after Putin departed the Kremlin, Kabayeva's name appeared on the passenger manifest of a private jet that flew from Switzerland to Prague and then to Sochi, the future site of the Olympics, where Putin would spend more and more of his time as he dispensed the contracts to build the facilities there. Also on the flight was Vladimir Kozhin, who since 2000 had served as the head of the Kremlin property administration office where Putin first worked when he moved to Moscow, and two businessmen and associates of Putin's: Dmitri Gorelov, an owner of the medical supply company Petromed, and Nikolai Shamalov, who had steered donations to it. What would not be known for two more years was that Shamalov and Gorelov were also the principal shareholders of an offshore company called Rosinvest, created on Putin's instructions in 2005. Among its supposed investments was the construction of an enormous villa on the Black Sea coast near Sochi, the one described as "fit for a tsar." It was surrounded by a wall and security gates adorned with the Russian state emblem; it contained three helicopter pads, a service building, a gymnasium, a bungalow, and an amphitheater, in addition to the main house. The private jet that carried them and a crew of three Finns from Switzerland to Sochi that day in May belonged to Airfix Aviation, which was then wholly owned by Gennady Timchenko.[27]

The surfacing of all these allegations at the end of Putin's presidency created an expectation—a vague hope, really—that the political transition would make change possible. The report by Nemtsov and Milov read like a policy platform for the opposition in a presidential campaign that never really took place. It called for the reforms that Putin had promised but never delivered: a fight against corruption among the police and prosecutors; new laws prohibiting conflicts of interest and business by lawmakers; the professionalization of the army; the construction of modern roads; the creation of a working health care system, whose absence had contributed to the demographic slump of the population and a life expectancy for men especially that, while now rising, remained far below the levels of Europe or North America. Putin, they argued, had squandered the rise in energy prices that fueled the undeniable boom, especially in Moscow, which glittered as it never had before. Even with Putin set to remain as prime minister, many wanted to believe that Putin planned eventually to cede political control to a new generation of leaders. With Medvedev at the helm, Putin could become Russia's Deng Xiaoping, officially handing over the reins while wielding power from behind the scenes to ensure the fulfillment of his policies—as Deng did for another five years until his death in 1997. Many people close to Putin believed it, and he did not tell them otherwise—even Medvedev, who had spent the previous eight years at his side in the Kremlin. Medvedev voiced many of the same concerns that these two critics had detailed. He believed in modernity, a transition to a freer market and political society, or at least he said so. "Freedom is better than non-freedom," he said so often it became a slogan of his presidency. It was a banal observation, but after Putin's tenure, it was enough to inspire hope.

When the public scandal broke over Putin's relationship with Kabayeva, the Duma promptly dusted off legislation that toughened the country's libel laws, equating the "dissemination of deliberately false information damaging individual honor and dignity" with the crimes of promoting terrorism or ethnic strife. The legislation not only prescribed civil penalties for the victims of libel, but allowed the government to shutter offending news organizations. A week after Putin denounced the article on the state of his marriage, the bill passed its first reading with 399 votes; only one deputy dared to vote against it. By the time the legislation passed in its final form, though, Medvedev had already been elected president. In one of the first signs he might try to demonstrate a degree of independence and perhaps chart a new course, he vetoed it.

PART FOUR

CHAPTER 19

The Regency

On the night of August 7, 2008, Dmitri Medvedev, now the third president of Russia, was on a sailboat on the Volga River with his wife, Svetlana, and their son, Ilya, then just a teenager. It was a working vacation in the languid holiday month. Medvedev had spent the day in the ancient city of Kazan, the capital of Tatarstan, a region conquered by Ivan the Terrible in the sixteenth century. There he reviewed preparations for the Universiade, the biennial international collegiate sporting competition, which would be held there in the summer of 2013, as a rehearsal for hosting the Winter Olympics in Sochi eight months later. He had traveled the day before in a neighboring region, Chuvashia, where he discussed plans to create a modern library network. The morning before that he attended the funeral of the Soviet dissident Aleksandr Solzhenitsyn, who had died in Moscow on August 3, thoroughly rehabilitated in post-Soviet culture as a state-decorated admirer of Vladimir Putin.[1]

Medvedev had been president for three months, but it seemed as if he were simply carrying on with the duties he had had as the unprepossessing first deputy prime minister, not the commander in chief of a resurgent, nuclear-armed state. His election in March had been no more in doubt than Putin's had four years before, even though he had no political base of his own, no particular platform, and no mandate from a populace hungry for change. On the contrary, the entirety of Medvedev's presidency rested on the premise that the people wanted not change, but stability. Had the voters been given the choice, they almost certainly would have elected Putin again, but they had accepted his choice as heir because Putin wished it so. So Medvedev cruised to a convincing victory in a managed election that saw prominent opponents of Putin's rule, including Mikhail Kasyanov and Garry Kasparov, blocked from registering as candidates, as they had been in the Duma elections in December

2007. Kasparov, despite his fame and financial resources, could not even manage to rent a hall large enough to hold a nominating convention, as required by law. Kasyanov was disqualified on the charge that his campaign had "forged" more than 13 percent of the signatures needed to nominate him. Another "liberal" candidate, Andrei Bogdanov, encountered no such obstacles with his signatures. He was a political strategist and a Free Mason from the very edge of obscurity, elected the previous year as the Grand Master of the Grand Lodge of Russia. The Kremlin orchestrated his candidacy as a fallback in the event no one else bothered to run.[2]

Medvedev performed his assigned role, eschewing retail campaigning and refusing to debate his challengers, who in addition to Bogdanov included the old stalwarts who had forgone a challenge against Putin in 2004: the Communist Gennady Zyuganov and the nationalist jester Vladimir Zhirinovsky. Medvedev simply went about his deputy ministerial duties, lionized by the state television channels, with his patron never far removed from the picture. He was Putin's choice, and therefore the only one. He was the heir, the tsarevich, simply awaiting popular affirmation. The short political campaign was so transparently contrived that Mikhail Gorbachev publicly rebuked the Kremlin. "Something is wrong with our elections," he said, but his was a moral voice of authority from a receding and discredited past, and few paid heed, certainly not the state media.[3] When the ballots were counted, Zyuganov trailed a distant second with 18 percent of the vote. Bogdanov received fewer than a million votes, fewer in fact than the number of spoiled or blank ballots. Medvedev, who had no political experience of his own, became the youngest elected president. He was only forty-three. He won 71.2 percent of the vote, a tally that was conspicuously—and widely seen as deliberately—a slight decrease from Putin's 71.9 percent four years before.

From the moment he took office in May, Medvedev struggled to emerge out of the shadow of the man who had elevated him to the heights of power. Yeltsin had quietly stepped out of the public limelight from the day he appointed Putin, but now Putin strode confidently through Medvedev's inauguration. He opened the ceremony in the Kremlin with an unprecedented valedictory speech that affirmed, unmistakably to the assembled elite in the Grand Palace, that he had no intention of disappearing from the public stage. Medvedev hoped to make a quick impression on the world stage, visiting Germany, Russia's closest trading partner in Europe, but Putin preempted his first official visit with his own visit to France. The chairman of the Federation Council's foreign affairs committee, Mikhail Margelov, told a visiting American official that Medvedev was a gifted, if yet unformed "student who had learned from his teachers," but the "dean of faculty" remained Putin.[4] Putin, he said, genuinely wanted to cede, albeit gradually, the duties of the head of state, especially foreign affairs, but Medvedev struggled to extend his authority over a bureaucracy conditioned after eight years to respond to Putin.

Yet with his mild, bookish temperament, Medvedev at least changed the tone of the Kremlin. During his campaign and his first weeks in office, he spoke of civil liberties, economic modernization, and the need to end rampant corruption and the "legal nihilism" that characterized Russian politics and society. Putin had offered similar pledges, but Medvedev proved far less bellicose, less conditional. He sounded eager to present a different image of leadership, to prove that the transition was a substantive, not purely symbolic, one. Where Putin was steely and brittle, Medvedev seemed gentle and open. He delighted in using modern devices (Steve Jobs would give him an iPhone in 2010) and opened accounts on social websites, where he posted photographs he took as a hobby.

Despite Putin's prominence as prime minister, many began to believe that Medvedev would carry out the liberalizing reforms that Putin had failed to deliver. One of those who found hope in Medvedev's promise remained in the Siberian cell where he had been confined: Mikhail Khodorkovsky. He was now eligible for parole, and his lawyers appealed in July for an early release.[5] Another was the American seeking to replace George Bush as president of the United States: Barack Obama. As Medvedev's boat rocked in the gentle flow of the Volga that night in August, his presidency seemed to be on the edge of an optimistic new era. Instead, he was about to face his gravest challenge. He had not even reached his hundredth day in office.

At one o'clock on the morning of August 8, the minister of defense, Anatoly Serdyukov, telephoned Medvedev with the news that war had erupted on Russia's southern flank. The armed forces of Georgia, led by the westernizing Mikheil Saakashvili, had begun an air and ground assault on the country's breakaway region of South Ossetia. Tensions with South Ossetia and another region, Abkhazia, had flared all year.

Both had split from Georgia during short violent conflicts in the early 1990s after the collapse of the Soviet Union and had remained in a diplomatic limbo ever since, recognized as part of Georgia but in fact independent statelets that sought closer relations—and financing—from Russia, which maintained peacekeeping forces in both regions under the mandate of the United Nations. In the wake of Kosovo's declaration of independence from Serbia in February 2008, Putin had increased assistance to the two regions. In one of his last official acts as president, he ordered a reinforcement of troops to the existing Russian peacekeeping mission in Abkhazia to oversee the reconstruction of the railroad that had once connected it to Sochi but since fallen into disrepair. The fate of the regions had become an acute focus of Putin's last weeks as president following a testy confrontation in Bucharest with President Bush and other NATO leaders debating whether to invite Georgia (and Ukraine) to join the military alliance.

Throughout the summer of 2008, Russia and Georgia traded accusations that the other intended to launch an invasion to resolve what had become known as "frozen conflicts." Medvedev held a series of meetings with Saakashvili, who also hoped that his presidency would represent a shift from his endless confrontations with Putin that had followed the "Rose Revolution," including a trade embargo in 2006 prompted by the arrest of four Russian intelligence agents. Saakashvili had proposed political settlements for the two regions, which Medvedev initially seemed amenable to, but when they met in Kazakhstan in July, he sensed that Medvedev was no longer interested in discussing them, as if he had been reined in by other powers in Moscow, that is, by Putin.[6] A conflict seemed inevitable, and the Russians had prepared for it thoroughly, though they suspected it would come in Abkhazia, not South Ossetia. The military had already drawn up plans for an intervention; Putin would later say that the plans had been in place as early as the end of 2006. In the summer, on Medvedev's orders, commanders amassed forces for a large training drill in the Northern Caucasus, within striking distance of either Abkhazia or South Ossetia, a feint that would become a signature of future military operations in Russia.

Nevertheless, Medvedev that night was surprised and skeptical of the urgent report interrupting his river cruise. "We should check this," he told Serdyukov on the telephone. He thought, "Is Saakashvili completely out of his mind? Maybe it's just a provocative act, maybe he is stressed, testing the Ossetians and trying to send us some kind of a message?" He asked the minister to call him back.

Putin had already left Moscow for Beijing where he, not the head of state, planned the next day to attend the opening ceremony of the Summer Olympics with dozens of other leaders, including President Bush. Serdyukov called Medvedev back an hour later to say that the reports were true. Georgia had begun an artillery barrage on South Ossetia's capital, Tskhinvali. "All right," Medvedev said. "I'll wait for another update."

He claimed he could not reach Putin in Beijing on a secure telephone line. That he felt the need to try showed he was uncertain whether to commit Russian forces to battle outside the country's borders for the first time since the collapse of the Soviet Union. His hesitancy would come to haunt him. Finally Serdyukov called a third time. A rocket had crashed through a tent full of Russian peacekeepers, "killing all of them." This would prove to be an exaggeration, the first of many that would be uttered in the days that followed,[7] but the fact was that Russian troops and their proxies in South Ossetia's irregular militia were under assault. More than four hours after the rockets began falling in and around Tskhinvali, Medvedev at last issued the orders to go to war.

"Return fire," he told Serdyukov, and then he rushed to fly back to Moscow.

By the time Medvedev arrived, Georgian battalions were moving into South Ossetia. Russia aircraft began striking not just inside the region, but in Georgia itself as well, hoping to forestall the advance. The word of the Georgian assault reached Putin in Beijing, and he was enraged—at Saakashvili primarily, but also at Medvedev's "lack of resolve."[8] Putin, speaking to reporters in the morning, made the first public statement on the crisis in China, vowing that Russia would retaliate for the Georgian incursion. He made repeated calls to Medvedev, who on the morning of August 8 met with his Security Council.[9] It was ten o'clock in the morning when Medvedev made his first public statement, well after Putin's. He declared that Georgia had breached international law and committed an act of aggression that had already cost lives, including those of Russian peacekeeping troops. "Civilians, women, children and old people are dying today in South Ossetia, and the majority of them are citizens of the Russian Federation," he said. "In accordance with the Constitution and the federal laws, as President of the Russian Federation it is my duty to protect the lives and dignity of Russian citizens wherever they may be."[10] By midday, Russian forces surged across the border.

President Bush was also in Beijing when an aide whispered into his ear that a "Russian offensive" had begun in Georgia.[11] He was standing in line at a diplomatic reception in the Great Hall of the People to greet China's president, Hu Jintao. Putin stood a few places ahead of him in line, but protocol mandated that Bush speak to his presidential counterpart first, so he waited until he returned to his hotel to call Medvedev, warning him to halt the counteroffensive. "We're going to be with them," Bush told him, referring to the Georgians.

What President Bush did not understand was the extent to which the Russians blamed his administration for the conflict. Even if he had not given a green light to Saakashvili's plan to seize South Ossetia, as the Russians suspected, Bush had bolstered Saakashvili with military training and the promise of NATO membership at the summit in Bucharest in April, despite Putin's personal warnings to him that an invitation would provoke Russia. What Saakashvili did not understand was that for all the effort he had used to win over the Americans, praising Bush and dispatching troops to serve in Iraq, neither the United States nor NATO was prepared to come to his aid in a war against Russia. The miscalculation cost Georgia dearly.

In his conversation with Bush, Medvedev compared Saakashvili to Saddam Hussein and told Bush that the Georgians had already killed 1,500 people, a glaring exaggeration.[12] It was clear now that Russia had no intention of pulling back. Bush eventually confronted Putin in Beijing at the "Bird Nest" stadium as they awaited the Olympics opening ceremony that night. They sat in the same row of VIP seats and Bush asked his wife and the king of Thailand to slide down so he could sit beside Putin to deliver a warning. With an interpreter leaning in awkwardly, Putin rose from his seat, momentarily looming over him until the taller Bush could stand fully upright, and told him Saakashvili was a war criminal.

"I've been warning you Saakashkili was hot-blooded," Bush said.

"I'm hot-blooded, too," Putin replied.

Bush later wrote that he had stared back at the man he had met with more times than any other world leader except Tony Blair. He had hoped to forge a new relationship with Russia, one that would overcome the mutual suspicions of the Cold War, only to realize he had misjudged the man when they first met in Slovenia in 2001.

"No, Vladimir, you're cold-blooded," he said.[13]

After meeting with Hu Jintao the morning after the opening ceremony, Putin left Beijing and flew back to Russia—not to Moscow, but to the bustling staging ground of Russia's full invasion force. He arrived on Saturday night at the headquarters of the 58th Army, in Vladikavkaz, the capital of North Ossetia, the Russian republic on the northern slope of the Caucasus that had been sundered from its compatriots on the Georgian side by a decree of Joseph Stalin. It was Putin who appeared on state media receiving the military updates from the generals in uniform on the ground, while Medvedev delivered pallid directions from his Kremlin office. Putin said Georgia, emboldened by its flirtation with the United States and NATO, was seeking to devour South Ossetia and now would lose it forever. "What's happening in Georgia is genocide," he said in a fury that overstated the reality on the ground.[14] By then Russian tanks had reached Tskhinvali and then pushed forward beyond Ossetia itself toward the Georgian city of Gori, Stalin's birthplace. Russian warships blockaded the port of Poti, south of the border with Abkhazia. Georgia's forces, despite years of American equipping and training, crumbled in disarray, unable to effectively communicate because the Russians had jammed or disrupted cell phone coverage, their only means of communication. A humiliated Saakashvili had to plead for help. The United States airlifted two thousand soldiers that Georgia had deployed to Iraq as part of the American war there, and President Bush later sent additional aid and equipment, but he also made it clear that the United States would not come to Georgia's side militarily. More than a hundred American military advisers who had remained in Georgia after the summer exercise withdrew to avoid becoming entangled in the fighting. With Georgia's fractured troops retreating in front of a Russian thrust toward the capital, Tbilisi, itself under bombardment, Saakashvili had no choice but to sue for peace.

Putin ostensibly accorded due deference to his protégé as the commander in chief, but the entire system—the bureaucracy, the military, the media—had become so conditioned to his role as paramount leader that it struggled to preserve the appearance that Medvedev was in charge. Putin himself was unable or unwilling to recede into the background, suggesting instructions in televised meetings during the crisis that Medvedev dutifully passed on. In public, Putin sought to emphasize Medvedev's preeminent post, but in private he hectored and cajoled his interlocutors, still very much the leader. When the French president, Nicolas Sarkozy, flew into Moscow to mediate a ceasefire on August 12, he found Medvedev calm and sanguine, able to negotiate. Putin also attended the meeting, however, and he was bombastic and crude, seething with a ferocity toward Saakashvili that seemed deeply personal.[15] Sarkozy pressed the Russians to call off an invasion that now seemed intent on reaching Georgia's capital and overthrowing its president. The foreign minister, Sergei Lavrov, had said as much to Bush's secretary of state, Condoleezza Rice, demanding Saakashvili's removal from power as a condition of peace.[16] Lavrov also belittled Medvedev in a conversation with the French ambassador, even as the leaders met in the Kremlin to resolve the conflict.[17] Sarkozy argued that the world would not accept the toppling of an elected leader, but this only further enraged Putin.

"Saakashvili—I'm going to hang him by the balls," Putin seethed, startling the French leader.

"Hang him?" he asked.

"Why not?" Putin replied, sounding petulant. "The Americans hanged Saddam Hussein."

The only thing that seemed to temper Putin was Sarkozy's asking him if he wanted to go down in history with a reputation like Bush's.[18]

It was early the next morning, after Sarkozy flew to Georgia's capital to seal Saakashvili's agreement, when Medvedev announced a ceasefire in the conflict's fifth day. He appeared alone in the Kremlin and adopted a Putinesque tone to declare that "the aggressor had been punished." He looked pale and tired. Despite the ceasefire, Russian forces consolidated their positions in the vacuum created by the routed Georgians, while the militias of South Ossetia conducted a campaign of pillaging and looting the homes of Georgian villagers inside the region, often under the eyes of the Russians.[19] Two days after the ceasefire, even as Condoleezza Rice flew into Georgia to deliver a pledge of political and humanitarian support from the United States, a Russian armored column pushed eastward toward the capital, stopping only 25 miles from Tbilisi's city limits. The last Russian troops would not withdraw from Georgian territory for another two months, and even then, they left reinforcements behind in South Ossetia and Abkhazia. On August 26, as the debris of the war was still being cleared, Medvedev announced that Russia would

recognize the two enclaves as independent nations. He and others cited
the precedent of Kosovo, whose declaration of independence six months
before the Russians had called illegitimate.

Despite some obvious shortcomings by its forces, the war fed a nationalist fervor in Russia, amplified by state media glorifying the actions of
the Russian liberators and vilifying the enemy with an intensity not seen
since the Great Patriotic War. The glory, however, redounded to Putin
as much as Medvedev, since it was clear to everyone that he remained
the paramount leader. Medvedev occupied a presidency with diminished
authority for the simple reason that Putin had effectively taken its powers with him—along with much of his presidential staff—to the prime
minister's office, located in the White House at the opposite end of Novy
Arbat from the Kremlin. Medvedev remained the nominal head of state,
but his handling of foreign affairs was muddled and confused because he
had to vet any fundamental decisions with his prime minister. His own
efforts to echo the commanding, aggressive, and unflinching tone that
Putin wielded so deftly often proved embarrassing instead.

On the day after voters in the United States elected Barack Obama
in November 2008, a moment widely celebrated around the world as
the end of the Bush era of unbridled American aggression, Medvedev
delivered his first national address since his inauguration. After the poi-
sonous relations at the end of the Bush presidency, in which Putin even
suggested that the United States had instigated the war in Georgia to
boost the chances of Obama's opponent, John McCain, it might have
been a moment to welcome the change in administrations. As he spoke
in the Grand Kremlin Palace, though, Medvedev did not even mention
Obama. He blamed the United States for the war in Georgia and threatened to deploy ballistic missiles in Kaliningrad, the Russian enclave in
Eastern Europe annexed as tribute after the Great Patriotic War, if the
Americans built their missile defense system in Europe. Instead of coming across as tough-minded, Medvedev sounded tone-deaf. It was not
even clear he believed his own bluster.

The making of Russia's foreign policy had been notoriously opaque
and unwieldy since Yeltsin's era, but with two centers of political power
it became even more so. Medvedev apologized for his remarks during
his first visit to Washington two weeks later, where he met President
Bush, though not the young president-elect. He claimed it had been
a simple oversight to deliver his provocative warning on the day that

leaders around the world were congratulating Barack Obama. "With all my respect for the United States, I absolutely forgot about the important political event that had to take place that day," he said, improbably. "There's nothing personal here."[20] As with the war in Georgia, Medvedev seemed to trip over his own feet—or Putin's.

A second crippling blow to Medvedev's nascent presidency came only weeks after the war in Georgia ended. The windfall from the steady increase in oil and gas revenues had stimulated the country's economic boom, driving up retail sales of everything from foreign cars to furniture and food. The economy had grown by an average of nearly 7 percent a year during Putin's presidency; Putin had paid off the country's foreign debt, amassed hundreds of billions of dollars in currency reserves, and, resisting pressure to spend freely, built a stabilization fund that would shield the country from any downturn. Newly installed in his post as prime minister, Putin acted as if his greatest legacy was irreversible. Coinciding with the political transition in 2008, however, Russia's economy began to slow. With inflation rising, the new prime minister sought to exert his will on the market and the oligarchs. In July, prodded by complaints from energy executives about the rising costs of steel for pipelines, he convened a meeting of the metals industry in Nizhny Novgorod, the purpose of which became clear when he singled out the billionaire owner of Russia's largest steel manufacturer, Mechel, for selling its coking coal on the domestic market for higher prices than abroad, thus avoiding taxes. (Igor Sechin was the one who had brought the matter to his attention, reportedly because of the economic pain Rosneft was feeling.) The company's owner, Igor Zyuzin, already under pressure from clients and competitors, made the mistake of skipping the conference and checking into a cardiac hospital. Putin's response was cutting. He suggested that perhaps the anti-monopoly authorities, even the prosecutor general, should inquire into the company's affairs. "Of course, illness is illness, but I think he should get well as soon as possible," he said. "Otherwise, we will have to send him a doctor and clean up all the problems." By the end of the day, Mechel's shares, traded on the New York Stock Exchange, lost more than a third of their value—nearly $6 billion—dragging down Russia's already slumping markets.

Mechel swiftly released a contrite statement promising to address the prime minister's concerns, but Putin had sent a clear message. He had no intention of taking his hands off the tiller of Russia's command economy, intervening whenever he felt the impulse and undercutting Medvedev's early efforts to nurture a more attractive climate for investments. Medvedev and his aides appeared surprised by Putin's assault. One of his senior aides, Arkady Dvorkovich, sought to calm the markets, but days later Putin reiterated his accusations that Mechel was evading taxes, sending its shares plummeting a second time. Putin acted as if Russia were invincible, an island of rising prosperity impervious to the financial storm that had been brewing all summer, from the moment the price of oil peaked at more than $140 a barrel.

The global economic crisis triggered by the mortgage defaults in the United States in 2008 seemed at first to pose little threat to Russia's economy since its banks had not issued the sort of subprime mortgages that had turned toxic. But the bankruptcy of the American investment bank Lehman Brothers on September 15—the same day oil slipped below $100 a barrel—reverberated around the world, and it hit Russia harder than most. By the end of the following day, the main stock index had dropped 17 percent. Panicked selling forced the suspension of trading repeatedly over the coming weeks, and even with government intervention to prop up shares, the market lost $1 trillion in a matter of months. Between October and December, $130 billion in capital flooded out of the country. While fewer Russians were invested in stocks compared, for example, to Americans, many of whom saw their life savings evaporate, the crisis hit Russians hard from the poorest to the richest. Disposable incomes fell almost immediately, as companies slashed costs, dragging down consumer spending, which only made production shrink more. Even the swaggering oligarchs "were pawning their yachts and selling their private jets."[21] Russia's booming economy went bust so precipitously that Putin found himself presiding over a meltdown as grave as the crisis of 1998. It seemed like a bookend to the decade of prosperity that had undergirded his presidency.

Within days, the government had approved $40 billion in credits to shore up banks and another $50 billion in loans for 295 companies that accounted for 80 percent of the country's economy. The Central Bank struggled to slow the decline in the ruble's value, draining nearly $200 billion from the currency reserves, a third of the peak of $598 billion reached in August. Putin's conservative macroeconomic policies—balancing budgets and building up reserves and a rainy-day fund, despite populist appeals from some in the Kremlin to spend more freely—proved prescient. Even now Putin felt pressure to bail out the

favored oligarchs and renationalize distressed companies ripe for taking over on the cheap. Yet he sided with the advisers who urged caution, "shifting more decision-making power to those who knew about
and could do something for the economy," as one of the government's
economic advisers, Sergei Guriev, later wrote.[22] The liberals allied with
Medvedev, including the finance minister, Andrei Kudrin, seemed to
have prevailed in the short term, and none of the worst predictions of
economic collapse came true. The effort was costly, though. Russia's
economy contracted 8 percent in 2009, the worst performance among
the world's twenty largest economies. For the first time Putin's popularity slipped significantly, dragged down by popular discontent that at
times spilled into the street as workers protested unpaid wages.

In his eight years as president, Putin had always been able to deflect
criticism toward the government, which was headed by the prime minister. Now he held the post, and he deflected the blame elsewhere. He
lashed out at what he saw as the external cause of Russia's woes: the
United States. In October, he took the unusual step of visiting the Duma
to meet the Communists as a bloc of delegates for the first time in all his
years in power. The gesture reflected his apprehension about the impact
of the crisis on voters—pensioners, laborers, and those still nostalgic
for the Soviet era—who supported the only opposition party holding
elected office. The Communist leader, Gennady Zyuganov, dutifully
called for more spending on key industries like agriculture, lamenting
that Russia's production of harvesters and tractors had fallen behind that
of Belarus, and denounced as ineffective Kudrin's "monetarist policy"
to control the circulation of rubles. (He also used the opportunity to
plead with Putin to ease up on the harassment of his party's candidates
in regional elections.) Putin had little interest in the Communist proposals, though. Zyuganov and his cadre were simply a foil for Putin
to deliver a populist message. When the United States plunged into
the Great Depression, Zyuganov noted in a long, rambling discourse,
Franklin Delano Roosevelt had sent "his best economic advisers" to the
Soviet Union to learn a thing or two, but now reckless American capitalist greed had brought calamity to the world. Putin, with the cameras
rolling, was happy to agree. "You made a good point when you said that
the faith in the United States as the leader of the free world and market
economy has been shaken, as well as the trust in Wall Street as the center
of this world," he told him. "And it will never be restored. I agree with
you here. Things will never be the same again."

The crisis highlighted the underlying structural weaknesses in Russia's economy, its dependence on energy resources, the crumbling industrial base, the pervasive corruption, the eroding infrastructure. (The country had fewer miles of paved roads in 2008 than it had had in 1997.)[23] Economists like Sergei Guriev argued that Russia should heed the lessons of the crisis and enact meaningful changes, and advisers to Medvedev's Kremlin, like Arkady Dvorkovich, agreed.[24] Russia's economy needed the rule of law, the protection of property rights and contracts, real competition and transparency, and some constraints on predatory and corrupt officials who would shake down companies and bleed their profits into their own pockets, hiding the illicit proceeds in foreign property and secret offshore accounts. Medvedev's team in the Kremlin had drafted proposals to address at least some of these issues. In his first national address, the one he delivered the day after Barack Obama's election, he called for a liberalization of the economy, freeing it from the bureaucracy that had grown under Putin's leadership. "The state bureaucracy, as 20 years ago, is being guided by the same old mistrust in the free individual and in free enterprise," he said in the speech, which had been twice postponed because of the financial crisis. "A strong state and an all-powerful bureaucracy is not the same thing. The former is an instrument which society needs to develop, to maintain order and strengthen democratic institutions. The latter is extremely dangerous."[25]

The twin crises of the summer and fall, however, deflated Medvedev's political aspirations. His closest aides blamed the crises for derailing his agenda, but Putin was the biggest obstacle. Putin had vetted drafts of Medvedev's first major address in November 2008, a role no prime minister had played when he was president. He insisted on hawkish language toward the United States and the West generally that made Medvedev uncomfortable—hence the threat to put missiles in Kaliningrad.[26]

Worried about the political fallout from the economic downturn, Putin had also insisted on inserting another proposal in his protégé's speech, one designed as a potential safety valve in the event the economic chaos threatened the political system itself. Early drafts did not include it; Putin had proposed it while meeting with Medvedev the day before the speech. When Medvedev dropped it into his remarks—almost as an aside, a single sentence in a speech of more than eight thousand words—not even his closest aides knew it was coming.[27] Medvedev called for revising the Constitution, something Putin had steadfastly resisted for years despite numerous entreaties, insisting that altering it would undermine political stability. The proposed change would extend the president's term in office from four years to six and the term of Duma members from four to five. Medvedev offered no explanation for the change, only the justification that many democracies, like France, had longer presidential terms. He later insisted that the amendments, the first changes to the Constitution since it was drafted in 1993, were only "adjustments" that did not "change the political and legal essence of the current institutions." In fact, they further strengthened the presidency and reduced the frequency of the election cycles that Putin had feared would become the focus for a "color revolution."

The proposal stunned the political elite, especially since no one then understood the rationale behind it. Speculation swirled that the ultimate goal was to clear the way for Putin's return to the presidency following a surprise Medvedev resignation. The change was carried out like other Putin special operations, swiftly and surreptitiously. Within nine days, the proposal barreled through the Duma, with only the Communists, his pliant prop only weeks before, opposing it. By the end of the year, the change had passed both houses of parliament with little debate, and certainly no input from the public. The beleaguered democrats tried to muster protests against the amendments, as well as against the government's failure to turn around the staggering economy, but they faced relentless harassment from the Kremlin and its proxies, especially the youth groups that the Kremlin had nurtured.

In that winter of discontent Garry Kasparov, Boris Nemtsov, and Vladimir Milov and others tried to form a new opposition coalition, hoping to use the economic crisis to fuse together a dissident movement. They called it Solidarity, after Poland's opposition group, formed in the grimmest years of martial law, but the opposition remained deeply atomized, consumed by personal rivalries and divided over tactics. Some of Putin's critics still hoped to work within the system to bring about change. Others wanted to spark a revolution. Still others refused to join out of a personal dislike for Kasparov or Kasyanov. Solidarity held a founding congress one weekend in December, but had to go to extraordinary lengths to keep its location and timing secret. Previous efforts to meet had been scuttled when venues canceled after phone calls from the authorities. The tactics against even a marginal opposition movement underscored the Kremlin's anxiety, but at the same time demonstrated its ability to smother any effort to organize anti-Putin sentiment. When Solidarity's leaders finally met at a conference center in the suburb of

Khimki, a busload of activists from the Youth Guard, affiliated with United Russia, arrived to harass the attendees. Their bus was loaded with sheep, wearing hats and T-shirts with Solidarity's emblem. Other protesters wore masks and threw bananas, the first of what would be many racist allusions to the new American president, the first of African heritage to hold the office. The message was crude but clear: Putin's opponents were animals shepherded by the nefarious hand of the United States. The activists pushed the sheep from the bus, many of them injured or ill. The sheep staggered bleating on the pavement, where several of them died.[28]

On December 30, just before the new year holidays, Medvedev signed the legislation that changed the Constitution. The most significant change in the country's political system since Putin's cancelation of gubernatorial elections in 2004 went from proposal to reality in less than two months. Less than a year into his presidency, it was clear that Medvedev was merely a junior partner in the "tandem" governing the country. Putin might outwardly defer to him as head of state, but he continuously upstaged him. In December, Putin went ahead with his annual appearance at the year-end call-in show, fielding seventy questions carefully screened from around the country. He vowed that the effects of the economic crisis would be minimal, promising to raise pensions and benefits for the unemployed. Putin's performances undermined Medvedev's political authority, making it harder for him to tame the bureaucracy that he wanted to change. Medvedev never betrayed his objections in public, but privately he expressed frustration, and his closest aides deeply resented the interference they constantly encountered from the prime minister's office. Medvedev struggled to enlist supporters in the bureaucracy, but Putin's loyalists occupied too many places, including within the Kremlin. After the war in Georgia, secret surveys of the Russian military showed the "absolute abysmal regard" commanding officers had for the new commander in chief. The final authority ultimately rested in the White House now, and everyone understood that. In the biting words of one American diplomat, Medvedev was "playing Robin to Putin's Batman."[29]

CHAPTER 20

Action Man

The only power plant that heated the town of Pikalevo shut off its furnaces on May 15, 2009. The owner of the plant had fallen in arrears to Gazprom on the order of $4.5 million, and in Putin's Russia, Gazprom's accounts always took precedence. Pikalevo, with twenty-two thousand people, was a "monotown," established in 1957 east of Petersburg, with a single enterprise that serviced the Soviet command economy. It consisted of three interlocking factories that made cement, potash, and alumina, a chemical compound used in the smelting of aluminum. The town's entire livelihood, in Soviet times as now, depended on the factories. Only now the factories had been privatized into three separate companies that were struggling even before the crisis hit in September. Crippled by the legacy of central planning and a convoluted dispute over prices in the wake of the global turmoil, production in Pikalevo was no longer economically viable.[1]

The cement factory went first, closing in October 2008 and laying off hundreds of workers. The potash plant shut down in February, followed in May by the alumina factory, which also owned the power plant. Most of the three factories' 4,500 workers were forced onto unpaid leave or let go. The governor of the region, still known as Leningrad, for it had not changed its name as the city had, appealed to Dmitri Medvedev to negotiate a resolution as early as February, but nothing happened. The shuttering of the power plant turned simmering discontent into a revolt, and the town's residents took to the streets.

The governor dismissed the protests, saying that the town's unions were merely fomenting a crisis. Every city shut off the hot water for periods of maintenance, he explained, as if it were a temporary inconvenience. "As for the heat, well, I don't think it's needed so much during the summer."[2] On May 20, several hundred residents stormed an emergency meeting at the mayor's office, demanding not only their hot water but also their jobs and unpaid salaries. The town's officials, though, had no more power over the factories than the residents did. Their owners were distant tycoons whose financial problems were far greater than the hardship of one remote town in the north. They included one of the country's richest men, Oleg Deripaska, an oligarch who had survived the end of the Yeltsin era and now enjoyed a favored status in Putin's. When the storming of the mayor's office failed to resolve anything, residents took their protest to the two-lane federal highway running from Vologda to Novaya Ladoga, near Petersburg, blocking the road for several hours and creating a traffic jam said to extend for 250 miles.

The protest was only one of many that had swept the country—from Baikalsk, where workers staged a hunger strike over unpaid wages at a paper mill, to Vladivostok, where protests erupted after new tariffs on automobile imports decimated the sales of used cars from Japan. The Kremlin monitored signs of discontent attentively. Medvedev and his top aides installed a program to track the unrest on their computers, showing troubled regions according to a matrix of measures that included, tellingly, the popularity of the new prime minister.[3]

Pikalevo was no worse off than the other struggling cities, but the spiraling protests there became so pronounced that they forced Putin to act, or perhaps were singled out to make the point that he would, if necessary. On June 4, Putin went to Pikalevo and summoned the owners of the shuttered factories to meet him there for a public dressing-down that even by his standards was impressively abrasive. "Why didn't you fix this before?" he scolded them when he met them in full view of the Kremlin's pool of television cameras. "You ran around like cockroaches when I said I was coming." Outside, hundreds of residents surrounded the factory where the meeting took place, waiting in the rain for word of what seemed like divine intervention. Putin, wearing a gray raincoat and a shirt unbuttoned at the neck, slouched at the table, seething with contempt. "You have taken these people hostage with your ambition, unprofessionalism, and, maybe, simple greed—thousands of people. It's absolutely unacceptable."

He gestured with a short stack of papers, an agreement already completed in advance of his arrival. Had everyone signed it? He stared at the unshaven Deripaska, whose fortunes had been battered by the economic crisis. Someone answered yes, but Deripaska nodded confusedly. There was really no document that needed a signature, but Putin summoned him to the front of the room anyway, humiliating him before everyone, most importantly the television viewers who would turn on the news that night and marvel at the force of the prime minister's will. Putin tossed his pen on the papers. Deripaska picked it up and made a pretense of skimming through the text before scribbling his signature. As he turned away, Putin cut him one bit lower: "And give me back my pen." Outside, the workers began to receive text messages on their telephones. They came from their banks. Their unpaid salaries—more than $1 million—would be deposited by the end of the day. Putin had made sure of that.

For months before, Putin had appeared increasingly detached; he worked more often at the residence at Novo-Ogaryovo than in his newly refurbished office in the government building, the White House. He delegated the day-to-day running of the government to one of his deputies, Igor Shuvalov. The drafting of a new state budget dragged on for months, while bureaucrats awaited decisions that he appeared to be in no rush to make.[4] With the performance in Pikalevo, however, he woke to the political threat of the economic crisis—and the prescription for salving it. On the very day Putin swept through Pikalevo, Medvedev warned that while the worst of the crisis had passed, it was not yet time "to open the champagne," but it was Putin who knew when a little succor was what the people needed.

The spectacle showed that Putin had no desire to release the levers of control—not to Medvedev and certainly not to people massed in the street. Putin's scolding of the plant owners had been harsh, but he also made it clear that he would not allow the rabble to establish a precedent for the airing of grievances against the government. Deripaska understood the charade, and accepted his public humiliation because he knew it was the cost of his privileged status in the Kremlin elite. He did not even come out the worst in the deal to restart the factories: the main supplier of the material the factory in Pikalevo needed, nepheline, was forced to sell it at a loss. Putin brokered even the details of its supply, delivered by Russian Railways, headed by Putin's old comrade from Petersburg, Vladimir Yakunin. The supplier, PhosAgro, would soon expand its holdings to include the fertilizer plant that Mikhail Khodorkovsky had been accused of pilfering, Apatit. One of its newest shareholders was the man who had approved Putin's disputed thesis in 1997, Vladimir Litvinenko. The agreement to reopen Pikalevo did nothing to solve the underlying problem with production there, nor the lack of demand for aluminum, which was compounded by the economic crisis, but that was not the point. Deripaska had already received billions in credits to help restructure his crippling debt—and even an extra loan to keep production open in Pikalevo. The public dressing-down nevertheless warned other tycoons that they should resolve any crises that could foment public unrest before Putin was forced to add new stops on his angry itinerary. Instead of using the economic crisis as an opportunity to address underlying weaknesses in the country's economy—which Medvedev would spell out in an online manifesto in September called "Russia, Forward!"—Putin intensified his role as the ultimate dispenser of the country's resources, punishing those who resisted his vision of how the money should be spent and rewarding those who went along. When the government established a mechanism for distributing funds from the stimulus package in 2009, Putin unilaterally decided which companies would receive them. This was how business worked in Putin's mind, through connections and deals, not through a liberalized economy where the market would make the decisions.

Putin's personal control of economic policy caused confusion at times. Even as he swaggered through Pikalevo in May, the Kremlin's economic advisers were putting the final touches on an agreement with the United States to advance Russia's stalled bid to join the World Trade Organization. Putin himself had criticized Russia's exclusion from the WTO and the talks had made progress, but only days later he unexpectedly announced that Russia would instead pursue an economic alliance with Belarus and Kazakhstan and only join the WTO with them as a bloc. The reversal made little sense economically since Russia had far more foreign trade with Europe and the United States than with others. Linking Russia's bid to a trade bloc that had not even been established would delay membership indefinitely. It also revealed the divisions within the Kremlin. Aleksei Kudrin, still the finance minister in Putin's cabinet, tried three times to talk Putin out of the announcement that week, but neither he nor Medvedev could prevail.[5]

Instead of opening up Russia's economy in response to the global crisis, Putin gave in to populist and autarkic instincts, cheered on by the hardliners who believed that the vagaries of the global market could be, and were being, manipulated to punish Russia. He did so because he believed he had chosen the wiser path to recovery. The economic crisis had been ruinous for Russia, but the Kremlin's emergency measures had managed to avert total collapse. By the middle of 2009, the price of oil had risen again, easing some of the pressures on the budget; the ruble regained some of its value, and the stock market began to recoup its losses. By 2010, Russia's economy was growing, bouncing back in fact with far more vigor than the economies of Europe and the United States. Far from encouraging a fuller embrace of economic modernization, the crisis only convinced Putin that Russia's economic security lay in the system of control that he had created—and in the power of his will. The dire predictions that Putin's system, and Putin himself, could not survive the economic and political tumult proved to be greatly exaggerated.

On September 28, 2009, the chief executive of Gazprom, Aleksei Miller, joined local and regional officials on a hill overlooking the Imereti Valley south of Sochi, the wide fluvial plain that Putin had approved as one of two main sites for the Winter Games, then less than five years away. They were there to break ground on a new power plant, which, when finished, would become the most visible structure on the coastal cityscape, topped with the company's logo. The necessity of building a power plant underscored just how underdeveloped the region had become. Beloved by Soviet leaders, especially Stalin, who built a dacha there, the resorts had fallen into disrepair even before the collapse of the Soviet Union. With prosperity trickling down to a burgeoning consumer class, millions and millions of Russians were lured instead by inexpensive vacation packages to Thailand, Turkey, and the Sinai, and Sochi became a backwater, left behind and often in the dark.

Having won the Olympics, Putin was determined to return Sochi to its previous glory, the Sochi he remembered from his first visits as a young man in the 1970s. The economic crisis had done nothing to smother those ambitions; in fact, they were an answer to it. With Sochi, he was reviving the legacy of the Soviet megaproject, the gigantic, top-down endeavors that industrialized the Soviet Union. These were the ideological triumphs of Putin's historical memory—from the Virgin Lands Campaign to boost agricultural output in the 1950s to the Baikal-Amur Mainline, or BAM, in the 1970s. As in Soviet times, the goal was ideological as much as economic, a demonstration of the country's progress and prestige in the world, even as the projects consumed enormous resources. Sochi became the largest single infrastructure project since the Soviet Union collapsed, though it was not the only one. Putin approved $20 billion to develop Vladivostok in the Far East—including a university on an island in the harbor that had been a closed military zone and a suspension bridge linking it to the city—in preparation for a two-day summit in 2012 of the Asia-Pacific Economic Cooperation nations. He spent $7 billion to rebuild much of Kazan to hold the 2013 Universiade, a biennial competition that hardly ranked as a major international event but justified an expensive redevelopment plan of the city. Flush from securing the Olympics, Putin drafted a bid to host the World Cup in 2018, promising to build or renovate stadiums in twelve cities, including the one in Kazan that would be used for the Universiade and the one in Sochi that would be the site of the opening and closing ceremonies in 2014. Each of these projects served multiple purposes for Putin, advertising Russia as a great power, providing economic stimulus to a faltering economy, and dispensing the resources of the state to those in a position to profit most.

Putin's attention to Sochi became so obsessive during his term as prime minister that the Olympics were called his pet project. It was not only a manifestation of his power, but also an instrument for keeping it. He had appointed one of his closest and most trusted advisers, Dmitri Kozak, to manage the project, and he created a new state company, Olympstroi, to build the venues that Sochi needed. By decree, Putin suspended legal and legislative oversight of the construction, including questions of cost and the environmental impact in an area that UNESCO had designated for protected status as one of "the only large mountain area in Europe that has not experienced significant human impact."[6] He also maintained formal control over the distribution of the contracts awarded to build the Olympic venues. He sat on the supervisory board of the state development agency, Vnesheconombank, which would end up providing the credits for the vast majority of the projects, whose contractors were also decided on by Putin. At Gazprom's groundbreaking ceremony, little was said about the companies that would build the plant or the pipeline—and nothing about the men who owned them. The contractor commissioned to build the pipeline was called Stroygazmontazh, which had not even existed until the year before. The company had emerged from the economic crisis in 2008, snatching up, for $400 million, various Gazprom subsidiaries and subcontractors that had built the country's vast network of pipelines. The man behind Stroygazmontazh happened to be Putin's judo sparring partner from his youth, Arkady Rotenberg.

By now, Rotenberg had parlayed his role in the state vodka monopoly, Rospiritprom, into a fortune. (One of his factories even produced a new brand, Putinka, a playful diminutive on Putin's name, which soon became one of the most popular and lucrative brands in Russia.[7]) Rotenberg's entry into the pipeline business made him wealthy on a whole new scale. Soon many of Gazprom's expansion projects went to his company—from the construction of North Stream, the pipeline that had entangled Gerhard Schröder in scandal, to the pipeline that would provide heat to the new island complex Putin was erecting in Vladivostok. In 2010 Rotenberg and his brother, Boris, occupied the final two spots on *Forbes*'s list of the hundred richest Russians, worth $700 million each. Arkady Rotenberg was so reclusive that he did not give an interview until his appearance among Russia's wealthiest began to raise speculation about the remarkable source of his wealth. "We didn't just come off the streets," he acknowledged in an interview with *Kommersant.*[8]

Putin's megaprojects only propelled Rotenberg's rise. In 2010, with his son, he took over the company building the power plant above the future Olympic Village, and received contract after contract for the games—twenty-one in all, worth nearly $7 billion, an amount equivalent to the entire cost of the 2010 Winter Olympics in Vancouver. He did not deny that his friendship with Putin had helped his meteoric rise, but he described their relationship as a duty, a burden, and as their judo coach had said, a matter of trust. "Knowing government officials of that high a level hasn't hurt anyone, but it certainly hasn't helped everyone either," he told the newspaper. "It's not a guarantee. I repeat, Putin has many more friends than those who are today famous and successful. Moreover, everyone for some reason forgets about the huge responsibility of such a friendship. For me, it is especially a responsibility. I try to behave in a way that I would never betray him."

As Putin's government parceled out contracts without public tenders and public scrutiny, the overwhelming majority went to those, like Rotenberg, whom Putin had elevated. Russian Railways, headed by Vladimir Yakunin, oversaw the single largest—and ultimately most expensive—project: the railroad spur that connected the coast to the mountains where the skiing events would be held. The project, called the "combined road," was at once an engineering marvel that overcame enormous geological challenges and, to critics, a boondoggle that created an environmental calamity in a once largely undisturbed valley. The railroad courses up the left bank of the Mzymta River, named after the word for "wild" in the lost Ubykh language that was spoken in the mountains before the Russian Empire conquered the region in the nineteenth century. The highway ran parallel to it and an old two-lane road on the right bank. The river gorge is so narrow in places that nearly twenty-four of the railroad's thirty miles had to run through tunnels (twelve in all, including one nearly three miles long) or over bridges, hundreds of piers of which were driven into the river or its banks, irreparably altering its wild state. Environmentalists mounted a campaign to challenge the project, but Putin had also suspended the laws that would have normally blocked the work; environmentalists who protested were harassed and ultimately jailed. Russian Railways subcontracted much of the work to companies that were also linked to Putin's friends, including the bridge builder, SK Most. A majority share of that company was subsequently purchased by Gennady Timchenko.

From the start, the Olympic construction was bedeviled by delays and soon by spiraling costs, forcing Putin to intervene, at times forcefully, to keep the project moving forward. Three times Putin fired the directors of Olympstroi, ostensibly because he was frustrated by slow progress and cost overruns. The priority Putin placed on the games invited the huge cost overruns—it had become so urgent a priority that no expense was spared and much was skimmed off the top. Because the allocation of contracts was so opaque, there was little accountability. A 2009 effort by the Communists in the Duma to impose oversight over the spiraling costs was blocked by United Russia.

There was ample evidence of corruption, with huge kickbacks factored into the contracts, but despite publicly chiding officials about the costs and dangers of corruption, Putin did nothing to punish it, even when it was exposed. In 2009, a Moscow businessman, Valery Morozov, complained publicly that an official in the Kremlin's Office of Presidential Affairs, Vladimir Leshchevsky, had shaken him down for 12 percent of a $500 million contract to refurbish a government-owned sanatorium in Sochi. He paid either in cash or through payments to an offshore company, but when he felt he was being squeezed out of the deal, he went to the police, who arranged a sting at Slivovitsa, a beer restaurant not far from the Kremlin. He even wore a hidden camera in his belt to record the last cash installment of $5 million. Leshchevsky took the cash but slipped away without being arrested. Frustrated by the failed sting, Morozov went public, appealing directly to Dmitri Medvedev's office and indirectly through the British and Russian press. Medvedev announced an investigation, but it quietly died two years later.[9] Instead prosecutors opened an investigation into Morozov's company. Morozov fled to Britain and detailed his accusations in a lengthy application for political asylum, which he received. The lesson was clear for anyone who dared challenge the system.

One man who did, Sergei Magnitsky, died in a cell in the Matross-kaya Tishina prison in Moscow on November 16, 2009. He had been transferred there for emergency medical treatment for pancreatitis and cholecystitis. He had already been in prison for nearly a year—the maximum he could be held without trial—on charges involving a massive tax fraud that he had uncovered and reported to the authorities. Instead of taking the ailing man to the prison's hospital, eight guards took him to an isolation cell, handcuffed him, and beat him with batons. He was only thirty-seven, an auditor so unprepossessing that no one would mistake him for a radical threatening Putin's system. He represented the post-Soviet generation that had come of age in the new Russia, highly educated and professional, a father of two, who believed in "the dictatorship of law" that Putin promised—as well as the end of "legal nihilism" that Medvedev had. After his arrest in 2008, he was sure the law would ultimately protect him. Instead he spent week after week transferred from dirty cell to dirty cell, allowed to see his wife and mother only once while in detention. He kept a meticulous diary of the abuses he experienced, as well as the steady decline of his health. To pass time, he read Shakespeare's tragedies.[10] His treatment in prison and finally his death might have been soon forgotten, as had so many others in Russia's horrid judicial system, where five thousand prisoners died that year, but Magnitsky had worked for a powerful patron, William Browder, once the country's most prominent foreign investor. Browder had been an early cheerleader for Putin's presidency, believing in the economic reforms he pledged, but by then he had become one of its most embittered foes.

Browder had amassed a fortune investing in shares in Russian companies and then using those shareholder stakes to lobby for good corporate governance and transparency. He was brash and aggressive, often suing companies, and though he almost always lost in court, he felt he shared a common goal with Putin to make Russia a truly competitive economy after the corrupted oligarchy of the 1990s. In 2005, however, he was unexpectedly turned away at the airport in Moscow, his visa revoked as a matter of national security. Browder's aggressive investment strategy had crossed some line—perhaps involving Gazprom or Surgutneftegaz, both with close links to Putin—but he would never know which one for certain. He initially hoped his deportation was a mistake that would be promptly sorted out. He appealed to the men he believed were his allies in the Kremlin, but by 2007, prosecutors had turned their attention to his company's offices in Moscow, and Browder began quietly divesting the assets of his investment fund, Hermitage Capital, and moving them to London. That June two dozen officers from the Interior Ministry raided Hermitage's skeletal office in Moscow and seized the company's corporate records: the certificates and stamps for the holding companies that had made up its portfolio.

By the end of the year three of the companies had been mysteriously reregistered under new owners, all of them convicted criminals. These owners then applied for $230 million in tax refunds, which were granted on a single day in December. Browder turned to a law firm in Moscow, Firestone Duncan, to figure out what had happened. The accountant who untangled the convoluted scheme was Sergei Magnitsky. He testified before the state's investigative committee, identifying the Interior Ministry officers, judges, and tax inspectors who had orchestrated the elaborate theft of the company seals and the subsequent tax fraud. The ministry ordered an investigation into the theft—and assigned as the lead investigator the major whom Magnitsky had accused of orchestrating it, Artyom Kuznetsov. Magnitsky was arrested eighteen days later.

Magnitsky's death deeply shocked Russia's elite. They had long been inured to the harsh measures used against political activists and wayward businessmen, but Magnitsky was neither. Even if Browder posed a threat to someone's powerful interests, Magnitsky was clearly a collateral victim. His death exposed a sweeping web of abuse and lies—about the case he investigated, his arrest and detention, the failure to treat his deteriorating health, the final beating that killed him. Dmitri Medvedev, too, seemed shocked; few cases illustrated as well the "legal nihilism" that he believed was stifling Russia's economic future. He ordered the prosecutor general to investigate and formed a working group to review the case independently, appointing prominent rights advocates whom Putin had increasingly marginalized when he was in the Kremlin. In December Medvedev dismissed twenty officials of the prison service, though most came from faraway regions; only one had any connection to Magnitsky's treatment in detention. Meanwhile, Browder poured his resources into tracing the proceeds from the $230 million in tax receipts. The lead investigator had purchased two apartments worth more than $2 million (registered in his parents' names), as well as a Mercedes-Benz, a Range Rover, and a Land Rover, each worth many times more than his annual salary of $10,200. The woman in the tax office who had approved the rebates had an estate in Moscow, a seaside villa in Dubai, and $11 million in cash in offshore accounts in her husband's name, according to Browder's investigators. The bureaucrats involved lived so far beyond their official means that it was clear that the embezzlement from Hermitage had been replicated in hundreds, perhaps thousands, of cases. Magnitsky had revealed not just the corrupted acts of a few officials but the corruption of the entire system.

For Medvedev, coming as it did only months after his "Russia, Forward!" exhortations, the case could have been an opportunity to set an example by punishing those involved in the embezzlement and the death of an innocent accountant. The official investigation, however, dragged on in silence, even as Browder made the case an international cause célèbre, petitioning the United States Congress and parliaments in Europe to impose sanctions on sixty people who had been involved. On the eve of the first anniversary of Magnitsky's death, the prosecutor's office at last announced the conclusion of its investigation, and it was as Kafkaesque as anything Medvedev had inveighed against: Magnitsky, the prosecutors announced triumphantly, had masterminded the embezzlement he uncovered.

It took nearly two years for the working group Medvedev had commissioned to present its final report. Its principal authors did so at a meeting with Medvedev in the Kremlin, concluding that his arrest had been unlawful, his death a crime, the investigation a cover-up, and the courts willing collaborators. Medvedev acknowledged in the meeting that crimes had been committed, but he was powerless to do anything about it. The next day the Ministry of Internal Affairs, ostensibly responsible to him as president and commander in chief, dismissed the group's report as irrelevant. Then the prosecutor's office announced that after a thorough investigation, it would reopen the criminal case against Magnitsky and charge him with tax fraud. Not even during the worst show trials of the Great Terror in the 1930s had the authorities put a dead man on trial. They would even call his mother to testify in court.

The United States under President Obama, in particular, vested inordinate hope in Dmitri Medvedev's presidency. Seeing his election as an evolutionary shift in Russia's political development, Obama promised a "reset" in relations after the disastrous end to the Bush years. Although realistic about Putin's continued political dominance, Obama and his aides went out of their way to court Medvedev directly, according to protocol, and hoped that he would over time build his own foundations of political power. Putin had "one foot in the old way of doing business," Obama said undiplomatically only weeks before he was to meet the new leader and the paramount one, but with Medvedev he hoped to move into a new era. No one in the White House or the State Department had any illusions that Medvedev could act without Putin's consent on important matters of state, but the initial embrace appeared to produce results. In 2009, the two leaders negotiated a treaty, New START, to replace the agreement Putin had negotiated with George Bush in 2002 and to further reduce the two nations' nuclear arsenals. Medvedev, as Putin had once done, helped the United States in Afghanistan, allowing the Americans to begin withdrawing thousands of matériel (though not weapons) by railroad through Russian territory.[11] When presented with evidence that Iran had developed a secret uranium enrichment program, Russia joined the United States at the United Nations Security Council and voted to impose new sanctions on the Iranian economy.

Making his own concession on one of Russia's bêtes noires, Obama abandoned plans to deploy missile defenses in the Czech Republic and Poland—the very deployments that had provoked Putin's ire before his Munich speech in 2007. The Obama administration even played down the American efforts to support democratic change in Ukraine and Georgia, which in neither place had succeeded very well anyway. Georgia remained a close American ally, but a fractured one after the war in 2008. Viktor Yanukovych, whose fraudulent victory in Ukraine in 2004 had been overturned, managed to exploit the infighting of his rivals and defeat Yulia Tymoshenko in an honest election in February 2010, after which she was tried and sent to jail, ironically, for having negotiated a deal with Putin to end a second shutoff of natural gas in the winter of 2009. The "reset" seemed to be working, but the warming of relations did not extend to Putin himself. And soon other events chilled the warming trend.

Only two months after Medvedev and Obama signed New START in April 2010, the FBI uncovered the existence of eleven sleeper agents who had lived covertly in the United States throughout Putin's rise to power. They were, in the parlance of espionage, "illegals," posing as ordinary suburban Americans, working and raising children near Boston, New York, and Washington without the protection of diplomatic immunity. As recently as 2009, Russia's FSB reminded these agents, in an encrypted message intercepted by the FBI "to search and develop ties in policymaking circles and sent intels to C."[12] The initial referred to the Center, where they sent reports, as well as pleas for reimbursements for the education and housing the agents felt they needed to live the American Dream. The FBI informed President Obama on the eve of Medvedev's second official visit to the United States, during which he visited Silicon Valley and promoted foreign investment and trade, but they did not move to make arrests until after Medvedev's meetings at the White House and a chummy lunch with Obama at a popular hamburger restaurant in Arlington, Virginia. Assisted by amused media coverage of what seemed to be a network of ineffective spies enjoying the perquisites of American life, Obama's aides dismissed the espionage as harmless efforts to glean information easily accessible from public sources, but the scope of the effort testified to the intensity of Russia's lingering distrust of American intentions.

Ten of the agents pleaded guilty in July. The eleventh had fled to Cyprus and apparently escaped back to Russia. The others were traded with Cold War–like drama at the airport in Vienna, exchanged for four Russians who had been imprisoned at home for spying for the West, though in at least one case, the man insisted he had never been a spy. Upon the sleepers' return, Putin met secretly with them, honoring those who had experienced the secret life he had once imagined for himself as a boy.

Together they sang songs, including the sentimental theme to *The Shield and the Sword,* the film that in 1968 propelled Putin into the KGB and even now seemed to serve as the foundation for his increasingly insulated and paranoid worldview. Putin still knew the words and had learned to play the music on the piano (which he would do at a charity auction a few months later). Whence does the Motherland begin, the song's lyrics ask, and the answer seemed rooted in Putin's own background:[13]

> *With good and trusted comrades*
> *Living in the neighboring yard*

Putin disclosed their meeting during an official visit in July to Sevastopol, the Crimea port that was the headquarters of the Black Sea Fleet.

He was attending an international motorcycle rally, featuring the Night Wolves, Russia's version of the Hell's Angels, bikers who blended patriotism, Russian Orthodoxy, and reverence for Putin. He rode with them, though on a three-wheeled motorcycle especially kitted out for him, the sort of photo opportunity that was again becoming more common. The betrayal of the illegals deeply angered him, and he vowed that the source—who, he said, was already known—would suffer for it. "Traitors always meet a bad end," he said. "As a rule, they die from either heavy drinking or drug abuse." He then alluded to Sergei Tretyakov, a senior intelligence officer who had defected to the United States in 2000. He was known to his American handlers as Comrade J, and among his disclosures were details about Putin's own chief of security, Viktor Zolotov. Tretyakov died only days before the spy ring was broken up, but his wife kept his death out of the news until the FBI could complete an autopsy, which showed no foul play. Having been head of intelligence activities at the United Nations before his defection, he might well have had a role in exposing the illegals, though his wife denied that.[14]

"Actually," Putin said of Tretyakov anyway, "his life was such a waste."

The stylistic contrasts between Medvedev and Putin prompted endless speculation about actual rifts within their tandem. Given Putin's expectation of loyalty, however, evidence of them rarely surfaced. Publicly at least, the two men and their aides portrayed their relationship as one united in a shared vision for Russia's future. "There cannot be, by definition, any disagreements in the Medvedev-Putin tandem," the speaker of the State Duma, Boris Gryzlov, declared in 2010.[15] At the start of the presidency, the two men had in fact reached an agreement to which few others were privy, respecting the responsibilities of their respective offices, though Putin retained a greater say in military and intelligence matters than any prime minster before him.[16] In the first half of his presidency, Medvedev never directly aired a word of criticism toward Putin himself or his policies, even as he struck a far more liberal tone in speeches that some read as implicit rebukes. Behind the scenes, though, rivalries hardened between the two offices and their cadres, the two centers of power. Medvedev had developed his own camp of advisers at the Kremlin who, like him, bristled at the obstacles that emerged to the president's policies and his vision of a more progressive society and economy. As they learned that Medvedev's authority extended only as far as Putin's forbearance allowed, their resentments became more and more pronounced. "There were disagreements—it is normal," one of Medvedev's closest advisers once said, though refusing to say even that much publicly.[17] In fact, on the issues that mattered most to him, Putin not only retained the ultimate veto but dictated the details as well.

In the eyes of the public, Medvedev became the man of words— "Russia, Forward!"—while Putin was the man of action. When pernicious peat fires shrouded Moscow and other cities in choking smoke in the summer of 2010, it was Putin who came to the rescue, as he had in Pikalevo. The fires, fueled by a heat wave, burned uncontrolled for weeks, killing dozens of people and destroying entire villages. Medvedev was on vacation on the Black Sea and slow to return even as the disaster worsened. The government seemed helpless to control them, prompting unusually fierce criticism. A blogger's profanity-laced diatribe, published on the website of Ekho Moskvy, was so incendiary that Putin had to respond.

"Where does our money go?" the blogger, who introduced himself as Aleksandr from a village near Tver, wrote. He complained that the village lost what meager equipment it had to fight the fires encroaching on residents' homes. He then went on to single out one of Medvedev's signature proposals: to create a Silicon Valley–like center for technological innovation in the Moscow suburb of Skolkovo. "Why do we every year slip farther and farther from even a primitive social system? What the fuck is your innovation center in Skolkovo to us, if we do not have basic fire trucks?"[18]

That the screed criticized a project closely associated with Medvedev's presidency, and not Putin himself, might have been the only reason it received the attention it did. A diatribe like that against Putin personally would have been too toxic for any media to discuss so openly, but it resonated widely and Putin was sensitive to shifts in public opinion. Nine days later, he appeared on television piloting an amphibious aircraft to fight the fires personally. The plane landed in the Oka River to load water and later dumped it on a smoldering bog southeast of Moscow.

"Was that OK?" Putin asked, turning toward the pilot.

"A direct hit!" the pilot replied.

These images, no matter how transparently staged by the Kremlin's media advisers and pliant television channels, proved remarkably effective. Putin was the ultimate celebrity of the Kremlin's own reality, the indispensable leader, even a "glamorous, elite sexual icon" whose stunts seemed intended to elicit "passionate, even sexualized reactions" from women.[19] Medvedev never enjoyed the same adulation, spontaneous or contrived. Where Putin once demurred at displays that suggested a cult of personality, saying manifestations of reverence for the nation's leader were inappropriately redolent of Stalinism, he now seemed to embrace them more than he ever had before.

The publicity stunts not only served Putin's politics; they played into his vanity. And he appeared to take his vanity very seriously. Only weeks after his fifty-eighth birthday, Putin appeared in public with his face so heavily caked with makeup that journalists noticed. He was in Kyiv, this time for talks to merge Ukraine's airline manufacturer with one of Russia's newly rebuilt state enterprises, the United Aviation Corporation. Ties with Ukraine had improved measurably after the election of Yanukovych in 2010, but Putin seemed uneasy, even avoiding looking at the television cameras. Beneath the makeup there were visible bruises under his eyes. "It's probably just the way the light fell," his spokesman, Dmitri Peskov, insisted. "The prime minister is tired." The bruises were undeniable, however, and they prompted speculation that Putin had begun a regime of cosmetic surgery.[20] The speculation—always denied, though never unequivocally—swelled as changes in Putin's appearance became evident in photographs and drew the attention of foreign officials who met him, at least one of whom spoke off the record of the cosmetic work as a matter of fact. The crow's feet on his temples disappeared, as did the deep creases in his forehead and the noticeable bags under his eyes. His skin was taut, his cheeks fuller. With his thinning but carefully groomed hair, his face seemed rounder, his eyes narrower. A plastic surgeon in Chelyabinsk, Aleksandr Pukhov, even came forward to claim he knew the doctor who had carried out the procedures, which included blepharoplasty. He said so approvingly. "Would you really want to see the president old and flabby?"[21]

Tensions within the tandem became more pronounced in the summer of 2010 when protests erupted over the construction of a new highway from Moscow to Petersburg. No one doubted the need for better roads, and the project, valued at $8 billion, was among the megaprojects Putin approved to stimulate economic growth, but a debate had raged for years over the route, and now, without public notice, the project suddenly moved forward. In July, bulldozers appeared and began clearing trees from Khimki Forest, a protected preserve on the edge of Moscow that many called the "lungs" of the city. The work prompted protests by the forest's neighbors, who were soon joined by local and foreign environmental activists. Wary after the public anger over the summer's fires, Medvedev announced in August that he would suspend the construction while the government considered alternate routes.

The controversy became an unexpected test of Medvedev's authority as president, and he failed. Moscow's mayor, Yuri Luzhkov, criticized the suspension of the project in the government's official newspaper, *Rossiskaya Gazeta,* a public rebuke he had never dared to make against Putin. Luzhkov, who had once opposed the highway for his own reasons, had shifted support to it. His reason was evidently that he knew the project had the support of Putin, who had awarded the contract for construction in 2008 and a year later waived the forest's protected status to allow construction to begin. Whether Medvedev knew that was never clear, but he acted as if he had the power to intervene now. Luzhkov, who had presided over Moscow for eighteen years, defiantly called for a restoration of "the true meaning and authority" of the government.[22] Many heard those words as a call for Putin to return to the presidency, a provocation that Medvedev could hardly ignore.

His aides in the Kremlin responded by unleashing state television on the mayor as fiercely as Boris Yeltsin's had more than a decade before when Luzhkov and Primakov appeared poised to emerge as the leaders of a post-Yeltsin coalition. After a week of that, Medvedev's chief of staff summoned Luzhkov and asked him to resign and "leave quietly." When he refused, the Kremlin told him to go on holiday for a week to think it over.[23] Medvedev, who privately denounced Luzhkov with an earthy vulgarity for loudmouth that roughly translates as "one who rings his balls," appeared unable to act without Putin's approval. Opposition leaders like Boris Nemtsov all but dared Medvedev to demonstrate his authority, but it was only when Luzhkov returned to Moscow and wrote a letter to Medvedev mocking his democratic pretensions and demanding the restoration of elections for mayors and governors (which Putin had taken away) that Medvedev finally received approval to dismiss him. Two weeks later, Putin forced Medvedev to appoint as mayor Putin's chief of staff, Sergei Sobyanin, a former governor from Siberia who had little experience or knowledge of the capital.

It seemed that Medvedev had triumphed, demonstrating resolve by removing Luzhkov from power, but the confrontation also illustrated the limits of his power as president. The highway construction later went ahead, as planned. The main contractor, the only bidder, was owned by a convoluted, overlapping chain of companies registered in Cyprus and the British Virgin Islands. One was called Croisette Investments, half of which was owned by another called Olpon Investments. Its sole owner was Arkady Rotenberg. When Medvedev was pressed on why the government had allowed the work to resume, he could only mutter that there were "private interests" involved.[24]

Medvedev's leadership disappointed Putin's critics, and the constraints on his authority left Medvedev himself frustrated. At the end of 2010, his resentments boiled over for the first time as the fate of Mikhail Khodorkovsky once again hung in the balance. With the end of his first prison sentence approaching, the authorities had launched a new investigation against Khodorkovsky and his partner, Platon Lebedev, intended to keep them in prison. The second trial had begun in 2009, this time on charges of embezzling profits that amounted to more than the worth of the oil Yukos had extracted over a period of six years.[25] It had dragged on for nineteen months. Resigned to a guilty verdict, Khodorkovsky's lawyers sought to highlight the political motives behind the case instead. They called as a witness Putin himself, as well as Igor Sechin; the finance minister, Aleksei Kudrin; and twenty other officials. The judge refused but did allow some prominent officials to testify, hoping, it seemed, to demonstrate some adherence to due process. They included one of Putin's oldest colleagues, German Gref, who appeared rattled by being questioned by Khodorkovsky himself through the glass enclosure, where the defendants sat. A crucial moment came when Gref conceded the point that was at the center of Khodorkovsky's defense: that it would have been impossible for him to have stolen what amounted to a year's worth of the entire country's oil production without somebody in the government noticing it at the time.

The courts in Russia had become so politicized by then that Khodorkovsky had no hope of prevailing. His defense was simply an exercise in delegitimizing the judicial process, and in that it succeeded. The prosecution was even more convoluted and confused than at his first trial, making a mockery of Medvedev's pledges to end "legal nihilism." The proceedings were riddled with procedural errors, conflated or contradictory accusations, and lacked any semblance of fairness. The spectacle was roundly condemned outside of Russia as an indication of the authoritarian state Russia had become.

On the eve of the judge's verdict, Putin even intervened forcefully

with one of his own. "It is my conviction that 'a thief should sit in jail,' "
he declared in his annual phone-in appearance on December 16, alluding to a line from a popular television serial from 1979, *The Meeting
Place Cannot Be Changed*. He spoke of Khodorkovsky's previous conviction as though it had already proved his guilt with regard to the new
charges and compared him to the American financier Bernard Madoff,
who had recently been sentenced to 150 years for running one of the
largest Ponzi schemes in history. Putin's response sounded deeply emotional, full of personal anger and indignation. He went even further than
the charges themselves, suggesting that Khodorkovsky had ordered his
chief of security to carry out the murder of the mayor of Nefteyugansk,
where Yukos's main oil fields were located. "One woman in Moscow
refused to hand over her small property, and they killed her, too. And
then they killed the assassin they hired to carry out those killings. All
they found was his brains, splattered all over his garage."

At this point, even Medvedev had to object. For the first time, he
openly criticized Putin, saying that no one, not the president, not the
prime minister, had a right to pronounce judgment before it was delivered by the court. His admonishment had no effect. In fact, the verdict
had already been decided, its 878 pages written for the judge to read,
as his own assistant would later disclose, describing recurrent meetings
and relentless pressure from senior officials. The trial did more than
expose the emptiness of Medvedev's pledges; it signaled an emerging
breach between the two that would only worsen, punctuating the end of
the "tandem" and the hopes so many had invested in it. The judge sentenced Khodorkovsky to thirteen years in prison, though the term was
later reduced slightly. This ensured that, with his time already served,
he would remain behind bars until 2016, well past the next parliamentary and presidential elections. Khodorkovsky responded with a series of
public and legal appeals, all futile. He taunted Medvedev for his lack of
authority and pitied Putin for his vindictiveness. In an open letter in the
Nezavisimaya Gazeta, he wrote that Putin "was incapable of tearing himself away from the already unmanageable 'oar' of the monstrous 'galley'
he himself has built, a galley that apathetically sails right over people's
destinies, a galley over which, more and more, the citizens of Russia
seem to see a black pirate flag flying."[26]

The Return

For a second day in the autumn of 2011 the delegates of the only political party that really mattered in Russia gathered in Luzhniki Stadium, the country's premier sporting arena, constructed in the 1950s at the height of Soviet might. It anchored the only Olympic Games ever held in the Soviet Union, in Moscow in 1980, and would soon be refurbished to serve as the main venue for the World Cup in 2018. In December 2010, Russia had won the competition to host the tournament despite a lackluster bid that appeared doomed until Putin personally intervened to oversee the proposal and tap the country's oligarchs for contributions. Russia was accused of trading votes with Qatar, which also bid and won the cup for 2022, votes that would remain a source of controversy and scandal for the sport's governing body, FIFA. There were even accusations that Russia had offered paintings from the storerooms of the State Hermitage Museum in Petersburg as gifts to delegates who would ultimately vote to award the cup. One painting was said to be a Picasso; the other was a landscape described by the recipient as "absolutely ugly."[1]

On that day in September, more than ten thousand delegates of United Russia filled grandstands adorned with party banners and red, white, and blue flags. The gathering resembled not an American-style party convention, but rather a display of fealty to party and state that more than a few observers noticed had an echo of the old Communist Party congresses with row after row of balding or gray-haired men and uniformed generals, festooned with medals from the glorious Soviet past. Only now the production was far slicker: a made-for-television affair that synthesized Soviet-like propaganda with state-of-the-art techniques and technology from the West.

It was just two and a half months before the newest round of parliamentary elections, which the party would, of course, win. Behind the orchestrated display, however, not all was well. The party's reputation had taken a dive after the Duma's failure to do much of anything beneficial for ordinary Russians during its last session, a turbulent period of economic and political crises. The party had by now become an object of ridicule, the brunt of jokes and scandal. The Duma had become a chamber filled with apparatchiks and opportunists, with Putin loyalists and celebrities like Alina Kabayeva or Andrei Lugovoi who were recruited and elected on party lists rather than politicians with genuine constituencies to answer to. In February 2011, Aleksei Navalny, a lawyer who had built a public following by exposing rampant corruption on a blog he kept, had called for a grassroots campaign to destroy United Russia for the sake of the country's democratic future. In a radio interview, he said that the party had become a manifestation of all that was wrong in Russia and added, almost as an aside, an appellation that proved to be catchy and, not suprisingly, durable: he called United Russia "the party of swindlers and thieves."[2]

Navalny had been active in democratic politics since the late 1990s, when he joined the Yabloko party, but he grew increasingly frustrated by that party's declining relevance and infighting. He was expelled after participating in the Russian March, an annual demonstration of nationalists that was anathema to Yabloko's liberals. He opened a law firm for a time, but only gained prominence when, like William Browder, he began to investigate the dealings of the opaque state corporations that dominated Russia's economy. His tactic was simple: acquire shares and investigate their books. As the owner of just two shares of Transneft, the oil-transport monopoly, he demanded to know why the company had donated $300 million to charity in 2007 and yet paid such paltry dividends to its shareholders.[3] He had, it seemed, uncovered the company's scheme to direct huge sums of money to the Kremlin, specifically the Federal Protective Service, which provided security to state officials and was headed by Putin's longtime bodyguard, Viktor Zolotov.

Navalny had no legal investigative power, but he used the last free space for public discourse in Russia, the Internet, to compile a virtual catalogue of malfeasance, conflicts of interest, and rapacious profiteering from the state's budget coffers. Expanding beyond Transneft, he highlighted the suspect and usually wildly inflated contracts of government agencies and corporations; the shady business activities of the Duma's deputies; and the luxurious properties they and government officials were able to acquire for themselves and their children despite their modest official salaries. He did what Sergei Magnitsky had done, piecing together a trail of evidence from public records that had become more open, if not exactly transparent, in part because of initiatives proposed by Medvedev, including one requiring that all government tenders be posted online. He created a website, RosPil.ru, that became a forum for scrutinizing these tenders and managed to create enough public scandal to force the cancelation of some contracts, though few meaningful government prosecutions ever resulted from his disclosures.

Navalny tapped into a simmering discontent with the Duma, with the system, even with Putin himself. It made him famous, and he made no secret of his ambition to lead a political movement that would steer Russia another way. Tall, blond, and handsome, with a chiseled jaw and a sense of joyous outrage, he seemed the first political figure to emerge from the atomized opposition who had the attributes to become a viable challenger to Putin himself. That could not go unnoticed for long. Nor could the role Medvedev's liberalizing reforms had played in enabling Navalny's dangerous and unexpected challenge to power.

Until the second Khodorkovsky trial, Medvedev had never openly contradicted Putin, never challenged him in any way, but as the end of his term as president approached, an undeclared campaign between the camps loyal to each man began to surface. In January 2011, one of Medvedev's advisers, Arkady Dvorkovich, publicly warned that the second Khodorkovsky trial had harmed the investment climate in Russia, reinforcing the perception that justice in Russia was capricious and deeply corrupted. Weeks later, Medvedev returned to Davos, where he had made his international debut four years before, and outlined ambitious plans to modernize Russia's economy, reassuring investors that, Khodorkovsky's case notwithstanding, the country welcomed foreign investors and capital. Only days before his trip to Davos, Medvedev had pushed the New START agreement negotiated with Barack Obama through the Duma, and while in Switzerland, he pledged to revive the talks to enter the World Trade Organization that Putin had upended in 2009. With the election of a new parliament scheduled for the end of the year and the presidential election three months after that, Medvedev presented a competing path for the future, and the insiders in the Kremlin and the government gravitated either toward his or toward Putin's.

The first question Medvedev faced at Davos was one he had not addressed in his remarks—and one that would prove decisive. It was about the Arab Spring, which had begun in Tunis in December 2010 and inspired protests that swept through the Arab world, toppling Hosni Mubarak in Egypt and threatening Colonel Muammar el-Qaddafi in Libya. Medvedev replied not only that he recognized the democratic aspirations of the thousands who had poured into Tunisia's streets to protest corruption, poverty, and lack of political rights, but also that governments had a responsibility to address those grievances. He went on to emphasize the importance of the relationship between governed and government in ways that could have applied equally to Russia, where the will of the people had been managed out of the electoral process. "When governments fail to keep up with social change and fail to meet people's hopes, disorganization and chaos ensue, sadly," Medvedev said, apparently warming to the theme. "This is a problem of governments themselves and the responsibility they bear. Even if governments in power find many of the demands made unacceptable they still must remain in dialogue with all the different groups because otherwise they lose their real foundation."

The protests in the Arab world had galvanized Russia's beleaguered opposition, at least in the still safe space of the Internet, and Medvedev's remarks sounded sympathetic to things that Putin feared most. Medvedev, while hardly endorsing protests at home, sounded irresolute. The American vice president, Joseph Biden, even had the audacity to quote him during a speech at Moscow State University in March 2011, in which he declared that Russians should have the same rights as anyone else. "Most Russians want to choose their national and local leaders in competitive elections," Biden said in what amounted to a endorsement in the undeclared campaign taking shape. "They want to be able to assemble freely, and they want a media to be independent of the state. And they want to live in a country that fights corruption. That's democracy. They're the ingredients of democracy. So I urge all of you students here: Don't compromise on the basic elements of democracy. You need not make that Faustian bargain."[4]

Behind the scenes, Biden used his visit to press Medvedev to support a United Nations Security Council resolution to authorize a military intervention in Libya, where peaceful protests had turned into an armed insurrection against the country's dictator, Muammar el-Qaddafi. The United States, its NATO allies, and some Arab nations wanted to establish a "no fly" zone over the country to prevent the bloody suppression of the rebels. Medvedev agreed, persuaded by the humanitarian case for intervention, despite the opposition of the Foreign Ministry and other security officials who saw the prospect of a NATO-led campaign outside its border as an extension of American hegemony to another part of the world. He had drifted dangerously far from Putin's path, making a confrontation seem inevitable.

Only weeks before, Putin had warned that the uprisings in Libya and other countries would fuel the rise of Islamic extremists allied with Al-Qaeda, aided and abetted by shortsighted sympathizers in the West trying to overthrow autocratic leaders. He was not wrong about the rise in extremism, which would later consume Libya and exacerbate a grinding civil war in Syria, a far more important ally of Russia in the Middle East. Putin's support for the autocratic dictators of Libya and Syria was widely viewed through the prism of Russia's geopolitical interests, including energy projects and a contract to build a railway linking Libya's coastal cities (negotiated by Putin's friend, Vladimir Yakunin), massive arms sales, and, in the case of Syria, Russia's only military base outside the former Soviet Union. In truth, his wariness ran much deeper. There existed a dark association in his mind between aspirations for democracy and the rise of radicalism, between elections and the chaos that would inevitably result. "Let's take a look back at history, if you don't mind," Putin said in Brussels in February. "Where did Khomeini, the mastermind of the Iranian revolution, live? He lived in Paris. And he was supported by most of Western society. And now the West is facing the Iranian nuclear program. I remember our partners calling for fair, democratic elections in the Palestinian territories. Excellent! Those elections were won by Hamas." Reflexively, instinctively, he imagined the uprising in Libya as simply another step toward a revolution being orchestrated for Moscow.

Perhaps it was because he was younger, perhaps because he never served in the security services, perhaps because of his convivial nature, but Medvedev did not share this bleak distrust of the West, of democracy, of human nature. He had spent the first three years of his presidency wooed by Barack Obama's administration, and now not only the United States but countries with much closer relations to Russia, including France and Italy, were appealing to him to help prevent a slaughter of civilians in Libya. And so, on his instruction, Russia abstained when the Security Council voted on United Nations Resolution 1973 on March 17, authorizing the use of military force to stop Qaddafi's forces from moving on the insurgents' stronghold in eastern Libya.

Medvedev's decision provoked a revolt among Russia's diplomats and security officials. Russia's ambassador to Libya, Vladimir Chamov, sent a cable to the president warning against the loss of an important ally. Medvedev fired him, but the ambassador returned to Moscow and declared publicly that the president was acting against Russia's interests. When NATO launched its first airstrikes two days later—a far more punishing initial barrage to destroy the country's air defenses than many expected—Medvedev seemed to many in Russia to be complicit in yet another American-led war.

One of the prime minister's closest advisers later claimed that Putin had not read the Security Council's resolution before the vote, deferring to the president and being preoccupied as he was with "economic diplomacy" rather than foreign affairs. Once the bombing started, however, Putin understood its import; the unstated goal of the NATO air war was not merely the protection of civilians caught in the crossfire, but rather the overthrow of Qaddafi's regime. He believed that Medvedev had been duped. "Putin read through the text of the resolution and saw that some countries could use the rubbery language to act the way they did," the adviser said.[5] As NATO bombs rained on Libya, Putin spoke out. Touring a weapons factory, he denounced the United Nations resolution as "flawed and inadequate." "If one reads it, then it immediately becomes clear that it authorizes anyone to take any measures against a sovereign state. All in all, it reminds me of a medieval call to crusade, when someone calls upon others to go somewhere and free someone else." He compared it to the American wars of the previous decade, the bombings of Serbia, Afghanistan, and, under a fabricated pretext, Iraq. "Now it's Libya's turn."

Putin's spokesman said he had merely expressed a personal opinion, but with Medvedev already facing criticism for the resolution, it was an unmistakable rebuke. Medvedev promptly assembled the Kremlin's press pool at his dacha outside Moscow to defend Russia's abstention and, at least obliquely, to criticize Putin. He wore a leather bomber jacket with a fur collar, zipped up tight. Appearing stern and a little uncomfortable, even nervous, he said the Security Council's action had been justified in light of Libya's actions. He sounded defensive. Russia's decision not to veto the resolution had been "a qualified decision" to help find a resolution to the exploding conflict. "Everything that is happening in Libya is a result of the Libyan leadership's absolutely intolerable behavior and the crimes that they have committed against their own people." Even as he expressed concern about the extent of the allied bombing campaign (which would continue for eight more months), he warned that Putin's language would not help end the fighting. "I think we need to be very careful in our choice of words. It is inadmissible to say anything that could lead to a clash of civilizations, talk of 'crusades' and so on. This is unacceptable."

As his term wound down, Medvedev redoubled his efforts to make liberalizing reforms in the economy, as if his time were running out. In one instance he decreed that government ministers could no longer serve on the boards of the state corporations that Putin had made a centerpiece of his economic policy. Medvedev himself had served on Gazprom's board while chief of staff and later deputy prime minister, but the move to bar officials from wearing two hats was an effort to weaken his chief rival in Putin's camp, Igor Sechin, who had served as deputy prime minister and chairman of Rosneft. (Putin ultimately agreed to the measure, but exempted Gazprom, where Putin's close ally and former prime minister Viktor Zubkov remained in place.) Medvedev's desire to remain as president for another term was palpable, though he could not risk openly declaring it. He and Putin may have been fighting a primary of sorts, but the only vote that mattered was Putin's, and Medvedev knew it.

In May, after three years in office, Medvedev held his first press conference, the event that Putin had used each year to great effect to demonstrate his mastery of politics and government. Medvedev's was a pale imitation of Putin's performances, though, and coming so late in his term, it seemed an act of political desperation. He held it at Skolkovo, the still evolving technological center he hoped would one day become a new Silicon Valley. Although he professed allegiance to Putin and praised their mutual commitment to the country's interests, he said he did not think that relations with NATO "were that bad," despite the war in Libya, and declared that Ukraine had every right to pursue its integration with Europe, something that Putin had viewed as a cataclysmic threat. In response to a question about replacing regional governors, he seemed to allude to the perpetuity of Putin's power, saying that leaders should not cling to office for too long, but rather make way for a new generation, as was happening in Tunisia and Egypt. "I think this is important because no one can stay in power forever," he said. "People who harbor such illusions usually come to a rather bad end, and the world has given us quite a few examples of late."

As the war in Libya dragged on, however, Medvedev's handling of the presidency became an open target for criticism in the media, signaled no doubt by Putin's own moves. In May, he announced the creation of a new organization, the All Russia People's Front, which was intended to expand the political coalition at the heart of his power and to distance him from the "party of swindlers and thieves." Within days, hundreds of organizations, unions, associations, and factories were rushing to join. The sole point of the project was to make Putin, not the country's sitting president, the "national leader" who would unite them. Medvedev pressed ahead with his proposals to reform the economy, freeing up capital and innovation, but he was losing ground. He met privately with twenty-seven of the country's leading businessmen—the oligarchs who like everyone else awaited the resolution of the presidential "primary" with growing alarm. He implored them to support his proposals, and by implication his candidacy, or to accept the stagnant status quo. Some of those in attendance interpreted Medvedev's remarks as an ultimatum for them to choose, but his message was so muddled that the participants could not be sure of his desire—or his ability—to fight to hold office. Afterward, they mocked his appeals, according to one of those who attended: "Have you already decided?"[6]

In June, in an interview with *The Financial Times,* Medvedev acknowledged for the first time that he wanted to return for a second term, but then he had to admit that it was not his decision alone. "I think that any leader who occupies such a post as president, simply must want to run," he said. "But another question is whether he is going to decide whether he's going to run for the presidency or not. So his decision is somewhat different from his willingness to run. So this is my answer."[7]

If Medvedev wanted to assert real political independence, he did not show it. He could have used any of his appearances or interviews to openly declare his intention to run, perhaps even against Putin himself, presenting a real choice to voters. Instead, he was left awkwardly not answering the question that by the summer of 2011 seemed to have dragged the country into a prolonged political crisis, recalling the uncertainties of the "2008 problem." Unnatural disasters unfolded, like sad symptoms of the country's paralysis, including the sinking of a ferryboat on the Volga River in July that drowned more than 120 people and the crash of an airplane carrying the players and coaches of one of the country's professional hockey teams, Lokomotiv Yaroslavl. Medvedev was scheduled days later to hold a conference in the team's hometown, Yaroslavl, and it seemed a terrible omen.

By then, even senior ministers were afraid to attend these conferences lest it be seen as an endorsement of Medvedev over Putin. Putin's steely charisma, his absolute determination, his ability to remain above the trials of Russian life, shielded him from blame when tragedies like these struck. Medvedev, though, looked overwhelmed as president. Perhaps by design, public blame for the sinking and the crash flowed toward him.

Putin's prominence in state media suddenly surged noticeably, an orchestrated campaign that seemed to highlight the personal, even physical, differences between the two men. Putin appeared at the summer camp of the youth group Nashi; he prayed at one of the holiest sites of Russian Orthodoxy; he dove in the Black Sea to the ruins of an ancient Greek city and, behold, surfaced clutching two amphorae. That his spokesman, Dmitri Peskov, later acknowledged that the "discovery" was staged was an unnoticed footnote to the televised image of a man in a tight wetsuit, still fit and very much in his prime.

By the time United Russia's delegates gathered at Luzhniki in September, there remained a shivering uncertainty, even bewilderment, as another political transition approached. Even as they drafted their party platform for the elections, then only ten weeks away, no one—not even the party leaders, or the closest aides of Putin or Medvedev—knew whether a choice had been made or whether the excruciating limbo ahead of the 2012 presidential campaign would continue. Inside the stadium on that Saturday morning, the delegates listened to speeches extolling the stunning transformation of an ideological empire that had rotted and collapsed and now risen again, presided over, it was made clear, by one man: Putin. Boris Gryzlov, the Duma's speaker, looked like an apparatchik of old, his face stern and pinched as he read the party's platform, droning on about pledges of prosperity and competence.

Eventually, the lights dimmed and the crowd hushed. From the wings, lit like rock stars, Putin and Medvedev entered the congress, striding side by side, their shoulders swaying in tandem. Putin had a look of utter assuredness, which is what his supporters have said the country always craved, not the shamed visage of a cowering leader of a diminished power. Putin spoke first, adhering to the protocol of political rank. He began by referring to "the most pressing challenges facing our nation," and then addressed the most acute question on the delegates' minds with an elaborate tease. He stopped short of revealing what exactly the answer was—just as he had done in the private councils he had held with his various aides in the preceding days. "I am aware that United Russia members, supporters, and the delegates of this conference are expecting the Russian president and prime minister to voice proposals on the country's power configuration and government structure after the elections," he said. "I want to tell you directly that we have long since reached an agreement on what we will be doing in the future. That agreement was reached several years ago. However, following this debate as observers, both Mr. Medvedev and I said that it is hardly the most important thing: who will do which job and occupy which position. What's more important is the quality of work, what results we achieve, and how our people perceive our efforts, what their reaction is to our proposals for the nation's future development and whether they support us."

Putin's words spoke volumes about his understanding of democracy: it is not for society to decide its leaders through some semblance of an electoral campaign, but to ratify those already chosen. He announced that Medvedev would, according to a "tradition" not even a decade old, head the party's ballot in the parliamentary elections in December and thus "guarantee its anticipated and honest victory." The applause that followed seemed rote; Putin had not yet clarified the fate of either man in the tandem.

Medvedev then followed him to the dais. "Naturally, it is a pleasure to speak here," he began, smiling awkwardly. Even after four years in office, he had not yet mastered the art of political speech. "There is a special energy in this room. It is simply charged with emotions." He praised Russia's democracy and the "new level of political culture" that it had achieved, but he went on to warn that "excessive formalism and bureaucracy" posed a danger to it. The delegates listened unemotionally; his relevance seemed to dim with each word. "They lead to the stagnation and degradation of the political system," he said. "And unfortunately, we have already witnessed this in our country's history." He outlined an eight-point political agenda, all of which he had promised for nearly four years and not yet delivered: modernizing the economy and industry; ensuring salaries, pensions, and health care, all precarious still; fighting corruption; strengthening the judiciary and criminal justice systems; combating illegal immigration while protecting the country's "interethnic and interreligious peace"; establishing a "modern political system"; building the nation's police and armed forces; and forging a strong "independent, sensible foreign policy."

With those words, he accepted Putin's nomination to head the party's list, and at last he addressed the agreement Putin had alluded to having reached years before. Medvedev spoke like a man reading his own political obituary; it was, in fact, one of the most bizarre resignation speeches in history. He was articulating and defending his vision for the country, even as he relinquished the post that might have made it achievable.

"I propose we decide on another very important issue which naturally concerns the party and all of our people who follow politics, namely the candidate for the role of president. In light of the proposal that I head the party list, do party work, and, if we perform well in the elections, my willingness to engage in practical work in the government, I think it's right that the party congress support the candidacy of the current prime minister, Vladimir Putin, in the role of the country's president."

In the end, perhaps, it was not a surprise. Medvedev's political stock had been sinking day by day for most of the year. Yet the shock was audible in the cavernous stadium, a collective gasp that soon turned to thunderous applause, wave after wave of it. Putin had succeeded in creating suspense and then releasing it at the moment of his choosing. He stood in front of his seat in the audience, basking in the spotlight, his eyes sparkling though his smile was tight, wry, and fleeting. He did not raise his arms in triumph or otherwise act like a candidate offered the chance to seek higher office. He simply nodded knowingly, as if his return to the presidency was preordained.

After Medvedev finished speaking, Putin strode to the dais a second time and delivered a lengthy, richly detailed, policy-laden address that outlined his plans to support veterans and farmers, doctors, teachers, scientists, soldiers. It was the nuts and bolts of governance, what the Russians had come to expect over years of watching him insist upon the right policy, the right decisions, on behalf of the people. He vowed to overcome the nagging hardships of the global economic crisis, the roots of which, he pointedly noted, again, "were not in Russia." He barely mentioned Medvedev's nomination to head the party list or his own return to the presidency, which in one sudden moment had become inexorable. "We have already entered a lengthy election cycle. The elections to the State Duma will take place on December 4, to be followed by the formation of its committees and government bodies. The presidential election is scheduled for next spring. I'd like to thank you for your positive response to the proposal for me to stand for president. This is a great honor for me." He spoke as if he had not decided everything himself.

The agreement was reached several years ago, Putin had explained. Medvedev suggested as much as well, though in fact it had not happened that way. Medvedev had nurtured the hope to return for a second term at least until the beginning of September, when his public demeanor started to suggest that it might not happen. He had only learned the details of Putin's final decision the night before during a late-night meeting at Novo-Ogaryovo. When the printers printed the ballots for the delegates to use to elevate Medvedev to the head of the party, the space for his name had been left blank, filled in only after the announcement. According to one account, Putin would not even let Medvedev tell his wife until the decision had been made public.[8] If Putin had known all along that he intended to reclaim the presidency, no one else in the government or in his inner circle had been allowed to know, let alone influence the outcome of his deliberations. He made the most momentous decision of his political career with his own counsel alone. One of Medvedev's loyalists, Arkady Dvorkovich, reacted with anguished sarcasm even as the events at the congress unfolded. In an interview the year before, Dvorkovich had acknowledged that Medvedev's plans—and really his entire presidency—had faced opposition from "those who thrive on the old system, on budget inefficiency and a resource-based economy."[9] He never named names, but he clearly referred to those arrayed around Putin. "Now," he tweeted from the floor of the party's congress, "it's time to switch to the sports channel."

Putin never bothered to explain his reasons for returning to the presidency, to the Kremlin. He could have remained the paramount leader, even with Medvedev serving another term as president. Perhaps there was no reason but the obvious one, though according to his most ardent supporters, he felt that his successor had not been a strong enough leader. In the days and months after the announcement, the same supporters set about demeaning Medvedev for the weaknesses he showed during the war in Georgia and failing to stop NATO's war in Libya. Even the anecdote about keeping Medvedev from telling his wife was laced with the insinuation that he was hardly man enough to trust his wife not to insist that he run again. These explanations sought to justify Putin's move, but they did not explain his motive. He never felt he had to. The position was his if he wanted it, which was, in his mind apparently, explanation enough.

Suddenly the significance of the constitutional change to lengthen the presidential term dawned on those who rued a new Putin presidency. Instead of four more years, Putin would serve six, until 2018. If he ran for another term after that—a fourth—he could be Russia's leader until 2024, surpassing Brezhnev in political longevity. Only Stalin, in power for thirty-one years, had remained in office longer. Putin's critics, and even some supporters, began to count the years of their own lives, envisioning their ages when, under the "managed democracy" the Kremlin had imposed, another leader might conceivably emerge in Russia. Photographs enhanced to show the aging process became popular memes on the Internet. The opposition newspaper *Novaya Gazeta* published pencil caricatures of Putin at the presumed end of his political career, his face creased with age, his hairline even further receded, his suit festooned with a field marshal's clusters of medals and ribbons. His senior aides were all there, too, those who had been with him from the beginning, looking like the hunched veterans of the Great Patriotic War, still revered and honored for deeds of a distant past.[10]

Medvedev, having been the hope of the liberals and reformers, faced even more ridicule than Putin. The decision to switch positions became known by the Russian word for castling in chess, *rokirovka,* in which the king swaps position with the rook, most often to solidify the defense of the king. No one doubted now who had always held the power, even those who had hoped that Medvedev would one day establish himself as an independent leader. Theirs was the bitter anger of disappointment. Whether or not the decision was made in 2008 or in 2011, Medvedev proved to be nothing more than a pawn in Putin's gambit to sidestep the letter of the law that limited a leader's term. Russians derisively reckoned his greatest accomplishments to be the reduction of Russia's eleven time zones to nine and the permanent shift to daylight saving time. A day after the announcement, a putative ally, the finance minister Aleksei Kudrin, publicly broke with Medvedev, saying he would refuse to remain in a cabinet with Medvedev as prime minister. Medvedev tried to explain "his" decision by saying that he and Putin had agreed to let opinion polls decide who would run—as if those in Russia were genuine reflections of voter sentiment—but he made matters worse by using the hated United States as a standard of comparison. It was inconceivable, he said, to imagine that Barack Obama and Hillary Clinton, being from the same party, would ever compete against each other. "They're both from the Democratic Party, so they made a decision based on who was capable of bringing the best result," he said, less than a week after the congress. "We made the same kind of decision." The fact that this ignored the heated Democratic primaries of 2008 only stoked the derision.[11]

Putin, having in his mind observed and respected the letter of Russia's Constitution, miscalculated the reaction to his return. He had grown increasingly isolated and detached from the popular sentiment he believed he understood intuitively. The successes he so often touted—stability and, despite the economic crisis, spreading affluence—were no longer sufficient to assuage a new generation that took them for granted. The chaos of the 1990s was a distant memory, and many of those who had benefited most from the Putin boom now expected a more modern, more open political culture as well. The Kremlin maintained its iron-clad grip on the television narrative, but the "videocracy" at the center of its mystique had grown stale, subject to the satire that has been a feature of Russian literature since Gogol. Opposition to the *rokirovka* churned in the arena still largely beyond the Kremlin's manipulations. Frustration and anger over Putin's return filled social media and online networks—Twitter, YouTube, Facebook and its Russian clone, VKontakte—and the animosity turned into an uprising, though for now a virtual one. The architects of the rebellion were disproportionately from the educated class, those with money and technical savvy, those who swam easily in the media that obliterated traditional borders of communication. They were called "Internet hamsters," and they produced a primal stream of denunciations and jeremiads, spoofs and mockery that freely ridiculed Putin, his antics, his evident cosmetic surgery, his humiliated sidekick, in ways that the official media had long ago stopped daring to do.

The discontent soon spread. When Putin appeared in the ring of an "ultimate fight" match at Olympic Stadium in Moscow in November, he was greeted by booing and whistling, though the Kremlin's supporters tried unconvincingly to suggest the audience's ire was directed at the loser of the bout, an American, or the long lines for the bathrooms. A heavily edited clip appeared on the evening news, with the booing muted, but the raw video spread online, picked up by Aleksei Navalny, who gleefully pronounced Putin's harsh reception from the fans as "the end of an era."[12] Putin had faced angry constituents before, but in this case, the booing came from a crowd that would presumably include his most ardent supporters. Putin's opponents took heart in the unseemly display, which challenged the myth that opposition to Putin existed only in the rarified elite, the intelligentsia, as they once were called, or the new generation who preferred a new adaptation from the West, *hipsteri*.

With the news of his return to the Kremlin, Putin's popularity actually slipped to the lowest levels since 2000. The party his strategists had constructed slipped even further, dismissed by its growing legion of critics as a badly reconstituted Communist Party of the Soviet Union—only more corrupt. By the time the parliamentary elections were held in December, it became clear that the foundation of Putin's power had fractured. The models that had worked since 2000 were no longer enough. The Kremlin's creation of a new pro-business "opposition" party called Right Cause, intended to inject a semblance of intrigue into the country's politics, became a farce when its recruited leader, the billionaire Mikhail Prokhorov, found his supporters barred from attending the party congress organized to nominate him. No one had given the party any chance of winning, but Medvedev had persuaded Prokhorov to take up politics, only to have the machinations of the Kremlin's political mastermind, Vladislav Surkov, shoulder him aside.[13] Prokhorov, a businessman who bought the New Jersey (later Brooklyn) Nets of the National Basketball Association in 2010, had naïvely assumed that he might exercise political independence. He claimed that Putin's power was not monolithic and that he had supporters inside its ranks, but his ouster made it clear they were losing out. "In Russia," he said, "all fights are on the inside."[14]

The parliamentary elections thus unfolded like those before, with the same stunted, state-sanctioned parties that had become grizzled fixtures of the political status quo. They became known as the "system opposition," nominally a check on power, but one wholly subservient to it: Zyuganov's Communists, Zhirinovsky's Liberal Democrats, and the rebranded version of the nationalists, now called Just Russia and led by Sergei Mironov, the Putin acolyte who had "challenged" him in the 2004. Other smaller parties that might have posed a challenge, like Yabloko or Boris Nemtsov's, were smothered by the electoral or legal bureaucracy, harassed or barred from registering at all. Even if they could have made it to the ballot, Putin's genuine opponents were so diverse and diffuse, so adrift after more than a decade on the political margins, that they failed to unite behind any one party or leader. Some had resigned themselves to boycott, but activists like Navalny urged them to vote anyway, for anyone but the "party of swindlers and thieves." The goal now was not to win; it was to expose elections in Russia for the Potemkin artifice they had become.

Putin remained defiant—to the point that he seemed oblivious to the dangerous discontent that seethed beneath Russia's chimera of progress and prosperity. "It's too early to organize my funeral," he told the Valdai gathering barely a week before the vote, brushing aside even the fawning or dutiful questions of those who attended.[15] The fate of United Russia was another matter. Its popularity had plummeted, and polls suggested that it would lose its constitutional majority; it might not even win a majority at all. All the bureaucrats and boyars who depended on Putin's system were increasingly haunted by the specter of the Orange Revolution, and now the Arab Spring, which had toppled strongman after strongman like dominoes. Suddenly, the armies of subversion seemed to be everywhere. Mubarak was in jail, Qaddafi was dead, and Assad was besieged by an armed rebellion that had fractured Syria along bloody fault lines. Putin would not be the next.

The Kremlin's anxiety manifested itself in heavy-handed efforts to ensure a high enough turnout and vote for United Russia. Even before election day, a voting-rights organization called Golos—the word for "vote," as well as "voice"—recorded thousands of violations of the country's election laws. Funded by foreign organizations supporting democracy, Golos annotated the violations on an online map that soon went viral, picked up by even relatively loyal newspapers and websites. Putin told steelworkers in Petersburg that election observers were the agents of foreign powers trying to destabilize the country. He even compared Golos to Judas. The group was promptly fined for violating the election law it was determined to enforce by publishing its map; its director was detained for hours at a Moscow airport the night before the election and released only after surrendering her laptop. The organization's website came under a computer attack that shut it down just as voting began. The same thing happened to other sites, including the popular and influential radio station Ekho Moskvy, which remained offline, almost certainly not coincidentally, until the polls closed.[16] The Kremlin, which had once acted as if the Internet were a harmless diversion of the spoiled elite, now moved decisively to curtail its influence.

Although all the previous elections of Putin's Russia had been marred by abuses and manipulation, the fraud that unfolded on December 4 was far more widespread and cynical. Despite the efforts of the authorities, the Internet now allowed evidence of violations to spread through the public consciousness. Official election observers could not be everywhere, but amateur videos taken with cell phones appeared online showing apparatchiks flagrantly stuffing ballot boxes, shepherding busloads of voters from polling station to polling station, even using invisible ink on ballots. In one video taken by a volunteer activist and promptly uploaded to YouTube, the elderly director of Polling Place No. 2501 in Moscow sat at a desk dutifully marking a stack of ballots. The international observers from the Organization for Security and Co-operation in Europe concluded that one in three polling stations experienced some sort of suspect activity—but that only counted the small percentage where observers were present.[17]

The flagrant disregard for electoral decency provoked outrage when unofficial results showed that United Russia had won just under 50 percent of the vote—enough, given the parties that did not make it to the threshold for winning seats, to allow it to retain a majority in the new Duma. It was clear that even that diminished result was a fraud, one that required the complicity of thousands upon thousands of people to carry out—from election officials like Vladimir Churov, a KGB colleague of Putin's from Petersburg, to state workers, forced by fear or favor to staff the polling stations, to the journalists of state media who struggled to report it all with straight faces. Even Putin, appearing to declare victory with Medvedev at United Russia's campaign headquarters, appeared less than exultant. The scale of the fraud at last was enough to stir thousands from the political apathy that had accompanied the rise of Putinism and the stultifying bureaucratic stagnation that it had produced.

On the night after the election, as the final and official results were announced, the small opposition party Solidarity held a rally at Chistye Prudy, near the center of Moscow. The party's periodic protests typically drew a few hundred people, who were always outnumbered by the police officers deployed to keep a close watch. This time, despite a cold rain, thousands showed up, drawn by appeals on the Internet. Speaker after speaker clutched a microphone and made demands and ultimatums. The people there were diverse, their ideas inchoate. Some of the old opposition leaders—the veterans of glasnost and the liberals of the Yeltsin years—were there, but others had never attended a protest before. The speaker who got the most attention was Aleksei Navalny, whose campaign against corruption arguably contributed most to this outburst of activism. He had an enormous following online, but now here he stood in the flesh, shouting into a microphone to a crowd that waved flags and handmade banners with slogans like "Putin—Thief" and the scarcely imaginable "Russia without Putin." "They can call us microbloggers or Internet hamsters," he roared. "I am an Internet hamster, and I'll be at the throats of those beasts!"[18]

Navalny and dozens of other protesters and protest organizers were arrested as they left the park to march toward the election commission's headquarters. He was jailed for fifteen days, charged with resisting arrest, and yet the protests continued. They even began to swell. The next Saturday tens of thousands showed up in Bolotnaya Square, across the river from the Kremlin. They proved undaunted by the arrests; undaunted by counterprotests that had been organized by the virulent youth group Nashi, which had been created after Ukraine's Orange Revolution for just this purpose; undaunted by veiled threats from the authorities, including a warning that young men of draft age would be picked up and inducted into the army. Two weeks later, on December 24, nearly a hundred thousand massed, this time on the avenue named after Andrei Sakharov, the nuclear physicist and Soviet dissident whose legacy of championing a democratic society had by then diminished significantly. Navalny was there this time; after his fifteen days in prison, he had emerged to a throng of supporters chanting his name on a dark, snowy evening. He said he had gone into prison in one country and come out into a new one. He turned his attention beyond the fraud in the parliamentary elections to the fraud in the presidential election scheduled for March 4. "What will happen on the fourth of March," he told them, "if it will happen, will be an illegal succession to the throne."[19]

The protests were the largest of the Putin era, the largest, in fact, since those in 1991 that had resisted the August putsch. They spread to other cities, attracting a broad spectrum of society: government workers, laborers, pensioners, students, the workers who filled the offices of new businesses that capitalism had brought. That the protests were peaceful made them even more terrifying to the Kremlin. Putin had said little at first, ignoring the allegations of fraud, but he greeted the prospect of a popular uprising with icy, sarcastic derision. Three days after the vote, speaking to organizers of his coming presidential campaign, he blamed the on-going protests on Secretary of State Hillary Rodham Clinton, who had criticized the conduct of the election. "She set the tone for some actors in our country and gave them a signal," he said. "They heard the signal and with the support of the State Department began active work." Even his use of the phrase "active work"—a term he had learned in the KGB—underscored his belief that the protests were neither indigenous nor spontaneous, but rather an intelligence operation. In his annual televised call-in show in December, he went further. He mocked the white ribbons that protesters had adopted as a symbol of their cause, saying they reminded him of condoms pinned to their coats. He compared the protesters to the Bandar-log, the wild monkeys of Rudyard Kipling's *The Jungle Book,* which had appeared as a Soviet television series when Putin was a teenager. You could not really reason with them, the monkeys, but they were afraid of the snake Kaa, who ultimately subdued them with his hypnotic power. "I've loved Kipling since I was a child," Putin said with an impish smile.

Despite his nonchalance, the vast bureaucracy beneath Putin seemed deeply shaken, and Putin's scorn seemed to embolden those protesting and attract even more. Protesters now showed up at rallies with condoms blown up like balloons, with stuffed animals and posters depicting monkeys and apes—and Putin as Kaa, strangling the nation. The government's outward unity began to show signs of the divisions inside. Medvedev first claimed that the viral videos of ballot stuffing were faked, but later he promised that the authorities would investigate any allegations. The speaker of the Duma, Boris Gryzlov, promised to allow members of opposition parties to serve as committee chairmen, hoping to temper the anger at United Russia's dominance. Then, under pressure, he resigned. The Kremlin demoted its "gray cardinal," Vladislav Surkov, the strategist who was credited—and reviled—for erecting the "managed democracy" that was the focus of the protesters' ire. Only days before, Surkov had said the protesters represented "the best part of our society, or, more accurately, the most productive part." Journalists at NTV, owned by Gazprom, refused to go on the air if the channel refused to cover the December 10 protest and, for the first time, the Kremlin's media masters relented, allowing the public display of dissent to appear on television channels broadcasting across the country (though without mentioning the anger directed toward Putin).[20] Members of the Putin elite—the academics, political strategists, bureaucrats, even the clerics of the Orthodox Church, who had always remained loyal—began to raise questions about the fraud, including Aleksei Kudrin, who spoke at the rally on December 24 and called on his former bosses to make the system more accountable.

Few, not even the protesters braving the cold, believed the protests would succeed in bringing about a new election or even a meaningful investigation of the fraud, and fewer still doubted that Putin would be reelected in March, but for the first time uncertainty haunted Putin's rule. The Russian stock market slumped after the election, and as in every crisis, capital flight accelerated. A fear crept into the elite, above all those most heavily invested in Putin's leadership. Vladimir Litvinenko, the rector of the Mining Institute in Petersburg where Putin had written his thesis, expressed the sentiments of many of them. He had remained close to his former student, and he had become a wealthy man, compensated, he claimed, for the consultation work he had done for the government with shares in PhosAgro, a company whose core asset had been seized from Mikhail Khodorkovsky's financial empire after his conviction. Only months before, the company had gone public on the London Stock Exchange. His fear now echoed Putin's of the past: the fear of the mob, the unruly hordes in the street, demanding respect and justice, the rabble toppling those in power and coating the street in blood. "I horribly fear the street," he said as the protests swelled. "This is an uprising. This is revolution, not evolution, with all the negative consequences of disorder on the street. This is the path to nowhere, I am certain. This is a catastrophe. We will do everything to prevent this in my country."[21]

PART FIVE

CHAPTER 22

The Restoration

On a cold gray morning in February 2012, less than two weeks before Putin's reelection, five young women appeared in the ornate, reconstructed church in Moscow that is, to believers, a landmark of the resurrection of the Orthodox faith after its repression by the Soviet state, the Cathedral of Christ the Savior. They mounted the elevated soleas in the front of the church's iconostasis and shed their winter coats to reveal colorful, sleeveless dresses and mismatched leggings. They pulled colorful balaclavas over their faces and began to dance and shout, their arms punching the air and their voices a discordant echo reverberating in the mostly empty church. One of them, Yekaterina Samutsevich, did not manage to slip the strap of her guitar over her shoulder before a guard ushered her off. The other four carried on, their words difficult to understand at times, though a few came through.

Virgin Mary, Mother of God, banish Putin!
Banish Putin!

The episode lasted less than a minute. The women, accompanied by a couple of men, hustled out of the church after being stopped by guards. By the end of the evening, a music video appeared online, spliced with material previously filmed in another church in Moscow, this time with lighting, sound, and a background that in the quick cuts could pass for Christ the Savior. It opened with a melodic hymnal chant, but then abruptly shifted to the grinding chords of the hardest punk, punctuated with vulgarities. The lyrics ridiculed the church and its priests as KGB collaborators, as mercantile and corrupted, repressive toward women, bigoted against gays and lesbians. The song was called "Punk Prayer," using a liturgical word for a special prayer service in times of national crisis, *moleben*.[1] It was the newest protest from a new amorphous guerrilla-art collective that—inspired by third-wave feminism, the Riot Grrrl movement in the United States, and Putin's return to the presidency—called itself Pussy Riot.

The women of Pussy Riot, roughly a dozen, though their membership and identities were kept secret, had created the group in the wake of Putin's announcement, joining the wave of dissent that spilled into the streets after the parliamentary election. The group included members of Voina, or War, an art collective that specialized in provocative, politically themed art performances. In one, they filmed five couples having sex in Moscow's museum of biology on the eve of Medvedev's election in 2008, mocking the government's appeals to increase birth rates to avert demographic collapse. In another, they painted a giant penis on a drawbridge in Petersburg, which, when raised, faced the Big House on Liteiny Prospekt, where Putin had once worked. Putin's imminent return to the Kremlin now focused the group's creative energy squarely on him.

Pussy Riot's first furtive performance in public occurred in October 2011, a month after the *rokirovka*. They filmed themselves at various locations inside Moscow's metro, at one point atop a workers' scaffold. Their faces covered with colorful balaclavas, they screamed as much as sang a song that alluded to the protests in Cairo that brought down Mubarak and called for the same in Red Square. In January, they performed in Red Square itself, atop the Lobnoye Mesto, a stone platform built in the sixteenth century and used to read out the tsars' decrees. This time, eight members of the group performed a song titled "Putin Pissed Himself," inspired by the government's palpable fear and confusion in the face of the protests. The song repeated Aleksei Navalny's exhortation from the night of the first protest, which they too had joined. "Riot in Russia," they sang, "we exist."

At first the authorities did not seem to be paying the group much attention. The performers were often detained and questioned, but they were careful to give false names and were usually let go after a few hours. Their videos, though, careered through the virtual world where Russia's protest movement now had the momentum. The group's protests and even its name—rendered in English because the equivalent expression in Russian would have sounded far more vulgar—perfectly suited the insurrectionary mood that had somehow survived the winter and carried on into the new year and the presidential election season. The Kremlin's foundations seemed to shudder in the face of it. Despite all expectation, there was a glimmer of hope that somehow the protests might forestall Putin's certain reelection in March.

He's a little less buoyant now," Henry Kissinger said not long after meeting Putin in Moscow in January 2012, as the protests continued.[2] The elder statesman of realpolitik had met regularly with Putin ever since he came to power. Putin admiringly recalled their first encounter when he picked Kissinger up from the airport in Petersburg in the 1990s and the older man flattered him by saying "all decent people get their start in intelligence." Putin considered Kissinger a trusted counselor, one who respected him and Russia's national interests, whatever the changing state of relations with the United States. Kissinger, the old Cold Warrior who had long advocated deeper cooperation with Russia, reciprocated the admiration. "Putin is not a Stalin who feels obliged to destroy anyone who might potentially at some future point disagree with him," he had once said. "Putin is somebody who wants to amass the power needed to accomplish his immediate task."[3] As Putin's reelection campaign began, the immediate task was to somehow contain the street protests. And Kissinger sensed that Putin's resolve—his usually steely assuredness—had waned at least a bit.

The Kremlin, still nominally headed by Dmitri Medvedev, initially offered concessions to defuse the protesters' anger. They included the restoration of the regional elections that Putin had abolished in 2004 and an easing of restrictions on forming new political parties, as well as securing a spot on the presidential ballot. Even the Orthodox Church called on the government to address the grievances of those in the streets. In an interview on state television on the Orthodox Christmas, January 7, the church's leader, Patriarch Kirill, said that a crackdown on the protesters would be as misguided as the repressions of the Soviet era. It was a startling statement from an institution that had allied itself so closely with the authorities.[4] Other church leaders began to echo similar sympathies, offering to mediate between the government and the protesters.

Then, abruptly, the church's tone shifted. Less than a month later, Putin convened the leaders of all the country's faiths—Orthodox, Jewish, Buddhist, Muslim, Roman Catholic, Armenian Catholic, even the Seventh-day Adventists, an evangelical faith that struggled without official recognition or support—at the Danilov Monastery in Moscow. Kirill, acting as host, now lavished praise on Putin, followed by the other clerics, rabbis, lamas, and muftis. Kirill recalled the hardships of the 1990s before Putin appeared on the scene, comparing the era to the Time of Troubles at the turn of the seventeenth century, and to Napoleon's invasion in 1812 and Hitler's in 1941. "What were the 2000s then?" he said. "Through a miracle of God, with the active participation of the country's leadership, we managed to exit this horrible, systemic crisis." He then spoke directly to Putin to thank him for the "massive role" he played in correcting "this crooked twist of our history."[5]

The church's support for Putin, an ostentatious if not deeply devout believer, was not surprising, but in a secular nation with a constitution that formally separated church and state, the choreographed display of fealty to Putin at the height of a turbulent election season provoked out-rage, including Pussy Riot's protest at Christ the Savior. Rumors swirled that the Kremlin had pressured the patriarch and the others to appear with Putin. Articles soon appeared in the opposition press recycling old rumors of Kirill's KGB affiliations, his commercial ventures importing tobacco in the 1990s, and his taste for finer luxuries, including a large dacha, a private yacht, and expensive watches. (He denied owning the latter until the unartful airbrushing of an official photograph left the reflection of a fancy watch on a glossy tabletop.) The church, once heav-ily repressed, had emerged from the Soviet collapse as one of the most respected institutions in the country, viewed by many of its adherents as an institution above the country's politics. Now Kirill led the faithful directly into an alliance with the state; just a month after expressing sym-pathy for the protesters, he now complained that their demands were the "ear-piercing shrieks" of those who valued a Western consumer culture incompatible with Russia's traditions.

Kirill's reversal was striking and to critics infuriating, but it reflected the emergence of a central narrative for Putin's return. It was a narrative rooted not in nostalgia for Soviet times but for the more distant tsarist past, one articulated in the writings of, among others, Ivan Ilyin, the political philosopher Putin had been citing in his speeches since 2005. In the face of mass unrest, Putin portrayed himself not just as the guar-antor of the gains achieved since the Soviet era, but also as the leader of the nation in a deeper way. He was the protector of its social and cultural values. In a series of seven campaign declarations reprinted in leading newspapers, he outlined a new starkly conservative vision of the country that referred to Russia's "civilizational model," one diametrically opposed to the decadent values of the West, represented in large part by those now protesting his rule on the streets. He had chosen a counter-attack, and it was strikingly effective.

At the height of the protests in December and January, opinion polls suggested that he might not win half the votes, which would force a runoff, but by February, his ratings began to climb again. The Kremlin's media apparatus remained at his service, portraying him as the steady master of a state under siege. His opponents were too feeble or too extreme, aided by the saboteurs within and their masters abroad, bent on destroying the nation. The arrival of a new American ambassador, Michael McFaul, and an ill-timed meeting with opposition leaders on his second day in the embassy became fodder for state television, which portrayed the protests as an alien incursion. The opposition wanted confrontation, Putin would say at the end of the month, even to the point of committing murder. "I know this," he said, alluding to the defense that had first circulated after the deaths of Anna Politkovskaya and Aleksandr Litvinenko, and using the language he had once used against the rebels in Chechnya. "They are even looking for a sacred victim, someone famous. They will waste him, if you will pardon the expression, and then blame the government."[6] The day before, the state television network Channel One had disclosed weeks-old arrests of two suspects in Ukraine who had allegedly been plotting to assassinate Putin, or perhaps other senior officials, by bombing their motorcades in Moscow. As the election approached, the choice facing Russians seemed stark and existential, as it was meant to: Putin or the abyss.

As in his previous elections Putin did not campaign directly, but his official duties increasingly had overtly military themes. In January, on the anniversary of the lifting of the siege of Leningrad, he visited the cemetery where a research organization had established that his brother, Viktor, was buried during the war. Days later he visited the scientists at the Sarov center (where the world's polonium-210 is made) and vowed to equip ten new regiments with new missiles capable of striking deep inside Europe. In February, he held his only public rally at Luzhniki on the old Red Army holiday, now rebranded as the Defenders of the Fatherland Day. The state channels reported that 130,000 attended, though the stadium's capacity was only 80,000, and many of those in attendance were government employees, some bused in from distant cities. All that mattered was the panorama shown over and over on the nation's television screens. Putin strode to the blue-carpeted platform at a midfield, wearing a black parka to ward off a light snow and clutching a microphone. Alone at the center of a sea of flags and banners, he began awkwardly. "Do we love Russia?" he shouted. As he lurched around the stage, a rage seemed to well up within him. He implored the audience "not to look overseas, not to run to the left or to the side, and not to betray your homeland, but to be with us, work for Russia and love her as we do—with our whole hearts." As Kirill had in their meeting, he invoked the Battle of Borodino that had defeated Napoleon on the outskirts of Moscow. He was appealing to the country's hallowed tradition of resistance to foreign invasion. He even quoted the famous poem of Mikhail Lermontov published on the twenty-fifth anniversary of Borodino, in which a colonel calls on his men to make the ultimate sacrifice to defend the Fatherland.

> *"Guys, is Moscow not for us?*
> *Then we shall die near Moscow*
> *As our brothers died"*
> *And we promised to die*

Two centuries later, the battle for Russia continued, Putin thundered in conclusion, his taut face wrenched into a grimace, but victory is "in our *genes.*"

By the night of March 4, Putin's victory had been secured, as almost everyone expected. He won 63 percent of the vote in the first round, less than in his or Medvedev's previous elections, but still a solid majority. Zyuganov, in his fourth run, finished a distant second, as usual, with 17 percent. To defuse the accusations that marred the parliamentary elections, Putin ordered cameras installed in nearly every polling station in the country, but evidence of fraud, including carousel voting and ballot stuffing, nonetheless cast doubt on the tally. By some estimates, millions of votes padded Putin's total, though even his harshest critics had to acknowledge that he had the support of most Russians. Putin won every region of the country except Moscow, the epicenter of the disgruntled elite, where he still won 47 percent. In his native Petersburg, where an outburst of political activism had also spread after the December voting, he drew 59 percent. Putin declared victory in a brief speech in Manezh Square with the towers of the Kremlin as a television-perfect backdrop. A large crowd gathered before a small platform. Many were from outside Moscow, as at his only campaign rally, bused into the heavily secured zone where Putin would appear. These were Putin's people, not the trendy *hipsteri,* the intellectuals and radicals, the "rootless cosmopolitans" who would drag Russia away from its historic roots and traditions. "We have demonstrated that our people are able to tell one thing from another," Putin said that night after Medvedev introduced him, "the genuine desire to achieve modernity despite the political provocations that have only one goal: to destroy Russia as a nation and usurp power." As he spoke, tears streamed down his face, the first he had shed in public since Anatoly Sobchak's funeral twelve years before. It appeared to be a genuine display of emotion, but the Kremlin later insisted it was just the bitter wind.

The election left Putin's opponents dispirited and disoriented. The celebratory mood of the first large protests faded into despair. The protesters were united by a cause, or a variety of them, but not by any strategy for achieving their goals. It became clear that nothing had changed, and perhaps nothing ever would. Except in the most abstract notions of a pluralistic, democratic society, who would step in if there were a "Russia without Putin"? A protest was planned for Pushkin Square the next evening, less than a mile from the Kremlin, but what now was the point? Instead of the masses who had surged to earlier protests, this time perhaps twenty thousand attended.

"We overestimated our force," Navalny said that night. By the end of the allotted two hours for protest, enough in the authorities' view to release some of the steam, fewer than two thousand remained in the square where they had gathered. They seemed uncertain whether to heed the calls by Navalny and a more aggressive opposition leader, Sergei Udaltsov, to remain in the streets, even to set up a tent camp the way the Ukrainians had in Kyiv in 2004, or the protesters in Cairo had the year before. Instead, the riot police swept through, swinging their truncheons. More than 250 people were arrested, dozens were injured. The streets of Moscow stayed clear.

Protests continued in the weeks and months ahead, but with each one the momentum dwindled. Many Russians wanted to end a system that had become so deeply cynical and corrupt, but only a very few, even among Putin's most ardent critics, wanted a revolution, which was what it would take to force a change. At the height of those protests, one of the Kremlin's political strategists, Sergei Markov, had compared the protesters to spoiled children demanding a toy, the Kremlin to a frustrated but firm parent. "It is not correct to go out and buy the child a toy," he said, "but rather to distract him with something else."[7]

Back in February, when she arrived at Christ the Savior Cathedral for Pussy Riot's performance, the guitarist Yekaterina Samustevich sensed that something had gone wrong with their clandestine plan. Men with video cameras were already in the church. The guards reacted so quickly that it seemed they had been expecting their arrival. Yekaterina—Katya, to her friends—suspected there had been a leak from one of the cameramen they brought along to record their performance. Or perhaps the FSB had begun monitoring them as their videos went viral through the protest movement. When they left the church, there were also journalists waiting for them outside.[8] She was never certain, but perhaps it was a setup all along. Either way it was clear that the authorities had taken an interest in their stunts and wanted to put an end to them.

The day after the video circulated, the church's spokesman, Archpriest Vsevelod Chaplin, denounced it as a mortal sin, a crime against God. Prosecutors promptly announced that they had opened an investigation, and it was only a matter of time before the full force of the state came down on Pussy Riot. On the day before Putin's reelection, the police arrested three women and a man; the following day, two more women were arrested. The police, still unsure of the group's identities, released four of them, but they had found two of the members who had been in the cathedral that day in February: Nadezhda Tolokonnikova and Maria Alyokhina. Katya was arrested two weeks later, on March 16. They were charged not with hooliganism, a petty violation that would normally not warrant more than a fine, but with hooliganism carried out by an organized group motivated by religious hatred, an ominous sign of the intent to make an example of their actions. The indictment that followed accused them of undermining "the spiritual foundations" not just of the church, but also "of the state." Conviction could mean as many as seven years in prison. The members of Pussy Riot had wanted to call attention to the communion of church and state, and they were about to learn how right they had been. All three were held without bail despite the fact that Nadezhda and Maria were both mothers of young children.

The arrests, and the gravity of the charges, provoked new outrage, now infused with dismay over the inability of the protests to do more than tarnish Putin's easy electoral victory. The three women became international celebrities, admired for their defiance of an authoritarian regime. Amnesty International declared them prisoners of conscience, while prominent musicians—Faith No More, Madonna, Pete Towns-hend, Paul McCartney—championed their cause. In Russia, however, their fate proved to be far more complicated: their protest divided the already fractured opposition and, with the Kremlin's gleeful connivance, did as much to discredit it in the eyes of the broader public as anything else. Aleksei Navalny, viewed warily by liberals for some of his national-istic views, denounced their detention but called their stunt idiotic. "I would not like it, to put it mildly, if at the moment I was in church some crazy girls ran in and began to run around the altar," he wrote on his blog.[9] Instead of provoking a debate over politics, as they had intended, the case fueled the culture war within society in a way that ultimately favored Putin. The church remained one of the most respected institu-tions in Russia, on a par with the presidency itself. More than 70 percent of Russians identified themselves as Orthodox, even if many wore their faith lightly, rarely practicing or attending church.

The "Punk Prayer" backfired. It rallied the faithful to the defense of the church, despite the scandals over its corruption and mercantile behavior. To believe was to be patriotic. To be patriotic was to believe. In April, on the Sunday after Easter, tens of thousands heeded a call by the patriarch for a special demonstration at Christ the Savior. The crowd swelled to sixty-five thousand, according to the official estimates. Even if those numbers were inflated, the demonstration was larger than any of the protests that continued to sputter on after Putin's election victory. Kirill emerged from the church that day in a procession of bishops and priests carrying icons that had been desecrated in Soviet times, including one with bullet holes dating to the 1920s. The "attack of persecutors" against the faith today could not be compared to Soviet repression, he said, but the liberalism of the West was a threat because it regarded "the very fact of blasphemy and sacrilege, of the mockery of shrines," as "the lawful manifestation of human freedom, as something that should be defended in modern society." He never mentioned Pussy Riot, but they had been turned into the symbol of a contagion seeping through the borders of Russia. As for the priests who called for forgive-ness for the three in prison, and they were some, citing the mercy of Jesus, Kirill called them "traitors in cassocks."[10]

On the eve of Putin's inauguration on May 7, the protest leaders planned one more rally, this one authorized to take place in Bolotnaya Square, across the river from the Kremlin where Medvedev would relinquish the reins of power that were never fully his own. The weather was warm with the onset of spring, which almost certainly swelled the crowds, as had the prosecution of Pussy Riot. So many people thronged the square that the phalanxes of police officers abruptly blocked the entrance, creating a scrum of protesters jammed on the streets. Those outside the blocked perimeter staged a sit-in; someone even pitched a tent, an ominous sign for the police, who had orders not to allow the kind of encampment seen in the Orange Revolution. For a time, the protest remained peaceful, but when the police began picking off protesters for arrest, it turned into a melee. The crowds began surging to the defense of those arrested, and the police responded by swinging truncheons; some in the crowd responded by throwing chunks of asphalt. Boris Nemstov was shouting, "Russia will be free," from atop a riser when officers led him away. When Navalny was arrested near the stage, he scolded the officer, his invective recorded by a microphone he was wearing for a documentary about the anti-Putin movement. "I will jail you later," he said, spitting out the names of Putin and his business cronies, Arkady Rotenberg and Gennady Timchenko. He vowed they would be on the wanted list when he came to power.[11] By evening, the protest had ended with more than four hundred arrests. Dozens were injured, including twenty-nine police officers. They were dutifully interviewed on state television lying on hospital gurneys, scenes that many believed had been staged. Putin's usually affable press secretary, Dmitri Peskov, a man known to channel his boss's sentiments, expressed disappointment that the police had acted with such restraint. "I would have liked them to act more harshly," he said.[12]

The crackdown continued the next day, even though the streets of central Moscow had been cleared of traffic for the inauguration ceremony. Police officers roaming the capital arrested dozens more, many for no apparent reason other than that they were wearing a white ribbon. A squadron of interior troops even raided what had become known as an unofficial headquarters of the opposition movement. It was a French restaurant, called Jean-Jacques, the sort of place that had sprung up in Moscow during the years of economic boom and made it seem more like a modern, vibrant European capital, full of young, creative Muscovites ordering foreign beers and wines off chalkboard menus. By the end of the day, more than seven hundred people were detained around Moscow. Scores of young men who haunted places like Jean-Jacques were taken to draft offices for induction into the army, just as they had been warned when the protests first started. "I think this is to show who is boss," said Oleg Orlov of Memorial, the human rights organization. "A new tsar has come."[13]

Putin's inauguration unfolded at midday with the pomp of the others, broadcast to the nation solemnly and ceremoniously, just as before. Only this time the cameras met Putin at the office of the prime minister in the White House, followed him down the carpeted stairs of the main entrance to a waiting Mercedes-Benz. For six minutes, an aerial camera followed the procession of police motorcycles escorting Putin's car and two others as it made its way to the Kremlin, where Medvedev waited, having already saluted the honor guard. The motorcade passed through streets that had been emptied not only of traffic but, eerily, of people, too. No one watched. No one waved or cheered that sunny morning. No one even dared be outside.

In 2000, Putin had taken his first oath of office against a backdrop of economic and political uncertainty and war in Chechnya. His second inauguration, more subdued, took place in the shadow of that war, amid the tightening of political freedoms and the dismantling of Yukos, but also in the midst of an economic revival that had trickled down to more Russians than at any time in the country's history. Medvedev took the oath in 2008 at a time of hope that Russia had overcome its turbulent history and would pass power to a new generation of leaders, soon perhaps to leaders who knew only modern Russia, not the Soviet Union. Now Putin returned to take the oath a third time, pledging to faithfully serve and protect the country for six more years. But he and the country had changed. He had returned to power by dividing the nation, by stoking fear of the enemies within that wanted to seize power and reverse all that had been accomplished since he first swore the oath. He had returned to power because he made himself the only real choice at the ballot. He no longer seemed to be president for all Russia but only for the Putin majority. For the opposition, it was a bitter pill to swallow.

He retraced the long walk through the Grand Kremlin Palace he had taken twelve years before. The defeated candidates were there, though not in the front. So were Mikhail Gorbachev and foreign leaders, like Silvio Berlusconi, a friend now, whose three terms as prime minister of Italy nearly matched his longevity, but whose political life had come to an end amid a swirl of inquiries into his finances and sex life. Medvedev spoke first, briefly, saying continuity was essential to Russia's future and, characteristically, as Yeltsin had but Putin had not, acknowledging the shortcomings of his presidency. "We did not succeed in doing everything we hoped and did not manage to complete everything we planned," he said. Putin appeared grave and unflappable. He was older, his face tightened by cosmetic surgery, his thinning hair having receded further, but at fifty-nine, he remained fit and lithe. "I see the whole sense and purpose of my life as being to serve our country and serve our people, whose support gives me the inspiration and help I need," he began. He said the coming years would be crucial in shaping the country Russia would become, a Russia that had, he said, restored its "dignity as a great nation" and would be the center of gravity for all of Eurasia. "The world has seen a Russia arisen anew."

After his brief remarks, he left the dais alone, striding directly past Lyudmila, who stood beside Medvedev's wife and Patriarch Kirill during the ceremony. She appeared pained at moments. Her disappearance from public life had become the source of speculation, sympathy, and ridicule. Putin stopped two paces beyond her, then turned around and returned to her. He leaned over a red rope and brushed her cheek with a kiss, and then departed.

If there was any expectation that Putin's third term would herald a softer, less authoritarian approach, it dissipated almost immediately. The authorities launched a sweeping investigation of the melee at Bolotnaya, which officials were now describing as a mass riot and even an attempted coup. Criminal charges were brought against twenty-seven people—not the leaders of the protest movement, not radicals, but ordinary people who had joined the protest in the heady desire to have their voices heard. They included students, a freelance journalist, a sales manager, an artist, a subway worker, and the press aide of one of the few opposition lawmakers in the Duma. One wanted activist, Leonid Razvozzhayev, fled to Ukraine but was arrested there by masked agents and returned to Moscow, where he claimed he had been kidnapped and tortured.[14] The defendants faced years in prison, often based on flimsy evidence from videos and the testimony of injured and aggrieved riot police officers. There were no mass arrests after Putin's inauguration, no Great Terror against dissidents, but rather a steady, selective accretion of prosecutorial pressure against those who stood against him. The authorities used the Bolotnaya investigation as a pretext to carry out investigations across the country for years to come, even in cases that had little connection to the melee that day, including one in 2013 against two human rights activists in Orel, hundreds of miles from Moscow.[15]

When opposition leaders planned a new rally for June 12, the holiday that marks Russia's declaration of independence from the Soviet Union in 1990, teams of police investigators swept through Moscow, raiding the apartments of the most prominent leaders of the opposition, including Aleksei Navalny, Boris Nemtsov, Ilya Yasin, and Ksenia Sobchak, the television star, socialite, and daughter of Putin's political mentor, a man once heralded as a symbol of Russia's fledgling democracy. Her role in the protests—which were viewed with skepticism by some because of her celebrity, her wealth, and her family connections to the man at the top—underscored the depth of the opposition Putin had faced in certain quarters upon his return to the Kremlin. "I never thought I would say this," a rattled Ksenia Sobchack told a television station after the search of her apartment, "but how good that my father wasn't here to see this."[16]

All of the protest leaders were summoned for questioning the next day, despite the holiday, to prevent them from attending the rally. Navalny encouraged the protest virtually, posting sarcastic messages on Twitter even as he was awaiting interrogation. More than fifty thousand people showed up, emboldened by the searches and arrests, and the speakers vowed to sustain the momentum. The pressure only intensified, though, and the harassment of the movement's most prominent figures—especially a celebrity like Sobchack—sent a message that not even personal connections to Putin would provide protection for anyone who rose up against him.

It was as if a signal had filtered through the ranks of the bureaucracy. The police, prosecutors, and the new deputies of the Duma and Federation Council, all now had license to staunch the contagion challenging Putin by any means. Within weeks of his inauguration, the Duma swiftly passed a law increasing fines for attending unauthorized protests from 5,000 rubles to 300,000 rubles, nearly $10,000 at the time and many times the average monthly salary. The city of Moscow prohibited the display of white ribbons on cars. The Duma passed one law giving the authorities the power to shut down websites, ostensibly for publishing information unsuitable for children, and another prohibiting the dissemination of "homosexual propaganda." In July, a new law required organizations that received foreign funding to register as "foreign agents"—a phrase with haunting echoes of Soviet-era persecutions—and another allowing a maximum prison sentence of twenty years for anyone "providing consultative assistance to a foreign organization" deemed to be acting against the state. Questioned by his own commission on human rights about the harshness and broad scope of the legislation, Putin said he would review it personally. He then signed it into law the very same day. It targeted not just overtly political groups, like Golos, but also others like the Environment Watch of the North Caucasus, which was trying to monitor the environmental damage caused by the Olympic construction in Sochi. In October, the Duma expanded the definition of treason so broadly that someone who unwillingly passed "state secrets" to a foreign state or international organization, even information that was available to the public, could be charged as a traitor.

There was no longer even the carefully choreographed illusion of considered debate, as the Duma and Federation Council spit out new laws one after another. Slander, which Medvedev had decriminalized, became a crime again, while penalties for it and for libel, especially against government officials, increased. Also criminalized were blasphemy and "offending religious feelings," inspired by the women of Pussy Riot. Those who dissented faced retribution. One Duma deputy who had dared to join the protesters was stripped of his immunity and his mandate. Ksenia Sobchak's mother, Lyudmila Narusova, was expelled from the seat she had held in the Federation Council for a decade, despite her relationship to Putin.

The flurry of legislating blended the harsh measures of an authoritarian crackdown with patriotic and religious appeals. The result was a potent brew, a cultural war born at the heart of Putin's new presidency. The trial of Pussy Riot was the first major battle. It opened on July 30, the day that Putin signed into law the legislation on libel and Internet restrictions. In their opening statements, delivered in a glass enclosure surrounded by guards and a snarling dog, the three young women apologized for causing offense but insisted theirs was not an expression of religious animosity. Rather it was a political protest protected by the freedom of speech. It was the core of a defense that no one expected to prevail. The trial was marred by judicial irregularities and the strenuous efforts of prosecuting lawyers to demonstrate the "moral damage" the brief performance inflicted, even on witnesses who had not been there but had only seen the video. One of the defense lawyers, Violetta Volkova, complained that the defendants had not been allowed to review the evidence against them, since it included hundreds of hours of videos they were not allowed to watch in their detention center. She added that documents for the prosecution had been forged; that she and her colleagues were not once allowed to meet confidentially with their clients; that the defense's expert witnesses had been barred from testifying; that the court simply ignored the defense's objections. "There's a sense right now that we're not in twenty-first century Russia, but in some alternative universe in a fairy tale like *Alice in Wonderland,* like *Alice Through the Looking-Glass,*" Volkova said, belittling the prosecution's claim that a few seconds of protest could shatter the foundations of a church with a millennium of history, "and right now this whole ludicrous reality will disappear and crumble like a house of cards."[17]

Theirs was a show trial that echoed those of Stalin's era or Brezhnev's, this time with each twist and statement chronicled on air or in print on the Internet. Although prosecutors did their best to portray the three women as ill-educated deviants, they appeared poised and courageous, well versed in history and religious thought. In their closing statements, they cited the intellectual and moral rebellions of thinkers from Socrates to Jesus, from Dostoyevsky (who once faced a mock execution) to Solzhenitsyn. In her closing statement, Maria Alyokhina compared prison to "Russia in miniature," where the people had lost the sense of themselves as anything other than hapless victims at the mercy of the prison's administration.

The trial intensified international outrage over the broader authoritarian turn that Putin had taken, and it dogged him whenever he traveled overseas. He made his first public remarks on the case as he visited London during the 2012 Summer Olympics, the last games to be held before those in Sochi. Putin claimed he had not raised the issue with the British prime minister, David Cameron, though the prime minister's aides said they had in fact discussed it. Putin's misstatements, his disregard for facts, were becoming harder to ignore.

"You know, there is nothing good about it," he said, when asked about the trial. "I do not really want to comment. But I think that if these young ladies went to, say, Israel and desecrated something there (many of you probably know that there are some very strong young men there), they would hardly be able to leave that easy." If they had done the performance in a mosque in the Northern Caucasus, he said, the police would not have arrested them in time to save them from a crueler fate. Magnanimously, he expressed hope that they would not be judged "too harshly," though the question of judgment was never really in doubt.

On August 17, to no one's surprise, the three were convicted, the judge having dismissed the defense that theirs had been a political protest against the state's leaders. The prosecutors had asked for three years, but almost certainly Putin's comments influenced the judge's decision to sentence them to only two years. Hundreds of the group's supporters had gathered outside the courthouse, while others swept through Moscow placing colorful balaclavas on statues. The police were prepared and unforgiving. Even before the verdict was read, Garry Kasparov was carried off from an impromptu press conference on the courthouse steps and beaten as the police forced him into van. Once news of the verdict spread, clashes erupted around the courthouse, with the police arresting dozens. It all played out on state television, fueling the anti-Western sentiment that had become a staple of the Kremlin's counterattack. In her final statement to the court, Nadezhda had bravely cited Solzhenitsyn's paean to the power of the word in his novel *The First Circle*. "Just like Solzhenitsyn, I believe the word will break through cement," she said. Pussy Riot's case instead had divided and deflated the opposition. The heady enthusiasm of the protests had now been thoroughly stifled, driven back underground or abroad. Pussy Riot became international stars but the movement that spawned them suffered. The two other performers who had been at the cathedral, identified only as Balaclava and Serafima, fled the country after the verdict.

In October, the three women appealed their sentences. Even Dmitri Medvedev, now installed as prime minister, said that while he was sickened by their protest, he believed their continued incarceration was unproductive and unnecessary. They had already been in detention for seven months by then anyway. Katya had hired a new lawyer, and rather than trying to justify the protest, she argued that her conviction should be reversed because she had not had time to even play the guitar before she was hustled off the soleas. Lawyers for the other two argued that comments by Putin and Medvedev had prejudiced the trial, thus justifying a dismissal or retrial. The judge accepted Katya's argument, releasing her on a suspended sentence, while dismissing the appeals of Nadezhda and Maria. Some suspected that Katya had made a separate deal, or perhaps that the Kremlin wanted to show that the judiciary was in fact free to deliberate fairly. Very few believed that Katya had won her appeal on its merits.

After her release, Katya retreated from public view. She still met the remaining members of Pussy Riot in Moscow, but they no longer performed. She was certain they remained under surveillance. In a vegetarian café in Moscow after her release, she explained that the meaning of their performances had been badly distorted for the Kremlin's political ends, but she also acknowledged that the broader public had not been receptive to the message.[18] The Russian people were not prepared to challenge the system that had slowly taken hold of society. Putin himself was not the villain in the prosecution against them, she believed. He simply represented the face of a conservative and deeply patriarchal society. The villain was the numbing conformity of a system, in culture and in politics, that made any deviation of thought too risky to contemplate. "The problem was not that everyone thought that we were innocent, that the charges brought against us were illegal, that Putin alone was bad, making phone calls and issuing demands in the case," Katya explained. "The problem was that *everyone* thought we were guilty."

CHAPTER 23

Alone on Olympus

Putin turned sixty in October 2012, reaching the official retirement age for Russian men. The limit had no bearing on the president or others holding high offices, but as president, Dmitri Medvedev had made a point of lowering the retirement age from sixty-five. The idea was to "rejuvenate" the ranks of the bulging bureaucracy by making room for younger people to rise up. With his birthday approaching—and with some of his closest allies in government already having passed the milestone—Putin now raised the retirement age to seventy. It seemed a minor adjustment, yet it was part of a pattern to reverse, step by step, whatever legacy Medvedev's presidency had left. In addition to the retirement age and the decriminalization of slander, Putin restored the two time zones that Medvedev had eliminated, and reversed his unpopular decision to stop changing the clocks twice a year. Medvedev's political reforms, announced as a concession amid the protests in the winter of 2011–2012 and signed into law as one of his last acts as president, were now diluted so that elections for regional leaders would only involve candidates screened by the Kremlin.

Although Medvedev remained prime minister and the leader of United Russia, the Kremlin seemed intent to airbrush him out of the pantheon of the country's leaders, as if Putin's presidency had never been interrupted. The Kremlin went so far as to belittle Medvedev's accomplishments, revising history in a Soviet style to emphasize Putin's ultimate responsibility for them. In August, on the fourth anniversary of the war in Georgia, a mysterious forty-seven-minute documentary appeared on YouTube and began to circulate widely. It was called "Lost Day," and, quoting senior military commanders, it claimed that Medvedev's indecisiveness in the opening hours of the war had resulted in higher casualties among the Ossetian and Russian forces. This was black PR, a stealthy technique Russian media strategists had wielded to chilling effect against political opponents and business rivals; only now it was turned on Putin's long-serving protégé. The film's details were contradictory, blatantly false in places, simply muddled in others. The film's core assertion, set to eerie music, was that Medvedev caused the deaths of a thousand people, even though the death toll from all sides in the war was 884. The harshest criticism in the film came from General Yuri Baluyevsky, who, though he stepped down two months before the war began, claimed that the Georgians had launched their attack in South Ossetia hours before they actually had and that Medvedev had acted only when Putin personally intervened from the Summer Olympics in Beijing. "Until there was a kick in the backside—first from Beijing, then a kick personally from, as you say, directly, Vladimir Vladimirovich—everyone, to put it mildly, was afraid of something," the general said.

The source of the film never became clear, and no one claimed credit; in black PR, anonymity reigns. It was posted on a YouTube account belonging to someone named Aslan Gudiev, and credited to a production company called Alfa, though no studio by that name existed in Russia. The Russian edition of *Forbes* linked the film to a television channel belonging to the National Media Group, partially owned and controlled by Bank Rossiya and its principal shareholder, Putin's old friend Yuri Kovalchuk.[1] As it began to circulate, a reporter in the Kremlin press pool queried Putin, who went on to embrace much of what the film asserted, including the claim that he had called Medvedev twice from Beijing, thus directly contradicting the narrative his protégé put forth. Given the Kremlin's tight control of questions from the press pool, the fact the question was even asked, by a reporter from the state news agency RIA Novosti, suggested that Putin wanted to draw attention to the film. He could easily have repudiated its worst insinuation about his old aide, his friend and protégé, but he did not.

The infighting among the courtiers that preceded Putin's return to the presidency intensified after Medvedev pressed ahead with plans to privatize the state's shares in hundreds of companies, but found he had no more independent power to act than he did the previous four years. His rivals in Putin's court remained Sergei Ivanov, who was now the Kremlin's chief of staff, and Igor Sechin and the other *siloviki*, whose financial interests in the state enterprises had become even more pronounced. Medvedev had already declared that he would not rule out a run for the presidency again in 2018, a position that was said to anger others in the Kremlin, many of whom held him responsible for the protests that marred Putin's return. Only months into his term as prime minister, the film and the rollback of several of his initiatives eroded what little political standing Medvedev had. His prized project to build a Silicon Valley on the edge of Moscow suddenly faced criminal investigations on grounds that its executives had channeled money to the protest movement. Criticism of Medvedev's work as prime minister began filtering even into the Kremlin-friendly media, while Putin himself harshly criticized the government's budget and its slow pace at instituting the ambitious and exceedingly detailed—and, some said, largely symbolic—targets he decreed at the beginning of his new term to improve housing, early childhood education, scientific research, and life expectancy.

The denigration of Medvedev's legacy extended to foreign affairs as well. Within days of his inauguration Putin signaled that the "reset" championed by the Obama administration had ended. He brusquely informed the White House that he would not attend the G8 summit that would be held near Washington later that month, a rebuff not just to the United States but also to the leaders of the other nations he had once courted. He sent Medvedev instead on the pretext that he would be too busy forming the new government. No one in the White House welcomed Putin's return to the Kremlin, but Obama had sent his national security adviser, Thomas Donilon, to Moscow after his election in hopes of securing Russia's support for continued reductions in nuclear weapons and for resolving the horrific civil war that had consumed Syria. In March, Obama, facing his own reelection campaign, had tried to reassure Medvedev that he and Putin could make progress overcoming Russia's opposition to missile defenses in Europe, but he needed to wait till after the election. Their exchange, at a meeting of world leaders on nuclear security, was inadvertently picked up on an open microphone.

"On all these issues, but particularly missile defense, this can be solved, but it's important for him to give me space," Obama told Medvedev.[2]

"Yeah, I understand," Medvedev replied. "I understand your message about space. Space for you . . ."

"This is my last election," Obama explained. "After my election I have more flexibility."

"I understand. I will transmit this information to Vladimir."

Obama's gaffe prompted his Republican challenger, Mitt Romney, to declare that Russia was "our No. 1 geopolitical foe"—worse than a nuclear-armed North Korea or an aspiring nuclear power in Iran because of the protection it provided to "the world's worst actors" through its veto at the United Nations Security Council. Obama misunderstood that while he might have more flexibility after his reelection, Putin would now be more inflexible than ever. By June, when Obama met Putin on the Baja California coast for the G20 summit, neither made much effort to conceal his disdain for the other. Putin kept Obama waiting for more than half an hour, and when the two emerged from their meeting, they did not smile or even speak to each other; both stared at the floor as they answered journalists' questions. They also made no progress on any of the difficult issues dividing them, especially the worsening conflict in Syria. Obama's aides had drafted a plan to negotiate the exile of Syria's president, Bashar al-Assad, but it was based on the assumption that Assad would step down—and that Putin would persuade him to do so. Mindful of Medvedev's "capitulation" on Libya at the United Nations in 2011, Putin made it clear that he would not allow the United States to lead another foreign intervention to topple a sovereign leader, no matter how many lives would be lost in an increasingly brutal conflict. Assad's government remained one of Russia's last allies in the Middle East, a major weapons purchaser and the host of a Russian naval base on the Mediterranean at Tartus, but Putin's primary concern was to prevent the United States from in his view unleashing the forces of radicalism once again. Some officials in Washington and other capitals played down the anti-Americanism of Putin's political campaign as a cynical appeal to patriotic resistance against Russia's external enemies, but they misjudged how deeply it now shaped Putin's thinking. The palpable international disappointment that greeted his return to the presidency, the consternation over the harsh crackdown on the protests, the denunciations of the trials of Pussy Riot and the Bolotnaya protesters—all served to harden Putin's view that the West was inimically opposed to him and his interests, and therefore inimically opposed to Russia itself.

Putin's language now echoed the worst periods of the Cold War, endorsed and amplified by the circle of strongmen who dominated his cabinet, pushing to the margins the more moderate voices who had gathered around Medvedev. The restoration of "foreign agents" as an appellation suggested that the Kremlin now viewed human rights advocacy or efforts like Navalny's to enforce government accountability as a crime

against state sovereignty. Navalny, after all, had participated at a graduate leadership fellowship at Yale University. That alone was grounds for
suspicion now.

In the summer of 2012, prosecutors had reopened a criminal investigation against Navalny, accusing him of "embezzling" $500,000 worth
of timber in the Kirov region while acting as an unpaid consultant to
the region's government. It came a week after he had published evidence
suggesting that the head of the investigative committee, Aleksandr Bastrykin, owned a business and apartment in the Czech Republic. Soon the
investigations expanded to other deals in which Navalny was involved,
forcing him to spend more of his time and energies defending himself
in court.

The opposition to Putinism that had emerged in the winter of 2011–
2012 slowly retreated from the streets, the rallies dwindling in size and
fervor as the Kremlin pressed harder and harder against its critics. Putin's
many opponents—the hamsters and hipsters, the "creative classes" who
had rallied behind Navalny—retreated instead back to the Internet,
where they raged on, helplessly.

In September, in still another sign of Russia's deteriorating relations with
the United States in particular, the Kremlin abruptly ended the work in
Russia of the U.S. Agency for International Development. USAID had
supported Golos and other civic organizations involved in politics but
also many other politically benign programs, including ones to develop
home mortgages and to fight AIDS. In October, a new law expanded the
definition of treason to include passing "financial, material and technical, consultative or other assistance" to a foreign state or international
organization. It was so broadly written that any critic of the government
who now had contact with a foreign NGO could be charged as a traitor.
Two prominent American organizations that supported election campaigns, the National Democratic Institute and the International Republican Institute, were forced to leave the country, as were similar groups
from Europe, lest their employees or contacts face charges that could
result in twenty years in prison.

It became a tit-for-tat cycle, each action taken by one country replicated in the other. In 2012, the United States Congress, over the opposition of the White House, which still hoped to maintain a semblance
of cooperation with Putin, adopted a new law named after Sergei Mag-

nitsky imposing travel bans and sanctions on Russian officials involved in his prosecution and death. American prosecutors ultimately traced some of the $230 million in illicit proceeds that Magnitsky had uncovered to four luxury condominiums and other commercial properties in Manhattan—and had a court seize them. They had been purchased by a real estate holding company in Cyprus, using money laundered through shell companies in the former Soviet republic of Moldova.[3] The Magnitsky Act infuriated Putin, who, while improbably denying knowledge of the details of Magnitsky's case, said that the United States would have sought to punish Russia regardless of the accountant's death in prison. "If Magnitsky did not exist," he said, "they would have found another pretext."

The Russians initially retaliated by imposing sanctions on eighteen American officials involved in the detention and torture of prisoners at the Guantánamo Bay prison and elsewhere. Like the Soviet propagandists of the past, Putin had used these parallels—however misplaced at times—to deflect criticism of Russia, but now he went further. He proposed legislation that would place sanctions on American judges and officials involved in cases of abuse against adopted children from Russia, a subject of periodic tensions with the United States that seemed to have been resolved by a bilateral agreement to allow greater oversight of the process. Amid the furor over the Magnitsky sanctions, however, the Duma then went further still, passing legislation that would ban *all* adoptions of Russian children by Americans. The final vote was nearly unanimous, even though the legislation was so cynical and cruel that even members of Putin's government objected. Russia's orphanages were full of children in dire need of families—by some estimates as many as 800,000 in a country where adoption remained stigmatized and thus rare. Americans had adopted nearly 50,000 children since 1999; the ban would freeze some adoptions already in progress. Russia's retaliation was not symmetrical, but asymmetrical and self-inflicted. The Americans had targeted corrupt bureaucrats for sanctions; Russia was now targeting its own orphans. The day before the Duma's final vote on the bill, Putin faced unusually sharp questions during his annual press conference. He was asked eight times why he would harm the interests of children in a political dispute with the United States. Putin lost his composure under the unexpected hostility of the questions, retorting angrily at one point that it was the United States that had been indifferent to the abuse of Russian adoptees. He claimed that American officials had rebuffed inquiries from Russian diplomats investigating instances where Russian children had been abused.

"Do you think this is normal?" he fumed at one reporter. "How can it be normal when you are humiliated? Do you like it? Are you a masochist?"

A week later, despite the unusual outpouring of protest at home, Putin signed the adoption ban into law.

Putin's sixtieth birthday on October 7, 2012, was celebrated across the nation in a manner befitting a cult of personality, something he always professed to find distasteful. No more, it seemed. In the days leading up to it, an exhibition of paintings was held in Moscow entitled, without irony, *Putin: The Most Kind-Hearted Man in the World.* A youth group affiliated with United Russia produced a four-minute, sexually charged video of beautiful women reenacting his most famous exploits: from riding a horse in the mountains to flying in a fighter jet to driving a yellow Lada in Siberia. There were poetry readings and essay contests for schoolchildren. The milestone had special political resonance in Soviet history, where the fate of the leader and the country seemed inexorably intertwined. Stalin's sixtieth birthday in 1939 had been treated as a national holiday that overshadowed the Winter War with Finland. He was awarded the Order of Lenin medal. Adolf Hitler even sent a telegram with his best wishes "for the prosperous future of the peoples of the friendly Soviet Union." Nikita Khrushchev received the same award on his sixtieth birthday in 1954, while Leonid Brezhnev was given the honor of Hero of the Soviet Union upon his.

Putin's sixtieth came with no medals, and there was something hollow in the fanfare. Despite the official adulation, there was an intangible sense of trepidation, among both his supporters and his critics, a realization of his age and mortality, a feeling that he had become indispensible but that no one could be forever. In September he appeared at the Asia-Pacific Economic Cooperation summit in Vladivostok with a visible limp that the Kremlin seemed unwilling to explain clearly. (He had pulled a muscle in his back while playing ice hockey, which he had recently taken up, one senior aide later explained.) After a tumultuous year, Putin had survived the wave of marches that sullied his reelection, but the uncertainty involving his health revealed a disquiet coursing through the system. The leader seemed to be struggling to regain the verve of his first presidency; it was as if he had returned to power with no clear goal, as if his election had been not a means to an end, but the end itself.

On his way to the summit he had flown on a motorized glider as part of a conservation program to return endangered Siberian cranes to the wild. Putin had charmed his supporters with various encounters with wild animals (some of them sedated), but his choreographed stunts no longer seemed convincing. He had stopped during the upheaval around his election, perhaps embarrassed by his "discovery" of the planted amphorae in the Black Sea, but now they had resumed, his strategists returning to the tactics that had worked for so long. Putin dressed in a willowy white jumpsuit and joined the glider's pilot to lead cranes raised in captivity near the river Ob in western Siberia toward their winter resting ground to the south. The aircraft, equipped with cameras, had to make two attempts before the birds would follow. Putin had reportedly paid for the glider and spent hours training for the flight, but the event was ridiculed as a twenty-first-century form of Soviet hagiography. Gleb Pavlovsky, the strategist who had fallen out of favor, described Putin's latest stunts as reflexive and unconvincing, as if the Kremlin had run out of new ideas. Pavlovsky had done as much as anyone to shape Putin's political image through the television stunts that had made him the political leader he became, but having returned to office, Putin seemed to know no other way to lead. Rather than drawing attention to conservation issues, the cranes now were simply another prop for Putin's vanity. "The leader went to the movies and never came back," Pavlovsky said. He sounded contrite.[4]

The hagiography continued on Putin's birthday itself. While he celebrated privately with close friends and family at the official residence in Petersburg all the state television channels organized special programming. On Rossiya's weekly news program, Dmitri Kiselyov compared him to Stalin and meant it as a compliment. "In terms of the scope of his activities, Putin as a politician is among his predecessors in the twentieth century comparable only to Stalin," he said in a thirteen-minute encomium that managed to mention rising salaries and pensions, the revival of the army, and the restoration of nuclear parity with the United States.[5] NTV broadcast a fifty-minute documentary that attempted to reintroduce a man who almost alone had been at the center of public attention for twelve years. Called *Visiting Putin*, it breathlessly claimed to show Putin as only "his closest circle" knew him, though it offered

little at all that was new. The presenter, Vadim Takmenev, followed the
president through a week at work, from his office at Novo-Ogaryovo to
the Kremlin, to a presidential visit to Tajikistan. In a series of interviews
conducted over the week, Putin simply restated his views on his election,
his critics, corruption, and foreign policy, dismissing criticisms as mere
annoyances.[6] The leaders of the protest movement—people like Na-
lavny, whose name Putin never seemed able to utter—were the "chaff"
that would fall away, he said, and make room for "truly charismatic and
interesting people" to emerge in public life and politics. Corruption was
overstated, and anyway, the average annual income for Russians had
risen from less than $1,000 a year when he took office to nearly $10,000
now. "It is extremely important for the self-perception of any person living in this territory that he should realize that he is not just living in this
territory but that he is a citizen of a strong powerful state which enjoys
the respect of the world." The most important thing, he too said, was
that only Russia had strategic nuclear parity with the United States.

Putin's answer ignored the daily humiliation and anger of Russians
forced to pay bribes for virtually any public service, the high graft that
Navalny made a specialty of exposing, the dismal rankings of Transparency International that placed Russia 133rd out of 176 countries. Only
two days before, NTV had aired a documentary accusing the protesters
who took to the streets of conspiring to overthrow the government, this
time with the assistance of oligarchs in Georgia and their patrons in
the West. The paired documentaries portrayed Putin as a simple, honest
patriot at work, tirelessly, exclusively devoted to the affairs of state, while
his critics were aliens who wanted anarchy. Amid the compounding
evidence of corruption and cronyism that had enriched his friends and
allies, Putin was shown living a modest, almost ascetic life in a residence
that, for all its comfort and amenities, was spare, with few ostentatious
displays of wealth. The latest white paper by Boris Nemtsov and his allies
on the corruption and wealth of Putin's inner circle had detailed the
twenty state residences the president had at his disposal, nine of them
built during his time in power, as well as dozens of yachts and aircraft.
Yet even these critics acknowledged that Putin cared less about the trap-
pings of wealth than about those of power.

Although reverential, *Visiting Putin* did provide a sketch of the official presidential routine that in the twelve years since Yeltsin's resignation
had by design remained something of a mystery to ordinary Russians.
Putin's days were scripted into what seemed a passionless series of meet-

ings and ceremonies. He began his morning late—waking at 8:30 on the second day of Takmenev's project—with his briefing folders, the daily compilations by the FSB and the foreign intelligence service, the SVR. Then, as on most days, he had a prolonged workout: first on the weight machines in the residence's gymnasium, watching television news programs, and then a kilometer swim in its indoor pool. It was noon before Putin ate breakfast, a simple meal of porridge, raw quail eggs, and cottage cheese, sent to him, he noted, by Patriarch Kirill from the church's own farms, and a juice from beets and horseradish. His working day therefore began late and lasted into the deepest night. His meetings with ministers often occurred when most people were already preparing for bed. It was nearly midnight one evening when he dismissed Takmenev in order to meet his anti-drug chief, Viktor Ivanov, and the minister of defense, Anatoly Serdyukov, who, like Takmenev, had to wait in the antechamber. Putin said his ministers were always on call, but he would only disturb them when he had to. When asked, he said he distrusted the mass media as biased, a curious admission given the Kremlin's obsessive control of virtually all channels. He claimed to prefer the information he received from his meetings with his men, like Serdyukov and Ivanov, which he considered "much more complete and much more accurate." The desk in his office had no computer linking him to the Internet where, were he so inclined, he might find information that would challenge what had become a circumscribed worldview, reinforced by the courtiers who rarely dared to challenge him.

Despite the adulatory tone, the documentary, like another one in German timed to coincide with his inauguration five months before, managed to be revealing nevertheless. They both showed him surrounded constantly by his aides and guards, but no one else. He worked out alone. He swam alone. He ate breakfast alone. No one from his family appeared in either film—neither his wife nor his daughters, Maria, who was then twenty-seven, and Katya, who was twenty-six—nor did any of his friends. His closest companion seemed to be his black Labrador, Koni, who waited poolside as he completed his laps. In NTV's film, the only sign of Medvedev, once his closest aide and still his prime minister, came when Putin pointed out a red tandem bicycle parked forlornly outside the gym. It had been a gift from Medvedev, Putin explained, while working out on the weights, "obviously as a joke." It did not seem to be used. One television critic thought the loneliness of the leader was an improbable invention, intended to convince viewers that he was not the corrupt, insensitive figure that the protesters made him out to be, but rather the dedicated public servant sacrificing himself for the nation.

Putin's personal life still remained a closely guarded secret to all but those who knew him best, a small and discreet circle, one that had been remarkably consistent over the years but also one that was increasingly insular. Everything Russians learned about Putin's life they learned like this, in small, measured glimpses that the Kremlin arranged or allowed to appear, always circumscribed, occasionally insightful. Putin's penchant for working late at night and keeping visitors waiting for hours had become notorious. Even his friends would wait to meet him in the wee hours. Igor Shadkhan, the filmmaker who had interviewed him two decades before, recalled meeting Putin the last time, at one o'clock in the morning, after waiting for hours as a line of officials and executives filed one at a time into Putin's office.[7] Putin no longer had the easy banter that had won Shadkhan over in 1991. He tried to tell a joke, but Putin did not laugh. "By the way," he said in an interview in 2013, "Stalin was also a night person." Echoing Solzhenitsyn's dramatization of Stalin's interior monologues in *The First Circle,* Shadkhan now described Putin as "terribly tired" and lonely, rigid in his dogma, distrusting and afraid even of those in his entourage who would "want revenge as soon as he steps down because many of them are humiliatingly dependent on him."

Those who had once occupied the outer orbits of Putin's life— ministers, businessmen, acquaintances—now met him less frequently. He seemed to have changed. German Gref, one of his liberal advisers since their days working together in Petersburg, had watched his old colleague for so long but nevertheless struggled to explain the evolution of his character. Asked once if Putin had changed, he paused uncomfortably, searching for an answer that would not offend. All he would say was "Power changes people."[8] Others who had been close found themselves excluded. Anatoly Sobchak's widow, Lyudmila Narusova, described Putin as a man who had changed from the time when her husband could jokingly call him Stirlitz, the double agent in the spy serial *Seventeen Moments in Spring.* "He has a good sense of humor—at least he used to," she told a newspaper after being ousted from the Federation Council in the fall of 2012. Her political exile was the price she paid for being a rare voice of opposition to the flurry of laws cracking down on protesters, her daughter Ksenia among them.[9] "The destruction of illusions that I have does not involve Vladimir Vladimirovich, whom I know to be an absolutely honest, decent, and devoted person, but to his entourage," Narusova said. "I have a feeling of disgust towards those he surrounds himself with." He had grown blind to the "very low moral standards" of the political leaders he relied on. "Is it possible they do not understand—small, fussy, and greedy as they are—that once they lie, they can never restore confidence again? They lie to each other, they lie to him, but nevertheless he relies on them." She said that in power a "certain *bronzoveniye* happens," using the word for "bronzing" that suggests an inflated sense of self-importance, hardening like a monument into something less than human. She recalled Sobchak's last meeting with Putin, when he headed to Kaliningrad to campaign for his election in 2000. "Volodya," he warned Putin, "don't become bronzed." And yet bronzed he seemed to have become.

As prime minister, Putin had continued to live in his official residence at Novo-Ogaryovo, but by the time he returned to the presidency, he was living alone. The oldest daughter, Maria, had married a Dutchman, Jorrit Faassen, who joined the executive ranks of Gazprom. His connection to the Putin family filtered into the public consciousness only after he was involved in a road-rage incident in November 2010 while driving his BMW on the traffic-clogged highway coursing through Rublyovka, the billionaire-studded suburb of Moscow's elite. After a near collision with a Mercedes carrying a young banker, Matvei Urin, several bodyguards piled out of a trailing Volkswagen van and beat Faassen badly. The attack was investigated not by the traffic police, but by the Presidential Security Service, and within weeks, not only were the bodyguards arrested, but so too was Urin. He was convicted of battery and sentenced to four and a half years in prison, compounded by subsequent convictions for embezzlement and fraud that dismantled his banking empire. Jorrit and Maria married in secrecy—it was never exactly clear when or where, though there were rumors of a ceremony on a Greek island—and in 2012, not long before Putin's sixtieth birthday, they had a son. Putin became a grandfather, a fact that was never reported in the Russian press.[10]

Even less was known about Putin's younger daughter, Katya, who was said to have majored in Asian studies at university. She was long rumored to be dating the son of a South Korean admiral—even to have married him, though that turned out not to be true. She took up competitive dancing, becoming vice president of the World Rock'n'Roll Confederation under the name Katerina Vladimirovna Tikhonova, the family name evidently taken from the patronymic of Lyudmila's mother. At the end of 2012, at the age of twenty-six, she became the director of the National Intellectual Development Fund, an organization building a $1.6 billion high-tech research center on the grounds of Moscow State University.[11] The fund's trustees included several of Putin's closest allies, now wealthy executives of state enterprises, including Igor Sechin and Sergei Chemezov. It was said she had married Kirill Shamalov, the son of Nikolai Shamalov, who had been a member of Putin's Ozero dacha cooperative. Kirill, too, had joined the executive ranks of Gazprom after graduating from the same university as Katerina. He then became an executive and ultimately a shareholder at Sibur, the country's largest petrochemical company, then owned in part by Gennady Timchenko. The interlocking, nepotistic ties of Putin's circle of friends and allies seemed to be trickling down to a new generation.

In the absence of official or even reliable information about the Putins' private lives, rumors festered, mostly in the more gossipy or conspiratorial quarters of the Internet. There was speculation about Lyudmila's health, including bouts of depression or addiction; a favorite tale had her living in a monastery near Pskov, banished as the wives of tsars had been throughout history. The truth was more pedestrian. Sergei Roldugin, one of Putin's oldest friends, said that the Putins had remained cordial, but had grown increasingly distant. Putin instead spent more time with the same circle of friends he had kept from his childhood, from the KGB, and from the businesses that took root in the 1990s. It was among these friends that Putin would relax, hosting late-night parties at his residence in Moscow or the official retreats that Boris Nemtsov detailed in his report on the presidential holdings. In these gatherings, Roldugin said, he never discussed business openly—those talks happened personally, one on one—and rarely politics. The discussions increasingly ranged through history and literature. Putin's interest could wane. He had little patience for tired subjects, but a thirst for new information. Roldugin revealed how after reading Pasternak's translation of *King Lear,* Putin quizzed his friends on whether they knew, as Pasternak wrote in his comments on the translation, that the historical inspiration for the tale dated to the ninth century. He would invite singers, preferring crooners like Grigory Leps and Philippe Kirkorov, for private concerts; the guests, even the host, would arrive at all hours by car or helicopter.

He once asked Roldugin to bring musicians from the House of Music in Petersburg, where his old friend now served as artistic director. The three musicians—a violinist, a pianist, and a clarinetist—played Mozart, Weber, and Tchaikovsky. Putin was moved and, with the grace of a tsar, invited them to play again the next night for the same small group of friends. These gatherings included the likes of Yuri Kovalchuk and Gennady Timchenko, but less and less often, Putin's wife.

Putin's obsessions remained work and sport. Ice hockey became a new hobby in 2011 after he attended a youth tournament. It was a sport that also occupied his friends Timchenko and the brothers Rotenberg, Boris and Arkady, who owned professional teams in Russia's Kontinental Hockey League. Putin spent hours learning to skate and handle a stick, an indication of the same zeal he showed in learning martial arts as a teenager, and soon was playing in games in arenas emptied of all but invited guests. His teammates and tutors were some of hockey's legends, like Slava Fetisov and Pavel Bure, as well as friends like the Rotenbergs, his own government ministers, and even the Belarusian president, Aleksandr Lukashenko. The bodyguards from his security detail and Medvedev's—though not Medvedev himself—filled out the squads. In the run-up to the Olympics, Putin decreed the creation of an amateur night league for men over forty, which expanded to include players of all ages. He saw it as part of the revitalization of the country through sports and fitness. The amateur games were soon opened to the public and featured in news reports that breathlessly tracked the president's growing prowess on the ice. Wearing number 11, he scored with astounding ease—six goals in one game! He was playing hockey, he said dismissively, on the night of the first mass protests in December 2011. On the day he was inaugurated in 2012, he left the Kremlin as the new president to play in an exhibition match against retired hockey legends, with two retired politicians, Silvio Berlusconi and Gerhard Schröder, among the spectators. Putin scored two goals, including the game winner on a penalty shot in overtime.[12]

It was on Putin's inauguration day that May that Lyudmila was last seen with him in public. Before that they had appeared together on election day at a polling station, where Putin pointedly joked at her expense. As a worker pointed out the candidate information posted on the wall, Putin replied that he did not need it but that she might. "She's not up to speed," he said.[13] Her absence in the new Putin presidency became striking, fueling new rumors of their separation. She was conspicuously absent at Easter services that year, when Putin appeared with Medvedev and his wife, accompanied by the mayor of Moscow, Sergei Sobyanin. Putin also avoided her fifty-fifth birthday on the eve of Orthodox Christmas in January 6, 2013; he was in Sochi, granting Gérard Depardieu a passport (so the actor could avoid paying taxes in France) and skiing at the newly groomed Olympic slopes.[14]

They did not appear together in public again until the following June, when they emerged after the first of three acts of a ballet being performed at the Kremlin, *La Esmeralda,* to answer a question from a journalist so impertinent that it could only have been as orchestrated as the performance they were attending. "How did you like *Esmeralda?*" the waiting correspondent from the all-news channel, Rossiya 24, began. After Putin and his wife made a few banal observations about the "beautiful" music and "airy" movements of the dancers, the correspondent then gently broached a subject that would have under any other circumstance provoked Putin's fury: "You so rarely appear together, and there are rumors that you do not live together. Is that so?"

Putin inhaled, glanced at Lyudmila, and after a moment answered: "It's true. All of my activity, my work, is public, absolutely public. Some like it. Others do not. Some are absolutely incompatible with it." He addressed her formally as Lyudmila Aleksandrovna, the way one would speak to a stranger or an elder. She was "done keeping watch," he said. "It's been eight years, or nine, yes, nine. So, to sum it up, it was a mutual decision." They stood slightly, awkwardly apart. Lyudmila appeared pained, Putin steely. "Our marriage is over because we barely see each other," she injected. "Vladimir Vladimirovich is engrossed in his work. Our children have grown up. They live their own lives. We all do." She expressed gratitude that he was "still supporting me and our children" and said they would remain friends. At a time when many Russian politicians and officials were fighting off revelations about their children living or studying abroad, Putin seized the opportunity to emphasize the point that their daughters had remained in Russia.

The correspondent seemed confused. Did this mean they were actually divorcing?

"You can call it a civilized divorce," Lyudmila said.

Putin's decision to lift the veil on his personal life coincided with the socially conservative turn of his policies, trumpeting Russian faith and morality in the struggle to define and defend the idea of the state. For the most part, Russians reacted with indifference, even sympathy. The only surprise was the timing. The divorce would not become official until the next year. Their separation, meanwhile, prompted a flurry of speculation that Putin was preparing to remarry—perhaps to Alina Kabayeva, who was rumored to have had his son in 2010 (and a daughter in 2012). Kabayeva, who appeared on the cover of the Russian edition of *Vogue* in January 2011, wearing a dazzling Balmain dress, repeatedly denied that she had children. (A boy who had appeared in her life, she said, was her nephew.) Rumors of other affairs emerged involving the sleeper spy Anna Chapman and Putin's official photographer, Yana Lapikova, a former model and a contestant in a Miss Moscow pageant. There was always something a little hollow about the rumors, all of which Putin's spokesman, Dmitri Peskov, denied. Stanislav Belkovsky, the political strategist and occasional columnist, claimed the rumors of a love life were themselves the invention of the Kremlin's PR machine, floated to enhance Putin's image. Belkovsky published a book, in Germany, that portrayed him as a lonely, distrustful leader, closer to his pet dogs than to any people, even among his friends. The book, simply titled *Putin,* blended speculation, hearsay, and fact—including accurate details, for example, about the daughters' lives—so seamlessly that it was impossible to distinguish one from the other, much as it was impossible to know the truth of Putin's private life. Even Belkovsky was not sure, however, distancing himself from the psychological portrait he had drawn.[15] Putin seemed no more genuine than any of the political stunts he had perfected. After more than twelve years in the public spotlight, he had become a more distant figure, as remote from the people as the general secretaries or tsars before him, as powerful and unknowable as the elusive authority Klamm in Kafka's *The Castle*. "You know, it's not about Putin anymore," Gleb Pavlovsky said. "We talk about Putin too much. Putin is our zero, a void, a screen where we project our desires, love, hate."[16]

CHAPTER 24

Putingrad

In February 2013, Putin led a large entourage of Russian officials and members of the International Olympic Committee to Sochi for two days of meetings exactly a year ahead of the planned Opening Ceremony. He did not appear pleased.

Five years of construction had transformed the sleepy coastal resort—Putin's aides said for the better, his critics said ruinously so. The circular site of the main Olympic arenas in the Imeretinskaya Valley had been drained, graded, and cleared of the hundreds of modest homes and dachas nestled among estuaries that had been the nesting grounds of migratory birds. The arenas rose from the plain like alien objects—sleek and modern compared to the neoclassical remnants of Sochi's glorious Soviet past. Yet the valley remained a scarred, muddied landscape, littered with construction debris, studded with construction cranes that pivoted day and night. The construction was equally intense in the mountains at Krasnaya Polyana, where the Mzymta River churned murkily past the still-incomplete railroad and highway. The scale of the work in the mountains and along Sochi's narrow coastline was staggering: two hundred miles of new roads; dozens of tunnels and bridges; eight new railroad stations and thirty-one smaller stops; the new power station that Gazprom built and a network of smaller substations; a new airport and a new seaport, built by Oleg Deripaska, the tycoon Putin had dressed down at Pikalevo in 2009; dozens of new hotels, schools, clinics. It was at the time the largest construction project on the planet, an effort that in Russia was compared to the reconstruction of ravaged cities after the Great Patriotic War. Anatoly Pakhomov, Sochi's mayor, said that one massive project, to tunnel a second bypass highway to relieve the city's congested traffic, was something that Stalin had proposed more than half a century before, but only now, under Putin, was it being realized.

Vladimir Yakunin, Putin's old friend, compared the railroad, built at an expense of nearly $10 billion, to an even older project to unify the nation: the Trans-Siberian Railway, built in the twilight of the Russian Empire by Tsar Alexander III and his son, Nicholas II.[1]

From the start, Putin had been intimately, obsessively, involved in the Olympic project, awarding contracts (often without competitive bidding), approving designs, and policing construction schedules. He visited Sochi repeatedly, on official visits as well as private ones to his dacha at Bocharov Ruchei, or to a new one built by Gazprom in the mountains. Far more than any other megaproject, Sochi was to symbolize the country's rising wealth, its international prestige, the triumph over terrorism and separatism in the turbulent Northern Caucasus, which was just over the mountain ridge from where the games would take place. For Putin, the Olympics had a purpose deeper than the merely political. He believed them to be a palliative for a country that had suffered so much over the previous decades. "After the collapse of the Soviet Union, after the dark and, let us be honest, bloody events in the Caucasus, the public attitude in Russia became very negative and pessimistic," Putin once told a group of foreign journalists. "We have to pull ourselves together and realize that we can deliver large-scale projects on time and with high standards, and by projects I mean not only stronger defense potential, but also developments in the humanitarian sphere, including high achievement in sport." The Olympics, he said, would strengthen "the nation's morale."

Even Putin's critics acknowledged the scale of the endeavor, though not always so favorably. Konstantin Remchukov, the publisher and editor in chief of the independent newspaper *Nezavisimaya Gazeta,* compared the reconstruction of Sochi to Peter the Great's creation of a new tsarist St. Petersburg in the eighteenth century not simply to replace Moscow as the nation's capital, but to haul the country out of backwardness. "We learned in school how it was built on bones, how many mumbled under their breath, how many had to cut off their beards, how unhappy Moscow was that Petersburg was created in some rotten and swampy place," he said. "Here, for Putin, it's his Petersburg. Look how he built Sochi, in Krasnodar! Fifty, sixty years will pass—I don't know—and those there will name it Putingrad."[2]

As with the nation's strategic industries, Putin had steered the biggest projects to people he trusted or controlled, making them even richer. He would brook no dissent, no delays. "After the journalists leave," he chided his assembled subordinates during an unhappy inspection tour photo op in 2012, "I will tell what failures to meet the deadlines will amount to. I do not want to frighten anyone, but I will speak with you as people I have known for many years now."

And still the construction suffered from delay, disaster, and scandal: cost overruns, accidents, theft, corruption, abuse. In 2009 a powerful winter storm had destroyed the cargo port built to unload construction materials, along with thousands of meters of barrier walls that would surround the site. Putin had had to fire three successive directors of the main contractor, Olympstroi, before the fourth hung on to the job. Tens of thousands of poorly paid guest workers poured in—from Moldova, Ukraine, and Central Asia, fueling resentment among Russians in the region—and many were horribly mistreated, poorly paid, cheated out of wages, and deported home. Dozens died in accidents.[3]

Putin wanted the Olympics to be a symbol of Russia, and they were. Corruption plagued every project, driving costs up so high that they became difficult to ignore, or hide. Early in 2013, Dmitri Kozak, his close aide and now the deputy prime minister he had put in charge of Sochi, let it slip in public remarks that the cost of preparing Sochi had ballooned from the $12 billion that Putin had promised the International Olympic Committee to a staggering $51 billion. It was the most expensive Olympics ever—more than seven times the amount Vancouver spent to host the Winter Games in 2010, more than Beijing spent to host the much larger Summer Games in 2008. In a country with an economy that was still struggling, the figure was so politically sensitive that Kozak and other ministers were ordered never to mention the figure again. The profligacy was ridiculed. The Russian edition of *Esquire* estimated that for the amount spent on the combined highway and railroad to the mountains engineers could have paved the route with a centimeter of black caviar, six centimeters of black truffles, and twenty-two centimeters of foie gras, among other luxuries.[4] The officials involved blamed the soaring expenses on difficult geological conditions or the demands of the International Olympic Committee, but virtually every project cost far more than comparable projects built elsewhere. There were widespread reports that contractors inflated their prices at every level in order to pay kickbacks to officials, as Valery Morozov had claimed in 2010. The pipeline that Arkady Rotenberg's company constructed under the Black Sea to power the games cost more than $5 million per kilometer, compared to $4 million for the Nord Stream pipeline in the Baltic Sea (which was itself several times more expensive than the European average).[5] Boris Nemtsov called Sochi "a festival of corruption," estimating in June 2013 in his newest report on corruption in the Putin era that as much as half of the $51 billion total was squandered or stolen. Even Russian officials acknowledged that enormous sums of money were lost. The Auditing Chamber estimated at least $500 million in spending was unaccounted for—and then promptly classified its quarterly reports as state secrets. Criminal charges never materialized, though, certainly not against any of Putin's allies, whom the Olympics made very, very wealthy.

The costs, and the assumption that much of the money had been stolen, made many question the wisdom of holding the Olympics. It was a backlash that many host cities experience, but in Russia the expense was coming at an inauspicious time. Russia's economy still relied heavily on natural resources, and after bouncing back from the worst of the economic crisis, it had stalled again. Growth had slowed from 3 percent in 2012 to barely over 1 percent in 2013. The consumer boom fueled by oil prices had not translated into better government services. Putin's approval ratings—an imperfect measurement given the state's grip on the media—slumped in 2013 to the lowest level recorded since he first became president in 2000. According to one agency, Putin's rating had peaked the month after the war in Georgia at 88 percent, but by now it bumped along at barely above 60.[6] Even fewer of those questioned had faith in the country's direction or the president's policies, certainly not in the rapacious and ineffective bureaucracy, which seemed to resist even Putin's decrees.

On the slopes of Krasnaya Polyana that day in February, Putin's frustration boiled over as he conducted his latest personal inspection tour of venues still scrambling to be ready on schedule. On these tours, said Mayor Pakhomov, Putin rarely expressed appreciation for a job well done; he was a taskmaster who set expectations and was furious when they were not met. Pakhomov spoke of these encounters with awe of the power of Putin's will. Putin was now determined to make a public spectacle of his displeasure. Dressed in a black overcoat, he stood amid a gaggle of his senior aides at the newly completed bobsled center. The head of the Sochi organizing committee, Dmitri Chernyshenko, was explaining the seating arrangements when Putin unexpectedly turned the conversation to another venue, the ski jump, which of all the examples of waste and delay was about to become the most notorious.

The project, called Gornaya Karusel, or Mountain Carousel, was overseen by Akhmed Bilalov, a vice president of the Russian Olympic Committee who also happened to have owned the land beneath it and, until recently, shares in the company that had been hired to do the construction. He had sold those to his brother. Bilalov, a businessman from Dagestan who had once served in the Duma, was close to Dmitri Medvedev and his team of advisers. He had been appointed to the Olympic committee during Medvedev's presidency, as well as to a project that Medvedev hoped would redevelop the Northern Caucasus by building a series of ski resorts, even one in Chechnya, as a way to tame the last remnants of the insurgency in the region by creating economic opportunities. The ski jump had been hampered by poor location, sloppy design, and construction techniques that, according to environmentalists, had probably caused a landslide in 2012 that nearly buried the site. Expensive new retaining walls had to be constructed, as well as a road to the site that had not been in the original contract. The budget for the project, which had begun at $40 million, had ballooned to more than $260 million, and yet only a year before the games it remained a muddy and unfinished construction site, littered with material and debris.

The men in Putin's entourage looked uncomfortable. Chernyshenko did not seem to know how to answer Putin's queries about the delays. Putin scanned the men, until Dmitri Kozak finally stepped forward to explain, under Putin's grilling, that it was two years behind schedule. Now Putin wanted to know who was responsible. "Comrade Bilalov," Kozak replied as the entourage shifted nervously around him.

"And what is he up to these days?"

Kozak stammered that he did not know. Putin turned and glared at the others. Someone said that he now ran the Northern Caucasus Resorts Company and was also on the Russian Olympic Committee, the head of which, Aleksandr Zhukov, also stood among them.

"So he's your vice president, is he?" he asked. Zhukov could only nod as Putin pressed on relentlessly. "And the vice president of the Olympic committee of the country is engaged in this kind of construction?"

"He owns a construction company of some sort," someone interjected from the back. Putin turned again to Kozak, leading him on like a prosecutor with a reluctant witness.

"Have there been increases in the cost of the facility's construction?" Putin asked. Kozak, now looking at the ground, seemingly unprepared for this interrogation or perhaps just nervous, detailed the costs generally and the sources of the money. Putin pressed for exact figures, though, and when Kozak gave them, he repeated them disgustedly.

"Well done, guys!" he said with icy sarcasm that would, of course, feature prominently on state television. "Let's move on." He then turned and walked off.

Bilalov, on Putin's orders, was sacked the next day from all his posts. A swarm of investigations began into his work at the Northern Caucasus Resorts, including lavish expenses for him to travel to the Summer Olympics in London in 2012. Bilalov, along with his brother, Magomed, promptly fled the country, surfacing briefly in April at a clinic in Baden-Baden, Germany, where he said he had elevated levels of mercury in his blood and suspected he had been deliberately poisoned. His doctors later claimed the poison in his body was arsenic and molybdenum.[7] The brothers Bilalov relocated to London, while Putin assigned the task of completing the ski jump to Sberbank, headed by German Gref. Putin had known Gref since the 1990s and, despite his intermittent oblique critiques of Putin's policies (testifying at Khodorkovsky's trial, for example), trusted him to finish the job.

The ski jump was not the only project behind schedule and over budget, and some suspected Putin of singling it out because its owners were tied to Medvedev's team and thus expendable.[8] Others, though, saw the performance as evidence that Putin was, at last, cracking down on the corruption gnawing at Russia, or at least making a show of it to deflect mounting criticism of the Olympic project. Justice remained selective, however, and there were no meaningful prosecutions, even in Bilalov's case. Corruption had become so pervasive it was institutionalized. That made it a tool of co-option and coercion. Anyone could be prosecuted, when necessary, because almost everyone was complicit—and even if they were not, they could be charged anyway. The threat of corruption hovered over anyone and thus tamed everyone. In Bilalov's case, Putin's concern was less about confronting corruption than with sending a very public warning to those involved in his Olympic dream that they had better finish on time. When he visited the ski jump again in December, this time with Gref in attendance, it had been completed—though ultimately at a great loss to Sberbank's bottom line.[9]

On June 23, 2013, an Aeroflot flight from Hong Kong landed in Moscow with what Putin would sardonically call "such a present for us for Christmas." On board was Edward Snowden, the young, deeply disillusioned contractor for the National Security Agency who had handed over to *The Guardian* and *The Washington Post* tens of thousands of highly classified documents detailing the pervasive American surveillance of telephones and computer networks, often in collaboration with its allies Canada, Britain, Australia, and New Zealand. Wanted by the United States on espionage charges after his disclosures, Snowden slipped out of Hong Kong after meeting with officials at the Russian consulate there, accompanied by a lawyer for WikiLeaks. Snowden had hoped merely to change planes in Moscow for a flight to Cuba, but the State Department revoked his passport in an effort to cut short his flight. The move backfired when the Chinese let him leave for Moscow anyway. When he arrived at Sheremetyevo Airport, he was effectively stranded without papers. As a result, he spent the next five weeks in a diplomatic limbo and under, presumably, the close watch of the FSB.

In Washington, officials panicked. They pleaded with Russia to put him on a plane for the United States, while fretting in private over the grave risk that Snowden might share even more of what he knew with the Russians. Putin seemed to relish the unexpected opportunity to chide the Americans. Snowden had committed no crime on Russian soil, he said during a visit to Finland two days later, acknowledging Snowden's presence in the airport's transit lounge. Snowden was a human rights defender who "struggles for the freedom of information," Putin said. "Ask yourself, do you need to put such people in jail, or not?" He said he did not want to trouble himself too much with the details of Snowden's case, leaving it to the director of the FSB, Aleksandr Bortnikov, an old colleague who had joined the KGB in Leningrad in 1975, the same year Putin had. "In any case, I would personally prefer not to engage in such matters, because it's like shearing a piglet: a lot of squealing, but little wool."

After years of facing criticism from the United States over his record on rights, the irony was sweet. The Russian media hailed Snowden as a hero, comparing him to Andrei Sakharov, his revelations against the United States as noble as Sakharov's against the Soviet Union. Three weeks into his limbo in the restricted transit area, the Kremlin allowed Snowden a platform to meet lawyers and leaders of rights organizations, including three—Human Rights Watch, Amnesty International, and Transparency International—whose offices had been raided by Russian investigators as part of the hunt for "foreign agents." Snowden read a written statement saying he would seek political asylum rather than return to a country that had violated its own laws. "A little over one month ago," he said, "I had family, a home in paradise, and I lived in great comfort. I also had the capability without any warrant to search for, seize, and read your communications—anyone's communications at any time. That is the power to change people's fates."[10]

Snowden's odyssey was a diplomatic and intelligence coup for Putin. Although the extent of Snowden's cooperation with Russian intelligence agencies remained unknown—and was fiercely disputed by his supporters—the FSB closely monitored this unexpected "gift." "He is actually surrounded by these people," said Andrei Soldatov, a journalist who wrote extensively about Russia's intelligence agencies and later complained that Snowden could not or would not meet with independent Russian journalists like him.[11] The Snowden affair gave Putin the evidence that confirmed his complaints about American hegemony and perfidy, the hypocrisy of the three American administrations he had now dealt with. Snowden's disclosures tarnished President Obama's reputation and undercut his foreign policy, souring relations even with allies like Germany, whose chancellor, Angela Merkel, learned that her own telephone conversations had been tapped. It also mitigated the disclosures that journalists like Soldatov and his wife, Irina Borogan, had been making about Russia's own extensive surveillance of its citizens through a program called SORM, or the System of Operative-Investigative Measures. They described SORM as "an Orwellian network that jeopardizes privacy and the ability to use telecommunications to oppose the government."[12] The effort expanded the reach of the intelligence services deeper and deeper into the Internet and social-media sites that had until recently seemed free of government interference. The number of intercepts had doubled since 2007, trapping communications of opposition leaders like Boris Nemtsov and Aleksei Navalny and leaking them to Kremlin-friendly news organizations. Given Snowden's disclosures, how could the United States object to Russia's creeping surveillance state?

Almost certainly with Putin's approval, Russia's migration service granted Snowden temporary asylum on August 1, giving him a permit to live and even work in the country; Snowden slipped out of the transit terminal and began a new life in Moscow's shadows. The decision, which the White House learned from news reports, drove a final nail in the "reset" in relations Obama had pursued with Medvedev, one that had been withering ever since Putin's return to the presidency. A week later Obama canceled plans to hold a separate meeting with Putin before the G20 summit that had been scheduled in Petersburg for September. Obama's frustration with Putin boiled over. At a press conference, he said there seemed little point in meeting Putin now given their differences over policies and worldviews—the disputes over missile defense, over the turmoil in the Middle East, over the crackdown on opposition in Russia, the banning of American adoptions, the passage of a new law barring the distribution to children of "homosexual propaganda"—not to mention the rising tide of anti-Americanism appearing on state television and in official statements. Obama described Putin as sullen and insolent, a taunt that infuriated Putin, according to an aide. "He's got that kind of slouch," Obama said, "looking like the bored kid in the back of the classroom." Obama's aides had convinced themselves that Putin craved the respect that such a meeting of the two world leaders would entail, but Putin acted as if he did not care nearly as much as they assumed. "You cannot dance tango alone," Putin's spokesman, Dmitri Peskov, declared.[13]

Within weeks, events in Syria proved Peskov right. In August a barrage of rockets loaded with nerve agents struck a suburb of Syria's capital, Damascus, killing 1,400 people. Obama had warned two years before that the use of chemical weapons by Syria's government would cross "a red line" that would prompt an American military response, and within a week the Pentagon had drafted plans for a retaliatory missile strike against Syria's army. Putin said nothing publicly, but Russian officials scrambled to muddy the debate, casting doubt on the evidence that President Bashar al-Assad's forces had been responsible. Putin told Britain's prime minister, David Cameron, that there was no evidence of "whether a chemical attack took place," and if so, who carried it out. Putin had little personal sympathy for Assad; what he vehemently opposed was another American-led attack in the Middle East. He was convinced that from the beginning the United States had been waiting for any pretext to attack and topple Assad, and he was far more resolved in that conviction than Obama was in his determination to punish Syria for the deadliest use of chemical weapons since the Iran-Iraq War in the 1980s.

Then, with American air strikes only hours away, Obama abruptly reversed course, saying he would seek authorization from Congress before mounting an attack. The coalition he had hoped to build had failed to materialize, with even close allies like Britain and Germany refusing to endorse a strike. By the time the leaders of the G20 nations met in Petersburg in September, Obama's international standing was as uncertain as the "red line" he had drawn against the use of chemical weapons. Putin had been isolated in defense of Assad's brutal crackdown, but now other leaders joined him in insisting that any intervention require the authorization of the United Nations Security Council, where Putin retained the advantage of Russia's veto. Even Pope Francis sent a letter to Putin urging the leaders "to lay aside the futile pursuit of a military solution."[14]

A month after pointedly canceling his plans to meet separately with Putin, Obama now pulled him aside at Constantine Palace during the G20 and the two sat down in armchairs, accompanied only by their translators. There Putin laid out a proposal to force Syria to dispose of its chemical stockpiles under international inspection, and Obama agreed. When the idea became public, what little support there had been for another American-led military intervention evaporated.

Putin, who had been vilified for his heavy hand after his reelection, was now hailed as a hero who had averted a potentially disastrous escalation of war. Even as Obama continued to seek congressional approval for potential military action—in part to keep the pressure on Assad's government to comply with the inspections—Putin drafted an article that the Kremlin's American public relations firm, Ketchum, managed to place in *The New York Times* on September 12. In it, he argued that it was the United States that threatened the international order established after the Great Patriotic War. Its interventions in Afghanistan, Iraq, and Libya had proved "ineffective and pointless." Russia did not want to protect Assad's regime so much as international law. Only the United Nations Security Council could authorize the use of force against another country. An American attack against Syria, or anything else, "would constitute an act of aggression," he argued. He ended by disputing Obama's claim to "American exceptionalism," made in a nationally televised address explaining his decision not to bomb Syria after all. "It is extremely dangerous to encourage people to see themselves as exceptional, whatever the motivation," Putin wrote. In fact, he concluded, "We are all different, but when we ask for the Lord's blessings, we must not forget that God created us equal."[15] The article—and its lecturing tone, its unmistakable allusion to the Declaration of Independence—infuriated officials in Washington. Many pointed out Russia's hypocrisy for not having sought authorization for its intervention in Georgia in 2008 and for continuing to supply weapons that allowed Assad's military to crush the rebels. Putin's article also included the unsubstantiated claim that the Syrian rebels had likely used chemical weapons and would use them next on Israel.

Yet Putin's gambit had offered a straw to a war-weary United States, and Obama, already facing opposition in Congress, clutched it. NTV began one broadcast by claiming that Putin should win the Nobel Prize for averting an American air strike. In Russia's controlled discourse, that was hardly surprising, but Putin's stance won plaudits in the United States, too—even if most of them came from conservatives happy to see Obama portrayed as a feckless leader, deftly outmaneuvered on the global stage. A month later *Forbes* magazine ranked Putin the most powerful person in the world, passing Obama for the first time; such rankings are meaningless, but Russia's media repeated it over and over. "Anyone watching this year's chess match over Syria and NSA leaks has a clear idea of the shifting individual power dynamics," the *Forbes* editors wrote.[16] The American blogger Matt Drudge called Putin "the leader of the free world."

An even bigger diplomatic triumph for Putin followed, this time in Ukraine. After years of negotiations that culminated in the fall of 2013, Ukraine had edged closer to an association agreement with the European Union, a treaty that would deepen trade and political ties between the two. Since his election in 2010, Ukraine's president, Viktor Yanukovych, had maintained closer relations with Russia, keeping his country in Russia's orbit. With his popularity fading ahead of the next election in 2015, however, he had revived the possibility of strengthening relations with Europe, something strongly supported by the country's opposition, and he pushed through political reforms that the Europeans had demanded as a condition of signing the agreement. The Europeans were negotiating similar agreements with Moldova, Georgia, and Armenia in the hopes of allowing them all access to the single market of Europe. For diplomats in Europe's capitals, the integration of these economies, with the prospect of full membership in the future, would steadily expand the peaceful, secure European space, an old idea that had become an article of faith in the twenty-first century.

For Putin, however, the expansion of "Europe" to include Ukraine amounted to an encroachment on Russia that would, in his mind, inevitably be followed by the further encroachment of NATO. Russia's own relations with the bloc had stalled, hampered by the suspicions of many European states, especially those once in the Soviet sphere, over energy policies and human rights; a summit in Yekaterinburg in May had failed to secure an agreement allowing visa-free travel for Russian government officials amid a debate over whether the American "Magnitsky sanctions" should be adopted on the continent. Putin's own efforts to knit Ukraine more closely to Russia, which he had first proposed to Leonid Kuchma on the eve of the Orange Revolution in 2004, had made little progress, blocked by the internal political divisions in Ukraine. Ten years later, Putin's vision of a trade and economic bloc with Moscow as its core had evolved beyond the technical customs agreements negotiated with Belarus and Kazakhstan. One of the first policy declarations he made in 2011 after announcing his return to the Kremlin was the establishment of a broader pact to reunify the economies that had drifted listlessly apart after the Soviet collapse. He called it the Eurasian Economic Union. Excluding the three Baltic nations, now ensconced in the EU and NATO, Putin envisioned the bloc not merely as a counterbalance to the European Union, but rather as a new empire unto itself, one that bridged European Russia and the vast steppe that stretched from the Black Sea to Central Asia and Siberia.

The Eurasian Union was the manifestation of an ideology that had taken hold among Putin and his inner circle, an ideology that had been missing from the pragmatism that had characterized Putin's rule until then. Eurasianism in Russia was a deeply conservative philosophy driven underground (or abroad) by the internationalist ideology of the Soviet Union. It had reemerged in the 1990s, blending the religious and monarchical ideas of exiles like Ivan Ilyin, the philosopher Putin took to quoting, with the geopolitical theories of those like Halford Mackinder, whose "Heartland Theory" made Eurasia the "pivot area" in the battle for control of the "World-Island," the European, Asian, and African landmass. These ideas, championed in articles and books by conservative strategists like Aleksandr Dugin, spread from the fringes of academic debate and became ever more prominent. They circulated among Putin's closest intimates and were discussed in their late-night meetings; increasingly they peppered the public remarks not only of Putin, but of his more powerful advisers.

The geopolitics coincided with the emerging conservatism in domestic politics that championed—and protected—the values of the Orthodox Church, as well as Islam, and resulted in new laws that made blasphemy a crime and that banned the dissemination of "homosexual propaganda" to children. Vladimir Yakunin, another Putin confidant, viewed efforts to impose the cultural values of the West as a new front in a historic geopolitical struggle between sea and land powers, with Russia (a vast land power) defending its very existence against the United States (the new sea power), much like Mackinder theorized. He described the American dominance of geopolitics and world finance as a conspiracy to suppress any potential competitors, which is what made the Eurasian Union, he believed, so threatening to the West. "Russia was, is, and will be some kind of geopolitical competitor to the interests of Anglo-Saxon civilization," he said.[17] The irony of the new ideology was that Russia's elite, especially those who could afford it, had become thoroughly westernized, taking vacations and owning properties in the nations whose values they reviled. Even Yakunin's son lived in London, prompting a satirical blog from Aleksei Navalny. "Down the voracious throat of the odious West, which is devoid of spiritual values, Vladimir Ivanovich Yakunin threw his dearest possession—excluding his love for Vladimir Putin—his family."[18]

In September, fresh from the diplomatic triumph over Syria's chemical weapons, Putin described the "Euro-Atlantic countries" as dangerously adrift from their Christian roots. "They are denying moral principles and all traditional identities: national, cultural, religious, and even sexual. They are implementing policies that equate large families with same-sex partnerships, belief in God with the belief in Satan. The excesses of political correctness have reached the point where people are seriously talking about registering political parties whose aim is to promote pedophilia." Worse, he said, these nations wanted to export these dangerous ideas. It was "a direct path to degradation and primitivism, resulting in a profound demographic and moral crisis."

Of all the countries Putin hoped to unite in the Eurasian Union, none was as important as Ukraine, with its deep historical, social, and religious ties to Russia. Many Ukrainians were ethnic Russians, sundered in Putin's view from their homeland by the "greatest geopolitical catastrophe" of the twentieth century. And now Ukraine was turning toward the embrace of the European Union, encouraged by the Europeans and the Americans, at the expense of his Eurasian Union. It was evidence enough for Putin when Hillary Rodham Clinton warned in December 2012 that the Eurasian Union was merely an attempt to subjugate its neighbors in a new Soviet-like alliance—and "we are trying to figure out effective ways to slow down or prevent it."[19]

The European Union set a deadline for Ukraine to adopt the trade agreement before its summit in Lithuania in November, and in the months leading up to it Putin exerted enormous effort to persuade Ukraine to resist. As he had before the Orange Revolution in 2004, he visited repeatedly. In July 2013, to highlight the religious ties that bound Ukraine to Russia, he attended a ceremony in Kyiv to commemorate the anniversary of the baptism of Prince Vladimir in 988. "We are all spiritual heirs of what happened here 1,025 years ago," Putin said, appearing with Yanukovych at the Monastery of the Caves, one of the holiest sites of Orthodoxy. He used economic levers, too. Within weeks of the anniversary, Russia banned the import of Ukrainian railcars and candies manufactured by Roshen, a confectionary owned by an oligarch and former minister, Petro Poroshenko, who favored closer integration with Europe. In August, Russia virtually halted all commercial traffic across its border with Ukraine by overzealously enforcing the customs rules of Russia's union with Belarus and Kazakhstan. It was a very public way of making the point that Ukraine's economic future would be much easier if it joined Russia's union, not Europe's. Putin's special envoy on Ukraine, the former presidential "challenger" Sergei Glazyev, traveled to Yalta in September and warned at a conference that Ukraine's embrace of Europe would amount to suicide. "Signing this treaty," he said, ominously, "will lead to political and social unrest."[20] He later provided Yanukovych with a Russian translation of the thousand pages of the European Union's agreement (which, evidently, the Ukrainians had not translated) and warned him that adopting it would mean that Russia would have to close its borders to avoid an influx of European goods.

Putin was said to dislike Yanukovych, a physically imposing but unprincipled leader who he felt was betraying him by flirting with the Europeans. Putin met him in late October and again in early November, icily explaining that an agreement with the European Union would cost Ukraine dearly. The losses it was already feeling because of the customs enforcement would pale in comparison to the billions of dollars in economic pain that the country would suffer from the new barriers to the Russian market and higher prices for natural gas.

After the last of those meetings, Yanukovych's negotiating partners in Europe noticed a change in his demeanor. They suspected Putin had threatened something more than economic pain, presenting him with *kompromat* that he would not want made public. Yanukovych's venality—the insider deals that enriched him, his family, and his close business associates—certainly made him vulnerable. It was not black-mail, a senior Kremlin adviser insisted later, but a sober analysis of how deeply intertwined the economies of the two countries were. In his meet-ings with the Europeans, Yanukovych now insisted that Ukraine stood to lose $160 billion in trade with Russia and higher energy prices, an improbable figure nearly equal to the country's gross domestic product.[21] It was a last, desperate ploy by Yanukovych to persuade the Europeans to sweeten their offer, but the Europeans balked. Putin had triumphed.

On November 21, a week before the summit in Lithuania, Yanu-kovych's government stunned his European counterparts, and many in Ukraine, by announcing that his country would back out of the agree-ment, a reversal that upended months of intensive talks. Yanukovych's announcement provoked outrage among those Ukrainians who envi-sioned closer ties with Europe as an inevitable evolution from their country's Soviet past. That night one thousand protesters rallied in Kyiv's main plaza, Maidan Nezalezhnosti. Yulia Tymoshenko issued a jailhouse statement urging people to react "as they would to a coup d'état" and take to the streets. The next day a few thousand more did.[22] By the weekend, the crowds had swelled, and tents were erected, as they had been after the fraudulent election in 2004—only this time the flags that fluttered in the streets were not orange, but blue with a circle of yellow stars, the banner of the European Union. They called their protest "EuroMaidan," and it reflected the clash of ideals among the country's 46 million people. The protesters soon turned their fury on the statue of Lenin that still stood at the end of Kyiv's main avenue. Lenin was not simply an anachronism; he was a manifestation of the lingering dominance of Moscow.

Yanukovich did little to defuse the protests at first, content to wait them out with the onset of winter. Early in December, as the protests intensified, he flew to China, touting trade deals he hoped would mol-lify the anger over rejecting an economic partnership with the Europe-ans. He stopped in Sochi to meet Putin on the way back, and there he secured a secret deal that would not be announced until December 17, when they again appeared together in the Kremlin. Putin announced that Russia would give Ukraine a cash infusion worth $15 billion by tapping Russia's National Wealth Fund to purchase Ukrainian bonds. Gazprom would slash the prince of natural gas from $400 per cubic meter to $268.

Putin emphasized, disingenuously, that he had not insisted that Ukraine join the Eurasian Union as a condition, though many suspected he and Yanukovych had agreed that this would happen at a later date, once the popular anger had subsided. Putin then made special note of his plans to celebrate the seventieth anniversary of the liberation of Sevastopol, the port city in Crimea, from the Nazis in 1944. Those celebrations would ultimately take place on May 9, 2014, though not in circumstances that anyone anticipated that wintry day in Moscow. Putin, once again, seemed to have outmaneuvered his rivals, securing a diplomatic victory over the Europeans.

Ahead of the Olympics, Putin sought to be magnanimous at home. After a year of harsh crackdowns and repressive new laws, the Kremlin signaled a thaw in the summer of 2013. In July, the court in Kirov had convicted Navalny of the embezzlement charges but then after a confusing night that included protests and frantic consultations between the Kremlin and the court, he was freed with only a suspended sentence. The Kremlin then allowed Navalny to campaign—at first furtively, then openly—as a candidate in Moscow's mayoral election in August against the incumbent, Sergei Sobyanin. It was the first campaign for the position since Putin had abolished elections for regional leaders after Beslan in 2004. Sobyanin, after Yuri Luzhkov's dismissal in 2010, hoped to establish his own political legitimacy and resigned early in order to win the office in what he vowed would be a free and fair election. Despite the by now familiar harassment of challengers and the use of government resources on behalf of the incumbent, the election that unfolded was certainly fairer than most had been in Russia for more than a decade, as even Putin's critics pointed out. Navalny modeled his campaign on one he had watched on the American television series *The Wire,* stumping for votes in speeches in public places around the city in a way that few candidates ever had in Russia.

Two years of diminishing public protests had done nothing to weaken Putin's grip on power. Now he seemed confident enough to relax some of the pressure he had exerted to suffocate the opposition. When the ballots in the mayor's race were counted, Sobyanin won, but Navalny drew 27 percent of the vote, a respectable showing that was far higher than polls had predicted. He thus established himself as the country's most prominent opposition leader—and yet not one who posed a formidable or imminent threat to Putin's political control.

The thaw continued in December, when at Putin's instigation the Duma adopted a law to grant amnesty to thousands of prisoners. Many of them had been convicted for economic "crimes" imposed to strip them of property or businesses, but the list of those eligible for amnesty included more prominent political prisoners, as well. The two members of Pussy Riot, Nadezhda Tolokonnikova and Maria Alyokhina, walked free a few months before their sentences ended, so did a few of those charged in the Bolotnaya Square protests. The courts then amnestied thirty Greenpeace International activists who had been arrested in September 2013 after their ship, *Arctic Sunrise,* mounted a high-seas protest against Russia's first offshore oil rig in the Kara Sea.

The biggest surprise of all, however, was the release of Mikhail Khodorkovsky in October. He marked his tenth year in prison, and Russian prosecutors had recently announced that they were pursuing yet another criminal case against him, suggesting he might never be freed. And yet two years of secret negotiations brokered by Germany cleared a path to freedom. As part of the deal, Khodorkovsky appealed to Putin in two letters that he had written in November. They have never been made public. Although Putin had at first demanded that Khodorkovsky acknowledge his guilt, he agreed to accept his plea for clemency on humanitarian grounds, citing his mother's declining health. "He has already spent more than ten years in confinement—this is a serious punishment," Putin said at his annual press conference in December. The broader amnesty appeared now, in hindsight, to have been engineered to accomplish the release of the man whose arrest in 2003 had signaled a dark turn in the country's modern history.

A few hours after Putin spoke in Moscow, Khodorkovsky was awoken at two o'clock in the morning in Karelia, where he had spent the last years of his detention. He was put on a plane and flown first to Petersburg and then to Berlin, another exile from the new Russia. The next day he appeared at the Checkpoint Charlie Museum, devoted to the dissident heroes of the Cold War and the victims of the divisions represented by the Berlin Wall. Grayer, his hair shorn, Khodorkovsky looked like someone who had walked "in from the cold and dark into a brightly lit and overheated room," a journalist who was there, Arkady Ostrovsky, wrote. Khodorkovsky, who had spent so much of his time in prison reading and writing, sounded neither broken nor bitter.[23] "In all these years, all the decisions about me were taken by one man: Vladimir Vladimirovich Putin. So today it is hard to say I am grateful. I have thought quite a bit about what words would express what I think. I am happy at his decision—I think that's it." As a condition of his release, he had agreed not to become involved in politics for a year, though he vowed to be active in forging a civil society in Russia—from afar. "The Russian problem is not just the president as a person," he said. "The problem is that our citizens in the large majority don't understand that they have to be responsible for their own fate. They are so happy to delegate it to, say, Vladimir Vladimirovich Putin, and then they will entrust it to somebody else, and I think that for such a big country as Russia this is the path to a dead end."

Khodorkovsky's release was intended to look less like an expulsion of a dissident than an act of mercy, the benevolence of a tsar. Many, including Khodorkovsky and the women of Pussy Riot, saw the amnesties as part of the Kremlin's efforts to take some of the edge off growing international criticism before the Olympics in Sochi, now less than two months away. Putin's pressure on Ukraine, the strengthening of laws against political opponents, the homophobic legislation and statements of some lawmakers and officials, the scandalously expensive preparations of the venues in Sochi, and the punitive anti-terrorist operations in the Caucasus leading up to it—all had come under withering attack. World leaders, including Barack Obama, Angela Merkel, and David Cameron, made it clear they would not be attending the games, lest their attendance be seen as endorsing Putin's rule. Polishing Russia's image was certainly part of the motive behind Putin's actions. They also demonstrated his singular power to bend branches of power to his will. Even other countries would succumb. Putin granted the amnesties the way he granted the contracts to build Sochi to the tycoons he trusted, the way he could, without debate, spend $15 billion of the nation's rainy day fund to keep Yanukovych's government under Moscow's sway. Khodorkovsky was right. Putin did what he did, on his own, because the people had "entrusted" him to rule, to be the ultimate leader, the tsar of a simulated democracy. There was no one now—from the ordinary Russian to the apparatchiks who were complicit in the political and economic system he had built—who would, or could, take the responsibility to change things.

On the night of February 7, 2014, Putin, in one short sentence prescribed by the Olympic Charter, opened the Winter Games in Sochi. Not everything had been completed in time, despite a breakneck effort

that continued even after the sporting events began: the unfinished
sidewalks were hastily covered; fields of construction debris were hidden behind crisp blue billboards. The failure to complete many hotels,
especially those where foreign journalists stayed, threatened to turn the
event into a public relations debacle. A campaign to round up stray
dogs, presumably to euthanize them, became the most prominent meme
of the pre-opening coverage in the media, after the colossal expense of
rebuilding Sochi and the threat of terrorism, punctuated at the end of
December by two suicide bombings in Volgograd that killed thirty-four
people. There was an element of schadenfreude in some of the coverage of Russia's bloated and brutal preparations; there was also genuine
international concern over Russia's regressive new laws—especially those
regarding blasphemy and "homosexual propaganda"—and the smother-
ing of protests that continued up to and through the opening ceremony.

Two days before the games commenced, more than two hundred writers from thirty countries published an open letter in *The Guardian* calling for the repeal of laws stifling free expression that had been passed
since Putin returned to the presidency. Four winners of the Nobel Prize—
Günter Grass, Wole Soyinka, Elfriede Jelinek, and Orhan Pamuk—
were among the signatories. Publicly, Putin feigned indifference to the
criticism, small and large, but it was said to have infuriated him. In an
interview in *Kommersant* Dmitri Peskov, his spokesman, dismissed the
complaints of corruption and waste as exaggerations.[24] Come to Sochi,
he said, and look at what had been built. It was proof enough that "at the
very least, not all the money was stolen." He recounted a conversation
with "a very wise person," clearly meaning Putin.

"This wise person said, 'Do you know when everyone will love us and
cease to criticize us, and so on, including criticizing us for no reason?'

"And I asked, 'When?'

"And he said, 'When we dissolve our army, when we concede all our
natural resources to them as a concession, and when we sell all of our
land to Western investors—that's when they will cease to criticize us.'"

In fact, the criticism waned once the games began. The opening ceremony was a lavish, dazzling expression of Putin's Russian ideal, choreographed by the head of Channel One, Konstantin Ernst, who also
directed the annual Victory Day parades on Red Square and Putin's
annual press conferences. The spectacle, called "Dreams of Russia," and
lasting nearly three hours, began with a young girl named Lyubov, or

Love, reciting the Cyrillic alphabet. With each letter came a projection representing famous artists, inventors, and places: Б for Baikal, С for Sputnik, П for the Periodic Table of Mendeleyev, and so on. Some were émigrés whose works had once been considered deviant or traitorous, including Chagall, Kandinsky, and Nabokov, but who were now reinstalled in the pantheon of a glorious Russian history. Lyubov was then swept through the country's vast history and geography, from the empire of Peter the Great (the letter И for *Imperiya*) to *War and Peace,* represented by a dazzling ballet, from the onion domes of St. Basil's Cathedral to a luminescent troika that Gogol made a metaphor for Russia in *Dead Souls:* "Russia, whither are you rushing? Answer! It gives no answer." The ceremony did not ignore the Bolsheviks, the Terror, or the Gulag completely, but it did not dwell on them. The ceremony was a manifestation of the "national idea" at the center of Putin's political construct, one that somehow adapted the best of the country's turbulent past and turned the arc of history into something people could be proud of, not ashamed. The only glitch in the ceremony came when five illuminated snowflakes unfolded into the rings of the Olympic symbol. One flake failed, but adroit television producers swiftly replaced the image with one from a rehearsal; no one watching on Russian television knew what had happened. The final journey of the Olympic torch, which in keeping with the superlative narrative of these games had traversed the country, from the bottom of Lake Baikal to outer space, included some of Russia's famous Olympians. The most noted of them was the gold medal winner from Athens in 2004, Alina Kabayeva.

The Olympics served the political purpose Putin intended. Even Aleksei Navalny, whose anti-corruption organization had published an interactive website on the titanic waste involved, found himself moved by the opening ceremony. "It's so sweet, and so uniting." As the attention turned to the sports, as Putin and his aides had always insisted it should, the Olympics even seemed to temper some of the harshest criticism of him and his rule. Putin himself rushed from event to event, reveling in the sports and the attention. He posed for photo ops with the athletes, drank beer at the Dutch house with King Willem-Alexander of the Netherlands, and even paid a visit to Team USA, ostentatiously making the point that despite his political differences with the United States, he welcomed their participation—and that he was a bigger man than Obama, who had declined to attend. He had achieved his dream: Russia was at the global center of gravity, a rich, indispensable, united nation playing host to the world. Russia, in his mind, had achieved the glory, the respect, that the Soviet Union had had when he was a boy, when Gagarin was in space, when the Red Army was formidable and feared.

And yet, beneath the spectacle and the sports, there was an undercurrent of unease and fear. The national unity on display in Sochi, however genuine, did nothing to keep the steady, firm hand of the state from throttling any sign of dissent. The protests in Ukraine, which had not dissipated over the winter, reverberated in Moscow like a distant earthquake, faintly but ominously shaking the ground. In the weeks before the games, Putin moved preemptively to quarantine any new outbreak of the protest contagion inside Russia. In December he decreed a makeover of RIA Novosti, the state news organization that under Medvedev had earned respect for balance and a diversity of points of view. In January, a liberal television station called Dozhd, or Rain, was dropped by the nation's cable providers after asking in an online poll whether more lives might have been saved in Leningrad if the Red Army had surrendered the city and retreated instead of enduring 872 days of siege at the cost of one million dead. Having reconstructed Putin's Olympian ideal of Russia's history, the Kremlin seemed determined to silence anyone who might contradict it.

In defiance of the Olympic charter's promotion of freedom of expression, the police from Petersburg to the Caucasus arrested scores of people who had tried to protest for one reason or another on the day of the opening ceremony. In the middle of the games, a court in Krasnodar sentenced an activist with Environmental Watch on the North Caucasus to three years in prison, while other members of the group were detained to keep them from presenting a report they had compiled on the ecological damage wrought by the construction in Sochi. The women of Pussy Riot reunited in Sochi with a new protest song, "Putin Will Teach You to Love the Motherland," and were immediately set upon by horsewhip-wielding Cossacks and then detained by the police, who claimed they were investigating a theft from their hotel. A documentary, *The Biochemistry of Betrayal*, appeared on Rossiya at the height of the games on February 18, equating the opposition in Russia to the Soviet commander Lieutenant General Andrei Vlasov, who collaborated with the Nazis after being captured in 1942. When the trial of eight arrested at the Bolotnaya protest in 2012 ended with convictions as the games climaxed, 212 people were arrested in the streets outside the courthouse; when their sentences were announced three days later, there were more protests and 232 more arrests, including, once again, Aleksei Navalny and the women of Pussy Riot.

Putin had invested so much in the Olympics that any criticism of it—any protest that might question its benefit—was treated as blasphemous, an act of treason against a resurgent state. In a column on the website of *Yezhednevny Zhurnal,* the satirist Viktor Shenderovich, whose portrayal of Putin had knocked his puppet show *Kukli* off the air in 2000, mused about the pride he felt in Russia during the Olympics, worrying that impulses like his would only enhance and even embolden Putin's power. He wondered whether a critic like himself could cheer guiltlessly for the Russian team, whose first gold medal in team figure skating came after a dazzling performance (and questionable voting by the judges) by a fifteen-year-old competitor, Yulia Lipnitskaya. Shenderovich's column explained that he, too, had enjoyed "the girl on skates," but he reminded readers of Germany's enthusiasm for Hans Wölke, a star in the 1936 Olympics in Berlin: "A smiling guy, a handsome man, symbolizing the youth of the new Germany! Something, however, prevents us from enjoying his victory today."[25]

He did not explain Wölke's fate explicitly, but he mentioned Dachau and the bombing of Coventry, the siege of Leningrad, and a lesser-known massacre at Khatyn, near Minsk, the capital of what is now Belarus. The entire village was brutally executed in 1943 in retaliation for a partisan attack on a convoy of the Nazis' 118th Auxiliary Police Battalion. Wölke, one of the battalion's officers, was killed in the attack. The Nazi massacre was a notorious war crime that the Soviet Union publicized and that Shenderovich's readers would certainly remember. "Not the fault of Hans, of course," he wrote, "but it turned out that he contributed." Shenderovich meant to be provocative—excessively so, perhaps—but his allusion to the Nazis provoked a furious backlash at a time when Russia was portraying the street protests in Ukraine as nothing less than an uprising of neo-Nazis. The reaction was swift and savage. Shenderovich was denounced in print and on air; the day after his column appeared the Rossiya channel broadcast snips of a video of him masturbating in bed with a woman who was not his wife.[26] A few weeks later, the journal's website was shut down, along with the opposition portals Grani.ru and Kasparov.ru. The Kremlin, having once largely ignored the permissive ethos of the Internet, had come to understand the threat it posed; it had tightened the screws with regulations against promoting "extremism," and now evoked them more vigorously than at any time in Putin's era. The crackdown against dissent—the campaign of denunciations so fulsome that it could only have been orchestrated by the Kremlin's media handlers—felt as if the country was being mobilized for war once again.

CHAPTER 25

Our Russia

Putin did not expect the crisis that exploded before the Olympics in Sochi ended. Even though he might have anticipated it six years before when he warned President George Bush that NATO should not consider Ukraine's membership, even though he had ordered a reorganization of Russia's conventional forces to address the shortcomings exposed by the war in Georgia in 2008, and even though he and his advisers had warily monitored the political convulsions in Kyiv caused by its refusal to embrace the European Union, Putin had not planned to take his country to war. Nor had he prepared the country for it. He did not consult with the country's diplomats or its military commanders, certainly not with its elected legislators, who no longer had any influence over how he governed.

On the night of February 18, the street protests in Kyiv, which had ebbed after Putin's $15 billion bailout of Yanukovych's flailing economy, erupted in an orgy of fire and violence as the riot police tried to clear the streets around Independence Square. By the end of the night, more than two dozen people had died, most of them protesters, but some of them police officers. By dawn the next day, there was open warfare in the center of the city, with police and protesters exchanging gunfire. The death toll soon climbed over a hundred, the worst violence in the city since the Great Patriotic War. The reports that filtered back to Putin in the Kremlin—and thus onto Russia's television networks—portrayed the clashes as an armed insurrection, prodded by American and European diplomats who had not only encouraged the protesters but even passed out food and cookies.

What had begun as largely peaceful demonstrations in favor of the agreement with the European Union had evolved since November into a broader movement to oust Yanukovych's corrupt regime. That there were radical groups in the square—masked gunmen from two fiercely nationalistic groups, Svoboda and Pravy Sektor—convinced Putin that Yanukovych had lost control to the forces of anarchy and fascism. Putin never understood the core grievances that kept the majority of the protesters in the streets during those winter months, the yearning to break the corrupted grip of a rapacious leader, the radicalization that had inevitably arisen when even their most basic demands went unheeded. Putin had thought he could buy off the president and thus the people, as he had succeeded in doing in Russia for fourteen years, with economic largess, dispensed at critical moments. As the writer James Meek wrote when the protests in Kyiv descended into violence that day in February, "It is the ideal of a complete cynic, Vladimir Putin, the one ideal a complete cynic can have—that people have no ideals."[1]

A troika of European diplomats—the foreign ministers of France, Germany, and Poland—rushed to Kyiv on February 20 to try to broker an end to the violence around Maidan. Still focused on the Olympics in Sochi, Putin said nothing at first, which left Russia's response confused and contradictory. Russia's foreign minister, Sergei Lavrov, denounced the Europeans' effort as an "uninvited mission," even as Yanukovych himself sat down to host the ministers. As they hashed out a political compromise they hoped would end the shooting outside—by holding accelerated presidential elections in 2014, as well as granting amnesty for the protesters—Yanukovych interrupted the talks to telephone Putin, who was then back in Moscow. Despite all his efforts to feign independence, he could make no deal without Putin's approval. He told Putin he would agree to step down for new elections and that he would order the withdrawal of the riot police from the burning barricades not far from the presidential office. In Putin's mind, that amounted to a humiliating abdication, a dangerous sign of weakness in the face of the mob.

"You will have anarchy," Putin claimed he told Yanukovych. "There will be chaos in the capital."

Yanukovych accepted the Europeans' compromise anyway, and it was announced at two o'clock on the afternoon of February 21. By that evening, Yanukovych's political allies had begun to abandon him, and his authority over the police and interior troops dissipated amid credible reports that a cache of weapons looted from police stations in western Ukraine was on its way to the capital.[2] After issuing a statement congratulating the women's biathlon relay team for winning the country's first gold medal in Sochi, Yanukovych fled the capital. He flew first to eastern Ukraine and then to Crimea before finally being secretly conveyed to refuge in southern Russia, in a special operation Putin ordered on February 23 after meeting all night with his advisers.[3] In Yanukovych's wake, the agreement that had been reached to end the fighting unraveled before it could even go into effect. Ukraine's parliament, with Yanukovych's loyalists having broken with him, promptly voted to "impeach" Yanukovych in a legally dubious procedure. Deputies then elected a new parliamentary leadership and appointed an interim president until new elections could be held. One of the first acts of the newly reconfigured parliament was to make Ukrainian the official language, reversing an earlier law passed by Yanukovych's government that had recognized Russian as well. The new acting president, Oleksandr Turchynov, blocked the proposal but not before it inflamed the ethnic divide in Ukraine, one that had never entirely been bridged in nearly a quarter century of independence. In Moscow, the events in Kyiv confirmed Putin's worst fears: what was happening was not a popular uprising against a weak, discredited leader, but a revolution hijacked by Ukrainian nationalists and radicals he compared to the Nazi storm trooper Ernst Röhm, and supported by the enemies of Russia, the Europeans and the Americans.[4]

Putin presided over the closing ceremonies in Sochi on the night of February 23, after first laying a wreath at the Tomb of the Unknown Soldiers in Moscow in the morning. The Olympics not only defied the most dire predictions of disaster, they ended with Russia's athletes winning the most gold medals—thirteen—and the most medals overall—thirty-three. Now, at Russia's moment of glory, years in the making, the convulsions in Ukraine overshadowed everything. That a sixteen-day sporting event had taken on such symbolic and ideological importance for Putin and for Russia only made the upheaval in Ukraine seem even more humiliating; some of Putin's supporters thought it really had been incited in order to sully the moment. Putin spent the hours before the closing ceremonies—another lavish ode to Russia, with even a knowing, self-deprecating wink to the snowflake gaffe in the opening ceremonies—complaining on the telephone to Angela Merkel that the Europeans had not enforced the agreement that Yanukovych had signed, as if they could have forced him to remain in Kyiv.

Putin said nothing publicly about Ukraine in Sochi that day, or the next, when he hosted a breakfast for the organizing committee, decorated Russia's medalists, and planted thirty-three trees, one for each medal. He would say nothing, in fact, for nine more days, even as he set in motion a secret operation that morning of February 23, one that not even his own ministers knew was coming. On February 25, he met with his national Security Council for the second time since the violence erupted in Kyiv. The council's twelve members included Medvedev, the ministers of defense, foreign affairs, and the interior, the leaders of both houses of parliament, and the directors of foreign intelligence and the FSB. One of them, Valentina Matviyenko, the chairwoman of the Federation Council, emerged from the meeting and declared that it was impossible that Russia would intervene militarily in Ukraine to halt the chaos.

Neither she nor many of the others in the Kremlin knew then that Russia already had. Putin would punish Ukraine by dismembering it. The next day, he announced a snap military exercise that mobilized tens of thousands of troops in western Russia, as well as the headquarters of the air force and air defense commands. The exercise had been planned for months, but the timing allowed the Kremlin to disguise the sudden deployment of thousands of Russia's elite special operations troops. Secrecy was essential, as was deniability. Putin could not be sure of the potential international response—from NATO, above all—and wanted to test the resolve of the world's leaders before he acknowledged the extent of his plan.

Before dawn on the morning of February 27, commandos from Russia and troops from the headquarters of the Black Sea Fleet and other bases in Crimea seized the Crimean regional parliament and other important buildings on the peninsula, as well as two airfields. The troops were well equipped and heavily armed, but their uniforms bore no insignia; the soldiers had been ordered to remove them. Within the next twenty-four hours, thousands more troops landed at the airfields and fanned out, securing the peninsula without significant violence, despite several tense confrontations with startled Ukrainian troops, who, amid the political havoc in Kyiv were under orders not to resist. The Russian commandos became known as "little green men," or "polite people," preserving Russia's increasingly unconvincing denials of any involvement. A hastily organized session of the regional parliament, which was held behind closed doors, elected a new government and declared, in violation of Ukrainian law, that a referendum would be held on May 25 on the question of giving Crimea greater autonomy.

Even Putin's supporters were surprised. Putin had acted after consul-

tations only with a small circle of aides that included the men he had
always trusted, the men whom he had kept by his side since they all
joined the KGB: Sergei Ivanov, Nikolai Patrushev, and Aleksandr Bortnikov. They shared his deepest thoughts, his suspicion of NATO's ambitions, and his rage over the culpability of Western nations in rushing to
embrace the new government that was taking shape after Yanukovych's
retreat. There were uncanny echoes of the decision in 1979 to invade
Afghanistan, which was also made by a close, cloistered cadre of the
Soviet leadership on false pretenses. The result of the secrecy was confusion among the country's political establishment, underscoring how
much decision making now rested solely in Putin's hands.

Ever since his return in 2012, Putin had narrowed the funnel of information that reached him to exclude the diplomats, economic ministers,
or others who might have offered advice on the possible consequences of
what was unfolding. Putin's actions now left his spokesman and even his
foreign minister, Sergei Lavrov, repeating falsehoods, denying there were
any Russians in Crimea, even as they seized its strategic sites, one by one.
When the United Nations Security Council met in emergency session in
New York on February 27, the day after the "little green men" appeared,
Russia's ambassador, Vitaly Churkin, was unprepared to explain even
the basic facts of what was happening, because, it seemed, he clearly
did not know them. That same day, Yanukovych finally resurfaced in
Russia, a week after fleeing Kyiv. He held a surreal press conference at
a shopping center in Rostov-on-Don in southern Russia, not far from
the Ukrainian border, where he claimed he remained the legitimate
president of Ukraine, even as protesters and journalists were combing
through his presidential estate outside of Kyiv, rifling through evidence
of his personal extravagance and professional corruption. Yanukovych
said he supported the territorial integrity of the country and opposed
any military intervention by Russia; he too was unaware that Putin had
already launched one.

The day after Yanukovych surfaced, Putin submitted a proposal to
the Federation Council to authorize the use of military force in Ukraine.
The council's speaker, Valentina Matviyenko, who had only three days
earlier ruled out any intervention, promptly convened a rare Saturday
session that with remarkable alacrity approved Putin's request. After a
vitriolic "debate" in which speaker after speaker railed against the evil of
Ukraine and the United States, the 90 (of 166) members who were present voted unanimously to give Putin free rein to invade its neighbor—

after he already had. It was only after that, on March 2, that Putin summoned Yanukovych to his residence outside Moscow and forced him to draft and sign a letter, dated the day before—that is, before the Federation Council's authorization vote—asking Russia to intervene. "Ukraine is on the brink of a civil war. In the country there is chaos and anarchy," the letter said, blending indisputable fact with the paranoia that infused Putin's closest circle of advisers. "Under the influence of Western countries there are open acts of terror and violence. People are being persecuted for language and political reasons. So in this regard I would call on the president of Russia, Mr. Putin, asking him to use the armed forces of the Russian Federation to establish legitimacy, peace, law and order, stability and defend the people of Ukraine."[5]

The day he pressed Yanukovych to sign the letter, Putin held a series of telephone calls with world leaders who strained to understand what exactly was unfolding. The most crucial was the one with Angela Merkel. Only two days before, he had told her that there were no Russian troops in Crimea, but now he acknowledged that there were—something no Russian official would admit publicly until Putin did in April, six weeks after the fact.[6] Putin repeated his warnings that ethnic Russians faced violence in Ukraine, forcing him to act. Merkel, the leader who remained Putin's best interlocutor on the continent, now turned sharply against him. She telephoned Barack Obama even as he was on the phone with Putin afterward, and when they spoke, she dropped her cautious approach to the crisis and took a far harsher stance. The United States, soon followed by the European Union and other members of the G8, warned that Russia risked its international standing and withering sanctions if it pressed a territorial claim on Crimea.

Putin's strategy at this point unfolded haphazardly, catching even his underlings off guard. He was making decisions alone and off the cuff. After conspicuously attending the snap military exercises at the Kirillovsky range north of Moscow, Putin returned to Moscow on March 4 and for the first time spoke publicly about the crisis that had gripped Ukraine—and the world—for the previous two weeks. He met with a small group of journalists from the Kremlin pool at Novo-Ogaryovo. Unlike his carefully orchestrated yearly press conferences, this one was hastily organized, and even he seemed ill-prepared. His answers were confused and, at times, contradictory. He appeared uncomfortable, alternately slouching and squirming in his seat. He declared Yanukovych the only legitimate president of Ukraine, but said there was no legitimate leader in Ukraine that he could talk to. ("I think he has no political future," he added regarding Yanukovych, condescendingly, "and I have told him so.") A change in power in Ukraine was "probably necessary," but what happened in Kyiv was an "armed seizure of power" that had, "like the genie suddenly let out of the bottle," flooded the capital with nationalists, swastika-wearing "semi-fascists," and anti-Semites—and yet, he added, "We have no enemies in Ukraine."

And again he raised the question of America's wars in Afghanistan, in Iraq and Libya, which were inextricably involved in this crisis only in his mind. Obama had, in fact, reacted slowly to the events in Ukraine, distracted by the crises in the Middle East, but Putin was convinced that the Americans, even more than the Europeans, had instigated the upheaval. "I sometimes get the feeling that somewhere across that huge puddle, in America, people sit in a lab and conduct experiments, as if with rats, without actually understanding the consequences of what they are doing." He obliquely acknowledged that Russia had reinforced its troops at the headquarters of the Black Sea Fleet in Sevastopol, but when pressed on the soldiers in Russian uniforms, though without insignia, who were occupying key buildings he dissembled, calling them "local self-defense units." "You can go to a store and buy any kind of uniform," he said.

Putin expressed support for the right of people in Crimea to hold a referendum but emphasized that he was not considering the possibility of Crimea joining Russia. And yet two days later, with international opposition growing, Crimea's new parliament abruptly announced that it had accelerated its plans and would hold the referendum on the peninsula's fate in a mere ten days, on March 16. Despite the opposition of ethnic Ukrainians and Crimean Tatars, once horribly repressed under Stalin and free to return openly only after the collapse of the Soviet Union, the results of the referendum were now merely a formality. The following day, despite Putin's own disavowal only days before, the Kremlin made it clear that Crimea was returning to the Motherland, as leaders of the Duma and the Federation met with a delegation from Crimea, while an officially sanctioned mass rally was held in Red Square, which swayed with Russian flags and banners. "Crimea is Russian Land," many signs said. The slogans, like the new mission of Vladimir Putin, was soon condensed into an incantation that simultaneously conveyed both pride and pique, Putin's rebuttal to what he considered years of mounting disrespect for Russia. It would become a rallying cry with surprisingly deep resonance, though one that Putin, forced by an unexpected sequence of events, did not anticipate would define his legacy and Russia's for years to come: *Krim nash! Crimea is ours!*

And on March 18, two days after a referendum that was held under the barrels of Russian rifles and widely denounced as a farce, it was. Putin appeared in the Grand Kremlin Palace before the country's political elite—to a one, publicly at least, fully behind him—and declared Crimea and, separately, Sevastopol to be new constituent parts of the Russian Federation. "Everything in Crimea speaks of our shared history and pride," he told them, invoking the legendary place where Prince Vladimir was baptized, thus begetting Rus itself, and the battles, from Balaklava to Sevastopol, that symbolize "Russian military glory and outstanding valor." The audience applauded and cheered, interrupting his speech repeatedly. Some had tears in their eyes. Putin appeared later that evening at a rally and concert in Red Square, organized as a national celebration that would become a hallowed holiday. "After a long, hard and exhaustive journey at sea, Crimea and Sevastopol are returning to their home harbor, to the native shores, to the home port, to Russia!" he told the pulsating crowd. Among the songs played that night was a sentimental Soviet song called "Sevastopol Waltz." It had been written after the Great Patriotic War in 1953, a year after Putin was born. Most Russians of a certain age and temperament could sing along.

> *We returned home*
> *On the edge of the Soviet land*
> *Again, as before, the chestnuts are in bloom*
> *And again, I was waiting for you . . .*
> *Along the boulevards we will walk*
> *And, as in youth, we will sing.*

The last nation to annex the territory of another was Iraq in 1990, when the armies of Saddam Hussein swept through Kuwait. Iraq's invasion, occupation, and annexation prompted universal condemnation and ultimately the formation of an American-led military coalition that, under the auspices of the United Nations and with no objection from the Soviet Union, expelled the Iraqis a mere seven months later. Putin understood that; he knew the risks he took by seizing foreign territory. Even in 2008, when Russia thrust into Georgia, South Ossetia and Abkhazia were disputed territories policed by Russian peacekeepers and under attack by the Georgian military. Crimea was indisputably part of Ukraine, however, and faced no military or security threat. Putin, in a matter of days, had not only violated the sovereignty of a neighboring nation, he upended what many had presumed to be the immutable post–Cold War order that had taken root after the violent breakup of Yugoslavia in the 1990s, one which many in Europe hoped would usher in an era of peaceful cooperation and integration after the bloodshed of the twentieth century. Putin himself had repeatedly advocated as much, denouncing the unilateral use of force by the United States and its allies as a threat to an international system that protected the rights of sovereign nations from attack. He had made this exact argument only months before when Barack Obama debated a military strike against Syria for its use of chemical weapons.

Putin understood what the reaction would be to the annexation, but he also calculated that the world would not dare to act as it had against Saddam Hussein in 1990. Iraq had been a weak nation, but Russia was a resurgent superpower. The West would not act against Russia—certainly not on behalf of Ukraine—just as it had not acted in 2008 to preserve Georgia's territorial integrity. Russia was no longer an enervated Soviet Union in its twilight, and Putin was now prepared to act in what he, and he alone, considered the country's national interest. He seized Crimea from Ukraine because he could—because he believed that a superpower had the legal and moral authority to do so, just as the United States had been doing ever since the end of the Cold War.

The operation Putin ordered in Crimea reflected the lessons the military had learned from the war in Georgia, as well as the benefits of the military modernization he had overseen since he was prime minister. Russia's military budget had nearly doubled since 2005, reaching an estimated $84 billion in 2014. It lagged behind only the United States and China but spent more as a percentage of its gross domestic product than any major economy.[7] The effects of the modernization were manifested in new weaponry, including ships and fighter jets that increasingly challenged American and NATO's air defenses, but also in the training and equipping of its most elite forces, like those ordered into Ukraine. The seizure of Crimea demonstrated a more capable—and to other neighbors in Europe, a more ominous—military machine than any since the Red Army disintegrated. It blended hard power with soft power, speed and stealth, obfuscation and relentless propaganda meant to deflect culpability until it was too late to do anything about it. By the time Putin acknowledged that Russian forces had in fact taken control of the entire peninsula before the referendum on its status, the annexation was already a fait accompli. And despite the international opprobrium, it would not soon be reversed.

Putin scrambled to justify the annexation, and his shifting arguments echoed throughout the diplomatic and military establishments and thus in the media the Kremlin controlled. He argued that Crimea had once been part of the historic Russian empire, that it had been administered in Soviet times from Moscow until Nikita Khrushchev bequeathed it to the Ukrainian Socialist Republic in 1954, that it remained home of the new Russia's Black Sea Fleet, that the new government in Ukraine was illegitimate, that the people of Crimea voted for independence from Ukraine, that they faced imminent danger from marauding fascists. Sometimes he simply asserted a moral equivalency that the United States had invaded other countries so why could not Russia? The most ominous rationale for many was that he had intervened to protect his Russian "compatriots" in Crimea—that is, not citizens of Russia, but those Russians who, as he often pointed out, found themselves adrift in "foreign countries" when the Soviet Union splintered in 1991 into separate successor nations. For years he had extolled the *Russki mir,* or Russian world, the community united across borders by language, culture, and faith, but never before had he used the notion as a rationale for military action. It was an argument that had uncomfortable parallels to those Adolf Hitler used in 1938 to claim Austria and later the Sudetenland in Czechoslovakia for the *Volksgenossen.* The question now was where would Putin's policy stop? Other parts of Ukraine included significant populations of ethnic Russians, as did Kazakhstan and the three former Soviet republics now in NATO and protected by a mutual defense pledge contained in Article 5 of the alliance's charter: Lithuania, Latvia, and Estonia. Few thought that Putin would risk a military confrontation with NATO by attacking one of its member states, but no one seemed certain that Putin's calculations were entirely rational anymore.

Within days of the annexation of Crimea, protesters in eastern Ukraine, incited or joined by Russian intelligence agents and volunteer fighters, began seizing administrative buildings in several cities. In two provincial capitals, Donetsk and Luhansk, they denounced the new central authorities in Kyiv and declared the creation of "People's Republics," scheduling their own referendums for May. The events unfolded just as officials in the regions had warned they would do after the political upheaval in 2004, supported by compatriots across the border in Russia. Both regions included large populations of ethnic Russians, though not outright majorities, whose political sympathies were far closer to Putin's Russia than to Kyiv, especially after the upheaval in the winter of 2013–2014. They were far more susceptible to the propaganda of the Kremlin-controlled media, which was widely available in eastern Ukraine and which portrayed those now in power as rabid nationalists who would deny Russians basic rights, who would suppress them, even torture and kill them. Although he stopped short of expressing explicit support for the protests, Putin repeatedly denounced the Ukrainian authorities and restated Russia's right to protect the interests of the Russian world. Within weeks, he used the term *Novorossiya,* or New Russia, to evoke a historical claim over the swath of Ukrainian territory from Odessa to the Russian border that imperial Russia seized in the eighteenth century from the declining Ottoman Empire. The ethnic fault lines that rived Ukraine—like others left behind by the messy breakup of the Soviet Union—now ruptured, perhaps irrevocably.

The Americans and Europeans were caught by surprise by the move on Crimea, as they had been by the bloodshed in Kyiv and by Yanukovych's abrupt flight on February 22. The initial international reaction to the annexation—and the unrest in eastern Ukraine—was confused and halting, hobbled by Putin's subterfuge and the startling ease with which thousands of Russian commandos managed to seize more than ten thousand square miles of territory populated by nearly two million people. In the days before Crimea's referendum, leaders in Europe and the United States hoped that diplomatic pressure would work; when the referendum went ahead anyway, they calculated that the threat of economic punishment—and international censure—would still be deterrent enough.

On March 17, the day after the referendum, the United States and European Union announced sanctions against nearly a dozen officials in Russia and in Crimea, but they included only those like Valentina Matviyenko of the Federation Council and the former Kremlin political strategist Vladislav Surkov, who, though prominent, had no influence over the decisions Putin was making now. Putin paid no heed to the initial response. He brushed aside the increasingly stern warnings not only of Barack Obama, whose relations with him after the adoption ban,

Edward Snowden, and Syria were already beyond repair, but also of leaders like Angela Merkel, who remained the counterpart on the continent most vested in maintaining close relations with Russia. He so strained credulity in his conversations with Merkel, denouncing the nefarious European actions against Russia, that she confided in Obama her belief that Putin was now living "in another world."[8]

Putin's intransigence proved to be unifying, shoring up international opposition. Russia was expelled from the G8, whose annual summit was to be held in the summer of 2014 in the newly rebuilt Sochi. Two days after the annexation, the United States ratcheted up the sanctions, followed by the European Union. This time the sanctions targeted those closest to Putin, intending to change his behavior by inflicting punishment on the friends who had amassed their fortunes during his presidency. They included his old judo partners, Arkady and Boris Rotenberg; Vladimir Yakunin, Yuri Kovalchuk, and Andrei Fursenko from the Ozero dacha cooperative; and Gennady Timchenko. Echoing the claims made by Putin's critics for years, the Treasury Department in Washington asserted that Putin himself had investments in Timchenko's company, Gunvor, and "may have access to Gunvor funds." The Americans accused Kovalchuk's Bank Rossiya of acting as the "personal banker" of senior officials in the Kremlin, including Putin.[9] The sanctions barred those targeted from traveling to the United States, froze their assets, and forbade American companies from doing business with them, effectively restricting their activities involving dollars almost anywhere. The American and European sanctions would continue to expand, singling out more officials and businesses, including the Rotenbergs' bank, SMP, the Russian abbreviation for the Northern Sea Route, which coursed through the Arctic, and ultimately entire sectors of the economy, including Rosneft and its ambitious plans to extract oil from the Arctic.

And yet these new sanctions had no more obvious effect than the sanctions against the aides and acolytes of the outer orbits of Putin's power, indeed, no more obvious effect than no sanctions at all. Putin's resolve could not be challenged even by those closest to him. All of those sanctioned—the high and the low, the close friends and the acquaintances, the agents of influence and the mere hangers-on—owed their places within the system to him. They were the new elite of the Putin era, above the law and thus protected by one man's justice. Their power and their fortunes relied on his power and their loyalty to him. Vladimir Yakunin, for whom the sanctions seemed a personal affront, said his

old friend would never let anyone try to dissuade him from any decision made in what he considered the best interests of Russia. He would
consider even the effort to do so an act of betrayal. "He will not forget
that—or forgive that," Yakunin said.[10]

And no one dared. One after another, those facing sanctions
expressed fealty and solidarity with the leader, proclaiming their willingness to make any sacrifice that was necessary. "You have to pay for
everything in this life," Gennady Timchenko said, rather richly, since he
had managed to sell his shares in Gunvor to his partner the day *before* the
sanctions were announced, suggesting that he had insider information
of the looming threat and moved quickly to protect his assets from seizure. Timchenko acknowledged his Gulfstream jet had been grounded
because he could no longer buy parts to service it, that his wife's credit
cards had been suspended, and that he could no longer safely vacation
in Europe with his family and their dog, Romi, the offspring of Putin's
beloved Koni. "But one can put up with business costs and personal
inconveniences when state interests are at stake. These are trifles on the
background of global problems."[11]

Protests like the ones that materialized in Simferopol and other cities
of Crimea in February spread across Ukraine. In Odessa, a violent
confrontation in May between pro-Russian protesters and government
supporters in the city's center ended in a fire at the old House of Trade
Unions that killed forty-eight people. The referendums held that month
by the people's republics of Donetsk and Luhansk were as hastily organized and legally dubious at the one in Crimea. Ukraine's security service
claimed to have captured a recording of one rebel leader, Dmitri Boitsov
of the Russian Orthodox Army, complaining that he could not oversee
a vote because a large force of Ukrainian troops and weaponry remained
in the region. "We can't conduct it lawfully as long as these cocksuckers
are here," he said. The man allegedly on the other end of the line was
Aleksandr Barkashov, a notorious neo-Nazi in Russia who in 1993 had
joined those who defended the White House in Moscow in defiance of
Boris Yeltsin's decrees. He told him to press ahead anyway, fixing a result
of, say, 89 percent. "Are you going to walk around collecting papers?"
Barkashov barked at him. "Are you fucking insane?"[12]

When the votes were counted, the total mirrored his recommendation—with 89 percent in favor—while in Luhansk the tally exceeded an
improbable 96 percent. The referendums were followed by escalating

violent clashes. The country descended into open war, one that the chief of Russia's general staff, Valery Gerasimov, seemingly anticipated the year before when he outlined a new military doctrine drafted after Putin's return to the presidency in reaction to the uprisings in the Arab world. "In the twenty-first century, we have seen a tendency toward blurring the lines between the states of war and peace," General Gerasimov wrote.[13] "Wars are no longer declared and, having begun, proceed according to an unfamiliar template. The experience of military conflicts—including those connected with the so-called colored revolutions in North Africa and the Middle East—confirm that a perfectly thriving state can, in a matter of months and even days, be transformed into an arena of fierce armed conflict, become a victim of foreign intervention, and sink into a web of chaos, humanitarian catastrophe, and civil war." And so it would be.

The annexation of Crimea had proved nearly effortless, but the situation in eastern Ukraine turned out to be far more complicated, and the uncertainty of Putin's intentions muddled the efforts by the insurgents. The newly elected president who replaced the self-exiled Yanukovych, the chocolate tycoon Petro Poroshenko, also acted with far greater determination to hold onto the rebellious regions in the east than the provisional government had been able to do in the case of Crimea in March. The Ukrainian military, joined by irregular militias that had formed during the events on the Maidan, counterattacked and moved to retake territory that was no longer government controlled, and with each passing day the fighting turned into civil war. Officially at least, Putin maintained an assiduous distance from those calling for independence in Donetsk and Luhansk; with the sanctions tightening further than he probably expected, he even called for postponing the votes on independence. The Americans and Europeans hoped that the diplomatic isolation facing Russia and the intensifying sanctions were, at last, altering Putin's choices, forcing him and other officials into more and more improbable denials of Russian involvement.

The insurgents nevertheless had ample support from Russia, both officially and unofficially. Their leaders at first were ethnic Russians, including a former or possible current military intelligence officer, Igor Girkin, who went by the nom de guerre Igor Strelkov. The militias that formed—and there were many, with unclear chains of command—included local fighters and "volunteers" from Russia who, the Kremlin insisted unconvincingly, joined the uprisings purely out of a fraternal desire to defend the *Russki mir*. Some had fought in the previous conflicts along the unravelling fringes of the Soviet empire in the early 1990s, like Abkhazia and South Ossetia in Georgia and the sliver of territory in Moldova known as Transnistria. They were bolstered by Russian commandos and intelligence officers and later regular troops, dispatched as "volunteers" by their commanders with the promise of extra payments and required on the Kremlin's orders to resign from the military and wear no Russian insignia. Putin did not want to risk an open Russian intervention, and the obfuscation masked the extent of Russia's activity enough to create confusion and, as he hoped, division and debate within Europe over how forcefully to respond. As Gerasimov predicted, the conflict in eastern Ukraine blurred the lines between war and peace, between instigator and defender. The Kremlin continued to deny the existence of Russian fighters and weaponry in Ukraine long after the first coffins of soldiers returned to Russia, buried in secrecy, just as the bodies of those who had died for the Soviet Union in Afghanistan. It would do so even after Russian soldiers were captured inside Ukraine and paraded by the authorities there.

On June 6, Putin traveled to France to attend ceremonies commemorating the seventieth anniversary of the Allied landings in Normandy on D-Day. His ostracism was palpable. The G7, having expelled Russia, met that week in Brussels instead of Sochi. Including him in the memorial ceremonies paid homage to the Soviet Union's contribution to the defeat of the Nazis, but Russia's intervention in a new war strained even that courtesy. The European leaders became increasingly frustrated with Putin's denials of culpability and his insistence that only a political resolution was possible, as he was equally frustrated by Ukrainian efforts to reassert control over the regions in the east. Angela Merkel and François Hollande tested his stated desire for a peaceful political solution in Ukraine by brokering peace talks. For the first time since the crisis began, he met Petro Poroshenko in Normandy, acting as proxy for the rebel regions he disavowed providing any support to. The fighting, however, intensified anyway, with government forces and insurgents trading fire with heavier weapons, including mortar and artillery.

A month later, Putin met again with Merkel in Brazil ahead of a World Cup final between Germany and Argentina. He was in attendance as the leader of the host nation for the tournament in 2018, a highly anticipated event for which he had already launched a new mega-project of stadium construction but one that would be dogged by questions over improprieties surrounding Russia's winning bid.[14] Even as they met again, pledging to negotiate a new ceasefire, there were new reports of Russian equipment crossing the border. A day later a Ukrainian AN-26 military cargo jet flying at an altitude of more than twenty-thousand feet was shot down along the Russian border near Luhansk; its downing, coming after the destruction of another military transport jet as it landed in June, was a portentous sign of the increasing firepower of the insurgents. Two days after that a Sukhoi fighter jet went down, hit by a sophisticated surface-to-air missile of a type the irregular fighters were not known to possess.

On the afternoon of July 17, the website used by Igor Strelkov posted a note announcing the downing of yet another AN-26, this one near the village of Torez, located between Donetsk and the Russian border. "We warned them—don't fly 'in our sky,'" the statement, attributed to Strelkov, declared triumphantly.[15] The Ukrainians later claimed to have intercepted telephone calls between a fighter and a Russian intelligence officer confirming the downing. It was not a Ukrainian military jet, though. The wreckage that fell from the sky belonged to a Boeing 777, carrying 283 passengers and 15 crew members on Malaysia Airways Flight 17 from Amsterdam to Kuala Lumpur. Their bodies landed amid the debris over several square miles of farmland, sown with wheat.

By all accounts except that of the Russians, a surface-to-air missile from a mobile battery known as a 9K37 Buk struck the airliner as it flew over the Donetsk region. Witnesses, including reporters from the Associated Press, reported seeing the battery moving through the villages nearby, while subsequent reports traced the unit to the Russian military, specifically the 53rd Anti-Aircraft Missile Brigade based in the city of Kursk. The unit was said to have crossed the border from Russia the night before and returned again, carrying only three of its four missiles. A preliminary investigation by the government of the Netherlands also concluded that the airline exploded in midair, the damage to its fuselage consistent with the explosion of a missile like the Buk, not a missile fired from a fighter jet, as Russia's Ministry of Defense quickly asserted.[16]

Putin, who was returning from his trip to Brazil when the tragedy occurred, spoke by telephone with Merkel and Obama that day, but made only terse statements in public. He said nothing about the evident source of the missile—neither to confirm nor deny Russian involvement—but blamed the tragedy on the resumption of fighting in eastern Ukraine, suggesting that it was the fault of the government of

Ukraine for trying to regain territory being held by armed insurgents. "No one should, and no one has the right, to use this tragedy to pursue his own political goals," he said in an unusual television address, delivered in the wee hours of the morning on July 21. He looked tired and drawn, standing shakily at his office desk, his eyes reddened. "Rather than dividing us, tragedies of this sort should bring people together. All those who are responsible for the situation in the region must take greater responsibility before their own peoples and before the peoples of the countries whose citizens were killed in this disaster." And yet he took no responsibility upon himself for any role in the tragedy, or in an increasingly deadly conflict that would kill thousands and drive hundreds of thousands of people from their homes on a continent that had dreamed of putting its bloody history behind it.

The world—at least much of the West—turned definitively against Putin after Flight 17. "Putin's missile," the British tabloid *The Sun* declared, and even more sober news organizations drew an inexorable line of responsibility. Without Putin, there would have been no annexation of Crimea, no war in eastern Ukraine, no wreckage scattered across the wheat fields. This was Putin's war, and the best efforts of the Kremlin's propagandists to muddy the waters—by broadcasting false claims and conspiracy theories—did nothing to obviate the blame. Even if he did not understand it, others around him did. He could have reined in the rebel leaders, withdrawn the Russian forces and equipment, facilitated the international investigation into the downing, and found and turned over to justice those responsible for the murder of 298 people. And yet he could no more do that than he could acknowledge the other failings of his presidency, the other sensational crimes, the corruption that erected the system of loyalty that he had created. Putin had made himself the symbol of the resurgent Russia, and the idea had to be maintained without acknowledgment of fault. Only in a cult of power can the leader be inseparable from the state. "There is Putin, and there is Russia," the man who had replaced Vladislav Surkov in 2011 as the Kremlin's political strategist, Vyacheslav Volodin, said in 2014. "No Putin—no Russia."[17]

The rift between Russia and the West now seemed irrevocable, and it was deliberate. The United States had already expanded its sanctions the day before the downing of Flight 17, and in the wake of the accident, opposition in Europe to intensifying its sanctions evaporated as well.

Entire sectors of the economy, including banking and energy, now faced sanctions, not just the officials and friends close to Putin. By the middle of 2014, capital flight had reached $75 billion for the year as those with cash sought safe harbors offshore; by the end of the year, $150 billion had fled the country. The economy, already slowing, slumped badly as investments withered. The value of the ruble crashed, despite efforts by the Central Bank to shore it up. The price of oil slumped—which Putin blamed on a conspiracy between the United States and Saudi Arabia—and that strained the budget, depleting the reserves that Putin had steadfastly built up throughout his years in power. Russia plunged into an economic crisis as bad as the ones in 1998 and 2009. Putin's tactics had backfired. Many in the West cheered, seeing the economic crisis as evidence of the self-inflicted pain of Putin's actions, but the isolation also fed Putin's view that the crises confronting Russia economically and diplomatically were part of a vast conspiracy effort to weaken Russia—to weaken his rule.

The day after the downing of Flight 17, the international arbitration court in the Hague finally issued its verdicts in the cases brought by the shareholders of Yukos over the expropriation of the company, ordering Russia to pay more than $50 billion in damages, citing Putin's own defense of the auction of the company's crown jewel a decade before as evidence of government collusion.[18] Each step against Russia he now believed to be a cynical, calculated attack against him. His actions belied a deep sense of grievance and betrayal, sharpened by the crisis that unfolded at the very moment Russia had achieved his Olympic dream. He was impervious to the threats of sanctions or international isolation because he now believed Russia's views, its interests, would never be respected, as he felt he had never been shown adequate respect, all the more so since he returned to the Kremlin in 2012 after the four-year interregnum as prime minister.

Putin had not miscalculated in his actions against Crimea and later in eastern Ukraine. He simply no longer cared how the West would respond. The change in Putin's demeanor became acute after the downing of Flight 17, according to his old friend, Sergei Roldugin. "I noticed that the more he is being teased the tougher he becomes," Roldugin said. It was as if the political upheaval in Ukraine affected Putin deeply and personally, like a taunt on the schoolyard that forced him to lash out. Merkel, according to Roldugin, infuriated him by being dismissive of the concerns he raised about the radicals in the ranks of Ukraine's new government, about the threats to the country's Russian minority, about the atrocities being committed by Ukrainian troops against civilians. Everyone wanted to blame him for the missile that destroyed the airliner, but what about the atrocities committed by the Ukrainian government against those in the east? Where once he had been patient with Merkel and other leaders, he was now annoyed; where once compromising, he was now unbending. "All this has annoyed him and he has become more—I don't want to say aggressive—but more indifferent," Roldugin explained. "He knows that we shall resolve it one way or another, but he does not want to compromise anymore."

For Putin, the personal had become policy. The pragmatism of his first two terms as president had long before ended, but now the upheaval in Ukraine signaled a fundamental break in the trajectory that he had followed since Yeltsin unexpectedly handed him the presidency at the dawn of the new millennium. For fourteen years in power, he had focused on restoring Russia to its place among the world's powers by integrating into a globalized economy, profiting from and exploiting the financial institutions of the free market—banks, stock markets, trading houses—to the benefit of those tycoons closest to him, of course, but also Russians generally. Now he would reassert Russia's power with or without the recognition of the West, shunning its "universal" values, its democracy and rule of law, as something alien to Russia, something intended not to include Russia but to subjugate it. The nation became "hostage to the psychosomatic quirks of its leader," the novelist Vladimir Sorokin wrote after the annexation. "All his fears, passions, weaknesses, and complexes become state policy. If he is paranoid, the whole country must fear enemies and spies; if he has insomnia, all the ministries must work at night; if he's a teetotaler, everyone must stop drinking; if he's a drunk, everyone should booze it up; if he doesn't like America, which his beloved KGB fought against, the whole population must dislike the United States."[19]

Opposition to Putin—to Putinism—continued to exist, but the events of 2014 drove it even further toward the margins of society. The leaders who did pose a challenge, or might once have, were under siege more than ever. Some left even before the events in Ukraine, including Garry Kasparov, who feared his imminent arrest after Aleksandr Bastrykin's investigative committee telephoned and spoke to his mother while he was traveling. A telephone call from the committee was now as ominous a warning as the KGB's knock on the door had once been.[20]

Kasparov was followed by others hounded out of Russia by investigators: the economist Sergei Guriev, who had advised Medvedev; a former central banker, Sergei Aleksashenko; and one of Aleksei Navalny's deputies who worked on his anti-corruption campaign, Vladimir Askurov, who received political asylum in Britain. Pavel Durov, the creator of Russia's version of Facebook, called VKontakte, and an example of a dynamic new generation of Russians, sold his remaining stake in the company and left the country, saying later, "Since I'm obviously a believer in free markets, it's hard for me to understand the current direction of the country."[21]

Boris Berezovsky, the man who claimed to be Putin's progenitor and became his biggest nemesis, died outside of London in 2013, ostensibly a suicide, hung by a cord in his bathroom. As ever when Berezovsky was involved, suspicion of a more nefarious end to his life never subsided entirely. Mikhail Khodorkovsky, amnestied by Putin in the winter of 2013, relocated to Switzerland and reopened his Open Russia once again to promote democracy in Russia. He offered himself as a potential leader of a provisional government that might one day serve as a transition to a new Russia, but he dared not return to the country.

At home, those who challenged the Kremlin's narrative on Ukraine were shunned. A prominent historian, Andrei Zubov, was fired from his post at the Moscow State Institute of International Relations for comparing the annexation of Crimea to Hitler's Anschluss in Austria in 1938, an event, he noted, that was followed by war and finally the fall of the Third Reich. "Friends," he implored in *Vedomosti*, "history repeats itself."[22] His ostracism was as swift and severe as the satirist Viktor Shenderovich's lament over a skater's gold at the Olympics. *Vedomosti's* founding editor, Leonid Bershidsky, announced his own exile in a newspaper column not long afterward, speaking for a generation of intelligentsia who saw Putin's Russia as no longer compatible with the relative freedoms to which they had grown accustomed. He wrote in *The Moscow Times* that he was not a panicked rat abandoning the sinking Russian ship. "I am more a sailor who, seeing that the captain had changed course toward a port of ill repute—and with loudspeakers blaring his intent—quietly, and without panicking, lowered the lifeboat and began rowing toward the port for which all of us had originally set sail."[23]

Others stayed on, fighting an increasingly lonely battle against Putin and the forces of nationalism he had unleashed. Alesksei Navalny, after being arrested while protesting the verdicts in the Bolotnaya cases at the closing of the Sochi Olympics, spent most of 2014 under house arrest, confined to his small apartment in a Soviet-era block in southern Moscow. The only opposition leader to have emerged from the grassroots of society—one who was not beholden to the Kremlin and charismatic enough to win a following independent of its influence—was forbidden for months from meeting anyone except his relatives and from using the Internet, the medium he had used so effectively to make himself a threat to Putin's system. With surveillance equipment brazenly installed around his apartment, he whiled away his days playing Grand Theft Auto, leaving only to attend court hearings, accompanied by a police escort. With prosecutors opening new cases—including one involving a "stolen" street poster as a gift and another that would send his brother, Oleg, to prison—his court appearances became more and more regular. The Kremlin's shadow loomed over him as it had the dissidents of the past.

"What have we won?" he said inside his apartment at the end of 2014, when the terms of his arrest were eased somewhat, musing on Putin's annexation of Crimea and the international demonization that followed in its wake. "Now literally no one likes us," he said. Even Ukraine, a natural ally, now hated Russia, if not Russians. The war overshadowed the work of Navalny's anticorruption campaign, which continued to expose the neo-feudal links between power and money. It became a war against all things Western, including those who would advocate for greater political openness and transparency. It permeated society, even the nightly weather reports Navalny watched on television, which took to warning that the situation in eastern Ukraine was "heating up." Putin had plunged the country into "a perpetual war" and thus "a perpetual mobilization," Navalny said. He rallied the country behind a manifest destiny that it had once lost, regardless of the cost in international standing. And yet, the more disastrous Putin's decisions were, the more powerful he became. With the country at war, his position seemed even more unassailable. It was a contradiction that Navalny, like others at home and abroad, struggled to understand. "In terms of strengthening his regime, Putin won," he said with an air of resignation. "In terms of Russia's strategic interests, we lost."[24]

Boris Nemtsov, who managed to get himself elected to the regional assembly in Yaroslavl, also continued to campaign against Putin, relying on the legal immunity that his legislative seat provided as some measure of protection. He fulminated against the war in postings on Facebook and Twitter, describing Putin as a ghoul who needed blood to survive. And yet he too acknowledged that Putin seemed resistant to the growing body of evidence that Russians were fighting and dying in Ukraine. He complained that the international sanctions and diplomatic isolation remained half-hearted. He wanted stronger international efforts to end Putin's regime, not to negotiate with it. "He's not in isolation," Nemtsov said. "He talks to Merkel. He talks to everyone." Nemtsov carried on undaunted, compiling evidence for another of his pamphlets, like those on Gazprom, on corruption, on Sochi. This time he would document the Russian involvement in the fighting in eastern Ukraine—on Putin's orders—and try to awaken the political conscience of the Russian people to the crimes being committed. He would call this one simply, "Putin. War." He would not finish it, though.[25] One night in February 2015, he was shot to death as he walked along the bridge leading from Red Square. He died within sight of the Kremlin, his death, like Politkovskaya's in 2006, a casualty of a larger war. It was no random act of violence, but a highly organized assassination carried out in the middle of one of the most heavily policed places on the planet. His murder was linked to assassins from Chechnya, some allegedly close to Ramzan Kadyrov, the man Putin had relied on to reestablish control over a region that once threatened to spin free of Russia but whose brutal rule now operated without constraints. Putin's indefatigable spokesman, Dmitri Peskov, let it be known that Putin was shocked by the tragedy but also that Nemtsov's influence had not been great. As with Politkovskaya's murder—or Aleksandr Litvinenko's or Sergei Magnitsky's—Putin may not have been personally involved or aware, as his supporters insisted. By then, however, it was difficult to argue that his epoch was not washed by the blood of his harshest critics.

On July 31, 2014, some of Russia's richest men gathered in Moscow at the headquarters of the Russian soccer federation to deal with an unexpected consequence of Putin's annexation of Crimea. They included the federation's officials, as well as the owners of its most prominent professional teams: Sergei Galitsky, the owner of a supermarket chain and the Krasnodar Football Club; Suleiman Kerimov, the tycoon who owned Anzhi Makhachkala in Dagestan; and Vladimir Yakunin, whose Russian Railways sponsored Lokomotiv Moskva. On the agenda was a vote by the foundation's executive committee to absorb Crimea's three clubs into the Russian league, and those gathered there harbored reservations about the risk of sanctions that could extend to them and their clubs. They could be barred from traveling to the West, expelled from competitions in Europe. "I don't have any doubts that we're all going to fall under sanctions," Galitsky complained, according to a transcript of their testy exchange, which was surreptitiously recorded and leaked to the newspaper *Novaya Gazata*.[26] He expressed frustration that everything he had built over the last quarter century—a chain of stores called Magnit that employed 250,000 people and was worth $30 billion—could be lost. Others in the committee's conference room shared his concern—as well as his fear of displeasing the "chief executive." Galitsky and the others clearly hoped to avoid having to vote, circuitously debating whether they needed to and whether a statement by the sports minister, Vitaly Mutko, could be as good as the word of Putin himself. None wanted to be put on the record with a vote, as the head of the union was insisting; nor did they want to risk disobeying Putin by not voting.

"It's obvious I'm ready to suffer," he said, but he would do so only if "the chief executive" made his choice on the matter clear. "Only after that would I be ready to ruin what I built over twenty-five years," Galitski declared.

When the president and co-owner of CSKA Moscow, Yevgeny Giner, echoed his reluctance, the head of the union and Yakunin turned on him sharply, calling his views "indecent." "Our country is under sanction," Yakunin told him. "Our president is standing alone on the parapet. And you're talking about screwing the country to the point they impose additional sanctions? They'll do it. No matter what you do, even if you crawl before them on your stomach—they'll do it! Understand? So either bug out of this country or behave appropriately, like a citizen of this country."

Nine days later, Putin having made his wishes clear, the union's executive committee accepted the three new teams into Russia's professional league. Sergei Stepashin, Putin's predecessor as prime minister and now a member of the union's executive committee, had warned them. "Directives aren't even needed. Crimea is a priori a territory of Russia!"

Crimea had become the new rallying cry around which the nation would unite behind Putin, the argument that ended all debate. The annexation drove his approval ratings above 85 percent, and the state of siege that followed—amplified by Orwellian agitprop on the state television—sustained Putin's popular support at home for months to come. After a quarter century of openness since the Soviet collapse, of economic and cultural exchange, most Russians again looked at the outside world as an enemy at the gates, to be feared and resisted. The siege mentality justified any sacrifice. "When a Russian feels any foreign pressure, he will never give up his leader," said one of Putin's deputy prime ministers, Igor Shuvalov, considered one of the liberals in his cabinet.[27] "We will survive any hardship in the country—eat less food, use less electricity."

Fear of censure, or worse, certainly silenced dissenting voices, but Putin had reasserted his place at the pinnacle of power, the indisputable leader of a country no longer a democracy except in periodic electoral simulation. After returning to power in 2012 with no clear purpose other than the exercise of power for its own sake, Putin now found the unifying factor for a large, diverse nation still in search of one. He found a millenarian purpose for the power that he held, one that shaped his country greater than any other leader had thus far in the twenty-first century. He had restored neither the Soviet Union nor the tsarist empire, but a new Russia with the characteristics and instincts of both, with himself as secretary general and sovereign, as indispensable as the country itself was exceptional. *No Putin, no Russia.* He had unified the country behind the only leader anyone could now imagine because he was, as in 2008 and 2012, unwilling to allow any alternative to emerge.

When he "disappeared" from public view for ten days in March 2015, the political elite seemed gripped by paralysis, the media filled with fevered speculation. Was Putin ill? Was there a coup? Was he grappling with an internal power struggle stemming from Nemtsov's assassination, whose killers were traced to the Chechnya he had kept in Russia's orbit under Ramzan Kadyrov? There were new rumors that he had fathered another child with Alina Kabayeva, who by then had resigned her seat in the Duma and joined the National Media Group, controlled by Bank Rossiya and Putin's old friend, Yuri Kovalchuk. Others contended he simply underwent a new round of medical treatment for a bad back—or cosmetic surgery. Whatever the explanation, his brief and ultimately inconsequential absence from public view proved that he alone provided the stability that kept the unwieldy, kleptocratic system in place, the factions of Putin's elite in stable equipoise.

Putin's rule was no more permanent now than it had been inevitable. Yet it seemed inexorable. He faced no obvious challenge to his power before the presidential election scheduled for 2018. He could by law serve six more years after that. When—if—he stepped down in 2024, he would not yet be seventy-two. Brezhnev had died in office at seventy-five; Stalin at seventy-four. He might then hand power to a new leader, Medvedev again perhaps or another member of the inner circle. It would ultimately be up to him. The fate of Russia was now entwined with his own, rushing forward as the troika in Gogol's *Dead Souls* to an unknown destiny. Putin probably did not know himself whither—except forward, impetuous, unrepentant, undaunted. "The air rumbles, shattered to pieces, and turns to wind," Gogol wrote of the troika.[28] "Everything on earth flies by, and, looking askance, other nations and states step aside to make way."

Acknowledgments

In the writing of this book, I am profoundly indebted to many, many people and two great institutions.

This book simply would not exist without *The New York Times,* where I have had the privilege to work since 1989. I am grateful to the editors who dispatched me as a correspondent to Moscow in 2002, and again in 2013, and who granted me leave to write the book. They include executive editors Joe Lelyveld, Howell Raines, Bill Keller, Jill Abramson, and Dean Baquet, and foreign editors Roger Cohen, Susan Chira, and Joe Kahn. The bones of this book were formed by my reporting for the *Times,* but also by that of colleagues past and present in the Moscow Bureau: Steven Erlanger (who first interviewed Vladimir Putin for the newspaper in April 1992), Frank Clines, Serge Schmemann, Felicity Barranger, Celestine Bohlen, Michael Specter, Alessandra Stanley, Michael Gordon, Michael Wines, Sabrina Tavernise, Sonia Kishkovsky, Seth Mydans, Erin Arvedlund, Rachel Thorner, Chris Chivers, Andrew Kramer, Michael Schwirtz, Cliff Levy, Ellen Berry, Andrew Roth, David Herszenhorn, Patrick Reevell, and, finally, James Hill, whose photographs are among those included in the preceding pages. None of our work would have been possible without the bureau's staff, particularly Natasha Bubenova, Oleg Shevchenko, Pavel Chervyakov, Alexandra Ordynova, and especially, the wonderful translators, fixers, traveling companions, and friends: Nikolay Khalip and Viktor Klimenko. I also thank Maria Goncharova for her assistance on a series of articles in 2014 on the economic pillars of Putin's rule, written with my colleagues Jo Becker and Jim Yardley.

The other institution is the Woodrow Wilson International Center for Scholars in Washington, D.C., which provided me a place to study

and write within its Kennan Institute, where the atmosphere was serious, nonpartisan, and thoroughly convivial. I thank the center's director,
Jane Harman, as well as Blair Ruble, Robert Litwak, and Will Pomeranz;
my research assistant there, Grace Kenneally; and the staff of the center's library—Janet Spikes, Dagne Gizaw, and Michelle Kamalich—who
guided me through not only the stacks of George Kennan's collection,
but also the Library of Congress, which extends the center's scholars
special access.

I relied on research by Almut Schoenfeld in Berlin and Dresden and
Noah Sneider in Moscow. Bryon MacWilliams, my old friend, author,
translator, and *banya* compatriot, also scoured obscure sources, while
acting as an expert on the nuances of the Russian language and culture.
Others read all or parts of the book and shared their insights, advice
and encouragement, including Nina Khrushcheva, Geraldine Fagan,
Frank Brown, Nathan Hodge, Max Trudolyubov, and Rory MacFar-
quhar. I also consulted many other experts on Russia, most of whom
have published their own books on subjects covered here, including
Anders Aslund, Harley Balzer, Karen Dawisha, Clifford Gaddy, Mark
Galeotti, Thane Gustafson, Fiona Hill, Oleg Kalugin, David Kramer,
Andrew Kuchins, Cliff Kupchan, Andrei Miroshnichenko, Robert Orttung, Peter Reddaway, Andrei Soldatov, and Dmitri Trenin.

There were several officials in Russia and the United States who provided information on condition that I not identify them; I appreciate
their confidence. Another source over the years—and a character in this
book—was Boris Nemtsov, who was assassinated near the Kremlin in
February 2015 just as I was finishing. He was a Russian patriot. May
justice prevail.

I owe a singular debt to Larry Weissman, the literary agent who
reached out more than a decade ago and planted the seed that grew into
this book. I would also like to thank the people at Alfred A. Knopf who
agreed to publish this book and who helped pull it together, especially a
fine editor, Andrew Miller.

Many others have supported me in ways large and small. I hesitate
to name them for fear of leaving someone out, but they include Boris
Shekhtman, who first taught me Russian, and Sveta Prudnikova, whose
irrepressible spirit never faltered as she tried to make my Russian better;
and my colleagues from the *Times* and elsewhere: Catherine Belton, Alan
Cowell, Alan Cullison, Peter Finn, Nicole Gaouette, Isabel Gorst, Nick

Kulish, Albina Kovalyova, Mark Mazzetti, Anna Nemtsova, Arkady Ostrovsky, and Sharon Weinberger. Finally, I thank my wife, Margaret Xavier Myers, and our daughters, Emma and Madeline, who tolerated the numerous inconveniences involved in this effort and to whom I have dedicated this book.

NOTES

EPIGRAPH

Fyodor Dostoevsky, *The Brothers Karamazov,* translated by Andrew R. MacAndrew (New York: Bantam Books, 1970), pp. 34–35.

CHAPTER 1: HOMO SOVIETICUS

1. The date of Vladimir Spiridonovich Putin's injury and the detail of his unit were reported by the official Russian Information Agency, during a memorial visit to the battlefield by Putin in 2004. The agency was rebranded as Sputnik in 2014; see http://sputniknews.com/onlinenews/20040127/39906137 .html.

2. Michael Jones, *Leningrad: State of Siege* (New York: Basic Books, 2008), p. 139.

3. Gevorkyan, Nataliya, Natalya Timakova, and Andrei Kolesnikov, *First Person: An Astonishingly Frank Self-Portrait by Russia's President Vladimir Putin* (New York: Public Affairs, 2000), p. 7. Putin recalls that "our guys" held the bridgehead throughout the war, which is not true.

4. Testimony at the Nuremburg trials, http://avalon.law.yale.edu/imt/02–22 –46.asp. Anna Reid, *Leningrad: The Epic Siege of World War II, 1941–1944* (New York: Walker, 2011), also cites the order, p. 135. In addition to Reid's and Jones's histories of the siege, see also Harrison E. Salisbury, *The 900 Days: The Siege of Leningrad* (New York: Harper & Row, 1969), and Alexander Werth, *Russia at War, 1941–1945* (New York: E. P. Dutton, 1964), part 3.

5. Reid, p. 114.

6. Gevorkyan et al., p. 3.

7. Christopher Andrew and Vasili Mitrokhin, *The Sword and the Shield: The Mitrokhin Archive and the Secret History of the KGB* (New York: Basic Books, 1999), p. 99.

8. Gevorkyan et al., p. 6.

9. Oleg M. Blotsky, *Vladmir Putin: Istoriya Zhizni* [Vladmir Putin: A Life Story] (Moscow: Mezhdunarodniye Otnosheniya, 2004), p. 83.

10. Werth, p. 308.

11. Max Hastings, *Inferno: The World at War, 1939–1945* (New York: Alfred A. Knopf, 2011), p. 169. Hastings notes that the privileged "escaped most of the suffering."

12. Gevorkyan et al., p. 5. The English translation mistakenly refers to Maria's brother as Peter, when in fact Putin did not name the brother. The captain was Ivan Ivanovich Shelomov. Maria did have a brother, Pyotr, who died on the front in the very first days of the war.

13. Gevorkyan et al., p. 6. Putin himself has retold this story repeatedly, though with shifting details that are impossible to verify. In 2012, he told Hillary Rodham Clinton that his father had found Maria in a stack of corpses, recognizing her by her shoes. He demanded to have her body and discovered she was still alive. Clinton recounts the anecdote in *Hard Choices* (New York: Simon & Schuster, 2014), p. 243.

14. Gevorkyan et al., pp. 8–9.

15. Jones, p. 249. Also see Werth, p. 309, and *Nezivisimoye Voyennoye Obozreniye* [Independent Military Review], March 14, 2003.

16. Jones, p. 141.

17. Gevorkyan et al., pp. 8–9.

18. Reid's *Leningrad* provides a wrenching history of the siege, as does Hastings's *Inferno*, pp. 164–171. See also Salisbury, and Jones.

19. Nikolai Zenkovich, *Putinskaya Entsiklopediya* (Moscow: Olma-Press, 2006), p. 363.

20. In 2012, a group in St. Petersburg found a record of his brother's death and burial in the cemetery, which Putin said he had not previously been told about, though he mentions it in Gevorkyan et al., *First Person;* and *New York Times,* Jan. 28, 2012.

21. The names of Putin's uncles who died during the war can be found in a searchable online catalogue of casualties from the war, www.obd-memorial.ru. Richard Sakwa, in *Putin: Russia's Choice* (London: Routledge, 2004), describes the losses to Putin's mother's family.

22. Russians use the patronymic of their father's first name: Vladimir Spiridonovich is the son of Spiridon; Vladimir Vladimirovich, the son of Vladimir; etc. The use of both first name and patronymic in address is a sign of respect and formality.

23. Reid, p. 402.

24. Gevorkyan et al., p. 3.

25. Ibid., p. 17.

26. A rumor has circulated for years that Putin was in fact born to another woman and later given up for adoption to distant relatives, Vladimir and

Maria Putin. The rumor resurfaced in 2008 when a woman in Georgia claimed to be his mother, but no evidence has emerged that would lend it credibility.

27. Putin has recounted this story on various occasions with different details. Of course, he would not remember himself and thus was relying on the story his mother told him. He told this version in remarks to reporters outside the cathedral at Christmas, 2000. See http://www.youtube.com /watch?feature=player_detailpage&v=u3d_yxJhmjk.

28. Sakwa, p. 3.

29. Gevorkyan et al., p. 11. In Putin's recollection of the neighbor, he did not seem impressed by the neighbor's faith, recalling him "droning on" in Hebrew. "Once, I could not hold back any longer and asked what he was chanting. He explained about the Talmud, and I immediately lost interest."

30. Ibid., p. 10.

31. Ibid., p. 18.

32. Ibid., p. 16.

33. Ibid., p. 11.

34. Viktor Borisenko, quoted in *Moskovsky Komsomolets,* Aug. 1, 2003; also Allen C. Lynch, *Vladimir Putin and Russian Statecraft* (Washington, DC: Potomac Books, 2011), p. 14.

35. Gevorkyan et al., p. 18.

36. Ibid., p. 18.

37. Ibid., p. 19.

38. *Moskovsky Komsomolets,* Aug. 1, 2003.

39. Interviewed in 2012 in a German documentary, *I, Putin,* which later appeared on NTV for Putin's inauguration for a third term on May 7, 2012.

40. *Moskovsky Komsomolets,* Aug. 1, 2003.

41. Vera Gurevich, *Bspominaniya o Budushchem Prezidente* [Recollections of the Future President] (Moscow: Mezhdunarodniye Otnosheniya, 2001), p. 31.

42. Vadim Kozhevnikov, *Shield and Sword* (London: MacGibbon & Kee, 1970).

43. *Kommersant,* July 25, 2010.

44. Gevorkyan et al., p. 22.

45. Chris Hutchins with Alexander Korobko, *Putin* (Leicester, UK: Matador, 2012), p. 26.

46. Gevorkyan et al., p. 23.

47. See http://www.scotsman.com/news/international/mccartney-rocking-back -in-the-ussr-1-1385940.

48. *Moskovsky Komsomolets,* Aug. 1, 2003.

49. Blotsky, *Vladimir Putin: Istoriya Zhizni,* p. 180.

50. Gevorkyan et al., p. 21.

51. *Komsomolskaya Pravda,* Oct. 4, 2007. In an interview, Mina Yuditskaya disclosed that Putin had given her an apartment during an official visit

to Israel, where she immigrated shortly after he finished school. See www
.kp.ru/daily/23979.3/74288.

52. *New York Times,* February 20, 2000.

53. Gevorkyan et al., p. 22. In an interview, Vera Gurevich said, "Volodya was
not especially interested in girls, but they were certainly interested in him."

54. See http://english.pravda.ru/society/stories/04–03–2006/76878-putin-0/.
See also Hutchins and Korobko, p. 27.

55. Gevorkyan et al., p. 22.

56. Lynch, p. 23; Masha Gessen, *The Man Without a Face: The Unlikely Rise of
Vladimir Putin* (New York: Riverhead Books, 2012), p. 55.

57. Putin recounted the story of his coat and the trip to Gagri during an interview with journalists in Abkhazia on Aug. 12, 2009, available, like virtually all his public remarks, at www.kremlin.ru or en.kremlin.ru. Hereafter,
unless otherwise noted, all of Putin's official remarks cited can be found by
searching these sites, by day or subject, in Russian and English. One word
of caution: the English versions of some speeches or comments can be truncated or edited, especially in cases of controversial comments.

58. Gevorkyan et al., p. 32.

59. Ibid., p. 36.

60. Ibid., p. 41.

61. Blotsky, *Vladimir Putin: Istoriya Zhizni,* p. 266.

62. Gevorkyan et al., p. 40.

63. Ibid., p. 42.

CHAPTER 2: A WARM HEART, A COOL HEAD, AND CLEAN HANDS

1. Gevorkyan et al., p. 42.

2. Blotsky, *Vladimir Putin: Istoriya Zhizni,* pp. 288–89.

3. J. Michael Waller, *Secret Empire: The KGB in Russia Today* (Boulder, CO:
Westview Press, 1994), pp. 14–17.

4. Yuri C. Bortsov, *Vladmir Putin* (Moscow: Fenix, 2001), p. 74.

5. Blotsky, *Vladimir Putin: Istoriya Zhizni,* p. 105.

6. A. A. Mukhin, *Kto Ect' Mister Putin i Kto c Nim Prishol* (Moscow: Gnom i
D, 2002), p. 27.

7. Andrew and Mitrokhin, p. 5.

8. Vladimir Usoltsev, *Sosluzhivets: Neizvestniye Stranitsi Zhizni Prezidenta*
[Comrade: The Unknown Pages of the President's Life] (Moscow: Eksmo,
2004), p. 186. Usoltsev, writing under a pseudonym, refers to Putin's work
in the Fifth Chief Directorate in an offhand manner and does not dwell on
it in an otherwise laudatory memoir of their time together in Dresden. Putin
denied working against dissidents, but the details of Usoltsev's recollections
have never been specifically refuted.

9. Koenraad De Wolf, *Dissident for Life: Alexander Ogorodnikov and the Struggle*

for Religious Freedom in Russia, translated by Nancy Forest-Flier (Grand Rapids, MI: William B. Eerdmans, 2013), pp. 116–17.

10. Gevorkyan et al., p. 40. The editors of the English translation note that Putin's description of informants did not appear in Russian newspaper articles based on the interviews.

11. Oleg Blotsky, *Vladimir Putin: Doroga k Vlasti* [Vladimir Putin: Path to Power] (Moscow: Osmos Press, 2002), p. 95.

12. Ibid., p. 113.

13. Yuri B. Shvets, *Washington Station: My Life as a KGB Spy in America* (New York: Simon & Schuster, 1994), p. 84.

14. Blotsky, *Vladimir Putin: Doroga k Vlasti,* p. 121.

15. Gevorkyan et al., p. 52.

16. Ibid., p. 44.

17. Andrew and Mitrokhin, p. 5.

18. Bortsov, p. 77; see also Kalugin, quoted in Lynch, p. 18.

19. Andrew and Mitrokhin, p. 214.

20. Christopher Andrew and Oleg Gordievsky, *KGB: The Inside Story of Its Foreign Operations from Lenin to Gorbachev* (New York: HarperCollins, 1990), p. 615.

21. Gevorkyan et al., p. 39.

22. Ibid., p. 56. The name of his first fiancée, Lyudmila Khmarina, was reported by Vladimir Pribylovsky on his website, *Antikomprimat,* http://www.anti compromat.org/putin/hmarina.html, and cited in Karen Dawisha, *Putin's Kleptocracy: Who Owns Russia* (New York: Simon & Schuster, 2014), p. 142.

23. Gevorkyan et al., p. 57.

24. Blotsky, *Vladimir Putin: Doroga k Vlasti,* p. 15.

25. Bortsov, p. 80.

26. Lyudmila Putina provides lengthy accounts of her experiences and courtship with Putin in Blotsky, *Vladimir Putin: Doroga k Vlasti,* p. 35.

27. Gevorkyan et al., p. 58.

28. Blotsky, *Vladimir Putin: Doroga k Vlasti,* p. 57.

29. Ibid., pp. 57–58.

30. Ibid., pp. 58–60.

31. Ibid., pp. 59–60.

32. Ibid., pp. 43–44.

33. Gevorkyan et al., pp. 59–60.

34. Blotsky, *Vladimir Putin: Doroga k Vlasti,* p. 53.

35. *New York Times,* February 20, 2000.

36. Andrew and Gordievsky, p. 612.

37. Gevorkyan et al., p. 68.

38. Andrew and Gordievsky, p. 613.

39. Gevorkyan et al., p. 53.

40. Andrew and Mitrokhin, p. 416.
41. Gevorkyan et al., p. 63.
42. Andrew and Gordievsky, p. 614.
43. Author interview with Sergei Roldugin, September 2014.
44. Gevorkyan et al., p. 55.

CHAPTER 3: THE DEVOTED OFFICER OF A DYING EMPIRE

1. Gary Bruce, *The Firm: The Inside Story of the Stasi* (Oxford: Oxford University Press, 2010), p. 12.
2. Gevorkyan et al., p. 73
3. Andrew and Mitrokhin, *The Sword and the Shield,* pp. 271–72.
4. Author interview with Herbert Wagner, former mayor of Dresden and director of the Stasi museum, December 2012.
5. Usoltsev, p. 50. "Why are you tempted by the West?" Usoltsev recalled saying to the Germans. "You already have a complete paradise here."
6. Ibid., p. 123.
7. Ibid., p. 105; Andrew and Gordievsky say the pressure from the KGB headquarters was so great that "in reports on particular topics they would commonly attribute to unnamed agents information obtained from the media or even invent details that they thought would please the Center" (p. 618).
8. Usoltsev, p. 68.
9. Ibid., p. 49.
10. Blotsky, *Vladimir Putin: Doroga k Vlasti,* pp. 234, 238.
11. Gevorkyan et al., p. 75.
12. Usoltsev, p. 64.
13. Author interview with Horst Jehmlich, Dresden, January 2013.
14. Usoltsev, pp. 124, 228.
15. Blotsky, *Vladimir Putin: Doroga k Vlasti,* pp. 251, 49.
16. Ibid., pp. 86, 256.
17. The report about the spy BALCONY was published by Erich Schmidt-Eenboom, a journalist who wrote extensively about the BND and Stasi, in *Berliner Zeitung* on Oct. 31, 2011, many years into Putin's presidency. A longer report on Putin's activities in Germany is available in German at http://www.geheimdienste.info/texte/beutezug.pdf. The authenticity of the account, based on access to highly classified reports, has never been verified.
18. Usoltsev, p. 110.
19. Correspondence with Uwe Müller, a former Stasi officer turned analyst.
20. Author interview with Siegfried Dannath, Dresden, November 2012.
21. Blotsky's *Doroga k Vlasti* includes a group photograph of the German and Russian intelligence officers in Dresden. Matveyev sits in the center, Putin far to his right. See photo insert.

22. Usoltsev made the comment in an interview with *Der Spiegel*, Oct. 20, 2003, before the publication of his memoir.

23. Usoltsev, p. 130.

24. Ibid., p. 211.

25. Ibid., p. 185.

26. Bortsov, p. 83.

27. Andrew and Gordievsky, p. 535.

28. Blotsky, *Vladimir Putin: Doroga k Vlasti*, p. 251.

29. *New York Times*, Oct. 7, 1989.

30. Gevorkyan et al., pp. 77, 85.

31. Blotsky, *Vladimir Putin: Doroga k Vlasti*, pp. 260–61.

32. Ibid., p. 260; Gevorkyan et al., p. 79.

33. Gevorkyan et al., p. 79, though the translation is slightly off.

34. Blotsky, *Vladimir Putin: Doroga k Vlasti*, pp. 261–63.

35. Author interview with Siegfried Dannath.

CHAPTER 4: DEMOCRACY FACES A HUNGRY WINTER

1. Gevorkyan et al., p. 80.

2. Ibid., p. 79.

3. Markus Wolf with Anne McElvoy, *The Man Without a Face: The Autobiography of Communism's Greatest Spy Master* (New York: Times Books, 1997), pp. 5, 224.

4. John O. Koehler, *Stasi: The Untold Story of the East German Secret Police* (Boulder, CO: Westview Press, 1999), p. 23. He gives the location of Böhm's death as his office, while news accounts put it in his apartment.

5. Author interview with Horst Jehmlich, Dresden, January 2013.

6. Interviewed in *Voyenno-Promishlenny Kuryur*, Feb. 14, 2005, vpk-news.ru/articles/3728. Putin in his own recollection of the destruction of the files refers to the furnace bursting; it is not clear if he was remembering the same incident or merely echoing the tales—perhaps exaggerated—that he had heard.

7. Zuchold, interviewed by Mark Franchetti in *The Sunday Times*, March 19, 2000. Aspects of news reports on Putin's last recruiting efforts in Dresden have been disputed, while other accounts confuse myth and fact, but Zuchold's own account has not been disputed.

8. Adam Tanner, Reuters, May 26, 2000, http://www.russialist.org/archives/4327.html#2.

9. Author interview with Sergei Roldugin, September 2014.

10. Author interview with Jörg Hoffman in Dresden in November 2012.

11. Gevorkyan et al., p. 87.

12. Blotsky, *Vladimir Putin: Doroga k Vlasti*, p. 271.

13. Gevorkyan et al., p. 86.

14. Fiona Hill and Clifford G. Gaddy, *Mr. Putin: Operative in the Kremlin* (Washington, DC: Brookings Institution Press, 2013), pp. 123–27. The authors argue that Putin's service in East Germany rendered him an outsider who did not absorb the changes in society into his DNA during those critical years. At the same time, they overstate his intellectual isolation in Dresden, and many Russians who did experience the changes firsthand ended up with views very much like his.

15. Gevorkyan et al., p. 89.

16. Blotsky, *Vladimir Putin: Doroga k Vlasti,* pp. 281–86.

17. Oleg Kalugin, *Spymaster: My Thirty-Two Years in Intelligence and Espionage Against the West* (New York: Basic Books, 2009), p. 336.

18. Olga B. Bain, *University Autonomy in the Russian Federation Since Perestroika* (New York: RoutledgeFalmer, 2003), pp. 139, 40.

19. Gevorkyan et al., p. 85.

20. *New York Times,* March 30, 1989.

21. Anatoly Sobchak, *For a New Russia: The Mayor of St. Petersburg's Own Story of the Struggle for Justice and Democracy* (New York: Free Press, 1992), p. 10.

22. Ibid., p. 13.

23. Ibid., chapter 5, "The Tbilisi Syndrome."

24. Robert W. Orttung, *From Leningrad to St. Petersburg* (New York: St. Martin's Press, 1995), p. 130. Orttung provides a thorough history of the political transition in the city before and after 1991; Putin, although an aide to Sobchak, does not appear in the book, an indication of his marginal role early on.

25. Author interview with Oleg Kalugin, October 2012.

26. Gevorkyan et al., pp. 88–89. The translation incorrectly refers to Merkuriev as president, instead of rector, as in the original, and makes the obscenity appropriate for a gentler audience.

27. Author interview with Carl M. Kuttler Jr., January 2013.

28. Sobchak, p. 10.

29. Kuttler interview.

30. Sobchak, pp. 158–59.

31. Leshchev quoted in Blotsky, *Vladimir Putin: Doroga k Vlasti,* pp. 310–11.

32. Associated Press, Nov. 13, 1990; also *Chicago Tribune,* Nov. 23, 1990.

33. Lisa A. Kirschenbaum, *The Legacy of the Siege of Leningrad, 1941–1995: Myth, Memories, and Monuments* (New York: Cambridge University Press, 2006), pp. 268–69.

34. Orttung, p. 137.

35. Andrei Piontovsky, "Stasi for President," *Russian Journal,* Jan. 17–23, 2000, quoting a television interview with Sergei Stepashin, a general in the Interior Ministry in Leningrad and future prime minister of Russia.

36. Gevorkyan et al., p. 91.

37. Blotsky, *Vladimir Putin: Doroga k Vlasti,* p. 319.

38. Sobchak, p. 178. David Remnick, *Lenin's Tomb: The Last Days of the Soviet Empire* (New York: Random House, 1993), recounts the coup as farce and includes details of Sobchak's role, pp. 462–63 and 468–69.

39. Orttung, p. 143.

40. *New York Times,* Sept. 10, 1991.

41. *St. Petersburg Times,* Aug. 17, 1991.

42. Sobchak, p. 180.

43. Lyudmila's account in Blotsky, *Vladimir Putin: Doroga k Vlasti,* p. 319.

44. Gevorkyan et al., pp. 93–94.

45. Remnick, p. 482.

46. *New York Times,* Sept. 10, 1991.

47. Foreign Broadcast Information Service, citing reporting by the newspaper *Smena,* Oct. 25, 1991.

48. Gevorkyan et al., p. 91.

49. Gevorkyan et al., p. 94.

50. Blotsky, *Vladimir Putin: Doroga k Vlasti,* pp. 310–11.

51. Ibid., p. 337.

CHAPTER 5: THE SPIES COME IN FROM THE COLD

1. Shadkhan interviewed in issue no. 21 of *Mishpokha,* a Belarusian magazine devoted to Jewish themes, www.mishpoha.org.

2. Orttung, p. 200.

3. Gevorkyan et al., p. 96.

4. Shadkhan in "Vecherny Razgovor [Evening Conversation]," broadcast on Oct. 7, 2002. The film included clips of Putin's interview in 1991.

5. *Mishpokha,* issue no. 21.

6. A translation of Yulian Semyonov's *Seventeen Moments of Spring* was published by Fredonia Books, Amsterdam, 2001.

7. Shadkhan, interviewed in *Moscow News,* Feb. 9, 2000.

8. "Vercheny Razgovor," Oct. 7, 2002.

9. *Chas Pik [Rush Hour],* Nov. 25, 1991.

10. "Vercheny Razgovor," Oct. 7, 2002.

11. Interfax, Oct. 4, 1991, also Orttung, p. 145.

12. Gevorkyan et al., p. 81. Kissinger meant his service as a private in military intelligence during World War II, which was quite different, but Putin told the anecdote often.

13. "The Rebirth of St. Petersburg," *Time,* Oct. 14, 1991.

14. Michael McFaul, *Russia's Unfinished Revolution* (Ithaca, NY: Cornell University Press, 2001), pp. 182–83.

15. Orttung, p. 202.

16. Yegor Gaidar, *The Collapse of an Empire: Lessons for Modern Russia* (Washington, DC: Brookings Institution Press, 2007), p. 239.

17. Yuri Felshtinsky and Vladimir Pribylovsky, *The Corporation: Russia and the KGB in the Age of President Putin* (New York: Encounter Books, 2008), p. 83. The authors reprint Sobchak's decree, dated Dec. 24, 1991.

18. Gevorkyan et al., p. 101.

19. Karen Dawisha, in *Putin's Kleptocracy*, pp. 126–32, details many of the relationships between organized crime and the casinos, though the extent of Putin's complicity remains unclear.

20. Gevorkyan et al., p. 102.

21. Felshtinsky and Pribylovsky, p. 72.

22. "Vercherny Razgovor," Oct. 7, 2002.

23. Smena, April 1, 1992.

24. Dmitri Vasilievich Kandoba, "Sankt-Peterburg v 1990–1996," www.gramota .net/materials/3/2011/6–3/21.html.

25. *New York Times,* April 27, 1992.

26. Felshtinsky and Pribylovsky, p. 78. Yakunin, in an interview in January 2014, said he first met Putin when he had set up business in the International Business Center Sobchak had created.

27. Gevorkyan et al., p. 99.

28. The report by Salye and Gladkov has been reproduced on an anti-Putin website, http://anticompromat.org/putin/salye92.html.

29. *Sankt Peterburgskiye Vedomosti,* May 14, 1992, reprinted by the Foreign Broadcast Information Service.

30. Kristie Macrakis, *Seduced by Secrets: Inside the Stasi's Spy-Tech World* (New York: Cambridge University Press, 2008), p. 49.

31. The photograph was included in files provided upon request by the German agency that oversees the Stasi archives, the Bundesbeauftragten, or BStU. The photograph (see insert) was included in file MfS BV Dresden, AKG No. 10852). Karen Dawisha also includes the photograph on p. 54 of *Putin's Kleptocracy.*

32. *New York Times,* April 5, 1992.

33. Author interview with Kaj Hober in February 2013.

34. Gevorkyan et al., p. 100.

35. Blotsky, *Vladimir Putin: Doroga k Vlasti,* p. 357.

36. Gevorkyan et al., p. 97.

37. Joyce Lasky Reed, Blair A. Ruble, and William Craft Brumfield, eds., *St. Petersburg, 1993–2003: The Dynamic Decade* (Washington, DC: St. Petersburg Conservancy, 2010), p. 8.

38. Hill and Gaddy, p. 165.

39. *Financial Times,* May 14, 2008.

40. Much has been written on Putin's connection to SPAG. Despite official

denials, Putin remained on the company's board until his inauguration as president. See http://www.newsweek.com/stain-mr-clean-152259, as well as Dawisha, *Putin's Kleptocracy,* pp. 132–41.

41. Thane Gustafson, *Wheel of Fortune: The Battle for Oil and Power in Russia* (Cambridge, MA: Belknap Press of Harvard University Press, 2012), p. 127. See also Dawisha; and Richard Sakwa, *The Crisis of Russian Democracy: The Dual State, Factionalism and the Medvedev Succession* (New York: Cambridge University Press, 2011), p. 174.

42. Timothy J. Colton, *Yeltsin: A Life* (New York: Basic Books, 2008), p. 277.

43. *Obshchaya Gazeta,* "'A Plague on Both Your Houses' Overtook Petersburg Last Week," Oct. 1, 1993.

44. Colton, p. 278. The written orders from the commander in chief proved crucial in establishing legal authority for the military to act. Mikhail Gorbachev did not issue written orders when he authorized force in Georgia, Lithuania, and Azerbaijan previously. See Robert V. Barylski, *The Soldier in Russian Politics: Duty, Dictatorship and Democracy Under Gorbachev and Yeltsin* (New Brunswick, NJ: Transaction Publishers, 1998).

45. "A Tried and True Official," *Vremya,* Aug. 10, 1999.

46. Gevorkyan et al., p. 96.

47. Sobchak's last interview, with Arkady Sonov, appears in "He Knew How to Make Himself Irreplaceable," *Russian Social Science Review* 41, no. 2 (March-April 2001): 91.

48. Roy Medvedev, *Vladimir Putin: Chetyre Goda v Kremle* [Four Years in the Kremlin] (Moscow: Vremya, 2004), p. 32.

CHAPTER 6: MISMANAGED DEMOCRACY

1. *Kommersant,* July 8, 1995.

2. Sobchak's interview in *Russian Social Science Review,* p. 90.

3. Blotsky, in *Vladimir Putin: Doroga k Vlasti,* described the date of the accident, which Putin later misstated as occurring in 1994.

4. Lyudmila recounts the accident and its aftermath in Gevorkyan et al., pp. 104–10, and also in Blotsky's *Vladimir Putin: Doroga k Vlasti.*

5. Gevorkyan et al., p. 108.

6. *The Wall Street Journal* disclosed the Stasi background of Warnig and his dealings with Putin in St. Petersburg, including Lyudmila's medical treatment after the car accident, Feb. 23, 2005; see also *Moscow Times,* Feb. 25, 2005.

7. Orttung, p. 210–12.

8. *Los Angeles Times,* Aug. 17, 1994.

9. *New York Times,* July 25, 1994.

10. Anatoly Sobchak, *Duzhina Nozhei v Spinu* [A Dozen Knives in the Back] (Moscow: Vagrius, 1999), p. 88.

11. Gevorkyan et al., p. 111.

12. Sobchak, p. 88.

13. Ibid., p. 76. Also in *Los Angeles Times,* May 16, 1996, Sobchak blames organized crime figures linked to his opponents.

14. Gevorkyan et al., p. 11.

15. Amy Knight, *Spies Without Cloaks: The KGB's Successors* (Princeton: NJ: Princeton University Press, 1996), p. 54.

16. Sobchak, *Duzhina Nozhei v Spinu,* p. 78; also *Nezavisimaya Gazeta,* Feb. 7, 1996.

17. Boris Vishnevski, a journalist and politician with the Yabloko party, recounts the details of Putin's arm-twisting at http://www.yabloko.ru/Publ/2006/2006_03/060321_kasp_vishn.html. Also see Timothy J. Colton and Michael McFaul, *Popular Choice and Managed Democracy: The Russian Elections of 1999 and 2000* (Washington, DC: Brookings Institution Press, 2003), p. 172.

18. Sobchak, *Duzhina Nozhei v Spinu,* p. 79.

19. Robert W. Orttung, ed., with Danielle N. Lussier and Anna Paretskaya, *The Republics and Regions of the Russian Federation: A Guide to Politics, Policies, and Leaders* (Armonk, NY: M. E. Sharpe, 2000), p. 467.

20. Gevorkyan et al., p. 112.

21. Zenkovich, p. 556.

22. Strobe Talbott, *The Russia Hand: A Memoir of Presidential Diplomacy* (New York: Random House, 2002), pp. 200–201.

23. Rosemary Mellor, "Through a Glass Darkly: Investigating the St. Petersburg Administration," *International Journal of Urban and Regional Research* 1, no. 3 (Sept. 1997): 482.

24. Colton and McFaul, p. 172.

25. Ibid.

26. Hill and Gaddy, pp. 178–79, also Felshtinsky and Pribylovsky, pp. 60–61.

27. Sobchak, *Duzhina Nozhei v Spinu,* p. 19.

28. Gazeta.ru, Sept. 8, 1999: http://gazeta.lenta.ru/daynews/09–08–1999/30bio.htm. Also *Moskovskiye Novosti,* May 26–June 2, 1996.

29. Hill and Gaddy, quoting Alexander Rahr, p. 178; and Gevorkyan et al., p. 113.

30. Sobchak, *Duzhina Nozhei v Spinu,* p. 92.

31. *Moscow News,* June 6, 1996.

32. Sobchak, *Duzhina Nozhei v Spinu,* p. 92.

33. Ibid., p. 88.

34. *New York Times,* June 4, 1996.

35. Sobchak, *Duzhina Nozhei v Spinu,* pp. 92–93.

36. Gevorkyan et al., p. 113.

37. Felshtinsky and Pribylovsky, p. 61.

38. Dawisha, p. 95.

39. Blotsky, *Vladimir Putin: Doroga k Vlasti,* p. 377.

40. Ibid., p. 365.

41. Gevorkyan et al., p. 122; Felshtinsky and Pribylovsky note the date of the fire on p. 106.

42. Ibid., p. 121.

43. Blotsky, *Vladimir Putin: Doroga k Vlasti,* p. 380.

44. Putin told the story to Larry King on CNN on Sept. 8, 2000 (transcripts .cnn.com/transcripts/0009/08/lkl.00.html) and to President George W. Bush in 2001. Bush writes, "He dramatically re-created the moment when a worker unfolded his hand and revealed the cross. It was, he said, 'as if it was meant to be.'" George W. Bush, *Decision Points* (New York: Crown, 2010), p. 196.

CHAPTER 7: AN UNEXPECTED PATH TO POWER

1. Boris Yeltsin, *Midnight Diaries* (New York: PublicAffairs, 2000), pp. 16–17.

2. Ibid., p. 21.

3. David M. Katz and Fred Weir, *Russia's Path from Gorbachev to Putin: The Demise of the Soviet System and the New Russia* (New York: Routledge, 2007), pp. 260–61; and Paul Klebnikov, *Godfather of the Kremlin: The Decline of Russia in the Age of Gangster Capitalism* (Orlando, FL: Harcourt, 2000), chapter 8.

4. Klebnikov, chapter 8. For the total campaign spending, he cites a report by the Center for Strategic and International Studies in Washington: *Russian Organized Crime: Global Organized Crime Project,* 1997.

5. Yeltsin, p. 70.

6. *New York Times,* June 28, 1996.

7. Yeltsin, pp. 61–62, 70.

8. Ibid., p. 32.

9. *The New York Times* conducted an exit poll during the vote. July 4, 1996.

10. Tim McDaniel, *The Agony of the Russian Idea* (Princeton, NJ: Princeton University Press, 1996), p. 163.

11. Hill and Gaddy, pp. 204–5.

12. Gevorkyan et al., pp. 192–94. In his interviews for the book Putin discussed Chubais at length. He acknowledged his skills as an administrator, but disparaged his privatization program and his decision to undo Putin's first appointment in Moscow. "Of course, I can't say I was overjoyed at the time," he said, then added magnanimously, "but I didn't feel angry at him." He noted that Chubais held "a bad credit record. I mean his public credit— the public's trust in him—is low."

13. Ibid., p. 127.

14. *St. Petersburg Times,* April 12, 2002.

15. Gevorkyan et al., p. 128.
16. Author interview with Dmitri S. Peskov, March 2014.
17. Gevorkyan et al., pp. 127–28.
18. Borodin news conference, March 11, 1997, transcript by Official Kremlin International Broadcast News; also Felshtinsky and Pribylovsky, pp. 111–15.
19. Colton, p. 327.
20. Ibid., p. 255.
21. Peter Baker and Susan Glasser, *Kremlin Rising: Vladimir Putin's Russia and the End of Revolution* (New York: Scribner, 2005), p. 48; and also author interview with John Evans, the American consul general in St. Petersburg. Borodin later emphasized his close ties with Putin and claimed, perhaps out of hopes for self-preservation, that he was the one who brought Putin to Moscow.
22. Alena V. Ledeneva, *Can Russia Modernise? Sistema, Power Networks, and Informal Governance* (Cambridge: Cambridge University Press, 2013), pp. 7–9.
23. Putin was interviewed as he left St. Petersburg in 1996, literally in the Pulkova airport as he boarded a plane to Moscow. A tape of the interview was broadcast in December 2012 on the television channel Kalamari (Squid). www.iarex.ru/news/32524.html.
24. Felshstinsky and Pribylovsky, p. 113.
25. Kalamari interview.
26. Blotsky, *Vladimir Putin: Doroga k Vlasti,* pp. 369–70.
27. Ibid., p. 397.
28. Gevorkyan et al., p. 128, and Blotsky, *Vladimir Putin: Doroga k Vlasti,* p. 368.
29. Felshtinsky and Pribylovsky, p. 112.
30. Interview with *Novaya Gazeta,* Dec. 27, 1999.
31. *Moskovskiye Novosti,* Aug. 11, 1998.
32. Felshtinsky and Pribylovsky, p. 115.
33. *Kommersant,* April 15, 1997.
34. Interfax, April 14, 1997.
35. Interfax, April 24, 1997; Rossiya TV, May 24, 1997, as monitored by the BBC; and Radio Rossiya, Sept. 17, 1997, as monitored by the BBC.
36. Hill and Gaddy, pp. 204–9.
37. The anecdote by Boris Nemtsov appeared posthumously, four days after his assassination in Moscow on Feb. 27, 2015, in an undated article, http://glavpost.com/post/3mar2015/History/18080-boris-nemcov-kak-putin-stal-preemnikom.html.
38. The United States government noted this aspect of Putin's character when comparing him to Dmitri Medvedev, who had a more established and

accomplished academic career. The analysis was contained in one of the State Department cables released by WikiLeaks in 2010: http://cablegatesearch.net/cable.php?id=07Moscow5800.

39. Gustafson, p. 247.

40. Vladimir Litvinenko described the roots of Putin's dissertation with the author's colleague, Andrew E. Kramer, who shared the transcript. See also Harley Balzer, "Vladimir Putin's Academic Writings and Russian Natural Resource Policy," *Problems of Post-Communism* 52, no. 1 (January–February 2006): 48.

41. The original of Putin's thesis for years proved difficult for researchers to track down. An English translation of Putin's dissertation appeared in *The Uppsala Yearbook of Eastern European Law* (London: Wildy, Simmonds & Hill Publishing, 2006). It was translated by Kaj Hober, a Swedish lawyer and arbitration expert who negotiated with Putin in Petersburg in the 1990s when Putin was deputy mayor. In 2005, Hober requested and received permission from Putin to publish the translation. The translation was reprinted in *The Journal of Eurasian Law* 2, no. 1 (2008). In an interview, Hober described the text as boring. "It was not a delight to translate it," he said.

42. Litvinenko's estranged daughter, Olga, became embroiled in a custody dispute with her father over her daughter, see http://ester-maria.com/olga. Harley Balzer, in "The Putin Thesis and Russian Energy Policy," *Post-Soviet Affairs* 21, no. 3 (2005): 215, suggested that Aleksei Kudrin might have helped with the writing as well.

43. Hill and Gaddy, p. 22; and *New York Times,* March 1, 2012.

44. The plagiarism was not widely publicized until 2006. Two researchers at the Brookings Institution in Washington, Igor Danchenko and Clifford Gaddy, found and scanned an original in a Moscow library and compared it to the Russian version of the King and Cleland textbook cited in the bibliography. Neither they nor other scholars have determined with certainty who wrote the thesis, but the general consensus is that it was ghostwritten, though with Putin's input and ultimate approval. See the Brookings presentation at http://www.brookings.edu/events/2006/03/30putin-dissertation. Gaddy shared a copy with the author.

45. Lynch, p. 36.

46. Harley Balzer, "Vladimir Putin on Russian Energy Policy," *The National Interest,* Dec. 1, 2005.

47. John Helmer, "US Law Firm Mines Legal Prospects in Russia Gold Project," *Journal of Commerce,* Nov. 18, 1997.

48. "Zapiski—Gorny Institut [Notes of the Mining Institute]," January 1999, reprinted and translated by Harley Balzer in "Vladimir Putin's Academic Writings and Russian Natural Resource Policy," *Problems of Post-Communism* 52, no. 1 (January–February 2006): 52. This essay has been widely confused

with Putin's thesis. Its themes are far broader than the narrow focus of his thesis and more representative of the policies he pursued.

49. *Literaturnaya Gazeta,* Nov. 26, 1997.

50. *Rossiyskaya Gazeta,* May 21, 1997.

51. Sobchak interviewed by Interfax, Jan. 18, 1997.

52. *Moscow Times,* Oct. 3, 1997.

53. Itar-Tass, Oct. 4, 1997.

54. Yeltsin, p. 234.

55. Felshtinsky and Pribylovsky, p. 232.

56. Gevorkyan et al., 118–19.

57. Yeltsin, pp. 234, 329.

CHAPTER 8: SWIMMING IN THE SAME RIVER TWICE

1. Gevorkyan et al., p. 128.

2. Roy Medvedev, *Post-Soviet Russia: A Journey Through the Yeltsin Era,* translated by George Shriver (New York: Columbia University Press, 2000), p. 288.

3. Yeltsin, *Midnight Diaries,* p. 88.

4. Medvedev, p. 285.

5. Yeltsin, p. 110.

6. Ibid., p. 113.

7. Klebnikov, p. 242.

8. Ibid., p. 278.

9. Gevorkyan et al., p. 129.

10. Interfax, June 4, 1998.

11. Medvedev, p. 294.

12. Andrei Soldatov and Irina Borogan, *The New Nobility: The Restoration of Russia's Security State and the Enduring Legacy of the KGB* (New York: Public-Affairs, 2010), pp. 12–13.

13. Yeltsin, p. 327.

14. Soldatov and Borogan, p. 25.

15. Alex Goldfarb with Marina Litvinenko, *Death of a Dissident: The Poisoning of Alexander Litvinenko and the Return of the KGB* (New York: Free Press, 2007), pp. 135–36.

16. Berezovsky interviewed in Gessen, *Man Without a Face,* p. 15.

17. Yeltsin, p. 326.

18. Gevorkyan et al., p. 130.

19. NTV, Sept. 3, 1997, as transcribed and translated by the BBC. The FSB's spokesman, Aleksandr Zdanovich, called the rumors "a canard" intended to "instill insecurity and create an element of instability." Within six weeks of Putin's appointment as FSB chief, he had to deny rumors that Putin was about to be sacked.

20. Gevorkyan et al., p. 130.

21. Lyudmila recounted the conversation in Gevorkyan et al., p. 132.

22. Itar-Tass, July 27, 1998.

23. Gevorkyan et al., p. 132.

24. *Kommersant,* July 30, 1998.

25. Yeltsin, p. 328. Putin, in his interview with *Kommersant* three days earlier, offered a slightly different account of the question of rank, saying it was up to Yeltsin to decide. He went on to add, however, "Honestly, rank doesn't bother me. The president showed confidence in me; that's obvious. After getting my degree 23 years ago, I joined the KGB in 1975 as a junior operative. And now I have risen to the top of the whole system. If the president tells me to be the first civilian director of the security service, I will accept the offer."

26. As of this writing, only two men have held the post after Putin, Nikolai Patrushev and Aleksander Bortnikov, both friends of Putin's who held the military rank of army general.

27. Goldfarb and Litvinenko, p. 163.

28. Yeltsin, p. 329.

29. Gevorkyan et al., p. 131.

30. Yelena Tregubova, *Baiky Kremlovskovo Diggera* [Tales of a Kremlin Digger] (Moscow: Marginem, 2003), p. 161.

31. *Segodnya,* Aug. 26, 1998; and *Moscow Times,* Aug. 28, 1998.

32. The case was discussed at a UNESCO conference held on May 3, 1999, in Bogota, Colombia, on the occasion of World Press Freedom Day. See archives -trim.un.org/webdrawer/rec/504045/view/item-in-KAAPressmatters—General 1999.pdf.

33. Colton, p. 416.

34. Interfax, Sept. 1, 1998.

35. Associated Press, Nov. 13, 1998.

36. Yeltsin, p. 328.

37. Medvedev offers a biographical portrait on pp. 323–35.

38. Andrew and Mitrokhin, *The Sword and the Shield,* p. 13.

39. Gevorkyan et al., p. 133.

40. Colton, p. 419.

41. *Kommersant,* Nov. 13, 1998.

42. Soldatov and Borogan, p. 17.

43. Transcript of the press conference by the Official Kremlin International News Broadcast, Nov. 17, 1998.

44. *Kommersant,* Nov. 17, 1998.

45. Litvinenko writing in *Mail on Sunday,* Nov. 25, 2006.

46. Goldfarb and Litvinenko, p. 136.

47. Official Kremlin International News Broadcast, Nov. 19, 1998.

48. *Argumenty I Fakty,* Dec. 9, 1998, as transcribed and translated by BBC Worldwide Monitoring.
49. Starovoitova interviewed on TV6 in Moscow, Sept. 19, 1998, as transcribed and translated by BBC.
50. Author interview with Ruslan Linkov, *New York Times,* Nov. 22, 2002.
51. *New York Times,* Nov. 23, 1998.
52. *New York Times,* Nov. 24, 1998.
53. *Washington Post,* Dec. 6, 1998.
54. Yeltsin, pp. 210–11.
55. Interfax, Dec. 18, 1998.

CHAPTER 9: *KOMPROMAT*

1. Irena Lesnevskaya, the president of REN TV, quoted in *Kommersant,* March 19, 1999.
2. *Kommersant,* March 19, 1999.
3. Yeltsin, *Midnight Diaries,* p. 223.
4. Ibid., pp. 222, 236.
5. *Washington Post,* March 8, 1999.
6. David Hoffman, *The Oligarchs: Wealth and Power in the New Russia* (New York: PublicAffairs, 2002), p. 459.
7. Yeltsin, p. 227.
8. Associated Press, March 17, 1999.
9. Yuri Skuratov, *Variant Drakona* [The Dragon Variation] (Moscow: Detectiv Press, 2000), p. 235.
10. Ibid., p. 147.
11. Ibid., p. 236.
12. *New York Times,* Dec. 20, 1998.
13. Skuratov, pp. 7–8.
14. Yeltsin, p. 225. For all the naked bitterness and controversy over the affair, the accounts of that meeting by Skuratov and Yeltsin do not differ substantively—only in tone and, of course, the meaning of what was said. Putin's version, though truncated, appears in Gevorkyan et al., *First Person,* pp. 198–99, and also broadly comports with theirs.
15. The popularity of chess in Russia makes it an easy metaphor for politics. The title of Skuratov's memoir, *Variant Drakona* [The Dragon Variation], is one of the main openings in the Sicilian Defense. Yeltsin referred to his frequent government shake-ups as akin to "castling," the move in which the king and rook exchange places; the term in Russian, *rokirovka,* would later be used in Putin's most significant gambit.
16. *New York Times,* March 24, 1999.
17. Yeltsin, p. 236.
18. *New York Times,* March 22, 1999.

19. Strobe Talbott's *The Russia Hand* offers an excellent firsthand account of the diplomacy between the United States and Russia during the Kosovo war. See chapters 12 and 13.

20. Ibid., p. 336.

21. Ibid., p. 335.

22. Years later, Strobe Talbott came to the conclusion that Putin had in fact lied. "What really struck my colleagues and me was the aplomb, smugness and brazenness with which Putin lied." See Strobe Talbott, "The Making of Vladimir Putin," *Politico,* Aug. 19, 2014.

23. The author witnessed this comical scene, having flown into Pristina's airport aboard NATO helicopters from Macedonia.

24. Wesley K. Clark, *Waging Modern War: Bosnia, Kosovo and the Future of Combat* (New York: PublicAffairs, 2001), p. 394.

25. Talbott, *Russia Hand,* p. 344.

26. Yeltsin, pp. 273–74.

27. Ibid., p. 276.

28. Ibid., p. 275.

29. Interfax, May 19, 1999.

30. *Komsomolskaya Pravda,* July 8, 1999.

31. Medvedev, p. 314.

32. Yeltsin, p. 329.

33. Colton, pp. 430, 586f. Colton says that Yeltsin's daughter and adviser, Tatyana, with whom he discussed all matters of political importance, had not discussed it with him in advance. Talbott writes that Israel's prime minister, Ehud Barak, visited Moscow—on August 2—and later telephoned President Bill Clinton to compare notes on this visit, which focused on the threat from Iran. Barak had been impressed with Stepashin but learned that he would be replaced imminently by "some guy whose name is Putin."

34. Associated Press, July 18, 1999.

35. Gevorkyan et al., p. 138.

36. Yeltsin, p. 331.

37. *New York Times,* Aug. 10, 1999.

38. Zenkovich, p. 364.

39. Gevorkyan et al., pp. 139–41.

CHAPTER 10: IN THE OUTHOUSE

1. *Nezavisimaya Gazeta,* Jan. 14, 2000.

2. Colton, p. 433.

3. Ibid., p. 432.

4. Matthew Evangelista, *The Chechen Wars: Will Russia Go the Way of the Soviet Union?* (Washington, DC: Brookings Institution Press, 2002), pp. 90–96. Basayev's main force evidently managed to withdraw from Dagestan with-

out overwhelming casualties, which added fodder to conspiracy theories that his fighters had been allowed safe passage as part of a vast plot to launch the second Chechen war. These theories ignore the intensity of the fighting in Dagestan, as evidenced by the destruction of the villages. They also presume that the Russian counteroffensive was more effective than it probably was.

5. NTV report, Aug. 27, 1999, as transcribed and translated by the BBC.

6. *New York Times,* Sept. 8, 1999.

7. *Moscow Times,* Sept. 11, 1999.

8. Talbott, p. 359.

9. Ibid., pp. 359–60.

10. Itar-Tass, Sept. 13, 1999.

11. *New York Times,* Sept. 20, 1999.

12. Itar-Tass, Sept. 10, 1999; *Moscow Times,* Sept. 11, 1999.

13. Quotation cited in *New York Review of Books,* Nov. 22, 2012.

14. *Moscow Times,* Sept. 17, 1999.

15. Interfax, Sept. 23, 1999. This is one of the most famous utterances of Putin's political life, the subject of endless quotation and even academic study. It is difficult to translate literally, and so many variations exist. Putin used the verb *zamochit,* which literally means "to (make) wet." In criminal slang, it evokes the spilling of blood. *Mocha* is also the word for "urine"; so "waste" seems the most appropriate. He went on to use Russian words with French roots, *pardon* and *v sortire,* the latter from the verb "to leave" or "go out," which in Russian slang has come to mean "the outhouse." It was widely understood in its most vulgar connotation. See *Kultura,* published by the University of Bremen in Germany, October 2006, p. 3. http://www.kultura-rus.uni-bremen.de/kultura_dokumente/ausgaben/englisch/kultura_10_2006_EN.pdf.

16. Many accounts have been written about the events in Ryazan, differing in the final analysis but not in the details. David Satter's *Darkness at Dawn: The Rise of the Russian Criminal State* (New Haven, CT: Yale University Press, 2003) includes a meticulous reconstruction of the case. John B. Dunlop also believes that the bombings were a government conspiracy to justify a second war in Chechnya. See *The Moscow Bombings of September 1999: Examinations of Russian Terrorist Attacks at the Outset of Vladimir Putin's Rule* (Stuttgart: Ibidem, 2012).

17. Soldatov and Borogan, p. 111.

18. *Moscow Times,* Sept. 25, 1999.

19. Evangelista, p. 68. Evangelista argues that Putin missed an opportunity to exploit the divisions between Maskhadov and Basayev before the second war began.

20. *New York Times,* Sept. 30, 1999.

21. Charles King, *The Ghost of Freedom: A History of the Caucasus* (Oxford: Oxford University Press, 2008), p. 238.

22. *Vremya,* Sept. 27, 1999.

23. Rossiya TV, Oct. 20, 1999, as transcribed by the BBC.

24. Primakov on TV6, transcript by the Official Kremlin International News Broadcast, Oct. 1, 1999.

25. Yeltsin, pp. 338, 344.

26. Goldfarb and Litvinenko, p. 191.

27. Hoffman, pp. 461–70.

28. *New York Times,* Oct. 14, 1999.

29. *Nezavisimaya Gazeta,* Nov. 19, 1999.

30. Colton and McFaul, p. 56.

31. *Sevodnya,* Nov. 25, 1999.

32. Yeltsin, p. 361.

33. *Vremya,* Sept. 27, 1999.

34. Colton, p. 434.

35. Yeltsin, p. 6. Putin, in Gevorkyan et al., p. 204, recounts a similar reaction: "I'm not ready for this."

36. Yeltsin, pp. 355–56.

37. Talbott, p. 7.

38. Yeltsin, pp. 7–8.

39. Ibid.

40. Interfax, Dec. 30, 1999.

41. Human Rights Watch's extensive reportage on Chechnya is available at the organization's website, www.hrw.org.

42. Interfax, Dec. 30, 1999.

43. Yeltsin's address and subsequent ones by Putin are translated and archived on the Kremlin's official website: http://archive.kremlin.ru.

44. Blotsky, *Vladimir Putin: Doroga k Vlast,* p. 417.

45. Gevorkyan et al., p. 138.

46. NTV report, Dec. 25, 2001.

47. The publication of the book in Germany was widely covered in the media at the time. See *St. Petersburg Times,* Feb. 23, 2001. And it was later published in Russia with the title translated as "Pikantnaya Friendship," as in "spicy" or "racy," reflecting its gossipy view of the Putin marriage.

48. Gevorkyan et al., p. 206.

49. Ibid., p. 189.

50. Yeltsin, p. 14.

51. Ibid., p. 366.

52. Gevorkyan et al., pp. 144–45.

CHAPTER 11: BECOMING PORTUGAL

1. Sakwa, *Putin: Russia's Choice,* p. 43.
2. Sakwa, *Putin: Russia's Choice,* includes a translation, pp. 251–62.
3. Ibid., p. 44.
4. *New York Times,* Feb. 5, 2000.
5. Colton and McFaul, pp. 176–77. Vasily Starodubtsev, the governor of Tula, was quoted in *The New York Times,* Jan. 6, 2000.
6. Interview with Natalya Timakova, one of the three who conducted the interviews, in March 2013. A former journalist, she began working for Putin's press office when he became prime minister in 1999. She continues to serve as spokeswoman for the current prime minister.
7. See Richard Torrence's essay in Lasky, Ruble, and Brumfield, *St. Petersburg, 1992–2003.*
8. Aleksandr Oslon, *Putinskoye Bolshinstvo Kak Socialni Fact* [The Putin Majority as a Social Fact], March 2001, Fund Obshchestvennoye Mneniye, the Public Opinion Fund.
9. The letter, available at the Kremlin's website, http://archive.kremlin.ru/eng, appeared in the newspapers *Izvestiya, Kommersant,* and *Komsomolskaya Pravda.*
10. Even now, the estimates of total Russian casualties in the war are disputed. The losses among Chechens—rebels and civilians—will never be known.
11. Michael Gordon, "The Grunts of Grozny," *New York Times Magazine,* Feb. 27, 2000.
12. In a television interview at the time of Babitsky's captivity, Putin pledged to support freedom of the press, but he also described Russia's media as beholden to special interests, rather than to the state. Early on, Putin understood the importance of controlling public opinion through the control of information. He considered it a primary lesson of his career in the KGB. "The intelligence service is basically an information service. It is first and foremost information work." Interviewed by ORT, Feb. 7, 2000, accessible at the Kremlin's archive.
13. *New York Times,* Feb. 3, 2000.
14. *New York Times,* Feb. 8, 2000.
15. BBC interview, March 5, 2000.
16. Ben Judah, *Fragile Empire: How Russia Fell In and Out of Love with Vladimir Putin* (New Haven, CT: Yale University Press, 2013), chapter 2.
17. *Moscow Times,* Sept. 9, 2000.
18. Medvedev, p. 360.
19. Satter in *Darkness at Dawn* identifies him as Aleksei Pinyaev, p. 30. Pinyaev later denied on state television that he had told the newspaper the story.
20. *Novaya Gazeta,* March 10, 2000.

21. *Moscow Times,* March 17, 2000.

22. Gevorkyan et al., pp. 143–44.

23. *Moskovskaya Pravda,* July 22, 1999.

24. *New York Review of Books,* April 13, 2000. Soros said he "could not quite believe" that the explosions were carried out to justify the war. "It was just too diabolical," he wrote, though he added that he could not entirely rule it out either. "From Berezovsky's point of view, the bombing makes perfect sense. Not only would such attacks help to elect a president who would provide immunity to Yeltsin and his family, but it would also give him, Berezovsky, a hold over Putin. So far, no evidence has surfaced which would contradict this theory."

25. Colton and McFaul, p. 191.

26. Author interview with Mikhail Kasyanov, March 2013.

27. Felshtinsky and Pribylovsky, in *The Corporation,* state, with no evidence, that he might not have been alone when he died. And they suggest that he had been poisoned by his own aide, Vladimir Putin: pp. 461–63. This seems preposterous, but Putin's critics by 2000 had begun to find patterns in untimely deaths.

28. *New York Times,* Aug. 10, 1996.

29. Yeltsin, p. 383.

30. Ibid., p. 384.

31. Gevorkyan et al., pp. 153–61.

32. Sergei Pugachev, a banker and businessman once close to the Putins and by 2010 in self-exile, said in an interview with the author in London in December 2014 that Lyudmila remained actively involved in business throughout her husband's presidency, though always discretely. This was also asserted by a former American intelligence official who spoke only on condition of anonymity, though no evidence of any investments or assets ever surfaced publicly.

33. *Novaya Gazeta,* Jan. 28, 2009.

34. Author interview with Vladimir Yakunin, January 2014.

35. Dawisha, p. 96.

36. Kremlin website, interview with ORT, Feb. 7, 2000.

37. Gevorkyan et al., p. 159.

38. Daniel Treisman, *The Return: Russia's Journey from Gorbachev to Medvedev* (New York: Free Press, 2011), p. 232.

39. Hoffman, p. 479.

40. Ibid., chapter 7, provides a biographical history.

41. Klebnikov, pp. 153–54. Berezovsky always denied that he had asked Korzhakov to organize the assassination.

42. *Los Angeles Times,* June 3, 2000; and *New York Times,* June 18, 2000.

43. See Putin's interview with Radio Mayak, March 18, 2000.

44. Talbott, p. 7. He offers an assessment of Putin's early presidency: "I wasn't sure whether he was hiding how many moves ahead he was thinking or how few. He seemed to have a knack for being in the right place at the right time with the right protector; he'd been promoted far beyond anything his experience or apparent abilities would have prepared him for. He was tactically adroit but, I suspected, strategically at sea. I still saw Putin as essentially a suave cop who had lucked into a very big job that would require a lot more than luck to pull off."

45. *New York Times,* Aug. 29, 2000.

46. The Kolesnikov letters were not found until October when the first bodies were retrieved from the submarine. His notes, displaying his bravery and his love for his wife, renewed the anguish of the Russians and resonated deeply in the culture. In 2007, the rock band DDT and Yuri Shevchuk recorded a poignant song based on the letters, "Captian Kolesnikov Wrote Us a Letter."

47. *Moscow Times,* Sept. 2, 2000.

48. Goldfarb and Litvinenko, p. 209.

49. Ibid., pp. 210–11.

50. Hoffman, p. 488. Hoffman's source is Berezovsky, whose version of their final meeting varied in some details with each telling, but not in substance.

51. Peter Truscott, *Kursk: The Gripping True Story of Russia's Worst Submarine Disaster* (London: Simon & Schuster, 2004), p. 85.

52. *The Moscow Times* published a translated transcript of the meeting on Sept. 12, 2000, available online at http://www.themoscowtimes.com/news /article/face-the-nation-putin-and-the-kursk-families/258935.html.

53. *Kommersant,* Aug. 24, 2000. The headline of the article was "How Putin Took Vidyayevo."

54. See Robert Brannon, *Russian Civil-Military Relations* (Farnham, UK: Ashgate, 2009), chapter 6.

55. Hill and Gaddy, p. 208.

56. Author interview with Sergei Pugachev, London, December 2014.

CHAPTER 12: PUTIN'S SOUL

1. Baker and Glasser, p. 122.

2. Condoleezza Rice, *No Higher Honor: A Memoir of My Years in Washington* (New York: Crown, 2011), p. 75. Earlier in her memoirs, Rice recalls meeting Putin in 1992 when she visited St. Petersburg as a Stanford professor to discuss the creation of a European university with Anatoly Sobchak. Sobchak hosted a reception that to her seemed populated by people named Tolstoy or Pushkin—and "one man who looked quite out of place, dressed in a suit befitting a high-ranking Soviet bureaucrat," that is, Putin (p. 61).

3. Kremlin archive, Sept. 11, 2001.

4. Bush, p. 196.

5. Karen Hughes, *Ten Minutes from Normal* (New York: Viking, 2004), p. 218.

6. Bush, p. 196.

7. See georgewbush-whitehouse.archives.gov/news/releases/2001/06/20010618 .html.

8. *New York Times,* June 16, 2001.

9. *Breakfast with David Frost,* BBC, March 5, 2000.

10. Dale R. Herspring, *The Kremlin and the High Command: Presidential Impact on the Russian Military from Gorbachev to Putin* (Lawrence: University Press of Kansas, 2006), p. 180.

11. Dmitri Trenin, "Military Reform: Can It Get off the Ground Under Putin?" *Demokratizatsiya,* March 22, 2001.

12. From the Kremlin website, Feb. 9, 2000. Putin returned to the phrase again five years later in an interview with German television, May 5, 2005. "People in Russia say that those who do not regret the collapse of the Soviet Union have no heart, and those that do regret it have no brain. We do not regret this. We simply state the fact and know that we need to look ahead, not backwards. We will not allow the past to drag us down and stop us from moving ahead." General Alexander Lebed used an almost identical phrase in his memoir, *My Life and My Country,* published in 1997, making clear Putin did not coin the phrase.

13. *New York Times,* Feb. 3, 2003. Putin attended the 60th anniversary of the victory at Stalingrad but avoided the use of the name. By the 70th, the city had adapted the old name ceremonially for six days each year to mark important dates in the war, and the old name peppered his remarks. "Stalingrad, of course, will always remain a symbol of the invincibility of the Russian people," he said, "the unity of the Russian people." *Volga-Media,* http:// www.vlg-media.ru/society/vladimir-putin-pozdravil-volgogradcev-2222 .html.

14. *Izvestiya,* Dec. 5, 2000, accessed through Johnson's Russia List, http:// russialist.org.

15. *Komsomolskaya Pravda,* Dec. 7, 2000.

16. *Kommersant,* March 21, 2001.

17. *Izvestiya,* Nov. 9, 2000. In an interview with reporters, including the author, in December 2006, Ivanov said they met in 1977 but added, "I don't want to go into the details."

18. Thomas Gomart, *Russian Civil-Military Relations: Putin's Legacy* (Washington, DC: Carnegie Endowment for International Peace, 2008), p. 52.

19. Rossiya TV, March 28, 2001, as transcribed and translated by BBC.

20. *New York Times,* Feb. 20, 2008. The Swiss arrested Adamov on an American arrest warrant in 2005, but the Russians resisted his extradition to the United States, fearing he would divulge nuclear secrets. Instead Russian prosecutors charged him with abuse of office and convicted him in a Russian court in

Feburary 2008. He was released on a suspended sentence two months later, however, and began a quiet retirement out of the public spotlight.

21. *Izvestiya,* March 29, 2001.

22. Associated Press, Sept. 14, 2001.

23. Schröder pressed Putin to intervene in one of the most notorious trials that came out of the war—one of the very few. On the night of Putin's election, Colonel Yuri Budanov, a decorated commander, kidnapped a Chechen woman, Elza Kungayeva, who had just turned eighteen. He took her to his quarters, ostensibly to question her, beat, raped, and then strangled her to death.

24. Peggy Noonan described the scene in a *Wall Street Journal* column, June 25, 2001.

25. Bush, p. 431.

26. Ibid., p. 200; Rice, p. 97.

27. Hughes, pp. 284–85.

28. Peter Pomerantsev, "Putin's Rasputin," *London Review of Books,* Oct. 20, 2011. Lenta.ru also has a detailed biography of his life and career. http://lenta.ru/lib/14159273/full.htm.

29. *Moscow Times,* April 4, 2002.

30. Human Rights Watch, "Swept Under: Torture, Forced Disappearances, and Extrajudicial Killings During Sweep Operations in Chechnya," February 2, 2002.

31. Pavel K. Baev, "Putin's War in Chechnya: Who Steers the Course?" Program on New Approaches to Russian Security, November 2004, http://www.ponarseurasia.org/sites/default/files/policy-memos-pdf/pm_0345.pdf.

32. Pavlov interviewed in *Nezavisimaya Gazeta,* Sept. 9, 2002.

33. *New York Times,* Aug. 23, 2002.

34. *Moscow Times,* Sept. 26, 2002.

35. See "Terror in Moscow," a British documentary film that appeared in 2003 on Channel 4 in Britain and HBO in the United States. Movsar's real name was Salamov, but he adopted the last name Barayev after his uncle's death.

36. RIA Novosti, Oct. 12, 2002. He had been erroneously reported killed in August 2001 as well.

37. Interview with a senior Russian official who was in the Kremlin with Putin during those three days, speaking on condition of anonymity.

38. Soldatov and Borogan, pp. 135–36.

39. "Terror in Moscow," the 2003 British documentary (see n. 33). Also, vivid accounts appear in Peter Baker and Susan Glasser's *Kremlin Rising;* Peter Truscott's *Putin's Progress: A Biography of Russia's Enigmatic President, Vladimir Putin* (London: Simon & Schuster, 2004); and Anna Politkovskaya's *A Russian Diary: A Journalist's Final Account of Life, Corruption and Death in Putin's Russia* (New York: Random House, 2007).

40. NTV's interview with the hostage takers on October 25, the second day of the siege, as transcribed by the BBC. NTV was forbidden by the Ministry of Communications to broadcast the audio of the interview during the siege and so showed only the images. The failure to include the sound irritated the terrorists.

41. Author interview with Mikhail Kasyanov; Angus Roxburgh, *The Strongman: Vladimir Putin and the Struggle for Russia* (London: I. B. Tauris, 2012), p. 70.

42. Yavlinsky interviewed on Radio Liberty, Oct. 28, 2002.

43. Anna Politkovskaya, *Is Journalism Worth Dying For?* (New York: Melville House, 2011), p. 229.

44. *New York Times,* Nov. 1, 2002.

45. Soldatov and Borogan, p. 142.

46. *New York Times,* Oct. 27, 2002.

47. Reports of the number of casualties were confused in the early days after the siege, but the final, reliable tally of the victims is kept by an organization, Nord-Ost, that represents the victims: www.nord-ost.org.

48. The European Court of Human Rights ruled in December 2011 that Russia had violated the rights of 64 victims by not providing adequate medical aid and ordered nearly $2 million in compensation. The court did not rule on whether the rescue itself violated any international standards.

49. *New York Times,* Nov. 13, 2002.

CHAPTER 13: THE GODS SLEPT ON THEIR HEADS

1. *Izvestiya,* Feb. 25, 2000.

2. Gustafson, p. 283.

3. Mikhail Khodorkovsky and Nataliya Gevorkyan, *Turma i Volya* [Prison and Will] (Moscow: Howard Roark, 2012), pp. 228–29.

4. Richard Sakwa, *Quality of Freedom: Khodorkovsky, Putin and the Yukos Affair* (Oxford: Oxford University Press, 2009), p. 143.

5. Khodorkovsky and Gevorkyan, p. 356.

6. Author interview with Andrei Illarionov, April 2013. The confrontation was televised and widely reported in the press. Gustafson, Sawka, and Baker and Glasser also recount the meeting. Khodorkovsky's coauthor, Nataliya Gevorkyan, describes it in *Turma i Volya* [Prison and Will], p. 52.

7. Illarionov interview.

8. Baker and Glasser, p. 282.

9. Viktor Gerashchenko interviewed in *Novaya Gazeta,* July 10, 2008, translated at Khodorkovsky's website, www.khodorkovsky.com.

10. Gustafson, p. 247.

11. Sakwa, *Quality of Freedom,* p. 97.

12. *New York Times,* May 31, 2001.

13. Gustafson, p. 320.
14. Ibid., p. 233.
15. Ibid., p. 234.
16. The United Nations formed an independent committee to investigate corruption in the "oil for food" program, see http://www.cfr.org/corruption -and-bribery/independent-inquiry-committee-report-manipulation-un -oil—food-programme/p9116. Its final report was made public in October 2005 and named Zhirinovsky and Voloshin as recipients of vouchers Saddam Hussein issued to allow companies and individuals to resell Iraqi oil at a large profit.
17. Charles Duelfer, *Hide and Seek: The Search for Truth in Iraq* (New York: PublicAffairs, 2009), p. 448.
18. Bush, p. 233.
19. Baker and Glasser, pp. 216.
20. Bush recalls the conversation in Bob Woodward's *Plan of Attack,* pp. 404–5.
21. *New York Times,* March 25, 2003.
22. *New York Times,* Jan. 16, 2003.
23. *New York Times,* April 23, 2003.
24. Kasyanov interview, March 2013.
25. *New York Times,* May 2, 2003.
26. Sakwa, *Quality of Freedom,* p. 91.
27. Ibid., p. 91.
28. Gustafson, p. 296.
29. Sakwa, *Quality of Freedom,* p. 144.
30. Ibid., p. 144.
31. Author interview with a fomer senior Kremlin official, April 2013. The same official told a similar version to correspondents in Moscow in the summer of 2003 as the case unfolded, calling it "a clearly organized assault," though by persons unknown.
32. The author joined other correspondents based in Moscow for the interview at Novo-Ogaryovo on Sept. 19, 2003.
33. Sakwa, *Quality of Freedom,* p. 89.
34. Gustafson, p. 304.
35. Khodorkovsky and Gevorkyan, p. 56.
36. Gustafson, pp. 299–300.
37. Khodorkovsky, interviewed by *New York Times,* October 2003.
38. John Browne with Philippa Anderson, *Beyond Business* (London: Phoenix, 2011), cited in David Remnick, "Gulag Lite," *The New Yorker,* Dec. 20, 2010.
39. A transcript of the interview, published Oct. 5, 2003, is available at www .nytimes.com/2003/10/05/international/06PTEXT-CND.html.
40. Interview with former senior Kremlin official, April 2013.

41. Anton Drel, quoted in *New York Times,* Nov. 1, 2003.
42. *New York Times,* Oct. 28, 2003.
43. Interview with former senior Kremlin official, April 2013.
44. Mikhail Kasyanov with Yevgeny Kiselyov, *Bez Putina* (Moscow: Novaya Gazeta, 2009), p. 222.
45. *New York Times,* Nov. 1, 2003.
46. Interview with senior Kremlin official, April 2013.
47. See the Permanent Arbitration Court's ruling on July 18, 2014, *Yukos Universal Limited v. The Russian Federation,* p. 64.
48. *New York Times* Dec. 7, 2003.
49. RIA Novosti, April 9, 2005.
50. *Express Gazeta,* Aug. 16, 2006, www.eg.ru/daily/animal/8134.
51. "The dog does not bother you, does it?" Putin asked Chancellor Angela Merkel when she visited Sochi in 2007, though he was surely aware of her fear of dogs. Koni then sat at Merkel's feet, to her evident discomfort. Merkel later told American officials of the encounter, including Putin's off-camera remark that she interpreted as a reference to the intelligence profile of her: "I know everything about you."
52. Bush, p. 433. Bush later retold the story to Prime Minister Stephen Harper of Canada, who replied, "You're lucky he only showed you his dog."
53. *New York Times,* Dec. 8, 2003.
54. *New York Times,* Dec. 8, 2003.

CHAPTER 14: ANNUS HORRIBILIS

1. See www.newsru.com, April 19, 2005.
2. The author visited the women's apartment and retraced parts of their story in Sept. 2004. *New York Times,* Sept. 10, 2004.
3. Paul J. Murphy, in *Allah's Angels: Chechen Women in War* (Annapolis, MD: Naval Institute Press, 2010), describes the fate of the four women and cites reports that Rosa Nagayeva had not been the bomber at the metro station, but rather was with Maryam Taburova at Beslan.
4. *Washington Post,* Oct. 27, 2003.
5. Gustafson, p. 264.
6. *Vedomosti,* Jan. 12, 2004.
7. Kasyanov, p. 226.
8. Vladimir Ryzhkov, "The Liberal Debacle," *Journal of Democracy* 15, no. 3 (July 2004).
9. *New York Times,* Jan. 9, 2004.
10. Itar-Tass, Feb. 13, 2004.
11. Goldfarb and Litvinenko, p. 308.
12. Interfax, Feb. 10, 2004.
13. *New York Times,* Feb. 3, 2004.

14. *Kommersant,* Nov. 11, 2006.
15. *New York Times,* March 6, 2004.
16. OSCE's Election Observer Mission Report, June 2, 2004.
17. Baker and Glasser, p. 325.
18. Kasyanov, p. 241.
19. Ibid., p. 241.
20. Anna Politkovskaya, *Putin's Russia* (London: Harvill Press, 2004), p. 274.
21. *Vedomosti,* March 2, 2004.
22. *Novaya Gazeta,* Oct. 11, 2007. Fradkov became the head of the foreign intelligence service in 2007, underscoring his presumed background.
23. Felshtinsky and Pribylovsky, p. 80.
24. Official Kremlin International Broadcast, March 16, 2004.
25. *Vremya Novosti,* March 15, 2004.
26. Ryzhkov, pp. 54, 57.
27. *Vedomosti,* March 29, 2004; Khodorkovsky reprinted the letter, including a translation, on his website, www.khodorkovsky.com.
28. The most authoritative and exhaustive account of the siege in Beslan is C. J. Chivers's horrifying reconstruction based on interviews with the hostages, "The School," *Esquire,* June 2006, p. 140.
29. *New York Times,* May 10, 2004.
30. *New York Times,* May 12, 2004.
31. *New York Times,* Sept. 2, 2004.
32. Aslambek Aslakhanov, Putin's chief adviser on Chechnya, quoted in Baker and Glasser, p. 23.
33. Hutchins and Korobko, p. 292.
34. Soldatov and Borogan, p. 159.
35. *Kommersant,* Sept. 3, 2004.
36. Ledeneva, p. 36. She cites an unnamed official who had been forced to repeat the lie about the number of hostages and, like others, had been "broken" by Beslan. He "had become a different person when he returned from Beslan," she writes.
37. Politkovskaya, *Is Journalism Worth Dying For?* pp. 251–52.
38. Soldatov and Borogan, p. 157.
39. *New York Times,* Sept. 4, 2004.
40. Ibid.
41. Soldatov and Borogan, p. 159.
42. Ibid., p. 162.
43. *New York Times,* Sept. 4, 2004.
44. Putin's full remarks, as translated by *The New York Times,* Sept. 5, 2004.
45. *Moskovskiye Novosti,* Sept. 17–23, 2004.
46. Author interview with Aleksandr Drozdov, executive director of the Yeltsin Center, in Moscow, June 2014.

47. Marie Mendras, *Russian Politics: The Paradox of a Weak State* (New York: Columbia University Press, 2012), p. 185. At the annual Valdai meeting in the wake of the attack, Putin made a similar comment; he recalled the election dispute he mediated in Karachayevo-Cherkessia as the head of Yeltsin's Security Council as an example of how dangerous elections were, according to Clifford Kupchan, one of those in attendance.

48. *New York Times,* Sept. 15, 2004.

CHAPTER 15: THE ORANGE CONTAGION

1. *New York Times,* Dec. 20, 2004.

2. J. V. Koshiw, *Abuse of Power: Corruption in the Office of the President* (n.p.: Artemia Press, 2013), p. 149.

3. Roxburgh, pp. 108–9.

4. Ibid., p. 116.

5. Ibid., p. 129.

6. Anders Aslund, *How Ukraine Became a Market Economy and Democracy* (Washington, DC: Peter G. Peterson Institute for International Economics, 2009), p. 170.

7. See also "It's a Gas—Funny Business in the Turkmen-Ukraine Gas Trade," a report by Global Witness, available on its website, www.globalwitness .co.uk.

8. *Kyiv Post,* July 29, 2004.

9. Koshiw, p. 136.

10. Boris Volodarsky, *The KGB's Poison Factory: From Lenin to Litvinenko* (Minneapolis: Zenith Press, 2009), p. 98.

11. Aslund, p. 180.

12. A full transcript of Putin's lengthy interview is on the Kremlin online archive, Oct. 27, 2004.

13. Mark MacKinnon, *The New Cold War: Revolutions, Rigged Elections and Pipeline Politics in the Former Soviet Union* (New York: Carroll & Graf, 2007), p. 181.

14. Nikolai Petrov and Andrei Ryabov, "Russia's Role in the Orange Revolution," in Anders Aslund and Michael McFaul, eds., *Revolution in Orange: The Origins of Ukraine's Democratic Breakthrough* (Washington, DC: Carnegie Endowment for International Peace, 2006), p. 158.

15. Ibid., p. 157.

16. *New York Times,* Nov. 22, 2004.

17. Roxburgh, p. 138.

18. *New York Times,* Dec. 3, 2005.

19. Author interview with Viktor Yushchenko, 2006.

20. *Kyiv Post,* Oct. 29, 2009.

21. RIA Novosti, Feb. 24, 2005.

22. Peter Baker, *Days of Fire: Bush and Cheney in the White House* (New York: Doubleday, 2013), p. 383.

23. Bush, p. 432.

24. Rice, p. 366.

25. *New York Times,* Oct. 9, 2005.

26. The passage comes from a translation online of a Russian newspaper in Paris, Возрождение (or *Revival*), published June 27, 1925. The translation, author unknown, appears at www.freerepublic.com/focus/news/30343571 /posts. Hill and Gaddy discuss Ilyin in *Mr. Putin,* pp. 106–107, as does Geraldine Fagan in *Believing in Russia—Religious Policy After Communism* (London: Routledge, 2013).

27. *New York Times,* July 3, 2005.

28. *New York Times,* May 17, 2005.

CHAPTER 16: KREMLIN, INC.

1. Interview with a former senior Kremlin official, who spoke only on condition of anonymity, April 2013. Both Thane Gustafson and Richard Sakwa argue that Putin's role in the assault on Yukos was less premeditated and more improvisational than often portrayed by his critics, though the result remained the same.

2. Gustafson's *Wheel of Fortune* provides an excellent history of the Soviet and Russian oil industry and the Yukos auction. See especially chapter 5, "The Russian 'Oil Miracle.'"

3. Cited in Baker and Glasser, p. 347.

4. A decade later, in July 2014, the Permanent Arbitration Court ruled that the case was "a deliberate and sustained effort to destroy Yukos, gain control over its assets and eliminate" Khodorkovsky as "a potential political opponent." See court's ruling, July 18, 2014, *Yukos Universal Limited v. The Russian Federation,* p. 30.

5. Sakwa, *Quality of Freedom,* p. 92. He argues that Putin did not initiate the prosecutorial assault, but was convinced by others that it was necessary. He describes the "politburo" as behind the dismantling of Yukos on p. 106.

6. Gustafson describes the history of Rosneft in *Wheel of Fortune,* chapter 8, "Russia's Accidental Oil Champion: The Rise of Rosneft."

7. *New York Times,* Oct. 28, 2004.

8. Gustafson, p. 343.

9. Ibid.

10. See Gustafson's chapter 8.

11. *New York Times,* Dec. 20, 2004.

12. *New York Times,* Dec. 21, 2004.

13. *Moscow Times,* Dec. 29, 2004.

14. Putin himself acknowledged this in an interview with Spanish journalists on February 7, 2006, available in the Kremlin's online archive.

15. Gustafson, p. 348.

16. The Permanent Arbitration Court cited Putin's statement as damning evidence that the auction was a vast conspiracy; see the court's ruling, July 18, 2014, *Yukos Universal Limited v. The Russian Federation*, p. 330. See also *The Financial Times Alphaville* blog, July 28, 2014, http://ftalphaville.ft.com/2014/07/28/1910622/yukos-putins-loose-lips/.

17. A translation was posted by Khodorkovsky's supporters during the trial at http://mikhail_khodorkovsky_society_three.blogspot.com/2005/04/final-statement-in-meshchansky-court.html.

18. Richard Sakwa, *Putin and the Oligarch: The Khodorkovsky-Yukos Affair* (London: I. B. Tauris, 2014), p. 107.

19. Associated Press, June 25, 2005.

20. Kraft recounted the pressure from the White House in remarks at a charity benefit in his honor at Carnegie Hall in New York, as reported by the *New York Post,* June 15, 2013.

21. *Boston Globe Magazine,* March 19, 2007.

22. A diplomatic cable by the American ambassador, William Burns, dated April 2, 2007, released by WikiLeaks in 2010.

23. Treisman, p. 115.

24. *Moscow Times,* April 19, 2005.

25. Marshall I. Goldman, *Petrostate: Putin, Power and the New Russia* (Oxford: Oxford University Press, 2008), p. 124.

26. Boris Nemstov and Vladimir Milov, both former government officials and opposition leaders, sharply questioned the sale in a series of white papers that began appearing in 2008. See "Putin and Gazprom," originally published in *Novaya Gazeta,* Aug. 28 and Sept. 4, 2008. Also Anders Aslund, in *Russia's Capitalist Revolution: Why Market Reform Succeeded and Democracy Failed* (Washington, DC: Peter G. Peterson Institute for International Economics, 2007), p. 253, and in other writings and interviews, argues that many of Gazprom's deals were corrupt.

27. The diplomatic cable, dated April 2, 2007, released by WikiLeaks.

28. Quoted in Edward Lucas, *The New Cold War: Putin's Russia and the Threat to the West* (New York: Palgrave Macmillan, 2008), p. 168. In the chapter "Pipeline Politics," he describes, ominously, the geopolitical consequences of Gazprom's rise.

29. *Wall Street Journal,* Dec. 16, 2005.

30. Tom Bower, *Oil: Money, Politics, and Power in the 21st Century* (New York: Grand Central Publishing, 2009), p. 375.

31. *New York Times,* Oct. 6, 2006.

32. Bower, p. 387.

33. *New York Times,* Dec. 22 and Dec. 29, 2006. The author attended the ceremony returning the Sakhalin project to the Kremlin's control.

34. A diplomatic cable, Dec. 8, 2008, "Ukraine: Firtash Makes His Case to the USG," released by WikiLeaks.

35. Koshiw, p. 65. Also the Jamestown Foundation, *Eurasian Daily Monitor,* March 25, 2009, "The Strange Ties Between Semion Mogilevich and Vladimir Putin."

36. Margarita M. Balmaceda, *Energy Dependency, Politics and Corruption in the Former Soviet Union: Russia's Power, Oligarchs' Profits and Ukraine's Missing Energy Policy, 1995–2006* (London: Routledge, 2008), p. 137.

37. Treisman, p. 116.

38. The disclosures about the palace and the allegations of the furtive financing of it and other investments did not become public until December 2010, when one of those involved, Sergei Kolsenikov, wrote an open letter to Dmitri Medvedev, disclosed in a column by David Ignatius in *The Washington Post.* Subsequent articles in *Novaya Gazeta* in February 2011 (http://en.novayagazeta.ru/politics/8779.html) and *The Financial Times* on Nov. 30, 2011, confirmed aspects of the deals, despite the Kremlin's consistent denials.

39. *Wall Street Journal,* Sept. 25, 2007.

40. Author interview with Mikhail Kasyanov, June 2014.

41. Lenta.ru's biography of Kovalchuk, at http://lenta.ru/lib/14149560.

42. Quoted in *Forbes Russia,* Aug. 3, 2008.

43. Mark Galeotti coined the phrase at http://inmoscowsshadows.wordpress .com/2013/08/10/the-rise-of-the-russian-judocracy/.

44. Mark Lawrence Schrad, *Vodka Politics: Alcohol, Autocracy and the Secret History of the Russian State* (Oxford: Oxford University Press, 2014), chapter 22.

45. Author interviews with Andrei Illarionov, October 2012 and August 2014.

46. Illarionov, quoted in *The New Times,* newtimes.ru, Nov. 4, 2011.

47. Republished in *New York Times,* Feb. 4, 2006.

48. Gustafson, p. 354.

49. The prospectus is available on the company's website, http://www.rosneft .com/attach/0/58/84/rosneft_prospectus.pdf.

50. Rosneft's annual report in 2006: http://www.rosneft.com/attach/0/58/80/a _report_2006_eng.pdf.

CHAPTER 17: POISON

1. *New York Times,* Nov. 25, 2006. The story here of Litvinenko's poisoning, one of the most intensely covered murders in history, is based on reporting at the time by the author and his colleagues in Moscow and London, espe-

cially Alan Cowell, who subsequently wrote *The Terminal Spy: The Life and Death of Alexander Litvinenko, a True Story of Espionage, Betrayal and Murder* (London: Doubleday, 2008). Other accounts that were useful include *The Death of a Dissident* by Alex Goldfarb and Marina Litvinenko, based on their personal relationships with him; *The Litvinenko File: The Life and Death of a Russian Spy* by Martin Sixsmith (New York: St. Martin's Press, 2007); and *Putin's Labyrinth: Spies, Murder, and the Dark Heart of the New Russia* by Steve LeVine (New York: Random House, 2008).

2. Goldfarb and Litvinenko, p. 330.

3. The book was published in English after Litvinenko's murder as *Blowing Up Russia: The Secret Plot to Bring Back KGB Terror* (New York: Encounter Books, 2007). The quote is on p. 3.

4. Skuratov, p. 147. This rumor was repeated to the author by a former KGB and FSB officer who was among those purged during Putin's time as director of the security service.

5. Author interview with Oleg Kalugin, October 2012.

6. Interviewed in Cowell, p. 209.

7. Cowell, p. 239.

8. Litvinenko's meetings and Grinda's views appeared in cables first disclosed by WikiLeaks, dated Aug. 31, 2009, and Feb. 8, 2010. Luke Harding details them in *Expelled: A Journalist's Descent into the Russian Mafia State* (New York: Palgrave Macmillan, 2012), pp. 235–39.

9. Politkovskaya, *Is Journalism Worth Dying For?* p. 5.

10. Diplomatic cable from WikiLeaks, dated Oct. 9, 2006.

11. LeVine, p. 125.

12. The details of the first attempt to poison Litvinenko at the office of Erinys were disclosed at the public inquiry held in Britain in 2015. Transcripts of the inquiry are available at www.litvinenkoinquiry.org.

13. The author interviewed Lugovoi and Kovtun in Moscow in March 2007 with Alan Cowell. *New York Times,* March 18, 2007.

14. Roxburgh, p. 177.

15. *Financial Times,* Nov. 25, 2006.

16. Sakwa, *Crisis of Russian Democracy,* p. 186; also *St. Petersburg Times,* Sept. 28, 2004.

17. Author interview with a British diplomatic official, April 2013.

18. Author interview with Lugovoi and Kovtun, March 18, 2007.

19. One of the first times he addressed the question of a third term—and dismissed it—was in December 2003. *New York Times,* Dec. 19, 2003.

20. This and other sources on Putin's succession struggle come from the author's reporting at the time for the article "Post-Putin," in *The New York Times Magazine,* Feb. 27, 2007.

21. The American ambassador, William J. Burns, expounded on the theory of

using the redistribution of assets to aid the candidates in the April 2, 2007, cable to Washington that was disclosed by WikiLeaks and already cited.

22. *Novaya Gazeta,* Oct. 11, 2007.

23. Sakwa, *Crisis of Russian Democracy,* pp. 188–89.

24. Roxburgh, p. 196. Roxburgh, a former journalist, worked for the public relations firm Ketchum, which the Kremlin had hired to burnish Russia's image, a frustrating experience he recounts in the book.

25. Available from the Kremlin's online archive, Feb. 10, 2007. This speech, one of Putin's most famous, also appears in numerous videos online.

26. *New York Times,* Feb. 11, 2007.

27. Cited and translated by *Der Speigel,* Feb. 12, 2007: http://www.spiegel.de /international/the-world-from-berlin-a-calculating-simulation-of-the-cold -war-a-465811.html.

28. *New York Times,* May 29, 2007.

29. *The Guardian,* April 12, 2007.

30. *New York Times,* June 1, 2007.

31. *New York Times,* July 19, 2007.

CHAPTER 18: THE 2008 PROBLEM

1. Boris Nemtsov recalled this anecdote in an interview with the author in December 2013.

2. Author interview with Anatoly Pakhomov, Sochi's mayor, December 2013.

3. Aleksandr Zhukov, interviewed by the author in January 2014, recounted the Politburo's deliberations over future Olympic sites, which were only revealed years later in a declassified report.

4. Associated Press, July 1, 2007.

5. Associated Press, July 4, 2007.

6. Sakwa, *Crisis of Russian Democracy,* p. 163.

7. Roxburgh, p. 208.

8. Ibid., p. 211.

9. Hill and Gaddy, pp. 181–82.

10. Ibid., p. 182. Richard Sakwa also attended; see *Crisis of Russian Democracy,* p. 178.

11. Sakwa, *Crisis of Russian Democracy,* p. 178.

12. *Kommersant,* Oct. 9, 2007.

13. As transcribed by Ekho Moskvy, Oct. 30, 2007.

14. One version of this analysis was revealed by WikiLeaks in a cable from the American ambassador, William Burns, dated Oct. 18, 2007. "In the absence of political institutions," he wrote, "the glue of the system created by Putin is his personalized power and the loyalty of those he appointed to key positions. Putin has attempted to preserve that power by keeping those jockeying for continued influence off balance."

15. Sakwa, *Crisis of Russian Democracy*, p. 197.

16. *Time,* Dec. 19, 2007. The full transcript of the interview is available at http://content.time.com/time/specials/2007/printout/0,29239,1690753 _1690757_1695787,00.html.

17. Transcript of the staged meeting can be found on the Kremlin online archive, Dec. 10, 2007.

18. Richard Sakwa argues that Sechin, to the end, favored a third term for Putin, though the famously reclusive Sechin never made his views public. *Crisis of Russian Democracy,* p. 272.

19. Author interview with Sergei Roldugin, St. Petersburg, September 2014.

20. Michael S. Gorham, *After Newspeak: Language, Culture, and Politics in Russia from Gorbachev to Putin* (Ithaca, NY: Cornell University Press, 2014), p. 157.

21. Julie A. Cassiday and Emily D. Johnson, "A Personality Cult for the Post-Modern Age," in Helena Goscilo, ed., *Putin as Celebrity and Cultural Icon* (London: Routledge, 2013), p. 43. The film *Potselui ne dlya Pressi* [A Kiss Off the Record] appeared for sale as a DVD on Valentine's Day 2008, though it had been filmed several years before. The fact that it did not appear in movie theaters suggested it was either too risky politically or, as some critics noted, pretty awful.

22. The newspaper *L'Espresso* published excerpts of conversations D'Addario secretly recorded during her tryst with Berlusconi on July 20, 2009. According to diplomatic cables published by WikiLeaks, American diplomats also took note of the deepening relations between and mutual admiration of Berlusconi and Putin, noting that they had to warily rebuff Berlusconi's efforts to serve as an intermediary when relations with the United States soured badly.

23. *Putin: Itogi* also appeared on Nemtsov's website, nemtsov.ru. An English translation by David Essel, cited here, appears on the *La Russophobe* blog, larussophobe.wordpress.com/2008/03/31/boris-nemtsovs-white-paper-in -full/, under the title "Putin: The Bottom Line."

24. *Wall Street Journal,* June 11, 2008.

25. The article about Timchenko and his company, Gunvor, appeared in *The Economist* on Nov. 29, 2008. After Timchenko sued for libel, the magazine ran a clarification on July 30, 2009, saying that it accepted "Gunvor's assurances that neither Vladimir Putin nor other senior Russian political figures have any ownership interest in Gunvor."

26. The existence of the CIA's study was disclosed to the author by two American government officials familiar with it, though it has never been made public and they would not discuss it in detail. Belkovsky first made his allegations about Putin's wealth in an interview with the German newspaper *Die Welt,* published on Nov. 12, 2007, and repeated them in December

to *The Daily Telegraph* and thereafter to pretty much anyone who would listen.

27. The details of the flight were first reported by Boris Nemtsov in his blog on Dec. 18 2010, when he was fighting a libel suit filed by Timchenko because of Nemtsov's description of him as a friend of Putin's in a subsequent paper on corruption in Russia: b-nemtsov.livejournal.com/93781.html. Reuters also described the flight and the construction of the palace in an article that was part of an investigative series called "Comrade Capitalism," May 21, 2014. The allegations—along with considerable evidence—came from one of their partners, Sergei Kolesnikov, who went public in late 2010 with an open letter to Dmitri Medvedev about the scheme. He has since described the palace in numerous interviews, including, especially, in *The Financial Times,* Nov. 11, 2013. Karen Dawisha also details the scandal in *Putin's Kleptocracy,* pp. 295–304; as does Ben Judah in *Fragile Empire,* pp. 116–21.

CHAPTER 19: THE REGENCY

1. See Solzhenitsyn's interview in *Der Spiegel* a year before his death, July 23, 2007, http://www.spiegel.de/international/world/spiegel-interview-with -alexander-solzhenitsyn-i-am-not-afraid-of-death-a-496003.html.
2. *New York Times,* Jan. 28; Sakwa, *Crisis of Russian Democracy,* p. 279.
3. *New York Times,* Jan. 29, 2008.
4. From a diplomatic cable by a senior State Department official, dated June 20, 2008, released by WikiLeaks.
5. *New York Times,* July 17, 2008.
6. Roxburgh, p. 237.
7. According to the subsequent investigations by the European Union and the Organization for Security and Co-operation in Europe (OSCE), only two Russian soldiers died in the initial barrage, while several others were wounded.
8. Yuri Ushakov, the former Russian ambassador who had returned to Moscow to serve as Putin's foreign policy adviser in the prime minister's office, cited in a diplomatic cable from the American ambassador in Moscow, John Beyrle, dated Aug. 26, 2008, released by WikiLeaks.
9. The timing of Putin's calls to Medvedev remains a matter of dispute. Medvedev has maintained that he issued the order to begin military action before he spoke with Putin, but Putin and other officials say there were repeated contacts between the two on the first morning, with Putin pushing for a more vigorous response.
10. Medvedev's remarks during his presidency are also archived at the Kremlin .ru archive, Aug. 8, 2009.
11. Bush, p. 434.

12. According to the European Union's report, which laid blame on both Russia and Georgia, the losses for all sides in the fighting totaled 844. South Ossetia reported 365 deaths, including uniformed personnel and civilians; Georgia lost 170 soldiers, 14 police officers, and 228 civilians; Russia 67. Many hundreds were wounded, and thousands displaced from their homes in South Ossetia and parts of Georgia.

13. Bush, p. 435.

14. RIA Novosti, Aug. 10, 2008.

15. *New York Times,* Aug. 21, 2008.

16. Rice, p. 688.

17. Diplomatic cable by John R. Beyrle, Aug. 26, 2008, released by WikiLeaks.

18. This conversation was reported by Sarkozy's adviser, Jean-David Levitte, in *Le Nouvel Observateur.* Although initially denied by Putin's spokesman, the entire article was later posted on the website of the prime minister's office: http://archive.premier.gov.ru/eng/premier/press/world/1182/print/.

19. Human Rights Watch's report on the conflict, "Up in Flames" (2009), p. 130. The organization reported war crimes by all parties in the conflict and called for investigations that never happened.

20. *New York Times,* Nov. 16, 2008.

21. Sergei Guriev and Aleh Tsyvinski, "Challenges Facing the Russian Economy After the Crisis," in Anders Aslund, et al., eds., *Russia After the Global Economic Crisis* (Washington, DC: Peter G. Peterson Institute for International Economics and the Center for Strategic and International Studies, 2010), p. 17. The study provides an overview of the crisis and the government response and many of the details cited here.

22. Ibid., p. 24.

23. Anders Aslund, Sergei Guriev, and Andrew Kuchins, "Russia's Course: Viable in the Short Term but Unsustainable in the Long Term," in Aslund et al., eds., *Russia After the Global Economic Crisis,* p. 259.

24. Roxburgh, p. 280.

25. *New York Times,* Nov. 6, 2008.

26. The derailing of Medvedev's agenda is based on an interview with a senior aide who would only speak on condition of anonymity. The vetting of the speech and Medvedev's discomfort with the language that was inserted was described in a State Department cable from the American ambassador, dated the day of the speech, which was disclosed by WikiLeaks.

27. *New York Times,* Nov. 6, 2008.

28. An account of the incident, with video, can be found on www.theother russia.org, in a post dated Dec. 14, 2008.

29. A State Department cable by the acting chief of mission in Moscow, Eric Rubin, dated Nov. 19, 2008, and released by WikiLeaks.

CHAPTER 20: ACTION MAN

1. Steven Fortescue, "Putin in Pikalevo," *Australian Slavonic and East European Studies* 23, no. 1–2 (2009).

2. The governor's remarks were quoted on the website www.theotherrussia.org, May 21, 2009. See also Anna Arutunyan, *The Putin Mystique: Inside Russia's Power Cult* (Northampton, MA: Olive Branch Press, 2014), which includes a detailed chapter on "The Pikalevo Effect"; and *New York Times,* June 5, 2009.

3. Daniel Treisman, "Russian Politics in a Time of Economic Turmoil," in Aslund et al., eds., *Russia After the Global Economic Crisis,* p. 54.

4. The reports of Putin's detachment in the initial months of 2009 were discussed in a State Department cable dated March 4, 2009, and disclosed by WikiLeaks.

5. The internal machinations over Putin's decision to upend the WTO talks were discussed by the officials themselves in discussions with frustrated American and European officials, as detailed in a State Department cable, dated June 19, 2009.

6. See UNESCO's website, whc.unesco.org/en/list/900.

7. Schrad, pp. 354–56.

8. *Kommersant,* April 28, 2010.

9. The closing of the investigation into Morozov's accusations was reported without comment by RIA Novosti on April 12, 2012. Morozov detailed his accusations in an interview with *Novaya Gazeta,* published June 4, 2010. Morozov's experience was also featured in a documentary, *Putin's Games,* released in 2014. The author has a copy of his appeal for political asylum, which was granted in April 2010.

10. Details of Sergei Magnitsky's case are from Ellen Barry's reconstruction in *The New York Times* on Dec. 23, 2010, along with interviews with William Browder and documents he provided to the author, as well as his book *Red Notice: A True Story of High Finance, Murder, and One Man's Fight for Justice* (New York: Simon & Schuster, 2015).

11. Angela Stent, *The Limits of Partnership: U.S.-Russian Relations in the Twenty-First Century* (Princeton, NJ: Princeton University Press, 2014), p. 231.

12. The FBI released hundreds of documents related to the investigation, code-named Operation Ghost Stories, on its website: http://vault.fbi.gov/ghost -stories-russian-foreign-intelligence-service-illegals/.

13. *Kommersant,* July 25, 2010.

14. Peter Earley, who wrote a biography of Tretyakov called *Comrade J: The Untold Secrets of Russia's Master Spy in America After the End of the Cold War* (New York: Berkley Books, 2007), and considered him a friend,

reported on the circumstances of his death on his website: www.pete earley.com/2010/07/09/sergei-tretyakov-comrade-j-has-died/. A year later, the Russians tried and convicted, in absentia, another intelligence officer, Aleksandr Poteyev, accusing him of having betrayed the sleeper agents.

15. Interviewed on Gazeta.ru, March 30, 2010.

16. Several officials who worked for one of the two leaders described their agreement to respect their responsibilities as prime minister and president, though no one maintained that Putin did not have the ultimate authority.

17. Senior official interviewed by the author, April 2013.

18. The blog appeared at top-lap.livejournal.com/1963.html.

19. See Helena Goscilo, "VVP as VIP *Objet d'Art*," p. 8; and Julie A. Cassiday and Emily D. Johnson, "A Personality Cult for the Postmodern Age," p. 43, both in Helena Goscilo, ed., *Putin as Celebrity and Cultural Icon.*

20. Gazeta.ru, Oct. 28, 2010.

21. The doctor's remarks—and the extent of Putin's cosmetic surgery— appeared in October 2012 on an industry website: http://tecrussia.ru /starplastica/308-vladimir-putin-plasticheske-operacii-foto.html.

22. *Rossiyskaya Gazeta,* Sept. 6, 2010.

23. Luzhkov's defiant letter appeared on Radio Free Europe/Radio Liberty on Sept. 29, 2010, http://www.rferl.org/content/Text_Of_Yury_Luzhkovs _Letter_To_President_Medvedev/2171682.html.

24. See a report on the project by CEE BankWatch, a non-governmental organization promoting corporate governance, at http://bankwatch.org/public -private-partnerships/case-studies/moscow-st-petersburg-motorway-section -15–58-km-deal-involvi.

25. Sakwa, in *Putin and the Oligarch,* details the second Khodorkovsky trial, pp. 136–45.

26. *Nezavisimaya Gazeta,* Dec. 24, 2010.

CHAPTER 21: THE RETURN

1. On November 30, 2014, *The Times* of London published a dossier written by former intelligence officers on the bids for the 2018 and 2022 World Cup championships. England's bid committee had hired the investigators after it applied for and lost out on the 2018 tournament. The accusations of corruption in the bids were investigated and rejected by FIFA, the sport's international governing body, amid much controversy. In May 2015, however, American and Swiss officials announced that the bids were the focus of a sprawling investigation that could yet force a reconsideration of the winning bids for Russia and Qatar.

2. In a radio interview on Finam FM, Feb. 2, 2011, available at www.stolica .fm/archive-view/3626.

3. *The New Yorker,* April 4, 2011.

4. At www.whitehouse.gov/the-press-office/2011/03/10/vice-president-bidens -remarks-moscow-state-university, March 10, 2011.

5. The security official spoke with the author in an interview in Moscow in December 2013 on condition of anonymity.

6. *Vedomosti,* July 13, 2011.

7. *The Financial Times* published a full transcript of the interview on June 19, 2011.

8. The final decision on Putin's return to the presidency was described by three people who were familiar with some of the details, though ultimately the full details of their final meeting the night before Medvedev's nomination are known only to the two men in the room.

9. He described and defended Medvedev's modernization program in a lengthy and largely favorable interview with *The Wall Street Journal,* July 10, 2011.

10. *Novaya Gazeta,* Sept. 26, 2011.

11. *New York Times,* Sept. 30, 2011.

12. Arutunyan, p. 207.

13. Prokhorov described Medvedev's recruitment of him in an interview in *New York Times,* Sept. 17, 2011.

14. *New York Times,* Dec. 13, 2011.

15. According to Serge Schmemman, who was among those attending. *New York Times,* Nov. 23, 2011.

16. See globalvoicesonline/2011/12/05/russia-election-day-ddos-alypse for a thorough account of the cyberattacks before and during the election.

17. The video of the old man filling in ballots was widely reported in the Russian media and cited in *New York Times,* Dec. 6, 2011. The OSCE's observer mission's final report on the elections is at www.osce.org/odihr/86959.

18. Quoted at www.opendemocracy.net, by Olga Breininger, March 28, 2013.

19. *New York Times,* Dec. 22, 2011.

20. *Kommersant,* Dec. 10, 2011.

21. Quotes from Litvinenko's interview were published in *The New York Times* on March 1, 2012; my colleague, Andrew Kramer, shared the full transcript.

CHAPTER 22: THE RESTORATION

1. Dmitry Uzlaner, "The Pussy Riot Case and the Peculiarities of Russian Post-Secularism," *State, Religion and Church* 1 (2014): 24. Uzlaner's study of the case and the role of the church and state in Russia provides useful background and translations by April French. See also Pussy Riot, *Pussy Riot! A Punk Prayer for Freedom* (New York: Feminist Press, 2013), which compiles the group's statements and testimony in court; Marc Bennetts, *Kicking the Kremlin: Russia's New Dissidents and the Battle to Topple Putin* (London: Oneworld, 2014); and Miriam Elder, "What Does Pussy Riot Mean Now,"

Buzzfeed, Feb. 7, 2014. There are many translations of the group's lyrics; the author chose those that seemed closest to their intended meaning.

2. Interviewed by the author in Washington, DC, in February 2012.
3. Kissinger in his interview with *Time* for the issue declaring him Man of the Year in 2007, available on his website, henrykissinger.com.
4. *New York Times,* Jan. 8, 2012.
5. Reuters, Feb. 8, 2013.
6. *Moscow News,* March 1, 2012.
7. *New York Times,* Dec. 8, 2011.
8. Author interview with Yekaterina Samustevich, March 2013.
9. Navalny's initial post on Pussy Riot, dated March 7, 2012, is at navalny .livejournal.com/690551.html.
10. Andrei Zolotov Jr. provided a detailed account of the special service for RIA Novosti, April 23, 2012. It is no longer available on the website of the agency, which was rebranded as Sputnik. It was reprinted, though, at http:// www.angelfire.com/pa/ImperialRussian/news/481news.html.
11. Bennetts, p. 164.
12. *New York Times,* March 7, 2012.
13. Ibid.
14. *New York Times,* Dec. 6, 2012.
15. Human Rights Watch report, "Laws of Attrition," published in April 2013.
16. *New York Times,* June 12, 2012.
17. Pussy Riot, p. 55.
18. Interview with Yekaterina Samustevich, March 2013.

CHAPTER 23: ALONE ON OLYMPUS

1. A seven-minute trailer of the film is still available at http://rutube.ru/video /eddef3b31e4bdff29de4db46ebdd4e44/. Forbes reported on the film and its mysterious production at http://www.forbes.ru/sobytiya/vlast/85216-kto -zdes-glavnokomanduyushchii.
2. See http://abcnews.go.com/blogs/politics/2012/03/president-obama-asks -medvedev-for-space-on-missile-defense-after-my-election-i-have-more -flexibility/.
3. http://www.justice.gov/usao/nys/pressreleases/September13/Prevezon HoldingsForfeiturePR.php.
4. *Novaya Gazeta,* Nov. 11, 2012; translated into English at http://en .novayagazeta.ru/politics/55288.html.
5. BBC Worldwide Monitoring, Oct. 9, 2012.
6. "Visiting Putin," NTV, Oct. 7, 2012, www.ntv.ru.novosti/348821.
7. *Bloomberg Business Week,* Aug. 27, 2013.
8. Interview with the author, April 2013.
9. Lyudmila Narusova's interview appeared in *Novaya Gazeta,* Nov. 11, 2012.

10. Sergei Roldugin, Maria's godfather, disclosed the marriage and birth of Putin's grandson in an interview in September 2013. Radio Netherlands Worldwide reported on the accident involving Jorrit Faassen on Jan. 12, 2011, http://www .rnw.org/archive/russias-mysterious-dutch-businessman. For details of Matvei Urin's legal troubles, see http://sobesednik.ru/kriminal/matvei-urin-sgorel -na-erunde and http://rapsinews.com/judicial_news/20140528/271420339 .html.

11. The details of Yekaterina Putina's affiliation with Moscow State University emerged in a report by the Russian newspaper *RBK* in January 2015, http:// top.rbc.ru/business/28/01/2015/54c8b4659a794730dbef8851. The journalist Oleg Kashin first identified her as Putin's daughter on his website in exile, http://kashin.guru/2015/01/29/ona/, and her identity was confirmed in the days that followed by Reuters on Jan. 29, 2015, and Bloomberg, Jan. 30, 2015.

12. *The Guardian* on May 9, 2012, posted a video of the match's highlights on its website, http://www.theguardian.com/world/video/2012/may/09/vladimir -putin-ice-hockey-russia-video.

13. *New York Times,* May 6, 2012.

14. *Daily Beast,* Jan. 13, 2013.

15. *Der Spiegel* reviewed the book, called *Putin,* on Dec. 2, 2013, http://www .spiegel.de/international/europe/new-book-on-vladimir-putin-claims -russian-president-flees-from-people-a-936801.html. Belkovsky distanced himself from some of his own conclusions in an interview in Moscow in September 2014.

16. *Novaya Gazeta,* Nov. 11, 2012.

CHAPTER 24: PUTINGRAD

1. Author interview with Vladimir Yakunin, January 2013. Details of the Sochi construction, including interviews with him and Anatoly Pakhomov, were also included in *The New York Times Magazine,* Jan. 22, 2014.

2. In an interview on Ekho Moskvy, Nov. 11, 2013.

3. See "Race to the Bottom," a report by Human Rights Watch, published Feb. 6, 2013, and available at its website.

4. *Esquire,* July 7, 2010, available at esquire.ru/sochi-road.

5. Boris Nemtsov and Leonid Martynuk detailed many cost overruns in a pamphlet, "Winter Olympics in the Sub-Tropics: Corruption and Abuse in Sochi," released May 20, 2013, and updated on Dec. 6, 2013. A translation by Catherine A. Fitzpatrick is available at www.interpretermag.com/winter -olympics-in-the-sub-tropics-corruption-and-abuse-in-sochi/. Nemtsov called it a "festival of corruption" in an interview with the author in Dec. 2013.

6. The Levada Center, one of the most trusted polling agencies, tracked Putin's

rating throughout his rule. After his approval rating peaked in 2008 at 88 percent, it bottomed out at 61 in November 2013, www.levada.ru/indeksy.

7. Interfax, April 29, 2013.

8. Tatiana Stanovaya, "Beware Medvedev," Institute of Modern Russia, March 6, 2013, http://imrussia.org/en/analysis/politics/405-beware-of -medvedev.

9. The Associated Press reported on Feb. 4, 2015, that Sberbank turned over the ski jump to the government, writing off a $1.7 billion loan.

10. Snowden's statement was released by WikiLeaks on its website, July 12, 2013.

11. Quoted in *The New York Times,* Nov. 1, 2013.

12. *World Policy Journal,* Fall 2013.

13. Interviewed by the author, cited in *The New York Times,* Aug. 2, 2013.

14. Available at the Vatican's website: http://w2.vatican.va/content/francesco /en/letters/2013/documents/papa-francesco_20130904_putin-g20.html.

15. *New York Times,* Sept. 12, 2013.

16. At http://www.forbes.com/sites/carolinehoward/2013/10/30/the-worlds -most-powerful-people-2013/.

17. Interviews with the author, January and March 2014.

18. *Moscow Times,* Oct. 8, 2013.

19. See Radio Free Europe/Radio Liberty, Dec. 7, 2012. www.rferl.org/content /clinton-calls-eurasian-integration-effort-to-resovietize/24791921.html.

20. *The Guardian,* Sept. 22, 2013.

21. *Der Spiegel,* Nov. 24, 2014, http://www.spiegel.de/international/europe /war-in-ukraine-a-result-of-misunderstandings-between-europe-and-russia -a-1004706–2.html. The remark of Putin's senior adviser was made in a briefing in Moscow in December 2013, conducted on condition of anonymity.

22. *New York Times,* Nov. 23, 2013.

23. *The Economist,* Dec. 23, 2013.

24. *Kommersant,* Feb. 6, 2014.

25. *Yezhednevny Zhurnal,* Feb. 10, 2014, http://ej.ru/?aote&id=24384.

26. Leonid Bershidsky, "Olympics Bring Back the 1980s in Russia," Bloomberg, Feb. 17, 2014.

CHAPTER 25: OUR RUSSIA

1. James Meek, "Romantics and Realists," *London Review of Books,* Feb. 20, 2014.

2. *New York Times,* Jan. 3, 2015.

3. Putin disclosed his secret order to evacuate Yanukovych from Crimea, along with other details about the crisis over Ukraine, during an interview for a

television documentary on the state channel Rossiya-1 that was broadcast on March 15, 2015, in time for the first anniversary of the annexation. It was called "Crimea: The Path to the Motherland" and is available online in various places, including at http://en.krymedia.ru/politics/3373711 -Documentary-Crimea-Path-to-Motherland-Call-and-Warning.

4. Putin made the comparison in his first public statements on the events in Ukraine on March 4, 2014.

5. Russia's representative at the United Nations read the letter at a meeting of the Security Council on March 3, 2014.

6. Andreas Rinke, "How Putin Lost Berlin," *IP Journal,* German Council on Foreign Relations, Sept. 29, 2014. Also Reuters, on March 20, 2014, reported Putin's admission to Merkel.

7. See the Stockholm International Peace Research Institute's "Trends in World Military Expenditure, 2014," available at books.sipri.org/files/FS /SIPRIFS1504.pdf.

8. *New York Times,* March 3, 2014.

9. The United States Treasury Department announced its second, more substantive round of sanctions on March 20, 2014, four days after the annexation of Crimea, http://www.treasury.gov/press-center/press-releases/Pages /jl23331.aspx.

10. Author interview with Vladimir Yakunin in March 2014.

11. Timchenko gave a lengthy interview to the Tass news agency, which was posted on Aug. 4, 2014, at tass.ru/en/Russia/743432.

12. The recording by the Ukrainian security service, known as the SBU, was widely cited in the international and Ukrainian media, part of an information war by both sides. Although the rebels denied fixing the results of the referendum, the recording itself of those involved did not appear to be in dispute, simply the meaning of it. A translated transcript appeared at http://ukrainianpolicy.com/sbu-audio-links-donetsk-republic-to-russian-involvement/.

13. Mark Galeotti discussed the doctrine, little noticed at the time of publication, and noted its relevance in the events in Ukraine in 2014 in an analysis that included this translation at https://inmoscowsshadows.wordpress .com/2014/07/06/the-gerasimov-doctrine-and-russian-non-linear-war/.

14. In May 2015, prosecutors in the United States and Switzerland announced the arrests of senior officials with FIFA as part of a years-long investigation into bribery in the awarding of World Cup bids. The scandal forced the resignation of FIFA's president, Sepp Blatter. Putin denounced the Americans in particular, saying the investigation was "another blatant attempt by the United States to extend its jurisdiction to other states."

15. Strelkov's posting on VKontakte was later removed, but versions of it

remained online, including a translation at http://www.interpretermag.com
/was-col-strelkovs-dispatch-about-a-downed-ukrainian-plane-authentic/.

16. The Dutch and Malaysian investigation into the destruction of Flight 17
was expected to be completed by the end of 2015. Overwhelming evidence
pointed to the Russian military's involvement. See https://www.bellingcat
.com/wp-content/uploads/2014/11/Origin-of-the-Separatists-Buk-A
-Bellingcat-Investigation1.pdf and http://interpretermag.com/evidence
-review-who-shot-down-mh17.

17. The phrase in Russian is simple, though difficult to translate literally, thus
there have been different versions. "Yest Putin, Yest Rossiya—nyet Putina,
nyet Rossii," http://izvestia.ru/news/578379.

18. See the Permanent Arbitration Court's ruling, July 18, 2014, *Yukos Universal Limited v. The Russian Federation,* p. 330, http://www.pca-cpa.org.

19. *New York Review of Books,* May 8, 2014.

20. Author interview with Garry Kasparov in Macau, June 2014, as part of
reporting for a *New York Times Magazine* article on his bid to become president of the international federation of chess, or FIDE, Aug. 6, 2014.

21. *New York Times,* Dec. 2, 2014.

22. *Vedomosti,* March 1, 2014.

23. *Moscow Times,* June 18, 2014.

24. Author interview with Aleksei Navalny, Dec. 2014.

25. Nemtsov's report was completed posthumously by colleagues in the opposition. It was released in the spring of 2015 and is available in English at
http://www.4freerussia.org/putin.war/.

26. *Novaya Gazeta,* Aug. 11, 2014, http://novayagazeta.ru/politics/64784.html.

27. *New York Times,* Jan. 24, 2015.

28. Nikolai Gogol, *Dead Souls,* translated by Richard Pevear and Larissa Volo-
khonsky (New York: Vintage, 1996), p. 253.

Bibliography

Albats, Yevgenia. *The State Within a State: The KGB and Its Hold on Russia—Past, Present and Future*. New York: Farrar, Straus and Giroux, 1994.

Albright, Madeleine, with Bill Woodward. *Madame Secretary: A Memoir.* New York: Miramax Books, 2003.

Alekperov, Vagit. *Oil of Russia: Past, Present and Future*. Minneapolis: East View Press, 2011.

Andrew, Christopher, and Oleg Gordievsky. *KGB: The Inside Story of Its Foreign Operations from Lenin to Gorbachev.* New York: HarperCollins, 1990.

Andrew, Christopher, and Vasili Mitrokhin. *The Sword and the Shield: The Mitrokhin Archive and the Secret History of the KGB.* New York: Basic Books, 1999.

———. *The World Was Going Our Way: The KGB and the Battle for the Third World.* New York: Basic Books, 2005.

Anthony, Ian, ed. *Russia and the Arms Trade.* Stockholm International Peace Research Institute (Sipri). Oxford: Oxford University Press, 1998.

Applebaum, Anne. *Gulag: A History.* New York: Anchor Books, 2003.

Arutunyan, Anna. *The Putin Mystique: Inside Russia's Power Cult.* Northampton, MA: Olive Branch Press, 2014.

Aslund, Anders. *How Ukraine Became a Market Economy and Democracy.* Washington, DC: Peter G. Peterson Institute for International Economics, 2009.

———. *Russia's Capitalist Revolution: Why Market Reform Succeeded and Democracy Failed.* Washington, DC: Peter G. Peterson Institute for International Economics, 2007.

Aslund, Anders, and Michael McFaul, eds. *Revolution in Orange: The Origins of Ukraine's Democratic Breakthrough.* Washington, DC: Carnegie Endowment for International Peace, 2006.

Aslund, Anders, Sergei Guriev, and Andrew Kuchins, eds. *Russia After the Global Economic Crisis.* Washington, DC: Peter G. Peterson Institute for International Economics and the Center for Strategic and International Studies, 2010.

Babchenko, Arkady. *One Soldier's War.* New York: Grove Press, 2007.

Bain, Olga B. *University Autonomy in the Russian Federation Since Perestroika.* New York: RoutledgeFalmer, 2003.

Baker, Peter. *Days of Fire: Bush and Cheney in the White House.* New York: Doubleday, 2013.

Baker, Peter, and Susan Glasser. *Kremlin Rising: Vladimir Putin's Russia and the End of Revolution.* New York: Scribner, 2005.

Balmaceda, Margarita M. *Energy Dependency, Politics and Corruption in the Former Soviet Union: Russia's Power, Oligarchs' Profits and Ukraine's Missing Energy Policy, 1995–2006.* London: Routledge, 2008.

Barylski, Robert V. *The Soldier in Russian Politics: Duty, Dictatorship and Democracy Under Gorbachev and Yeltsin.* New Brunswick, NJ: Transaction Publishers, 1998.

Bennetts, Marc. *Kicking the Kremlin: Russia's New Dissidents and the Battle to Topple Putin.* London: Oneworld, 2014.

Blotsky, Oleg M. *Vladimir Putin: Doroga k Vlasti* [Vladimir Putin: The Road to Power]. Moscow: Osmos Press, 2002.

———. *Vladimir Putin: Istoriya Zhizni* [Vladimir Putin: A Life History]. Moscow: Mezhdunarodniye Otnosheniya, 2001.

Bortsov, Yuri C. *Vladimir Putin.* Moscow: Feniks, 2001.

Bower, Tom. *Oil: Money, Politics, and Power in the 21st Century.* New York: Grand Central Publishing, 2009.

Brannon, Robert. *Russian Civil-Military Relations.* Farnham, UK: Ashgate, 2009.

Browder, Bill. *Red Notice: A True Story of High Finance, Murder, and One Man's Fight for Justice.* New York: Simon & Schuster, 2015.

Browne, John, with Philippa Anderson. *Beyond Business: An Inspirational Memoir from a Remarkable Leader.* London: Phoenix, 2011.

Bruce, Gary. *The Firm: The Inside Story of the Stasi.* New York: Oxford University Press, 2010.

Bush, George W. *Decision Points.* New York: Crown, 2010.

Clark, Westley K., *Waging Modern War: Bosnia, Kosovo and the Future of Combat.* New York: PublicAffairs, 2001

Clinton, Hillary Rodham. *Hard Choices.* New York: Simon & Schuster, 2014.

Cohen, Stephen F. *Soviet Fates and Lost Alternatives: From Stalinism to the New Cold War.* New York: Columbia University Press, 2009.

Coll, Steve. *Private Empire: ExxonMobile and American Power.* New York: Penguin, 2012.

Colton, Timothy J. *Yeltsin: A Life.* New York: Basic Books, 2008.

Colton, Timothy J., and Michael McFaul. *Popular Choice and Managed Democracy: The Russian Elections of 1999 and 2000.* Washington, DC: Brookings Institution Press, 2003.

Cornell, Svante E., and S. Frederick Starr, eds. *The Guns of August 2008: Russia's War in Georgia*. Armonk, NY: M.E. Sharpe, 2009.

Cowell, Alan. *The Terminal Spy: The Life and Death of Alexander Litvinenko, a True Story of Espionage, Betrayal and Murder*. London: Doubleday, 2008.

Dawisha, Karen. *Putin's Kleptocracy: Who Owns Russia?* New York: Simon & Schuster, 2014.

De Waal, Thomas. *The Caucasus: An Introduction*. Oxford: Oxford University Press, 2010.

De Wolf, Koenraad. *Dissident for Life: Alexander Ogorodnikov and the Struggle for Religious Freedom in Russia*. Translated by Nancy Forest-Flier. Grand Rapids, MI: William B. Eerdmans, 2013.

Dorofeyev, Vladislav, et al. *Dmitri Medvedev: Chelovek, Kotory Ostanovil Vremya* [The Man Who Stopped Time]. Moscow: Eksmo, 2012.

Duelfer, Charles. *Hide and Seek: The Search for Truth in Iraq*. New York: Public-Affairs, 2009.

Dunlop, John B. *The 2002 Dubrovka and 2004 Beslan Hostage Crises: A Critique of Russian Counter-Terrorism*. Stuttgart: Ibidem, 2006.

———. *The Moscow Bombings of September 1999: Examinations of Russian Terrorist Attacks at the Onset of Vladimir Putin's Rule*. Stuttgart: Ibidem, 2012.

Earley, Pete. *Comrade J: The Untold Secrets of Russia's Master Spy in America After the End of the Cold War*. New York: Berkley Books, 2007.

Evangelista, Matthew. *The Chechen Wars: Will Russia Go the Way of the Soviet Union?* Washington, DC: Brookings Institution Press, 2002.

Fagan, Geraldine. *Believing in Russia—Religious Policy After Communism*. London: Routledge, 2013.

Felshtinsky, Yuri, ed. *Boris Berezovsky: The Art of the Impossible*. 3 vols. Falmouth, MA: Terra-USA, 2006.

Felshtinsky, Yuri, and Vladimir Pribylovsky. *The Corporation: Russia and the KGB in the Age of President Putin*. New York: Encounter Books, 2008.

Freeland, Chrystia. *Sale of the Century: Russia's Wild Ride from Communism to Capitalism*. New York: Crown Business, 2000.

Gaidar, Yegor. *Collapse of an Empire: Lessons for Modern Russia*. Washington, DC: Brookings Institution Press, 2007.

Gessen, Masha. *The Man Without a Face: The Unlikely Rise of Vladimir Putin*. New York: Riverhead Books, 2012.

———. *Words Will Break Cement: The Passion of Pussy Riot*. New York: Riverhead Books, 2014.

Gevorkyan, Nataliya, Natalya Timakova, and Andrei Kolesnikov. *First Person: An Astonishingly Frank Self-Portrait by Russia's President Vladimir Putin*. New York: PublicAffairs, 2000. Originally published in Russian as *Ot Pervovo Litsa: Razgovory c Vladimirom Putinim*.

Gilligan, Emma. *Terror in Chechnya: Russia and the Tragedy of Civilians in War.* Princeton, NJ: Princeton University Press, 2010.

Goldfarb, Alex, with Marina Litvinenko. *Death of a Dissident: The Poisoning of Alexander Litvinenko and the Return of the KGB.* New York: Free Press, 2007.

Goldman, Marshall I. *Petrostate: Putin, Power and the New Russia.* Oxford: Oxford University Press, 2008.

———. *The Piratization of Russia: Russian Reform Goes Awry.* London: Routledge, 2003.

Gomart, Thomas. *Russian Civil-Military Relations: Putin's Legacy.* Washington, DC: Carnegie Endowment for International Peace, 2008.

Gorham, Michael S. *After Newspeak: Language, Culture and Politics in Russia from Gorbachev to Putin.* Ithaca, NY: Cornell University Press, 2014.

Goscilo, Helena, ed. *Putin as Celebrity and Cultural Icon.* London: Routledge, 2013.

Greene, Samuel A. *Moscow in Movement: Power and Opposition in Putin's Russia.* Stanford, CA: Stanford University Press, 2014.

Gurevich, Vera. *Bspominaniya o Budushchem Prezidente* [Recollections of the Future President]. Moscow: Mezhdunarodniye Otnosheniya, 2001.

Gustafson, Thane. *Wheel of Fortune: The Battle for Oil and Power in Russia.* Cambridge, MA: Belknap Press of Harvard University Press, 2012.

Harding, Luke. *Expelled: A Journalist's Descent into the Russian Mafia State.* New York: Palgrave Macmillan, 2012.

Hastings, Max. *Inferno: The World at War, 1939–1945.* New York: Alfred A. Knopf, 2011.

Herspring, Dale R., ed. *The Kremlin and the High Command: Presidential Impact on the Russian Military from Gorbachev to Putin.* Lawrence: University Press of Kansas, 2006.

———. *Putin's Russia: Past Imperfect, Future Uncertain.* Lanham, MD: Rowman & Littlefield, 2003.

Hill, Fiona, and Clifford G. Gaddy. *Mr. Putin: Operative in the Kremlin.* Washington, DC: Brookings Institution Press, 2013. Updated and expanded in paperback in 2015.

Hoffman, David E. *The Oligarchs: Wealth and Power in the New Russia.* New York: PublicAffairs, 2002.

Hughes, Karen. *Ten Minutes from Normal.* New York: Viking, 2004.

Hutchins, Chris, with Alexander Korobko. *Putin.* Leicester, UK: Matador, 2012.

Jack, Andrew. *Inside Putin's Russia: Can There Be Reform Without Democracy?* Oxford: Oxford University Press, 2004.

Jones, Michael. *Leningrad: State of Siege.* New York: Basic Books, 2008.

Judah, Ben. *Fragile Empire: How Russia Fell In and Out of Love with Vladimir Putin.* New Haven, CT: Yale University Press, 2013.

Kalugin, Oleg. *Spymaster: My Thirty-Two Years in Intelligence and Espionage Against the West*. New York: Basic Books, 2009.

Kasyanov, Mikhail, with Yevgeny Kiselyov. *Bez Putina* [Without Putin]. Moscow: Novaya Gazeta, 2009.

Katz, David M., and Fred Weir. *Russia's Path from Gorbachev to Putin: The Demise of the Soviet System and the New Russia*. New York: Routledge, 2007.

Khodorkovsky, Mikhail, and Nataliya Gevorkyan. *Turma i Volya* [Prison and Will]. Moscow: Howard Roark, 2012.

King, Charles. *The Ghost of Freedom: A History of the Caucasus*. Oxford: Oxford University Press, 2008.

King, William R., and David I. Cleland. *Strategic Planning and Policy*. New York: Van Nostrand Reinhold, 1978.

Kirschenbaum, Lisa A. *The Legacy of the Siege of Leningrad, 1941–1995: Myth, Memories, and Monuments*. New York: Cambridge University Press, 2006.

Klebnikov, Paul. *Godfather of the Kremlin: The Decline of Russia in the Age of Gangster Capitalism*. Orlando, FL: Harcourt, 2000.

Knight, Amy. *Spies Without Cloaks: The KGB's Successors*. Princeton, NJ: Princeton University Press, 1996.

Koehler, John O. *Stasi: The Untold Story of the East German Secret Police*. Boulder, CO: Westview Press, 1999.

Koenker, Diane P., and Ronald D. Bachman, eds. *Revelations from the Russian Archives: Documents in English Translation*. Washington, DC: Library of Congress, 1997.

Konitzer, Andrew. *Voting for Russia's Governors: Regional Elections and Accountability Under Yeltsin and Putin*. Washington, DC: Woodrow Wilson Center Press, 2005.

Koplanov, Andrei, and Andrei Yudin. *Tainy Bolshovo Doma* [Secrets of the Big House]. Moscow: Astrel-SPB, 2007.

Koshiw, J. V. *Abuse of Power: Corruption in the Office of the President*. n.p.: Artemia Press, 2013.

Kotkin, Stephen. *Armageddon Averted: The Soviet Collapse, 1970–2000*. Oxford: Oxford University Press, 2001.

Kozhevnikov, Vadim. *Shield and Sword*. London: MacGibbon & Kee, 1970.

Lebed, Alexander. *My Life and My Country*. Washington, DC: Regnery Publishing, 1997.

Ledeneva, Alena V. *Can Russia Modernise? Sistema, Power Networks and Informal Governance*. Cambridge: Cambridge University Press, 2013.

LeVine, Steve. *Putin's Labyrinth: Spies, Murder, and the Dark Heart of the New Russia*. New York: Random House, 2008.

Litvinenko, Alexander, and Yuri Felshtinsky. *Blowing Up Russia: The Secret Plot to Bring Back KGB Terror*. New York: Encounter Books, 2007.

Lucas, Edward. *Deception: The Untold Story of East-West Espionage Today.* New York: Walker, 2012.

———. *The New Cold War: Putin's Russia and the Threat to the West.* New York: Palgrave Macmillan, 2008. Updated 2009.

Lynch, Allen C. *Vladimir Putin and Russian Statecraft.* Washington, DC: Potomac Books, 2011.

MacKinnon, Mark. *The New Cold War: Revolutions, Rigged Elections and Pipeline Politics in the Former Soviet Union.* New York: Carroll & Graf, 2007.

Macrakis, Kristie. *Seduced by Secrets: Inside the Stasi's Spy-Tech World.* New York: Cambridge University Press, 2008.

McDaniel, Tim. *The Agony of the Russian Idea.* Princeton, NJ: Princeton University Press, 1996.

McFaul, Michael. *Russia's Unfinished Revolution: Political Change from Gorbachev to Putin.* Ithaca, NY: Cornell University Press, 2001.

Medvedev, Roy. *Post-Soviet Russia: A Journey Through the Yeltsin Era.* Translated and edited by George Shriver. New York: Columbia University Press, 2000.

———. *Vladimir Putin: Chetyre Goda v Kremle* [Vladimir Putin: Four Years in the Kremlin]. Moscow: Vremya, 2004.

Mendras, Marie. *Russian Politics: The Paradox of a Weak State.* New York: Columbia University Press, 2012.

Merridale, Catherine. *Night of Stone: Death and Memory in Twentieth-Century Russia.* New York: Penguin, 2000.

Moore, Robert. *A Time to Die: The Untold Story of the Kursk Tragedy.* New York: Three Rivers Press, 2002.

Mukhin, A. A. *Kto Ect' Mister Putin i Kto c Nim Prishol* [Who Is Mister Putin and Who Came with Him]. Moscow: Gnom i D, 2002.

Murphy, Paul J. *Allah's Angels: Chechen Women in War.* Annapolis, MD: Naval Institute Press, 2010.

O'Cleary, Conor. *Moscow, December 25, 1991: The Last Day of the Soviet Union.* New York: PublicAffairs, 2011.

Orttung, Robert W. *From Leningrad to St. Petersburg.* New York: St. Martin's Press, 1995.

Orttung, Robert W., ed., with Danielle N. Lussier and Anna Paretskaya. *The Republics and Regions of the Russian Federation: A Guide to Politics, Policies, and Leaders.* Armonk, NY: M. E. Sharpe, 2000.

Pepper, John. *Russian Tide: Building a Leadership Business in the Midst of Unprecedented Change.* Cincinnati: John Pepper, 2012.

Piontkovsky, Andrei. *Treti Put k Rabstvu* [The Third Road Is to Serfdom]. Boston: M- Graphics, 2010.

Politkovskaya, Anna. *Is Journalism Worth Dying For?* New York: Melville House, 2011. First published as *Za Chto,* Moscow: Novaya Gazeta, 2007.

———. *Putin's Russia.* London: Harvill Press, 2004.

————. *A Russian Diary: A Journalist's Final Account of Life, Corruption and Death in Putin's Russia.* New York: Random House, 2007.

————. *A Small Corner of Hell: Dispatches from Chechnya.* Chicago: University of Chicago Press, 2003.

Pomerantsev, Peter. *Nothing Is True and Everything Is Possible: The Surreal Heart of the New Russia.* New York: PublicAffairs, 2014.

Primakov, Yevgeny. *Vocem Mesyatsev Plus . . .* [Eight Months Plus . . .]. Moscow: Mysl, 2001.

Pussy Riot. *Pussy Riot: A Punk Prayer for Freedom.* New York: Feminist Press, 2013.

Reddaway, Peter, and Dmitri Glinski. *The Tragedy of Russia's Reforms: Market Bolshevism Against Democracy.* Washington, DC: United States Institute of Peace, 2001.

Reed, Joyce Lasky, Blair A. Ruble, and William Craft Brumfield, eds. *St. Petersburg, 1993–2003: The Dynamic Decade.* Washington, DC: St. Petersburg Conservancy, 2010.

Reid, Anna. *Leningrad: The Epic Siege of World War II, 1941–1944.* New York: Walker, New York, 2011.

Remnick, David, *Lenin's Tomb: The Last Days of the Soviet Empire,* Random House, New York, 1993.

————. *Resurrection: The Struggle for a New Russia.* New York: Random House, 1997.

Rice, Condoleezza. *No Higher Honor: A Memoir of My Years in Washington.* New York: Crown, 2011.

Rose, Richard, William Mishler, and Neil Munro. *Popular Support for an Undemocratic Regime: The Changing Views of Russians.* Cambridge: Cambridge University Press, 2011.

Roxburgh, Angus. *The Strongman: Vladimir Putin and the Struggle for Russia.* London: I. B. Tauris, 2012.

Sakwa, Richard. *The Crisis of Russian Democracy: The Dual State, Factionalism and the Medvedev Succession.* New York: Cambridge University Press, 2011.

————. *Putin and the Oligarch: The Khodorkovsky-Yukos Affair.* London: I. B. Tauris, 2014.

————. *Putin: Russia's Choice.* London: Routledge, 2004.

————. *The Quality of Freedom: Khodorkovsky, Putin and the Yukos Affair.* Oxford: Oxford University Press, 2009.

Salisbury, Harrison E. *The 900 Days: The Siege of Leningrad.* New York: Harper & Row, 1969.

Satter, David. *Darkness at Dawn: The Rise of the Russian Criminal State.* New Haven, CT: Yale University Press, 2003.

————. *It Was a Long Time Ago, and It Never Happened Anyway: Russia and the Communist Past.* New Haven, CT: Yale University Press, 2012.

Schrad, Mark Lawrence. *Vodka Politics: Alcohol, Autocracy and the Secret History of the Russian State.* Oxford: Oxford University Press, 2014.

Semyonov, Yulian. *Seventeen Moments of Spring.* Amsterdam: Fredonia Books, 2001.

Service, Robert. *A History of Modern Russia: From Tsarism to the Twenty-First Century.* 3rd ed. Cambridge, MA: Harvard University Press, 2009.

Shevtsova, Lilia. *Putin's Russia.* Washington, DC: Carnegie Endowment for International Peace, 2005.

———. *Russia—Lost in Transition: The Yeltsin and Putin Legacies.* Washington, DC: Carnegie Endowment for International Peace, 2007.

Shlapentokh, Vladimir, and Anna Arutunyan. *Freedom, Repression, and Private Property in Russia.* New York: Cambridge University Press, 2013.

Shvets, Yuri B. *Washington Station: My Life as a KGB Spy in America.* New York: Simon & Schuster, 1994.

Sixsmith, Martin. *The Litvinenko File: The Life and Death of a Russian Spy.* New York: St. Martin's Press, 2007.

Skuratov, Yuri. *Variant Drakona* [The Dragon Variation]. Moscow: Detectiv Press, 2000. Republished in modified form as part of the series *Proekt Putin, Putin—Ispolnitel Zloi Voli* [Putin—Executor of Evil Will]. Moscow: Algorithm, 2012.

Sobchak, Anatoly. *Duzhina Nozhei v Spinu* [A Dozen Knives in the Back]. Moscow: Vagrius, 1999.

———. *For a New Russia: The Mayor of St. Petersburg's Own Story of the Struggle for Justice and Democracy.* New York: Free Press, 1992.

Soldatov, Andrei, and Irina Borogan. *The New Nobility: The Restoration of Russia's Security State and the Enduring Legacy of the KGB.* New York: PublicAffairs, 2010.

Solovyov, Vladimir, and Elena Klepikova. *Behind the High Kremlin Walls.* New York: Dodd, Mead, 1986.

Stent, Angela E. *The Limits of Partnership: U.S.-Russian Relations in the Twenty-First Century.* Princeton, NJ: Princeton University Press, 2014.

Stuermer, Michael. *Putin and the Rise of Russia.* New York: Pegasus Books, 2009.

Svanidze, Nikolai and Marina. *Medvedev.* St. Petersburg: Amfora, 2008.

Talbott, Strobe. *The Russia Hand: A Memoir of Presidential Diplomacy.* New York: Random House, 2002.

Tregubova, Yelena. *Baiki Kremlyovskaya Diggera* [Tales of a Kremlin Digger]. Moscow: Ad Marginem, 2003.

———. *Proshchaniye Kremlyovskaya Diggera* [Farewell of the Kremlin Digger]. Moscow: Ad Marginem, 2004.

Treisman, Daniel. *The Return: Russia's Journey from Gorbachev to Medvedev.* New York: Free Press, 2011.

Trenin, Dmitri. *Post-Imperium: A Eurasian Story.* Washington, DC: Carnegie Endowment for International Peace, 2011.

Trenin, Dmitri V., and Aleksei V. Malashenko, with Anatol Lieven. *Russia's Restless Frontier: The Chechnya Factor in Post-Soviet Russia.* Washington, DC: Carnegie Endowment for International Peace, 2004.

Truscott, Peter. *Kursk: The Gripping True Story of Russia's Worst Submarine Disaster.* London: Simon & Schuster, 2004.

———. *Putin's Progress: A Biography of Russia's Enigmatic President, Vladimir Putin.* London: Simon & Schuster, 2004.

Usoltsev, Vladimir. *Sosluzhivets: Neizvestniye Stranitsi Zhizni Prezidenta* [Comrade: Unknown Pages in the President's Life]. Moscow: Eksmo, 2004.

Van Herpen, Marcel H. *Putin's Wars: The Rise of Russia's New Imperialism.* Lanham, MD: Rowman & Littlefield, 2014.

Volkov, Vadim. *Violent Entrepreneurs: The Use of Force in the Making of Russian Capitalism.* Ithaca and London: Cornell University Press, 2002.

Volodarsky, Boris. *The KGB's Poison Factory: From Lenin to Litvinenko.* Minneapolis: Zenith Press, 2009.

Waller, J. Michael. *Secret Empire: The KGB in Russia Today.* Boulder, CO: Westview Press, 1994.

Werth, Alexander. *Russia at War, 1941–1945.* New York: E. P. Dutton, 1964.

White, Stephen, ed. *Politics and the Ruling Group in Putin's Russia.* New York: Palgrave Macmillan, 2008.

Wolf, Markus, with Anne McElvoy. *The Man Without a Face: The Autobiography of Communism's Greatest Spymaster.* New York: Times Books, 1997.

Woodward, Bob. *Plan of Attack.* New York: Simon & Schuster, 2004.

Yeltsin, Boris. *Midnight Diaries.* New York: PublicAffairs, 2000.

———. *The Struggle for Russia.* New York: Times Books, 1994.

Zenkovich, Nikolai. *Putinskaya Entsiklopediya* [Putin Encyclopedia]. Moscow: Olma-Press, 2006.

Index

ILLUSTRATION CREDITS

Putin with his mother: Kremlin (http://putin.kremlin.ru/bio)

Putin in 1960: Getty

In elementary school in Leningrad: Kremlin (http://putin.kremlin.ru/bio)

Joined the KGB in 1975: Kremlin (http://putin.kremlin.ru/bio)

Working for the KGB in Leningrad: Rossiya Segodnya (Rian)

Stasi: Stasi archives, MfS BV Dresden, AKG Nr. 10852

Putin and Lyudmila Shkrebneva wedding photo: Kremlin (http://putin.kremlin.ru/bio)

The Putins with daughter Maria in 1985: Kremlin (http://putin.kremlin.ru/bio)

Daughters Yekaterina and Maria: Kremlin (http://putin.kremlin.ru/bio)

Leningrad, 1990: Associated Press

Aleksandr Litvinenko: Associated Press

In Dagestan: Associated Press

Putin and Boris Yeltsin: Kremlin (http://putin.kremlin.ru/bio)

Putin and his dog Koni: James Hill

Mikhail Khodorkovsky: James Hill

Aleksei Miller: Getty

Shirtless: Getty

Dmitri Medvedev: James Hill

Arkady Rotenburg: Getty

Aleksei Navalny: James Hill

Putin and Lyudmila: Associated Press

Alina Kabayeva: Kremlin (http://putin.kremlin.ru/bio)

Flags with Putin's image: James Hill

A NOTE ABOUT THE AUTHOR

Steven Lee Myers has worked at *The New York Times* since 1989. Beginning in 2002, he spent more than seven years, in two stints, as a correspondent based in Russia during the reign of Vladimir Putin, covering many of the events in this book: from the war in Chechnya to the preparations for the Sochi Olympics, from the Orange Revolution in Ukraine to the annexation of Crimea. He has previously worked in New York, Washington, D.C., and, during the winding down of the American war in Iraq, in Baghdad. He now writes about foreign affairs and national security issues from Washington. This is his first book.

A NOTE ON THE TYPE

This book was set in Adobe Garamond. Designed for the Adobe Corporation by Robert Slimbach, the fonts are based on types first cut by Claude Garamond (ca. 1480–1561). Garamond was a pupil of Geoffroy Tory and is believed to have followed the Venetian models, although he introduced a number of important differences, and it is to him that we owe the letter we now know as old style. He gave to his letters a certain elegance and feeling of movement that won their creator an immediate reputation and the patronage of Francis I of France.

Composed by North Market Street Graphics,
Lancaster, Pennsylvania

Printed and bound by Berryville Graphics,
Berryville, Virginia

Designed by Betty Lew